2003 Supplement to

AMERICAN CRIMINAL PROCEDURE

CASES AND COMMENTARY
Sixth Edition

By

Stephen A. Saltzburg

Howrey Professor of Trial Advocacy,
Litigation and Professional Responsibility
George Washington University Law School

Daniel J. Capra

Philip D. Reed Professor of Law
Fordham University School of Law

AMERICAN CASEBOOK SERIES®

THOMSON
TM
WEST

Mat #40152681

COPYRIGHT © 1996 WEST PUBLISHING CO.
COPYRIGHT © 1997, 1998, 1999, 2000, 2001 By WEST GROUP
COPYRIGHT © 2003 By West, a Thomson business
             610 Opperman Drive
             P.O. Box 64526
             St. Paul, MN 55164–0526
             1–800–328–9352

ISBN 0–314–14684–9

TEXT IS PRINTED ON 10% POST CONSUMER RECYCLED PAPER

Table of Contents

Table of Cases

The principal cases are in bold type. Cases cited or discussed in the text are roman type. References are to pages. Cases cited in principal cases and within other quoted materials are not included.

*

2003 Supplement to

AMERICAN CRIMINAL PROCEDURE

CASES AND COMMENTARY

Sixth Edition

*

Part I

RECENT DEVELOPMENTS

Chapter One

BASIC PRINCIPLES

I. A CRIMINAL CASE

Page 5. Add the following after the headnote on Kansas v. Hendricks:

An "As Applied" Challenge to Confinement of a Sexual Predator: Seling v. Young

In Seling v. Young, 531 U.S. 250 (2001), a person incarcerated as a sexual predator challenged his confinement on double jeopardy and ex post facto grounds. His challenge therefore depended on whether he was subject to civil or criminal confinement. The sexual predator statute challenged by Young was virtually identical to that upheld as civil rather than criminal in *Hendricks*. He argued, however, that *Hendricks* had upheld a facial challenge to the sexual predator statute, while his challenge went to the statute *as applied*. He contended that the state's sexual offender program in fact provided no treatment and in fact resulted in conditions worse than confinement on a criminal charge. The Court, in an opinion by Justice O'Connor, rejected the possibility of an as applied challenge to the sexual predator statute as "fundamentally flawed." Justice O'Connor reasoned as follows:

> We hold that respondent cannot obtain release through an "as-applied" challenge to the Washington Act on double jeopardy and *ex post facto* grounds. We agree with petitioner that an "as-applied" analysis would prove unworkable. Such an analysis would never conclusively resolve whether a particular scheme is punitive and would thereby prevent a final determination of the scheme's validity under the Double Jeopardy and *Ex Post Facto* Clauses. Unlike a fine, confinement is not a fixed event. As petitioner notes, it extends over time under conditions that are subject to change. The particular

1

features of confinement may affect how a confinement scheme is evaluated to determine whether it is civil rather than punitive, but it remains no less true that the query must be answered definitively. The civil nature of a confinement scheme cannot be altered based merely on vagaries in the implementation of the authorizing statute.

Justice Scalia wrote a concurring opinion joined by Justice Souter. He elaborated on the problems of an as applied challenge:

> The short of the matter is that, for Double Jeopardy and *Ex Post Facto* Clause purposes, the question of criminal penalty *vel non* depends upon the intent of the legislature; and harsh executive implementation cannot transform what was clearly intended as a civil remedy into a criminal penalty, any more than compassionate executive implementation can transform a criminal penalty into a civil remedy. This is not to say that there is no relief from a system that administers a facially civil statute in a fashion that would render it criminal. The remedy, however, is not to invalidate the legislature's handiwork under the Double Jeopardy Clause, but to eliminate whatever excess in administration contradicts the statute's civil character. When, as here, a state statute is at issue, the remedy for implementation that does not comport with the civil nature of the statute is resort to the traditional state proceedings that challenge unlawful executive action; if those proceedings fail, and the state courts authoritatively interpret the state statute as permitting impositions that are indeed punitive, then and only then can federal courts pronounce a statute that on its face is civil to be criminal. Such an approach protects federal courts from becoming enmeshed in the sort of intrusive inquiry into local conditions at state institutions that are best left to the State's own judiciary, at least in the first instance. And it avoids federal invalidation of state statutes on the basis of executive implementation that the state courts themselves, given the opportunity, would find to be ultra vires. Only this approach, it seems to me, is in accord with our sound and traditional reluctance to be the initial interpreter of state law.

Justice Thomas wrote an opinion concurring in the judgment. Justice Stevens wrote a dissent.

Registration of Sex Offenders–Civil Regulation or Criminal Punishment?: Smith v. Doe

In Smith v. Doe, 123 S.Ct. 1140 (2003), the Court upheld Alaska's version of a "Megan's Law" against a challenge that it violated the Ex Post Facto Clause. Megan's Laws, adopted by legislatures throughout the country, require those convicted as sex offenders to register with their state of residence. Information about the offenders is then published over the internet. Alaska's version required sex offenders to register even if they were convicted before the date of the legislation. The Court, in an opinion by Justice Kennedy for five Justices, held that the statutory scheme was civil rather than punitive, and therefore the Ex Post Facto Clause did not apply. The Court noted that the purpose of the law, as expressed in the statutory text, was to protect the public from sex offenders. Justice Kennedy cited *Hendricks* and declared that "an imposition of restrictive measures on sex offenders adjudged to be dangerous is a legitimate nonpunitive governmental objective" and that "nothing on the face of the statute suggests that the legislature sought to create anything other than a civil scheme designed to protect the public from harm." The Court also noted that the Alaska law simply requires registration; it "imposes no physical restraint, and so does not resemble the punishment of imprisonment, which is the paradigmatic affirmative disability or restraint."

Justice Kennedy rejected the argument that the registration system was punitive because it was tantamount to probation or supervised release, which clearly are aspects of the criminal justice system. He distinguished registration from probation or supervised release as follows:

> Probation and supervised release entail a series of mandatory conditions and allow the supervising officer to seek the revocation of probation or release in case of infraction. By contrast, offenders subject to the Alaska statute are free to move where they wish and to live and work as other citizens, with no supervision. Although registrants must inform the authorities after they change their facial features (such as growing a beard), borrow a car, or seek psychiatric treatment, they are not required to seek permission to do so. A sex offender who fails to comply with the reporting requirement may be subjected to a criminal prosecution for that failure, but any prosecution is a proceeding separate from the individual's original offense. Whether other constitutional objections can be raised to a mandatory reporting requirement, and how those questions might be resolved, are concerns beyond the scope of this opinion. It suffices to say the registration requirements make a valid regulatory program effective and do not impose punitive restraints in violation of the *Ex Post Facto* Clause.

Justice Thomas wrote a short concurring opinion.

Justice Souter concurred in the judgment. He noted that the Alaska scheme did contain some aspects of punishment. For example, some of the provisions were located in the criminal code; the touchstone for regulation was the commission of a past crime rather than current dangerousness; and the statute made written notification of the registration requirement a condition of a guilty plea to any sex offense. He also noted that the publication of sex offender status on the internet might be seen to bear "some resemblance to shaming punishments that were used earlier in our history to disable offenders from living normally in the community." Justice Souter, however, concluded as follows:

> To me, the indications of punitive character stated above and the civil indications weighed heavily by the Court are in rough equipoise. * * * What tips the scale for me is the presumption of constitutionality normally accorded a State's law. That presumption gives the State the benefit of the doubt in close cases like this one, and on that basis alone I concur in the Court's judgment.

Justice Stevens dissented. He declared as follows:

> No matter how often the Court may repeat and manipulate multifactor tests that have been applied in wholly dissimilar cases involving only one or two of these three aspects of these statutory sanctions, it will never persuade me that the registration and reporting obligations that are imposed on convicted sex offenders *and on no one else* as a result of their convictions are not part of their punishment. In my opinion, a sanction that (1) is imposed on everyone who commits a criminal offense, (2) is not imposed on anyone else, and (3) severely impairs a person's liberty is punishment.

Justice Ginsburg, joined by Justice Breyer, wrote a separate dissent. She argued that the registration and reporting requirements are comparable to conditions of supervised release or parole, and that the public notification regimen called to mind the shaming punishments of the past. She concluded as follows:

> What ultimately tips the balance for me is the Act's excessiveness in relation to its nonpunitive purpose. * * * [T]he Act has a legitimate civil purpose: to promote public safety by alerting the public to potentially recidivist sex offenders in the community. But its scope notably exceeds this purpose. The Act applies to all convicted sex offenders, without regard to their future dangerousness. And the duration of the reporting requirement is keyed not to any determination of a particular offender's risk of reoffending, but to whether the offense of conviction qualified as aggravated. The reporting requirements themselves are exorbitant: The Act requires aggravated offenders to engage in perpetual quarterly reporting, even if their personal information has not changed. And meriting heaviest weight in my judgment, the Act makes no provision whatever for the possibility of rehabilitation: Offenders cannot shorten their registration or notification period, even on the clearest demonstration of rehabilitation or conclusive proof of physical incapacitation. However plain it may be that a former sex offender currently poses no threat of recidivism, he will remain subject to long-term monitoring and inescapable humiliation.

III. TWO SPECIAL ASPECTS OF CONSTITU-TIONAL LAW: THE INCORPORATION DOC-TRINE AND PROSPECTIVE DECISIONMAK-ING

B. RETROACTIVITY

4. *Current Supreme Court Approach to Retroactivity*

Page 30.   After the runover paragraph, add the following:

In Williams v. Taylor, 529 U.S. 362 (2000), the Court, in an opinion by Justice O'Connor, declared that the AEDPA essentially codified a standard of review of state court decisions that is equivalent to the "new rule" jurisprudence of *Teague*. Under AEDPA, a federal court cannot grant relief unless the state court decision is "contrary to, or involved an unreasonable application of, clearly established Federal law, as determined by the Supreme Court of the United States." In *Williams*, Justice O'Connor declared that "whatever would qualify as an old rule under our *Teague* jurisprudence will constitute 'clearly established Federal law, as determined by the Supreme Court of the United States' under § 2254(d)(1). The one caveat, as the statutory language makes clear, is that § 2254(d)(1) restricts the source of clearly established law to this Court's jurisprudence." Consequently, if a habeas petitioner is claiming that a state court misapplied constitutional law that was not clearly established by the United States Supreme Court at the time, the habeas petition must be denied—because the state court decision is not "contrary to" clearly established law as defined by the Supreme Court. It follows that the *Teague* "new rule" jurisprudence has been codified, for all practical purposes, by AEDPA.

Chapter Two

SEARCHES AND SEIZURES OF PERSONS AND THINGS

II. THRESHOLD REQUIREMENTS FOR FOURTH AMENDMENT PROTECTIONS: WHAT IS A "SEARCH"? WHAT IS A "SEIZURE"?

C. APPLICATIONS OF THE *KATZ* PRINCIPLE

3. *Access by Members of the Public*

h. *Manipulation of Bags in Public Transit*

Page 57. At the end of the section, add the following case:

The Supreme Court overruled the Fifth Circuit's holding in *Bond* that Agent Cantu's squeezing of the bag did not constitute a search.

BOND v. UNITED STATES

Supreme Court of the United States, 2000.
529 U.S. 334.

CHIEF JUSTICE REHNQUIST delivered the opinion of the Court.

This case presents the question whether a law enforcement officer's physical manipulation of a bus passenger's carry-on luggage violated the Fourth Amendment's proscription against unreasonable searches. We hold that it did.

Petitioner Steven Dewayne Bond was a passenger on a Greyhound bus that left California bound for Little Rock, Arkansas. The bus stopped, as it was required to do, at the permanent Border Patrol checkpoint in Sierra Blanca, Texas. Border Patrol Agent Cesar Cantu boarded the bus to check the immigration status of its passengers. After reaching the back of the bus, having satisfied himself that the passengers were lawfully in the United States, Agent Cantu began walking toward the front. Along the way, he squeezed the soft luggage which passengers had placed in the overhead storage space above the seats.

Petitioner was seated four or five rows from the back of the bus. As Agent Cantu inspected the luggage in the compartment above petitioner's seat, he squeezed a green canvas bag and noticed that it contained a "brick-like" object. Petitioner admitted that the bag was his and agreed to allow Agent Cantu to open it. [The Government has not argued here that petitioner's consent to Agent Cantu's opening the bag is a basis for admitting the evidence.] Upon opening the bag, Agent Cantu discovered a "brick" of methamphetamine. The brick had been wrapped in duct tape until it was oval-shaped and then rolled in a pair of pants.

Petitioner was indicted for conspiracy to possess, and possession with intent to distribute, methamphetamine in violation of 21 U.S.C. § 841(a)(1). He moved to suppress the drugs, arguing that Agent Cantu conducted an illegal search of his bag. Petitioner's motion was denied, and the District Court found him guilty on both counts and sentenced him to 57 months in prison. On appeal, he conceded that other passengers had access to his bag, but contended that Agent Cantu manipulated the bag in a way that other passengers would not. The Court of Appeals rejected this argument, stating that the fact that Agent Cantu's manipulation of petitioner's bag was calculated to detect contraband is irrelevant for Fourth Amendment purposes. Thus, the Court of Appeals affirmed the denial of the motion to suppress, holding that Agent Cantu's manipulation of the bag was not a search within the meaning of the Fourth Amendment. We granted certiorari, and now reverse.

The Fourth Amendment provides that "[t]he right of the people to be secure in their persons, houses, papers, and effects, against unreasonable searches and seizures, shall not be violated...." A traveler's personal luggage is clearly an "effect" protected by the Amendment. See United States v. Place, 462 U.S. 696 (1983). Indeed, it is undisputed here that petitioner possessed a privacy interest in his bag.

But the Government asserts that by exposing his bag to the public, petitioner lost a reasonable expectation that his bag would not be physically manipulated. The Government relies on our decisions in California v. Ciraolo, and Florida v. Riley, for the proposition that matters open to public observation are not protected by the Fourth Amendment. In *Ciraolo*, we held that police observation of a backyard from a plane flying at an altitude of 1,000 feet did not violate a reasonable expectation of privacy. Similarly, in *Riley*, we relied on *Ciraolo* to hold that police observation of a greenhouse in a home's curtilage from a helicopter passing at an altitude of 400 feet did not violate the Fourth Amendment. We reasoned that the property was "not necessarily protected from inspection that involves no physical invasion," and determined that because any member of the public could have lawfully observed the defendants' property by flying overhead, the defendants' expectation of privacy was "not reasonable and not one that society is prepared to honor."

But *Ciraolo* and *Riley* are different from this case because they involved only visual, as opposed to tactile, observation. Physically invasive inspection is simply more intrusive than purely visual inspection. For example, in Terry v. Ohio, we stated that a "careful [tactile] exploration of the outer surfaces of a person's clothing all over his or her body" is a "serious intrusion upon the sanctity of the person, which may inflict great indignity and arouse strong resentment, and is not to be undertaken lightly." Although Agent Cantu did not "frisk" petitioner's person, he did conduct a probing tactile examination of petitioner's carry-on luggage. Obviously, petitioner's bag was not part of his person. But travelers are particularly concerned about their carry-on luggage; they generally use it to transport personal items that, for whatever reason, they prefer to keep close at hand.

Here, petitioner concedes that, by placing his bag in the overhead compartment, he could expect that it would be exposed to certain kinds of touching and handling. But petitioner argues that Agent Cantu's physical manipulation of his luggage "far exceeded the casual contact [petitioner] could have expected from other passengers." The Government counters that it did not.

Our Fourth Amendment analysis embraces two questions. First, we ask whether the individual, by his conduct, has exhibited an actual expectation of privacy; that is, whether he has shown that "he [sought] to preserve [something] as private." Smith v. Maryland, 442 U.S. 735 (1979) (internal quotation marks omitted). Here, petitioner sought to preserve privacy by using an opaque bag and placing that bag directly above his seat. Second, we

inquire whether the individual's expectation of privacy is "one that society is prepared to recognize as reasonable." When a bus passenger places a bag in an overhead bin, he expects that other passengers or bus employees may move it for one reason or another. Thus, a bus passenger clearly expects that his bag may be handled. He does not expect that other passengers or bus employees will, as a matter of course, feel the bag in an exploratory manner. But this is exactly what the agent did here. We therefore hold that the agent's physical manipulation of petitioner's bag violated the Fourth Amendment.

The judgment of the Court of Appeals is

Reversed.

Justice Breyer, with whom Justice Scalia joins, dissenting.

Does a traveler who places a soft-sided bag in the shared overhead storage compartment of a bus have a "reasonable expectation" that strangers will not push, pull, prod, squeeze, or otherwise manipulate his luggage? Unlike the majority, I believe that he does not.

Petitioner argues—and the majority points out—that, even if bags in overhead bins are subject to general "touching" and "handling," this case is special because "Agent Cantu's physical manipulation of [petitioner's] luggage far exceeded the casual contact [he] could have expected from other passengers." But the record shows the contrary. Agent Cantu testified that border patrol officers (who routinely enter buses at designated checkpoints to run immigration checks) "conduct an inspection of the overhead luggage by squeezing the bags as we're going out." On the occasion at issue here, Agent Cantu "felt a green bag" which had "a brick-like object in it." He explained that he felt "the edges of the brick in the bag," and that it was a "[b]rick-like object . . . that, when squeezed, you could feel an outline of something of a different mass inside of it." Although the agent acknowledged that his practice was to "squeeze [bags] very hard," he testified that his touch ordinarily was not "[h]ard enough to break something inside that might be fragile." Petitioner also testified that Agent Cantu "reached for my bag, and he shook it a little, and squeezed it."

How does the "squeezing" just described differ from the treatment that overhead luggage is likely to receive from strangers in a world of travel that is somewhat less gentle than it used to be? I think not at all. See United States v. McDonald, 100 F.3d 1320, 1327 (C.A.7 1996) (" '[A]ny person who has travelled on a common carrier knows that luggage placed in an overhead compartment is always at the mercy of all people who want to rearrange or move previously placed luggage' "); Eagan, Familiar Anger Takes Flight with Airline Tussles, Boston Herald, Aug. 15, 1999, p. 8 ("It's dog-eat-dog trying to cram half your home into overhead compartments"); Massingill, Airlines Ride on the Wings of High–Flying Economy and Travelers Pay Price in Long Lines, Cramped Airplanes, Kansas City Star, May 9, 1999, p. F4 ("[H]undreds of passengers fill overhead compartments with bulky carry-on bags that they have to cram, recram, and then remove"); Flynn, Confessions of a Once–Only Carry–On

Guy, San Francisco Examiner, Sept. 6, 1998, p. T2 (flight attendant "rearranged the contents of three different overhead compartments to free up some room" and then "shoved and pounded until [the] bag squeezed in"). The trial court, which heard the evidence, saw nothing unusual, unforeseeable, or special about this agent's squeeze. It found that Agent Cantu simply "felt the outside of Bond's softside green cloth bag," and it viewed the agent's activity as "minimally intrusive touching."

* * * Privacy itself implies the exclusion of uninvited strangers, not just strangers who work for the Government. Hence, an individual cannot reasonably expect privacy in respect to objects or activities that he knowingly exposes to the public.

Indeed, the Court has said that it is not objectively reasonable to expect privacy if "[a]ny member of the public . . . could have" used his senses to detect "everything that th[e] officers observed." California v. Ciraolo, 476 U.S. 207 (1986). Thus, it has held that the fact that strangers may look down at fenced-in property from an aircraft or sift through garbage bags on a public street can justify a similar police intrusion. Florida v. Riley, 488 U.S. 445 (1989) (plurality opinion); California v. Greenwood, 486 U.S. 35 (1988). The comparative likelihood that strangers will give bags in an overhead compartment a hard squeeze would seem far greater. See *Riley* (O'Connor, J., concurring in judgment) (reasonableness of privacy expectation depends on whether intrusion is a "sufficiently routine part of modern life"). * * *

Of course, the agent's purpose here—searching for drugs—differs dramatically from the intention of a driver or fellow passenger who squeezes a bag in the process of making more room for another parcel. But in determining whether an expectation of privacy is reasonable, it is the effect, not the purpose, that matters. Few individuals with something to hide wish to expose that something to the police, however careless or indifferent they may be in respect to discovery by other members of the public. Hence, a Fourth Amendment rule that turns on purpose could prevent police alone from intruding where other strangers freely tread. And the added privacy protection achieved by such an approach would not justify the harm worked to law enforcement—at least that is what this Court's previous cases suggest. See *Greenwood* ("[T]he police cannot reasonably be expected to avert their eyes from evidence of criminal activity that could have been observed by any member of the public"); *Ciraolo* (rejecting petitioner's argument that the police should be restricted solely because their actions are "motivated by a law enforcement purpose, and not the result of a causal, accidental observation").

Nor can I accept the majority's effort to distinguish "tactile" from "visual" interventions, even assuming that distinction matters here.

Whether tactile manipulation (say, of the exterior of luggage) is more intrusive or less intrusive than visual observation (say, through a lighted window) necessarily depends on the particular circumstances.

If we are to depart from established legal principles, we should not begin here. At best, this decision will lead to a constitutional jurisprudence of "squeezes," thereby complicating further already complex Fourth Amendment law, increasing the difficulty of deciding ordinary criminal matters, and hindering the administrative guidance (with its potential for control of unreasonable police practices) that a less complicated jurisprudence might provide. At worst, this case will deter law enforcement officers searching for drugs near borders from using even the most non-intrusive touch to help investigate publicly exposed bags. At the same time, the ubiquity of non-governmental pushes, prods, and squeezes (delivered by driver, attendant, passenger, or some other stranger) means that this decision cannot do much to protect true privacy. Rather, the traveler who wants to place a bag in a shared overhead bin and yet safeguard its contents from public touch should plan to pack those contents in a suitcase with hard sides, irrespective of the Court's decision today.

For these reasons, I dissent.

4. *Investigation That Can Only Uncover Illegal Activity*

c. *Thermal Detection Devices*

Page 62.   At the end of the section, add the following case:

KYLLO v. UNITED STATES

United States Supreme Court, 2001.
533 U.S. 27.

JUSTICE SCALIA **delivered the opinion of the Court.**

This case presents the question whether the use of a thermal-imaging device aimed at a private home from a public street to detect relative amounts of heat within the home constitutes a "search" within the meaning of the Fourth Amendment.

I

In 1991 Agent William Elliott of the United States Department of the Interior came to suspect that marijuana was being grown in the home belonging to petitioner Danny Kyllo, part of a triplex on Rhododendron Drive in Florence, Oregon. Indoor marijuana growth typically requires high-intensity lamps. In order to determine whether an amount of heat was emanating from petitioner's home consistent with the use of such lamps, at 3:20 a.m. on January 16, 1992, Agent Elliott and Dan Haas used an Agema Thermovision 210 thermal imager to scan the triplex. Thermal imagers detect infrared radiation, which virtually all objects emit but which is not visible to the naked eye. The imager converts radiation into images based on relative warmth—black is cool, white is hot, shades of gray connote relative differences; in that respect, it operates somewhat like a video camera showing heat images. The scan of Kyllo's home took only a few minutes and was performed from the passenger seat of Agent Elliott's vehicle across the street from the front of the house and also from the street in back of the house. The scan showed that the roof over the garage and a side wall of petitioner's home were relatively hot compared to the rest of the home and substantially warmer than neighboring homes in the triplex. Agent Elliott concluded that petitioner was using halide lights to grow marijuana in his house, which indeed he was. Based on tips from informants, utility bills, and the thermal imaging, a Federal Magistrate Judge issued a warrant authorizing a search of petitioner's home, and the agents found an indoor growing operation involving more than 100 plants. Petitioner was indicted on one count of manufacturing marijuana, in violation of 21 U.S.C. § 841(a)(1). He unsuccessfully moved to suppress the evidence seized from his home and then entered a conditional guilty plea.

The Court of Appeals for the Ninth Circuit remanded the case for an evidentiary hearing regarding the intrusiveness of thermal imaging. On remand the District Court found that the Agema 210 "is a non-intrusive device which emits no rays or beams and shows a crude visual image of the heat being radiated from the outside of the house"; it "did not show any people or activity within the walls of the structure"; "[t]he device used cannot penetrate walls or windows to reveal conversations or human activities"; and "[n]o intimate details of the home were observed." Based on these findings, the District Court upheld the validity of the warrant that relied in part upon the thermal imaging, and reaffirmed its denial of the motion to suppress. A divided Court of Appeals initially reversed, but that opinion was withdrawn and the panel (after a change in composition) affirmed, with Judge Noonan dissenting. The court held that petitioner had shown no subjective expectation of privacy because he had made no attempt to conceal the heat escaping from his home, and even if he had, there was no objectively reasonable expectation of privacy because the imager "did not expose any intimate details of Kyllo's life," only "amorphous 'hot spots' on the roof and exterior wall." We granted certiorari.

II

The Fourth Amendment provides that "[t]he right of the people to be secure in their persons, houses, papers, and effects, against unreasonable searches and seizures, shall not be violated." "At the very core" of the Fourth Amendment "stands the right of a man to retreat into his own home and there be free from unreasonable governmental intrusion." Silverman v. United States, 365 U.S. 505, 511 (1961). With few exceptions, the question whether a warrantless search of a home is rea-

sonable and hence constitutional must be answered no. See Illinois v. Rodriguez, 497 U.S. 177, 181 (1990); Payton v. New York, 445 U.S. 573, 586 (1980).

On the other hand, the antecedent question of whether or not a Fourth Amendment "search" has occurred is not so simple under our precedent. The permissibility of ordinary visual surveillance of a home used to be clear because, well into the 20th century, our Fourth Amendment jurisprudence was tied to common-law trespass. Visual surveillance was unquestionably lawful because "the eye cannot by the laws of England be guilty of a trespass." Boyd v. United States, 116 U.S. 616, 628 (1886). We have since decoupled violation of a person's Fourth Amendment rights from trespassory violation of his property, see Rakas v. Illinois, 439 U.S. 128 (1978), but the lawfulness of warrantless visual surveillance of a home has still been preserved. As we observed in California v. Ciraolo, 476 U.S. 207, 213 (1986), "[t]he Fourth Amendment protection of the home has never been extended to require law enforcement officers to shield their eyes when passing by a home on public thoroughfares."

One might think that the new validating rationale would be that examining the portion of a house that is in plain public view, while it is a "search" despite the absence of trespass, is not an "unreasonable" one under the Fourth Amendment. See Minnesota v. Carter, 525 U.S. 83, 104 (1998) (BREYER, J., concurring in judgment). But in fact we have held that visual observation is no "search" at all—perhaps in order to preserve somewhat more intact our doctrine that warrantless searches are presumptively unconstitutional. See Dow Chemical Co. v. United States, 476 U.S. 227, 234–235, 239 (1986). In assessing when a search is not a search, we have applied somewhat in reverse the principle first enunciated in Katz v. United States, 389 U.S. 347 (1967). *Katz* involved eavesdropping by means of an electronic listening device placed on the outside of a telephone booth—a location not within the catalog ("persons, houses, papers, and effects") that the Fourth Amendment protects against unreasonable searches. We held that the Fourth Amendment nonetheless protected Katz from the warrantless eavesdropping because he "justifiably relied" upon the privacy of the telephone booth. As Justice Harlan's oft-quoted concurrence described it, a Fourth Amendment search occurs when the government violates a subjective expectation of privacy that society recognizes as reasonable. We have subsequently applied this principle to hold that a Fourth Amendment search does not occur—even when the explicitly protected location of a house is concerned—unless "the individual manifested a subjective expectation of privacy in the object of the challenged search," and "society [is] willing to recognize that expectation as reasonable." *Ciraolo*, supra, at 211. We have applied this test in holding that it is not a search for the police to use a pen register at the phone company to determine what numbers were dialed in a private home, Smith v. Maryland, 442 U.S. 735, 743–744 (1979), and we have applied the test on two different occasions in holding that aerial surveillance of private homes and surrounding areas does not constitute a search, *Ciraolo*, supra; Florida v. Riley, 488 U.S. 445 (1989).

The present case involves officers on a public street engaged in more than naked-eye surveillance of a home. We have previously reserved judgment as to how much technological enhancement of ordinary perception from such a vantage point, if any, is too much. While we upheld enhanced aerial photography of an industrial complex in *Dow Chemical*, we noted that we found "it important that this is not an area immediately adjacent to a private home, where privacy expectations are most heightened."

III

It would be foolish to contend that the degree of privacy secured to citizens by the Fourth Amendment has been entirely unaffected by the advance of technology. For example, as the cases discussed above make clear, the technology enabling human flight has exposed to public view (and hence, we have said, to official observation) uncovered portions of the house and its curtilage that once were private. The question we confront today is what limits there are upon this power of technology to shrink the realm of guaranteed privacy.

The *Katz* test—whether the individual has an expectation of privacy that society is prepared to recognize as reasonable—has often been criticized as circular, and hence subjective and unpredictable. See Posner, The Uncertain Protection of Privacy by the Supreme Court, 1979 S. Ct. Rev. 173, 188; *Carter*, supra, at 97 (SCALIA, J., concurring). While it may be difficult to refine *Katz* when the search of areas such as telephone booths, automobiles, or even the curtilage and uncovered portions of residences are at issue, in the case of the search of the interior of homes—the prototypical and hence most commonly litigated area of protected privacy—there is a ready criterion, with roots deep in the common law, of the minimal expectation of privacy that exists, and that is acknowledged to be reasonable. To withdraw protection of this minimum expectation would be to permit police technology to erode the privacy guaranteed by the Fourth Amendment. We think that obtaining by sense-enhancing technology any information regarding the interior of the home that could not otherwise have been obtained without physical "intrusion into a constitutionally protected area," *Silverman*, 365 U.S., at 512, constitutes a search—at least where (as here) the technology in question is not in general public use. This assures preservation of that degree of privacy against government that existed when the Fourth Amendment was adopted. On the basis of this criterion, the information obtained by the thermal imager in this case was the product of a search.[2]

The Government maintains, however, that the thermal imaging must be upheld because it detected "only heat radiating from the external surface of the house." The dissent

makes this its leading point, contending that there is a fundamental difference between what it calls "off-the-wall" observations and "through-the-wall surveillance." But just as a thermal imager captures only heat emanating from a house, so also a powerful directional microphone picks up only sound emanating from a house-and a satellite capable of scanning from many miles away would pick up only visible light emanating from a house. We rejected such a mechanical interpretation of the Fourth Amendment in *Katz*, where the eavesdropping device picked up only sound waves that reached the exterior of the phone booth. Reversing that approach would leave the homeowner at the mercy of advancing technology—including imaging technology that could discern all human activity in the home. While the technology used in the present case was relatively crude, the rule we adopt must take account of more sophisticated systems that are already in use or in development. The dissent's reliance on the distinction between "off-the-wall" and "through-the-wall" observation is entirely incompatible with the dissent's belief, which we discuss below, that thermal-imaging observations of the intimate details of a home are impermissible. The most

---

2. The dissent's repeated assertion that the thermal imaging did not obtain information regarding the interior of the home is simply inaccurate. A thermal imager reveals the relative heat of various rooms in the home. The dissent may not find that information particularly private or important, but there is no basis for saying it is not information regarding the interior of the home. The dissent's comparison of the thermal imaging to various circumstances in which outside observers might be able to perceive, without technology, the heat of the home—for example, by observing snow-

melt on the roof—is quite irrelevant. The fact that equivalent information could sometimes be obtained by other means does not make lawful the use of means that violate the Fourth Amendment. The police might, for example, learn how many people are in a particular house by setting up year-round surveillance; but that does not make breaking and entering to find out the same information lawful. In any event, on the night of January 16, 1992, no outside observer could have discerned the relative heat of Kyllo's home without thermal imaging.

sophisticated thermal imaging devices continue to measure heat "off-the-wall" rather than "through-the-wall"; the dissent's disapproval of those more sophisticated thermal-imaging devices, is an acknowledgement that there is no substance to this distinction. As for the dissent's extraordinary assertion that anything learned through "an inference" cannot be a search, that would validate even the "through-the-wall" technologies that the dissent purports to disapprove. Surely the dissent does not believe that the through-the-wall radar or ultrasound technology produces an 8–by–10 Kodak glossy that needs no analysis (i.e., the making of inferences). And, of course, the novel proposition that inference insulates a search is blatantly contrary to United States v. Karo, 468 U.S. 705 (1984), where the police "inferred" from the activation of a beeper that a certain can of ether was in the home. The police activity was held to be a search, and the search was held unlawful.

The Government also contends that the thermal imaging was constitutional because it did not "detect private activities occurring in private areas." It points out that in *Dow Chemical* we observed that the enhanced aerial photography did not reveal any "intimate details." *Dow Chemical*, however, involved enhanced aerial photography of an industrial complex, which does not share the Fourth Amendment sanctity of the home. The Fourth Amendment's protection of the home has never been tied to measurement of the quality or quantity of information obtained. In *Silverman*, for example, we made clear that any physical invasion of the structure of the home, "by even a fraction of an inch," was too much, 365 U.S., at 512, and there is certainly no exception to the warrant requirement for the officer who barely cracks open the front door and sees nothing but the nonintimate rug on the vestibule floor. In the home, our cases show, all details are intimate details, because the entire area is held safe from prying government eyes. Thus, in *Karo*, supra, the only thing detected was a can of ether in the home; and in Arizona v. Hicks, 480 U.S. 321 (1987), the only thing detected by a physical search that went beyond what officers lawfully present could observe in "plain view" was the registration number of a phonograph turntable. These were intimate details because they were details of the home, just as was the detail of how warm—or even how relatively warm—Kyllo was heating his residence.

Limiting the prohibition of thermal imaging to "intimate details" would not only be wrong in principle; it would be impractical in application, failing to provide "a workable accommodation between the needs of law enforcement and the interests protected by the Fourth Amendment," Oliver v. United States, 466 U.S. 170, 181 (1984). To begin with, there is no necessary connection between the sophistication of the surveillance equipment and the "intimacy" of the details that it observes—which means that one cannot say (and the police cannot be assured) that use of the relatively crude equipment at issue here will always be lawful. The Agema Thermovision 210 might disclose, for example, at what hour each night the lady of the house takes her daily sauna and bath—a detail that many would consider "intimate"; and a much more sophisticated system might detect nothing more intimate than the fact that someone left a closet light on. We could not, in other words, develop a rule approving only that through-the-wall surveillance which identifies objects no smaller than 36 by 36 inches, but would have to develop a jurisprudence specifying which home activities are "intimate" and which are not. And even when (if ever) that jurisprudence were fully developed, no police officer would be able to know in advance whether his through-the-wall surveillance picks up "intimate" details—and thus would be unable to know in advance whether it is constitutional.

The dissent's proposed standard—whether the technology offers the "functional equivalent of actual presence in the area being searched"—would seem quite similar to our own at first blush. The dissent concludes that *Katz* was such a case, but then inexplicably asserts that if the same listening device only revealed the volume of the conversation, the surveillance would be permissible. Yet if, without technology, the police could not discern volume without being actually present in the phone booth, JUSTICE STEVENS should conclude a search has occurred. The same should hold for the interior heat of the home if only a person present in the home could discern the heat. Thus the driving force of the dissent, despite its recitation of the above standard, appears to be a distinction among different types of information—whether the "homeowner would even care if anybody noticed." The dissent offers no practical guidance for the application of this standard, and for reasons already discussed, we believe there can be none. The people in their houses, as well as the police, deserve more precision.[6]

We have said that the Fourth Amendment draws "a firm line at the entrance to the house," *Payton*, 445 U.S., at 590. That line, we think, must be not only firm but also bright—which requires clear specification of those methods of surveillance that require a warrant. While it is certainly possible to conclude from the videotape of the thermal imaging that occurred in this case that no "significant" compromise of the homeowner's privacy has occurred, we must take the long view, from the original meaning of the Fourth Amendment forward.

Where, as here, the Government uses a device that is not in general public use, to explore details of the home that would previously have been unknowable without physical intrusion, the surveillance is a "search" and is presumptively unreasonable without a warrant.

Since we hold the Thermovision imaging to have been an unlawful search, it will remain for the District

---

6. The dissent argues that we have injected potential uncertainty into the constitutional analysis by noting that whether or not the technology is in general public use may be a factor. That quarrel, however, is not with us but with this Court's precedent. See *Ciraolo*, supra, at 215 ("In an age where private and commercial flight in the public airways is routine, it is unreasonable for respondent to expect that his marijuana plants were constitutionally protected from being observed with the naked eye from an altitude of 1,000 feet"). Given that we can quite confidently say that thermal imaging is not "routine," we decline in this case to reexamine that factor.

Court to determine whether, without the evidence it provided, the search warrant issued in this case was supported by probable cause—and if not, whether there is any other basis for supporting admission of the evidence that the search pursuant to the warrant produced.

* * *

The judgment of the Court of Appeals is reversed; the case is remanded for further proceedings consistent with this opinion.

JUSTICE STEVENS, with whom THE CHIEF JUSTICE, JUSTICE O'CONNOR, and JUSTICE KENNEDY join, dissenting.

There is, in my judgment, a distinction of constitutional magnitude between "through-the-wall surveillance" that gives the observer or listener direct access to information in a private area, on the one hand, and the thought processes used to draw inferences from information in the public domain, on the other hand. The Court has crafted a rule that purports to deal with direct observations of the inside of the home, but the case before us merely involves indirect deductions from "off-the-wall" surveillance, that is, observations of the exterior of the home. Those observations were made with a fairly primitive thermal imager that gathered data exposed on the outside of petitioner's home but did not invade any constitutionally protected interest in privacy. Moreover, I believe that the supposedly "bright-line" rule the Court has created in response to its concerns about future technological developments is unnecessary, unwise, and inconsistent with the Fourth Amendment.

I

* * *

While the Court "take[s] the long view" and decides this case based largely on the potential of yet-to-be-developed technology that might allow "through-the-wall surveillance," this case involves nothing more than off-the-wall surveillance by law enforcement officers to gather information exposed to the general public from the outside of petitioner's home. All that the infrared camera did in this case was passively measure heat emitted from the exterior surfaces of petitioner's home; all that those measurements showed were relative differences in emission levels, vaguely indicating that some areas of the roof and outside walls were warmer than others. As still images from the infrared scans show, no details regarding the interior of petitioner's home were revealed. Unlike an x-ray scan, or other possible "through-the-wall" techniques, the detection of infrared radiation emanating from the home did not accomplish "an unauthorized physical penetration into the premises," Silverman v. United States, 365 U.S. 505, 509 (1961), nor did it "obtain information that it could not have obtained by observation from outside the curtilage of the house," United States v. Karo, 468 U.S. 705, 715 (1984).

Indeed, the ordinary use of the senses might enable a neighbor or passerby to notice the heat emanating from a building, particularly if it is vented, as was the case here. Additionally, any member of the public might notice that one part of a house is warmer than another part or a nearby building if, for example, rainwater evaporates or snow melts at different rates across its surfaces. Such use of the senses would not convert into an unreasonable search if, instead, an adjoining neighbor allowed an officer onto her property to verify her perceptions with a sensitive thermometer. Nor, in my view, does such observation become an unreasonable search if made from a distance with the aid of a device that merely discloses that the exterior of one house, or one area of the house, is much warmer than another. Nothing more occurred in this case.

Thus, the notion that heat emissions from the outside of a dwelling is a private matter implicating the protections of the Fourth Amendment (the text of which guarantees the right of people "to be secure in their . . . houses" against unreasonable searches and seizures (emphasis added)) is not only unprecedented but also quite difficult to take seriously. Heat waves, like aromas that are generated in a kitchen, or in a laboratory or opium den, enter the public domain if and when they leave a building. A subjective expectation that they would remain private is not only implausible but also surely not "one that society is prepared to recognize as reasonable."

To be sure, the homeowner has a reasonable expectation of privacy concerning what takes place within the home, and the Fourth Amendment's protection against physical invasions of the home should apply to their functional equivalent. But the equipment in this case did not penetrate the walls of petitioner's home, and while it did pick up "details of the home" that were exposed to the public, it did not obtain "any information regarding the interior of the home." In the Court's own words, based on what the thermal imager "showed" regarding the outside of petitioner's home, the officers "concluded" that petitioner was engaging in illegal activity inside the home. It would be quite absurd to characterize their thought processes as "searches," regardless of whether they inferred (rightly) that petitioner was growing marijuana in his house, or (wrongly) that "the lady of the house [was taking] her daily sauna and bath." In either case, the only conclusions the officers reached concerning the interior of the home were at least as indirect as those that might have been inferred from the contents of discarded garbage, see California v. Greenwood, 486 U.S. 35 (1988), or pen register data, see Smith v. Maryland, 442 U.S. 735 (1979) * * *. For the first time in its history, the Court assumes that an inference can amount to a Fourth Amendment violation.

Notwithstanding the implications of today's decision, there is a strong public interest in avoiding constitutional litigation over the monitoring of emissions from homes, and over the inferences drawn from such monitoring. Just as "the police cannot reasonably be expected to avert their eyes from evidence of criminal activity that could have been observed by any member of the public," Greenwood, 486 U.S., at 41, so too public officials should not have to avert their senses or their equipment from detecting emissions in the public domain such as excessive heat, traces of smoke, suspicious odors, odorless gases, airborne particulates, or radioactive emissions, any of which could identify hazards to the community. In my judgment, monitoring such emissions with "sense-enhancing technology," and drawing useful conclusions from such monitoring, is an entirely reasonable public service.

On the other hand, the countervailing privacy interest is at best trivial. After all, homes generally are insulated to keep heat in, rather than to prevent the detection of heat going out, and it does not seem to me that society will suffer from a rule requiring the rare homeowner who both intends to engage in uncommon activities that produce extraordinary amounts of heat, and wishes to conceal that production from outsiders, to make sure that the surrounding area is well insulated. The interest in concealing the heat escaping from one's house pales in significance to the "the chief evil against which the wording of the Fourth Amendment is directed," the "physical entry of the home," and it is hard to believe that it is an interest the Framers sought to protect in our Constitution.

Since what was involved in this case was nothing more than drawing inferences from off-the-wall surveillance, rather than any "through-the-wall" surveillance, the officers' conduct did not amount to a search and was perfectly reasonable.

II

* * *

Despite the Court's attempt to draw a line that is "not only firm but also bright," the contours of its new rule are uncertain because its protection apparently dissipates as soon as the relevant technology is "in general public use." Yet how much use is general public use is not even hinted at by the Court's opinion, which makes the somewhat doubtful assumption that the thermal imager used in this case does not satisfy that criterion. In any event, putting aside its lack of clarity, this criterion is somewhat perverse because it seems likely that the threat to privacy will grow, rather than recede, as the use of intrusive equipment becomes more readily available.

It is clear, however, that the category of "sense-enhancing technology" covered by the new rule is far too broad. It would, for example, embrace potential mechanical substitutes for dogs trained to react when they sniff narcotics. But in United States v. Place, 462 U.S. 696, 707 (1983), we held that a dog sniff that "discloses only the presence or absence of narcotics" does "not constitute a search within the meaning of the Fourth Amendment," and it must follow that sense-enhancing equipment that identifies nothing but illegal activity is not a search either. Nevertheless, the use of such a device would be unconstitutional under the Court's rule, as would the use of other new devices that might detect the odor of deadly bacteria or chemicals for making a new type of high explosive, even if the devices (like the dog sniffs) are "so limited in both the manner in which" they obtain information and "in the content of the information" they reveal. * * *

The application of the Court's new rule to "any information regarding the interior of the home," is also unnecessarily broad. If it takes sensitive equipment to detect an odor that identifies criminal conduct and nothing else, the fact that the odor emanates from the interior of a home should not provide it with constitutional protection. The criterion, moreover, is too sweeping in that information "regarding" the interior of a home apparently is not just information obtained through its walls, but also information concerning the outside of the building that could lead to (however many) inferences "regarding" what might be inside. Under that expansive view, I suppose, an officer using an infrared camera to observe a man silently entering the side door of a house at night carrying a pizza might conclude that its interior is now occupied by someone who likes pizza, and by doing so the officer would be guilty of conducting an unconstitutional "search" of the home.

Because the new rule applies to information regarding the "interior" of the home, it is too narrow as well as too broad. Clearly, a rule that is designed to protect individuals from the overly intrusive use of sense-enhancing equipment should not be limited to a home. If such equipment did provide its user with the functional equivalent of access to a private place—such as, for example, the telephone booth involved in *Katz*, or an office building—then the rule should apply to such an area as well as to a home.

* * *

The two reasons advanced by the Court as justifications for the adoption of its new rule are both unpersuasive. First, the Court suggests that its rule is compelled by our holding in *Katz*, because in that case, as in this, the surveillance consisted of nothing more than the monitoring of waves emanating from a private area into the public

domain. Yet there are critical differences between the cases. In *Katz*, the electronic listening device attached to the outside of the phone booth allowed the officers to pick up the content of the conversation inside the booth, making them the functional equivalent of intruders because they gathered information that was otherwise available only to someone inside the private area; it would be as if, in this case, the thermal imager presented a view of the heat-generating activity inside petitioner's home. By contrast, the thermal imager here disclosed only the relative amounts of heat radiating from the house; it would be as if, in *Katz*, the listening device disclosed only the relative volume of sound leaving the booth, which presumably was discernible in the public domain. Surely, there is a significant difference between the general and well-settled expectation that strangers will not have direct access to the contents of private communications, on the one hand, and the rather theoretical expectation that an occasional homeowner would even care if anybody noticed the relative amounts of heat emanating from the walls of his house, on the other. It is pure hyperbole for the Court to suggest that refusing to extend the holding of *Katz* to this case would leave the homeowner at the mercy of "technology that could discern all human activity in the home."

Second, the Court argues that the permissibility of "through-the-wall surveillance" cannot depend on a distinction between observing "intimate details" such as "the lady of the house [taking] her daily sauna and bath," and noticing only "the nonintimate rug on the vestibule floor" or "objects no smaller than 36 by 36 inches." This entire argument assumes, of course, that the thermal imager in this case could or did perform "through-the-wall surveillance" that could identify any detail "that would previously have been unknowable without physical intrusion." In fact, the device could not, and did not, enable its user to identify either the lady of the house, the rug on the vestibule floor, or anything else inside the house, whether smaller or larger than 36 by 36 inches. * * * But even if the device could reliably show extraordinary differences in the amounts of heat leaving his home, drawing the inference that there was something suspicious occurring inside the residence—a conclusion that officers far less gifted than Sherlock Holmes would readily draw—does not qualify as "through-the-wall surveillance," much less a Fourth Amendment violation.

III

Although the Court is properly and commendably concerned about the threats to privacy that may flow from advances in the technology available to the law enforcement profession, it has unfortunately failed to heed the tried and true counsel of judicial restraint. Instead of concentrating on the rather mundane issue that is actually presented by the case before it, the Court has endeavored to craft an all-encompassing rule for the future. It would be far wiser to give legislators an unimpeded opportunity to grapple with these emerging issues rather than to shackle them with prematurely devised constitutional constraints.

I respectfully dissent.

V. TO APPLY OR NOT TO APPLY THE WARRANT CLAUSE

A. ARRESTS IN PUBLIC AND IN THE HOME

2. *Arrest Versus Summons*

Page 153. Replace the second and third full paragraphs with the following:

In Atwater v. City of Lago Vista, 532 U.S. 318 (2001), the Court opted for a bright-line rule that a custodial arrest is always reasonable if the officer has probable cause of a criminal violation. Atwater was arrested for a minor traffic offense that was punishable only by a fine. The Court reasoned that it would be too difficult to distinguish among offenses that could be subject to custodial arrest and those that could not. *Atwater* is set forth in full in the section on arrest powers, *infra*. It is clear after *Atwater* that the decision to proceed by arrest or summons is totally within the police officer's discretion.

Atwater holds that an officer does not need to proceed by summons, even for minor offenses. Is it possible to argue, on the other hand, that there are certain offenses that *must not* proceed by summons? Should the officer be *required* to arrest a suspect for certain types of offenses?

B. STOP AND FRISK

2. *When Does the Seizure Occur: The Line Between "Stop" and "Encounter"*

Page 208. At the bottom of the page, after the section entitled "Questions After Bostick", add the following:

In the following case, the Court once again addressed whether, and under what circumstances, a bus sweep might be a seizure under the Fourth Amendment. Once again, the Court refused to impose any *per se* rules on police officers.

UNITED STATES v. DRAYTON

Supreme Court of the United States, 2002.
536 U.S. 194.

JUSTICE KENNEDY **delivered the opinion of the Court.**

The Fourth Amendment permits police officers to approach bus passengers at random to ask questions and to request their consent to searches, provided a reasonable person would understand that he or she is free to refuse. *Florida v. Bostick,* 501 U.S. 429 (1991). This case requires us to determine whether officers must advise bus passengers during these encounters of their right not to cooperate.

I

On February 4, 1999, respondents Christopher Drayton and Clifton Brown, Jr., were traveling on a Greyhound bus en route from Ft. Lauderdale, Florida, to Detroit, Michigan. The bus made a scheduled stop in Tallahassee, Florida. The passengers were required to disembark so the bus could be refueled and cleaned. As the passengers reboarded, the driver checked their tickets and then left to complete paperwork inside the terminal. As he left, the driver allowed three members of the Tallahassee Police Department to board the bus as part of a routine drug and weapons interdiction effort. The officers were dressed in plain clothes and carried concealed weapons and visible badges.

Once onboard Officer Hoover knelt on the driver's seat and faced the rear of the bus. He could observe the passengers and ensure the safety of the two other officers without blocking the aisle or otherwise obstructing the bus exit. Officers Lang and Blackburn went to the rear of the bus. Blackburn remained stationed there, facing forward. Lang worked his way toward the front of the bus, speaking with individual passengers as he went. He asked the passengers about their travel plans and sought to match passengers with luggage in the overhead racks. To avoid blocking the aisle, Lang stood next to or just behind each passenger with whom he spoke.

According to Lang's testimony, passengers who declined to cooperate with him or who chose to exit the bus at any time would have been allowed to do so without argument. In Lang's experience, however, most people are willing to cooperate. Some passengers go so far as to commend the police for their efforts to ensure the safety of their travel. Lang could recall five to six instances in the previous year in which passengers had declined to have their luggage searched. It also was common for passengers to leave the bus for a cigarette or a snack while the officers were on board. Lang sometimes informed passengers of their right to refuse to cooperate. On the day in question, however, he did not.

Respondents were seated next to each other on the bus. Drayton was in the aisle seat, Brown in the seat next to the window. Lang approached respondents from the rear and leaned over Drayton's shoulder. He held up his badge long enough for respondents to identify him as a police officer. With his face 12–to–18 inches away from Drayton's, Lang spoke in a voice just loud enough for respondents to hear:

> I'm Investigator Lang with the Tallahassee Police Department. We're conducting bus interdiction [sic], attempting to deter drugs and illegal weapons being transported on the bus. Do you have any bags on the bus?

Both respondents pointed to a single green bag in the overhead luggage rack. Lang asked, "Do you mind if I check it?," and Brown responded, "Go ahead." Lang handed the bag to Officer Blackburn to check. The bag contained no contraband.

Officer Lang noticed that both respondents were wearing heavy jackets and baggy pants despite the warm weather. In Lang's experience drug traffickers often use baggy clothing to conceal weapons or nar-

cotics. The officer thus asked Brown if he had any weapons or drugs in his possession. And he asked Brown: "Do you mind if I check your person?" Brown answered, "Sure," and cooperated by leaning up in his seat, pulling a cell phone out of his pocket, and opening up his jacket. Lang reached across Drayton and patted down Brown's jacket and pockets, including his waist area, sides, and upper thighs. In both thigh areas, Lang detected hard objects similar to drug packages detected on other occasions. Lang arrested and handcuffed Brown. Officer Hoover escorted Brown from the bus.

Lang then asked Drayton, "Mind if I check you?" Drayton responded by lifting his hands about eight inches from his legs. Lang conducted a pat-down of Drayton's thighs and detected hard objects similar to those found on Brown. He arrested Drayton and escorted him from the bus. A further search revealed that respondents had duct-taped plastic bundles of powder cocaine between several pairs of their boxer shorts. Brown possessed three bundles containing 483 grams of cocaine. Drayton possessed two bundles containing 295 grams of cocaine.

Respondents were charged with conspiring to distribute cocaine, in violation of 21 U.S.C. §§ 841(a)(1) and 846, and with possessing cocaine with intent to distribute it, in violation of § 841(a)(1). They moved to suppress the cocaine, arguing that the consent to the pat-down search was invalid. Following a hearing at which only Officer Lang testified, the United States District Court for the Northern District of Florida denied their motions to suppress. The District Court determined that the police conduct was not coercive and respondents' consent to the search was voluntary. The District Court pointed to the fact that the officers were dressed in plain clothes, did not brandish their badges in an authoritative manner, did not make a general announcement to the entire bus, and did not address anyone in a menacing tone of voice. It noted that the officers did not block the aisle or the exit, and stated that it was "obvious that [respondents] can get up and leave, as can the people ahead of them." The District Court concluded: "[E]verything that took place between Officer Lang and Mr. Drayton and Mr. Brown suggests that it was cooperative. There was nothing coercive, there was nothing confrontational about it."

The Court of Appeals for the Eleventh Circuit reversed and remanded with instructions to grant respondents' motions to suppress. The court held that this disposition was compelled by its previous decisions in *United States v. Washington*, 151 F. 3d 1354 (1998), and *United States v. Guapi*, 144 F. 3d 1393 (1998). Those cases had held that bus passengers do not feel free to disregard police officers' requests to search absent "some positive indication that consent could have been refused."

We granted certiorari. The respondents, we conclude, were not seized and their consent to the search was voluntary; and we reverse.

II

Law enforcement officers do not violate the Fourth Amendment's prohibition of unreasonable seizures merely by approaching individuals on the street or in other public places and putting questions to them if they are willing to listen. Even when law enforcement officers have no basis for suspecting a particular individual, they may pose questions, ask for identification, and request consent to search luggage—provided they do not induce cooperation by coercive means. See *Florida v. Bostick*, 501 U.S., at 434–435. If a reasonable person would feel free to terminate the encounter, then he or she has not been seized.

The Court has addressed on a previous occasion the specific question of drug interdiction efforts on buses. In *Bostick*, two police officers requested a bus passenger's consent to a search of his luggage. The passenger agreed, and the resulting search revealed cocaine in his suitcase. The Florida Supreme Court suppressed the cocaine. In doing so it adopted a *per se* rule that due to the cramped confines onboard a bus the act of questioning would deprive a person of his or her freedom of movement and so constitute a seizure under the Fourth Amendment.

This Court reversed. *Bostick* first made it clear that for the most part *per se* rules are inappropriate in the Fourth Amendment context. The proper inquiry necessitates a consideration of "all the circumstances surrounding the encounter." The Court noted next that the traditional rule, which states that a seizure does not occur so long as a reasonable person would feel free "to disregard the police and go about his business," is not an accurate measure of the coercive effect of a bus encounter. A passenger may not want to get off a bus if there is a risk it will depart before the opportunity to reboard. A bus rider's movements are confined in this sense, but this is the natural result of choosing to take the bus; it says nothing about whether the police conduct is coercive. The proper inquiry "is whether a reasonable person would feel free to decline the officers' requests or otherwise terminate the encounter." Finally, the Court rejected Bostick's argument that he must have been seized because no reasonable person would consent to a search of luggage containing drugs. The reasonable person test, the Court explained, is objective and "presupposes an *innocent* person."

In light of the limited record, *Bostick* refrained from deciding whether a seizure occurred. The Court, however, identified two factors "particularly worth noting" on remand. First, although it was obvious that an officer was armed, he did not remove the gun from its pouch or use it in a threatening way. Second, the officer advised the passenger that he could refuse consent to the search.

Relying upon this latter factor, the Eleventh Circuit has adopted what is in effect a *per se* rule that evidence obtained during suspicionless drug interdiction efforts aboard buses must be suppressed unless the officers have advised passengers of their right not to cooperate and to refuse consent to a search. In *United States v. Guapi, supra,* the Court of Appeals described "[t]he most glaring difference" between the encounters in *Guapi* and in *Bostick* as "the complete lack of any notification to the passengers that they were in fact free to decline the

search request.... .Providing [this] simple notification ... is perhaps the most efficient and effective method to ensure compliance with the Constitution." The Court of Appeals then listed other factors that contributed to the coerciveness of the encounter: (1) the officer conducted the interdiction before the passengers disembarked from the bus at a scheduled stop; (2) the officer explained his presence in the form of a general announcement to the entire bus; (3) the officer wore a police uniform; and (4) the officer questioned passengers as he moved from the front to the rear of the bus, thus obstructing the path to the exit.

After its decision in *Guapi* the Court of Appeals decided *United States v. Washington* and the instant case. The court suppressed evidence obtained during similar drug interdiction efforts despite the following facts: (1) the officers in both cases conducted the interdiction after the passengers had re-boarded the bus; (2) the officer in the present case did not make a general announcement to the entire bus but instead spoke with individual passengers; (3) the officers in both cases were not in uniform; and (4) the officers in both cases questioned passengers as they moved from the rear to the front of the bus and were careful not to obstruct passengers' means of egress from the bus.

Although the Court of Appeals has disavowed a *per se* requirement, the lack of an explicit warning to passengers is the only element common to all its cases. Under these cases, it appears that the Court of Appeals would suppress any evidence obtained during suspicion-less drug interdiction efforts aboard buses in the absence of a warning that passengers may refuse to coop-erate. The Court of Appeals erred in adopting this approach.

Applying the *Bostick* framework to the facts of this particular case, we conclude that the police did not seize respondents when they board-ed the bus and began questioning passengers. The officers gave the passengers no reason to believe that they were required to answer the officers' questions. When Officer Lang approached respondents, he did not brandish a weapon or make any intimidating movements. He left the aisle free so that respondents could exit. He spoke to passengers one by one and in a polite, quiet voice. Nothing he said would sug-gest to a reasonable person that he or she was barred from leaving the bus or otherwise terminating the encounter.

There were ample grounds for the District Court to conclude that "everything that took place between Officer Lang and [respondents] sug-gests that it was cooperative" and that there "was nothing coercive [or] confrontational" about the en-counter. There was no application of force, no intimidating movement, no overwhelming show of force, no brandishing of weapons, no block-ing of exits, no threat, no com-mand, not even an authoritative tone of voice. It is beyond question that had this encounter occurred on the street, it would be constitution-al. The fact that an encounter takes place on a bus does not on its own transform standard police question-ing of citizens into an illegal sei-zure. Indeed, because many fellow passengers are present to witness officers' conduct, a reasonable per-son may feel even more secure in his or her decision not to cooperate with police on a bus than in other circumstances.

Respondents make much of the fact that Officer Lang displayed his badge. In *Florida v. Rodriguez,* 469 U.S., at 5–6, however, the Court rejected the claim that the defen-dant was seized when an officer ap-proached him in an airport, showed him his badge, and asked him to answer some questions. Likewise, in *INS v. Delgado,* 466 U.S. 210, 212–213 (1984), the Court held that INS agents' wearing badges and ques-tioning workers in a factory did not constitute a seizure. And while nei-ther Lang nor his colleagues were in uniform or visibly armed, those fac-tors should have little weight in the analysis. Officers are often required to wear uniforms and in many cir-cumstances this is cause for assur-ance, not discomfort. Much the same can be said for wearing side-arms. That most law enforcement officers are armed is a fact well known to the public. The presence of a holstered firearm thus is unlike-ly to contribute to the coerciveness of the encounter absent active brandishing of the weapon.

Officer Hoover's position at the front of the bus also does not tip the scale in respondents' favor. Hoover did nothing to intimidate passengers, and he said nothing to suggest that people could not exit and indeed he left the aisle clear. In *Delgado,* the Court determined there was no seizure even though several uniformed INS officers were stationed near the exits of the facto-ry. The Court noted: "The presence of agents by the exits posed no reasonable threat of detention to these workers, ... the mere possibility that they would be questioned if they sought to leave the buildings should not have resulted in any reasonable apprehension by any of them that they would be seized or detained in any meaningful way."

Finally, the fact that in Officer Lang's experience only a few passengers have refused to cooperate does not suggest that a reasonable person would not feel free to terminate the bus encounter. In Lang's experience it was common for passengers to leave the bus for a cigarette or a snack while the officers were questioning passengers. And of more importance, bus passengers answer officers' questions and otherwise cooperate not because of coercion but because the passengers know that their participation enhances their own safety and the safety of those around them. * * *

Drayton contends that even if Brown's cooperation with the officers was consensual, Drayton was seized because no reasonable person would feel free to terminate the encounter with the officers after Brown had been arrested. The Court of Appeals did not address this claim; and in any event the argument fails. The arrest of one person does not mean that everyone around him has been seized by police. If anything, Brown's arrest should have put Drayton on notice of the consequences of continuing the encounter by answering the officers' questions. Even after arresting Brown, Lang addressed Drayton in a polite manner and provided him with no indication that he was required to answer Lang's questions.

We turn now from the question whether respondents were seized to whether they were subjected to an unreasonable search, *i.e.*, whether their consent to the suspicionless search was involuntary. In circumstances such as these, where the question of voluntariness pervades both the search and seizure inquiries, the respective analyses turn on very similar facts. And, as the facts above suggest, respondents' consent to the search of their luggage and their persons was voluntary. Nothing Officer Lang said indicated a command to consent to the search. Rather, when respondents informed Lang that they had a bag on the bus, he asked for their permission to check it. And when Lang requested to search Brown and Drayton's persons, he asked first if they objected, thus indicating to a reasonable person that he or she was free to refuse. Even after arresting Brown, Lang provided Drayton with no indication that he was required to consent to a search. To the contrary, Lang asked for Drayton's permission to search him ("Mind if I check you?"), and Drayton agreed.

The Court has rejected in specific terms the suggestion that police officers must always inform citizens of their right to refuse when seeking permission to conduct a warrantless consent search. See, *e.g., Ohio v. Robinette,* 519 U.S. 33, 39–40 (1996); *Schneckloth v. Bustamonte,* 412 U.S. 218, 227 (1973). "While knowledge of the right to refuse consent is one factor to be taken into account, the government need not establish such knowledge as the *sine qua non* of an effective consent." Nor do this Court's decisions suggest that even though there are no *per se* rules, a presumption of invalidity attaches if a citizen consented without explicit notification that he or she was free to refuse to cooperate. Instead, the Court has repeated that the totality of the circumstances must control, without giving extra weight to the absence of this type of warning. Although Officer Lang did not inform respondents of their right to refuse the search, he did request permission to search, and the totality of the circumstances indicates that their consent was voluntary, so the searches were reasonable.

In a society based on law, the concept of agreement and consent should be given a weight and dignity of its own. Police officers act in full accord with the law when they ask citizens for consent. It reinforces the rule of law for the citizen to advise the police of his or her wishes and for the police to act in reliance on that understanding. When this exchange takes place, it dispels inferences of coercion.

We need not ask the alternative question whether, after the arrest of Brown, there were grounds for a *Terry* stop and frisk of Drayton, though this may have been the case. It was evident that Drayton and Brown were traveling together—Officer Lang observed the pair reboarding the bus together; they were each dressed in heavy, baggy clothes that were ill-suited for the day's warm temperatures; they were seated together on the bus; and they each claimed responsibility for the single piece of green carry-on luggage. Once Lang had identified Brown as carrying what he believed to be narcotics, he may have had reasonable suspicion to conduct a *Terry* stop and frisk on Drayton as well. That question, however, has

not been presented to us. The fact the officers may have had reasonable suspicion does not prevent them from relying on a citizen's consent to the search. It would be a paradox, and one most puzzling to law enforcement officials and courts alike, were we to say, after holding that Brown's consent was voluntary, that Drayton's consent was ineffectual simply because the police at that point had more compelling grounds to detain him. After taking Brown into custody, the officers were entitled to continue to proceed on the basis of consent and to ask for Drayton's cooperation.

The judgment of the Court of Appeals is reversed, and the case is remanded for further proceedings consistent with this opinion.

JUSTICE SOUTER, with whom JUSTICE STEVENS and JUSTICE GINSBURG join, dissenting.

Anyone who travels by air today submits to searches of the person and luggage as a condition of boarding the aircraft. It is universally accepted that such intrusions are necessary to hedge against risks that, nowadays, even small children understand. The commonplace precautions of air travel have not, thus far, been justified for ground transportation, however, and no such conditions have been placed on passengers getting on trains or buses. There is therefore an air of unreality about the Court's explanation that bus passengers consent to searches of their luggage to "enhanc[e] their own safety and the safety of those around them." * * *

Florida v. Bostick, 501 U.S. 429 (1991), established the framework for determining whether the bus passengers were seized in the constitutional sense. In that case, we rejected the position that police questioning of bus passengers was a *per se* seizure, and held instead that the issue of seizure was to be resolved under an objective test considering all circumstances: whether a reasonable passenger would have felt "free to decline the officers' requests or otherwise terminate the encounter." * * *

Before applying the standard in this case, it may be worth getting some perspective from different sets of facts. A perfect example of police conduct that supports no colorable claim of seizure is the act of an officer who simply goes up to a pedestrian on the street and asks him a question. A pair of officers questioning a pedestrian, without more, would presumably support the same conclusion. Now consider three officers, one of whom stands behind the pedestrian, another at his side toward the open sidewalk, with the third addressing questions to the pedestrian a foot or two from his face. Finally, consider the same scene in a narrow alley. On such barebones facts, one may not be able to say a seizure occurred, even in the last case, but one can say without qualification that the atmosphere of the encounters differed significantly from the first to the last examples. * * * The police not only carry legitimate authority but also exercise power free from immediate check, and when the attention of several officers is brought to bear on one civilian the imbalance of immediate power is unmistakable. We all understand this, as well as we understand that a display of power * * * may overbear a normal person's ability to act freely, even in the absence of explicit commands

or the formalities of detention. As common as this understanding is, however, there is little sign of it in the Court's opinion. * * *

* * * [F]or reasons unexplained, the driver with the tickets entitling the passengers to travel had yielded his custody of the bus and its seated travelers to three police officers, whose authority apparently superseded the driver's own. The officers took control of the entire passenger compartment, one stationed at the door keeping surveillance of all the occupants, the others working forward from the back. With one officer right behind him and the other one forward, a third officer accosted each passenger at quarters extremely close and so cramped that as many as half the passengers could not even have stood to face the speaker. None was asked whether he was willing to converse with the police or to take part in the enquiry. Instead the officer said the police were "conducting bus interdiction," in the course of which they "would like . . . cooperation." The reasonable inference was that the "interdiction" was not a consensual exercise, but one the police would carry out whatever the circumstances; that they would prefer "cooperation" but would not let the lack of it stand in their way. There was no contrary indication that day, since no passenger had refused the cooperation requested, and there was no reason for any passenger to believe that the driver would return and the trip resume until the police were satisfied. The scene was set and an atmosphere of obligatory participation was established by this introduction. Later requests to search prefaced with "Do you mind . . ." would naturally have been un-

derstood in the terms with which the encounter began.

It is very hard to imagine that either Brown or Drayton would have believed that he stood to lose nothing if he refused to cooperate with the police, or that he had any free choice to ignore the police altogether. No reasonable passenger could have believed that, only an uncomprehending one. It is neither here nor there that the interdiction was conducted by three officers, not one, as a safety precaution. The fact was that there were three, and when Brown and Drayton were called upon to respond, each one was presumably conscious of an officer in front watching, one at his side questioning him, and one behind for cover, in case he became unruly, perhaps, or "cooperation" was not forthcoming. The situation is much like the one in the alley, with civilians in close quarters, unable to move effectively, being told their cooperation is expected. While I am not prepared to say that no bus interrogation and search can pass the *Bostick* test without a warning that passengers are free to say no, the facts here surely required more from the officers than a quiet tone of voice. A police officer who is certain to get his way has no need to shout.

* * *

3. *Grounds for a Stop: Reasonable Suspicion*

a.   *Source of Information*

Anonymous Tips Concerning Gun Possession

Page 220.   At the end of the discussion of *Gibson*, add the following case:

The Court rejected the analysis in *Gibson*, which distinguished gun tips from other tips, in the following case.

FLORIDA v. J.L.

Supreme Court of the United States, 2000.
529 U.S. 266.

JUSTICE GINSBURG delivered the opinion of the Court.

The question presented in this case is whether an anonymous tip that a person is carrying a gun is, without more, sufficient to justify a police officer's stop and frisk of that person. We hold that it is not.

I

On October 13, 1995, an anonymous caller reported to the Miami–Dade Police that a young black male standing at a particular bus stop and wearing a plaid shirt was carrying a gun. So far as the record reveals, there is no audio recording of the tip, and nothing is known about the informant. Sometime after the police received the tip—the record does not say how long—two officers were instructed to respond. They arrived at the bus stop about six minutes later and saw three black males "just hanging out [there]." One of the three, respondent J.L., was wearing a plaid shirt. Apart from the tip, the officers had no reason to suspect any of the three of illegal conduct. The officers did not see a firearm, and J.L. made no threatening or otherwise unusual movements. One of the officers approached J.L., told him to put his hands up on the bus stop, frisked him, and seized a gun from J.L.'s pocket. The second officer frisked the other two individuals, against whom no allegations had been made, and found nothing. J.L., who was at the time of the frisk 10 days shy of his 16th birthday, was charged under state law with carrying a concealed firearm without a license and possessing a firearm while under the age of 18. He moved to suppress the gun as the fruit of an unlawful search, and the trial court granted his motion. The intermediate appellate court reversed, but the Supreme Court of Florida quashed that decision and held the search invalid under the Fourth Amendment.

Anonymous tips, the Florida Supreme Court stated, are generally less reliable than tips from known informants and can form the basis for reasonable suspicion only if accompanied by specific indicia of reliability, for example, the correct forecast of a subject's "not easily predicted" movements. The tip leading to the frisk of J.L., the court observed, provided no such predictions, nor did it contain any other qualifying indicia of reliability. Two justices dissented. The safety of the police and the public, they maintained, justifies a "firearm exception" to the general rule barring investigatory stops and frisks on the basis of bare-boned anonymous tips.

* * * We granted certiorari, and now affirm the judgment of the Florida Supreme Court.

II

* * *

In the instant case, the officers' suspicion that J.L. was carrying a weapon arose not from any observations of their own but solely from a call made from an unknown location by an unknown caller. Unlike a tip from a known informant whose reputation can be assessed and who can be held responsible if her allegations turn out to be fabricated, see Adams v. Williams, 407 U.S. 143 (1972), "an anonymous tip alone seldom demonstrates the informant's basis of knowledge or veracity," Alabama v. White, 496 U.S., at 329. As we have recognized, however, there are situations in which an anonymous tip, suitably corroborated, exhibits "sufficient indicia of reliability to provide reasonable suspicion to make the investigatory stop." The question we here confront is whether the tip pointing to J.L. had those indicia of reliability.

In *White*, the police received an anonymous tip asserting that a woman was carrying cocaine and predicting that she would leave an apartment building at a specified time, get into a car matching a particular description, and drive to a named motel. Standing alone, the tip would not have justified a *Terry* stop. Only after police observation showed that the informant had accurately predicted the woman's movements, we explained, did it become reasonable to think the tipster had inside knowledge about the suspect and therefore to credit his assertion about the cocaine. Although the Court held that the suspicion in *White* became reasonable after police surveillance, we regarded the case as borderline. Knowledge about a person's future movements indicates some familiarity with that person's affairs, but having such knowledge does not necessarily imply that the informant knows, in particular, whether that person is carrying hidden contraband. We accordingly classified *White* as a "close case."

The tip in the instant case lacked the moderate indicia of reliability present in *White* and essential to the Court's decision in that case. The anonymous call concerning J.L. provided no predictive information and therefore left the police without means to test the informant's knowledge or credibility. That the allegation about the gun turned out to be correct does not suggest that the officers, prior to the frisks, had a reasonable basis for suspecting J.L. of engaging in unlawful conduct: The reasonableness of official suspicion must be measured by what the officers knew before they conducted their search. All the police had to go on in this case was the bare report of an unknown, unaccountable informant who neither explained how he knew about the gun nor supplied any basis for believing he had inside information about J.L. If *White* was a close case on the reliability of anonymous tips, this one surely falls on the other side of the line.

Florida contends that the tip was reliable because its description of the suspect's visible attributes proved accurate: There really was a young black male wearing a plaid shirt at the bus stop. The United States as amicus curiae makes a similar argument, proposing that a stop and frisk should be permitted "when (1) an anonymous tip provides a description of a particular person at a particular location illegally carrying a concealed firearm, (2) police promptly verify the pertinent details of the tip except the existence of the firearm, and (3) there are no factors that cast doubt on the reliability of the tip." * * * These contentions misapprehend the reliability needed for a tip to justify a *Terry* stop.

An accurate description of a subject's readily observable location and appearance is of course reliable in this limited sense: It will help the police correctly identify the person whom the tipster means to accuse. Such a tip, however, does not show that the tipster has knowledge of concealed criminal activity. The reasonable suspicion here at issue requires that a tip be reliable in its assertion of illegality, not just in its tendency to identify a determinate person.

A second major argument advanced by Florida and the United States as amicus is, in essence, that the standard *Terry* analysis should be modified to license a "firearm exception." Under such an exception, a tip alleging an illegal gun would justify a stop and frisk even if the accusation would fail standard pre-search reliability testing. We decline to adopt this position.

Firearms are dangerous, and extraordinary dangers sometimes justify unusual precautions. Our decisions recognize the serious threat that armed criminals pose to public safety; *Terry's* rule, which permits protective police searches on the basis of reasonable suspicion rather than demanding that officers meet the higher standard of probable cause, responds to this very concern. But an automatic firearm exception to our established reliability analysis would rove too far. Such an exception would enable any person seeking to harass another to set in motion an intrusive, embarrassing police search of the targeted person simply by placing an anonymous call falsely reporting the target's unlawful carriage of a gun. Nor could one securely confine such an exception to allegations involving firearms. Several Courts of Appeals have held it per se foreseeable for people carrying significant amounts of illegal drugs to be carrying guns as well. If police officers may properly conduct *Terry* frisks on the basis of bare-boned tips about guns, it would be reasonable to maintain under the above-cited decisions that the police should similarly have discretion to frisk based on bare-boned tips about narcotics. As we clarified when we made indicia of reliability critical in *Adams* and *White*, the Fourth Amendment is not so easily satisfied. Cf. Richards v. Wisconsin, 520 U.S. 385 (1997) (rejecting a per se exception to the "knock and announce" rule for narcotics cases partly because "the reasons for creating an exception in one category [of Fourth Amendment cases] can, relatively easily, be applied to others," thus allowing the exception to swallow the rule).

The facts of this case do not require us to speculate about the circumstances under which the danger alleged in an anonymous tip might be so great as to justify a search even without a showing of reliability. We do not say, for example, that a report of a person carrying a bomb need bear the indicia of reliability we demand for a report of a person carrying a firearm before the police can constitutionally conduct

a frisk. Nor do we hold that public safety officials in quarters where the reasonable expectation of Fourth Amendment privacy is diminished, such as airports, see Florida v. Rodriguez, 469 U.S. 1 (1984) (per curiam), and schools, see New Jersey v. T.L.O., 469 U.S. 325 (1985), cannot conduct protective searches on the basis of information insufficient to justify searches elsewhere.

Finally, the requirement that an anonymous tip bear standard indicia of reliability in order to justify a stop in no way diminishes a police officer's prerogative, in accord with *Terry*, to conduct a protective search of a person who has already been legitimately stopped. We speak in today's decision only of cases in which the officer's authority to make the initial stop is at issue. In that context, we hold that an anonymous tip lacking indicia of reliability of the kind contemplated in *Adams* and *White* does not justify a stop and frisk whenever and however it alleges the illegal possession of a firearm.

The judgment of the Florida Supreme Court is affirmed.

JUSTICE KENNEDY, with whom THE CHIEF JUSTICE joins, concurring.

On the record created at the suppression hearing, the Court's decision is correct. The Court says all that is necessary to resolve this case, and I join the opinion in all respects. It might be noted, however, that there are many indicia of reliability respecting anonymous tips that we have yet to explore in our cases.

When a police officer testifies that a suspect aroused the officer's suspicion, and so justifies a stop and frisk, the courts can weigh the officer's credibility and admit evidence seized pursuant to the frisk even if no one, aside from the officer and defendant themselves, was present or observed the seizure. An anony- mous telephone tip without more is different, however; for even if the officer's testimony about receipt of the tip is found credible, there is a second layer of inquiry respecting the reliability of the informant that cannot be pursued. If the telephone call is truly anonymous, the infor- mant has not placed his credibility at risk and can lie with impunity. The reviewing court cannot judge the credibility of the informant and the risk of fabrication becomes un- acceptable.

On this record, then, the Court is correct in holding that the tele- phone tip did not justify the arrest- ing officer's immediate stop and frisk of respondent. There was testi- mony that an anonymous tip came in by a telephone call and nothing more. The record does not show whether some notation or other documentation of the call was made either by a voice recording or trac- ing the call to a telephone number. The prosecution recounted just the tip itself and the later verification of the presence of the three young men in the circumstances the Court describes.

It seems appropriate to observe that a tip might be anonymous in some sense yet have certain other features, either supporting reliabili- ty or narrowing the likely class of informants, so that the tip does pro- vide the lawful basis for some po- lice action. One such feature, as the Court recognizes, is that the tip pre- dicts future conduct of the alleged criminal. There may be others. For example, if an unnamed caller with a voice which sounds the same each time tells police on two successive nights about criminal activity which in fact occurs each night, a similar call on the third night ought not be treated automatically like the tip in the case now before us. In the in- stance supposed, there would be a plausible argument that experience cures some of the uncertainty sur- rounding the anonymity, justifying a proportionate police response. In today's case, however, the State provides us with no data about the reliability of anonymous tips. Nor do we know whether the dispatcher or arresting officer had any objec- tive reason to believe that this tip had some particular indicia of relia- bility.

If an informant places his ano- nymity at risk, a court can consider this factor in weighing the reliability of the tip. An instance where a tip might be considered anonymous but nevertheless sufficiently reliable to justify a proportionate police re- sponse may be when an unnamed person driving a car the police offi- cer later describes stops for a mo- ment and, face to face, informs the police that criminal activity is occur- ring. This too seems to be different from the tip in the present case. See United States v. Sierra–Hernandez, 581 F.2d 760 (C.A.9 1978).

Instant caller identification is widely available to police, and, if anonymous tips are proving unrelia- ble and distracting to police, squad cars can be sent within seconds to the location of the telephone used by the informant. Voice recording of telephone tips might, in appropri- ate cases, be used by police to lo- cate the caller. It is unlawful to make false reports to the police, and the ability of the police to trace the identity of anonymous telephone informants may be a factor which lends reliability to what, years earlier, might have been considered unreliable anonymous tips.

These matters, of course, must await discussion in other cases, where the issues are presented by the record.

---

b. *Quantum of Suspicion*

Page 229. At the end of the section "Examples of Reasonable Suspicion" add the following case:

UNITED STATES v. ARVIZU

Supreme Court of the United States, 2002.
534 U.S. 266.

CHIEF JUSTICE REHNQUIST **delivered the opinion of the Court**.

Respondent Ralph Arvizu was stopped by a border patrol agent while driving on an unpaved road in a remote area of southeastern Arizona. A search of his vehicle turned up more than 100 pounds of marijuana. The District Court for the District of Arizona denied respondent's motion to suppress, but the Court of Appeals for the Ninth Circuit reversed. In the course of its opinion, it categorized certain factors relied upon by the District Court as simply out of bounds in deciding whether there was "reasonable suspicion" for the stop. We hold that the Court of Appeals' methodology was contrary to our prior decisions and that it reached the wrong result in this case.

On an afternoon in January 1998, Agent Clinton Stoddard was working at a border patrol checkpoint along U.S. Highway 191 approximately 30 miles north of Douglas, Arizona. Douglas has a population of about 13,000 and is situated on the United States–Mexico border in the southeastern part of the State. Only two highways lead north from Douglas. See App. 157. Highway 191 leads north to Interstate 10, which passes through Tucson and Phoenix. State Highway 80 heads northeast through less populated areas toward New Mexico, skirting south and east of the portion of the Coronado National Forest that lies approximately 20 miles northeast of Douglas.

The checkpoint is located at the intersection of 191 and Rucker Canyon Road, an unpaved east-west road that connects 191 and the Coronado National Forest. When the checkpoint is operational, border patrol agents stop the traffic on 191 as part of a coordinated effort to stem the flow of illegal immigration and smuggling across the international border. Agents use roving patrols to apprehend smugglers trying to circumvent the checkpoint by taking the backroads, including those roads through the sparsely populated area between Douglas and the national forest. Magnetic sensors, or "intrusion devices," facilitate agents' efforts in patrolling these areas. Directionally sensitive, the sensors signal the passage of traffic that would be consistent with smuggling activities.

Sensors are located along the only other northbound road from Douglas besides Highways 191 and 80: Leslie Canyon Road. Leslie Canyon Road runs roughly parallel to 191, about halfway between 191 and the border of the Coronado National Forest, and ends when it intersects Rucker Canyon Road. It is unpaved beyond the 10–mile stretch leading out of Douglas and is very rarely traveled except for use by local ranchers and forest service personnel. Smugglers commonly try to avoid the 191 checkpoint by heading west on Rucker Canyon Road from Leslie Canyon Road and thence to Kuykendall Cutoff Road, a primitive dirt road that leads north approximately 12 miles east of 191. From there, they can gain access to Tucson and Phoenix.

Around 2:15 p.m., Stoddard received a report via Douglas radio that a Leslie Canyon Road sensor had triggered .. This was significant to Stoddard for two reasons. First, it suggested to him that a vehicle might be trying to circumvent the checkpoint. Second, the timing coincided with the point when agents begin heading back to the checkpoint for a shift change, which leaves the area unpatrolled. Stoddard knew that alien smugglers did extensive scouting and seemed to be most active when agents were en route back to the checkpoint. Another border patrol agent told Stoddard that the same sensor had gone off several weeks before and that he had apprehended a minivan using the same route and witnessed the occupants throwing bundles of marijuana out the door.

Stoddard drove eastbound on Rucker Canyon Road to investigate. As he did so, he received another radio report of sensor activity. It indicated that the vehicle that had triggered the first sensor was heading westbound on Rucker Canyon Road. He continued east, passing Kuykendall Cutoff Road. He saw the dust trail of an approaching vehicle about a half mile away. Stoddard had not seen any other vehicles and, based on the timing, believed that this was the one that had tripped the sensors. He pulled off to the side of the road at a slight slant so he could get a good look at the oncoming vehicle as it passed by.

It was a minivan, a type of automobile that Stoddard knew smugglers used. As it approached, it slowed dramatically, from about 50–55 to 25–30 miles per hour. He saw five occupants inside. An adult man was driving, an adult woman sat in the front passenger seat, and three children were in the back .. The driver appeared stiff and his posture very rigid. He did not look at Stoddard and seemed to be trying to pretend that Stoddard was not there. Stoddard thought this suspicious because in his experience on patrol most persons look over and see what is going on, and in that area most drivers give border patrol agents a friendly wave. Stoddard noticed that the knees of the two children sitting in the very back seat were unusually high, as if their feet were propped up on some cargo on the floor.

At that point, Stoddard decided to get a closer look, so he began to follow the vehicle as it continued westbound on Rucker Canyon Road toward Kuykendall Cutoff Road.

Shortly thereafter, all of the children, though still facing forward, put their hands up at the same time and began to wave at Stoddard in an abnormal pattern. It looked to Stoddard as if the children were being instructed. Their odd waving continued on and off for about four to five minutes.

Several hundred feet before the Kuykendall Cutoff Road intersection, the driver signaled that he would turn. At one point, the driver turned the signal off, but just as he approached the intersection he put it back on and abruptly turned north onto Kuykendall. The turn was significant to Stoddard because it was made at the last place that would have allowed the minivan to avoid the checkpoint. Also, Kuykendall, though passable by a sedan or van, is rougher than either Rucker Canyon or Leslie Canyon roads, and the normal traffic is four-wheel-drive vehicles. Stoddard did not recognize the minivan as part of the local traffic agents encounter on patrol and he did not think it likely that the minivan was going to or coming from a picnic outing. He was not aware of any picnic grounds on Turkey Creek, which could be reached by following Kuykendall Cutoff all the way up. He knew of picnic grounds and a Boy Scout camp east of the intersection of Rucker Canyon and Leslie Canyon roads, but the minivan had turned west at that intersection. And he had never seen anyone picnicking or sightseeing near where the first sensor went off.

Stoddard radioed for a registration check and learned that the minivan was registered to an address in Douglas that was four blocks north of the border in an area notorious for alien and narcotics smuggling. After receiving the information, Stoddard decided to make a vehicle stop. He approached the driver and learned that his name was Ralph Arvizu. Stoddard asked if respondent would mind if he looked inside and searched the vehicle. Respondent agreed, and Stoddard discovered marijuana in a black duffel bag under the feet of the two children in the back seat. Another bag containing marijuana was behind the rear seat. In all, the van contained 128.85 pounds of marijuana, worth an estimated $99,080.

Respondent was charged with possession with intent to distribute marijuana in violation of 21 U.S.C. § 841(a)(1) (1994 ed.). He moved to suppress the marijuana, arguing among other things that Stoddard did not have reasonable suspicion to stop the vehicle as required by the Fourth Amendment. After holding a hearing where Stoddard and respondent testified, the District Court for the District of Arizona ruled otherwise. It pointed to a number of the facts described above and noted particularly that any recreational areas north of Rucker Canyon would have been accessible from Douglas via 191 and another paved road, making it unnecessary to take a 40–to–50–mile trip on dirt roads.

The Court of Appeals for the Ninth Circuit reversed. In its view, fact-specific weighing of circumstances or other multifactor tests introduced "a troubling degree of uncertainty and unpredictability" into the Fourth Amendment analysis. It therefore "attempt[ed] ... to describe and clearly delimit the extent to which certain factors may be considered by law enforcement officers in making stops such as the stop involv[ing]" respondent. After characterizing the District Court's analysis as relying on a list of 10 factors, the Court of Appeals proceeded to examine each in turn. It held that 7 of the factors, including respondent's slowing down, his failure to acknowledge Stoddard, the raised position of the children's knees, and their odd waving carried little or no weight in the reasonable-suspicion calculus. The remaining factors—the road's use by smugglers, the temporal proximity between respondent's trip and the agents' shift change, and the use of minivans by smugglers—were not enough to render the stop permissible. We granted certiorari to review the decision of the Court of Appeals because of its importance to the enforcement of federal drug and immigration laws.

The Fourth Amendment prohibits "unreasonable searches and seizures" by the Government, and its protections extend to brief investigatory stops of persons or vehicles that fall short of traditional arrest. Terry v. Ohio, 392 U.S. 1, 9 (1968). Because the "balance between the public interest and the individual's right to personal security," United States v. Brignoni–Ponce, 422 U.S. 873, 878 (1975), tilts in favor of a standard less than probable cause in such cases, the Fourth Amendment is satisfied if the officer's action is supported by reasonable suspicion to believe that criminal activity " 'may be afoot,' " United States v. Sokolow, 490 U.S. 1, 7 (1989).

When discussing how reviewing courts should make reasonable-sus-

picion determinations, we have said repeatedly that they must look at the "totality of the circumstances" of each case to see whether the detaining officer has a "particularized and objective basis" for suspecting legal wrongdoing. This process allows officers to draw on their own experience and specialized training to make inferences from and deductions about the cumulative information available to them that "might well elude an untrained person." See also Ornelas v. United States, 517 U.S. 690, 699 (1996) (reviewing court must give "due weight" to factual inferences drawn by resident judges and local law enforcement officers). Although an officer's reliance on a mere "hunch" is insufficient to justify a stop, the likelihood of criminal activity need not rise to the level required for probable cause, and it falls considerably short of satisfying a preponderance of the evidence standard.

Our cases have recognized that the concept of reasonable suspicion is somewhat abstract. But we have deliberately avoided reducing it to " 'a neat set of legal rules,' " *Ornelas, supra,* at 695–696 (quoting Illinois v. Gates, 462 U.S. 213, 232 (1983)). In *Sokolow,* for example, we rejected a holding by the Court of Appeals that distinguished between evidence of ongoing criminal behavior and probabilistic evidence because it "create[d] unnecessary difficulty in dealing with one of the relatively simple concepts embodied in the Fourth Amendment."

We think that the approach taken by the Court of Appeals here departs sharply from the teachings of these cases. The court's evaluation and rejection of seven of the listed factors in isolation from each other does not take into account the "totality of the circumstances," as our cases have understood that phrase. The court appeared to believe that each observation by Stoddard that was by itself readily susceptible to an innocent explanation was entitled to "no weight." *Terry*, however, precludes this sort of divide-and-conquer analysis. The officer in *Terry* observed the petitioner and his companions repeatedly walk back and forth, look into a store window, and confer with one another. Although each of the series of acts was "perhaps innocent in itself," we held that, taken together, they "warranted further investigation." See also *Sokolow*, supra, at 9 (holding that factors which by themselves were "quite consistent with innocent travel" collectively amounted to reasonable suspicion).

The Court of Appeals' view that it was necessary to "clearly delimit" an officer's consideration of certain factors to reduce "troubling . . . uncertainty," also runs counter to our cases and underestimates the usefulness of the reasonable-suspicion standard in guiding officers in the field. In Ornelas v. United States, we held that the standard for appellate review of reasonable-suspicion determinations should be de novo, rather than for "abuse of discretion." There, we reasoned that *de novo* review would prevent the affirmance of opposite decisions on identical facts from different judicial districts in the same circuit, which would have been possible under the latter standard, and would allow appellate courts to clarify the legal principles. Other benefits of the approach, we said, were its tendency

to unify precedent and greater capacity to provide law enforcement officers with the tools to reach correct determinations beforehand: Even if in many instances the factual "mosaic" analyzed for a reasonable-suspicion determination would preclude one case from squarely controlling another, "two decisions when viewed together may usefully add to the body of law on the subject."

But the Court of Appeals' approach would go considerably beyond the reasoning of *Ornelas* and seriously undercut the "totality of the circumstances" principle which governs the existence vel non of "reasonable suspicion." Take, for example, the court's positions that respondent's deceleration could not be considered because "slowing down after spotting a law enforcement vehicle is an entirely normal response that is in no way indicative of criminal activity" and that his failure to acknowledge Stoddard's presence provided no support because there were "no 'special circumstances' rendering 'innocent avoidance . . . improbable.' "We think it quite reasonable that a driver's slowing down, stiffening of posture, and failure to acknowledge a sighted law enforcement officer might well be unremarkable in one instance (such as a busy San Francisco highway) while quite unusual in another (such as a remote portion of rural southeastern Arizona). Stoddard was entitled to make an assessment of the situation in light of his specialized training and familiarity with the customs of the area's inhabitants. To the extent that a totality of the circumstances approach may render appellate review less circumscribed by precedent than otherwise, it is the nature of the totality rule.

In another instance, the Court of Appeals chose to dismiss entirely the children's waving on grounds that odd conduct by children was all too common to be probative in a particular case. See 232 F.3d, at 1249 ("If every odd act engaged in by one's children . . . could contribute to a finding of reasonable suspicion, the vast majority of American parents might be stopped regularly within a block of their homes"). Yet this case did not involve simply any odd act by children. At the suppression hearing, Stoddard testified about the children's waving several times, and the record suggests that he physically demonstrated it as well. The District Court Judge, who saw and heard Stoddard, then characterized the waving as "methodical," "mechanical," "abnormal," and "certainly . . . a fact that is odd and would lead a reasonable officer to wonder why they are doing this." Though the issue of this case does not turn on the children's idiosyncratic actions, the Court of Appeals should not have casually rejected this factor in light of the District Court's superior access to the evidence and the well-recognized inability of reviewing courts to reconstruct what happened in the courtroom.

Having considered the totality of the circumstances and given due weight to the factual inferences drawn by the law enforcement officer and District Court Judge, we hold that Stoddard had reasonable suspicion to believe that respondent was engaged in illegal activity. It was reasonable for Stoddard to infer from his observations, his reg-istration check, and his experience as a border patrol agent that respondent had set out from Douglas along a little-traveled route used by smugglers to avoid the 191 checkpoint. Stoddard's knowledge further supported a commonsense inference that respondent intended to pass through the area at a time when officers would be leaving their backroads patrols to change shifts. The likelihood that respondent and his family were on a picnic outing was diminished by the fact that the minivan had turned away from the known recreational areas accessible to the east on Rucker Canyon Road. Corroborating this inference was the fact that recreational areas farther to the north would have been easier to reach by taking 191, as opposed to the 40–to–50–mile trip on unpaved and primitive roads. The children's elevated knees suggested the existence of concealed cargo in the passenger compartment. Finally, for the reasons we have given, Stoddard's assessment of respondent's reactions upon seeing him and the children's mechanical-like waving, which continued for a full four to five minutes, were entitled to some weight.

Respondent argues that we must rule in his favor because the facts suggested a family in a minivan on a holiday outing. A determination that reasonable suspicion exists, however, need not rule out the possibility of innocent conduct. See Illinois v. Wardlow, 528 U.S. 119, 125 (2000) (that flight from police is not necessarily indicative of ongoing criminal activity does not establish Fourth Amendment violation). Undoubtedly, each of these factors alone is susceptible to innocent explanation, and some factors are more probative than others. Taken together, we believe they sufficed to form a particularized and objective basis for Stoddard's stopping the vehicle, making the stop reasonable within the meaning of the Fourth Amendment.

The judgment of the Court of Appeals is therefore reversed, and the case is remanded for further proceedings consistent with this opinion.

It is so ordered.

[The concurring opinion of Justice Scalia is omitted.]

---

5. Brief and Limited Detentions: The Line Between "Stop" and "Arrest"

f. Interrogations and Fingerprinting Pursuant to a Terry Stop

The Court in Kaupp v. Texas, 123 S.Ct. 1843 (2003) (per curiam) confirmed that a forced transportation and interrogation of a suspect constitutes an arrest for which probable cause is required. Police officers suspected Kaupp, an adolescent, of involvement in a murder, but did not have probable cause to arrest him. The officers entered Kaupp's house at 3 a.m., went to his bedroom, woke him up, placed him in handcuffs, and transported him in a patrol car while he was still in his underwear. The patrol car stopped for 5 to 10 minutes at the site where the victim's body had been found, and then went on to the sheriff's headquarters, where police removed Kaupp's handcuffs, gave him *Miranda* warnings, and told him that the victim's brother had confessed to the crime and implicated him as an accomplice. Kaupp then admitted to some part in the crime.

The state courts held that Kaupp had not been arrested, because he answered "okay" when he was told in his bedroom that he needed to go with the officers. The state courts brushed off the officers' use of handcuffs as "routine" practice of the police department. The Court reversed, finding it clear that Kaupp had been arrested without probable cause. The Court reasoned as follows:

> Although certain seizures may be justified on something less than probable cause, see, *e.g.*, Terry v. Ohio, 392 U.S. 1 (1968), we have never "sustained against Fourth Amendment challenge the involuntary removal of a suspect from his home to a police station and his detention there for investigative purposes . . . absent probable cause or judicial authorization." Hayes v. Florida, 470 U.S. 811, 815 (1985). Such involuntary transport to a police station for questioning is "sufficiently like arrest to invoke the traditional rule that arrests may constitutionally be made only on probable cause." *Hayes, supra*, at 816.

> The state does not claim to have had probable cause here, and a straightforward application of the test just mentioned shows beyond cavil that Kaupp was arrested within the meaning of the Fourth Amendment * * * . A 17–year-old boy was awakened in his bedroom

at three in the morning by at least three police officers, one of whom stated "we need to go and talk." He was taken out in handcuffs, without shoes, dressed only in his underwear in January, placed in a patrol car, driven to the scene of a crime and then to the sheriff's offices, where he was taken into an interrogation room and questioned. This evidence points to arrest even more starkly than the facts in Dunaway v. New York, 442 U.S. 200, 212 (1979), where the petitioner "was taken from a neighbor's home to a police car, transported to a police station, and placed in an interrogation room." There we held it clear that the detention was "in important respects indistinguishable from a traditional arrest" and therefore required probable cause or judicial authorization to be legal. *Ibid.* The same is, if anything, even clearer here.

Contrary reasons mentioned by the state courts are no answer to the facts. Kaupp's " 'Okay' " in response to Pinkins's statement [telling Kaupp to come with them to "have a talk"] is no showing of consent under the circumstances. Pinkins offered Kaupp no choice, and a group of police officers rousing an adolescent out of bed in the middle of the night with the words "we need to go and talk" presents no option but "to go." * * * If reasonable doubt were possible on this point, the ensuing events would resolve it: removal from one's house in handcuffs on a January night with nothing on but underwear for a trip to a crime scene on the way to an interview room at law enforcement headquarters. Even "an initially consensual encounter ... can be transformed into a seizure or detention within the meaning of the Fourth Amendment." INS v. Delgado, 466 U.S. 210, 215 (1984); see *Hayes, supra,* at 815–816 ("At some point in the investigative process, police procedures can qualitatively and quantitatively be so intrusive with respect to a suspect's freedom of movement and privacy interests as to trigger the full protection of the Fourth and Fourteenth Amendments"). It cannot seriously be suggested that when the detectives began to question Kaupp, a reasonable person in his situation would have thought he was sitting in the interview room as a matter of choice, free to change his mind and go home to bed.

Nor is it significant, as the state court thought, that the sheriff's department "routinely" transported individuals, including Kaupp on one prior occasion, while handcuffed for safety of the officers, or that Kaupp "did not resist the use of handcuffs or act in a manner consistent with anything other than full cooperation." The test is an objective one, and stressing the officers' motivation of self-protection does not speak to how their actions would reasonably be understood. As for the lack of resistance, failure to struggle with a cohort of deputy sheriffs is not a waiver of Fourth Amendment protection, which does not require the perversity of resisting arrest or assaulting a police officer.

Page 264. **At the end of the section on Stop and Frisk, add the following section:**

8. Application of the Terry Reasonableness Analysis Outside the Stop and Frisk Context

The *Terry* analysis balances the nature of the individual interest at stake in a search and seizure against the interest of the government in investigating and preventing crime. *Terry* applied this reasonableness analysis in the context of the limited intrusion known as stop and frisk. But it is apparent that the balancing analysis could be applied in a wide variety of contexts to allow intrusions on less than probable cause and without a warrant. In the following case, the Court applied the *Terry* analysis to a full-blown search of the residence of a probationer.

UNITED STATES v. KNIGHTS

Supreme Court of the United States, 2001.
534 U.S. 112.

CHIEF JUSTICE REHNQUIST **delivered the opinion of the Court.**

A California court sentenced respondent Mark James Knights to summary probation for a drug offense. The probation order included the following condition: that Knights would "[s]ubmit his ... person, property, place of residence, vehicle, personal effects, to search at anytime, with or without a search warrant, warrant of arrest or reasonable cause by any probation officer or law enforcement officer." Knights signed the probation order, which stated immediately above his signature that "I HAVE RECEIVED A COPY, READ AND UNDERSTAND THE ABOVE TERMS AND CONDITIONS OF PROBATION AND AGREE TO ABIDE BY SAME." In this case, we decide whether a search pursuant to this probation condition, and supported by reasonable suspicion, satisfied the Fourth Amendment.

Three days after Knights was placed on probation, a Pacific Gas & Electric (PG & E) power transformer and adjacent Pacific Bell telecommunications vault near the Napa County Airport were pried open and set on fire, causing an estimated $1.5 million in damage. Brass padlocks had been removed and a gasoline accelerant had been used to ignite the fire. This incident was the latest in more than 30 recent acts of vandalism against PG & E facilities in Napa County. Suspicion for these acts had long focused on Knights and his friend, Steven Simoneau. The incidents began after PG & E had filed a theft-of-services complaint against Knights and discontinued his electrical service for failure to pay his bill. Detective Todd Hancock of the Napa County Sheriff's Department had noticed that the acts of vandalism coincided with Knights's court appearance dates concerning the theft of PG & E services. And just a week before the arson, a sheriff's deputy had stopped Knights and Simoneau near a PG & E gas line and observed pipes and gasoline in Simoneau's pickup truck.

After the PG & E arson, a sheriff's deputy drove by Knights's residence, where he saw Simoneau's truck parked in front. The deputy felt the hood of the truck. It was warm. Detective Hancock decided to set up surveillance of Knights's apartment. At about 3:10 the next morning, Simoneau exited the apartment carrying three cylindrical items. Detective Hancock believed the items were pipe bombs. Simoneau walked across the street to the bank of the Napa River, and Hancock heard three splashes. Simoneau returned without the cylinders and drove away in his truck. Simoneau then stopped in a driveway, parked, and left the area. Detective Hancock entered the driveway and observed a number of suspicious objects in the truck: a Molotov cocktail and explosive materials, a gasoline can, and two brass padlocks that fit the description of those removed from the PG & E transformer vault.

After viewing the objects in Simoneau's truck, Detective Hancock decided to conduct a search of Knights's apartment. Detective Hancock was aware of the search condition in Knights's probation order and thus believed that a warrant was not necessary. The search revealed a detonation cord, ammunition, liquid chemicals, instruction manuals on chemistry and electrical circuitry, bolt cutters, telephone pole-climbing spurs, drug paraphernalia, and a brass padlock stamped "PG & E."

Knights was arrested, and a federal grand jury subsequently indicted him for conspiracy to commit arson, for possession of an unregistered destructive device, and being a felon in possession of ammunition. Knights moved to suppress the evidence obtained during the search of his apartment. The District Court held that Detective Hancock had

"reasonable suspicion" to believe that Knights was involved with incendiary materials. The District Court nonetheless granted the motion to suppress on the ground that the search was for "investigatory" rather than "probationary" purposes. The Court of Appeals for the Ninth Circuit affirmed. The Court of Appeals relied on its earlier decisions holding that the search condition in Knights's probation order "must be seen as limited to probation searches, and must stop short of investigation searches."

The Supreme Court of California has rejected this distinction and upheld searches pursuant to the California probation condition "whether the purpose of the search is to monitor the probationer or to serve some other law enforcement purpose." People v. Woods, 21 Cal.4th 668, 681, 88 Cal.Rptr.2d 88, 981 P.2d 1019, 1027 (1999). We granted certiorari, to assess the constitutionality of searches made pursuant to this common California probation condition.

Certainly nothing in the condition of probation suggests that it was confined to searches bearing upon probationary status and nothing more. The search condition provides that Knights will submit to a search "by any probation officer or law enforcement officer" and does not mention anything about purpose. The question then is whether the Fourth Amendment limits searches pursuant to this probation condition to those with a "probationary" purpose.

Knights argues that this limitation follows from our decision in Griffin v. Wisconsin, 483 U.S. 868 (1987) [see the discussion of *Griffin* in the section on "special needs" searches, page 364 of the Casebook]. In *Griffin*, we upheld a search of a probationer conducted pursuant to a Wisconsin regulation permitting "any probation officer to search a probationer's home without a warrant as long as his supervisor approves and as long as there are 'reasonable grounds' to believe the presence of contraband," The Wisconsin regulation that authorized the search was not an express condition of Griffin's probation; in fact, the regulation was not even promulgated at the time of Griffin's sentence. The regulation applied to all Wisconsin probationers, with no need for a judge to make an individualized determination that the probationer's conviction justified the need for warrantless searches. We held that a State's operation of its probation system presented a "special need" for the "exercise of supervision to assure that [probation] restrictions are in fact observed." That special need for supervision justified the Wisconsin regulation and the search pursuant to the regulation was thus reasonable.

In Knights's view, apparently shared by the Court of Appeals, a warrantless search of a probationer satisfies the Fourth Amendment only if it is just like the search at issue in *Griffin*—i.e., a "special needs" search conducted by a probation officer monitoring whether the probationer is complying with probation restrictions. This dubious logic—that an opinion upholding the constitutionality of a particular search implicitly holds unconstitutional any search that is not like it— runs contrary to *Griffin's* express statement that its "special needs"

holding made it "unnecessary to consider whether" warrantless searches of probationers were otherwise reasonable within the meaning of the Fourth Amendment.

We now consider that question in assessing the constitutionality of the search of Knights's apartment. The Government * * * contends that the search satisfied the Fourth Amendment under the "consent" rationale of cases such as * * * Schneckloth v. Bustamonte, 412 U.S. 218 (1973) [see the discussion of *Bustamonte* in the section on consent searches, page 413 of the Casebook]. In the Government's view, Knights's acceptance of the search condition was voluntary because he had the option of rejecting probation and going to prison instead, which the Government argues is analogous to the voluntary decision defendants often make to waive their right to a trial and accept a plea bargain.

We need not decide whether Knights's acceptance of the search condition constituted consent in the *Schneckloth* sense of a complete waiver of his Fourth Amendment rights, however, because we conclude that the search of Knights was reasonable under our general Fourth Amendment approach of "examining the totality of the circumstances," Ohio v. Robinette, 519 U.S. 33, 39 (1996) [Casebook page 420], with the probation search condition being a salient circumstance.

The touchstone of the Fourth Amendment is reasonableness, and the reasonableness of a search is determined "by assessing, on the one hand, the degree to which it intrudes upon an individual's privacy and, on the other, the degree to which it is needed for the promotion of legitimate governmental interests." Wyoming v. Houghton, 526 U.S. 295, 300 (1999) [Casebook page 327]. Knights's status as a probationer subject to a search condition informs both sides of that balance. "Probation, like incarceration, is a form of criminal sanction imposed by a court upon an offender after verdict, finding, or plea of guilty." *Griffin, supra,* at 874. Probation is "one point . . . on a continuum of possible punishments ranging from solitary confinement in a maximum-security facility to a few hours of mandatory community service." 483 U.S., at 874. Inherent in the very nature of probation is that probationers "do not enjoy the absolute liberty to which every citizen is entitled." Ibid. (quoting Morrissey v. Brewer, 408 U.S. 471, 480 (1972)). Just as other punishments for criminal convictions curtail an offender's freedoms, a court granting probation may impose reasonable conditions that deprive the offender of some freedoms enjoyed by law-abiding citizens.

The judge who sentenced Knights to probation determined that it was necessary to condition the probation on Knights's acceptance of the search provision. It was reasonable to conclude that the search condition would further the two primary goals of probation—rehabilitation and protecting society from future criminal violations. The probation order clearly expressed the search condition and Knights was unambiguously informed of it. The probation condition thus significantly diminished Knights's reasonable expectation of privacy.[6]

In assessing the governmental interest side of the balance, it must be remembered that "the very assumption of the institution of probation" is that the probationer "is more likely than the ordinary citizen to violate the law." *Griffin,* 483 U.S., at 880. The recidivism rate of probationers is significantly higher than the general crime rate. See U.S. Dept. of Justice, Office of Justice Programs, Bureau of Justice Statistics, Recidivism of Felons on Probation, 1986–89, pp. 1, 6 (Feb.1992) (reporting that 43% of 79,000 felons placed on probation in 17 States were rearrested for a felony within three years while still on probation). And probationers have even more of an incentive to conceal their criminal activities and quickly dispose of incriminating evidence than the ordinary criminal because probationers are aware that they may be subject to supervision and face revocation of probation, and possible incarceration, in proceedings in which the trial rights of a jury and proof beyond a reasonable doubt, among other things, do not apply, see 18 U.S.C. § 3583(e).

The State has a dual concern with a probationer. On the one hand is the hope that he will successfully complete probation and be integrated back into the community. On the other is the concern, quite justified,

---

6. We do not decide whether the probation condition so diminished, or completely eliminated, Knights's reasonable expectation of privacy (or constituted consent, see supra, at 6) that a search by a law enforcement officer without any individualized suspicion would have satisfied the reasonableness requirement of the Fourth Amendment. The terms of the probation condition permit such a search, but we need not address the constitutionality of a suspicionless search because the search in this case was supported by reasonable suspicion.

that he will be more likely to engage in criminal conduct than an ordinary member of the community. The view of the Court of Appeals in this case would require the State to shut its eyes to the latter concern and concentrate only on the former. But we hold that the Fourth Amendment does not put the State to such a choice. Its interest in apprehending violators of the criminal law, thereby protecting potential victims of criminal enterprise, may therefore justifiably focus on probationers in a way that it does not on the ordinary citizen.

We hold that the balance of these considerations requires no more than reasonable suspicion to conduct a search of this probationer's house. The degree of individualized suspicion required of a search is a determination of when there is a sufficiently high probability that criminal conduct is occurring to make the intrusion on the individual's privacy interest reasonable. See United States v. Cortez, 449 U.S. 411, 418 (1981) (individualized suspicion deals "with probabilities"). Although the Fourth Amendment ordinarily requires the degree of probability embodied in the term "probable cause," a lesser degree satisfies the Constitution when the balance of governmental and private interests makes such a standard reasonable. See, e.g., Terry v. Ohio, 392 U.S. 1 (1968). Those interests warrant a lesser than probable-cause standard here. When an officer has reasonable suspicion that a probationer subject to a search condition is engaged in criminal activity, there is enough likelihood that criminal conduct is occurring that an intrusion on the probationer's

significantly diminished privacy interests is reasonable.

The same circumstances that lead us to conclude that reasonable suspicion is constitutionally sufficient also render a warrant requirement unnecessary. See Illinois v. McArthur, 531 U.S. 326, 330 (2001) (noting that general or individual circumstances, including "diminished expectations of privacy," may justify an exception to the warrant requirement).

Because our holding rests on ordinary Fourth Amendment analysis that considers all the circumstances of a search, there is no basis for examining official purpose. With the limited exception of some special needs and administrative search cases, see Indianapolis v. Edmond, 531 U.S. 32, 45 (2000), "we have been unwilling to entertain Fourth Amendment challenges based on the actual motivations of individual officers." Whren v. United States, 517 U.S. 806, 813 (1996).

The District Court found, and Knights concedes, that the search in this case was supported by reasonable suspicion. We therefore hold that the warrantless search of Knights, supported by reasonable suspicion and authorized by a condition of probation, was reasonable within the meaning of the Fourth Amendment. The judgment of the Court of Appeals is reversed, and the cause is remanded for further proceedings not inconsistent with this opinion.

It is so ordered.

Justice Souter, concurring.

As this case was originally presented to us, the dispute centered on whether Knights's agreement to the search condition included in his terms of probation covered only those searches with a probation-related purpose, or rather extended to searches with an investigatory or law-enforcement purpose. At that time, the Government argued that Whren v. United States, 517 U.S. 806 (1996), precluded any inquiry into the motives of the individual officers conducting the search. We now hold that law-enforcement searches of probationers who have been informed of a search condition are permissible upon individualized suspicion of criminal behavior committed during the probationary period, thus removing any issue of the subjective intention of the investigating officers from the case. I would therefore reserve the question whether *Whren's* holding, that "[s]ubjective intentions play no role in ordinary, probable-cause Fourth Amendment analysis," id., at 813 should extend to searches based only upon reasonable suspicion.

C. SEARCH INCIDENT TO ARREST: THE ARREST POWER RULE

3. Searches of the Person Incident to Arrest

Custodial Arrests for Minor Offenses

Page 279.   Add the following case at the end of the runover paragraph:

The Supreme Court in the following case affirmed the Fifth Circuit's en banc opinion.

ATWATER v. CITY OF LAGO VISTA

United States Supreme Court, 2001.
532 U.S. 318.

JUSTICE SOUTER delivered the opinion of the Court.

The question is whether the Fourth Amendment forbids a warrantless arrest for a minor criminal offense, such as a misdemeanor seatbelt violation punishable only by a fine. We hold that it does not.

I

A

In Texas, if a car is equipped with safety belts, a front-seat passenger must wear one, Tex. Tran. Code Ann. § 545.413(a) (1999), and the driver must secure any small child riding in front, § 545.413(b). Viola-tion of either provision is "a misdemeanor punishable by a fine not less than $25 or more than $50." § 545.413(d). Texas law expressly authorizes "[a]ny peace officer [to] arrest without warrant a person found committing a violation" of these seatbelt laws, § 543.001, although it permits police to issue citations in lieu of arrest, §§ 543.003–543.005.

In March 1997, Petitioner Gail Atwater was driving her pickup truck in Lago Vista, Texas, with her 3–year-old son and 5–year-old daughter in the front seat. None of them was wearing a seatbelt. Respondent

Bart Turek, a Lago Vista police officer at the time, observed the seatbelt violations and pulled Atwater over. According to Atwater's complaint (the allegations of which we assume to be true for present purposes), Turek approached the truck and "yell [ed]" something to the effect of "[w]e've met before" and "[y]ou're going to jail." [Turek had previously stopped Atwater for what he had thought was a seatbelt violation, but then had realized that Atwater's son, although seated on the vehicle's armrest, was in fact belted in. Atwater acknowledged that her son's seating position was unsafe, and Turek had issued a verbal warning.] He then called for backup and asked to see Atwater's driver's license and insurance documentation, which state law required her to carry. When Atwater told Turek that she did not have the papers because her purse had been stolen the day before, Turek said that he had "heard that story two-hundred times." Atwater asked to take her "frightened, upset, and crying" children to a friend's house nearby, but Turek told her, "[y]ou're not going anywhere." As it turned out, Atwater's friend learned what was going on and soon arrived to take charge of the children. Turek then handcuffed Atwater, placed her in his squad car, and drove her to the local police station, where booking officers had her remove her shoes, jewelry, and eyeglasses, and empty her pockets. Officers took Atwater's "mug shot" and placed her, alone, in a jail cell for about one hour, after which she was taken before a magistrate and released on $310 bond. Atwater was charged with driving without her seatbelt fastened, failing to secure her children in seatbelts, driving without a license, and failing to provide proof of insurance. She ultimately pleaded no contest to the misdemeanor seatbelt offenses and paid a $50 fine; the other charges were dismissed.

B

Atwater and her husband * * * filed suit * * * under 42 U.S.C. § 1983 against Turek and respondents City of Lago Vista and Chief of Police Frank Miller. So far as concerns us, petitioners (whom we will simply call Atwater) alleged that respondents (for simplicity, the City) had violated Atwater's Fourth Amendment "right to be free from unreasonable seizure," and sought compensatory and punitive damages. * * * Given Atwater's admission that she had "violated the law" * * * the District Court ruled the Fourth Amendment claim "meritless" and granted the City's summary judgment motion. A panel of the United States Court of Appeals for the Fifth Circuit reversed. It concluded that "an arrest for a first-time seat belt offense" was an unreasonable seizure within the meaning of the Fourth Amendment * * *. Sitting en banc, the Court of Appeals vacated the panel's decision and affirmed the District Court's summary judgment for the City. Relying on Whren v. United States, 517 U.S. 806 (1996), the en banc court observed that, although the Fourth Amendment generally requires a balancing of individual and governmental interests, where "an arrest is based on probable cause then with rare exceptions * * * the result of that balancing is not in doubt." Because "[n]either party dispute[d] that Officer Turek had probable cause to arrest Atwater," and because "there [was] no evidence in the record that Officer Turek conducted the arrest in an extraordinary manner, unusually harmful to Atwater's privacy interests," the en banc court held that the arrest was not unreasonable for Fourth Amendment purposes. * * *

We granted certiorari to consider whether the Fourth Amendment, either by incorporating common-law restrictions on misdemeanor arrests or otherwise, limits police officers' authority to arrest without warrant for minor criminal offenses. We now affirm.

II

The Fourth Amendment safeguards "[t]he right of the people to be secure in their persons, houses, papers, and effects, against unreasonable searches and seizures." In reading the Amendment, we are guided by "the traditional protections against unreasonable searches and seizures afforded by the common law at the time of the framing," Wilson v. Arkansas, 514 U.S. 927, 931 (1995), since "[a]n examination of the common-law understanding of an officer's authority to arrest sheds light on the obviously relevant, if not entirely dispositive, consideration of what the Framers of the Amendment might have thought to be reasonable," Payton v. New York, 445 U.S. 573, 591 (1980). Thus, the first step here is to assess Atwater's claim that peace officers' authority to make warrantless arrests for misdemeanors was restricted at common law * * * . Atwater's specific contention is that "founding-era common-law rules" forbade peace officers to make warrantless misdemeanor arrests except in cases of "breach of the peace," a category she claims was then understood narrowly as covering only those nonfelony offenses "involving or tending toward violence." Although her historical argument is by no means insubstantial, it ultimately fails.

A

[Justice Souter engaged in an extensive and detailed analysis of pre-founding English common law and concluded that, "the common-law commentators (as well as the sparsely reported cases) reached divergent conclusions with respect to officers' warrantless misdemeanor arrest power. Moreover, in the years leading up to American independence, Parliament repeatedly extended express warrantless arrest authority to cover misdemeanor-level offenses not amounting to or involving any violent breach of the peace."]

B

An examination of specifically American evidence is to the same effect. Neither the history of the framing era nor subsequent legal development indicates that the Fourth Amendment was originally understood, or has traditionally been read, to embrace Atwater's position.

1

To begin with, Atwater has cited no particular evidence that those who framed and ratified the Fourth Amendment sought to limit peace officers' warrantless misdemeanor arrest authority to instances of actual breach of the peace, and our own review of the recent and respected compilations of framing-era documentary history has likewise failed to reveal any such design. See The Complete Bill of Rights 223–263 (N. Cogan ed. 1997) (collecting original sources); 5 The Founders' Constitution 219–244 (P. Kurland & R. Lerner eds. 1987) (same). Nor have we found in any of the modern historical accounts of the Fourth Amendment's adoption any substantial indication that the Framers intended such a restriction. See, e.g., L. Levy, Origins of the Bill of Rights 150–179 (1999); T. Taylor, Two Studies in Constitutional Interpretation 19–93 (1969); J. Landynski, Search and Seizure and the Supreme Court 19–48 (1966); N. Lasson, History and Development of the Fourth Amendment to the United States Constitution 79–105 (1937); Davies, Recovering the Original Fourth Amendment, 98 Mich. L.Rev. 547 (1999); Amar, Fourth Amendment First Principles, 107 Harv. L.Rev. 757 (1994); Bradley, Constitutional Theory of the Fourth Amendment, 38 DePaul L.Rev. 817 (1989). Indeed, to the extent these modern histories address the issue, their conclusions are to the contrary. See Landynski, supra, at 45 (Fourth Amendment arrest rules are based on common-law practice, which "dispensed with a warrant requirement for misdemeanors committed in the presence of the arresting officer").

The evidence of actual practice also counsels against Atwater's position. During the period leading up to and surrounding the framing of the Bill of Rights, colonial and state legislatures, like Parliament before them, regularly authorized local peace officers to make warrantless misdemeanor arrests without conditioning statutory authority on breach of the peace. [Justice Souter cites more than ten statutes from colonial and state legislatures.]

What we have here, then, is just the opposite of what we had in Wilson v. Arkansas. There, we emphasized that during the founding era a number of States had "enacted statutes specifically embracing" the common-law knock-and-announce rule; here, by contrast, those very same States passed laws extending warrantless arrest authority to a host of nonviolent misdemeanors, and in so doing acted very much inconsistently with Atwater's claims about the Fourth Amendment's object. Of course, the Fourth Amendment did not originally apply to the States, see Barron v. Mayor of Baltimore, 7 Pet. 243 (1833), but that does not make state practice irrelevant in unearthing the Amendment's original meaning. A number of state constitutional search-and-seizure provisions served as models for the Fourth Amendment, see, e.g., N. H. Const. of 1784, pt. I, Art. XIX; Pa. Const. of 1776 (Declaration of Rights), Art. X, and the fact that many of the original States with such constitutional limitations continued to grant their own peace officers broad warrantless misdemeanor arrest authority undermines Atwater's contention that the founding generation meant to bar federal law enforcement officers from exercising the same authority. Given the early state practice, it is likewise troublesome for Atwater's view that just one year after the ratification of the Fourth Amendment, Congress vested federal marshals with "the same powers in executing the laws of the United States, as sheriffs and their deputies in the several states have by law, in executing the laws of their respective states." Act of May 2, 1792, ch. 28, § 9, 1 Stat. 265.

Thus, as we have said before in only slightly different circumstances, the Second Congress apparently "saw no inconsistency between the Fourth Amendment and legislation giving United States marshals the same power as local peace officers" to make warrantless arrests. United States v. Watson, 423 U.S. 411, 420 (1976). We simply cannot conclude that the Fourth Amendment, as originally understood, forbade peace officers to arrest without a warrant for misdemeanors not amounting to or involving breach of the peace.

2

Nor does Atwater's argument from tradition pick up any steam from the historical record as it has unfolded since the framing, there being no indication that her claimed rule has ever become "woven * * * into the fabric" of American law. The story, on the contrary, is of two centuries of uninterrupted (and largely unchallenged) state and federal practice permitting warrantless arrests for misdemeanors not amounting to or involving breach of the peace. First, there is no support for Atwater's position in this Court's cases * * *. Although the Court has not had much to say about warrantless misdemeanor arrest authority, what little we have said tends to cut against Atwater's argument. In discussing this authority, we have focused on the circumstance that an offense was committed in an officer's presence, to the omission of any reference to a breach-of-the-peace limitation. See,

e.g., United States v. Watson, supra, at 418 ("The cases construing the Fourth Amendment thus reflect the ancient common-law rule that a peace officer was permitted to arrest without a warrant for a misdemeanor or felony committed in his presence * * *."); United States v. Carroll, 267 U.S., at 156–157 ("The usual rule is that a police officer may arrest without a warrant one * * * guilty of a misdemeanor if committed in his presence").

Second, and again in contrast with *Wilson*, it is not the case here that "[e]arly American courts ... embraced" an accepted common-law rule with anything approaching unanimity. [Justice Souter engages in an extensive analysis of the early American cases cited by Atwater and distinguishes each of them.] The reports may well contain early American cases more favorable to Atwater's position than the ones she has herself invoked. But more to the point, we think, are the numerous early-and mid–19th-century decisions expressly sustaining (often against constitutional challenge) state and local laws authorizing peace officers to make warrantless arrests for misdemeanors not involving any breach of the peace. See, e.g., Mayo v. Wilson, 1 N.H. 53 (1817) (upholding statute authorizing warrantless arrests of those unnecessarily traveling on Sunday against challenge based on state due process and search-and-seizure provisions); Holcomb v. Cornish, 8 Conn. 375 (1831) (upholding statute permitting warrantless arrests for "drunkenness, profane swearing, cursing or sabbath-breaking" against argument that "[t]he power of a justice of the peace to arrest and detain a citizen without complaint or warrant against him, is surely not given by the common law"); Davis v. American Soc. for Prevention of Cruelty to Animals, 75 N.Y. 362 (1878) (upholding statute permitting warrantless arrest for misdemeanor violation of cruelty-to-animals prohibition). See generally Wilgus, Arrest Without a Warrant, 22 Mich. L.Rev. 541, 550, and n. 54 (1924) (collecting cases and observing that "[t]he states may, by statute, enlarge the common law right to arrest without a warrant, and have quite generally done so or authorized municipalities to do so, as for example, an officer may be authorized by statute or ordinance to arrest without a warrant for various misdemeanors and violations of ordinances, other than breaches of the peace, if committed in his presence").

Finally, both the legislative tradition of granting warrantless misdemeanor arrest authority and the judicial tradition of sustaining such statutes against constitutional attack are buttressed by legal commentary that, for more than a century now, has almost uniformly recognized the constitutionality of extending warrantless arrest power to misdemeanors without limitation to breaches of the peace. [Justice Souter provides copious citations to a number of treatises.] Small wonder, then, that today statutes in all 50 States and the District of Columbia permit warrantless misdemeanor arrests by at least some (if not all) peace officers without requiring any breach of the peace, as do a host of congressional enactments. The American Law Institute has long endorsed the validity of such legislation, see American Law Institute, Code of Criminal Procedure § 21(a), p. 28 (1930); American Law Institute, Model Code of Pre–Arraignment Procedure § 120.1(1)(c), p. 13 (1975), and the consensus, as stated in the current literature, is that statutes "removing the breach of the peace limitation and thereby permitting arrest without warrant for any misdemeanor committed in the arresting officer's presence have never been successfully challenged and stand as the law of the land." 3 W. LaFave, Search and Seizure § 5.1(b), pp. 13–14, and n. 76 (1996). This, therefore, simply is not a case in which the claimant can point to "a clear answer [that] existed in 1791 and has been generally adhered to by the traditions of our society ever since." County of Riverside v. McLaughlin, 500 U.S. 44, 60 (1991) (SCALIA, J., dissenting).

III

While it is true here that history, if not unequivocal, has expressed a decided, majority view that the police need not obtain an arrest warrant merely because a misdemeanor stopped short of violence or a threat of it, Atwater does not wager all on history. Instead, she asks us to mint a new rule of constitutional law on the understanding that when historical practice fails to speak conclusively to a claim grounded on the Fourth Amendment, courts are left to strike a current balance between individual and societal interests by subjecting particular contemporary circumstances to traditional standards of reasonableness. Atwater accordingly argues for a modern arrest rule, one not necessarily requiring violent breach of the peace, but nonetheless forbidding custodial arrest, even upon probable cause, when conviction could not ultimately carry any jail time and when the government shows no compelling need for immediate detention.

If we were to derive a rule exclusively to address the uncontested facts of this case, Atwater might well prevail. She was a known and established resident of Lago Vista with no place to hide and no incentive to flee, and common sense says she would almost certainly have buckled up as a condition of driving off with a citation. In her case, the physical incidents of arrest were merely gratuitous humiliations imposed by a police officer who was (at best) exercising extremely poor judgment. Atwater's claim to live free of pointless indignity and confinement clearly outweighs anything the City can raise against it specific to her case.

But we have traditionally recognized that a responsible Fourth Amendment balance is not well served by standards requiring sensitive, case-by-case determinations of government need, lest every discretionary judgment in the field be converted into an occasion for constitutional review. *See, e.g.,* United States v. Robinson, 414 U.S. 218, 234–235 (1973). Often enough, the Fourth Amendment has to be applied on the spur (and in the heat) of the moment, and the object in implementing its command of reasonableness is to draw standards sufficiently clear and simple to be applied with a fair prospect of sur-

viving judicial second-guessing months and years after an arrest or search is made. Courts attempting to strike a reasonable Fourth Amendment balance thus credit the government's side with an essential interest in readily administrable rules. See New York v. Belton, 453 U.S. 454, 458 (1981) (Fourth Amendment rules "ought to be expressed in terms that are readily applicable by the police in the context of the law enforcement activities in which they are necessarily engaged" * * *).[16]

At first glance, Atwater's argument may seem to respect the values of clarity and simplicity, so far as she claims that the Fourth Amendment generally forbids warrantless arrests for minor crimes not accompanied by violence or some demonstrable threat of it (whether "minor crime" be defined as a fine-only traffic offense, a fine-only offense more generally, or a misdemeanor). But the claim is not ultimately so simple, nor could it be, for complications arise the moment we begin to think about the possible applications of the several criteria Atwater proposes for drawing a line between minor crimes with limited arrest authority and others not so restricted.

One line, she suggests, might be between "jailable" and "fine-only" offenses, between those for which conviction could result in commitment and those for which it could not. The trouble with this distinc-

---

16. Terry v. Ohio, 392 U.S. 1 (1968), upon which the dissent relies, is not to the contrary. *Terry* certainly supports a more finely tuned approach to the Fourth Amendment when police act without the traditional justification that either a warrant (in the case of a search) or probable

cause (in the case of arrest) provides; but at least in the absence of "extraordinary" circumstances, Whren v. United States, 517 U.S. 806, 818 (1996), there is no comparable cause for finicking when police act with such justification.

tion, of course, is that an officer on the street might not be able to tell. It is not merely that we cannot expect every police officer to know the details of frequently complex penalty schemes, but that penalties for ostensibly identical conduct can vary on account of facts difficult (if not impossible) to know at the scene of an arrest. Is this the first offense or is the suspect a repeat offender? Is the weight of the marijuana a gram above or a gram below the fine-only line? Where conduct could implicate more than one criminal prohibition, which one will the district attorney ultimately decide to charge? And so on. But Atwater's refinements would not end there. She represents that if the line were drawn at nonjailable traffic offenses, her proposed limitation should be qualified by a proviso authorizing warrantless arrests where "necessary for enforcement of the traffic laws or when [an] offense would otherwise continue and pose a danger to others on the road." * * * The proviso only compounds the difficulties. Would, for instance, either exception apply to speeding? At oral argument, Atwater's counsel said that "it would not be reasonable to arrest a driver for speeding unless the speeding rose to the level of reckless driving." But is it not fair to expect that the chronic speeder will speed again despite a citation in his pocket, and should that not qualify as showing that the "offense would * * * continue" under Atwater's rule? And why, as a constitutional matter, should we assume that only reckless driving will "pose a danger to others on the road" while speeding will not?

There is no need for more examples to show that Atwater's general rule and limiting proviso promise very little in the way of administrability. It is no answer that the police routinely make judgments on grounds like risk of immediate repetition; they surely do and should. But there is a world of difference between making that judgment in choosing between the discretionary leniency of a summons in place of a clearly lawful arrest, and making the same judgment when the question is the lawfulness of the warrantless arrest itself. It is the difference between no basis for legal action challenging the discretionary judgment, on the one hand, and the prospect of evidentiary exclusion or (as here) personal § 1983 liability for the misapplication of a constitutional standard, on the other. Atwater's rule therefore would not only place police in an almost impossible spot but would guarantee increased litigation over many of the arrests that would occur. For all these reasons, Atwater's various distinctions between permissible and impermissible arrests for minor crimes strike us as very unsatisfactory lines to require police officers to draw on a moment's notice. One may ask, of course, why these difficulties may not be answered by a simple tie breaker for the police to follow in the field: if in doubt, do not arrest. The first answer is that in practice the tie breaker would boil down to something akin to a least-restrictive-alternative limitation, which is itself one of those "ifs, ands, and buts" rules, New York v. Belton, 453 U.S., at 458, generally thought inappropriate in working out Fourth Amendment protection. *See, e.g.,* United States v. Martinez–Fuerte, 428 U.S. 543, 557–558, n. 12 (1976)

("The logic of such elaborate less-restrictive-alternative arguments could raise insuperable barriers to the exercise of virtually all search-and-seizure powers"). Beyond that, whatever help the tie breaker might give would come at the price of a systematic disincentive to arrest in situations where even Atwater concedes that arresting would serve an important societal interest. An officer not quite sure that the drugs weighed enough to warrant jail time or not quite certain about a suspect's risk of flight would not arrest, even though it could perfectly well turn out that, in fact, the offense called for incarceration and the defendant was long gone on the day of trial. Multiplied many times over, the costs to society of such underenforcement could easily outweigh the costs to defendants of being needlessly arrested and booked * * *.

Just how easily the costs could outweigh the benefits may be shown by asking, as one Member of this Court did at oral argument, "how bad the problem is out there." The very fact that the law has never jelled the way Atwater would have it leads one to wonder whether warrantless misdemeanor arrests need constitutional attention, and there is cause to think the answer is no. So far as such arrests might be thought to pose a threat to the probable-cause requirement, anyone arrested for a crime without formal process, whether for felony or misdemeanor, is entitled to a magistrate's review of probable cause within 48 hours, County of Riverside v. McLaughlin, 500 U.S., at 55–58, and there is no reason to think the procedure in this case atypical in giving the suspect a prompt opportunity to request release. Many jurisdictions, moreover, have chosen to impose more restrictive safeguards through statutes limiting warrantless arrests for minor offenses. See, e.g., Ala. Code § 32–1–4 (1999); Cal. Veh. Code Ann. § 40504 (West 2000); Ky. Rev. Stat. Ann. §§ 431.015(1), (2) (Michie 1999); La. Rev. Stat. Ann. § 32:391 (West 1989); Md. Transp. Code Ann. § 26–202(a)(2) (1999); S. D. Codified Laws § 32–33–2 (1998); Tenn. Code Ann. § 40–7–118(b)(1) (1997); Va. Code Ann. § 46.2–936 (Supp. 2000). It is of course easier to devise a minor-offense limitation by statute than to derive one through the Constitution, simply because the statute can let the arrest power turn on any sort of practical consideration without having to subsume it under a broader principle. It is, in fact, only natural that States should resort to this sort of legislative regulation, for, as Atwater's own amici emphasize, it is in the interest of the police to limit petty-offense arrests, which carry costs that are simply too great to incur without good reason. Finally, and significantly, under current doctrine the preference for categorical treatment of Fourth Amendment claims gives way to individualized review when a defendant makes a colorable argument that an arrest, with or without a warrant, was "conducted in an extraordinary manner, unusually harmful to [his] privacy or even physical interests." Whren v. United States, 517 U.S., at 818; see also Graham v. Connor, 490 U.S. 386, 395–396 (1989) (excessive force actionable under § 1983). The upshot of all these influences, combined with the good sense (and, failing that, the political accountability) of most local lawmakers and law-enforcement officials, is a dearth of horribles demanding redress. Indeed, when Atwater's counsel was asked at oral argument for any indications of comparably foolish, warrantless misdemeanor arrests, he could offer only one. We are sure that there are others, but just as surely the country is not confronting anything like an epidemic of unnecessary minor-offense arrests. That fact caps the reasons for rejecting Atwater's request for the development of a new and distinct body of constitutional law.

Accordingly, we confirm today what our prior cases have intimated: the standard of probable cause "applies to all arrests, without the need to balance the interests and circumstances involved in particular situations." Dunaway v. New York, 442 U.S. 200, 208 (1979). If an officer has probable cause to believe that an individual has committed even a very minor criminal offense in his presence, he may, without violating the Fourth Amendment, arrest the offender.

IV

Atwater's arrest satisfied constitutional requirements. There is no dispute that Officer Turek had probable cause to believe that Atwater had committed a crime in his presence. She admits that neither she nor her children were wearing seat belts, as required by Tex. Tran. Code Ann. § 545.413 (1999). Turek was accordingly authorized (not required, but authorized) to make a custodial arrest without balancing costs and benefits or determining whether or not Atwater's arrest was in some sense necessary.

Nor was the arrest made in an "extraordinary manner, unusually harmful to [her] privacy or * * * physical interests." Whren v. United States, 517 U. S., at 818. As our citations in *Whren* make clear, the question whether a search or seizure is "extraordinary" turns, above all else, on the manner in which the search or seizure is executed. See id., at 818 (citing Tennessee v. Garner, 471 U.S. 1 (1985) ("seizure by means of deadly force"), Wilson v. Arkansas, 514 U.S. 927 (1995) ("unannounced entry into a home"), Welsh v. Wisconsin, 466 U.S. 740 (1984) ("entry into a home without a warrant"), and Winston v. Lee, 470 U.S. 753 (1985) ("physical penetration of the body")). Atwater's arrest was surely "humiliating," as she says in her brief, but it was no more "harmful to privacy or physical interests" than the normal custodial arrest. She was handcuffed, placed in a squad car, and taken to the local police station, where officers asked her to remove her shoes, jewelry, and glasses, and to empty her pockets. They then took her photograph and placed her in a cell, alone, for about an hour, after which she was taken before a magistrate, and released on $310 bond. The arrest and booking were inconvenient and embarrassing to Atwater, but not so extraordinary as to violate the Fourth Amendment.

The Court of Appeals's en banc judgment is affirmed.

JUSTICE O'CONNOR, with whom JUSTICE STEVENS, JUSTICE GINSBURG, and JUSTICE BREYER join, dissenting.

* * * The Court recognizes that the arrest of Gail Atwater was a "pointless indignity" that served no discernible state interest, and yet

holds that her arrest was constitutionally permissible. Because the Court's position is inconsistent with the explicit guarantee of the Fourth Amendment, I dissent.

I

A full custodial arrest, such as the one to which Ms. Atwater was subjected, is the quintessential seizure. When a full custodial arrest is effected without a warrant, the plain language of the Fourth Amendment requires that the arrest be reasonable. It is beyond cavil that the touchstone of our analysis under the Fourth Amendment is always "the reasonableness in all the circumstances of the particular governmental invasion of a citizen's personal security." Pennsylvania v. Mimms, 434 U.S. 106, 108–109 (1977) (per curiam). We have "often looked to the common law in evaluating the reasonableness, for Fourth Amendment purposes, of police activity." Tennessee v. Garner, 471 U.S. 1, 13 (1985). But history is just one of the tools we use in conducting the reasonableness inquiry. And when history is inconclusive, as the majority amply demonstrates it is in this case, we will evaluate the search or seizure under traditional standards of reasonableness by assessing, on the one hand, the degree to which it intrudes upon an individual's privacy and, on the other, the degree to which it is needed for the promotion of legitimate governmental interests. In other words, in determining reasonableness, each case is to be decided on its own facts and circumstances.

The majority gives a brief nod to this bedrock principle of our Fourth Amendment jurisprudence, and even acknowledges that "Atwa-

ter's claim to live free of pointless indignity and confinement clearly outweighs anything the City can raise against it specific to her case." But instead of remedying this imbalance, the majority allows itself to be swayed by the worry that "every discretionary judgment in the field [will] be converted into an occasion for constitutional review." It therefore mints a new rule that "[i]f an officer has probable cause to believe that an individual has committed even a very minor criminal offense in his presence, he may, without violating the Fourth Amendment, arrest the offender." This rule is not only unsupported by our precedent, but runs contrary to the principles that lie at the core of the Fourth Amendment.

* * * While probable cause is surely a necessary condition for warrantless arrests for fine-only offenses, any realistic assessment of the interests implicated by such arrests demonstrates that probable cause alone is not a sufficient condition.

Our decision in Whren v. United States, 517 U.S. 806 (1996), is not to the contrary. The specific question presented there was whether, in evaluating the Fourth Amendment reasonableness of a traffic stop, the subjective intent of the police officer is a relevant consideration. We held that it is not, and stated that the making of a traffic stop "is governed by the usual rule that probable cause to believe the law has been broken 'outbalances' private interest in avoiding police contact." We of course did not have occasion in Whren to consider the constitutional preconditions for warrantless arrests for fine-only offenses. Nor should our words be taken beyond their context. There are significant qualitative differences between a traffic stop and a full custodial arrest. While both are seizures that fall within the ambit of the Fourth Amendment, the latter entails a much greater intrusion on an individual's liberty and privacy interests. * * * [W]hen there is probable cause to believe that a person has violated a minor traffic law, there can be little question that the state interest in law enforcement will justify the relatively limited intrusion of a traffic stop. It is by no means certain, however, that where the offense is punishable only by fine, "probable cause to believe the law has been broken [will] 'outbalanc[e]' private interest in avoiding" a full custodial arrest. Whren v. United States, supra, at 818. Justifying a full arrest by the same quantum of evidence that justifies a traffic stop—even though the offender cannot ultimately be imprisoned for her conduct—defies any sense of proportionality and is in serious tension with the Fourth Amendment's proscription of unreasonable seizures.

A custodial arrest exacts an obvious toll on an individual's liberty and privacy, even when the period of custody is relatively brief. The arrestee is subject to a full search of her person and confiscation of her possessions. If the arrestee is the occupant of a car, the entire passenger compartment of the car, including packages therein, is subject to search as well. The arrestee may be detained for up to 48 hours without having a magistrate determine whether there in fact was probable cause for the arrest. Because people arrested for all types of violent and nonviolent offenses may be housed together awaiting such review, this detention period is potentially dangerous. And once the period of custody is over, the fact of the arrest is a permanent part of the public record. We have said that "the penalty that may attach to any particular offense seems to provide the clearest and most consistent indication of the State's interest in arresting individuals suspected of committing that offense." Welsh v. Wisconsin, 466 U.S. 740, 754, n. 14 (1984). If the State has decided that a fine, and not imprisonment, is the appropriate punishment for an offense, the State's interest in taking a person suspected of committing that offense into custody is surely limited, at best. This is not to say that the State will never have such an interest. A full custodial arrest may on occasion vindicate legitimate state interests, even if the crime is punishable only by fine. Arrest is the surest way to abate criminal conduct. It may also allow the police to verify the offender's identity and, if the offender poses a flight risk, to ensure her appearance at trial. But when such considerations are not present, a citation or summons may serve the State's remaining law enforcement interests every bit as effectively as an arrest.

Because a full custodial arrest is such a severe intrusion on an individual's liberty, its reasonableness hinges on "the degree to which it is needed for the promotion of legitimate governmental interests." Wyoming v. Houghton, 526 U.S., at 300. In light of the availability of citations to promote a State's interests when a fine-only offense has been committed, I cannot concur in a rule which deems a full custodial arrest to be reasonable in every circumstance. * * * Instead, I would require that when there is probable cause to believe that a fine-only offense has been committed, the police officer should issue a citation unless the officer is "able to point to specific and articulable facts which, taken together with rational inferences from those facts, reasonably warrant [the additional] intrusion" of a full custodial arrest. Terry v. Ohio, 392 U.S., at 21.

The majority insists that a bright-line rule focused on probable cause is necessary to vindicate the State's interest in easily administrable law enforcement rules. Probable cause itself, however, is not a model of precision. "The quantum of information which constitutes probable cause—evidence which would warrant a man of reasonable caution in the belief that a [crime] has been committed—must be measured by the facts of the particular case." Wong Sun v. United States, 371 U.S. 471, 479 (1963). The rule I propose—which merely requires a legitimate reason for the decision to escalate the seizure into a full custodial arrest—thus does not undermine an otherwise "clear and simple" rule. While clarity is certainly a value worthy of consideration in our Fourth Amendment jurisprudence, it by no means trumps the values of liberty and privacy at the heart of the Amendment's protections. What the *Terry* rule lacks in precision it makes up for in fidelity to the Fourth Amendment's command of reasonableness and sensitivity to the competing values protected by that Amendment. Over the past 30 years, it appears that the *Terry* rule has been workable and easily applied by officers on the street.

At bottom, the majority offers two related reasons why a bright-line rule is necessary: the fear that officers who arrest for fine-only offenses will be subject to "personal [42 U.S.C.] § 1983 liability for the misapplication of a constitutional standard,"and the resulting "systematic disincentive to arrest * * * where arresting would serve an important societal interest." These concerns are certainly valid, but they are more than adequately resolved by the doctrine of qualified immunity. Qualified immunity was created to shield government officials from civil liability for the performance of discretionary functions so long as their conduct does not violate clearly established statutory or constitutional rights of which a reasonable person would have known. * * * In Anderson v. Creighton, 483 U.S. 635 (1987), we made clear that the standard of reasonableness for a search or seizure under the Fourth Amendment is distinct from the standard of reasonableness for qualified immunity purposes. If a law enforcement officer "reasonably but mistakenly conclude[s]" that the constitutional predicate for a search or seizure is present, he "should not be held personally liable." This doctrine thus allays any concerns about liability or disincentives to arrest. If, for example, an officer reasonably thinks that a suspect poses a flight risk or might be a danger to the community if released, he may arrest without fear of the legal consequences. Similarly, if an officer reasonably concludes that a suspect may possess more than four ounces of marijuana and thus might be guilty of a felony, the officer will be insulated from liability for arresting the suspect even if the initial assessment turns out to be factually incorrect. Of course, even the specter of liability can entail substantial social costs, such as inhibiting public officials in the discharge of their duties. We may not ignore the central command of the Fourth Amendment, however, to avoid these costs.

II

The record in this case makes it abundantly clear that Ms. Atwater's arrest was constitutionally unreasonable. * * * While Turek was justified in stopping Atwater, neither law nor reason supports his decision to arrest her instead of simply giving her a citation. The officer's actions cannot sensibly be viewed as a permissible means of balancing Atwater's Fourth Amendment interests with the State's own legitimate interests. There is no question that Officer Turek's actions severely infringed Atwater's liberty and privacy. [Justice O'Connor reprises the facts of Atwater's arrest and incarceration.]. Ms. Atwater ultimately pleaded no contest to violating the seatbelt law and was fined $50. Even though that fine was the maximum penalty for her crime, and even though Officer Turek has never articulated any justification for his actions, the city contends that arresting Atwater was constitutionally reasonable because it advanced two legitimate interests: "the enforcement of child safety laws and encouraging [Atwater] to appear for trial."

It is difficult to see how arresting Atwater served either of these goals any more effectively than the issuance of a citation. With respect to the goal of law enforcement generally, Atwater did not pose a great danger to the community. She had been driving very slowly—approximately 15 miles per hour—in broad daylight on a residential street that had no other traffic. Nor was she a repeat offender; until that day, she had received one traffic citation in her life—a ticket, more than 10 years earlier, for failure to signal a lane change. Moreover, Atwater immediately accepted responsibility and apologized for her conduct. Thus, there was every indication that Atwater would have buckled herself and her children in had she been cited and allowed to leave.

With respect to the related goal of child welfare, the decision to arrest Atwater was nothing short of counterproductive. Atwater's children witnessed Officer Turek yell at their mother and threaten to take them all into custody. Ultimately, they were forced to leave her behind with Turek, knowing that she was being taken to jail. Understandably, the 3-year-old boy was "very, very, very traumatized." After the incident, he had to see a child psychologist regularly, who reported that the boy "felt very guilty that he couldn't stop this horrible thing * * * he was powerless to help his mother or sister." Both of Atwater's children are now terrified at the sight of any police car. According to Atwater, the arrest "just never leaves us. It's a conversation we have every other day, once a week, and it's—it raises its head constantly in our lives."

Citing Atwater surely would have served the children's interests well. It would have taught Atwater to ensure that her children were buckled up in the future. It also would have taught the children an important lesson in accepting responsibility and obeying the law. Arresting Atwater, though, taught the children an entirely different lesson: that "the bad person could just as easily be the policeman as it could be the most horrible person they could imagine."

Respondents also contend that the arrest was necessary to ensure Atwater's appearance in court. Atwater, however, was far from a flight risk. A 16–year resident of Lago Vista, population 2,486, Atwater was not likely to abscond. Although she was unable to produce her driver's license because it had been stolen, she gave Officer Turek her license number and address. In addition, Officer Turek knew from their previous encounter that Atwater was a local resident. The city's justifications fall far short of rationalizing the extraordinary intrusion on Gail Atwater and her children. Measuring the degree to which Atwater's custodial arrest was needed for the promotion of legitimate governmental interests, against the degree to which it intruded upon her privacy, it can hardly be doubted that Turek's actions were disproportionate to Atwater's crime. The majority's assessment that "Atwater's claim to live free of pointless indignity and confinement clearly outweighs anything the City can raise against it specific to her case," is quite correct. In my view, the Fourth Amendment inquiry ends there.

III

The Court's error, however, does not merely affect the disposition of this case. The per se rule that the Court creates has potentially serious consequences for the everyday lives of Americans. A broad range of conduct falls into the category of fine-only misdemeanors. In Texas alone, for example, disobeying any sort of traffic warning sign is a misdemeanor punishable only by fine, as is failing to pay a highway toll, and driving with expired license plates. Nor are fine-only crimes limited to the traffic context. In several States, for example, littering is a criminal offense punishable only by fine. To be sure, such laws are valid and wise exercises of the States' power to protect the public health and welfare. My concern lies not with the decision to enact or enforce these laws, but rather with the manner in which they may be enforced. Under today's holding, when a police officer has probable cause to believe that a fine-only misdemeanor offense has occurred, that officer may stop the suspect, issue a citation, and let the person continue on her way. Or, if a traffic violation, the officer may stop the car, arrest the driver, search the driver, see United States v. Robinson, 414 U.S., at 235, search the entire passenger compartment of the car including any purse or package inside, see New York v. Belton, 453 U.S., at 460, and impound the car and inventory all of its contents, see Colorado v. Bertine, 479 U.S. 367, 374 (1987). Although the Fourth Amendment expressly requires that the latter course be a reasonable and proportional response to the circumstances of the offense, the majority gives officers unfettered discretion to choose that course without articulating a single reason why such action is appropriate.

Such unbounded discretion carries with it grave potential for abuse. The majority takes comfort in the lack of evidence of "an epidemic of unnecessary minor-offense arrests." But the relatively small number of published cases dealing with such arrests proves little and should provide little solace. Indeed, as the recent debate over racial profiling demonstrates all too clearly, a relatively minor traffic infraction may often serve as an excuse for stopping and harassing an individual. After today, the arsenal available to any officer extends to a full arrest and the searches permissible concomitant to that arrest. An officer's subjective motivations for making a traffic stop are not relevant considerations in determining the reasonableness of the stop. But it is precisely because these motivations are beyond our purview that we must vigilantly ensure that officers' post-stop actions—which are properly within our reach—comport with the Fourth Amendment's guarantee of reasonableness.

The Court neglects the Fourth Amendment's express command in the name of administrative ease. In so doing, it cloaks the pointless indignity that Gail Atwater suffered with the mantle of reasonableness. I respectfully dissent.

D. PRETEXTUAL STOPS AND ARRESTS

Page 294. After the *Whren* case, add the following:

Whren Reaffirmed: Arkansas v. Sullivan

The Court made it clear that it was committed to the *Whren* "objective" approach to questions of pretext in the per curiam opinion in Arkansas v. Sullivan, 532 U.S. 769 (2001). Sullivan was stopped by Officer Taylor for speeding and for having an improperly tinted windshield. The officer approached Sullivan's vehicle, explained the reason for the stop, and requested Sullivan's license, registration, and insurance documentation. Upon seeing Sullivan's license, Taylor realized that he was aware of "intelligence on [Sullivan] regarding narcotics." When Sullivan opened his car door in an (unsuccessful) attempt to locate his registration and insurance papers, Taylor noticed a rusted roofing hatchet on the car's floorboard. Taylor then arrested Sullivan for speeding, driving without his registration and insurance documentation, carrying a weapon (the roofing hatchet), and improper window tinting. After another officer arrived and placed Sullivan in his squad car, Officer Taylor conducted an inventory search of Sullivan's vehicle pursuant to the Conway Police Department's Vehicle Inventory Policy. Drugs were discovered in the car, and Sullivan was charged with a drug offense.

The Arkansas courts found the search illegal because it was pretextual. The Arkansas Supreme Court declined to follow *Whren* on the ground that "much of it is dicta." The Supreme Court unanimously reversed, concluding that the Arkansas ruling "is flatly contrary to this Court's controlling precedent." Justice Ginsburg, joined by Justices Stevens, O'Connor and Breyer, wrote a short concurring opinion emphasizing that her opinion on the *Whren* rule might change if "experience demonstrates anything like an epidemic of unnecessary minor-offense arrests."

G. EXIGENT CIRCUMSTANCES

8. Seizing Premises in the Absence of Exigent Circumstances

Page 351. Add the following case at the end of the section

Prohibiting Entry While a Warrant Is Being Obtained: Illinois v. McArthur

In the following case, the Court expanded upon the analysis in *Segura* and firmly established the authority of police officers to maintain the status quo while a warrant is being obtained.

ILLINOIS v. McARTHUR

Supreme Court of the United States, 2001.
531 U.S. 326.

JUSTICE BREYER delivered the opinion of the Court.

Police officers, with probable cause to believe that a man had hidden marijuana in his home, prevented that man from entering the home for about two hours while they obtained a search warrant. We must decide whether those officers violated the Fourth Amendment. We conclude that the officers acted reasonably. They did not violate the Amendment's requirements. And we reverse an Illinois court's holding to the contrary.

I

A

On April 2, 1997, Tera McArthur asked two police officers to accompany her to the trailer where she lived with her husband, Charles, so that they could keep the peace while she removed her belongings. The two officers, Assistant Chief John Love and Officer Richard Skidis, arrived with Tera at the trailer at about 3:15 p.m. Tera went inside, where Charles was present. The officers remained outside.

When Tera emerged after collecting her possessions, she spoke to Chief Love, who was then on the porch. She suggested he check the trailer because "Chuck had dope in there." She added (in Love's words) that she had seen Chuck "slid[e] some dope underneath the couch."

Love knocked on the trailer door, told Charles what Tera had said, and asked for permission to search the trailer, which Charles denied. Love then sent Officer Skidis with Tera to get a search warrant.

Love told Charles, who by this time was also on the porch, that he could not reenter the trailer unless a police officer accompanied him. Charles subsequently reentered the trailer two or three times (to get cigarettes and to make phone calls), and each time Love stood just inside the door to observe what Charles did.

Officer Skidis obtained the warrant by about 5 p.m. He returned to the trailer and, along with other officers, searched it. The officers found under the sofa a marijuana pipe, a box for marijuana (called a "one-hitter" box), and a small amount of marijuana. They then arrested Charles.

B

Illinois subsequently charged Charles McArthur with unlawfully possessing drug paraphernalia and marijuana (less than 2.5 grams), both misdemeanors. McArthur moved to suppress the pipe, box, and marijuana on the ground that they were the "fruit" of an unlawful police seizure, namely, the refusal to let him reenter the trailer unaccompanied, which would have permitted him, he said, to "have destroyed the marijuana."

The trial court granted McArthur's suppression motion. The Appellate Court of Illinois affirmed, and the Illinois Supreme Court denied the State's petition for leave to appeal. We granted certiorari to determine whether the Fourth Amendment prohibits the kind of temporary seizure at issue here.

II

A

The Fourth Amendment says that the "right of the people to be secure in their persons, houses, papers, and effects, against unreasonable searches and seizures, shall not be violated." Its "central requirement" is one of reasonableness. In order to enforce that requirement, this Court has interpreted the Amendment as establishing rules and presumptions designed to control conduct of law enforcement officers that may significantly intrude upon privacy interests. Sometimes those rules require warrants. We have said, for example, that in "the ordinary case," seizures of personal property are "unreasonable within the meaning of the Fourth Amendment," without more, "unless ... accomplished pursuant to a judicial

warrant," issued by a neutral magistrate after finding probable cause. United States v. Place, 462 U.S. 696 (1983).

We nonetheless have made it clear that there are exceptions to the warrant requirement. When faced with special law enforcement needs, diminished expectations of privacy, minimal intrusions, or the like, the Court has found that certain general, or individual, circumstances may render a warrantless search or seizure reasonable. See, e.g., Pennsylvania v. Labron, 518 U.S. 938, 940–941 (1996) *(per curiam)* (search of automobile supported by probable cause); Michigan Dept. of State Police v. Sitz, 496 U.S. 444, 455 (1990) (suspicionless stops at drunk driver checkpoint); United States v. Place, *supra*, at 706, (temporary seizure of luggage based on reasonable suspicion); Michigan v. Summers, 452 U.S. 692, 702–705 (1981) (temporary detention of suspect without arrest warrant to prevent flight and protect officers while executing search warrant); Terry v. Ohio, 392 U.S. 1 (1968) (temporary stop and limited search for weapons based on reasonable suspicion).

In the circumstances of the case before us, we cannot say that the warrantless seizure was *per se* unreasonable. It involves a plausible claim of specially pressing or urgent law enforcement need, *i.e.,* "exigent circumstances." Moreover, the restraint at issue was tailored to that need, being limited in time and scope, and avoiding significant intrusion into the home itself. Consequently, rather than employing a *per se* rule of unreasonableness, we balance the privacy-related and law enforcement-related concerns to determine if the intrusion was reasonable.

We conclude that the restriction at issue was reasonable, and hence lawful, in light of the following circumstances, which we consider in combination. First, the police had probable cause to believe that McArthur's trailer home contained evidence of a crime and contraband, namely, unlawful drugs. The police had had an opportunity to speak with Tera McArthur and make at least a very rough assessment of her reliability. They knew she had had a firsthand opportunity to observe her husband's behavior, in particular with respect to the drugs at issue. And they thought, with good reason, that her report to them reflected that opportunity. Cf. Massachusetts v. Upton, 466 U.S. 727, 732–734 (1984) *(per curiam)* (upholding search warrant issued in similar circumstances).

Second, the police had good reason to fear that, unless restrained, McArthur would destroy the drugs before they could return with a warrant. They reasonably might have thought that McArthur realized that his wife knew about his marijuana stash; observed that she was angry or frightened enough to ask the police to accompany her; saw that after leaving the trailer she had spoken with the police; and noticed that she had walked off with one policeman while leaving the other outside to observe the trailer. They reasonably could have concluded that McArthur, consequently suspecting an imminent search, would, if given the chance, get rid of the drugs fast.

Third, the police made reasonable efforts to reconcile their law enforcement needs with the demands of personal privacy. They neither searched the trailer nor arrested McArthur before obtaining a warrant. Rather, they imposed a significantly less restrictive restraint, preventing McArthur only from entering the trailer unaccompanied. They left his home and his belongings intact—until a neutral Magistrate, finding probable cause, issued a warrant.

Fourth, the police imposed the restraint for a limited period of time, namely, two hours. Cf. Terry v. Ohio, *supra,* at 28 (manner in which police act is a vital part of the inquiry). As far as the record reveals, this time period was no longer than reasonably necessary for the police, acting with diligence, to obtain the warrant. Compare United States v. Place, *supra,* at 709–710, (holding 90–minute detention of luggage unreasonable based on nature of interference with person's travels and lack of diligence of police), with United States v. Van Leeuwen, 397 U.S. 249, 253 (1970) (holding 29–hour detention of mailed package reasonable given unavoidable delay in obtaining warrant and minimal nature of intrusion). Given the nature of the intrusion and the law enforcement interest at stake, this brief seizure of the premises was permissible.

B

Our conclusion that the restriction was lawful finds significant support in this Court's case law. In Segura v. United States, 468 U.S. 796 (1984), the Court considered the admissibility of drugs which the police had found in a lawful, warrant-based search of an apartment, but only after unlawfully entering the apartment and occupying it for 19 hours. The majority held that the drugs were admissible because, had the police acted lawfully throughout, they could have discovered and seized the drugs pursuant to the validly issued warrant. The minority disagreed. However, when describing alternative lawful search and seizure methods, both majority and minority assumed, at least for argument's sake, that the police, armed with reliable information that the apartment contained drugs, might lawfully have sealed the apartment from the outside, restricting entry into the apartment while waiting for the warrant. See also Mincey v. Arizona, 437 U.S. 385, 394 (1978) (exigent circumstances do not justify search where police guard at door could prevent loss of evidence).

In various other circumstances, this Court has upheld temporary restraints where needed to preserve evidence until police could obtain a warrant. See, *e.g.,* United States v. Place, 462 U.S. 696, at 706 (reasonable suspicion justifies brief detention of luggage pending further investigation); Carroll v. United States, 267 U.S. 132 (1925) (warrantless search of automobile constitutionally permissible).

We have found no case in which this Court has held unlawful a temporary seizure that was supported by probable cause and was designed to prevent the loss of evidence while the police diligently obtained a warrant in a reasonable period of time. But cf. Welsh v. Wisconsin, 466 U.S. 740 (1984) (holding warrantless entry into and arrest in home unreasonable despite possibility that evidence of noncriminal offense would be lost while warrant was being obtained).

C

Nor are we persuaded by the countervailing considerations that the parties or lower courts have raised. * * * The Appellate Court of Illinois concluded that the police could not order McArthur to stay outside his home because McArthur's porch, where he stood at the time, was part of his home; hence the order "amounted to a constructive eviction" of McArthur from his residence. This Court has held, however, that a person standing in the doorway of a house is "in a 'public' place," and hence subject to arrest without a warrant permitting entry of the home. United States v. Santana, 427 U.S. 38 (1976). Regardless, we do not believe the difference to which the Appellate Court points—porch versus, *e.g.,* front walk—could make a significant difference here as to the reasonableness of the police restraint; and that, from the Fourth Amendment's perspective, is what matters.

The Appellate Court also found negatively significant the fact that Chief Love, with McArthur's consent, stepped inside the trailer's doorway to observe McArthur when McArthur reentered the trailer on two or three occasions. McArthur, however, reentered simply for his own convenience, to make phone calls and to obtain cigarettes. Under these circumstances, the reasonableness of the greater restriction (preventing reentry) implies the reasonableness of the lesser (permitting reentry conditioned on observation).

Finally, McArthur points to a case (and we believe it is the only case) that he believes offers direct support, namely, Welsh v. Wisconsin, *supra*. In *Welsh*, this Court held that police could not enter a home without a warrant in order to prevent the loss of evidence (namely, the defendant's blood alcohol level) of the "nonjailable traffic offense" of driving while intoxicated. McArthur notes that his two convictions are for misdemeanors, which, he says, are as minor, and he adds that the restraint, keeping him out of his home, was nearly as serious.

We nonetheless find significant distinctions. The evidence at issue here was of crimes that were "jailable," not "nonjailable." See Ill. Comp. Stat., ch. 720, § 550/4(a) (1998); ch. 730, § 5/5–8–3(3) (possession of less than 2.5 grams of marijuana punishable by up to 30 days in jail); ch. 720, § 600/3.5; ch. 730, § 5/5–8–3(1) (possession of drug paraphernalia punishable by up to one year in jail). In *Welsh*, we noted that, "[g]iven that the classification of state crimes differs widely among the States, the penalty that may attach to any particular offense seems to provide the clearest and most consistent indication of the State's interest in arresting individuals suspected of committing that offense." The same reasoning applies here, where class C misdemeanors include such widely diverse offenses as drag racing, drinking alcohol in a railroad car or on a railroad platform, bribery by a candidate for public office, and assault.

And the restriction at issue here is less serious. Temporarily keeping a person from entering his home, a consequence whenever police stop a person on the street, is considerably less intrusive than police entry into the home itself in order to make a warrantless arrest or conduct a search.

We have explained above why we believe that the need to preserve evidence of a "jailable" offense was sufficiently urgent or pressing to justify the restriction upon entry that the police imposed. We need not decide whether the circumstances before us would have justified a greater restriction for this type of offense or the same restriction were only a "nonjailable" offense at issue.

III

In sum, the police officers in this case had probable cause to believe that a home contained contraband, which was evidence of a crime. They reasonably believed that the home's resident, if left free of any restraint, would destroy that evidence. And they imposed a restraint that was both limited and tailored reasonably to secure law enforcement needs while protecting privacy interests. In our view, the restraint met the Fourth Amendment's demands.

The judgment of the Illinois Appellate Court is reversed, and the case is remanded for further proceedings not inconsistent with this opinion.

JUSTICE SOUTER, concurring.

I join the Court's opinion subject to this afterword on two points: the constitutionality of a greater intrusion than the one here and the permissibility of choosing impoundment over immediate search. Respondent McArthur's location made the difference between the exigency that justified temporarily barring him from his own dwelling and circumstances that would have supported a greater interference with his privacy and property. As long as he was inside his trailer, the police had probable cause to believe that he had illegal drugs stashed as his wife had reported and that with any sense he would flush them down the drain before the police could get a warrant to enter and search. This probability of destruction in anticipation of a warrant exemplifies the kind of present risk that undergirds the accepted exigent circumstances exception to the general warrant requirement. That risk would have justified the police in entering McArthur's trailer promptly to make a lawful, warrantless search. When McArthur stepped outside and left the trailer uninhabited, the risk abated and so did the reasonableness of entry by the police for as long as he was outside. This is so because the only justification claimed for warrantless action here is the immediate risk, and the limit of reasonable response by the police is set by the scope of the risk.

Since, however, McArthur wished to go back in, why was it reasonable to keep him out when the police could perfectly well have let him do as he chose, and then enjoyed the ensuing opportunity to follow him and make a warrantless search justified by the renewed danger of destruction? The answer is not that the law officiously insists on safeguarding a suspect's privacy from search, in preference to respecting the suspect's liberty to enter his own dwelling. Instead, the legitimacy of the decision to impound the dwelling follows from the law's strong preference for warrants, which underlies the rule that a search with a warrant has a stronger claim to justification on later, judi-

cial review than a search without one. The law can hardly raise incentives to obtain a warrant without giving the police a fair chance to take their probable cause to a magistrate and get one.

JUSTICE STEVENS, dissenting.

The Illinois General Assembly has decided that the possession of less than 2.5 grams of marijuana is a class C misdemeanor. In so classifying the offense, the legislature made a concerted policy judgment that the possession of small amounts of marijuana for personal use does not constitute a particularly significant public policy concern. While it is true that this offense—like feeding livestock on a public highway or offering a movie for rent without clearly displaying its rating—may warrant a jail sentence of up to 30 days, the detection and prosecution of possessors of small quantities of this substance is by no means a law enforcement priority in the State of Illinois.

Because the governmental interest implicated by the particular criminal prohibition at issue in this case is so slight, this is a poor vehicle for probing the boundaries of the government's power to limit an individual's possessory interest in his or her home pending the arrival of a search warrant. Given my preference, I would, therefore, dismiss the writ of certiorari as improvidently granted.

Compelled by the vote of my colleagues to reach the merits, I would affirm. As the majority explains, the essential inquiry in this case involves a balancing of the "privacy-related and law enforcement-related concerns to determine if the intrusion was reasonable."

Under the specific facts of this case, I believe the majority gets the balance wrong. Each of the Illinois jurists who participated in the decision of this case placed a higher value on the sanctity of the ordinary citizen's home than on the prosecution of this petty offense. They correctly viewed that interest—whether the home be a humble cottage, a secondhand trailer, or a stately mansion—as one meriting the most serious constitutional protection. Following their analysis and the reasoning in our decision in Welsh v. Wisconsin (holding that some offenses may be so minor as to make it unreasonable for police to undertake searches that would be constitutionally permissible if graver offenses were suspected), I would affirm.

H. ADMINISTRATIVE SEARCHES AND OTHER SEARCHES AND SEIZURES BASED ON "SPECIAL NEEDS"

3. Searches and Seizures of Individuals Pursuant to "Special Needs"

b. Suspicionless Searches of Persons on the Basis of "Special Needs"

Page 388.   After *Chandler*, add the following case:

Expansion of Suspicionless Drug–Testing in the Schools: Board of Education v. Earls

In the following case, the Court virtually ignored the limitations of *Chandler* and extended *Vernonia* to permit suspicionless testing of all schoolchildren who wish to participate in "competitive" extracurricular activities.

BOARD OF EDUCATION OF INDEPENDENT SCHOOL DISTRICT NO. 92 OF POTTAWATOMIE COUNTY v. EARLS

Supreme Court of the United States, 2002.
536 U.S. 822

JUSTICE THOMAS delivered the opinion of the Court.

The Student Activities Drug Testing Policy implemented by the Board of Education of Independent School District No. 92 of Pottawatomie County (School District) requires all students who participate in competitive extracurricular activities to submit to drug testing. Because this Policy reasonably serves the School District's important interest in detecting and preventing drug use among its students, we hold that it is constitutional.

I

The city of Tecumseh, Oklahoma, is a rural community located approximately 40 miles southeast of Oklahoma City. The School District administers all Tecumseh public schools. In the fall of 1998, the School District adopted the Student Activities Drug Testing Policy (Policy), which requires all middle and high school students to consent to drug testing in order to participate in any extracurricular activity. In practice, the Policy has been applied only to competitive extracurricular activities sanctioned by the Oklahoma Secondary Schools Activities Association, such as the Academic Team, Future Farmers of America, Future Homemakers of America, band, choir, pom pon, cheerleading, and athletics. Under the Policy, students are required to take a drug test before participating in an extracurricular activity, must submit to random drug testing while participating in that activity, and must agree to be tested at any time upon reasonable suspicion. The urinalysis tests are designed to detect only the use of illegal drugs, including amphetamines, marijuana, cocaine, opiates, and barbiturates, not medical conditions or the presence of authorized prescription medications.

At the time of their suit, both respondents attended Tecumseh High School. Respondent Lindsay Earls was a member of the show choir, the marching band, the Academic Team, and the National Honor Society. Respondent Daniel James sought to participate in the Academic Team. Together with their parents, Earls and James brought a 42 U.S.C. § 1983 action against the School District, challenging the Policy both on its face and as applied to their participation in extracurricular activities. They alleged that the Policy violates the Fourth Amendment as incorporated by the Fourteenth Amendment and requested injunctive and declarative relief. They also argued that the School District failed to identify a special need for testing students who participate in extracurricular activities, and that the "Drug Testing Policy neither addresses a proven problem nor promises to bring any benefit to students or the school."

Applying the principles articulated in Vernonia School Dist. 47J v. Acton, 515 U.S. 646 (1995), in which we upheld the suspicionless drug testing of school athletes, the United States District Court for the Western District of Oklahoma rejected respondents' claim that the Policy was unconstitutional and granted summary judgment to the School District. The court noted that "special needs" exist in the public school context and that, although the School District did "not show a drug problem of epidemic proportions," there was a history of drug abuse starting in 1970 that presented "legitimate cause for concern." The District Court also held that the Policy was effective because "[i]t can scarcely be disputed that the drug problem among the student body is effectively addressed by making sure that the large number of students participating in competitive, extracurricular activities do not use drugs."

The United States Court of Appeals for the Tenth Circuit reversed, holding that the Policy violated the Fourth Amendment. The Court of Appeals agreed with the District Court that the Policy must be evaluated in the "unique environment of the school setting," but reached a different conclusion as to the Policy's constitutionality. Before imposing a suspicionless drug testing program, the Court of Appeals concluded that a school "must demonstrate that there is some identifiable drug abuse problem among a sufficient number of those subject to the testing, such that testing that group of students will actually redress its drug problem." The Court of Appeals then held that because the School District failed to demonstrate such a problem existed among Tecumseh students participating in competitive extracurricular activities, the Policy was unconstitutional. We granted certiorari, and now reverse.

II

* * * Searches by public school officials, such as the collection of urine samples, implicate Fourth Amendment interests. We must therefore review the School District's Policy for "reasonableness," which is the touchstone of the constitutionality of a governmental search.

In the criminal context, reasonableness usually requires a showing of probable cause. The probable-cause standard, however, "is peculiarly related to criminal investigations" and may be unsuited to determining the reasonableness of administrative searches where the "Government seeks to *prevent* the development of hazardous conditions." Treasury Employees v. Von Raab, 489 U.S. 656, 667–668 (1989). The Court has also held that a warrant and finding of probable cause are unnecessary in the public school context because such requirements "would unduly interfere with the maintenance of the swift and informal disciplinary procedures that are needed." *Vernonia, supra,* at 653.

Given that the School District's Policy is not in any way related to the conduct of criminal investigations, see Part II–B, *infra,* respondents do not contend that the

School District requires probable cause before testing students for drug use. Respondents instead argue that drug testing must be based at least on some level of individualized suspicion. It is true that we generally determine the reasonableness of a search by balancing the nature of the intrusion on the individual's privacy against the promotion of legitimate governmental interests. But we have long held that "the Fourth Amendment imposes no irreducible requirement of [individualized] suspicion." United States v. Martinez—Fuerte, 428 U.S. 543, 561 (1976). "[I]n certain limited circumstances, the Government's need to discover such latent or hidden conditions, or to prevent their development, is sufficiently compelling to justify the intrusion on privacy entailed by conducting such searches without any measure of individualized suspicion." *Von Raab, supra,* at 668. Therefore, in the context of safety and administrative regulations, a search unsupported by probable cause may be reasonable "when 'special needs, beyond the normal need for law enforcement, make the warrant and probable-cause requirement impracticable.'" Griffin v. Wisconsin, 483 U.S. 868, 873 (1987).

Significantly, this Court has previously held that "special needs" inhere in the public school context. See *Vernonia, supra,* at 653. While schoolchildren do not shed their constitutional rights when they enter the schoolhouse, "Fourth Amendment rights ... are different in public schools than elsewhere; the 'reasonableness' inquiry cannot disregard the schools' custodial and tutelary responsibility for children." *Vernonia, supra,* at 656. In particular, a finding of individualized suspicion may not be necessary when a school conducts drug testing.

In *Vernonia,* this Court held that the suspicionless drug testing of athletes was constitutional. The Court, however, did not simply authorize all school drug testing, but rather conducted a fact-specific balancing of the intrusion on the children's Fourth Amendment rights against the promotion of legitimate governmental interests. Applying the principles of *Vernonia* to the somewhat different facts of this case, we conclude that Tecumseh's Policy is also constitutional.

A

We first consider the nature of the privacy interest allegedly compromised by the drug testing. As in *Vernonia,* the context of the public school environment serves as the backdrop for the analysis of the privacy interest at stake and the reasonableness of the drug testing policy in general.

A student's privacy interest is limited in a public school environment where the State is responsible for maintaining discipline, health, and safety. Schoolchildren are routinely required to submit to physical examinations and vaccinations against disease. Securing order in the school environment sometimes requires that students be subjected to greater controls than those appropriate for adults.

Respondents argue that because children participating in nonathletic extracurricular activities are not subject to regular physicals and communal undress, they have a stronger expectation of privacy than the athletes tested in *Vernonia.* This

distinction, however, was not essential to our decision in *Vernonia,* which depended primarily upon the school's custodial responsibility and authority.

In any event, students who participate in competitive extracurricular activities voluntarily subject themselves to many of the same intrusions on their privacy as do athletes. Some of these clubs and activities require occasional off-campus travel and communal undress. All of them have their own rules and requirements for participating students that do not apply to the student body as a whole. For example, each of the competitive extracurricular activities governed by the Policy must abide by the rules of the Oklahoma Secondary Schools Activities Association, and a faculty sponsor monitors the students for compliance with the various rules dictated by the clubs and activities. This regulation of extracurricular activities further diminishes the expectation of privacy among schoolchildren. Cf. *Vernonia, supra,* at 657 ("Somewhat like adults who choose to participate in a closely regulated industry, students who voluntarily participate in school athletics have reason to expect intrusions upon normal rights and privileges, including privacy"). We therefore conclude that the students affected by this Policy have a limited expectation of privacy.

B

Next, we consider the character of the intrusion imposed by the Policy. Urination is an excretory function traditionally shielded by great privacy. But the "degree of intrusion" on one's privacy caused by collecting a urine sample "depends upon the manner in which production of the urine sample is monitored." *Vernonia, supra,* at 658.

Under the Policy, a faculty monitor waits outside the closed restroom stall for the student to produce a sample and must "listen for the normal sounds of urination in order to guard against tampered specimens and to insure an accurate chain of custody." The monitor then pours the sample into two bottles that are sealed and placed into a mailing pouch along with a consent form signed by the student. This procedure is virtually identical to that reviewed in *Vernonia,* except that it additionally protects privacy by allowing male students to produce their samples behind a closed stall. Given that we considered the method of collection in *Vernonia* a "negligible" intrusion, the method here is even less problematic.

In addition, the Policy clearly requires that the test results be kept in confidential files separate from a student's other educational records and released to school personnel only on a "need to know" basis. Respondents nonetheless contend that the intrusion on students' privacy is significant because the Policy fails to protect effectively against the disclosure of confidential information and, specifically, that the school "has been careless in protecting that information: for example, the Choir teacher looked at students' prescription drug lists and left them where other students could see them." But the choir teacher is someone with a "need to know," because during off-campus trips she needs to know what medications are taken by her students.

Even before the Policy was enacted the choir teacher had access to this information. In any event, there is no allegation that any other student did see such information. This one example of alleged carelessness hardly increases the character of the intrusion.

Moreover, the test results are not turned over to any law enforcement authority. Nor do the test results here lead to the imposition of discipline or have any academic consequences. Rather, the only consequence of a failed drug test is to limit the student's privilege of participating in extracurricular activities. Indeed, a student may test positive for drugs twice and still be allowed to participate in extracurricular activities. After the first positive test, the school contacts the student's parent or guardian for a meeting. The student may continue to participate in the activity if within five days of the meeting the student shows proof of receiving drug counseling and submits to a second drug test in two weeks. For the second positive test, the student is suspended from participation in all extracurricular activities for 14 days, must complete four hours of substance abuse counseling, and must submit to monthly drug tests. Only after a third positive test will the student be suspended from participating in any extracurricular activity for the remainder of the school year, or 88 school days, whichever is longer.

Given the minimally intrusive nature of the sample collection and the limited uses to which the test results are put, we conclude that the invasion of students' privacy is not significant.

C

Finally, this Court must consider the nature and immediacy of the government's concerns and the efficacy of the Policy in meeting them. See *Vernonia,* 515 U.S., at 660. This Court has already articulated in detail the importance of the governmental concern in preventing drug use by schoolchildren. The drug abuse problem among our Nation's youth has hardly abated since *Vernonia* was decided in 1995. In fact, evidence suggests that it has only grown worse.[5] As in *Vernonia,* "the necessity for the State to act is magnified by the fact that this evil is being visited not just upon individuals at large, but upon children for whom it has undertaken a special responsibility of care and direction." The health and safety risks identified in *Vernonia* apply with equal force to Tecumseh's children. Indeed, the nationwide drug epidemic makes the war against drugs a pressing concern in every school.

Additionally, the School District in this case has presented specific evidence of drug use at Tecumseh schools. Teachers testified that they had seen students who appeared to be under the influence of drugs and that they had heard students speaking openly about using drugs. A drug dog found marijuana cigarettes near the school parking lot. Police officers once found drugs or drug paraphernalia in a car driven by a Future Farmers of America member. And the school board president reported that people in the community were calling the board to discuss the "drug situation." We decline to second-guess the finding of the District Court that "[v]iewing the evidence as a whole, it cannot be reasonably disputed that the [School District] was faced with a 'drug problem' when it adopted the Policy."

Respondents consider the proffered evidence insufficient and argue that there is no "real and immediate interest" to justify a policy of drug testing nonathletes. We have recognized, however, that "[a] demonstrated problem of drug abuse ... [is] not in all cases necessary to the validity of a testing regime," but that some showing does "shore up an assertion of special need for a suspicionless general search program." Chandler v. Miller, 520 U.S. 305, 319 (1997). The School District has provided sufficient evidence to shore up the need for its drug testing program.

Furthermore, this Court has not required a particularized or pervasive drug problem before allowing the government to conduct suspicionless drug testing. For instance, in *Von Raab* the Court upheld the drug testing of customs officials on a purely preventive basis, without any documented history of drug use by such officials. In response to the lack of evidence relating to drug use, the Court noted generally that "drug abuse is one of the most serious problems confronting our society today," and that programs to prevent and detect drug use among customs officials could not be deemed unreasonable. Likewise,

---

5. For instance, the number of 12th graders using any illicit drug increased from 48.4 percent in 1995 to 53.9 percent in 2001. The number of 12th graders reporting they had used marijuana jumped from 41.7 percent to 49.0 percent during that same period. See Department of Health and Human Services, Monitoring the Future: National Results on Adolescent Drug Use, Overview of Key Findings (2001) (Table 1).

the need to prevent and deter the substantial harm of childhood drug use provides the necessary immediacy for a school testing policy. Indeed, it would make little sense to require a school district to wait for a substantial portion of its students to begin using drugs before it was allowed to institute a drug testing program designed to deter drug use.

Given the nationwide epidemic of drug use, and the evidence of increased drug use in Tecumseh schools, it was entirely reasonable for the School District to enact this particular drug testing policy. We reject the Court of Appeals' novel test that "any district seeking to impose a random suspicionless drug testing policy as a condition to participation in a school activity must demonstrate that there is some identifiable drug abuse problem among a sufficient number of those subject to the testing, such that testing that group of students will actually redress its drug problem." Among other problems, it would be difficult to administer such a test. As we cannot articulate a threshold level of drug use that would suffice to justify a drug testing program for schoolchildren, we refuse to fashion what would in effect be a constitutional quantum of drug use necessary to show a "drug problem."

Respondents also argue that the testing of nonathletes does not implicate any safety concerns, and that safety is a "crucial factor" in applying the special needs framework. They contend that there must be "surpassing safety interests," or "extraordinary safety and national security hazards," *Von Raab, supra,* at 674, in order to override the usual protections of the Fourth

Amendment. Respondents are correct that safety factors into the special needs analysis, but the safety interest furthered by drug testing is undoubtedly substantial for all children, athletes and nonathletes alike. We know all too well that drug use carries a variety of health risks for children, including death from overdose.

We also reject respondents' argument that drug testing must presumptively be based upon an individualized reasonable suspicion of wrongdoing because such a testing regime would be less intrusive. In this context, the Fourth Amendment does not require a finding of individualized suspicion, and we decline to impose such a requirement on schools attempting to prevent and detect drug use by students. Moreover, we question whether testing based on individualized suspicion in fact would be less intrusive. Such a regime would place an additional burden on public school teachers who are already tasked with the difficult job of maintaining order and discipline. A program of individualized suspicion might unfairly target members of unpopular groups. The fear of lawsuits resulting from such targeted searches may chill enforcement of the program, rendering it ineffective in combating drug use. See *Vernonia,* 515 U.S., at 663–664 (offering similar reasons for why "testing based on 'suspicion' of drug use would not be better, but worse"). In any case, this Court has repeatedly stated that reasonableness under the Fourth Amendment does not require employing the least intrusive means, because "[t]he logic of such elaborate less-restrictive-alternative arguments could raise insuperable barriers to the exercise of virtually all search-and-seizure powers." *Martinez—Fuerte,* 428 U.S., at 556–557, n. 12.

Finally, we find that testing students who participate in extracurricular activities is a reasonably effective means of addressing the School District's legitimate concerns in preventing, deterring, and detecting drug use. While in *Vernonia* there might have been a closer fit between the testing of athletes and the trial court's finding that the drug problem was "fueled by the 'role model' effect of athletes' drug use," such a finding was not essential to the holding. *Vernonia* did not require the school to test the group of students most likely to use drugs, but rather considered the constitutionality of the program in the context of the public school's custodial responsibilities. Evaluating the Policy in this context, we conclude that the drug testing of Tecumseh students who participate in extracurricular activities effectively serves the School District's interest in protecting the safety and health of its students.

III

Within the limits of the Fourth Amendment, local school boards must assess the desirability of drug testing schoolchildren. In upholding the constitutionality of the Policy, we express no opinion as to its wisdom. Rather, we hold only that Tecumseh's Policy is a reasonable means of furthering the School District's important interest in preventing and deterring drug use among its schoolchildren. Accordingly, we reverse the judgment of the Court of Appeals.

It is so ordered.

JUSTICE BREYER, concurring.

I agree with the Court that Vernonia School Dist. 47J v. Acton, 515 U.S. 646 (1995), governs this case and requires reversal of the Tenth Circuit's decision. The school's drug testing program addresses a serious national problem by focusing upon demand, avoiding the use of criminal or disciplinary sanctions, and relying upon professional counseling and treatment. In my view, this program does not violate the Fourth Amendment's prohibition of "unreasonable searches and seizures." I reach this conclusion primarily for the reasons given by the Court, but I would emphasize several underlying considerations, which I understand to be consistent with the Court's opinion.

I

In respect to the school's need for the drug testing program, I would emphasize the following: First, the drug problem in our Nation's schools is serious in terms of size, the kinds of drugs being used, and the consequences of that use both for our children and the rest of us. See, *e.g.,* White House Nat. Drug Control Strategy 25 (Feb. 2002) (drug abuse leads annually to about 20,000 deaths, $160 billion in economic costs); Department of Health and Human Services, L. Johnston et al., Monitoring the Future: National Results on Adolescent Drug Use, Overview of Key Findings 5 (2001) (Monitoring the Future) (more than one-third of all students have used illegal drugs before completing the eighth grade; more than half before completing high school); *ibid.* (about 30% of all students use drugs *other than mari-*

juana prior to completing high school (emphasis added)); National Center on Addiction and Substance Abuse, Malignant Neglect: Substance Abuse and America's Schools 15 (Sept.2001) (Malignant Neglect) (early use leads to later drug dependence).

Second, the government's emphasis upon supply side interdiction apparently has not reduced teenage use in recent years. Compare R. Perl, CRS Issue Brief for Congress, Drug Control: International Policy and Options CRS–1 (Dec. 12, 2001) (supply side programs account for 66% of the federal drug control budget), with Partnership for a Drug–Free America, 2001 Partnership Attitude Tracking Study: Key Findings 1 (showing increase in teenage drug use in early 1990's, peak in 1997, holding steady thereafter); 2000–2001 PRIDE National Summary: Alcohol, Tobacco, Illicit Drugs, Violence and Related Behaviors, Grades 6 thru 12 (Apr. 5, 2002), http://www.pridesurveys.com/us00.pdf (slight rise in high school drug use in 2000–2001); Monitoring the Future, Table 1 (lifetime prevalence of drug use increasing over last 10 years).

Third, public school systems must find effective ways to deal with this problem. Today's public expects its schools not simply to teach the fundamentals, but "to shoulder the burden of feeding students breakfast and lunch, offering before and after school child care services, and providing medical and psychological services," all in a school environment that is safe and encourages learning. Brief for National School Boards Association et al. as *Amici Curiae* 3–4. The law itself recognizes these responsibili-

ties with the phrase *in loco parentis*—a phrase that draws its legal force primarily from the needs of younger students (who here are necessarily grouped together with older high school students) and which reflects, not that a child or adolescent lacks an interest in privacy, but that a child's or adolescent's school-related privacy interest, when compared to the privacy interests of an adult, has different dimensions. A public school system that fails adequately to carry out its responsibilities may well see parents send their children to private or parochial school instead—with help from the State.

Fourth, the program at issue here seeks to discourage demand for drugs by changing the school's environment in order to combat the single most important factor leading school children to take drugs, namely, peer pressure. Malignant Neglect 4 (students "whose friends use illicit drugs are more than 10 times likelier to use illicit drugs than those whose friends do not"). It offers the adolescent a nonthreatening reason to decline his friend's drug-use invitations, namely, that he intends to play baseball, participate in debate, join the band, or engage in any one of half a dozen useful, interesting, and important activities.

II

In respect to the privacy-related burden that the drug testing program imposes upon students, I would emphasize the following: First, not everyone would agree with this Court's characterization of the privacy-related significance of urine sampling as "negligible." Some find the procedure no more intrusive than a routine medical examination, but others are seriously embarrassed by the need to provide a urine sample with someone listening "outside the closed restroom stall." When trying to resolve this kind of close question involving the interpretation of constitutional values, I believe it important that the school board provided an opportunity for the airing of these differences at public meetings designed to give the entire community "the opportunity to be able to participate" in developing the drug policy. The board used this democratic, participatory process to uncover and to resolve differences, giving weight to the fact that the process, in this instance, revealed little, if any, objection to the proposed testing program.

Second, the testing program avoids subjecting the entire school to testing. And it preserves an option for a conscientious objector. He can refuse testing while paying a price (nonparticipation) that is serious, but less severe than expulsion from the school.

Third, a contrary reading of the Constitution, as requiring "individualized suspicion" in this public school context, could well lead schools to push the boundaries of "individualized suspicion" to its outer limits, using subjective criteria that may "unfairly target members of unpopular groups," or leave those whose behavior is slightly abnormal stigmatized in the minds of others. See Belsky, Random vs. Suspicion–Based Drug Testing in the Public Schools—A Surprising Civil Liberties Dilemma, 27 Okla. City U.L.Rev. 1, 20–21 (forthcoming 2002) (listing court-approved factors justifying suspicion-based drug

testing, including tiredness, overactivity, quietness, boisterousness, sloppiness, excessive meticulousness, and tardiness). If so, direct application of the Fourth Amendment's prohibition against "unreasonable searches and seizures" will further that Amendment's liberty-protecting objectives at least to the same extent as application of the mediating "individualized suspicion" test, where, as here, the testing program is neither criminal nor disciplinary in nature.

* * *

I cannot know whether the school's drug testing program will work. But, in my view, the Constitution does not prohibit the effort. Emphasizing the considerations I have mentioned, along with others to which the Court refers, I conclude that the school's drug testing program, constitutionally speaking, is not "unreasonable." And I join the Court's opinion.

Justice O'Connor, **with whom** Justice Souter **joins, dissenting.**

I dissented in Vernonia School Dist. 47J v. Acton, 515 U.S. 646 (1995), and continue to believe that case was wrongly decided. Because *Vernonia* is now this Court's precedent, and because I agree that petitioners' program fails even under the balancing approach adopted in that case, I join Justice GINSBURG's dissent.

Justice Ginsburg, **with whom** Justice Stevens, Justice O'Connor, **and** Justice Souter **join, dissenting.**

Seven years ago, in Vernonia School Dist. 47J v. Acton, 515 U.S. 646 (1995), this Court determined that a school district's policy of randomly testing the urine of its student athletes for illicit drugs did not violate the Fourth Amendment. In so ruling, the Court emphasized that drug use "increase[d] the risk of sports—related injury" and that Vernonia's athletes were the "leaders" of an aggressive local "drug culture" that had reached "'epidemic proportions.'" *Id.,* at 649. Today, the Court relies upon *Vernonia* to permit a school district with a drug problem its superintendent repeatedly described as "not ... major," to test the urine of an academic team member solely by reason of her participation in a nonathletic, competitive extracurricular activity—participation associated with neither special dangers from, nor particular predilections for, drug use.

"[T]he legality of a search of a student," this Court has instructed, "should depend simply on the reasonableness, under all the circumstances, of the search." *New Jersey v. T.L.O.,* 469 U.S. 325, 341 (1985). Although "special needs" inhere in the public school context, those needs are not so expansive or malleable as to render reasonable any program of student drug testing a school district elects to install. The particular testing program upheld today is not reasonable, it is capricious, even perverse: Petitioners' policy targets for testing a student population least likely to be at risk from illicit drugs and their damaging effects. I therefore dissent.

I

A

A search unsupported by probable cause nevertheless may be consistent with the Fourth Amendment "when special needs, beyond the normal need for law enforcement, make the warrant and probable-cause requirement impracticable." *Griffin v. Wisconsin,* 483 U.S. 868, 873 (1987). * * * The *Vernonia* Court concluded that a public school district facing a disruptive and explosive drug abuse problem sparked by members of its athletic teams had "special needs" that justified suspicionless testing of district athletes as a condition of their athletic participation.

This case presents circumstances dispositively different from those of *Vernonia.* True, as the Court stresses, Tecumseh students participating in competitive extracurricular activities other than athletics share two relevant characteristics with the athletes of *Vernonia.* First, both groups attend public schools. * * * Concern for student health and safety is basic to the school's caretaking, and it is undeniable that "drug use carries a variety of health risks for children, including death from overdose."

Those risks, however, are present for *all* schoolchildren. *Vernonia* cannot be read to endorse invasive and suspicionless drug testing of all students upon any evidence of drug use, solely because drugs jeopardize the life and health of those who use them. Many children, like many adults, engage in dangerous activities on their own time; that the children are enrolled in school scarcely allows government to monitor all such activities. If a student has a reasonable subjective expectation of privacy in the personal items she brings to school, see *T.L.O.,* 469 U.S., at 338–339, surely she has a similar expectation regarding the chemical composition of her urine. Had the *Vernonia* Court agreed that public school attendance, in and of itself, permitted the State to test each student's blood or urine for drugs, the opinion in *Vernonia* could have saved many words. See, *e.g.,* 515 U.S., at 662 ("[I]t must not be lost sight of that [the Vernonia School District] program is directed ... to drug use by school athletes, where the risk of immediate physical harm to the drug user or those with whom he is playing his sport is particularly high.").

The second commonality to which the Court points is the voluntary character of both interscholastic athletics and other competitive extracurricular activities. "By choosing to 'go out for the team,' [school athletes] voluntarily subject themselves to a degree of regulation even higher than that imposed on students generally." *Id.,* at 657. Comparably, the Court today observes, "students who participate in competitive extracurricular activities voluntarily subject themselves to" additional rules not applicable to other students.

The comparison is enlightening. While extracurricular activities are "voluntary" in the sense that they are not required for graduation, they are part of the school's educational program; for that reason, the petitioner (hereinafter School District) is justified in expending public resources to make them available. Participation in such activities is a key component of school life, essential in reality for students applying to college, and, for all participants, a significant contributor to the breadth and quality of the educational experience. Students "volunteer" for extracurricular pursuits in the same way they might volunteer for honors classes: They subject themselves to additional requirements, but they do so in order to take full advantage of the education offered them.

Voluntary participation in athletics has a distinctly different dimension: Schools regulate student athletes discretely because competitive school sports by their nature require communal undress and, more important, expose students to physical risks that schools have a duty to mitigate. For the very reason that schools cannot offer a program of competitive athletics without intimately affecting the privacy of students, *Vernonia* reasonably analogized school athletes to "adults who choose to participate in a closely regulated industry." Industries fall within the closely regulated category when the nature of their activities requires substantial government oversight. Interscholastic athletics similarly require close safety and health regulation; a school's choir, band, and academic team do not.

In short, *Vernonia* applied, it did not repudiate, the principle that "the legality of a search of a student should depend simply on the reasonableness, *under all the circumstances,* of the search." Enrollment in a public school, and election to participate in school activities beyond the bare minimum that the curriculum requires, are indeed factors relevant to reasonableness, but they do not on their own justify intrusive, suspicionless searches. *Vernonia,* accordingly, did not rest upon these factors; instead, the Court performed what today's majority aptly describes as a "fact-specific balancing." Balancing of that order, applied to the facts now before the Court, should yield a result other than the one the Court announces today.

B

* * *

[T]he "nature and immediacy of the governmental concern," *Vernonia*, 515 U.S., at 660, faced by the Vernonia School District dwarfed that confronting Tecumseh administrators. Vernonia initiated its drug testing policy in response to an alarming situation: "[A] large segment of the student body, particularly those involved in interscholastic athletics, was in a state of rebellion ... fueled by alcohol and drug abuse as well as the student[s'] misperceptions about the drug culture." *Id.*, at 649. Tecumseh, by contrast, repeatedly reported to the Federal Government during the period leading up to the adoption of the policy that "types of drugs [other than alcohol and tobacco] including controlled dangerous substances, are present [in the schools] but have not identified themselves as major problems at this time." 1998–1999 Tecumseh School's Application for Funds under the Safe and Drug–Free Schools and Communities Program. As the Tenth Circuit observed, "without a demonstrated drug abuse problem among the group being tested, the efficacy of the District's solution to its perceived problem is ... greatly diminished."

The School District cites Treasury Employees v. Von Raab, 489 U.S. 656, 673–674 (1989), in which this Court permitted random drug testing of customs agents absent "any perceived drug problem among Customs employees," given that

"drug abuse is one of the most serious problems confronting our society today." See also Skinner v. Railway Labor Executives' Assn., 489 U.S. 602, 607, and n. 1 (1989) (upholding random drug and alcohol testing of railway employees based upon industry-wide, rather than railway-specific, evidence of drug and alcohol problems). The tests in *Von Raab* and *Railway Labor Executives*, however, were installed to avoid enormous risks to the lives and limbs of others, not dominantly in response to the health risks to users invariably present in any case of drug use. See *Von Raab*, 489 U.S., at 674 (drug use by customs agents involved in drug interdiction creates "extraordinary safety and national security hazards"); *Railway Labor Executives*, 489 U.S., at 628 (railway operators "discharge duties fraught with such risks of injury to others that even a momentary lapse of attention can have disastrous consequences"); see also *Chandler v. Miller*, 520 U.S. 305, 321 (1997) ("*Von Raab* must be read in its unique context").

Not only did the Vernonia and Tecumseh districts confront drug problems of distinctly different magnitudes, they also chose different solutions: Vernonia limited its policy to athletes; Tecumseh indiscriminately subjected to testing all participants in competitive extracurricular activities. Urging that "the safety interest furthered by drug testing is undoubtedly substantial for all children, athletes and nonathletes alike," the Court cuts out an element essential to the *Vernonia* judgment. Citing medical literature on the effects of combining illicit drug use with physical exertion, the *Vernonia* Court emphasized that "the particular drugs screened by [Vernonia's] Policy have been demonstrated to pose substantial physical risks to athletes." 515 U.S., at 662; see also *id.*, at 666 (GINSBURG, J., concurring) (*Vernonia* limited to "those seeking to engage with others in team sports"). We have since confirmed that these special risks were necessary to our decision in *Vernonia*. See *Chandler*, 520 U.S., at 317 (*Vernonia* "emphasized the importance of deterring drug use by schoolchildren and the risk of injury a drug-using student athlete cast on himself and those engaged with him on the playing field").

At the margins, of course, no policy of *random* drug testing is perfectly tailored to the harms it seeks to address. The School District cites the dangers faced by members of the band, who must "perform extremely precise routines with heavy equipment and instruments in close proximity to other students," and by Future Farmers of America, who "are required to individually control and restrain animals as large as 1500 pounds." For its part, the United States acknowledges that "the linebacker faces a greater risk of serious injury if he takes the field under the influence of drugs than the drummer in the halftime band," but parries that "the risk of injury to a student who is under the influence of drugs while playing golf, cross country, or volleyball (sports covered by the policy in *Vernonia*) is scarcely any greater than the risk of injury to a student ... handling a 1500–pound steer (as [Future Farmers of America] members do) or working with cutlery or other sharp instruments (as [Future Homemakers of America] members do)."

Brief for United States as *Amicus Curiae* 18. One can demur to the Government's view of the risks drug use poses to golfers, for golfers were surely as marginal among the linebackers, sprinters, and basketball players targeted for testing in *Vernonia* as steer-handlers are among the choristers, musicians, and academic-team members subject to urinalysis in Tecumseh. Notwithstanding nightmarish images of out-of-control flatware, livestock run amok, and colliding tubas disturbing the peace and quiet of Tecumseh, the great majority of students the School District seeks to test in truth are engaged in activities that are not safety sensitive to an unusual degree. There is a difference between imperfect tailoring and no tailoring at all.

The Vernonia district, in sum, had two good reasons for testing athletes: Sports team members faced special health risks and they "were the leaders of the drug culture." *Vernonia*, 515 U.S., at 649. No similar reason, and no other tenable justification, explains Tecumseh's decision to target for testing all participants in every competitive extracurricular activity. See *Chandler*, 520 U.S., at 319 (drug testing candidates for office held incompatible with Fourth Amendment because program was "not well designed to identify candidates who violate anti-drug laws").

Nationwide, students who participate in extracurricular activities are significantly less likely to develop substance abuse problems than are their less-involved peers. See, *e.g.*, N. Zill, C. Nord, & L. Loomis, Adolescent Time Use, Risky Behavior, and Outcomes 52 (1995) (tenth graders "who reported spending no time in school-sponsored activities were ... 49 percent more likely to have used drugs" than those who spent 1–4 hours per week in such activities). Even if students might be deterred from drug use in order to preserve their extracurricular eligibility, it is at least as likely that other students might forgo their extracurricular involvement in order to avoid detection of their drug use. Tecumseh's policy thus falls short doubly if deterrence is its aim: It invades the privacy of students who need deterrence least, and risks steering students at greatest risk for substance abuse away from extracurricular involvement that potentially may palliate drug problems.

To summarize, this case resembles *Vernonia* only in that the School Districts in both cases conditioned engagement in activities outside the obligatory curriculum on random subjection to urinalysis. The defining characteristics of the two programs, however, are entirely dissimilar. The Vernonia district sought to test a subpopulation of students distinguished by their reduced expectation of privacy, their special susceptibility to drug-related injury, and their heavy involvement with drug use. The Tecumseh district seeks to test a much larger population associated with none of these factors. It does so, moreover, without carefully safeguarding student confidentiality and without regard to the program's untoward effects. A program so sweeping is not sheltered by *Vernonia;* its unreasonable reach renders it impermissible under the Fourth Amendment.

II

In *Chandler,* this Court inspected "Georgia's requirement that candidates for state office pass a drug test"; we held that the requirement "d[id] not fit within the closely guarded category of constitutionally permissible suspicionless searches." Georgia's testing prescription, the record showed, responded to no "concrete danger," was supported by no evidence of a particular problem, and targeted a group not involved in "high-risk, safety-sensitive tasks." We concluded:

> "What is left, after close review of Georgia's scheme, is the image the State seeks to project. By requiring candidates for public office to submit to drug testing, Georgia displays its commitment to the struggle against drug abuse.... The need revealed, in short, is symbolic, not 'special,' as that term draws meaning from our case law."

Close review of Tecumseh's policy compels a similar conclusion. That policy was not shown to advance the " 'special needs' [existing] in the public school context [to maintain] ... swift and informal disciplinary procedures ... [and] order in the schools," *Vernonia,* 515 U.S., at 653. What is left is the School District's undoubted purpose to heighten awareness of its abhorrence of, and strong stand against, drug abuse. But the desire to augment communication of this message does not trump the right of persons—even of children within the schoolhouse gate—to be "secure in their persons ... against unreasonable searches and seizures." U.S. Const., Amdt. 4.

In *Chandler,* the Court referred to a pathmarking dissenting opinion in which "Justice Brandeis recognized the importance of teaching by example: 'Our Government is the potent, the omnipresent teacher. For good or for ill, it teaches the whole people by its example.' "520 U.S., at 322 (quoting *Olmstead v. United States*, 277 U.S. 438, 485 (1928)). That wisdom should guide decisionmakers in the instant case: The government is nowhere more a teacher than when it runs a public school.

* * *

For the reasons stated, I would affirm the judgment of the Tenth Circuit declaring the testing policy at issue unconstitutional.

4. Roadblocks and Suspicionless Seizures

Page 390. At the end of the section, add the following:

Drug-Testing of Pregnant Mothers

In the following case the Court continued along the difficult path of distinguishing which searches serve special needs beyond ordinary criminal law enforcement and which do not.

FERGUSON v. CITY OF CHARLESTON

Supreme Court of the United States, 2001.
532 U.S. 67.

JUSTICE STEVENS **delivered the opinion of the Court.**

In this case, we must decide whether a state hospital's performance of a diagnostic test to obtain evidence of a patient's criminal conduct for law enforcement purposes is an unreasonable search if the patient has not consented to the procedure. More narrowly, the question is whether the interest in using the threat of criminal sanctions to deter pregnant women from using cocaine can justify a departure from the general rule that an official non-consensual search is unconstitutional if not authorized by a valid warrant.

I

In the fall of 1988, staff members at the public hospital operated in the city of Charleston by the Medical University of South Carolina (MUSC) became concerned about an apparent increase in the use of cocaine by patients who were receiving prenatal treatment. In response to this perceived increase, as of April 1989, MUSC began to order drug screens to be performed on urine samples from maternity patients who were suspected of using cocaine. If a patient tested positive, she was then referred by MUSC staff to the county substance abuse commission for counseling and treatment. However, despite the referrals, the incidence of cocaine use among the patients at MUSC did not appear to change.

Some four months later, Nurse Shirley Brown, the case manager for the MUSC obstetrics department, heard a news broadcast reporting that the police in Greenville, South Carolina, were arresting pregnant users of cocaine on the theory that such use harmed the fetus and was therefore child abuse. Nurse Brown discussed the story with MUSC's general counsel, Joseph C. Good,

Jr., who then contacted Charleston Solicitor Charles Condon in order to offer MUSC's cooperation in prosecuting mothers whose children tested positive for drugs at birth.

After receiving Good's letter, Solicitor Condon took the first steps in developing the policy at issue in this case. He organized the initial meetings, decided who would participate, and issued the invitations, in which he described his plan to prosecute women who tested positive for cocaine while pregnant. The task force that Condon formed included representatives of MUSC, the police, the County Substance Abuse Commission and the Department of Social Services. Their deliberations led to MUSC's adoption of a 12–page document entitled "POLICY M–7," dealing with the subject of "Management of Drug Abuse During Pregnancy." The first three pages of Policy M–7 set forth the procedure to be followed by the hospital staff to "identify/assist pregnant patients suspected of drug abuse." The first section, entitled the "Identification of Drug Abusers," provided that a patient should be tested for cocaine through a urine drug screen if she met one or more of nine criteria.[4] It also stated that a chain of custody should be followed when obtaining and testing urine samples, presumably to make sure that the results could be used in subsequent criminal proceedings. The policy also provided

for education and referral to a substance abuse clinic for patients who tested positive. Most important, it added the threat of law enforcement intervention that "provided the necessary leverage to make the [p]olicy effective." That threat was, as respondents candidly acknowledge, essential to the program's success in getting women into treatment and keeping them there.

The threat of law enforcement involvement was set forth in two protocols, the first dealing with the identification of drug use during pregnancy, and the second with identification of drug use after labor. Under the latter protocol, the police were to be notified without delay and the patient promptly arrested. Under the former, after the initial positive drug test, the police were to be notified (and the patient arrested) only if the patient tested positive for cocaine a second time or if she missed an appointment with a substance abuse counselor. In 1990, however, the policy was modified at the behest of the solicitor's office to give the patient who tested positive during labor, like the patient who tested positive during a prenatal care visit, an opportunity to avoid arrest by consenting to substance abuse treatment.

The last six pages of the policy contained forms for the patients to sign, as well as procedures for the police to follow when a patient was arrested. The policy also prescribed

---

4.   Those criteria were as follows:

   1.   No prenatal care
   2.   Late prenatal care after 24 weeks gestation
   3.   Incomplete prenatal care
   4.   Abruptio placentae
   5.   Intrauterine fetal death

6.   Preterm labor of no obvious cause

7.   IUGR [intrauterine growth retardation] of no obvious cause

8.   Previously known drug or alcohol abuse

9.   Unexplained congenital anomalies.

in detail the precise offenses with which a woman could be charged, depending on the stage of her pregnancy. If the pregnancy was 27 weeks or less, the patient was to be charged with simple possession. If it was 28 weeks or more, she was to be charged with possession and distribution to a person under the age of 18—in this case, the fetus. If she delivered "while testing positive for illegal drugs," she was also to be charged with unlawful neglect of a child. Under the policy, the police were instructed to interrogate the arrestee in order "to ascertain the identity of the subject who provided illegal drugs to the suspect." Other than the provisions describing the substance abuse treatment to be offered to women who tested positive, the policy made no mention of any change in the prenatal care of such patients, nor did it prescribe any special treatment for the newborns.

II

Petitioners are 10 women who received obstetrical care at MUSC and who were arrested after testing positive for cocaine. Four of them were arrested during the initial implementation of the policy; they were not offered the opportunity to receive drug treatment as an alternative to arrest. The others were arrested after the policy was modified in 1990; they either failed to comply with the terms of the drug treatment program or tested positive for a second time. Respondents include the city of Charleston, law enforcement officials who helped develop and enforce the policy, and representatives of MUSC.

Petitioners' complaint challenged the validity of the policy under vari-

ous theories, including the claim that warrantless and nonconsensual drug tests conducted for criminal investigatory purposes were unconstitutional searches. Respondents advanced two principal defenses to the constitutional claim: (1) that, as a matter of fact, petitioners had consented to the searches; and (2) that, as a matter of law, the searches were reasonable, even absent consent, because they were justified by special non-law-enforcement purposes. The District Court rejected the second defense because the searches in question "were not done by the medical university for independent purposes. [Instead,] the police came in and there was an agreement reached that the positive screens would be shared with the police." Accordingly, the District Court submitted the factual defense to the jury with instructions that required a verdict in favor of petitioners unless the jury found consent. The jury found for respondents.

Petitioners appealed, arguing that the evidence was not sufficient to support the jury's consent finding. The Court of Appeals for the Fourth Circuit affirmed, but without reaching the question of consent. Disagreeing with the District Court, the majority of the appellate panel held that the searches were reasonable as a matter of law under our line of cases recognizing that "special needs" may, in certain exceptional circumstances, justify a search policy designed to serve non-law—enforcement ends. On the understanding "that MUSC personnel conducted the urine drug screens for medical purposes wholly independent of an intent to aid law enforcement efforts," the majority applied the balancing test used in Treasury Employees v. Von Raab, 489 U.S. 656 (1989), and Vernonia School Dist. 47J v. Acton, 515 U.S. 646 (1995), and concluded that the interest in curtailing the pregnancy complications and medical costs associated with maternal cocaine use outweighed what the majority termed a minimal intrusion on the privacy of the patients. In dissent, Judge Blake concluded that the "special needs" doctrine should not apply and that the evidence of consent was insufficient to sustain the jury's verdict.

We granted certiorari to review the appellate court's holding on the "special needs" issue. Because we do not reach the question of the sufficiency of the evidence with respect to consent, we necessarily assume for purposes of our decision—as did the Court of Appeals— that the searches were conducted without the informed consent of the patients. We conclude that the judgment should be reversed and the case remanded for a decision on the consent issue.

III

Because MUSC is a state hospital, the members of its staff are government actors, subject to the strictures of the Fourth Amendment. Moreover, the urine tests conducted by those staff members were indisputably searches within the meaning of the Fourth Amendment. Skinner v. Railway Labor Executives' Assn., 489 U.S. 602 (1989). Neither the District Court nor the Court of Appeals concluded that any of the nine criteria used to identify the women to be searched provided either probable cause to believe that they were using cocaine, or even

the basis for a reasonable suspicion of such use. Rather, the District Court and the Court of Appeals viewed the case as one involving MUSC's right to conduct searches without warrants or probable cause. Furthermore, given the posture in which the case comes to us, we must assume for purposes of our decision that the tests were performed without the informed consent of the patients.

Because the hospital seeks to justify its authority to conduct drug tests and to turn the results over to law enforcement agents without the knowledge or consent of the patients, this case differs from the four previous cases in which we have considered whether comparable drug tests "fit within the closely guarded category of constitutionally permissible suspicionless searches." Chandler v. Miller, 520 U.S. 305 (1997). In three of those cases, we sustained drug tests for railway employees involved in train accidents, Skinner v. Railway Labor Executives' Assn., 489 U.S. 602 (1989), for United States Customs Service employees seeking promotion to certain sensitive positions, Treasury Employees v. Von Raab, 489 U.S. 656 (1989), and for high school students participating in interscholastic sports, Vernonia School Dist. 47J v. Acton, 515 U.S. 646 (1995). In the fourth case, we struck down such testing for candidates for designated state offices as unreasonable. Chandler v. Miller, 520 U.S. 305 (1997). In each of those cases, we employed a balancing test that weighed the intrusion on the individual's interest in privacy against the "special needs" that supported the program. As an initial matter, we note that the invasion of privacy in this case is far more substantial than in those cases. In the previous four cases, there was no misunderstanding about the purpose of the test or the potential use of the test results, and there were protections against the dissemination of the results to third parties. The use of an adverse test result to disqualify one from eligibility for a particular benefit, such as a promotion or an opportunity to participate in an extracurricular activity, involves a less serious intrusion on privacy than the unauthorized dissemination of such results to third parties. The reasonable expectation of privacy enjoyed by the typical patient undergoing diagnostic tests in a hospital is that the results of those tests will not be shared with nonmedical personnel without her consent. In none of our prior cases was there any intrusion upon that kind of expectation.

The critical difference between those four drug-testing cases and this one, however, lies in the nature of the "special need" asserted as justification for the warrantless searches. In each of those earlier cases, the "special need" that was advanced as a justification for the absence of a warrant or individualized suspicion was one divorced from the State's general interest in law enforcement. * * * In this case, however, the central and indispensable feature of the policy from its inception was the use of law enforcement to coerce the patients into substance abuse treatment. This fact distinguishes this case from circumstances in which physicians or psychologists, in the course of ordinary medical procedures aimed at helping the patient herself, come across information that under

rules of law or ethics is subject to reporting requirements, which no one has challenged here. *See, e.g.,* Ark.Code Ann. § 12–12–602 (1999) (requiring reporting of intentionally inflicted knife or gunshot wounds); Ariz.Rev.Stat. Ann. § 13–3620 (Supp.2000) (requiring "any ... person having responsibility for the care or treatment of children" to report suspected abuse or neglect to a peace officer or child protection agency).

Respondents argue in essence that their ultimate purpose—namely, protecting the health of both mother and child—is a beneficent one. In *Chandler*, however, we did not simply accept the State's invocation of a "special need." Instead, we carried out a "close review" of the scheme at issue before concluding that the need in question was not "special," as that term has been defined in our cases. In this case, a review of the M–7 policy plainly reveals that the purpose actually served by the MUSC searches "is ultimately indistinguishable from the general interest in crime control." Indianapolis v. Edmond, [infra, this Supplement, in the section on roadblocks].

In looking to the programmatic purpose, we consider all the available evidence in order to determine the relevant primary purpose. In this case, as Judge Blake put it in her dissent below, "it * * * is clear from the record that an initial and continuing focus of the policy was on the arrest and prosecution of drug-abusing mothers." Tellingly, the document codifying the policy incorporates the police's operational guidelines. It devotes its attention to the chain of custody, the range of possible criminal charges, and the logistics of police notification and arrests. Nowhere, however, does the document discuss different courses of medical treatment for either mother or infant, aside from treatment for the mother's addiction.

Moreover, throughout the development and application of the policy, the Charleston prosecutors and police were extensively involved in the day-to-day administration of the policy. Police and prosecutors decided who would receive the reports of positive drug screens and what information would be included with those reports. Law enforcement officials also helped determine the procedures to be followed when performing the screens. In the course of the policy's administration, they had access to Nurse Brown's medical files on the women who tested positive, routinely attended the substance abuse team's meetings, and regularly received copies of team documents discussing the women's progress. Police took pains to coordinate the timing and circumstances of the arrests with MUSC staff, and, in particular, Nurse Brown.

While the ultimate goal of the program may well have been to get the women in question into substance abuse treatment and off of drugs, the immediate objective of the searches was to *generate evidence for law enforcement purposes* in order to reach that goal.[21] The threat of law enforcement may ultimately have been intended as a means to an end, but the direct and primary purpose of MUSC's policy was to ensure the use of those means. In our opinion, this distinction is critical. Because law enforcement involvement always serves some broader social purpose or objective, under respondents' view, virtually any nonconsensual suspicionless search could be immunized under the special needs doctrine by defining the search solely in terms of its ultimate, rather than immediate, purpose. Such an approach is inconsistent with the Fourth Amendment. Given the primary purpose of the Charleston program, which was to use the threat of arrest and prosecution in order to force women into treatment, and given the extensive involvement of

21. Accordingly, this case differs from New York v. Burger, 482 U.S. 691 (1987), in which the Court upheld a scheme in which police officers were used to carry out administrative inspections of vehicle dismantling businesses. That case involved an industry in which the expectation of privacy in commercial premises was "particularly attenuated" given the extent to which the industry in question was closely regulated. More important for our purposes, the Court relied on the "plain administrative purposes" of the scheme to reject the contention that the statute was in fact "designed to gather evidence to enable convictions under the penal laws." The discovery of evidence of other violations would have been merely incidental to the purposes of the administrative search. In contrast, in this case, the policy was specifically designed to gather evidence of violations of penal laws.

This case also differs from the handful of seizure cases in which we have applied a balancing test to determine Fourth Amendment reasonableness. *See, e.g.,* Michigan Dept. of State Police v. Sitz, 496 U.S. 444, 455 (1990); United States v. Martinez–Fuerte, 428 U.S. 543 (1976). First, those cases involved roadblock seizures, rather than "the intrusive search of the body or the home." See Indianapolis v. Edmond (REHNQUIST, C. J., dissenting); *Martinez-Fuerte,* 428 U.S., at 561 ("[W]e deal neither with searches nor with the sanctity of private dwellings, ordinarily afforded the most stringent Fourth Amendment protection"). Second, the Court explicitly distinguished the cases dealing with checkpoints from those dealing with "special needs." *Sitz,* 496 U.S., at 450.

law enforcement officials at every stage of the policy, this case simply does not fit within the closely guarded category of "special needs."

The fact that positive test results were turned over to the police does not merely provide a basis for distinguishing our prior cases applying the "special needs" balancing approach to the determination of drug use. It also provides an affirmative reason for enforcing the strictures of the Fourth Amendment. While state hospital employees, like other citizens, may have a duty to provide the police with evidence of criminal conduct that they inadvertently acquire in the course of routine treatment, when they undertake to obtain such evidence from their patients for the specific purpose of incriminating those patients, they have a special obligation to make sure that the patients are fully informed about their constitutional rights, as standards of knowing waiver require.[24]

As respondents have repeatedly insisted, their motive was benign rather than punitive. Such a motive, however, cannot justify a departure from Fourth Amendment protections, given the pervasive involvement of law enforcement with the

development and application of the MUSC policy. The stark and unique fact that characterizes this case is that Policy M–7 was designed to obtain evidence of criminal conduct by the tested patients that would be turned over to the police and that could be admissible in subsequent criminal prosecutions. While respondents are correct that drug abuse both was and is a serious problem, the gravity of the threat alone cannot be dispositive of questions concerning what means law enforcement officers may employ to pursue a given purpose. The Fourth Amendment's general prohibition against nonconsensual, warrantless, and suspicionless searches necessarily applies to such a policy.

Accordingly, the judgment of the Court of Appeals is reversed, and the case is remanded for further proceedings consistent with this opinion.

JUSTICE KENNEDY, concurring in the judgment.

I agree that the search procedure in issue cannot be sustained under the Fourth Amendment. My reasons for this conclusion differ somewhat from those set forth by the Court, however, leading to this separate opinion.

---

24. The dissent * * * mischaracterizes our opinion as holding that "material which a person voluntarily entrusts to someone else cannot be given by that person to the police and used for whatever evidence it may contain." But * * * given the posture of the case, we must assume for purposes of decision that the patients did not consent to the searches, and we leave the question of consent for the Court of Appeals to determine.

The dissent further argues that our holding "leaves law enforcement officials entirely in the dark as to when they can use incriminating evidence obtained from trusted sources." With all due respect, we dis-

agree. We do not address a case in which doctors independently complied with reporting requirements. Rather, as we point out above, in this case, medical personnel used the criteria set out in n. 4, supra, to collect evidence for law enforcement purposes, and law enforcement officers were extensively involved in the initiation, design, and implementation of the program. In such circumstances, the Fourth Amendment's general prohibition against nonconsensual, warrantless, and suspicionless searches applies in the absence of consent. We decline to accept the dissent's invitation to make a foray into dicta and address other situations not before us.

I

The Court does not dispute that the search policy at some level serves special needs, beyond those of ordinary law enforcement, such as the need to protect the health of mother and child when a pregnant mother uses cocaine. Instead, the majority characterizes these special needs as the "ultimate goal[s]" of the policy, as distinguished from the policy's "immediate purpose," the collection of evidence of drug use, which, the Court reasons, is the appropriate inquiry for the special needs analysis.

* * * The distinction the Court makes, however, lacks foundation in our special needs cases. All of our special needs cases have turned upon what the majority terms the policy's ultimate goal. For example, in Skinner v. Railway Labor Executives' Assn., 489 U.S. 602 (1989), had we employed the majority's distinction, we would have identified as the relevant need the collection of evidence of drug and alcohol use by railway employees. Instead, we identified the relevant need as "[t]he Government's interest in regulating the conduct of railroad employees to ensure [railroad] safety." In Treasury Employees v. Von Raab, 489 U.S. 656 (1989), the majority's distinction should have compelled us to isolate the relevant need as the gathering of evidence of drug abuse by would-be drug interdiction officers. Instead, the special needs the Court identified were the necessities "to deter drug use among those eligible for promotion to sensitive positions within the [United States Customs] Service and to prevent the promotion of drug users to those positions." In Vernonia School Dist. 47J v. Acton, 515 U.S. 646 (1995), the majority's distinction would have required us to identify the immediate purpose of gathering evidence of drug use by student-athletes as the relevant "need" for purposes of the special needs analysis. Instead, we sustained the policy as furthering what today's majority would have termed the policy's ultimate goal: "[d]eterring drug use by our Nation's schoolchildren," and particularly by student-athletes, because "the risk of immediate physical harm to the drug user or those with whom he is playing his sport is particularly high."

It is unsurprising that in our prior cases we have concentrated on what the majority terms a policy's ultimate goal, rather than its proximate purpose. By very definition, in almost every case the immediate purpose of a search policy will be to obtain evidence. The circumstance that a particular search, like all searches, is designed to collect evidence of some sort reveals nothing about the need it serves. Put a different way, although procuring evidence is the immediate result of a successful search, until today that procurement has not been identified as the special need which justifies the search.

II

While the majority's reasoning seems incorrect in the respects just discussed, I agree with the Court that the search policy cannot be sustained. As the majority demonstrates and well explains, there was substantial law enforcement involvement in the policy from its inception. None of our special needs precedents has sanctioned the routine inclusion of law enforcement, both in the design of the policy and in using arrests, either threatened or real, to implement the system designed for the special needs objectives. The special needs cases we have decided do not sustain the active use of law enforcement, including arrest and prosecutions, as an integral part of a program which seeks to achieve legitimate, civil objectives. The traditional warrant and probable-cause requirements are waived in our previous cases on the explicit assumption that the evidence obtained in the search is not intended to be used for law enforcement purposes. Most of those tested for drug use under the policy at issue here were not brought into direct contact with law enforcement. This does not change the fact, however, that, as a systemic matter, law enforcement was a part of the implementation of the search policy in each of its applications. Every individual who tested positive was given a letter explaining the policy not from the hospital but from the solicitor's office. Everyone who tested positive was told a second positive test or failure to undergo substance abuse treatment would result in arrest and prosecution. As the Court holds, the hospital acted, in some respects, as an institutional arm of law enforcement for purposes of the policy. Under these circumstances, while the policy may well have served legitimate needs unrelated to law enforcement, it had as well a penal character with a far greater connection to law enforcement than other searches sustained under our special needs rationale.

In my view, it is necessary and prudent to be explicit in explaining the limitations of today's decision.

The beginning point ought to be to acknowledge the legitimacy of the State's interest in fetal life and of the grave risk to the life and health of the fetus, and later the child, caused by cocaine ingestion. * * * There can be no doubt that a mother's ingesting this drug can cause tragic injury to a fetus and a child. There should be no doubt that South Carolina can impose punishment upon an expectant mother who has so little regard for her own unborn that she risks causing him or her lifelong damage and suffering. The State, by taking special measures to give rehabilitation and training to expectant mothers with this tragic addiction or weakness, acts well within its powers and its civic obligations.

The holding of the Court, furthermore, does not call into question the validity of mandatory reporting laws such as child abuse laws which require teachers to report evidence of child abuse to the proper authorities, even if arrest and prosecution is the likely result. That in turn highlights the real difficulty. As this case comes to us * * * we must accept the premise that the medical profession can adopt acceptable criteria for testing expectant mothers for cocaine use in order to provide prompt and effective counseling to the mother and to take proper medical steps to protect the child. If prosecuting authorities then adopt legitimate procedures to discover this information and prosecution follows, that ought not to invalidate the testing. One of the ironies of the case, then, may be that the program now under review, which gives the cocaine user a second and third chance, might be replaced by some more rigorous system. We must, however, take the case as it comes to us; and the use of handcuffs, arrests, prosecutions, and police assistance in designing and implementing the testing and rehabilitation policy cannot be sustained under our previous cases concerning mandatory testing.

III

An essential, distinguishing feature of the special needs cases is that the person searched has consented, though the usual voluntariness analysis is altered because adverse consequences, (e.g., dismissal from employment or disqualification from playing on a high school sports team), will follow from refusal. The person searched has given consent, as defined to take into account that the consent was not voluntary in the full sense of the word. The consent, and the circumstances in which it was given, bear upon the reasonableness of the whole special needs program. Here, on the other hand, the question of consent, even with the special connotation used in the special needs cases, has yet to be decided. Indeed, the Court finds it necessary to take the unreal step of assuming there was no voluntary consent at all. Thus, we have erected a strange world for deciding the case. My discussion has endeavored to address the permissibility of a law enforcement purpose in this artificial context. The role played by consent might have affected our assessment of the issues. My concurrence in the judgment, furthermore, should not be interpreted as having considered or resolved the important questions raised by JUSTICE SCALIA with reference to whether limits might be imposed on the use of the evidence if in fact it were obtained with the patient's consent and in the context of the special needs program. Had we the prerogative to discuss the role played by consent, the case might have been quite a different one. All are in agreement, of course, that the Court of Appeals will address these issues in further proceedings on remand.

With these remarks, I concur in the judgment.

JUSTICE SCALIA, with whom THE CHIEF JUSTICE and JUSTICE THOMAS join as to Part II, dissenting.

There is always an unappealing aspect to the use of doctors and nurses, ministers of mercy, to obtain incriminating evidence against the supposed objects of their ministration—although here, it is correctly pointed out, the doctors and nurses were ministering not just to the mothers but also to the children whom their cooperation with the police was meant to protect. But whatever may be the correct social judgment concerning the desirability of what occurred here, that is not the issue in the present case. The Constitution does not resolve all difficult social questions, but leaves the vast majority of them to resolution by debate and the democratic process—which would produce a decision by the citizens of Charleston, through their elected representatives, to forbid or permit the police action at issue here. The question before us is a narrower one: whether, whatever the desirability of this police conduct, it violates the Fourth Amendment's prohibition of unreasonable searches and seizures. In my view, it plainly does not.

I

The first step in Fourth Amendment analysis is to identify the search or seizure at issue. What petitioners, the Court, and to a lesser extent the concurrence really object to is not the urine testing, but the hospital's reporting of positive drug-test results to police. But the latter is obviously not a search. At most it may be a "derivative use of the product of a past unlawful search," which, of course, "work[s] no new Fourth Amendment wrong" and "presents a question, not of rights, but of remedies." United States v. Calandra, 414 U.S. 338 (1974). There is only one act that could conceivably be regarded as a search of petitioners in the present case: the taking of the urine sample. I suppose the testing of that urine for traces of unlawful drugs could be considered a search of sorts, but the Fourth Amendment protects only against searches of citizens' "persons, houses, papers, and effects"; and it is entirely unrealistic to regard urine as one of the "effects" (i.e., part of the property) of the person who has passed and abandoned it. Some would argue, I suppose, that testing of the urine is prohibited by some generalized privacy right "emanating" from the "penumbras" of the Constitution (a question that is not before us); but it is not even arguable that the testing of urine that has been lawfully obtained is a Fourth Amendment search. * * *

It is rudimentary Fourth Amendment law that a search which has been consented to is not unreasonable. There is no contention in the present case that the urine samples were extracted forcibly. The only conceivable bases for saying that

they were obtained without consent are the contentions (1) that the consent was coerced by the patients' need for medical treatment, (2) that the consent was uninformed because the patients were not told that the tests would include testing for drugs, and (3) that the consent was uninformed because the patients were not told that the results of the tests would be provided to the police.* * *

Under our established Fourth Amendment law, the last two contentions would not suffice, even without reference to the special-needs doctrine. [Fourth amendment jurisprudence] shows that using lawfully (but deceivingly) obtained material for purposes other than those represented, and giving that material or information derived from it to the police, is not unconstitutional. In Hoffa v. United States, 385 U.S. 293 (1966), "[t]he argument [was] that [the informant's] failure to disclose his role as a government informant vitiated the consent that the petitioner gave" for the agent's access to evidence of criminal wrongdoing. We rejected that argument, because "the Fourth Amendment [does not protect] a wrongdoer's misplaced belief that a person to whom he voluntarily confides his wrongdoing will not reveal it." Because the defendant had voluntarily provided access to the evidence, there was no reasonable expectation of privacy to invade. Abuse of trust is surely a sneaky and ungentlemanly thing, and perhaps there should be (as there are) laws against such conduct by the government. That, however, is immaterial for Fourth Amendment purposes, for "however strongly a defendant may trust an apparent colleague, his expectations in this respect are not protected by the Fourth Amendment when it turns out that the colleague is a government agent regularly communicating with the authorities." United States v. White, 401 U.S. 745, 749 (1971). * * *

Until today, we have never held—or even suggested—that material which a person voluntarily entrusts to someone else cannot be given by that person to the police, and used for whatever evidence it may contain. Without so much as discussing the point, the Court today opens a hole in our Fourth Amendment jurisprudence, the size and shape of which is entirely indeterminate. * * * Since the Court declines even to discuss the issue, it leaves law enforcement officials entirely in the dark as to when they can use incriminating evidence obtained from "trusted" sources. Presumably the lines will be drawn in the case-by-case development of a whole new branch of Fourth Amendment jurisprudence, taking yet another social judgment (which confidential relationships ought not be invaded by the police) out of democratic control, and confiding it to the uncontrolled judgment of this Court—uncontrolled because there is no common-law precedent to guide it. I would adhere to our established law, which says that information obtained through violation of a relationship of trust is obtained consensually, and is hence not a search.

There remains to be considered the first possible basis for invalidating this search, which is that the patients were coerced to produce their urine samples by their necessitous circumstances, to-wit, their need for medical treatment of their pregnancy. If that was coercion, it was not coercion applied by the government—and if such nongovernmental coercion sufficed, the police would never be permitted to use the ballistic evidence obtained from treatment of a patient with a bullet wound. And the Fourth Amendment would invalidate those many state laws that require physicians to report gunshot wounds, evidence of spousal abuse, and evidence of child abuse.

II

I think it clear, therefore, that there is no basis for saying that obtaining of the urine sample was unconstitutional. The special-needs doctrine is thus quite irrelevant, since it operates only to validate searches and seizures that are otherwise unlawful. In the ensuing discussion, however, I shall assume (contrary to legal precedent) that the taking of the urine sample was (either because of the patients' necessitous circumstances, or because of failure to disclose that the urine would be tested for drugs, or because of failure to disclose that the results of the test would be given to the police) coerced. Indeed, I shall even assume (contrary to common sense) that the testing of the urine constituted an unconsented search of the patients' effects. On those assumptions, the special-needs doctrine would become relevant; and, properly applied, would validate what was done here.

The conclusion of the Court that the special-needs doctrine is inapplicable rests upon its contention that respondents "undert[ook] to obtain [drug] evidence from their patients" not for any medical purpose, but "for the specific purpose of incriminating those patients." In other words, the purported medical rationale was merely a pretext; there was no special need. This contention contradicts the District Court's finding of fact that the goal of the testing policy "was not to arrest patients but to facilitate their treatment and protect both the mother and unborn child." * * *

The cocaine tests started in April 1989, neither at police suggestion nor with police involvement. Expectant mothers who tested positive were referred by hospital staff for substance-abuse treatment—an obvious health benefit to both mother and child. * * * Thus, in their origin—before the police were in any way involved—the tests had an immediate, not merely an "ultimate," purpose of improving maternal and infant health. Several months after the testing had been initiated, a nurse discovered that local police were arresting pregnant users of cocaine for child abuse, the hospital's general counsel wrote the county solicitor to ask "what, if anything, our Medical Center needs to do to assist you in this matter," the police suggested ways to avoid tainting evidence, and the hospital and police in conjunction used the testing program as a means of securing what the Court calls the "ultimate" health benefit of coercing drug-abusing mothers into drug treatment. Why would there be any reason to believe that, once this policy of using the drug tests for their "ultimate" health benefits had been adopted, use of them for their original, immediate, benefits somehow disappeared, and testing somehow became in its entirety nothing more than a "pretext" for obtaining grounds for arrest? On the face of it,

this is incredible. The only evidence of the exclusively arrest-related purpose of the testing adduced by the Court is that the police-cooperation policy itself does not describe how to care for cocaine-exposed infants. But of course it does not, since that policy, adopted months after the cocaine testing was initiated, had as its only health object the "ultimate" goal of inducing drug treatment through threat of arrest. Does the Court really believe (or even hope) that, once invalidation of the program challenged here has been decreed, drug testing will cease?

* * *

As I indicated at the outset, it is not the function of this Court—at least not in Fourth Amendment cases—to weigh petitioners' privacy interest against the State's interest in meeting the crisis of "crack babies" that developed in the late 1980's. I cannot refrain from observing, however, that the outcome of a wise weighing of those interests is by no means clear. The initial goal of the doctors and nurses who conducted cocaine-testing in this case was to refer pregnant drug addicts to treatment centers, and to prepare for necessary treatment of their possibly affected children. When the doctors and nurses agreed to the program providing test results to the police, they did so because (in addition to the fact that child abuse was required by law to be reported) they wanted to use the sanction of arrest as a strong incentive for their addicted patients to undertake drug-addiction treatment. And the police themselves used it for that benign purpose, as is shown by the fact that only 30 of 253 women testing positive for cocaine were ever arrested, and only 2 of those prosecuted. It would not be unreasonable to conclude that today's judgment, authorizing the assessment of damages against the county solicitor and individual doctors and nurses who participated in the program, proves once again that no good deed goes unpunished.

4. Roadblocks and Suspicionless Seizures

Page 396.   At the end of the section, add the following:

Roadblock for Purposes of Ordinary Criminal Law Enforcement

In the following case, the Court invalidates a roadblock program because its primary purpose was to enforce the criminal law. How is a court supposed to determine whether the state has an improper purpose after this case?

CITY OF INDIANAPOLIS v. EDMOND

Supreme Court of the United States, 2000.
531 U.S. 32.

JUSTICE O'CONNOR **delivered the opinion of the Court.**

In Michigan Dept. of State Police v. Sitz, 496 U.S. 444, and United States v. Martinez—Fuerte, 428 U.S. 543 (1976), we held that brief, suspicionless seizures at highway checkpoints for the purposes of combating drunk driving and intercepting illegal immigrants were constitutional. We now consider the constitutionality of a highway checkpoint program whose primary purpose is the discovery and interdiction of illegal narcotics.

I

In August 1998, the city of Indianapolis began to operate vehicle checkpoints on Indianapolis roads in an effort to interdict unlawful drugs. The city conducted six such roadblocks between August and November that year, stopping 1,161 vehicles and arresting 104 motorists. Fifty-five arrests were for drug-related crimes, while 49 were for offenses unrelated to drugs. The overall "hit rate" of the program was thus approximately nine percent.

The parties stipulated to the facts concerning the operation of the checkpoints by the Indianapolis Police Department (IPD) for purposes of the preliminary injunction proceedings instituted below. At each checkpoint location, the police stop a predetermined number of vehicles. Approximately 30 officers are stationed at the checkpoint. Pursuant to written directives issued by the chief of police, at least one officer approaches the vehicle, advises the driver that he or she is being stopped briefly at a drug checkpoint, and asks the driver to produce a license and registration. The officer also looks for signs of impairment and conducts an open-view examination of the vehicle from the outside. A narcotics-detection dog walks around the outside of each stopped vehicle.

The directives instruct the officers that they may conduct a search only by consent or based on the appropriate quantum of particularized suspicion. The officers must conduct each stop in the same manner until particularized suspicion develops, and the officers have no discretion to stop any vehicle out of sequence. The city agreed in the stipulation to operate the checkpoints in such a way as to ensure that the total duration of each stop, absent reasonable suspicion or probable cause, would be five minutes or less.

* * * [C]heckpoint locations are selected weeks in advance based on such considerations as area crime statistics and traffic flow. The checkpoints are generally operated during daylight hours and are identified with lighted signs reading, "NARCOTICS CHECKPOINT —— MILE AHEAD, NARCOTICS K–9 IN USE, BE PREPARED TO STOP." Once a group of cars has been stopped, other traffic proceeds without interruption until all the stopped cars have been processed or diverted for further processing. * * * [T]he average stop for a vehicle not subject to further processing lasts two to three minutes or less.

Respondents James Edmond and Joell Palmer were each stopped at a narcotics checkpoint in late September 1998. Respondents then filed a lawsuit on behalf of themselves and the class of all motorists who had been stopped or were subject to being stopped in the future at the Indianapolis drug checkpoints. Respondents claimed that the roadblocks violated the Fourth Amendment of the United States Constitution and the search and seizure provision of the Indiana Con-

stitution. Respondents requested declaratory and injunctive relief for the class, as well as damages and attorney's fees for themselves.

Respondents then moved for a preliminary injunction. * * * The United States District Court for the Southern District of Indiana agreed to class certification and denied the motion for a preliminary injunction, holding that the checkpoint program did not violate the Fourth Amendment. A divided panel of the United States Court of Appeals for the Seventh Circuit reversed, holding that the checkpoints contravened the Fourth Amendment. We granted certiorari, and now affirm.

II

The Fourth Amendment requires that searches and seizures be reasonable. A search or seizure is ordinarily unreasonable in the absence of individualized suspicion of wrongdoing. Chandler v. Miller, 520 U.S. 305, 308 (1997). While such suspicion is not an "irreducible" component of reasonableness, Martinez–Fuerte, 428 U.S., at 561, we have recognized only limited circumstances in which the usual rule does not apply. For example, we have upheld certain regimes of suspicionless searches where the program was designed to serve "special needs, beyond the normal need for law enforcement." See, e.g., Vernonia School Dist. 47J v. Acton, 515 U.S. 646 (1995) (random drug testing of student-athletes); Treasury Employees v. Von Raab, 489 U.S. 656 (1989) (drug tests for United States Customs Service employees seeking transfer or promotion to certain positions); Skinner v. Railway Labor Executives' Assn., 489 U.S. 602 (1989) (drug and alcohol

tests for railway employees involved in train accidents or found to be in violation of particular safety regulations). We have also allowed searches for certain administrative purposes without particularized suspicion of misconduct, provided that those searches are appropriately limited. See, *e.g.,* New York v. Burger, 482 U.S. 691, 702–704 (1987) (warrantless administrative inspection of premises of "closely regulated" business); Camara v. Municipal Court of City and County of San Francisco, 387 U.S. 523 (1967) (administrative inspection to ensure compliance with city housing code).

We have also upheld brief, suspicionless seizures of motorists at a fixed Border Patrol checkpoint designed to intercept illegal aliens, *Martinez-Fuerte,* supra, and at a sobriety checkpoint aimed at removing drunk drivers from the road, Michigan Dept. of State Police v. Sitz, 496 U.S. 444 (1990). In addition, in Delaware v. Prouse, 440 U.S. 648 (1979), we suggested that a similar type of roadblock with the purpose of verifying drivers' licenses and vehicle registrations would be permissible. In none of these cases, however, did we indicate approval of a checkpoint program whose primary purpose was to detect evidence of ordinary criminal wrongdoing.

In *Martinez-Fuerte,* we entertained Fourth Amendment challenges to stops at two permanent immigration checkpoints located on major United States highways less than 100 miles from the Mexican border. We noted at the outset the particular context in which the constitutional question arose, describing in some detail the "formidable law enforcement problems" posed by the northbound tide of illegal entrants into the United States. * * * In *Martinez-Fuerte,* we found that the balance tipped in favor of the Government's interests in policing the Nation's borders. In so finding, we emphasized the difficulty of effectively containing illegal immigration at the border itself. We also stressed the impracticality of the particularized study of a given car to discern whether it was transporting illegal aliens, as well as the relatively modest degree of intrusion entailed by the stops.

Our subsequent cases have confirmed that considerations specifically related to the need to police the border were a significant factor in our *Martinez-Fuerte* decision. For example, in United States v. Montoya de Hernandez, 473 U.S. 531, 538 (1985), we counted *Martinez-Fuerte* as one of a number of Fourth Amendment cases that "reflect longstanding concern for the protection of the integrity of the border." Although the stops in *Martinez-Fuerte* did not occur at the border itself, the checkpoints were located near the border and served a border control function made necessary by the difficulty of guarding the border's entire length.

In *Sitz,* we evaluated the constitutionality of a Michigan highway sobriety checkpoint program. The *Sitz* checkpoint involved brief suspicionless stops of motorists so that police officers could detect signs of intoxication and remove impaired drivers from the road. Motorists who exhibited signs of intoxication were diverted for a license and registration check and, if warranted, further sobriety tests. This checkpoint program was clearly aimed at reducing the immediate hazard posed by the presence of drunk drivers on the highways, and there was an obvious connection between the imperative of highway safety and the law enforcement practice at issue. The gravity of the drunk driving problem and the magnitude of the State's interest in getting drunk drivers off the road weighed heavily in our determination that the program was constitutional.

In *Prouse*, we invalidated a discretionary, suspicionless stop for a spot check of a motorist's driver's license and vehicle registration. The officer's conduct in that case was unconstitutional primarily on account of his exercise of "standardless and unconstrained discretion." We nonetheless acknowledged the States' "vital interest in ensuring that only those qualified to do so are permitted to operate motor vehicles, that these vehicles are fit for safe operation, and hence that licensing, registration, and vehicle inspection requirements are being observed." Accordingly, we suggested that "[q]uestioning of all oncoming traffic at roadblock-type stops" would be a lawful means of serving this interest in highway safety.

We further indicated in *Prouse* that we considered the purposes of such a hypothetical roadblock to be distinct from a general purpose of investigating crime. The State proffered the additional interests of "the apprehension of stolen motor vehicles and of drivers under the influence of alcohol or narcotics" in its effort to justify the discretionary spot check. We attributed the entirety of the latter interest to the State's interest in roadway safety. We also noted that the interest in apprehending stolen vehicles may

be partly subsumed by the interest in roadway safety. We observed, however, that "[t]he remaining governmental interest in controlling automobile thefts is not distinguishable from the general interest in crime control." Not only does the common thread of highway safety thus run through *Sitz* and *Prouse*, but *Prouse* itself reveals a difference in the Fourth Amendment significance of highway safety interests and the general interest in crime control.

III

It is well established that a vehicle stop at a highway checkpoint effectuates a seizure within the meaning of the Fourth Amendment. The fact that officers walk a narcotics-detection dog around the exterior of each car at the Indianapolis checkpoints does not transform the seizure into a search. See United States v. Place, 462 U.S. 696, 707 (1983). Just as in *Place*, an exterior sniff of an automobile does not require entry into the car and is not designed to disclose any information other than the presence or absence of narcotics. * * * Rather, what principally distinguishes these checkpoints from those we have previously approved is their primary purpose.

As petitioners concede, the Indianapolis checkpoint program unquestionably has the primary purpose of interdicting illegal narcotics. In their stipulation of facts, the parties repeatedly refer to the checkpoints as "drug checkpoints" and describe them as "being operated by the City of Indianapolis in an effort to interdict unlawful drugs in Indianapolis." In addition, the first document attached to the parties' stipulation is entitled "DRUG CHECKPOINT CONTACT OFFICER DIRECTIVES BY ORDER OF THE CHIEF OF POLICE.". These directives instruct officers to "[a]dvise the citizen that they are being stopped briefly at a drug checkpoint." * * * Further, * * * the checkpoints are identified with lighted signs reading, "NARCOTICS CHECKPOINT ___ MILE AHEAD, NARCOTICS K–9 IN USE, BE PREPARED TO STOP." Finally, both the District Court and the Court of Appeals recognized that the primary purpose of the roadblocks is the interdiction of narcotics.

We have never approved a checkpoint program whose primary purpose was to detect evidence of ordinary criminal wrongdoing. Rather, our checkpoint cases have recognized only limited exceptions to the general rule that a seizure must be accompanied by some measure of individualized suspicion. * * * [E]ach of the checkpoint programs that we have approved was designed primarily to serve purposes closely related to the problems of policing the border or the necessity of ensuring roadway safety. Because the primary purpose of the Indianapolis narcotics checkpoint program is to uncover evidence of ordinary criminal wrongdoing, the program contravenes the Fourth Amendment.

Petitioners propose several ways in which the narcotics-detection purpose of the instant checkpoint program may instead resemble the primary purposes of the checkpoints in *Sitz* and *Martinez-Fuerte*. Petitioners state that the checkpoints in those cases had the same ultimate purpose of arresting those suspected of committing crimes. Se-

curing the border and apprehending drunk drivers are, of course, law enforcement activities, and law enforcement officers employ arrests and criminal prosecutions in pursuit of these goals. If we were to rest the case at this high level of generality, there would be little check on the ability of the authorities to construct roadblocks for almost any conceivable law enforcement purpose. Without drawing the line at roadblocks designed primarily to serve the general interest in crime control, the Fourth Amendment would do little to prevent such intrusions from becoming a routine part of American life.

Petitioners also emphasize the severe and intractable nature of the drug problem as justification for the checkpoint program. There is no doubt that traffic in illegal narcotics creates social harms of the first magnitude. The law enforcement problems that the drug trade creates likewise remain daunting and complex, particularly in light of the myriad forms of spin-off crime that it spawns. The same can be said of various other illegal activities, if only to a lesser degree. But the gravity of the threat alone cannot be dispositive of questions concerning what means law enforcement officers may employ to pursue a given purpose. Rather, in determining whether individualized suspicion is required, we must consider the nature of the interests threatened and their connection to the particular law enforcement practices at issue. We are particularly reluctant to recognize exceptions to the general rule of individualized suspicion where governmental authorities primarily pursue their general crime control ends.

Nor can the narcotics-interdiction purpose of the checkpoints be rationalized in terms of a highway safety concern similar to that present in *Sitz*. The detection and punishment of almost any criminal offense serves broadly the safety of the community, and our streets would no doubt be safer but for the scourge of illegal drugs. Only with respect to a smaller class of offenses, however, is society confronted with the type of immediate, vehicle-bound threat to life and limb that the sobriety checkpoint in *Sitz* was designed to eliminate.

Petitioners also liken the anticontraband agenda of the Indianapolis checkpoints to the antismuggling purpose of the checkpoints in *Martinez-Fuerte*. Petitioners cite this Court's conclusion in *Martinez-Fuerte* that the flow of traffic was too heavy to permit "particularized study of a given car that would enable it to be identified as a possible carrier of illegal aliens," and claim that this logic has even more force here. The problem with this argument is that the same logic prevails any time a vehicle is employed to conceal contraband or other evidence of a crime. This type of connection to the roadway is very different from the close connection to roadway safety that was present in *Sitz* and *Prouse*. Further, the Indianapolis checkpoints are far removed from the border context that was crucial in *Martinez-Fuerte*. While the difficulty of examining each passing car was an important factor in validating the law enforcement technique employed in *Martinez-Fuerte*, this factor alone cannot justify a regime of suspicionless searches or seizures. Rather, we must look more closely at the na-

ture of the public interests that such a regime is designed principally to serve.

* * * We decline to suspend the usual requirement of individualized suspicion where the police seek to employ a checkpoint primarily for the ordinary enterprise of investigating crimes. We cannot sanction stops justified only by the generalized and ever-present possibility that interrogation and inspection may reveal that any given motorist has committed some crime.

Of course, there are circumstances that may justify a law enforcement checkpoint where the primary purpose would otherwise, but for some emergency, relate to ordinary crime control. For example, as the Court of Appeals noted, the Fourth Amendment would almost certainly permit an appropriately tailored roadblock set up to thwart an imminent terrorist attack or to catch a dangerous criminal who is likely to flee by way of a particular route. The exigencies created by these scenarios are far removed from the circumstances under which authorities might simply stop cars as a matter of course to see if there just happens to be a felon leaving the jurisdiction. While we do not limit the purposes that may justify a checkpoint program to any rigid set of categories, we decline to approve a program whose primary purpose is ultimately indistinguishable from the general interest in crime control.

Petitioners argue that our prior cases preclude an inquiry into the purposes of the checkpoint program. For example, they cite Whren v. United States, 517 U.S. 806 (1996), and Bond v. United States,

529 U.S. 334 (2000), to support the proposition that "where the government articulates and pursues a legitimate interest for a suspicionless stop, courts should not look behind that interest to determine whether the government's 'primary purpose' is valid." These cases, however, do not control the instant situation.

In *Whren*, we held that an individual officer's subjective intentions are irrelevant to the Fourth Amendment validity of a traffic stop that is justified objectively by probable cause to believe that a traffic violation has occurred. We observed that our prior cases "foreclose any argument that the constitutional reasonableness of traffic stops depends on the actual motivations of the individual officers involved." In so holding, we expressly distinguished cases where we had addressed the validity of searches conducted in the absence of probable cause. See *Whren* (distinguishing Florida v. Wells, 495 U.S. 1, 4 (1990) (stating that "an inventory search must not be a ruse for a general rummaging in order to discover incriminating evidence"), Colorado v. Bertine, 479 U.S. 367, 372 (1987) (suggesting that the absence of bad faith and the lack of a purely investigative purpose were relevant to the validity of an inventory search), and Burger, 482 U.S., at 716–717, n. 27 (observing that a valid administrative inspection conducted with neither a warrant nor probable cause did not appear to be a pretext for gathering evidence of violations of the penal laws)).

Whren therefore reinforces the principle that, while "[s]ubjective intentions play no role in ordinary, probable-cause Fourth Amendment analysis," programmatic purposes

may be relevant to the validity of Fourth Amendment intrusions undertaken pursuant to a general scheme without individualized suspicion. Accordingly, *Whren* does not preclude an inquiry into programmatic purpose in such contexts. It likewise does not preclude an inquiry into programmatic purpose here.

Last Term in *Bond*, we addressed the question whether a law enforcement officer violated a reasonable expectation of privacy in conducting a tactile examination of carry-on luggage in the overhead compartment of a bus. In doing so, we simply noted that the principle of *Whren* rendered the subjective intent of an officer irrelevant to this analysis. While, as petitioners correctly observe, the analytical rubric of *Bond* was not "ordinary, probable-cause Fourth Amendment analysis," nothing in *Bond* suggests that we would extend the principle of *Whren* to all situations where individualized suspicion was lacking. Rather, subjective intent was irrelevant in *Bond* because the inquiry that our precedents required focused on the objective effects of the actions of an individual officer. By contrast, our cases dealing with intrusions that occur pursuant to a general scheme absent individualized suspicion have often required an inquiry into purpose at the programmatic level.

Petitioners argue that the Indianapolis checkpoint program is justified by its lawful secondary purposes of keeping impaired motorists off the road and verifying licenses and registrations. If this were the case, however, law enforcement authorities would be able to establish checkpoints for virtually any purpose so long as they also included a license or sobriety check. For this reason, we examine the available evidence to determine the primary purpose of the checkpoint program. While we recognize the challenges inherent in a purpose inquiry, courts routinely engage in this enterprise in many areas of constitutional jurisprudence as a means of sifting abusive governmental conduct from that which is lawful. As a result, a program driven by an impermissible purpose may be proscribed while a program impelled by licit purposes is permitted, even though the challenged conduct may be outwardly similar. While reasonableness under the Fourth Amendment is predominantly an objective inquiry, our special needs and administrative search cases demonstrate that purpose is often relevant when suspicionless intrusions pursuant to a general scheme are at issue.[2]

It goes without saying that our holding today does nothing to alter the constitutional status of the sobriety and border checkpoints that we approved in *Sitz* and *Martinez-Fuerte*, or of the type of traffic checkpoint that we suggested would be lawful in *Prouse*. The constitutionality of such checkpoint programs still depends on a balancing of the competing interests at stake and the effectiveness of the program. When law enforcement authorities pursue primarily general

crime control purposes at checkpoints such as here, however, stops can only be justified by some quantum of individualized suspicion.

Our holding also does not affect the validity of border searches or searches at places like airports and government buildings, where the need for such measures to ensure public safety can be particularly acute. Nor does our opinion speak to other intrusions aimed primarily at purposes beyond the general interest in crime control. Our holding also does not impair the ability of police officers to act appropriately upon information that they properly learn during a checkpoint stop justified by a lawful primary purpose, even where such action may result in the arrest of a motorist for an offense unrelated to that purpose. Finally, we caution that the purpose inquiry in this context is to be conducted only at the programmatic level and is not an invitation to probe the minds of individual officers acting at the scene.

Because the primary purpose of the Indianapolis checkpoint program is ultimately indistinguishable from the general interest in crime control, the checkpoints violate the Fourth Amendment. The judgment of the Court of Appeals is accordingly affirmed.

CHIEF JUSTICE REHNQUIST, **with whom** JUSTICE THOMAS **joins, and with whom** JUSTICE SCALIA **joins as to Part I, dissenting.**

---

2. Because petitioners concede that the primary purpose of the Indianapolis checkpoints is narcotics detection, we need not decide whether the State may establish a checkpoint program with the primary purpose of checking licenses or driver sobriety and a secondary purpose of interdicting narcotics. Specifically, we express no view on the question whether police may expand the scope of a license or sobriety checkpoint seizure in order to detect the presence of drugs in a stopped car.

The State's use of a drug-sniffing dog, according to the Court's holding, annuls what is otherwise plainly constitutional under our Fourth Amendment jurisprudence: brief, standardized, discretionless, roadblock seizures of automobiles, seizures which effectively serve a weighty state interest with only minimal intrusion on the privacy of their occupants. Because these seizures serve the State's accepted and significant interests of preventing drunken driving and checking for driver's licenses and vehicle registrations, and because there is nothing in the record to indicate that the addition of the dog sniff lengthens these otherwise legitimate seizures, I dissent.

I

* * *

This case follows naturally from *Martinez-Fuerte* and *Sitz*. Petitioners acknowledge that the "primary purpose" of these roadblocks is to interdict illegal drugs, but this fact should not be controlling. Even accepting the Court's conclusion that the checkpoints at issue in *Martinez-Fuerte* and *Sitz* were not primarily related to criminal law enforcement, the question whether a law enforcement purpose could support a roadblock seizure is not presented in this case. The District Court found that another "purpose of the checkpoints is to check driver's licenses and vehicle registrations," and the written directives state that the police officers are to "[l]ook for signs of impairment." The use of roadblocks to look for signs of impairment was validated by *Sitz*, and the use of roadblocks to check for driver's licenses and vehicle registrations was expressly

recognized in Delaware v. Prouse, 440 U.S. 648, 663 (1979). That the roadblocks serve these legitimate state interests cannot be seriously disputed, as the 49 people arrested for offenses unrelated to drugs can attest. And it would be speculative to conclude—given the District Court's findings, the written directives, and the actual arrests—that petitioners would not have operated these roadblocks but for the State's interest in interdicting drugs.

Because of the valid reasons for conducting these roadblock seizures, it is constitutionally irrelevant that petitioners also hoped to interdict drugs. In Whren v. United States, 517 U.S. 806 (1996), we held that an officer's subjective intent would not invalidate an otherwise objectively justifiable stop of an automobile. The reasonableness of an officer's discretionary decision to stop an automobile, at issue in *Whren*, turns on whether there is probable cause to believe that a traffic violation has occurred. The reasonableness of highway checkpoints, at issue here, turns on whether they effectively serve a significant state interest with minimal intrusion on motorists. The stop in *Whren* was objectively reasonable because the police officers had witnessed traffic violations; so too the roadblocks here are objectively reasonable because they serve the substantial interests of preventing drunken driving and checking for driver's licenses and vehicle registrations with minimal intrusion on motorists.

Once the constitutional requirements for a particular seizure are satisfied, the subjective expectations of those responsible for it, be it police officers or members of a city council, are irrelevant. Cf. Scott v. United States, 436 U.S. 128 (1978) ("Subjective intent alone ... does not make otherwise lawful conduct illegal or unconstitutional"). It is the objective effect of the State's actions on the privacy of the individual that animates the Fourth Amendment. Because the objective intrusion of a valid seizure does not turn upon anyone's subjective thoughts, neither should our constitutional analysis.

* * * The only difference between this case and *Sitz* is the presence of the dog. We have already held, however, that a "sniff test" by a trained narcotics dog is not a "search" within the meaning of the Fourth Amendment because it does not require physical intrusion of the object being sniffed and it does not expose anything other than the contraband items. And there is nothing in the record to indicate that the dog sniff lengthens the stop. Finally, the checkpoints' success rate—49 arrests for offenses unrelated to drugs—only confirms the State's legitimate interests in preventing drunken driving and ensuring the proper licensing of drivers and registration of their vehicles. These stops effectively serve the State's legitimate interests; they are executed in a regularized and neutral manner; and they only minimally intrude upon the privacy of the motorists. They should therefore be constitutional.

II

The Court, unwilling to adopt the straightforward analysis that these precedents dictate, adds a new non-law-enforcement primary purpose test lifted from a distinct area of Fourth Amendment jurisprudence relating to the *searches* of homes and businesses. As discussed above, the question that the Court answers is not even posed in this case given the accepted reasons for the seizures. But more fundamentally, whatever sense a non-law-enforcement primary purpose test may make in the search setting, it is ill suited to brief roadblock seizures, where we have consistently looked at "the scope of the stop" in assessing a program's constitutionality.

* * *

The "special needs" doctrine, which has been used to uphold certain suspicionless searches performed for reasons unrelated to law enforcement, is an exception to the general rule that a search must be based on individualized suspicion of wrongdoing. The doctrine permits intrusions into a person's body and home, areas afforded the greatest Fourth Amendment protection. But there were no such intrusions here.

"[O]ne's expectation of privacy in an automobile and of freedom in its operation are significantly different from the traditional expectation of privacy and freedom in one's residence." *Martinez-Fuerte,*supra. This is because "[a]utomobiles, unlike homes, are subjected to pervasive and continuing governmental regulation and controls." South Dakota v. Opperman, 428 U.S. 364 (1976). The lowered expectation of privacy in one's automobile is coupled with the limited nature of the intrusion: a brief, standardized, nonintrusive seizure. The brief seizure of an automobile can hardly be compared to the intrusive search of the body or the home. * * *

Because of these extrinsic limitations upon roadblock seizures, the Court's newfound non-law-enforcement primary purpose test is both unnecessary to secure Fourth Amendment rights and bound to produce wide-ranging litigation over the "purpose" of any given seizure. Police designing highway roadblocks can never be sure of their validity, since a jury might later determine that a forbidden purpose exists. Roadblock stops identical to the one that we upheld in *Sitz* 10 years ago, or to the one that we upheld 24 years ago in *Martinez-Fuerte,* may now be challenged on the grounds that they have some concealed forbidden purpose.

Efforts to enforce the law on public highways used by millions of motorists are obviously necessary to our society. The Court's opinion today casts a shadow over what had been assumed, on the basis of *stare decisis,* to be a perfectly lawful activity. Conversely, if the Indianapolis police had assigned a different purpose to their activity here, but in no way changed what was done on the ground to individual motorists, it might well be valid. See majority opinion, n. 2. The Court's non-law-enforcement primary purpose test simply does not serve as a proxy for anything that the Fourth Amendment is, or should be, concerned about in the automobile seizure context.

Petitioners' program complies with our decisions regarding roadblock seizures of automobiles, and the addition of a dog sniff does not add to the length or the intrusion of the stop. Because such stops are consistent with the Fourth Amendment, I would reverse the decision of the Court of Appeals.

JUSTICE THOMAS, dissenting.

Taken together, our decisions in Michigan Dept. of State Police v. Sitz, 496 U.S. 444 (1990), and United States v. Martinez–Fuerte, 428 U.S. 543 (1976), stand for the proposition that suspicionless roadblock seizures are constitutionally permissible if conducted according to a plan that limits the discretion of the officers conducting the stops. I am not convinced that *Sitz* and *Martinez-Fuerte* were correctly decided. Indeed, I rather doubt that the Framers of the Fourth Amendment would have considered "reasonable" a program of indiscriminate stops of individuals not suspected of wrongdoing.

Respondents did not, however, advocate the overruling of *Sitz* and *Martinez-Fuerte,* and I am reluctant to consider such a step without the benefit of briefing and argument. For the reasons given by THE CHIEF JUSTICE, I believe that those cases compel upholding the program at issue here. I, therefore, join his opinion.

VI. WIRETAPPING, UNDERCOVER ACTIVITY, AND THE OUTER REACHES OF THE FOURTH AMENDMENT

C. WIRETAPPING AND EAVESDROPPING STATUTES

Page 438. At the beginning of the discussion of Title III, add the following:

The USA PATRIOT ACT, passed in response to the terrorist attacks of September 11, made some amendments to Title III and to the Foreign Intelligence Surveillance Act. These changes generally make it easier to obtain authorization of electronic surveillance against suspected terrorists. The statutory changes are set forth in Part IV of this Supplement.

Page 444. At the end of the section, add the following:

If a communication is intercepted in violation of Title III, can it be published by someone who did not take part in the illegality? This was the question faced by the Court in Bartnicki v. Vopper, 532 U.S. 514 (2001). The defendant in *Bartnicki* was a radio commentator who broadcast illegally intercepted communications on a matter of public interest. The defendant knew that the communications had been intercepted illegally, but he did not take part in their interception. The District Court concluded that, under the statutory language, an individual violates Title III by intentionally disclosing the contents of an electronic communication when he or she knows or has reason to know that the information was obtained through an illegal interception, even if the individual was not involved in that interception. The Supreme Court agreed with that interpretation of the statute, but held that the First Amendment protected the disclosures by the defendant. The Court held that the purposes of the statute could not be extended in these circumstances to someone who was a broadcaster uninvolved in the illegal interception.

VII. REMEDIES FOR FOURTH AMENDMENT VIOLATIONS

D. THE EXCLUSIONARY RULE IN DETAIL: PROCEDURES, SCOPE AND PROBLEMS

6. *The Fruits of the Search: Causation and Attenuation*

Page 494. At the end of the headnote on "Statements Tainted by an Illegal Arrest" add the following:

The Court applied *Brown*, *Dunaway* and *Taylor* in Kaupp v. Texas, 123 S.Ct. 1843 (2003) (per curiam) as it held that a suspect's confession was, on the record before it, the fruit of an arrest without probable Police officers suspected Kaupp, an adolescent, of involvement in a murder, but did not have probable cause to arrest him. The officers entered Kaupp's house at 3 a.m., went to his bedroom, woke him up, placed him in handcuffs, and took him in his underwear in a patrol car. They stopped for 5 to 10 minutes at the site where the victim's body had been found, and then went on to the sheriff's headquarters, where they removed his handcuffs, gave him *Miranda* warnings, and told him that the victim's brother had confessed to the crime and implicated him as an accomplice. Kaupp then admitted to some part in the crime.

The state courts held that Kaupp had not been arrested, because he voluntarily accompanied the officers. But the Court found this conclusion to be error, holding that the "evidence points to arrest even more starkly than the facts in *Dunaway v. New York,* 442 U.S. 200, 212 (1979), where the petitioner was taken from a neighbor's home to a police car, transported to a police station, and placed in an interrogation room." On the question of admissibility of the confession, the Court declared as follows:

> Since Kaupp was arrested before he was questioned, and because the state does not even claim that the sheriff's department had probable cause to detain him at that point, well-established precedent requires suppression of the confession unless that confession was "an act of free will [sufficient] to purge the primary taint of the unlawful invasion." *Wong Sun* v. *United States,* 371 U.S. 471, 486 (1963). Demonstrating such purgation is, of course, a function of circumstantial evidence, with the burden of persuasion on the state. See *Brown,* 422 U.S., at 604. Relevant considerations include observance of *Miranda,* "the temporal proximity of the arrest and the confession, the presence of intervening circumstances, and, particularly, the purpose and flagrancy of the official misconduct." 422 U.S., at 603–604.

> The record before us shows that only one of these considerations, the giving of *Miranda* warnings, supports the state, and we held in *Brown* that "*Miranda* warnings, *alone* and *per se,* cannot always ... break, for Fourth Amendment purposes, the causal connection between the illegality and the confession."; see also *Taylor* v. *Alabama,* 457 U.S. 687, 699 (1982) (O'CONNOR, J., dissenting) (noting that, although *Miranda* warnings are an important factor, "they are, standing alone, insufficient"). All other factors point the opposite way. There is no indication from the record that any substantial time passed between Kaupp's removal from his home in handcuffs and his confession after only 10 or 15 minutes of interrogation. In the interim, he remained in his partially clothed state in the physical custody of a number of officers, some of whom, at least, were conscious that they lacked probable cause to arrest. See *Brown, supra,* at 604–605. In fact, the state has not even alleged "any meaningful intervening event" between the illegal arrest and Kaupp's confession. *Taylor, supra,* at 691. Unless, on remand, the state can point to testimony undisclosed on the record before us, and weighty enough to carry the state's burden despite the clear force of the evidence shown here, the confession must be suppressed.

Chapter Three

SELF–INCRIMINATION AND CONFESSIONS

I. THE PRIVILEGE AGAINST COMPELLED SELF–INCRIMINATION

B. SCOPE OF THE PRIVILEGE

Page 569.   Add the following section:

4. *Compulsion of Statements Never Admitted at a Criminal Trial*

In *Chavez v. Martinez,* 123 S.Ct. 1994 (2003), the Court considered whether the Fifth Amendment is violated when police compel a statement from a suspect during interrogation , but the statement is never admitted against the suspect in a criminal trial. Martinez brought a 1983 action for violation of his Fifth Amendment rights. Chavez was a police officer who interrogated Martinez after Martinez was shot in a fight with police officers. The interrogation session occurred while Martinez was in the hospital being treated for bullet wounds. Martinez made some inculpatory statements. For purposes of the appeal, all of the Justices on the Court assumed that the statements made by Martinez would have been excluded under the Fifth Amendment as compelled self-incrimination, had the statements been offered at a criminal trial. However, Martinez was never charged with a crime, and the statements were never used against him in a criminal prosecution.

A majority of the Justices found that the Fifth Amendment does not protect against statements compelled during interrogation that are never admitted in a criminal case, but there was no opinion for the Court on this question. Justice Thomas, joined by Chief Justice Rehnquist and Justices O'Connor and Scalia, provided the broadest opinion, declaring that the Fifth Amendment simply did not apply because Martinez's confession was ever admitted against him in a criminal case. Justice Thomas reasoned as follows:

> Although Martinez contends that the meaning of "criminal case" should encompass the entire criminal investigatory process,

including police interrogations, we disagree. In our view, a "criminal case" at the very least requires the initiation of legal proceedings. We need not decide today the precise moment when a "criminal case" commences; it is enough to say that police questioning does not constitute a "case" any more than a private investigator's precomplaint activities constitute a "civil case." Statements compelled by police interrogations of course may not be used against a defendant at trial, but it is not until their use in a criminal case that a violation of the Self–Incrimination Clause occurs, see United States v. Verdugo–Urquidez, 494 U.S. 259, 264 (1990) ("The privilege against self-incrimination guaranteed by the Fifth Amendment is *a fundamental trial right* of criminal defendants. Although conduct by law enforcement officials prior to trial may ultimately impair that right, *a constitutional violation occurs only at trial*"). * * * Here, Martinez was never made to be a "witness" against himself in violation of the Fifth Amendment's Self–Incrimination Clause because his statements were never admitted as testimony against him in a criminal case. Nor was he ever placed under oath and exposed to " 'the cruel trilemma of self-accusation, perjury or contempt.' " Michigan v. Tucker, 417 U.S. 433, 445 (1974). The text of the Self–Incrimination Clause simply cannot support the Ninth Circuit's view that the mere use of compulsive questioning, without more, violates the Constitution. * * *

We fail to see how Martinez was any more "compelled in any criminal case to be a witness against himself" than an immunized witness forced to testify on pain of contempt. One difference, perhaps, is that the immunized witness *knows* that his statements will not, and may not, be used against him, whereas Martinez likely did not. But this does not make the statements of the immunized witness any less "compelled" and lends no support to the Ninth Circuit's conclusion that coercive police interrogations, absent the use of the involuntary statements in a criminal case, violate the Fifth Amendment's Self–Incrimination Clause.

Justice Thomas recognized that citizens have a right to receive immunity *before,* for example, an incriminating statement is compelled from them in a grand jury proceeding. Justice Thomas distinguished the immunity cases from the present one in the following passage:

By allowing a witness to insist on an immunity agreement *before* being compelled to give incriminating testimony in a noncriminal case, the privilege preserves the core Fifth Amendment right from invasion by the use of that compelled testimony in a subsequent criminal case. Because the failure to assert the privilege will often forfeit the right to exclude the evidence in a subsequent "criminal case," it is necessary to allow assertion of the privilege prior to the commencement of a "criminal case" to safeguard the core Fifth Amendment trial right. If the privilege could not be asserted in such situations, testimony given in those judicial proceedings would be deemed "voluntary," hence, insistence on a prior grant of immunity is essential to memorialize the fact that the testimony had indeed been compelled and therefore protected from use against the speaker in any "criminal case."

Rules designed to safeguard a constitutional right, however, do not extend the scope of the constitutional right itself, just as violations of judicially crafted prophylactic rules do not violate the constitutional rights of any person. As we explained, we have allowed the Fifth Amendment privilege to be asserted by witnesses in noncriminal cases in order to safeguard the core constitutional right defined by the Self–Incrimination Clause—the right not to be compelled in any criminal case to be a witness against oneself. * * *

Justice Thomas also recognized that the Court has held that the Fifth Amendment is violated if the government imposes a penalty on a citizen who invokes her constitutional right to silence, even if no compelled statement is offered against the person in a criminal trial. For example, a person cannot be debarred from a government contract for properly invoking his right to silence. Justice Thomas explained these cases as follows:

Once an immunity waiver is signed, the signatory is unable to assert a Fifth Amendment objection to the subsequent use of his statements in a criminal case, even if his statements were in fact compelled. A waiver of immunity is therefore a prospective waiver of the core self-incrimination right in any subsequent criminal proceeding, and States cannot condition public employment on the waiver of constitutional rights.

Justice Souter, joined by Justice Breyer, concurred in the judgment, agreeing with the general proposition that the Fifth Amendment does not protect against compulsion of statements that are never used in a criminal case. Justice Souter expressed concern over the stopping point for a rule of law providing that compelled confessions are actionable in themselves.

The most obvious drawback inherent in Martinez's purely Fifth Amendment claim to damages is its risk of global application in every instance of interrogation producing a statement inadmissible under Fifth and Fourteenth Amendment principles, or violating one of the complementary rules we have accepted in aid of the privilege against evidentiary use. If obtaining Martinez's statement is to be treated as a stand-alone violation of the privilege subject to compensation, why should the same not be true whenever the police obtain any involuntary self-incriminating statement, or whenever the government so much as threatens a penalty in derogation of the right to immunity, or whenever the police fail to honor *Miranda?* Martinez offers no limiting principle or reason to foresee a stopping place short of liability in all such cases.

Recognizing an action for damages in every such instance not only would revolutionize Fifth and Fourteenth Amendment law, but would beg the question that must inform every extension or recognition of a complementary rule in service of the core privilege: why is this new rule necessary in aid of the basic guarantee? Martinez has offered no reason to believe that the guarantee has been ineffective in all or many of those circumstances in which its vindication has depended on excluding testimonial admissions or barring penalties. And I have no reason to believe the law has been systemically defective in this respect.

Justice Kennedy, joined by Justice Stevens and in part by Justice Ginsburg, dissented. He argued as follows:

Our cases and our legal tradition establish that the Self–Incrimination Clause is a substantive constraint on the conduct of the government, not merely an evidentiary rule governing the work of the courts. The Clause must provide more than mere assurance that a compelled statement will not be introduced against its declarant in a criminal trial. Otherwise there will be too little protection against the compulsion the Clause prohibits. The Clause protects an individual from being forced to give answers demanded by an official in any context when the answers might give rise to criminal liability in the future. "It can be asserted in any proceeding, civil or criminal, administrative or judicial, investigatory or adjudicatory; and it protects against any disclosures that the witness reasonably believes could be used in a criminal prosecution or could lead to other evidence that might be so used." Kastigar v. United States, 406 U.S. 441, 444–445 (1972). The decision in *Kastigar* described the Self–Incrimination Clause as an exemption from the testimonial duty. As the duty is immediate, so must be the privilege. Furthermore, the exercise of the privilege depends on what the witness reasonably believes will be the future use of a statement. Again, this indicates the existence of a present right. * * *

The conclusion that the Self–Incrimination Clause is not violated until the government seeks to use a statement in some later criminal proceeding strips the Clause of an essential part of its force and meaning. This is no small matter. It should come as an unwelcome surprise to judges, attorneys, and the citizenry as a whole that if a legislative committee or a judge in a civil case demands incriminating testimony without offering immunity, and even imposes sanctions for failure to comply, that the witness and counsel cannot insist the right against compelled self-incrimination is applicable then and there. JUSTICE SOUTER and JUSTICE THOMAS, I submit, should be more respectful of the understanding that has prevailed for generations now. To tell our whole legal system that when conducting a criminal investigation police officials can use severe compulsion or even torture with no present violation of the right against compelled self-incrimination can only diminish a celebrated provision in the Bill of Rights. A Constitution survives over time because the people share a common, historic commitment to certain simple but fundamental principles which preserve their freedom. Today's decision undermines one of those respected precepts.

Justice Stevens and Justice Ginsburg each added a separate opinion concurring in part and dissenting in part.

While a majority of the Court held that Martinez could claim no Fifth Amendment violation because the compelled statements were not admitted against him in a criminal case, a different majority of the Court voted to remand the case for a determination of whether the interrogation session so "shocked the conscience" as to constitute a violation of Martinez's right to substantive due process. The Justices agreed that if a police officer's misconduct rises to the level of a substantive due process violation, it would not matter whether the suspect's statements were ever admitted at trial. Justice Thomas, joined by the Chief Justice and Justice Scalia, declared that Chavez's conduct did not shock the conscience and therefore dissented from a remand on this question.

C.   WHAT IS COMPULSION?

2.   *Other State–Imposed Sanctions*

Page 574.   At the end of the section, add the following:

The Benefit–Penalty Distinction and Penalties Imposed on Incarcerated Sex Offenders: McKune v. Lile

In the following case, a divided Court considers whether the benefit-penalty distinction works when applied to a program for rehabilitating incarcerated sex offenders.

McKUNE v. LILE

Supreme Court of the United States, 2002.
536 U.S. 24.

JUSTICE KENNEDY **announced the judgment of the Court and delivered an opinion, in which** THE CHIEF JUSTICE, JUSTICE SCALIA, **and** JUSTICE THOMAS **join.**

Respondent Robert G. Lile is a convicted sex offender in the custody of the Kansas Department of Corrections (Department). A few years before respondent was scheduled to reenter society, Department officials recommended that he enter a prison treatment program so that he would not rape again upon release. While there appears to be some difference of opinion among experts in the field, Kansas officials and officials who administer the United States prison system have made the determination that it is of considerable importance for the program participant to admit having committed the crime for which he is being treated and other past offenses. The first and in many ways most crucial step in the Kansas rehabilitation program thus requires the participant to confront his past crimes so that he can begin to understand his own motivations and weaknesses. As this initial step can be a most difficult one, Kansas offers sex offenders incentives to participate in the program.

Respondent contends this incentive system violates his Fifth Amendment privilege against self-incrimination. Kansas' rehabilitation program, however, serves a vital penological purpose, and offering inmates minimal incentives to participate does not amount to compelled self-incrimination prohibited by the Fifth Amendment.

I

In 1982, respondent lured a high school student into his car as she was returning home from school. At gunpoint, respondent forced the victim to perform oral sodomy on him and then drove to a field where he raped her. After the sexual assault, the victim went to her school, where, crying and upset, she reported the crime. The police arrested respondent and recovered on his person the weapon he used to facilitate the crime. Although respondent maintained that the sexual intercourse was consensual, a jury convicted him of rape, aggravated sodomy, and aggravated kidnaping. * * *

In 1994, a few years before respondent was scheduled to be released, prison officials ordered him to participate in a Sexual Abuse Treatment Program (SATP). As part of the program, participating inmates are required to complete and sign an "Admission of Responsibility" form, in which they discuss and accept responsibility for the crime for which they have been sentenced. Participating inmates also are required to complete a sexual history form, which details all prior sexual activities, regardless of whether such activities constitute uncharged criminal offenses. A polygraph examination is used to verify the accuracy and completeness of the offender's sexual history.

While information obtained from participants advances the SATP's rehabilitative goals, the information is not privileged. Kansas leaves open the possibility that new evidence might be used against sex offenders in future criminal proceedings. In addition, Kansas law requires the SATP staff to report any uncharged sexual offenses involving minors to law enforcement authorities. Although there is no evidence that incriminating information has ever been disclosed under the SATP, the release of information is a possibility.

Department officials informed respondent that if he refused to participate in the SATP, his privilege status would be reduced from Level III to Level I. As part of this reduction, respondent's visitation rights, earnings, work opportunities, ability to send money to family, canteen expenditures, access to a personal television, and other privileges automatically would be curtailed. In addition, respondent would be transferred to a maximum-security unit, where his movement would be more limited, he would be moved from a two-person to a four-person cell, and he would be in a potentially more dangerous environment.

Respondent refused to participate in the SATP on the ground that the required disclosures of his criminal history would violate his Fifth Amendment privilege against self-incrimination. He brought this action under 42 U.S.C. § 1983 against the warden and the secretary of the Department, seeking an injunction to prevent them from withdrawing his prison privileges and transferring him to a different housing unit.

After the parties completed discovery, the United States District Court for the District of Kansas en-. tered summary judgment in respondent's favor. The District Court noted that because respondent had testified at trial that his sexual intercourse with the victim was consensual, an acknowledgement of responsibility for the rape on the "Admission of Guilt" form would subject respondent to a possible charge of perjury. After reviewing the specific loss of privileges and change in conditions of confinement that respondent would face for refusing to incriminate himself, the District Court concluded that these consequences constituted coercion in violation of the Fifth Amendment.

The Court of Appeals for the Tenth Circuit affirmed. It held that the compulsion element of a Fifth Amendment claim can be established by penalties that do not constitute deprivations of protected liberty interests under the Due Process Clause. It held that the reduction in prison privileges and housing accommodations was a penalty, both because of its substantial impact on the inmate and because that impact was identical to the punishment imposed by the Department for serious disciplinary infractions. In the Court of Appeals' view, the fact that the sanction was automatic, rather than conditional, supported the conclusion that it constituted compulsion. Moreover, because all SATP files are subject to disclosure by subpoena, and an admission of culpability regarding the crime of conviction would create a

risk of a perjury prosecution, the court concluded that the information disclosed by respondent was sufficiently incriminating. The Court of Appeals recognized that the Kansas policy served the State's important interests in rehabilitating sex offenders and promoting public safety. It concluded, however, that those interests could be served without violating the Constitution, either by treating the admissions of the inmates as privileged communications or by granting inmates use immunity.

II

Sex offenders are a serious threat in this Nation. In 1995, an estimated 355,000 rapes and sexual assaults occurred nationwide. Between 1980 and 1994, the population of imprisoned sex offenders increased at a faster rate than for any other category of violent crime. In 1995, for instance, a majority of reported forcible sexual offenses were committed against persons under 18 years of age. Nearly 4 in 10 imprisoned violent sex offenders said their victims were 12 or younger.

When convicted sex offenders reenter society, they are much more likely than any other type of offender to be rearrested for a new rape or sexual assault. See Sex Offenses 27; U.S. Dept. of Justice, Bureau of Justice Statistics, Recidivism of Prisoners Released in 1983, p. 6 (1997). States thus have a vital interest in rehabilitating convicted sex offenders.

Therapists and correctional officers widely agree that clinical rehabilitative programs can enable sex offenders to manage their impulses and in this way reduce recidivism. An important component of those rehabilitation programs requires participants to confront their past and accept responsibility for their misconduct. "Denial is generally regarded as a main impediment to successful therapy," and "[t]herapists depend on offenders' truthful descriptions of events leading to past offences in order to determine which behaviours need to be targeted in therapy." H. Barbaree, Denial and Minimization Among Sex Offenders: Assessment and Treatment Outcome, 3 Forum on Corrections Research, No. 4, p. 30 (1991). Research indicates that offenders who deny all allegations of sexual abuse are three times more likely to fail in treatment than those who admit even partial complicity.

The critical first step in the Kansas Sexual Abuse Treatment Program (SATP), therefore, is acceptance of responsibility for past offenses. This gives inmates a basis to understand why they are being punished and to identify the traits that cause such a frightening and high risk of recidivism. As part of this first step, Kansas requires each SATP participant to complete an "Admission of Responsibility" form, to fill out a sexual history form discussing their offending behavior, and to discuss their past behavior in individual and group counseling sessions.

The District Court found that the Kansas SATP is a valid "clinical rehabilitative program," supported by a "legitimate penological objective" in rehabilitation. The SATP lasts for 18 months and involves substantial daily counseling. It helps inmates address sexual addiction; under-

stand the thoughts, feelings, and behavior dynamics that precede their offenses; and develop relapse prevention skills. Although inmates are assured of a significant level of confidentiality, Kansas does not offer legal immunity from prosecution based on any statements made in the course of the SATP. According to Kansas, however, no inmate has ever been charged or prosecuted for any offense based on information disclosed during treatment. There is no contention, then, that the program is a mere subterfuge for the conduct of a criminal investigation.

As the parties explain, Kansas' decision not to offer immunity to every SATP participant serves two legitimate state interests. First, the professionals who design and conduct the program have concluded that for SATP participants to accept full responsibility for their past actions, they must accept the proposition that those actions carry consequences. Although no program participant has ever been prosecuted or penalized based on information revealed during the SATP, the potential for additional punishment reinforces the gravity of the participants' offenses and thereby aids in their rehabilitation. If inmates know society will not punish them for their past offenses, they may be left with the false impression that society does not consider those crimes to be serious ones. The practical effect of guaranteed immunity for SATP participants would be to absolve many sex offenders of any and all cost for their earlier crimes. This is the precise opposite of the rehabilitative objective.

Second, while Kansas as a rule does not prosecute inmates based upon information revealed in the course of the program, the State confirms its valid interest in deterrence by keeping open the option to prosecute a particularly dangerous sex offender. Kansas is not alone in declining to offer blanket use immunity as a condition of participation in a treatment program. The Federal Bureau of Prisons and other States conduct similar sex offender programs and do not offer immunity to the participants.

The mere fact that Kansas declines to grant inmates use immunity does not render the SATP invalid. Asking at the outset whether prison administrators can or should offer immunity skips the constitutional inquiry altogether. If the State of Kansas offered immunity, the self-incrimination privilege would not be implicated. The State, however, does not offer immunity. So the central question becomes whether the State's program, and the consequences for nonparticipation in it, combine to create a compulsion that encumbers the constitutional right. If there is compulsion, the State cannot continue the program in its present form; and the alternatives, as will be discussed, defeat the program's objectives.

The SATP does not compel prisoners to incriminate themselves in violation of the Constitution. The Fifth Amendment Self–Incrimination Clause, which applies to the States via the Fourteenth Amendment, provides that no person "shall be compelled in any criminal case to be a witness against himself." The "Amendment speaks of compulsion," and the Court has insisted that the "constitutional guarantee is only that the witness not be *compelled* to give self-incriminating testimony." The consequences in question here—a transfer to another prison where television sets are not placed in each inmate's cell, where exercise facilities are not readily available, and where work and wage opportunities are more limited—are not ones that compel a prisoner to speak about his past crimes despite a desire to remain silent. The fact that these consequences are imposed on prisoners, rather than ordinary citizens, moreover, is important in weighing respondent's constitutional claim.

The privilege against self-incrimination does not terminate at the jailhouse door, but the fact of a valid conviction and the ensuing restrictions on liberty are essential to the Fifth Amendment analysis. A broad range of choices that might infringe constitutional rights in free society fall within the expected conditions of confinement of those who have suffered a lawful conviction.

The Court has instructed that rehabilitation is a legitimate penological interest that must be weighed against the exercise of an inmate's liberty. Since "most offenders will eventually return to society, [a] paramount objective of the corrections system is the rehabilitation of those committed to its custody." Pell v. Procunier, 417 U.S. 817, 823 (1974). Acceptance of responsibility in turn demonstrates that an offender "is ready and willing to admit his crime and to enter the correctional system in a frame of mind that affords hope for success in rehabilitation over a shorter period of time than might otherwise be necessary."

Brady v. United States, 397 U.S. 742, 753 (1970).

The limitation on prisoners' privileges and rights also follows from the need to grant necessary authority and capacity to federal and state officials to administer the prisons. See, e.g., Turner v. Safley, 482 U.S. 78 (1987). "Running a prison is an inordinately difficult undertaking that requires expertise, planning, and the commitment of resources, all of which are peculiarly within the province of the legislative and executive branches of government." Id., at 84–85. To respect these imperatives, courts must exercise restraint in supervising the minutiae of prison life. Ibid. * * *

* * * The compulsion inquiry must consider the significant restraints already inherent in prison life and the State's own vital interests in rehabilitation goals and procedures within the prison system. A prison clinical rehabilitation program, which is acknowledged to bear a rational relation to a legitimate penological objective, does not violate the privilege against self-incrimination if the adverse consequences an inmate faces for not participating are related to the program objectives and do not constitute atypical and significant hardships in relation to the ordinary incidents of prison life.

Along these lines, this Court has recognized that lawful conviction and incarceration necessarily place limitations on the exercise of a defendant's privilege against self-incrimination. See, e.g., Baxter v. Palmigiano, 425 U.S. 308 (1976). Baxter declined to extend to prison disciplinary proceedings the rule of Griffin v. California, 380 U.S. 609 (1965), that the prosecu-

tion may not comment on a defendant's silence at trial. As the Court explained, "[d]isciplinary proceedings in state prisons ... involve the correctional process and important state interests other than conviction for crime." Id., at 319. The inmate in Baxter no doubt felt compelled to speak in one sense of the word. The Court, considering the level of compulsion in light of the prison setting and the State's interests in rehabilitation and orderly administration, nevertheless rejected the inmate's self-incrimination claim.

In the present case, respondent's decision not to participate in the Kansas SATP did not extend his term of incarceration. Nor did his decision affect his eligibility for good-time credits or parole. Respondent instead complains that if he remains silent about his past crimes, he will be transferred from the medium-security unit—where the program is conducted—to a less desirable maximum-security unit. No one contends, however, that the transfer is intended to punish prisoners for exercising their Fifth Amendment rights. Rather, the limitation on these rights is incidental to Kansas' legitimate penological reason for the transfer: Due to limited space, inmates who do not participate in their respective programs will be moved out of the facility where the programs are held to make room for other inmates. As the Secretary of Corrections has explained, "it makes no sense to have someone who's not participating in a program taking up a bed in a setting where someone else who may be willing to participate in a program could occupy that bed and participate in a program."

It is well settled that the decision where to house inmates is at the core of prison administrators' expertise. See Meachum v. Fano, 427 U.S. 215, 225 (1976). For this reason the Court has not required administrators to conduct a hearing before transferring a prisoner to a bed in a different prison, even if "life in one prison is much more disagreeable than in another." *Ibid.* The Court has considered the proposition that a prisoner in a more comfortable facility might begin to feel entitled to remain there throughout his term of incarceration. The Court has concluded, nevertheless, that this expectation "is too ephemeral and insubstantial to trigger procedural due process protections as long as prison officials have discretion to transfer him for whatever reason or for no reason at all." *Id.,* at 228. This logic has equal force in analyzing respondent's self-incrimination claim.

Respondent also complains that he will be demoted from Level III to Level I status as a result of his decision not to participate. This demotion means the loss of his personal television; less access to prison organizations and the gym area; a reduction in certain pay opportunities and canteen privileges; and restricted visitation rights. An essential tool of prison administration, however, is the authority to offer inmates various incentives to behave. The Constitution accords prison officials wide latitude to bestow or revoke these perquisites as they see fit. Accordingly, Hewitt v. Helms, 459 U.S. 460, 467, n. 4 (1983), held that an inmate's transfer to another facility did not in itself implicate a liberty

interest, even though that transfer resulted in the loss of "access to vocational, educational, recreational, and rehabilitative programs." Respondent concedes that no liberty interest is implicated in this case. To be sure, cases like *Meachum* and *Hewitt* involved the Due Process Clause rather than the privilege against compelled self-incrimination. Those cases nevertheless underscore the axiom that, by virtue of their convictions, inmates must expect significant restrictions, inherent in prison life, on rights and privileges free citizens take for granted.

Respondent fails to cite a single case from this Court holding that the denial of discrete prison privileges for refusal to participate in a rehabilitation program amounts to unconstitutional compulsion. Instead, relying on the so-called penalty cases, respondent treats the fact of his incarceration as if it were irrelevant. See, e.g., Garrity v. New Jersey, 385 U.S. 493 (1967); Spevack v. Klein, 385 U.S. 511 (1967). Those cases, however, involved free citizens given the choice between invoking the Fifth Amendment privilege and sustaining their economic livelihood. Those principles are not easily extended to the prison context, where inmates surrender upon incarceration their rights to pursue a livelihood and to contract freely with the State, as well as many other basic freedoms. * * * It would come as a surprise if *Spevack* stands for the proposition that when a lawyer has been disbarred by reason of a final criminal conviction, the court or agency considering reinstatement of the right to practice law could not consider that the disbarred attorney has admitted his guilt and expressed contrition. Indeed, this consideration is often given dispositive weight by this Court itself on routine motions for reinstatement. The current case is more complex, of course, in that respondent is also required to discuss other criminal acts for which he might still be liable for prosecution. On this point, however, there is still a critical distinction between the instant case and *Garrity* or *Spevack*. Unlike those cases, respondent here is asked to discuss other past crimes as part of a legitimate rehabilitative program conducted within prison walls.

To reject out of hand these considerations would be to ignore the State's interests in offering rehabilitation programs and providing for the efficient administration of its prisons. There is no indication that the SATP is an elaborate attempt to avoid the protections offered by the privilege against compelled self-incrimination. Rather, the program serves an important social purpose. It would be bitter medicine to treat as irrelevant the State's legitimate interests and to invalidate the SATP on the ground that it incidentally burdens an inmate's right to remain silent.

Determining what constitutes unconstitutional compulsion involves a question of judgment: Courts must decide whether the consequences of an inmate's choice to remain silent are closer to the physical torture against which the Constitution clearly protects or the *de minimis* harms against which it does not. [In the prison context, the question is] whether the response of prison administrators to correctional and rehabilitative necessities are so out of the ordinary that one could sensibly say they rise to the level of unconstitutional compulsion.

Prison context or not, respondent's choice is marked less by compulsion than by choices the Court has held give no rise to a self-incrimination claim. The "criminal process, like the rest of the legal system, is replete with situations requiring the making of difficult judgments as to which course to follow. Although a defendant may have a right, even of constitutional dimensions, to follow whichever course he chooses, the Constitution does not by that token always forbid requiring him to choose." McGautha v. California, 402 U.S. 183, 213 (1971). It is well settled that the government need not make the exercise of the Fifth Amendment privilege cost free. See, e.g., Jenkins v. Anderson, 447 U.S. 231, 238 (1980) (a criminal defendant's exercise of his Fifth Amendment privilege prior to arrest may be used to impeach his credibility at trial); Williams v. Florida, 399 U.S. 78, 84–85 (1970) (a criminal defendant may be compelled to disclose the substance of an alibi defense prior to trial or be barred from asserting it).

The cost to respondent of exercising his Fifth Amendment privilege— denial of certain perquisites that make his life in prison more tolerable—is much less than that borne by the defendant in *McGautha*. There, the Court upheld a procedure that allowed statements, which were made by a criminal defendant to mitigate his responsibility and avoid the death penalty, to be used against him as evidence of his guilt. The Court likewise has held that plea bargaining does not violate the

Fifth Amendment, even though criminal defendants may feel considerable pressure to admit guilt in order to obtain more lenient treatment. See, e.g., Bordenkircher v. Hayes, 434 U.S. 357 (1978); *Brady*, 397 U.S., at 751.

Nor does reducing an inmate's prison wage and taking away personal television and gym access pose the same hard choice faced by the defendants in Baxter v. Palmigiano, 425 U.S. 308 (1976), Ohio Adult Parole Authority v. Woodard, 523 U.S. 272 (1998), and Minnesota v. Murphy, 465 U.S. 420 (1984). In *Baxter*, a state prisoner objected to the fact that his silence at a prison disciplinary hearing would be held against him. The Court acknowledged that Griffin v. California, held that the Fifth Amendment prohibits courts from instructing a criminal jury that it may draw an inference of guilt from a defendant's failure to testify. The Court nevertheless refused to extend the *Griffin* rule to the context of state prison disciplinary hearings because those proceedings "involve the correctional process and important state interests other than conviction for crime." Whereas the inmate in the present case faces the loss of certain privileges, the prisoner in *Baxter* faced 30 days in punitive segregation as well as the subsequent downgrade of his prison classification status.

In *Murphy,* the defendant feared the possibility of additional jail time as a result of his decision to remain silent. The defendant's probation officer knew the defendant had committed a rape and murder unrelated to his probation. One of the terms of the defendant's probation required him to be truthful with the probation officer in all matters.

Seizing upon this, the officer interviewed the defendant about the rape and murder, and the defendant admitted his guilt. The Court found no Fifth Amendment violation, despite the defendant's fear of being returned to prison for 16 months if he remained silent.

In *Woodard,* the plaintiff faced not loss of a personal television and gym access, but loss of life. In a unanimous opinion just four Terms ago, this Court held that a death row inmate could be made to choose between incriminating himself at his clemency interview and having adverse inferences drawn from his silence. The Court reasoned that it "is difficult to see how a voluntary interview could 'compel' respondent to speak. He merely faces a choice quite similar to the sorts of choices that a criminal defendant must make in the course of criminal proceedings, none of which has ever been held to violate the Fifth Amendment." As here, the inmate in *Woodard* claimed to face a Hobson's choice: He would damage his case for clemency no matter whether he spoke and incriminated himself, or remained silent and the clemency board construed that silence against him. Unlike here, the Court nevertheless concluded that the pressure the inmate felt to speak to improve his chances of clemency did not constitute unconstitutional compulsion.

Woodard, Murphy, and *Baxter* illustrate that the consequences respondent faced here did not amount to unconstitutional compulsion. Respondent and the dissent attempt to distinguish *Baxter, Murphy,* and *Woodard* on the dual grounds that (1) the penalty here followed automatically from respondent's decision to remain silent, and (2) respondent's participation in the SATP was involuntary. Neither distinction would justify departing from this Court's precedents, and the second is question begging in any event.

It is proper to consider the nexus between remaining silent and the consequences that follow. Plea bargains are not deemed to be compelled in part because a defendant who pleads not guilty still must be convicted. States may award good-time credits and early parole for inmates who accept responsibility because silence in these circumstances does not automatically mean the parole board, which considers other factors as well, will deny them parole. While the automatic nature of the consequence may be a necessary condition to finding unconstitutional compulsion, however, that is not a sufficient reason alone to ignore *Woodard, Murphy,* and *Baxter.* Even if a consequence follows directly from a person's silence, one cannot answer the question whether the person has been compelled to incriminate himself without first considering the severity of the consequences.

Nor can *Woodard* be distinguished on the alternate ground that respondent's choice to participate in the SATP was involuntary, whereas the death row inmate in *Woodard* chose to participate in clemency proceedings. This distinction assumes the answer to the compulsion inquiry. If respondent was not compelled to participate in the SATP, his participation was voluntary in the only sense necessary for our present inquiry. Kansas asks sex offenders to participate in SATP

because, in light of the high rate of recidivism, it wants all, not just the few who volunteer, to receive treatment. Whether the inmates are being asked or ordered to participate depends entirely on the consequences of their decision not to do so. The parties in *Woodard, Murphy,* and *Baxter* all were faced with ramifications far worse than respondent faces here, and in each of those cases the Court determined that their hard choice between silence and the consequences was not compelled. It is beyond doubt, of course, that respondent would prefer not to choose between losing prison privileges and accepting responsibility for his past crimes. It is a choice, nonetheless, that does not amount to compulsion, and therefore one Kansas may require respondent to make.

The Federal Government has filed an *amicus* brief describing its sex offender treatment program. Were respondent's position to prevail, the constitutionality of the federal program would be cast into serious doubt. The fact that the offender in the federal program can choose to participate without being given a new prisoner classification is not determinative. For, as the Government explains, its program is conducted at a single, 112–bed facility that is more desirable than other federal prisons. Inmates choose at the outset whether to enter the federal program. Once accepted, however, inmates must continue to discuss and accept responsibility for their crimes if they wish to maintain the status quo and remain in their more comfortable accommodations. Otherwise they will be expelled from the program and sent to a less desirable facility. Thus the federal program is different from Kansas' SATP only in that it does not require inmates to sacrifice privileges besides housing as a consequence of nonparticipation. The federal program is comparable to the Kansas program because it does not offer participants use immunity and because it conditions a desirable housing assignment on inmates' willingness to accept responsibility for past behavior. Respondent's theory cannot be confined in any meaningful way, and state and federal courts applying that view would have no principled means to determine whether these similarities are sufficient to render the federal program unconstitutional.

Respondent is mistaken as well to concentrate on the so-called reward/penalty distinction and the illusory baseline against which a change in prison conditions must be measured. The answer to the question whether the government is extending a benefit or taking away a privilege rests entirely in the eye of the beholder. For this reason, emphasis of any baseline, while superficially appealing, would be an inartful addition to an already confused area of jurisprudence. The prison warden in this case stated that it is largely a matter of chance where in a prison an inmate is assigned. Even if Inmates A and B are serving the same sentence for the same crime, Inmate A could end up in a medium-security unit and Inmate B in a maximum-security unit based solely on administrative factors beyond their control. Under respondent's view, however, the Constitution allows the State to offer Inmate B the opportunity to live in the medium-security unit conditioned on his participation in the SATP, but does not allow the State to offer Inmate A the opportunity to live in that same medium-security unit subject to the same conditions. The consequences for Inmates A and B are identical: They may participate and live in medium security or refuse and live in maximum security. Respondent, however, would have us say the Constitution puts Inmate A in a superior position to Inmate B solely by the accident of the initial assignment to a medium-security unit.

This reasoning is unsatisfactory. * * * Respondent's reasoning would provide States with perverse incentives to assign all inmates convicted of sex offenses to maximum security prisons until near the time of release, when the rehabilitation program starts. The rule would work to the detriment of the entire class of sex offenders who might not otherwise be placed in maximum-security facilities. And prison administrators would be forced, before making routine prison housing decisions, to identify each inmate's so-called baseline and determine whether an adverse effect, however marginal, will result from the administrative decision. The easy alternatives that respondent predicts for prison administrators would turn out to be not so trouble free.

Respondent's analysis also would call into question the constitutionality of an accepted feature of federal criminal law: the downward adjustment for acceptance of criminal responsibility provided in § 3E1.1 of the United States Sentencing Guidelines (Nov. 2002). If the Constitution does not permit the government to condition the use of a personal television on the acceptance of responsibility for past crimes, it is unclear how it could permit the government to reduce the length of a prisoner's term of incarceration based upon the same factor. By rejecting respondent's theory, we do not, in this case, call these policies into question.

Acceptance of responsibility is the beginning of rehabilitation. And a recognition that there are rewards for those who attempt to reform is a vital and necessary step toward completion. The Court of Appeals' ruling would defeat these objectives. If the State sought to comply with the ruling by allowing respondent to enter the program while still insisting on his innocence, there would be little incentive for other SATP participants to confess and accept counseling; indeed, there is support for Kansas' view that the dynamics of the group therapy would be impaired. If the State had to offer immunity, the practical effect would be that serial offenders who are incarcerated for but one violation would be given a windfall for past bad conduct, a result potentially destructive of any public or state support for the program and quite at odds with the dominant goal of acceptance of responsibility. If the State found it was forced to graduate prisoners from its rehabilitation program without knowing what other offenses they may have committed, the integrity of its program would be very much in doubt. If the State found it had to comply by allowing respondent the same perquisites as those who accept counseling, the result would be a dramatic illustration that obduracy has the same rewards as acceptance, and so the program itself would become self-defeating, even hypocritical, in the eyes of those whom it

seeks to help. The Fifth Amendment does not require the State to suffer these programmatic disruptions when it seeks to rehabilitate those who are incarcerated for valid, final convictions.

The Kansas SATP represents a sensible approach to reducing the serious danger that repeat sex offenders pose to many innocent persons, most often children. The State's interest in rehabilitation is undeniable. There is, furthermore, no indication that the SATP is merely an elaborate ruse to skirt the protections of the privilege against compelled self-incrimination. Rather, the program allows prison administrators to provide to those who need treatment the incentive to seek it.

The judgment of the Court of Appeals is reversed, and the case is remanded for further proceedings.

JUSTICE O'CONNOR, **concurring in the judgment.**

The Court today is divided on the question of what standard to apply when evaluating compulsion for the purposes of the Fifth Amendment privilege against self-incrimination in a prison setting. I write separately because, although I agree with Justice STEVENS that the Fifth Amendment compulsion standard is broader than the "atypical and significant hardship" standard we have adopted for evaluating due process claims in prisons, I do not believe that the alterations in respondent's prison conditions as a result of his failure to participate in the Sexual Abuse Treatment Program (SATP) were so great as to constitute compulsion for the purposes of the Fifth Amendment privilege against self-incrimination. I therefore agree with the plurality that the decision below should be reversed.

The text of the Fifth Amendment does not prohibit all penalties levied in response to a person's refusal to incriminate himself or herself—it prohibits only the compulsion of such testimony. Not all pressure necessarily "compel[s]" incriminating statements.

* * * Our precedents establish that certain types of penalties are capable of coercing incriminating testimony: termination of employment, Uniformed Sanitation Men Ass'n, Inc. v. Commissioner of Sanitation of City of New York, 392 U.S. 280 (1968), the loss of a professional license, Spevack v. Klein, 385 U.S. 511 (1967), ineligibility to receive government contracts, Lefkowitz v. Turley, 414 U.S. 70 (1973), and the loss of the right to participate in political associations and to hold public office, Lefkowitz v. Cunningham, 431 U.S. 801 (1977). All of these penalties, however, are far more significant than those facing respondent here.

* * *

I do not believe the consequences facing respondent in this case are serious enough to compel him to be a witness against himself. These consequences involve a reduction in incentive level, and a corresponding transfer from a medium-security to a maximum-security part of the prison. In practical terms, these changes involve restrictions on the personal property respondent can keep in his cell, a reduction in his visitation privileges, a reduction in the amount of money he can spend in the canteen, and a reduction in the wage he can earn through prison employment. These

changes in living conditions seem to me minor. Because the prison is responsible for caring for respondent's basic needs, his ability to support himself is not implicated by the reduction in wages he would suffer as a result. While his visitation is reduced as a result of his failure to incriminate himself, he still retains the ability to see his attorney, his family, and members of the clergy. The limitation on the possession of personal items, as well as the amount that respondent is allowed to spend at the canteen, may make his prison experience more unpleasant, but seems very unlikely to actually compel him to incriminate himself.

Justice STEVENS also suggests that the move to the maximum-security area of the prison would itself be coercive. Although the District Court found that moving respondent to a maximum-security section of the prison would put him "in a more dangerous environment occupied by more serious offenders," there was no finding about how great a danger such a placement posed. Because it is respondent's burden to prove compulsion, we may assume that the prison is capable of controlling its inmates so that respondent's personal safety is not jeopardized by being placed in the maximum-security area of the prison, at least in the absence of proof to the contrary.

* * *

Although I do not think the penalties respondent faced were sufficiently serious to compel his testimony, I do not agree with the suggestion in the plurality opinion that these penalties could permissibly rise to the level of those in cases like McGautha v. California, 402 U.S. 183 (1971) (holding that statements made in the mitigation phase of a capital sentencing hearing may be used as evidence of guilt), Bordenkircher v. Hayes, 434 U.S. 357 (1978) (holding that plea bargaining does not violate the Fifth Amendment privilege against self-incrimination), and Ohio Adult Parole Authority v. Woodard, 523 U.S. 272 (1998) (holding that there is no right to silence at a clemency interview). The penalties potentially faced in these cases—longer incarceration and execution—are far greater than those we have already held to constitute unconstitutional compulsion in the penalty cases. Indeed, the imposition of such outcomes as a penalty for refusing to incriminate oneself would surely implicate a "liberty interest."

Justice STEVENS attempts to distinguish these cases because, in each, the negative outcome did not follow directly from the decision to remain silent, and because none of these cases involved a direct order to testify. As the plurality's opinion makes clear, however, these two factors do not adequately explain the difference between these cases and the penalty cases, where we have found compulsion based on the imposition of penalties far less onerous.

I believe the proper theory should recognize that it is generally acceptable to impose the risk of punishment, however great, so long as the actual imposition of such punishment is accomplished through a fair criminal process. Forcing defendants to accept such consequences seems to me very different than imposing penalties for the refusal to incriminate oneself that go beyond the criminal process and appear, starkly, as government attempts to compel testimony; in the latter context, any penalty that is capable of compelling a person to be a witness against himself is illegitimate. But even this explanation of the privilege is incomplete, as it does not fully account for all of the Court's precedents in this area. Compare Griffin v. California, 380 U.S. 609 (1965) (holding that prosecutor may not comment on a defendant's failure to testify), with Ohio Adult Parole Authority v. Woodard, (holding that there is no right to silence at a clemency interview).

Complicating matters even further is the question of whether the denial of benefits and the imposition of burdens ought to be analyzed differently in this area. This question is particularly important given the existence of United States Sentencing Commission, Guidelines Manual § 3E1.1 (Nov.2000), which can be read to offer convicted criminals the benefit of a lower sentence in exchange for accepting responsibility for their crimes.

I find the plurality's failure to set forth a comprehensive theory of the Fifth Amendment privilege against self-incrimination troubling. But because this case indisputably involves burdens rather than benefits, and because I do not believe the penalties assessed against respondent in response to his failure to incriminate himself are compulsive on any reasonable test, I need not resolve this dilemma to make my judgment in this case.

* * *

JUSTICE STEVENS, with whom JUSTICE SOUTER, JUSTICE GINSBURG, and JUSTICE BREYER join, dissenting.

No one could possibly disagree with the plurality's statement that "offering inmates minimal incentives to participate [in a rehabilitation program] does not amount to compelled self-incrimination prohibited by the Fifth Amendment." The question that this case presents, however, is whether the State may punish an inmate's assertion of his Fifth Amendment privilege with the same mandatory sanction that follows a disciplinary conviction for an offense such as theft, sodomy, riot, arson, or assault. Until today the Court has never characterized a threatened harm as "a minimal incentive." Nor have we ever held that a person who has made a valid assertion of the privilege may nevertheless be ordered to incriminate himself and sanctioned for disobeying such an order. This is truly a watershed case.

Based on an ad hoc appraisal of the benefits of obtaining confessions from sex offenders, balanced against the cost of honoring a bedrock constitutional right, the plurality holds that it is permissible to punish the assertion of the privilege with what it views as modest sanctions, provided that those sanctions are not given a "punitive" label. As I shall explain, the sanctions are in fact severe, but even if that were not so, the plurality's policy judgment does not justify the evisceration of a constitutional right. Despite the plurality's meandering attempt to justify its unprecedented departure from a rule of law that has been settled since the days of John Marshall, I respectfully dissent.

I

* * * Putting to one side the plurality's evaluation of the policy judgments made by Kansas, its central submission is that the threatened withdrawal of respondent's Level III and medium-security status is not sufficiently harmful to qualify as unconstitutional compulsion. In support of this position, neither the plurality nor Justice O'CONNOR cites a single Fifth Amendment case in which a person invoked the privilege and was nevertheless required to answer a potentially incriminating question.

* * *

The plurality's suggestion that our decision in Meachum v. Fano, 427 U.S. 215 (1976), supports a novel interpretation of the Fifth Amendment, is inconsistent with the central rationale of that case. In *Meachum*, a group of prison inmates urged the Court to hold that the Due Process Clause entitled them to a hearing prior to their transfer to a substantially less favorable facility. Relying on the groundbreaking decisions in Morrissey v. Brewer, 408 U.S. 471 (1972), and Wolff v. McDonnell, 418 U.S. 539 (1974), which had rejected the once-prevailing view that a prison inmate had no more rights than a "slave of the State," the prisoners sought to extend those holdings to require judicial review of "any substantial deprivation imposed by prison authorities." The Court recognized that after *Wolff* and its progeny, convicted felons retain "a variety of important rights that the courts must be alert to protect." Although *Meachum* refused to expand the constitutional rights of inmates, we did not narrow the protection of any established right. Indeed, Justice White explicitly limited the holding to prison conditions that "do not otherwise violate the Constitution."

Not a word in our discussion of the privilege in Ohio Adult Parole Authority v. Woodard, 523 U.S. 272 (1998), requires a heightened showing of compulsion in the prison context to establish a Fifth Amendment violation. That case is wholly unlike this one because Woodard was not ordered to incriminate himself and was not punished for refusing to do so. He challenged Ohio's clemency procedures, arguing, *inter alia,* that an interview with members of the clemency board offered to inmates one week before their clemency hearing presented him with a Hobson's choice that violated the privilege against self-incrimination. He could either take advantage of the interview and risk incriminating himself, or decline the interview, in which case the clemency board might draw adverse inferences from his decision not to testify. We concluded that the prisoner who was offered "a voluntary interview" is in the same position as any defendant faced with the option of either testifying or accepting the risk that adverse inferences may be drawn from his silence.

Respondent was directly ordered by prison authorities to participate in a program that requires incriminating disclosures, whereas no one ordered Woodard to do anything. Like a direct judicial order to answer questions in the courtroom, an order from the State to participate in the SATP is inherently coercive. Moreover, the penalty for re-

fusing to participate in the SATP is automatic. Instead of conjecture and speculation about the indirect consequences that may flow from a decision to remain silent, we can be sure that defiance of a direct order carries with it the stigma of being a lawbreaker or a problem inmate, as well as other specified penalties. The penalty involved in this case is a mandated official response to the assertion of the privilege.

* * *

II

The plurality and Justice O'CONNOR hold that the consequences stemming from respondent's invocation of the privilege are not serious enough to constitute compulsion. The threat of transfer to Level I and a maximum-security unit is not sufficiently coercive in their view—either because the consequence is not really a penalty, just the loss of a benefit, or because it is a penalty, but an insignificant one. I strongly disagree.

It took respondent several years to acquire the status that he occupied in 1994 when he was ordered to participate in the SATP. Because of the nature of his convictions, in 1983 the Department initially placed him in a maximum-security classification. Not until 1989 did the Department change his "security classification to 'medium by exception' because of his good behavior." Thus, the sanction at issue threatens to deprive respondent of a status in the prison community that it took him six years to earn and which he had successfully maintained for five more years when he was ordered to incriminate himself. Moreover, abruptly "busting" his custody back to Level I would impose the same stigma on him as would a disciplinary conviction for any of the most serious offenses described in petitioners' formal statement of Internal Management Policy and Procedure (IMPP). As the District Court found, the sanctions imposed on respondent "mirror the consequences imposed for serious disciplinary infractions." This same loss of privileges is considered serious enough by prison authorities that it is used as punishment for theft, drug abuse, assault, and possession of dangerous contraband.

The punitive consequences of the discipline include not only the dignitary and reputational harms flowing from the transfer, but a serious loss of tangible privileges as well. Because he refused to participate in the SATP, respondent's visitation rights will be restricted. He will be able to earn only $0.60 per day, as compared to Level III inmates, who can potentially earn minimum wage. His access to prison organizations and activities will be limited. He will no longer be able to send his family more than $30 per pay period. He will be prohibited from spending more than $20 per payroll period at the canteen, rather than the $140 he could spend at Level III, and he will be restricted in what property he can keep in his cell. In addition, because he will be transferred to a maximum-security unit, respondent will be forced to share a cell with three other inmates rather than one, and his movement outside the cell will be substantially curtailed. The District Court found that the maximum-security unit is "a more dangerous environment occupied by more serious offenders." Perhaps most importantly, respondent will no longer be able to earn his way back up to Level III status through good behavior during the remainder of his sentence.

The plurality's glib attempt to characterize these consequences as a loss of potential benefits rather than a penalty is wholly unpersuasive. The threatened transfer to Level I and to a maximum-security unit represents a significant, adverse change from the status quo. * * *

* * * We have recognized that the government can extend a benefit in exchange for incriminating statements, but cannot threaten to take away privileges as the cost of invoking Fifth Amendment rights. Based on this distinction, nothing that I say in this dissent calls into question the constitutionality of *downward* adjustments for acceptance of responsibility under the United States Sentencing Guidelines. Although such a reduction in sentence creates a powerful incentive for defendants to confess, it completely avoids the constitutional issue that would be presented if the Guidelines operated like the scheme here and authorized an *upward* adjustment whenever a defendant refused to accept responsibility. Similarly, taking into account an attorney's acceptance of responsibility or contrition in deciding whether to reinstate his membership to the bar of this Court is obviously different from disbarring an attorney for invoking his privilege. By obscuring the distinction between penalties and incentives, it is the plurality that calls into question both the Guidelines and plea bargaining.

It is curious that the plurality asserts the impracticality of drawing such a distinction, given that in this case a majority of the Court agrees that it is perfectly clear the consequences facing respondent represent a burden, rather than the denial of a benefit. Our cases reveal that it is not only possible, but necessary to draw the distinction. For even Bordenkircher v. Hayes, 434 U.S. 357 (1978), conditioned its entire analysis of plea bargaining on the assumption that the defendant had been charged with the greater offense prior to plea bargaining and, therefore, faced the denial of leniency rather than an enhanced penalty.

Even if the change in respondent's status could properly be characterized as a loss of benefits to which he had no entitlement, the question at hand is not whether the Department could have refused to extend those benefits in the first place, but rather whether revoking them at this point constitutes a penalty for asserting the Fifth Amendment privilege. The plurality contends that the transfer from medium to maximum security and the associated loss of Level III status is not intended to punish prisoners for asserting their Fifth Amendment rights, but rather is merely incidental to the prison's legitimate interest in making room for participants in the program. Of course, the Department could still house participants together without moving those who refuse to participate to more restrictive conditions of confinement and taking away their privileges. Moreover, petitioners have not alleged that respondent is taking up a bed in a unit devoted to the SATP; therefore, all the Department would have to do is allow respondent to stay in his current

medium-security cell. If need be, the Department could always transfer respondent to another medium-security unit. Given the absence of evidence in the record that the Department has a shortage of medium-security beds, or even that there is a separate unit devoted to participants in the SATP, the only plausible explanation for the transfer to maximum security and loss of Level III status is that it serves as punishment for refusing to participate in the program.

Justice O'CONNOR recognizes that the transfer is a penalty, but finds insufficient coercion because the "changes in [respondent's] living conditions seem to [her] minor." The coerciveness of the penalty in this case must be measured not by comparing the quality of life in a prison environment with that in a free society, but rather by the contrast between the favored and disfavored classes of prisoners. It is obviously impossible to measure precisely the significance of the difference between being housed in a four-person, maximum-security cell in the most dangerous area of the prison, on the one hand, and having a key to one's own room, the right to take a shower, and the ability to move freely within adjacent areas during certain hours, on the other—or to fully appreciate the importance of visitation privileges, being able to send more than $30 per pay period to family, having access to the yard for exercise, and the opportunity to participate in group activities. What is perfectly clear, however, is that it is the aggregate effect of those penalties that creates compulsion. Nor is it coincidental that petitioners have selected this same group of sanctions as the punishment to be imposed for the most serious violations of prison rules. * * *

III

The SATP clearly serves legitimate therapeutic purposes. The goal of the program is to rehabilitate sex offenders, and the requirement that participants complete admission of responsibility and sexual history forms may well be an important component of that process. * * * The program's laudable goals, however, do not justify reduced constitutional protection for those ordered to participate. * * * The benefits of obtaining confessions from sex offenders may be substantial, but "claims of overriding interests are not unusual in Fifth Amendment litigation," and until today at least "they have not fared well." *Turley,* 414 U.S., at 78. The State's interests in law enforcement and rehabilitation are present in every criminal case. If those interests were sufficient to justify impinging on prisoners' Fifth Amendment right, inmates would soon have no privilege left to invoke.

The plurality's willingness to sacrifice prisoners' Fifth Amendment rights is also unwarranted because available alternatives would allow the State to achieve the same objectives without impinging on inmates' privilege. The most obvious alternative is to grant participants use immunity. Petitioners have not provided any evidence that the program's therapeutic aims could not be served equally well by granting use immunity. Participants would still obtain all the therapeutic benefits of accepting responsibility and admitting past misconduct; they simply would not incriminate

themselves in the process. At least one State already offers such protection, see Ky.Rev.Stat. Ann. § 197.440 (2001) ("Communications made in the application for or in the course of a sexual offender's diagnosis and treatment ... shall be privileged from disclosure in any civil or criminal proceeding"), and there is no indication that its choice is incompatible with rehabilitation. In fact, the program's rehabilitative goals would likely be furthered by ensuring free and open discussion without the threat of prosecution looming over participants' therapy sessions.

The plurality contends that requiring immunity will undermine the therapeutic goals of the program because once "inmates know society will not punish them for their past offenses, they may be left with the false impression that society does not consider those crimes to be serious ones." The idea that an inmate who is confined to prison for almost 20 years for an offense could be left with the impression that his crimes are not serious or that wrongdoing does not carry consequences is absurd. Moreover, the argument starts from a false premise. Granting use immunity does not preclude prosecution; it merely prevents the State from using an inmate's own words, and the fruits thereof, against him in a subsequent prosecution. The plurality's concern might be justified if the State were required to grant *transactional* immunity, but we have made clear since *Kastigar* that use immunity is sufficient to alleviate a potential Fifth Amendment violation, 406 U.S., at 453. Nor is a State *required* to grant use immunity in order to have a sex offender treatment program that involves admission of responsibility.

Alternatively, the State could continue to pursue its rehabilitative goals without violating participants' Fifth Amendment rights by offering inmates a voluntary program. The United States points out that an inmate's participation in the sexual offender treatment program operated by the Federal Bureau of Prisons is entirely voluntary. * * * Although the inmates in the federal program are not granted use immunity, they are not compelled to participate. Indeed, there is reason to believe successful rehabilitation is more likely for voluntary participants than for those who are compelled to accept treatment. See Abel, Mittelman, Becker, Rathner & Rouleau, Predicting Child Molesters' Response to Treatment, 528 Annals N.Y. Acad. of Sciences 223 (1988) (finding that greater perceived pressure to participate in treatment is strongly correlated with the dropout rate).

Through its treatment program, Kansas seeks to achieve the admirable goal of reducing recidivism among sex offenders. In the process, however, the State demands an impermissible and unwarranted sacrifice from the participants. No matter what the goal, inmates should not be compelled to forfeit the privilege against self-incrimination simply because the ends are legitimate or because they have been convicted of sex offenses. Particularly in a case like this one, in which respondent has protested his innocence all along and is being compelled to confess to a crime that he still insists he did not commit, we ought to ask ourselves— what if this is one of those rare cases in which the jury made a mistake and he is actually innocent? And in answering that question, we should consider that even members of the Star Chamber thought they were pursuing righteous ends. I respectfully dissent.

E. WHAT IS PROTECTED?

2. Documents

Page 599.   Add the following section at the bottom of the page, before the material on *Braswell*:

Interaction of Document Production, Incrimination, and Immunity

In the following case, the Court revisited the question of the extent of Fifth Amendment protection when a person is compelled to produce incriminating documents. The concurring opinion is especially notable for its willingness to consider whether *Fisher* should be overruled in favor of a return to the rule that the Fifth Amendment protects against compelled disclosure of the content of incriminating documents.

UNITED STATES v. HUBBELL

Supreme Court of the United States, 2000.
530 U.S. 27.

JUSTICE STEVENS **delivered the opinion of the Court.**

* * *

I

This proceeding arises out of the second prosecution of respondent, Webster Hubbell, commenced by the Independent Counsel appointed in August 1994 to investigate possible violations of federal law relating to the Whitewater Development Corporation. The first prosecution was terminated pursuant to a plea bargain. In December 1994, respondent pleaded guilty to charges of mail fraud and tax evasion arising out of his billing practices as a member of an Arkansas law firm from 1989 to 1992, and was sentenced to 21 months in prison. In the plea agreement, respondent promised to provide the Independent Counsel with "full, complete, accurate, and truthful information" about matters relating to the Whitewater investigation.

The second prosecution resulted from the Independent Counsel's attempt to determine whether respondent had violated that promise. In October 1996, while respondent was incarcerated, the Independent Counsel served him with a subpoena duces tecum calling for the production of 11 categories of documents before a grand jury sitting in Little Rock, Arkansas. [See the Appendix, infra]. On November 19, he appeared before the grand jury and invoked his Fifth Amendment privilege against self-incrimination. In response to questioning by the prosecutor, respondent initially refused "to state whether there are documents within my possession, custody, or control responsive to

the Subpoena." Thereafter, the prosecutor produced an order, which had previously been obtained from the District Court * * * directing him to respond to the subpoena and granting him immunity "to the extent allowed by law." Respondent then produced 13,120 pages of documents and records and responded to a series of questions that established that those were all of the documents in his custody or control that were responsive to the commands in the subpoena, with the exception of a few documents he claimed were shielded by the attorney-client and attorney work-product privileges.

The contents of the documents produced by respondent provided the Independent Counsel with the information that led to this second prosecution. On April 30, 1998, a grand jury in the District of Columbia returned a 10–count indictment charging respondent with various tax-related crimes and mail and wire fraud. The District Court dismissed the indictment relying, in part, on the ground that the Independent Counsel's use of the subpoenaed documents [was illegal] because all of the evidence he would offer against respondent at trial derived either directly or indirectly from the testimonial aspects of respondent's immunized act of producing those documents. Noting that the Independent Counsel had admitted that he was not investigating tax-related issues when he issued the subpoena, and that he had learned about the unreported income and other crimes from studying the records' contents, the District Court characterized the subpoena as "the quintessential fishing expedition."

The Court of Appeals vacated the judgment and remanded for further proceedings. The majority concluded that the District Court had incorrectly relied on the fact that the Independent Counsel did not have prior knowledge of the contents of the subpoenaed documents. The question the District Court should have addressed was the extent of the Government's independent knowledge of the documents' existence and authenticity, and of respondent's possession or control of them. It explained:

> On remand, the district court should hold a hearing in which it seeks to establish the extent and detail of the [G]overnment's knowledge of Hubbell's financial affairs (or of the paperwork documenting it) on the day the subpoena issued. It is only then that the court will be in a position to assess the testimonial value of Hubbell's response to the subpoena. Should the Independent Counsel prove capable of demonstrating with reasonable particularity a prior awareness that the exhaustive litany of documents sought in the subpoena existed and were in Hubbell's possession, then the wide distance evidently traveled from the subpoena to the substantive allegations contained in the indictment would be based upon legitimate intermediate steps. To the extent that the information conveyed through Hubbell's compelled act of production provides the necessary linkage, however, the indictment deriving therefrom is tainted.

* * *

On remand, the Independent Counsel acknowledged that he could not satisfy the "reasonable particularity" standard prescribed by the Court of Appeals and entered into a conditional plea agreement with respondent. In essence, the agreement provides for the dismissal of the charges unless this Court's disposition of the case makes it reasonably likely that respondent's "act of production immunity" would not pose a significant bar to his prosecution. * * *

II

* * *

[It is settled that] a person may be required to produce specific documents even though they contain incriminating assertions of fact or belief because the creation of those documents was not "compelled" within the meaning of the privilege. Our decision in Fisher v. United States, 425 U.S. 391 (1976), dealt with summonses issued by the Internal Revenue Service (IRS) seeking working papers used in the preparation of tax returns. Because the papers had been voluntarily prepared prior to the issuance of the summonses, they could not be"said to contain compelled testimonial evidence, either of the taxpayers or of anyone else." Accordingly, the taxpayer could not "avoid compliance with the subpoena merely by asserting that the item of evidence which he is required to produce contains incriminating writing, whether his own or that of someone else." See also United States v. Doe, 465 U.S. 605 (1984). It is clear, therefore, that respondent Hubbell could not avoid compliance with the subpoena served on him merely because the demanded documents contained incriminating evidence, whether written by others or voluntarily prepared by himself.

On the other hand, we have also made it clear that the act of producing documents in response to a subpoena may have a compelled testimonial aspect. We have held that the act of production itself may implicitly communicate "statements of fact." By producing documents in compliance with a subpoena, the witness would admit that the papers existed, were in his possession or control, and were authentic. Moreover, as was true in this case, when the custodian of documents responds to a subpoena, he may be compelled to take the witness stand and answer questions designed to determine whether he has produced everything demanded by the subpoena. The answers to those questions, as well as the act of production itself, may certainly communicate information about the existence, custody, and authenticity of the documents. Whether the constitutional privilege protects the answers to such questions, or protects the act of production itself, is a question that is distinct from the question whether the unprotected contents of the documents themselves are incriminating.

* * *

III

* * *

IV

The Government correctly emphasizes that the testimonial aspect of a response to a subpoena duces tecum does nothing more than establish the existence, authenticity, and custody of items that are produced. We assume that the Government is also entirely correct in its submission that it would not have to advert to respondent's act of production in order to prove the existence, authenticity, or custody of any documents that it might offer in evidence at a criminal trial; indeed, the Government disclaims any need to introduce any of the documents produced by respondent into evidence in order to prove the charges against him. It follows, according to the Government, that it has no intention of making improper "use" of respondent's compelled testimony.

The question, however, is not whether the response to the subpoena may be introduced into evidence at his criminal trial. That would surely be a prohibited "use" of the immunized act of production. But the fact that the Government intends no such use of the act of production leaves open the separate question whether it has already made "derivative use" of the testimonial aspect of that act in obtaining the indictment against respondent and in preparing its case for trial. It clearly has.

It is apparent from the text of the subpoena itself that the prosecutor needed respondent's assistance both to identify potential sources of information and to produce those sources. Given the breadth of the description of the 11 categories of documents called for by the subpoena, the collection and production of the materials demanded was tantamount to answering a series of interrogatories asking a witness to disclose the existence and location of particular documents fitting certain broad descriptions. The assembly of literally hundreds of pages of material in response to a request for "any and all documents reflecting, referring, or relating to any direct or indirect sources of money or other things of value received by or provided to" an individual or members of his family during a 3–year period, is the functional equivalent of the preparation of an answer to either a detailed written interrogatory or a series of oral questions at a discovery deposition. Entirely apart from the contents of the 13,‑120 pages of materials that respondent produced in this case, it is undeniable that providing a catalog of existing documents fitting within any of the 11 broadly worded subpoena categories could provide a prosecutor with a lead to incriminating evidence, or a link in the chain of evidence needed to prosecute.

Indeed, the record makes it clear that that is what happened in this case. The documents were produced before a grand jury sitting in the Eastern District of Arkansas in aid of the Independent Counsel's attempt to determine whether respondent had violated a commitment in his first plea agreement. The use of those sources of information eventually led to the return of an indictment by a grand jury sitting in the District of Columbia for offenses that apparently are unrelated to that plea agreement. What the District Court characterized as a "fishing expedition" did produce a fish, but not the one that the Independent Counsel expected to hook. It is abundantly clear that the testimonial aspect of respondent's act of producing subpoenaed documents was the first step in a chain of evidence that led to this prosecution. The documents did not magically appear in the prosecutor's office like "manna from heaven." They arrived there only after respondent asserted his constitutional privilege, received a grant of immunity, and—under the compulsion of the District Court's order—took the mental and physical steps necessary to provide the prosecutor with an accurate inventory of the many sources of potentially incriminating evidence sought by the subpoena. It was only through respondent's truthful reply to the subpoena that the Government received the incriminating documents of which it made substantial use in the investigation that led to the indictment.

For these reasons, we cannot accept the Government's submission that respondent's immunity did not preclude its derivative use of the produced documents because its possession of the documents was the fruit only of a simple physical act—the act of producing the documents. It was unquestionably necessary for respondent to make extensive use of "the contents of his own mind" in identifying the hundreds of documents responsive to the requests in the subpoena. See Curcio v. United States, 354 U.S. 118 (1957); Doe v. United States, 487 U.S., at 210. The assembly of those documents was like telling an inquisitor the combination to a wall safe, not like being forced to surrender the key to a strongbox. * * *

In sum, we have no doubt that the constitutional privilege against self-incrimination protects the target of a grand jury investigation from being compelled to answer questions designed to elicit information about the existence of sources of potentially incriminating evidence. That constitutional privilege has the same application to the testimonial aspect of a response to a subpoena seeking discovery of those sources. * * * [T]he Government has argued that the communicative aspect of respondent's act of producing ordinary business records is insufficiently "testimonial" to support a claim of privilege because the existence and possession of such records by any businessman is a "foregone conclusion" under our decision in Fisher v. United States, 425 U.S., at 411. This argument both misreads *Fisher* and ignores our subsequent decision in United States v. Doe, 465 U.S. 605 (1984).

* * * *Fisher* involved summonses seeking production of working papers prepared by the taxpayers' accountants that the IRS knew were in the possession of the taxpayers' attorneys. In rejecting the taxpayers' claim that these documents were protected by the Fifth Amendment privilege, we stated:

> It is doubtful that implicitly admitting the existence and possession of the papers rises to the level of testimony within the protection of the Fifth Amendment. The papers belong to the accountant, were prepared by him, and are the kind usually prepared by an accountant working on the tax returns of his client. Surely the Government is in no way relying on the "truthtelling" of the taxpayer to prove the existence of or

his access to the documents.... The existence and location of the papers are a foregone conclusion and the taxpayer adds little or nothing to the sum total of the Government's information by conceding that he in fact has the papers.

Whatever the scope of this "foregone conclusion" rationale, the facts of this case plainly fall outside of it. While in *Fisher* the Government already knew that the documents were in the attorneys' possession and could independently confirm their existence and authenticity through the accountants who created them, here the Government has not shown that it had any prior knowledge of either the existence or the whereabouts of the 13,120 pages of documents ultimately produced by respondent. The Government cannot cure this deficiency through the overbroad argument that a businessman such as respondent will always possess general business and tax records that fall within the broad categories described in this subpoena. The *Doe* subpoenas also sought several broad categories of general business records, yet we upheld the District Court's finding that the act of producing those records would involve testimonial self-incrimination.

* * *

Accordingly, the indictment against respondent must be dismissed. The judgment of the Court of Appeals is affirmed.

APPENDIX TO OPINION OF THE COURT

On October 31, 1996, upon application by the Independent Counsel, a subpoena was issued commanding respondent to appear and testify before the grand jury of the United States District Court for the Eastern District of Arkansas on November 19, 1996, and to bring with him various documents described in a "Subpoena Rider" as follows:

A. Any and all documents reflecting, referring, or relating to any direct or indirect sources of money or other things of value receive by or provided to Webster Hubbell, his wife, or children from January 1, 1993 to the present, including but not limited to the identity of employers or clients of legal or any other type of work.

B. Any and all documents reflecting, referring, or relating to any direct or indirect sources of money of other things of value received by or provided to Webster Hubbell, his wife, or children from January 1, 1993 to the present, including but not limited to billing memoranda, draft statements, bills, final statements, and/or bills for work performed or time billed from January 1, 1993 to the present.

C. Copies of all bank records of Webster Hubbell, his wife, or children for all accounts from January 1, 1993 to the present, including but not limited to all statements, registers and ledgers, cancelled checks, deposit items, and wire transfers.

D. Any and all documents reflecting, referring, or relating to time worked or billed by Webster Hubbell from January 1, 1993 to the present, including but not limited to original time sheets, books, notes, papers, and/or computer records.

E. Any and all documents reflecting, referring, or relating to expenses incurred by and/or disbursements of money by Webster Hubbell during the course of any work performed or to be performed by Mr. Hubbell from January 1, 1993 to the present.

F. Any and all documents reflecting, referring, or relating to Webster Hubbell's schedule of activities, including but not limited to any and all calendars, day-timers, time books, appointment books, diaries, records of reverse telephone toll calls, credit card calls, telephone message slips, logs, other telephone records, minutes, databases, electronic mail messages, travel records, itineraries, tickets for transportation of any kind, payments, bills, expense backup documentation, schedules, and/or any other document or database that would disclose Webster Hubbell's activities from January 1, 1993 to the present.

G. Any and all documents reflecting, referring, or relating to any retainer agreements or contracts for employment of Webster Hubbell, his wife, or his children from January 1, 1993 to the present.

H. Any and all tax returns and tax return information, including but not limited to all W–2s, form 1099s, schedules, draft returns, work papers, and backup documents filed, created or held by or on behalf of Webster Hubbell, his wife, his children, and/or any business in which he, his wife, or his children holds or has held an interest, for the tax years 1993 to the present.

I. Any and all documents reflecting, referring, or relating to work performed or to be performed or on behalf of the City of Los Angeles, California, the Los Angeles Department of Airports or any other Los Angeles municipal Governmental entity, Mary Leslie, and/or Alan S. Arkatov, including but not limited to correspondence, retainer agreements, contracts, time sheets, appointment calendars, activity calendars, diaries, billing statements, billing memoranda, telephone records, telephone message slips, telephone credit card statements, itineraries, tickets for transportation, payment records, expense receipts, ledgers, check registers, notes, memoranda, electronic mail, bank deposit items, cashier's checks, traveler's checks, wire transfer records and/or other records of financial transactions.

J. Any and all documents reflecting, referring, or relating to work performed or to be performed by Webster Hubbell, his wife, or his children on the recommendation, counsel or other influence of Mary Leslie and/or Alan S. Arkatov, including but not limited to correspondence, retainer agreements, contracts, time sheets, appointment calendars, activity calendars, diaries, billing statements, billing memoranda, telephone records, telephone message slips, telephone credit card statements, itineraries, tickets for transportation, payment records, expense receipts, ledgers, check registers, notes, memoranda, electronic mail, bank deposit items, cashier's checks, traveler's checks, wire transfer records and/or other records of financial transactions.

K. Any and all documents related to work performed or to be performed for or on behalf of Lippo Ltd. (formerly Public Finance (H.K.) Ltd.), the Lippo Group, the Lippo Bank, Mochtar Riady, James Riady, Stephen Riady, John Luen Wai Lee, John Huang, Mark W. Grobmyer, C. Joseph Giroir, Jr., or any affiliate, subsidiary, or corporation owned or controlled by or related to the aforementioned entities or individuals, including but not limited to correspondence, retainer agreements, contracts, time sheets, appointment calendars, activity calendars, diaries, billing statements, billing memoranda, telephone records, telephone message slips, telephone credit card statements, itineraries, tickets for transportation, payment records, expense receipts, ledgers, check registers, notes, memoranda, electronic mail, bank deposit items, cashier's checks, traveler's checks, wire transfer records and/or other records of financial transactions. App. 47–49.

CHIEF JUSTICE REHNQUIST dissents and would reverse the judgment of the Court of Appeals in part, for the reasons given by Judge Williams in his dissenting opinion in that court, 167 F.3d 552, 597 (C.A.D.C.1999).

JUSTICE THOMAS, **with whom JUSTICE SCALIA joins, concurring**.

Our decision today involves the application of the act-of-production doctrine, which provides that persons compelled to turn over incriminating papers or other physical evidence pursuant to a subpoena duces tecum or a summons may invoke the Fifth Amendment privilege against self-incrimination as a bar to production only where the act of producing the evidence would contain "testimonial" features. I join the opinion of the Court because it properly applies this doctrine, but I write separately to note that this doctrine may be inconsistent with the original meaning of the Fifth Amendment's Self–Incrimination Clause. A substantial body of evidence suggests that the Fifth Amendment privilege protects against the compelled production not just of incriminating testimony, but of any incriminating evidence. In a future case, I would be willing to reconsider the scope and meaning of the Self–Incrimination Clause.

I

The Fifth Amendment provides that "[n]o person ... shall be compelled in any criminal case to be a witness against himself." The key word at issue in this case is "witness." The Court's opinion, relying on prior cases, essentially defines "witness" as a person who provides testimony, and thus restricts the Fifth Amendment's ban to only those communications that are "testimonial" in character. None of this Court's cases, however, has undertaken an analysis of the meaning of the term at the time of the founding. A review of that period reveals substantial support for the view that

the term "witness" meant a person who gives or furnishes evidence, a broader meaning than that which our case law currently ascribes to the term. If this is so, a person who responds to a subpoena duces tecum would be just as much a "witness" as a person who responds to a subpoena ad testificandum.

Dictionaries published around the time of the founding included definitions of the term "witness" as a person who gives or furnishes evidence. Legal dictionaries of that period defined "witness" as someone who "gives evidence in a cause." 2 G. Jacob, A New Law–Dictionary (8th ed. 1762); 2 T. Cunningham, New and Complete Law–Dictionary (2d ed. 1771); T. Potts, A Compendious Law Dictionary 612 (1803); 6 G. Jacob, The Law–Dictionary 450 (T. Tomlins 1st American ed. 1811). * * * The term "witness" apparently continued to have this meaning at least until the first edition of Noah Webster's dictionary, which defined it as "[t]hat which furnishes evidence or proof." An American Dictionary of the English Language (1828).

Such a meaning of "witness" is consistent with, and may help explain, the history and framing of the Fifth Amendment. The 18th century common-law privilege against self-incrimination protected against the compelled production of incriminating physical evidence such as papers and documents. * * *

Against this common-law backdrop, the privilege against self-incrimination was enshrined in the Virginia Declaration of Rights in 1776. That document provided that no one may "be compelled to give evidence against himself." Following Virginia's lead, seven of the other original States included specific provisions in their Constitutions granting a right against compulsion "to give evidence" or "to furnish evidence." And during ratification of the Federal Constitution, the four States that proposed bills of rights put forward draft proposals employing similar wording for a federal constitutional provision guaranteeing the right against compelled self-incrimination. Each of the proposals broadly sought to protect a citizen from "be[ing] compelled to give evidence against himself." Similarly worded proposals to protect against compelling a person "to furnish evidence" against himself came from prominent voices outside the conventions.

In response to such calls, James Madison penned the Fifth Amendment. In so doing, Madison substituted the phrase "to be a witness" for the proposed language "to give evidence" and "to furnish evidence." But it seems likely that Madison's phrasing was synonymous with that of the proposals. The definitions of the word "witness" and the background history of the privilege against self-incrimination, both discussed above, support this view. And this may explain why Madison's unique phrasing— phrasing that none of the proposals had suggested—apparently attracted no attention, much less opposition, in Congress, the state legislatures that ratified the Bill of Rights, or anywhere else. * * *

II

This Court has not always taken the approach to the Fifth Amendment that we follow today. The first case interpreting the Self–Incrimination Clause—Boyd v. United States—was decided, though not explicitly, in accordance with the understanding that "witness" means one who gives evidence. In *Boyd*, this Court unanimously held that the Fifth Amendment protects a defendant against compelled production of books and papers. And the Court linked its interpretation of the Fifth Amendment to the common-law understanding of the self-incrimination privilege.

But this Court's decision in Fisher v. United States, 425 U.S. 391 (1976), rejected this understanding, permitting the Government to force a person to furnish incriminating physical evidence and protecting only the "testimonial" aspects of that transfer. In so doing, *Fisher* not only failed to examine the historical backdrop to the Fifth Amendment, it also required—as illustrated by extended discussion in the opinions below in this case—a difficult parsing of the act of responding to a subpoena duces tecum.

None of the parties in this case has asked us to depart from *Fisher*, but in light of the historical evidence that the Self–Incrimination Clause may have a broader reach than *Fisher* holds, I remain open to a reconsideration of that decision and its progeny in a proper case.

F. PROCEDURAL ASPECTS OF SELF–INCRIMINATION CLAIMS

1. Determining the Risk of Incrimination

Page 609.   Add the following at the end of the section:

The Risk of Incrimination and Denial of Guilt: Ohio v. Reiner

Can a witness invoke the Fifth Amendment privilege if she denies guilt of any crime? This question was faced by the Court in Ohio v. Reiner, 532 U.S. 17 (2001) (per curiam). Reiner was charged with involuntary manslaughter in connection with the death of his infant son. He blamed it on the babysitter. The babysitter refused to testify, claiming a Fifth Amendment privilege. She was granted immunity, then testified as a prosecution witness that she had nothing to do with the infant's death or with other injuries to the infant's brother. Reiner was convicted but the state court reversed, on the ground that the babysitter should not have been granted immunity. In the state court's view, the babysitter's testimony "did not incriminate her, because she denied any involvement in the abuse. Thus, she did not have a valid Fifth Amendment privilege."

The Supreme Court reinstated the conviction; it found that the babysitter faced a risk of self-incrimination even though she denied wrongdoing, and therefore the grant of immunity was not unlawful. The Court reasoned as follows:

> We have held that the privilege's protection extends only to witnesses who have "reasonable cause to apprehend danger from a direct answer." Hoffman v. United States, 341 U.S. 479, 486 (1951). That inquiry is for the court; the witness' assertion does not by itself establish the risk of incrimination. A danger of "imaginary and unsubstantial character" will not suffice. Mason v. United States, 244 U.S. 362, 366 (1917). But we have never held, as the Supreme Court of Ohio did, that the privilege is unavailable to those who claim innocence. To the contrary, we have emphasized that one of the Fifth Amendment's "basic functions * * * is to protect innocent men * * * who otherwise might be ensnared by ambiguous circumstances." Grunewald v. United States, 353 U.S. 391, 421 (1957). In *Grunewald,* we recognized that truthful responses of an innocent witness, as well as those of a wrongdoer, may provide the government with incriminating evidence from the speaker's own mouth.

> The Supreme Court of Ohio's determination that Batt [the babysitter] did not have a valid Fifth Amendment privilege because she denied any involvement in the abuse of the children clearly conflicts with *Hoffman* and *Grunewald*. Batt had "reasonable cause" to apprehend danger from her answers if questioned at respondent's trial. Batt spent extended periods of time alone with [the infant in the weeks before his death]. She was with Alex within

the potential timeframe of the fatal trauma. The defense's theory of the case was that Batt, not respondent, was responsible for Alex's death and his brother's uncharged injuries. In this setting, it was reasonable for Batt to fear that answers to possible questions might tend to incriminate her. Batt therefore had a valid Fifth Amendment privilege against self-incrimination.

IV. FIFTH AMENDMENT LIMITATIONS ON CONFESSIONS

B. DID CONGRESS OVERRULE *MIRANDA?*

Page 660.   Add at the end of the section.

In the following case, the Court reversed the Fourth Circuit's decision that section 3501, and not *Miranda* governed the admissibility of confessions in federal courts. The Court did so by holding that the *Miranda* safeguards are constitutionally-based. And yet the Court appears to preserve its many decisions establishing exceptions to *Miranda*. Read the opinion and ask yourself: was the Court successful in walking the tightrope that it had created? Or is Justice Scalia right that the Court is walking on thin air?

DICKERSON v. UNITED STATES

United States Supreme Court, 2000.
530 U.S. 428.

CHIEF JUSTICE REHNQUIST **delivered the opinion of the Court.**

In Miranda v. Arizona, 384 U.S. 436 (1966), we held that certain warnings must be given before a suspect's statement made during custodial interrogation could be admitted in evidence. In the wake of that decision, Congress enacted 18 U.S.C. § 3501, which in essence laid down a rule that the admissibility of such statements should turn only on whether or not they were voluntarily made. We hold that *Miranda*, being a constitutional decision of this Court, may not be in effect overruled by an Act of Congress, and we decline to overrule *Miranda* ourselves. We therefore hold that *Miranda* and its progeny in this Court govern the admissibility of statements made during custodial interrogation in both state and federal courts.

Petitioner Dickerson was indicted for bank robbery, conspiracy to commit bank robbery, and using a firearm in the course of committing a crime of violence, all in violation of the applicable provisions of Title 18 of the United States Code. Before trial, Dickerson moved to suppress a statement he had made at a Federal Bureau of Investigation field office, on the grounds that he had not received "*Miranda* warnings" before being interrogated. The District Court granted his motion to suppress, and the Government took an interlocutory appeal to the United States Court of Appeals for the Fourth Circuit. That court, by a divided vote, reversed the District Court's suppression order. It agreed with the District Court's conclusion that petitioner had not received *Miranda* warnings before making his statement. But it went on to hold that § 3501, which in effect makes the admissibility of statements such as Dickerson's turn solely on whether they were made voluntarily, was satisfied in this case. It then concluded that our decision in *Miranda* was not a constitutional holding, and that therefore Congress could by statute have the final say on the question of admissibility.

Because of the importance of the questions raised by the Court of Appeals' decision, we granted certiorari, and now reverse.

We begin with a brief historical account of the law governing the admission of confessions. Prior to *Miranda*, we evaluated the admissibility of a suspect's confession under a voluntariness test. The roots of this test developed in the common law, as the courts of England and then the United States recognized that coerced confessions are inherently untrustworthy. Hopt v. Territory of Utah, 110 U.S. 574 (1884); Pierce v. United States, 160 U.S. 355 (1896). Over time, our cases recognized two constitutional bases for the requirement that a confession be voluntary to be admitted into evidence: the Fifth Amendment right against self-incrimination and the Due Process Clause of the Fourteenth Amendment. See, e.g., Bram v. United States, 168 U.S. 532, 542 (1897) (stating that the voluntariness test "is controlled by that portion of the Fifth Amendment ... commanding that no person 'shall be compelled in any criminal case to be a witness against himself' "); Brown v. Missis-

sippi, 297 U.S. 278 (1936) (reversing a criminal conviction under the Due Process Clause because it was based on a confession obtained by physical coercion).

While *Bram* was decided before *Brown* and its progeny, for the middle third of the 20th century our cases based the rule against admitting coerced confessions primarily, if not exclusively, on notions of due process. We applied the due process voluntariness test in some 30 different cases decided during the era that intervened between *Brown* and Escobedo v. Illinois, 378 U.S. 478 (1964). See, e.g., Haynes v. Washington, 373 U.S. 503 (1963); Ashcraft v. Tennessee, 322 U.S. 143 (1944); Chambers v. Florida, 309 U.S. 227 (1940). Those cases refined the test into an inquiry that examines "whether a defendant's will was overborne" by the circumstances surrounding the giving of a confession. The due process test takes into consideration "the totality of all the surrounding circumstances—both the characteristics of the accused and the details of the interrogation." The determination "depends upon a weighing of the circumstances of pressure against the power of resistance of the person confessing."

We have never abandoned this due process jurisprudence, and thus continue to exclude confessions that were obtained involuntarily. But our decisions in Malloy v. Hogan, 378 U.S. 1 (1964), and *Miranda* changed the focus of much of the inquiry in determining the admissibility of suspects' incriminating statements. In *Malloy*, we held that the Fifth Amendment's Self-Incrimination Clause is incorporated in the Due Process Clause of the Fourteenth Amendment and thus applies to the States. We decided *Miranda* on the heels of *Malloy*.

In *Miranda*, we noted that the advent of modern custodial police interrogation brought with it an increased concern about confessions obtained by coercion. Because custodial police interrogation, by its very nature, isolates and pressures the individual, we stated that "[e]ven without employing brutality, the 'third degree' or [other] specific stratagems, ... custodial interrogation exacts a heavy toll on individual liberty and trades on the weakness of individuals." We concluded that the coercion inherent in custodial interrogation blurs the line between voluntary and involuntary statements, and thus heightens the risk that an individual will not be "accorded his privilege under the Fifth Amendment ... not to be compelled to incriminate himself." Accordingly, we laid down "concrete constitutional guidelines for law enforcement agencies and courts to follow." Those guidelines established that the admissibility in evidence of any statement given during custodial interrogation of a suspect would depend on whether the police provided the suspect with four warnings. These warnings (which have come to be known colloquially as "*Miranda* rights") are: a suspect "has the right to remain silent, that anything he says can be used against him in a court of law, that he has the right to the presence of an attorney, and that if he cannot afford an attorney one will be appointed for him prior to any questioning if he so desires."

Two years after *Miranda* was decided, Congress enacted § 3501. That section provides, in relevant part:

(a) In any criminal prosecution brought by the United States or by the District of Columbia, a confession ... shall be admissible in evidence if it is voluntarily given. Before such confession is received in evidence, the trial judge shall, out of the presence of the jury, determine any issue as to voluntariness. If the trial judge determines that the confession was voluntarily made it shall be admitted in evidence and the trial judge shall permit the jury to hear relevant evidence on the issue of voluntariness and shall instruct the jury to give such weight to the confession as the jury feels it deserves under all the circumstances.

(b) The trial judge in determining the issue of voluntariness shall take into consideration all the circumstances surrounding the giving of the confession, including (1) the time elapsing between arrest and arraignment of the defendant making the confession, if it was made after arrest and before arraignment, (2) whether such defendant knew the nature of the offense with which he was charged or of which he was suspected at the time of making the confession, (3) whether or not such defendant was advised or knew that he was not required to make any statement and that any such statement could be used against him, (4) whether or not such defendant had been advised prior to questioning of his right to the assistance of counsel; and (5) whether or not such defendant was without the assistance of counsel when questioned and when giving such confession.

The presence or absence of any of the above—mentioned factors to be taken into consideration by the judge need not be conclusive on the issue of voluntariness of the confession.

Given § 3501's express designation of voluntariness as the touchstone of admissibility, its omission of any warning requirement, and the instruction for trial courts to consider a nonexclusive list of factors relevant to the circumstances of a confession, we agree with the Court of Appeals that Congress intended by its enactment to overrule *Miranda*. Because of the obvious conflict between our decision in *Miranda* and § 3501, we must address whether Congress has constitutional authority to thus supersede *Miranda*. If Congress has such authority, § 3501's totality-of-the-circumstances approach must prevail over *Miranda's* requirement of warnings; if not, that section must yield to *Miranda's* more specific requirements.

The law in this area is clear. This Court has supervisory authority over the federal courts, and we may use that authority to prescribe rules of evidence and procedure that are binding in those tribunals. However, the power to judicially create and enforce nonconstitutional rules of procedure and evidence for the federal courts exists only in the absence of a relevant Act of Congress. Congress retains the ultimate authority to modify or set aside any judicially created rules of evidence and procedure that are not required by the Constitution. But Congress may not legislatively supersede our decisions interpreting and applying the Constitution. This case therefore turns on whether the *Miranda* Court announced a constitutional rule or merely exercised its supervisory authority to regulate evidence in the absence of congressional direction.

Recognizing this point, the Court of Appeals surveyed *Miranda* and its progeny to determine the constitutional status of the *Miranda* decision. Relying on the fact that we have created several exceptions to *Miranda's* warnings requirement and that we have repeatedly referred to the *Miranda* warnings as "prophylactic," New York v. Quarles, 467 U.S. 649, 653 (1984), and "not themselves rights protected by the Constitution," Michigan v. Tucker, 417 U.S. 433, 444 (1974), the Court of Appeals concluded that the protections announced in *Miranda* are not constitutionally required.

We disagree with the Court of Appeals' conclusion, although we concede that there is language in some of our opinions that supports the view taken by that court. But first and foremost of the factors on the other side—that *Miranda* is a constitutional decision—is that both *Miranda* and two of its companion cases applied the rule to proceedings in state courts—to wit, Arizona, California, and New York. Since that time, we have consistently applied *Miranda's* rule to prosecutions arising in state courts. See, e.g., Stansbury v. California, 511 U.S. 318 (1994) (per curiam); Minnick v. Mississippi, 498 U.S. 146 (1990); Arizona v. Roberson, 486 U.S. 675 (1988); Edwards v. Arizona, 451

U.S. 477, 481–482 (1981). It is beyond dispute that we do not hold a supervisory power over the courts of the several States.

The *Miranda* opinion itself begins by stating that the Court granted certiorari "to explore some facets of the problems . . . of applying the privilege against self-incrimination to in-custody interrogation, and to give concrete constitutional guidelines for law enforcement agencies and courts to follow." In fact, the majority opinion is replete with statements indicating that the majority thought it was announcing a constitutional rule. Indeed, the Court's ultimate conclusion was that the unwarned confessions obtained in the four cases before the Court in *Miranda* "were obtained from the defendant under circumstances that did not meet constitutional standards for protection of the privilege." Additional support for our conclusion that *Miranda* is constitutionally based is found in the *Miranda* Court's invitation for legislative action to protect the constitutional right against coerced self-incrimination. After discussing the "compelling pressures" inherent in custodial police interrogation, the *Miranda* Court concluded that, "[i]n order to combat these pressures and to permit a full opportunity to exercise the privilege against self-incrimination, the accused must be adequately and effectively appraised of his rights and the exercise of those rights must be fully honored." However, the Court emphasized that it could not foresee "the potential alternatives for protecting the privilege which might be devised by Congress or the States," and it accordingly opined that the Constitution would not preclude legislative solutions that differed from the prescribed *Miranda* warnings but which were "at least as effective in apprising accused persons of their right of silence and in assuring a continuous opportunity to exercise it."

The Court of Appeals also relied on the fact that we have, after our *Miranda* decision, made exceptions from its rule in cases such as New York v. Quarles, 467 U.S. 649 (1984), and Harris v. New York, 401 U.S. 222 (1971). But we have also broadened the application of the *Miranda* doctrine in cases such as Doyle v. Ohio, 426 U.S. 610 (1976), and Arizona v. Roberson, 486 U.S. 675 (1988). These decisions illustrate the principle—not that *Miranda* is not a constitutional rule—but that no constitutional rule is immutable. No court laying down a general rule can possibly foresee the various circumstances in which counsel will seek to apply it, and the sort of modifications represented by these cases are as much a normal part of constitutional law as the original decision.

The Court of Appeals also noted that in Oregon v. Elstad, 470 U.S. 298 (1985), we stated that "[t]he Miranda exclusionary rule . . . serves the Fifth Amendment and sweeps more broadly than the Fifth Amendment itself." Our decision in that case—refusing to apply the traditional "fruits" doctrine developed in Fourth Amendment cases—does not prove that *Miranda* is a non-constitutional decision, but simply recognizes the fact that unreasonable searches under the Fourth Amendment are different from unwarned interrogation under the Fifth Amendment.

As an alternative argument for sustaining the Court of Appeals' decision, the court-invited amicus curiae contends that the section complies with the requirement that a legislative alternative to *Miranda* be equally as effective in preventing coerced confessions. See Brief for Paul G. Cassell as Amicus Curiae 28–39. We agree with the amicus' contention that there are more remedies available for abusive police conduct than there were at the time *Miranda* was decided, see, e.g., Wilkins v. May, 872 F. 2d 190, 194 (C.A.7 1989) (applying Bivens v. Six Unknown Fed. Narcotics Agents, 403 U.S. 388 (1971), to hold that a suspect may bring a federal cause of action under the Due Process Clause for police misconduct during custodial interrogation). But we do not agree that these additional measures supplement § 3501's protections sufficiently to meet the constitutional minimum. *Miranda* requires procedures that will warn a suspect in custody of his right to remain silent and which will assure the suspect that the exercise of that right will be honored. As discussed above, § 3501 explicitly eschews a requirement of pre-interrogation warnings in favor of an approach that looks to the administration of such warnings as only one factor in determining the voluntariness of a suspect's confession. The additional remedies cited by amicus do not, in our view, render them, together with § 3501 an adequate substitute for the warnings required by *Miranda*.

The dissent argues that it is judicial overreaching for this Court to hold § 3501 unconstitutional unless we hold that the *Miranda* warnings are required by the Constitution, in the sense that nothing else will suffice to satisfy constitutional requirements. But we need not go farther than *Miranda* to decide this case. In *Miranda*, the Court noted that reliance on the traditional totality-of-the-circumstances test raised a risk of overlooking an involuntary custodial confession, a risk that the Court found unacceptably great when the confession is offered in the case in chief to prove guilt. The Court therefore concluded that something more than the totality test was necessary. As discussed above, § 3501 reinstates the totality test as sufficient. Section 3501 therefore cannot be sustained if *Miranda* is to remain the law.

Whether or not we would agree with *Miranda's* reasoning and its resulting rule, were we addressing the issue in the first instance, the principles of stare decisis weigh heavily against overruling it now. See, e.g., Rhode Island v. Innis, 446 U.S. 291, 304 (1980) (Burger, C. J., concurring in judgment) ("The meaning of *Miranda* has become reasonably clear and law enforcement practices have adjusted to its strictures; I would neither overrule *Miranda*, disparage it, nor extend it at this late date"). While "stare decisis is not an inexorable command, particularly when we are interpreting the Constitution, even in constitutional cases, the doctrine carries such persuasive force that we have always required a departure from precedent to be supported by some 'special justification.' "

We do not think there is such justification for overruling *Miranda*. *Miranda* has become embedded in routine police practice to the point where the warnings have become part of our national culture. While we have overruled our precedents when subsequent cases have undermined their doctrinal underpinnings, we do not believe that this has happened to the *Miranda* decision. If anything, our subsequent cases have reduced the impact of the *Miranda* rule on legitimate law enforcement while reaffirming the decision's core ruling that unwarned statements may not be used as evidence in the prosecution's case in chief.

The disadvantage of the *Miranda* rule is that statements which may be by no means involuntary, made by a defendant who is aware of his "rights," may nonetheless be excluded and a guilty defendant go free as a result. But experience suggests that the totality-of-the-circumstances test which § 3501 seeks to revive is more difficult than *Miranda* for law enforcement officers to conform to, and for courts to apply in a consistent manner. See, e.g., Haynes v. Washington, 373 U.S., at 515 ("The line between proper and permissible police conduct and techniques and methods offensive to due process is, at best, a difficult one to draw"). The requirement that *Miranda* warnings be given does not, of course, dispense with the voluntariness inquiry. But as we said in Berkemer v. McCarty, 468 U.S. 420 (1984), "[c]ases in which a defendant can make a colorable argument that a self-incriminating statement was 'compelled' despite the fact that the law enforcement authorities adhered to the dictates of *Miranda* are rare."

In sum, we conclude that *Miranda* announced a constitutional rule that Congress may not supersede legislatively. Following the rule of stare decisis, we decline to overrule *Miranda* ourselves. The judgment of the Court of Appeals is therefore

Reversed.

JUSTICE SCALIA, with whom JUSTICE THOMAS joins, dissenting.

Those to whom judicial decisions are an unconnected series of judgments that produce either favored or disfavored results will doubtless greet today's decision as a paragon of moderation, since it declines to overrule Miranda v. Arizona, 384 U.S. 436 (1966). Those who understand the judicial process will appreciate that today's decision is not a reaffirmation of *Miranda*, but a radical revision of the most significant element of *Miranda* (as of all cases): the rationale that gives it a permanent place in our jurisprudence.

Marbury v. Madison, 1 Cranch 137 (1803), held that an Act of Congress will not be enforced by the courts if what it prescribes violates the Constitution of the United States. That was the basis on which *Miranda* was decided. One will search today's opinion in vain, however, for a statement (surely simple enough to make) that what 18 U.S.C. § 3501 prescribes—the use at trial of a voluntary confession, even when a *Miranda* warning or its equivalent has failed to be given—violates the Constitution. The reason the statement does not appear is not only (and perhaps not so much) that it would be absurd, inasmuch as § 3501 excludes from trial precisely what the Constitution excludes from trial, viz., compelled confessions; but also that Justices whose votes are needed to compose today's majority are on record as believing that a violation of *Miranda* is not a violation of the Constitution. See Davis v. United States, 512 U.S. 452, 457–458 (1994) (opinion of the Court, in which Kennedy, J., joined); Duckworth v. Eagan, 492 U.S. 195, 203 (1989) (opinion of the Court, in which Kennedy, J., joined); Oregon v. Elstad, 470 U.S. 298 (1985) (opinion of the Court by O'Connor, J.); New York v. Quarles, 467 U.S. 649 (1984) (opinion of the Court by Rehnquist, J.). And so, to justify today's agreed-upon result, the Court must adopt a significant new, if not entirely comprehensible, principle of constitutional law. As the Court chooses to describe that principle, statutes of Congress can be disregarded, not only when what they prescribe violates the Constitution, but when what they prescribe contradicts a decision of this Court that "announced a constitutional rule." As I shall discuss in some detail, the only thing that can possibly mean in the context of this case is that this Court has the power, not merely to apply the Constitution but to expand it, imposing what it regards as useful "prophylactic" restrictions upon Congress and the States. That is an immense and frightening anti-democratic power, and it does not exist. It takes only a small step to bring today's opinion out of the realm of power-judging and into the mainstream of legal reasoning: The Court need only go beyond its carefully couched iterations that "*Miranda* is a constitutional decision," that "*Miranda* is constitutionally based," that *Miranda* has "constitutional underpinnings," and come out and say quite clearly: "We reaffirm today that custodial interrogation that is not preceded by *Miranda* warnings or their equivalent violates the Constitution of the United States." It cannot say that, because a majority of the Court does not believe it. The Court therefore acts in plain violation of the Constitution when it denies effect to this Act of Congress.

I

* * *

It was once possible to characterize the so-called *Miranda* rule as resting (however implausibly) upon the proposition that what the statute here before us permits—the admission at trial of un-*Mirandized* confessions—violates the Constitution. That is the fairest reading of the *Miranda* case itself. * * * Having extended the privilege into the confines of the station house, the Court liberally sprinkled throughout its sprawling 60–page opinion suggestions that, because of the compulsion inherent in custodial interrogation, the privilege was violated by any statement thus obtained that did not conform to the rules set forth in *Miranda*, or some functional equivalent. * * *

So understood, *Miranda* was objectionable for innumerable reasons, not least the fact that cases spanning more than 70 years had rejected its core premise that, absent the warnings and an effective waiver of the right to remain silent and of the (hitherto unknown) right to have an attorney present, a statement obtained pursuant to custodial interrogation was necessarily the product of compulsion. Moreover, history and precedent aside, the decision in *Miranda*, if read as an explication of what the Constitution requires, is preposterous. There is, for example, simply no basis in reason for concluding that a response to the very first question asked, by a suspect who already knows all of the rights described in the *Miranda* warning, is anything other than a volitional act. And even if one assumes that the elimination of compulsion absolutely requires informing even the most knowledgeable suspect of his right to remain silent, it cannot conceivably require the right to have counsel present. There is a world of difference, which the Court recognized under the traditional voluntariness test but ignored in *Miranda*, between compelling a suspect to incriminate himself and preventing him from foolishly doing so of his own accord. Only the latter (which is not required by the Constitution) could explain the Court's inclusion of a right to counsel and the requirement that it, too, be knowingly and intelligently waived. Counsel's presence is not required to tell the suspect that he need not speak; the interrogators can do that. The only good reason for having counsel there is that he can be counted on to advise the suspect that he should not speak. * * * Thus, what is most remarkable about the *Miranda* decision—and what made it unacceptable as a matter of straightforward constitutional interpretation in the *Marbury* tradition—is its palpable hostility toward the act of confession per se, rather than toward what the Constitution abhors, compelled confession.

For these reasons, and others more than adequately developed in the *Miranda* dissents and in the subsequent works of the decision's many critics, any conclusion that a violation of the *Miranda* rules necessarily amounts to a violation of the privilege against compelled self-incrimination can claim no support in history, precedent, or common sense, and as a result would at least presumptively be worth reconsidering even at this late date. But that is unnecessary, since the Court has (thankfully) long since abandoned the notion that failure to comply with *Miranda's* rules is itself a violation of the Constitution.

II

As the Court today acknowledges, since *Miranda* we have explicitly, and repeatedly, interpreted that decision as having announced, not the circumstances in which custodial interrogation runs afoul of the Fifth or Fourteenth Amendment, but rather only "prophylactic" rules that go beyond the right against compelled self-incrimination. Of course the seeds of this "prophylactic" interpretation of *Miranda* were present in the decision itself. In subsequent cases, the seeds have sprouted and borne fruit: The Court has squarely concluded that it is possible—indeed not uncommon—for the police to violate *Miranda* without also violating the Constitution. Michigan v. Tucker, 417 U.S. 433 (1974), an opinion for the Court written by then-Justice Rehnquist, rejected the * * * failure-to-warn-as-constitutional-violation interpretation of *Miranda*. It held that exclusion of the "fruits" of a *Miranda* violation—the statement of a witness whose identity the defendant had revealed while in custody—was not required. The opinion explained that the question whether the "police conduct complained of directly infringed upon respondent's right against compulsory self-incrimination" was a "separate question" from "whether it instead violated only the prophylactic rules developed to protect that right." The "procedural safeguards" adopted in *Miranda*, the Court said, "were not themselves rights protected by the Constitution but were instead measures to insure that the right against compulsory self-incrimination was protected," and to "provide practical reinforcement for the right." * * * [T]he Court concluded, unequivocally, that the defendant's statement could not be termed "involuntary as that term has been defined in the decisions of this Court," and thus that there had been no constitutional violation, notwithstanding the clear violation of the "procedural rules later established in *Miranda*." * * * It is clear from our cases, of course, that if the statement in *Tucker* had been obtained in violation of the Fifth Amendment, the statement and its fruits would have been excluded. See also Mincey v. Arizona, 437 U.S. 385, 397–398 (1978) (holding that while statements obtained in violation of *Miranda* may be used for impeachment if otherwise trustworthy, the Constitution prohibits "any criminal trial use against a defendant of his involuntary statement").

[Justice Scalia discusses other cases in which the Court stated that the *Miranda* warnings are prophylactic safeguards rather than constitutional rights, including New York v. Quarles and Oregon v. Elstad.]

In light of these cases, * * * it is simply no longer possible for the Court to conclude, even if it wanted to, that a violation of *Miranda's* rules is a violation of the Constitution. But as I explained at the outset, that is what is required before the Court may disregard a law of Congress governing the admissibility of evidence in federal court. The Court today insists that the decision in *Miranda* is a "constitutional" one, that it has "constitutional underpinnings," * * * and that it announced a "constitutional rule." It is fine to play these word games; but what makes a decision "constitutional" in the only sense relevant here—in the sense that renders it impervious to supersession by congressional legislation such as § 3501—is the determination that the Constitution requires the result that the decision announces and the statute ignores. By disregarding congressional action that concededly does not violate the Constitution, the Court flagrantly offends fundamental principles of separation of powers, and arrogates to itself prerogatives reserved to the representatives of the people.

The Court seeks to avoid this conclusion in two ways: First, by misdescribing these post-*Miranda* cases as mere dicta. The Court concedes only "that there is language in some of our opinions that supports the view" that *Miranda's* protections are not "constitutionally required." It is not a matter of language; it is a matter of holdings. The proposition that failure to comply with *Miranda's* rules does not establish a constitutional violation was central to the holdings of *Tucker, Hass, Quarles, and Elstad*.

The second way the Court seeks to avoid the impact of these cases is simply to disclaim responsibility for reasoned decisionmaking. It says:

These decisions illustrate the principle—not that *Miranda* is not a constitutional rule—but that no constitutional rule is immutable. No court laying down a general rule can possibly foresee the various circumstances in which counsel will seek to apply it, and the sort of modifications represented by these cases are as much a normal part of constitutional law as the original decision.

The issue, however, is not whether court rules are "mutable"; they assuredly are. It is not whether, in the light of "various circumstances," they can be "modifi[ed]"; they assuredly can. The issue is whether, as mutated and modified, they must make sense. The requirement that they do so is the only thing that prevents this Court from being some sort of nine-headed Caesar, giving thumbs-up or thumbs-down to whatever outcome, case by case, suits or offends its collective fancy. And if confessions procured in violation of *Miranda* are confessions "compelled" in violation of the Constitution, the post-*Miranda* decisions I have discussed do not make sense. The only reasoned basis for their outcome was that a violation of *Miranda* is not a violation of the Constitution. If, for example, as the Court acknowledges was the holding of *Elstad*, "the traditional 'fruits' doctrine developed in Fourth Amendment cases" (that the fruits of evidence obtained unconstitutionally must be excluded from trial) does not apply to the fruits of *Miranda* violations; and if the reason for the difference is not that *Miranda* violations are not constitutional violations (which is plainly and flatly what *Elstad* said); then the Court must come up with some other explanation for the

difference. (That will take quite a bit of doing, by the way, since it is not clear on the face of the Fourth Amendment that evidence obtained in violation of that guarantee must be excluded from trial, whereas it is clear on the face of the Fifth Amendment that unconstitutionally compelled confessions cannot be used.) To say simply that "unreasonable searches under the Fourth Amendment are different from unwarned interrogation under the Fifth Amendment," is true but supremely unhelpful.

Finally, the Court asserts that *Miranda* must be a "constitutional decision" announcing a "constitutional rule," and thus immune to congressional modification, because we have since its inception applied it to the States. If this argument is meant as an invocation of stare decisis, it fails because, though it is true that our cases applying *Miranda* against the States must be reconsidered if *Miranda* is not required by the Constitution, it is likewise true that our cases (discussed above) based on the principle that *Miranda* is not required by the Constitution will have to be reconsidered if it is. So the stare decisis argument is a wash. If, on the other hand, the argument is meant as an appeal to logic rather than stare decisis, it is a classic example of begging the question: Congress's attempt to set aside *Miranda*, since it represents an assertion that violation of *Miranda* is not a violation of the Constitution, also represents an assertion that the Court has no power to impose *Miranda* on the States. To answer this assertion—not by showing why violation of *Miranda* is a violation of the Constitution—but by asserting that *Mi-*

randa does apply against the States, is to assume precisely the point at issue. In my view, our continued application of the *Miranda* code to the States despite our consistent statements that running afoul of its dictates does not necessarily—or even usually—result in an actual constitutional violation, represents not the source of *Miranda's* salvation but rather evidence of its ultimate illegitimacy.
* * *

III

There was available to the Court a means of reconciling the established proposition that a violation of *Miranda* does not itself offend the Fifth Amendment with the Court's assertion of a right to ignore the present statute. That means of reconciliation was argued strenuously by both petitioner and the United States, who were evidently more concerned than the Court is with maintaining the coherence of our jurisprudence. It is not mentioned in the Court's opinion because, I assume, a majority of the Justices intent on reversing believes that incoherence is the lesser evil. They may be right.

* * *

Where the Constitution has wished to lodge in one of the branches of the Federal Government some limited power to supplement its guarantees, it has said so. See Amdt. 14, § 5 ("The Congress shall have power to enforce, by appropriate legislation, the provisions of this article"). The power with which the Court would endow itself under a "prophylactic" justification for *Miranda* goes far beyond what it has permitted Congress to

do under authority of that text. Whereas we have insisted that congressional action under § 5 of the Fourteenth Amendment must be "congruent" with, and "proportional" to, a constitutional violation, the *Miranda* nontextual power to embellish confers authority to prescribe preventive measures against not only constitutionally prohibited compelled confessions, but also (as discussed earlier) foolhardy ones.

I applaud, therefore, the refusal of the Justices in the majority to enunciate this boundless doctrine of judicial empowerment as a means of rendering today's decision rational. In nonetheless joining the Court's judgment, however, they overlook two truisms: that actions speak louder than silence, and that (in judge-made law at least) logic will out. Since there is in fact no other principle that can reconcile today's judgment with the post-*Miranda* cases that the Court refuses to abandon, what today's decision will stand for, whether the Justices can bring themselves to say it or not, is the power of the Supreme Court to write a prophylactic, extra-constitutional Constitution, binding on Congress and the States.

IV

Thus, while I agree with the Court that § 3501 cannot be upheld without also concluding that *Miranda* represents an illegitimate exercise of our authority to review state-court judgments, I do not share the Court's hesitation in reaching that conclusion. For while the Court is also correct that the doctrine of stare decisis demands some "special justification" for a departure from longstanding precedent—even precedent of the constitutional variety—that criterion is more than met here. * * * Despite the Court's Orwellian assertion to the contrary, it is undeniable that later cases (discussed above) have undermined *Miranda's* doctrinal underpinnings, denying constitutional violation and thus stripping the holding of its only constitutionally legitimate support. *Miranda's* critics and supporters alike have long made this point. See Office of Legal Policy, U.S. Dept. of Justice, Report to Attorney General on Law of Pre–Trial Interrogation 97 (Feb. 12, 1986) ("The current Court has repudiated the premises on which *Miranda* was based, but has drawn back from recognizing the full implications of its decisions"); id., at 78 ("Michigan v. Tucker accordingly repudiated the doctrinal basis of the *Miranda* decision"); Sonenshein, *Miranda* and the Burger Court: Trends and Countertrends, 13 Loyola U. Chi. L. J. 405, 407–408 (1982) ("Although the Burger Court has not overruled *Miranda*, the Court has consistently undermined the rationales, assumptions, and values which gave *Miranda* life").

Neither am I persuaded by the argument for retaining *Miranda* that touts its supposed workability as compared with the totality-of-the-circumstances test it purported to replace. *Miranda's* proponents cite ad nauseam the fact that the Court was called upon to make difficult and subtle distinctions in applying the "voluntariness" test in some 30–odd due process "coerced confessions" cases in the 30 years between Brown v. Mississippi, 297 U.S. 278 (1936), and *Miranda*. It is not immediately apparent, however, that the judicial burden has been eased by the "bright-line" rules

adopted in *Miranda*. In fact, in the 34 years since *Miranda* was decided, this Court has been called upon to decide nearly 60 cases involving a host of *Miranda* issues, most of them predicted with remarkable prescience by Justice White in his *Miranda* dissent. * * * But even were I to agree that the old totality-of-the-circumstances test was more cumbersome, it is simply not true that *Miranda* has banished it from the law and replaced it with a new test. Under the current regime, which the Court today retains in its entirety, courts are frequently called upon to undertake both inquiries. That is because, as explained earlier, voluntariness remains the constitutional standard, and as such continues to govern the admissibility for impeachment purposes of statements taken in violation of *Miranda*, the admissibility of the "fruits" of such statements, and the admissibility of statements challenged as unconstitutionally obtained despite the interrogator's compliance with *Miranda*.

Finally, I am not convinced by petitioner's argument that *Miranda* should be preserved because the decision occupies a special place in the "public's consciousness." As far as I am aware, the public is not under the illusion that we are infallible. I see little harm in admitting that we made a mistake in taking away from the people the ability to decide for themselves what protections (beyond those required by the Constitution) are reasonably affordable in the criminal investigatory process.

Today's judgment converts *Miranda* from a milestone of judicial overreaching into the very Cheops' Pyramid (or perhaps the Sphinx would be a better analogue) of judicial arrogance. In imposing its Court-made code upon the States, the original opinion at least asserted that it was demanded by the Constitution. Today's decision does not pretend that it is—and yet still asserts the right to impose it against the will of the people's representatives in Congress. Far from believing that stare decisis compels this result, I believe we cannot allow to remain on the books even a celebrated decision—especially a celebrated decision—that has come to stand for the proposition that the Supreme Court has power to impose extraconstitutional constraints upon Congress and the States. This is not the system that was established by the Framers, or that would be established by any sane supporter of government by the people.

I dissent from today's decision, and, until § 3501 is repealed, will continue to apply it in all cases where there has been a sustainable finding that the defendant's confession was voluntary.

Can a Miranda Violation Occur If the Statement Is Never Admitted? Chavez v. Martinez

In Chavez v. Martinez, 123 S.Ct. 1994 (2003), the Court held that a person's *Miranda* rights are not violated if his confession is never admitted at trial. Martinez brought a 1983 action after Chavez, a police officer, questioned Martinez in a hospital after Martinez had been shot. Martinez received no *Miranda* warnings, and he made some incriminating admissions. But charges were never brought and these statements were never admitted against Martinez. Martinez nonetheless argued that his Fifth Amendment rights were violated by the custodial questioning itself. The Court, in a number of separate opinions, held that the *Miranda* rule is a trial right that is not implicated until the government offers *Miranda*-defective statements against the defendant at trial. The Court also held that the Fifth Amendment provided no protection because the statements were never admitted in a "criminal case."

Justice Thomas, in an opinion for four Justices in *Chavez*, declared that *Miranda* simply provides a "prophylactic safeguard." While this declaration seems at odds with the Court's ruling in *Dickerson*, it did not command a majority of the Court. For more extensive treatment of *Chavez*, see *supra* in the section on the Fifth Amendment.

C. THE CONSEQUENCES OF HOLDING THAT THE *MIRANDA* SAFEGUARDS ARE NOT REQUIRED BY THE CONSTITUTION: EXCEPTIONS TO THE *MIRANDA* RULE OF EXCLUSION

Page 660. Add the following note at the beginning of the section:

In Dickerson v. United States, 530 U.S. 428 (2000), the Court held that the *Miranda* safeguards are constitutionally-based; therefore Congress could not abrogate them. Such a holding would appear to require the Court to overrule the cases discussed in the following section, all of which were based on the premise that a violation of the *Miranda* warnings requirement is not itself a violation of the Constitution. Yet the Court in *Dickerson* explicitly adhered to its decisions carving out exceptions to *Miranda*. The Court justifies these decisions as based on "the principle—not that *Miranda* is not a constitutional rule—but that no constitutional rule is immutable." The Court explained that "[n]o court laying down a general rule can possibly foresee the various circumstances in which counsel will seek to apply it, and the sort of modifications represented by these cases are as much a normal part of constitutional law as the original decision." Thus, the cases that follow in this section are essentially rewritten as "modifying" *Miranda's* constitutional rules, as opposed to depriving the *Miranda* safeguards of constitutional status. Though this might not make logical sense, it makes for an easy bottom line–the holdings of *Miranda*, as well as the cases limiting *Miranda*, apparently have been preserved. The majority and dissenting opinions in *Dickerson* are set forth *supra* in this Supplement.

V.   CONFESSIONS AND THE SIXTH AMENDMENT RIGHT TO COUNSEL

E.   WAIVER OF SIXTH AMENDMENT PROTECTIONS

Page 742.   Replace the Material in the Headnote "Which Crimes Are Related to the Crime Charged" with the following material:

Which Crimes Are Related to the Crime Charged?

McNeil holds that the Sixth Amendment is "offense-specific" and that the suspect-initiation requirement of *Jackson* applies only for questions concerning the offenses on which the accused has been formally charged. But in any criminal transaction, a number of different crimes may be charged. What happens when an officer approaches a suspect who is charged with a crime, and questions the suspect about uncharged crimes that arise out of the same criminal transaction? The following case discusses this problem.

TEXAS v. COBB

Supreme Court of the United States, 2001.
532 U.S. 162.

CHIEF JUSTICE REHNQUIST **delivered the opinion of the Court.**

The Texas Court of Criminal Appeals held that a criminal defendant's Sixth Amendment right to counsel attaches not only to the offense with which he is charged, but to other offenses "closely relat-ed factually" to the charged offense. We hold that our decision in McNeil v. Wisconsin, 501 U.S. 171 (1991), meant what it said, and that the Sixth Amendment right is "offense specific."

In December 1993, Lindsey Owings reported to the Walker County, Texas, Sheriff's Office that the home he shared with his wife, Margaret, and their 16–month-old daughter, Kori Rae, had been burglarized. He also informed police that his wife and daughter were missing. Respondent Raymond Levi Cobb lived across the street from the Owings. Acting on an anonymous tip that respondent was involved in the burglary, Walker County investigators questioned him about the events. He denied involvement. In July 1994, while under arrest for an unrelated offense, respondent was again questioned about the incident. Respondent then gave a written statement confessing to the burglary, but he denied knowledge relating to the disappearances. Respondent was subsequently indicted for the burglary, and Hal Ridley was appointed in August 1994 to represent respondent on that charge.

Shortly after Ridley's appointment, investigators asked and received his permission to question respondent about the disappearances. Respondent continued to deny involvement. Investigators repeated this process in September 1995, again with Ridley's permission and again with the same result.

In November 1995, respondent, free on bond in the burglary case, was living with his father in Odessa, Texas. At that time, respondent's father contacted the Walker County Sheriff's Office to report that respondent had confessed to him that he killed Margaret Owings in the course of the burglary. Walker County investigators directed respondent's father to the Odessa police station, where he gave a statement. Odessa police then faxed the statement to Walker County, where

investigators secured a warrant for respondent's arrest and faxed it back to Odessa. Shortly thereafter, Odessa police took respondent into custody and administered warnings pursuant to Miranda v. Arizona, 384 U.S. 436 (1966). Respondent waived these rights.

After a short time, respondent confessed to murdering both Margaret and Kori Rae. Respondent explained that when Margaret confronted him as he was attempting to remove the Owings' stereo, he stabbed her in the stomach with a knife he was carrying. Respondent told police that he dragged her body to a wooded area a few hundred yards from the house. Respondent then stated:

"I went back to her house and I saw the baby laying on its bed. I took the baby out there and it was sleeping the whole time. I laid the baby down on the ground four or five feet away from its mother. I went back to my house and got a flat edge shovel. That's all I could find. Then I went back over to where they were and I started digging a hole between them. After I got the hole dug, the baby was awake. It started going toward its mom and it fell in the hole. I put the lady in the hole and I covered them up. I remember stabbing a different knife I had in the ground where they were. I was crying right then."

Respondent later led police to the location where he had buried the victims' bodies.

Respondent was convicted of capital murder for murdering more than one person in the course of a single criminal transaction. He was sentenced to death. On appeal to the Court of Criminal Appeals of Texas, respondent argued * * * that his confession should have been suppressed because it was obtained in violation of his Sixth Amendment right to counsel. Relying on Michigan v. Jackson, 475 U.S. 625 (1986), respondent contended that his right to counsel had attached when Ridley was appointed in the burglary case and that Odessa police were therefore required to secure Ridley's permission before proceeding with the interrogation.

The Court of Criminal Appeals reversed respondent's conviction by a divided vote and remanded for a new trial. The court held that "once the right to counsel attaches to the offense charged, it also attaches to any other offense that is very closely related factually to the offense charged." Finding the capital murder charge to be "factually interwoven with the burglary," the court concluded that respondent's Sixth Amendment right to counsel had attached on the capital murder charge even though respondent had not yet been charged with that offense. The court further found that respondent had asserted that right by accepting Ridley's appointment in the burglary case. See ibid. Accordingly, it deemed the confession inadmissible and found that its introduction had not been harmless error. Three justices dissented, finding Michigan v. Jackson to be distinguishable and concluding that respondent had made a valid unilateral waiver of his right to counsel before confessing.

* * * [W]e granted certiorari to consider first whether the Sixth Amendment right to counsel extends to crimes that are "factually

related" to those that have actually been charged, and second whether respondent made a valid unilateral waiver of that right in this case. Because we answer the first question in the negative, we do not reach the second.

The Sixth Amendment provides that "[i]n all criminal prosecutions, the accused shall enjoy the right ... to have the Assistance of Counsel for his defence." In McNeil v. Wisconsin, we explained when this right arises:

> "The Sixth Amendment right [to counsel] ... is offense specific. It cannot be invoked once for all future prosecutions, for it does not attach until a prosecution is commenced, that is, at or after the initiation of adversary judicial criminal proceedings—whether by way of formal charge, preliminary hearing, indictment, information, or arraignment."

Accordingly, we held that a defendant's statements regarding offenses for which he had not been charged were admissible notwithstanding the attachment of his Sixth Amendment right to counsel on other charged offenses.

Some state courts and Federal Courts of Appeals, however, have read into *McNeil's* offense-specific definition an exception for crimes that are "factually related" to a charged offense. Several of these courts have interpreted Brewer v. Williams, 430 U.S. 387 (1977), and Maine v. Moulton, 474 U.S. 159 (1985)—both of which were decided well before *McNeil*—to support this view, which respondent now invites us to approve. We decline to do so.

In *Brewer*, a suspect in the abduction and murder of a 10–year-old girl had fled from the scene of the crime in Des Moines, Iowa, some 160 miles east to Davenport, Iowa, where he surrendered to police. An arrest warrant was issued in Des Moines on a charge of abduction, and the suspect was arraigned on that warrant before a Davenport judge. Des Moines police traveled to Davenport, took the man into custody, and began the drive back to Des Moines. Along the way, one of the officers persuaded the suspect to lead police to the victim's body. The suspect ultimately was convicted of the girl's murder. This Court upheld the federal habeas court's conclusion that police had violated the suspect's Sixth Amendment right to counsel. We held that the officer's comments to the suspect constituted interrogation and that the suspect had not validly waived his right to counsel by responding to the officer.

Respondent suggests that *Brewer* implicitly held that the right to counsel attached to the factually related murder when the suspect was arraigned on the abduction charge. The Court's opinion, however, simply did not address the significance of the fact that the suspect had been arraigned only on the abduction charge, nor did the parties in any way argue this question. Constitutional rights are not defined by inferences from opinions which did not address the question at issue.

Moulton is similarly unhelpful to respondent. That case involved two individuals indicted for a series of thefts, one of whom had secretly agreed to cooperate with the police investigation of his codefendant, Moulton. At the suggestion of police, the informant recorded several telephone calls and one face-to-face conversation he had with Moulton during which the two discussed their criminal exploits and possible alibis. In the course of those conversations, Moulton made various incriminating statements regarding both the thefts for which he had been charged and additional crimes. In a superseding indictment, Moulton was charged with the original crimes as well as burglary, arson, and three additional thefts. At trial, the State introduced portions of the recorded face-to-face conversation, and Moulton ultimately was convicted of three of the originally charged thefts plus one count of burglary. Moulton appealed his convictions to the Supreme Judicial Court of Maine, arguing that introduction of the recorded conversation violated his Sixth Amendment right to counsel. That court agreed, holding:

"Those statements may be admissible in the investigation or prosecution of charges for which, at the time the recordings were made, adversary proceedings had not yet commenced. But as to the charges for which Moulton's right to counsel had already attached, his incriminating statements should have been ruled inadmissible at trial, given the circumstances in which they were acquired."

We affirmed.

Respondent contends that, in affirming reversal of both the theft and burglary charges, the *Moulton* Court must have concluded that Moulton's Sixth Amendment right to counsel attached to the burglary charge. But the *Moulton* Court did not address the question now before us, and to the extent *Moulton* spoke to the matter at all, it expressly referred to the offense-specific nature of the Sixth Amendment right to counsel:

> "The police have an interest in the thorough investigation of crimes for which formal charges have already been filed. They also have an interest in investigating new or additional crimes. Investigations of either type of crime may require surveillance of individuals already under indictment. Moreover, law enforcement officials investigating an individual suspected of committing one crime and formally charged with having committed another crime obviously seek to discover evidence useful at trial of either crime. In seeking evidence pertaining to pending charges, however, the Government's investigative powers are limited by the Sixth Amendment rights of the accused. . . . On the other hand, to exclude evidence pertaining to charges as to which the Sixth Amendment right to counsel had not attached at the time the evidence was obtained, simply because other charges were pending at that time, would unnecessarily frustrate the public's interest in the investigation of criminal activities."

Thus, respondent's reliance on *Moulton* is misplaced and, in light of the language employed there and subsequently in *McNeil,* puzzling.

Respondent predicts that the offense-specific rule will prove "disastrous" to suspects' constitutional rights and will "permit law enforcement officers almost complete and total license to conduct unwanted and uncounseled interrogations."

Besides offering no evidence that such a parade of horribles has occurred in those jurisdictions that have not enlarged upon *McNeil*, he fails to appreciate the significance of two critical considerations. First, there can be no doubt that a suspect must be apprised of his rights against compulsory self-incrimination and to consult with an attorney before authorities may conduct custodial interrogation. See Miranda v. Arizona, 384 U.S., at 479; Dickerson v. United States, 530 U.S. 428, 435 (2000). In the present case, police scrupulously followed *Miranda's* dictates when questioning respondent. Second, it is critical to recognize that the Constitution does not negate society's interest in the ability of police to talk to witnesses and suspects, even those who have been charged with other offenses.

It is also worth noting that, contrary to the dissent's suggestion, there is no "background principle" of our Sixth Amendment jurisprudence establishing that there may be no contact between a defendant and police without counsel present. The dissent would expand the Sixth Amendment right to the assistance of counsel in a criminal prosecution into a rule which "exists to prevent lawyers from taking advantage of uncounseled laypersons and to preserve the integrity of the lawyer-client relationship." Every profession is competent to define the standards of conduct for its members, but such standards are obviously not controlling in interpretation of constitutional provisions. The Sixth Amendment right to counsel is personal to the defendant and specific to the offense.

Although it is clear that the Sixth Amendment right to counsel attaches only to charged offenses, we have recognized in other contexts that the definition of an "offense" is not necessarily limited to the four corners of a charging instrument. In Blockburger v. United States, 284 U.S. 299 (1932), we explained that "where the same act or transaction constitutes a violation of two distinct statutory provisions, the test to be applied to determine whether there are two offenses or only one, is whether each provision requires proof of a fact which the other does not." We have since applied the *Blockburger* test to delineate the scope of the Fifth Amendment's Double Jeopardy Clause, which prevents multiple or successive prosecutions for the "same offence." We see no constitutional difference between the meaning of the term "offense" in the contexts of double jeopardy and of the right to counsel. Accordingly, we hold that when the Sixth Amendment right to counsel attaches, it does encompass offenses that, even if not formally charged, would be considered the same offense under the *Blockburger* test.

While simultaneously conceding that its own test "lacks the precision for which police officers may hope," the dissent suggests that adopting *Blockburger's* definition of "offense" will prove difficult to administer. But it is the dissent's vague iterations of the " 'closely related to' " or " 'inextricably intertwined with' "test that would defy simple application. The dissent seems to presuppose that officers will possess complete knowledge of the circumstances surrounding an incident, such that the officers will be able to tailor their investigation to avoid addressing factually related offenses. Such an assumption, however, ignores the reality that police often are not yet aware of the exact sequence and scope of events they are investigating—indeed, that is why police must investigate in the first place. Deterred by the possibility of violating the Sixth Amendment, police likely would refrain from questioning certain defendants altogether.

It remains only to apply these principles to the facts at hand. At the time he confessed to Odessa police, respondent had been indicted for burglary of the Owings residence, but he had not been charged in the murders of Margaret and Kori Rae. As defined by Texas law, burglary and capital murder are not the same offense under *Blockburger*. Compare Texas Penal Code Ann. § 30.02(a) (1994) (requiring entry into or continued concealment in a habitation or building) with § 19.03(a)(7)(A) (requiring murder of more than one person during a single criminal transaction). Accordingly, the Sixth Amendment right to counsel did not bar police from interrogating respondent regarding the murders, and respondent's confession was therefore admissible.

The judgment of the Court of Criminal Appeals of Texas is reversed.

JUSTICE KENNEDY, with whom JUSTICE SCALIA and JUSTICE THOMAS join, concurring.

The Court's opinion is altogether sufficient to explain why the decision of the Texas Court of Criminal Appeals should be reversed for failure to recognize the offense-specific nature of the Sixth Amendment right to counsel. It seems advisable, however, to observe that the Court has reached its conclusion without the necessity to reaffirm or give approval to the decision in Michigan v. Jackson, 475 U.S. 625 (1986). This course is wise, in my view, for the underlying theory of *Jackson* seems questionable.

As the facts of the instant case well illustrate, it is difficult to understand the utility of a Sixth Amendment rule that operates to invalidate a confession given by the free choice of suspects who have received proper advice of their *Miranda* rights but waived them nonetheless. The *Miranda* rule, and the related preventative rule of Edwards v. Arizona, 451 U.S. 477 (1981), serve to protect a suspect's voluntary choice not to speak outside his lawyer's presence. The parallel rule announced in *Jackson*, however, supersedes the suspect's voluntary choice to speak with investigators. * * *

In the instant case, Cobb at no time indicated to law enforcement authorities that he elected to remain silent about the double murder. By all indications, he made the voluntary choice to give his own account. Indeed, even now Cobb does not assert that he had no wish to speak at the time he confessed. While the *Edwards* rule operates to preserve the free choice of a suspect to remain silent, if *Jackson* were to apply it would override that choice.

There is further reason to doubt the wisdom of the *Jackson* holding. Neither *Miranda* nor *Edwards* enforces the Fifth Amendment right unless the suspect makes a clear and unambiguous assertion of the right to the presence of counsel during custodial interrogation. * * *

The Sixth Amendment right to counsel attaches quite without reference to the suspect's choice to speak with investigators after a *Miranda* warning. It is the commencement of a formal prosecution, indicated by the initiation of adversary judicial proceedings, that marks the beginning of the Sixth Amendment right. These events may be quite independent of the suspect's election to remain silent, the interest which the *Edwards* rule serves to protect with respect to *Miranda* and the Fifth Amendment, and it thus makes little sense for a protective rule to attach absent such an election by the suspect. We ought to question the wisdom of a judge-made preventative rule to protect a suspect's desire not to speak when it cannot be shown that he had that intent.

Even if *Jackson* is to remain good law, its protections should apply only where a suspect has made a clear and unambiguous assertion of the right not to speak outside the presence of counsel, the same clear election required under *Edwards*. Cobb made no such assertion here, yet Justice BREYER's dissent rests upon the assumption that the *Jackson* rule should operate to exclude the confession no matter. There would be little justification for this extension of a rule that, even in a more limited application, rests on a doubtful rationale.

Justice BREYER defends *Jackson* by arguing that, once a suspect has accepted counsel at the commencement of adversarial proceedings, he should not be forced to confront the police during interrogation without the assistance of counsel. But the acceptance of counsel at an arraignment or similar proceeding only begs the question: acceptance of counsel for what? It is quite unremarkable that a suspect might want the assistance of an expert in the law to guide him through hearings and trial, and the attendant complex legal matters that might arise, but nonetheless might choose to give on his own a forthright account of the events that occurred. A court-made rule that prevents a suspect from even making this choice serves little purpose, especially given the regime of *Miranda* and *Edwards*.

With these further remarks, I join in full the opinion of the Court.

JUSTICE BREYER, **with whom** JUSTICE STEVENS, JUSTICE SOUTER, **and** JUSTICE GINSBURG **join, dissenting.**

This case focuses upon the meaning of a single word, "offense," when it arises in the context of the Sixth Amendment. Several basic background principles define that context.

First, the Sixth Amendment right to counsel plays a central role in ensuring the fairness of criminal proceedings in our system of justice. Second, the right attaches when adversary proceedings, triggered by the government's formal accusation of a crime, begin. Third, once this right attaches, law enforcement officials are required, in most circumstances, to deal with the defendant through counsel, rather than directly, even if the defendant has waived his Fifth Amendment rights. See Michigan v. Jackson, 475 U.S. 625 (1986) (waiver of right to presence of counsel is assumed invalid unless accused initiates communication); Maine v.

Moulton, 474 U.S. 159 (1985) (Sixth Amendment gives defendant right "to rely on counsel as a 'medium' between him and the State"). Cf. ABA Model Rule of Professional Conduct 4.2 (2001) (lawyer is generally prohibited from communicating with a person known to be represented by counsel "about the subject of the representation" without counsel's "consent"); Green, A Prosecutor's Communications with Defendants: What Are the Limits?, 24 Crim. L. Bull. 283, 284, and n. 5 (1988) (version of Model Rule 4.2 or its predecessor has been adopted by all 50 States).

Fourth, the particular aspect of the right here at issue—the rule that the police ordinarily must communicate with the defendant through counsel—has important limits. In particular, recognizing the need for law enforcement officials to investigate "new or additional crimes" not the subject of current proceedings, this Court has made clear that the right to counsel does not attach to any and every crime that an accused may commit or have committed, see McNeil v. Wisconsin, 501 U.S. 171, 175–176 (1991). The right "cannot be invoked once for all future prosecutions," and it does not forbid "interrogation unrelated to the charge." In a word, as this Court previously noted, the right is "offense specific."

This case focuses upon the last-mentioned principle, in particular upon the meaning of the words "offense specific." These words appear in this Court's Sixth Amendment case law, not in the Sixth Amendment's text. See U.S. Const., Amdt. 6 (guaranteeing right to counsel "[i]n all criminal prosecutions"). The definition of these words is not self-evident. * * * This case requires us to determine whether an "offense"—for Sixth Amendment purposes—includes factually related aspects of a single course of conduct other than those few acts that make up the essential elements of the crime charged.

We should answer this question in light of the Sixth Amendment's basic objectives as set forth in this Court's case law. At the very least, we should answer it in a way that does not undermine those objectives. But the Court today decides that "offense" means the crime set forth within "the four corners of a charging instrument," along with other crimes that "would be considered the same offense" under the test established by Blockburger v. United States, 284 U.S. 299 (1932). In my view, this unnecessarily technical definition undermines Sixth Amendment protections while doing nothing to further effective law enforcement.

For one thing, the majority's rule, while leaving the Fifth Amendment's protections in place, threatens to diminish severely the additional protection that, under this Court's rulings, the Sixth Amendment provides when it grants the right to counsel to defendants who have been charged with a crime and insists that law enforcement officers thereafter communicate with them through that counsel.

Justice KENNEDY, Justice SCALIA, and Justice THOMAS, if not the majority, apparently believe these protections constitutionally unimportant, for, in their view, "the underlying theory of *Jackson* seems questionable." Both the majority and concurring opinions suggest that a suspect's ability to invoke his Fifth Amendment right and "refuse any police questioning" offers that suspect adequate constitutional protection. But that is not so.

Jackson focuses upon a suspect—perhaps a frightened or uneducated suspect—who, hesitant to rely upon his own unaided judgment in his dealings with the police, has invoked his constitutional right to legal assistance in such matters. *Jackson* says that, once such a request has been made, the police may not simply throw that suspect—who does not trust his own unaided judgment—back upon his own devices by requiring him to rely for protection upon that same unaided judgment that he previously rejected as inadequate. In a word, the police may not force a suspect who has asked for legal counsel to make a critical legal choice without the legal assistance that he has requested and that the Constitution guarantees. The Constitution does not take away with one hand what it gives with the other. See Michigan v. Jackson, supra, at 633, 635 (presuming "that the defendant requests the lawyer's services at every critical stage of the prosecution" even if the defendant fails to invoke his Fifth Amendment rights at the time of interrogation); ABA Ann. Model Rule of Professional Conduct 4.2, p. 398, comment. (4th ed. 1999) ("Rule 4.2 . . . exists to prevent lawyers from taking advantage of uncounseled laypersons and to preserve the integrity of the lawyer-client relationship").

For these reasons, the Sixth Amendment right at issue is independent of the Fifth Amendment's protections; and the importance of this Sixth Amendment right has been repeatedly recognized in our cases. *See, e.g.*, Michigan v. Jackson, supra, at 636 ("We conclude that the assertion [of the right to counsel] is no less significant, and the need for additional safeguards no less clear, when the request for counsel is made at an arraignment and when the basis for the claim is the Sixth Amendment").

* * *

Justice KENNEDY also criticizes *Jackson* on the ground that it prevents a suspect "from . . . making th[e] choice" to "give . . . a forthright account of the events that occurred." But that is not so. A suspect may initiate communication with the police, thereby avoiding the risk that the police induced him to make, unaided, the kind of critical legal decision best made with the help of counsel, whom he has requested.

Unlike Justice KENNEDY, the majority does not call *Jackson* itself into question. But the majority would undermine that case by significantly diminishing the Sixth Amendment protections that the case provides. That is because criminal codes are lengthy and highly detailed, often proliferating "overlapping and related statutory offenses" to the point where prosecutors can easily "spin out a startlingly numerous series of offenses from a single * * * criminal transaction." Ashe v. Swenson, 397 U.S. 436, 445, n. 10 (1970). Thus, an armed robber who reaches across a store counter, grabs the cashier, and demands "your money or your life," may through that single instance of conduct have committed several "offenses," in the majority's sense of the term, including armed robbery, assault, battery, trespass, use of a firearm to commit a felony, and perhaps possession of a firearm by a felon, as well. A person who is using and selling drugs on a single occasion might be guilty of possessing various drugs, conspiring to sell drugs, being under the influence of illegal drugs, possessing drug paraphernalia, possessing a gun in relation to the drug sale, and, depending upon circumstances, violating various gun laws as well. A protester blocking an entrance to a federal building might also be trespassing, failing to disperse, unlawfully assembling, and obstructing Government administration all at one and the same time.

The majority's rule permits law enforcement officials to question those charged with a crime without first approaching counsel, through the simple device of asking questions about any other related crime not actually charged in the indictment. Thus, the police could ask the individual charged with robbery about, say, the assault of the cashier not yet charged, or about any other uncharged offense (unless under *Blockburger's* definition it counts as the "same crime"), all without notifying counsel. Indeed, the majority's rule would permit law enforcement officials to question anyone charged with any crime in any one of the examples just given about his or her conduct on the single relevant occasion without notifying counsel unless the prosecutor has charged every possible crime arising out of that same brief course of conduct. What Sixth Amendment sense—what common sense—does such a rule make? What is left of the "communicate through counsel" rule?

The majority's approach is inconsistent with any common understanding of the scope of counsel's representation. It will undermine the lawyer's role as "medium" between the defendant and the government. And it will, on a random basis, remove a significant portion of the protection that this Court has found inherent in the Sixth Amendment.

In fact, under the rule today announced by the majority, two of the seminal cases in our Sixth Amendment jurisprudence would have come out differently. In Maine v. Moulton, * * * we treated burglary and theft as the same offense for Sixth Amendment purposes. Despite the opinion's clear statement that "[i]ncriminating statements pertaining to other crimes, as to which the Sixth Amendment right has not yet attached, are, of course, admissible at a trial of those offenses," the Court affirmed the lower court's reversal of both burglary and theft charges even though, at the time that the incriminating statements at issue were made, Moulton had been charged only with theft by receiving. Under the majority's rule, in contrast, because theft by receiving and burglary each required proof of a fact that the other did not, only Moulton's theft convictions should have been overturned. Compare Me.Rev.Stat. Ann., Tit. 17–A, § 359 (1981) (theft) (requiring knowing receipt, retention, or disposal of stolen property with the intent to deprive the owner thereof), with § 401 (burglary) (requiring entry of a structure without permission and with the intent to commit a crime).

In Brewer v. Williams, the effect of the majority's rule would have been even more dramatic. Because first-degree murder and child abduction each required proof of a fact not required by the other, and because at the time of the impermissible interrogation Williams had been charged only with abduction of a child, Williams' murder conviction should have remained undisturbed. Compare Iowa Code § 690.2 (1950 and Supp.1978) (first-degree murder) (requiring a killing) with Iowa Code § 706.2 (1950) (repealed 1978) (child-stealing) (requiring proof that a child under 16 was taken with the intent to conceal the child from his or her parent or guardian). This is not to suggest that this Court has previously addressed and decided the question presented by this case. Rather, it is to point out that the Court's conception of the Sixth Amendment right at the time that *Moulton* and *Brewer* were decided naturally presumed that it extended to factually related but uncharged offenses.

At the same time, the majority's rule threatens the legal clarity necessary for effective law enforcement. That is because the majority, aware that the word "offense" ought to encompass something beyond "the four corners of the charging instrument," imports into Sixth Amendment law the definition of "offense" set forth in Blockburger v. United States, 284 U.S. 299 (1932), a case interpreting the Double Jeopardy Clause of the Fifth Amendment, which Clause uses the word "offence" but otherwise has no relevance here. Whatever Fifth Amendment virtues *Blockburger* may have, to import it into this Sixth Amendment context will work havoc.

In theory, the test says that two offenses are the "same offense" unless each requires proof of a fact that the other does not. That means that most of the different crimes mentioned above are not the "same offense." Under many States' laws, for example, the statute defining assault and the statute defining robbery each requires proof of a fact that the other does not. Compare, e.g., Cal.Penal Code Ann. § 211 (West 1999) (robbery) (requiring taking of personal property of another) with § 240 (assault) (requiring attempt to commit violent injury). Hence the extension of the definition of "offense" that is accomplished by the use of the *Blockburger* test does nothing to address the substantial concerns about the circumvention of the Sixth Amendment right that are raised by the majority's rule.

But, more to the point, the simple-sounding *Blockburger* test has proved extraordinarily difficult to administer in practice. Judges, lawyers, and law professors often disagree about how to apply it. *Compare* United States v. Dixon, 509 U.S. 688 (1993) (opinion of SCALIA, J.) (applying *Blockburger* and concluding that contempt is same offense as underlying substantive crime), with 509 U.S., at 716–720 (REHNQUIST, C. J., concurring in part and dissenting in part) (applying *Blockburger* and deciding that the two are separate offenses). The test has emerged as a tool in an area of our jurisprudence that THE CHIEF JUSTICE has described as "a veritable Sargasso Sea which could not fail to challenge the most intrepid judicial navigator." Albernaz v. United States, 450 U.S. 333, 343 (1981). Yet the Court now asks, not

the lawyers and judges who ordinarily work with double jeopardy law, but police officers in the field, to navigate *Blockburger* when they question suspects. Cf. New York v. Belton, 453 U.S. 454 (1981) (noting importance of clear rules to guide police behavior). Some will apply the test successfully; some will not. Legal challenges are inevitable. The result, I believe, will resemble not so much the Sargasso Sea as the criminal law equivalent of Milton's "Serbonian Bog ... Where Armies whole have sunk."

There is, of course, an alternative. We can, and should, define "offense" in terms of the conduct that constitutes the crime that the offender committed on a particular occasion, including criminal acts that are "closely related to" or "inextricably intertwined with" the particular crime set forth in the charging instrument. This alternative is not perfect. The language used lacks the precision for which police officers may hope; and it requires lower courts to specify its meaning further as they apply it in individual cases. Yet virtually every lower court in the United States to consider the issue has defined "offense" in the Sixth Amendment context to encompass such closely related acts. These courts have found offenses "closely related" where they involved the same victim, set of acts, evidence, or motivation. They have found offenses unrelated where time, location, or factual circumstances significantly separated the one from the other. See, e.g., Commonwealth v. Rainwater, 425 Mass. 540, 547–549 (1997) (vehicle theft charge and earlier vehicle thefts in same area); Whittlesey v. State, 340 Md. 30, 56–57, 665 A.2d

223, 236 (1995) (murder and making false statements charges) (1996); People v. Dotson, 214 Ill. App.3d 637, 646, 574 N.E.2d 143, 149 (murder and weapons charges).

One cannot say in favor of this commonly followed approach that it is perfectly clear—only that, because it comports with common sense, it is far easier to apply than that of the majority. One might add that, unlike the majority's test, it is consistent with this Court's assumptions in previous cases. See Maine v. Moulton, 474 U.S., at 162 (affirming reversal of both burglary and theft convictions); Brewer v. Williams, 430 U.S., at 389 (affirming grant of habeas which vacated murder conviction). And, most importantly, the "closely related" test furthers, rather than undermines, the Sixth Amendment's "right to counsel," a right so necessary to the realization in practice of that most "noble ideal," a fair trial. Gideon v. Wainwright, 372 U.S., at 344.

The Texas Court of Criminal Appeals, following this commonly accepted approach, found that the charged burglary and the uncharged murders were "closely related." All occurred during a short period of time on the same day in the same basic location. The victims of the murders were also victims of the burglary. Cobb committed one of the murders in furtherance of the robbery, the other to cover up the crimes. The police, when questioning Cobb, knew that he already had a lawyer representing him on the burglary charges and had demonstrated their belief that this lawyer also represented Cobb in respect to the murders by asking his permission to question Cobb about the murders on previous occasions. The relatedness of the crimes is well illustrated by the impossibility of questioning Cobb about the murders without eliciting admissions about the burglary. Nor, in my view, did Cobb waive his right to counsel. These considerations are sufficient. The police officers ought to have spoken to Cobb's counsel before questioning Cobb. I would affirm the decision of the Texas court.

Consequently, I dissent.

Chapter Five

THE RIGHT TO COUNSEL

III. A NEW AND SWEEPING RIGHT AND ITS LIMITS

B. THE RIGHT TO APPOINTED COUNSEL IN MISDEMEANOR CASES

Page 793. At the end of the section, add the following:

Uncounseled Convictions and Suspended Sentences: Alabama v. Shelton

In the following case, the Court considered whether *Argersinger* or *Scott* applies when the defendant receives a suspended sentence.

ALABAMA v. SHELTON

Supreme Court of the United States, 2002.
535 U.S. 654.

JUSTICE GINSBURG **delivered the opinion of the Court.**

This case concerns the Sixth Amendment right of an indigent defendant charged with a misdemeanor punishable by imprisonment, fine, or both, to the assistance of court-appointed counsel. Two prior decisions control the Court's judgment. First, in Argersinger v. Hamlin, 407 U.S. 25 (1972), this Court held that defense counsel must be appointed in any criminal prosecution, "whether classified as petty, misdemeanor, or felony," "that actually leads to imprisonment even for a brief period." Later, in Scott v.

Illinois, 440 U.S. 367, 373–374 (1979), the Court drew the line at "actual imprisonment," holding that counsel need not be appointed when the defendant is fined for the charged crime, but is not sentenced to a term of imprisonment.

Defendant-respondent LeReed Shelton, convicted of third-degree assault, was sentenced to a jail term of 30 days, which the trial court immediately suspended, placing Shelton on probation for two years. The question presented is whether the Sixth Amendment right to appointed counsel, as delineated in *Argersinger* and *Scott,* applies to a

172

defendant in Shelton's situation. We hold that a suspended sentence that may "end up in the actual deprivation of a person's liberty" may not be imposed unless the defendant was accorded "the guiding hand of counsel" in the prosecution for the crime charged.

I

After representing himself at a bench trial in the District Court of Etowah County, Alabama, Shelton was convicted of third-degree assault, a class A misdemeanor carrying a maximum punishment of one year imprisonment and a $2000 fine. He invoked his right to a new trial before a jury in Circuit Court, where he again appeared without a lawyer and was again convicted. The court repeatedly warned Shelton about the problems self-representation entailed, but at no time offered him assistance of counsel at state expense.

The Circuit Court sentenced Shelton to serve 30 days in the county prison. As authorized by Alabama law, however, the court suspended that sentence and placed Shelton on two years' unsupervised probation, conditioned on his payment of court costs, a $500 fine, reparations of $25, and restitution in the amount of $516.69.

Shelton appealed his conviction and sentence on Sixth Amendment grounds, and the Alabama Court of Criminal Appeals affirmed. * * * A suspended sentence, the court concluded, does not trigger the Sixth Amendment right to appointed counsel unless there is "evidence in the record that the [defendant] has actually been deprived of liberty." Because Shelton remained on probation, the court held that he had

not been denied any Sixth Amendment right at trial.

The Supreme Court of Alabama reversed the Court of Criminal Appeals in relevant part. Referring to this Court's decisions in *Argersinger* and *Scott,* the Alabama Supreme Court reasoned that a defendant may not be "sentenced to a term of imprisonment" absent provision of counsel .. In the Alabama high court's view, a suspended sentence constitutes a "term of imprisonment" * * * even though incarceration is not immediate or inevitable. And because the State is constitutionally barred from activating the conditional sentence, the Alabama court concluded, " 'the threat itself is hollow and should be considered a nullity.' " Accordingly, the court affirmed Shelton's conviction and the monetary portion of his punishment, but invalidated "that aspect of his sentence imposing 30 days of suspended jail time." By reversing Shelton's suspended sentence, the State informs us, the court also vacated the two-year term of probation.

* * *

II

Three positions are before us in this case. In line with the decision of the Supreme Court of Alabama, Shelton argues that an indigent defendant may not receive a suspended sentence unless he is offered or waives the assistance of state-appointed counsel. Alabama now concedes that the Sixth Amendment bars *activation* of a suspended sentence for an uncounseled conviction, but maintains that the Constitution does not prohibit *imposition* of such a sentence as a method of effectuating probationary punishment. To assure full airing of the question presented, we invited an *amicus curiae* ("*amicus*") to argue in support of a third position, one Alabama has abandoned: Failure to appoint counsel to an indigent defendant "does not bar the imposition of a suspended or probationary sentence upon conviction of a misdemeanor, even though the defendant might be incarcerated in the event probation is revoked."

A

In Gideon v. Wainwright, 372 U.S. 335, 344–345 (1963), we held that the Sixth Amendment's guarantee of the right to state-appointed counsel, firmly established in federal-court proceedings in Johnson v. Zerbst, 304 U.S. 458 (1938), applies to state criminal prosecutions through the Fourteenth Amendment. We clarified the scope of that right in *Argersinger,* holding that an indigent defendant must be offered counsel in any misdemeanor case "that actually leads to imprisonment." Seven Terms later, *Scott* confirmed *Argersinger's* "delimit[ation]." Although the governing statute in *Scott* authorized a jail sentence of up to one year, we held that the defendant had no right to state-appointed counsel because the sole sentence actually imposed on him was a $50 fine. "Even were the matter *res nova,*" we stated, "the central premise of *Argersinger*—that actual imprisonment is a penalty different in kind from fines or the mere threat of imprisonment—is eminently sound and warrants adoption of actual imprisonment as the line defining the constitutional

right to appointment of counsel" in nonfelony cases.

* * *

B

Applying the "actual imprisonment" rule to the case before us, we take up first the question we asked *amicus* to address: Where the State provides no counsel to an indigent defendant, does the Sixth Amendment permit activation of a suspended sentence upon the defendant's violation of the terms of probation? We conclude that it does not. A suspended sentence is a prison term imposed for the offense of conviction. Once the prison term is triggered, the defendant is incarcerated not for the probation violation, but for the underlying offense. The uncounseled conviction at that point "result[s] in imprisonment"; it "end[s] up in the actual deprivation of a person's liberty." This is precisely what the Sixth Amendment, as interpreted in *Argersinger* and *Scott,* does not allow.

* * *

Amicus * * * contends that "practical considerations clearly weigh against" the extension of the Sixth Amendment appointed-counsel right to a defendant in Shelton's situation .. He cites figures suggesting that although conditional sentences are commonly imposed, they are rarely activated. Tr. of Oral Arg. 20–21 (speculating that "hundreds of thousands" of uncounseled defendants receive suspended sentences, but only "thousands" of that large number are incarcerated upon violating the terms of their probation). Based on these estimations, *amicus* argues that a rule requiring appointed counsel in every case involving a suspended sentence would unduly hamper the States' attempts to impose effective probationary punishment. A more "workable solution," he contends, would permit imposition of a suspended sentence on an uncounseled defendant and require appointment of counsel, if at all, only at the probation revocation stage, when incarceration is imminent.

Amicus observes that probation is "now a critical tool of law enforcement in low level cases." Even so, it does not follow that preservation of that tool warrants the reduction of the Sixth Amendment's domain that would result from the regime *amicus* hypothesizes. *Amicus* does not describe the contours of the hearing that, he suggests, might precede revocation of a term of probation imposed on an uncounseled defendant. In Alabama, however, the character of the probation revocation hearing currently afforded is not in doubt. The proceeding is an "informal" one, at which the defendant has no right to counsel, and the court no obligation to observe customary rules of evidence.

More significant, the sole issue at the hearing—apart from determinations about the necessity of confinement—is whether the defendant breached the terms of probation. The validity or reliability of the underlying conviction is beyond attack.

We think it plain that a hearing so timed and structured cannot compensate for the absence of trial counsel, for it does not even address the key Sixth Amendment inquiry: whether the adjudication of guilt corresponding to the prison sentence is sufficiently reliable to permit incarceration. Deprived of

counsel when tried, convicted, and sentenced, and unable to challenge the original judgment at a subsequent probation revocation hearing, a defendant in Shelton's circumstances faces incarceration on a conviction that has never been subjected to "the crucible of meaningful adversarial testing.". The Sixth Amendment does not countenance this result.

In a variation on *amicus'* position, the dissent would limit review in this case to the question whether the *imposition* of Shelton's suspended sentence required appointment of counsel, answering that question "plainly no" because such a step "does not deprive a defendant of his personal liberty." Only if the sentence is later activated, the dissent contends, need the Court "ask whether the procedural safeguards attending the imposition of [Shelton's] sentence comply with the Constitution."

Severing the analysis in this manner makes little sense. One cannot assess the constitutionality of imposing a suspended sentence while simultaneously walling off the procedures that will precede its activation. The dissent imagines a set of safeguards Alabama might provide at the probation revocation stage sufficient to cure its failure to appoint counsel prior to sentencing, including, perhaps, "complete retrial of the misdemeanor violation with assistance of counsel." But there is no cause for speculation about Alabama's procedures; they are established by Alabama statute and decisional law, and they bear no resemblance to those the dissent invents in its effort to sanction the prospect of Shelton's imprisonment on an uncounseled conviction. Assessing the issue before us in light of actual circumstances, we do not comprehend how the procedures Alabama in fact provides at the probation revocation hearing could bring Shelton's sentence within constitutional bounds.

Nor do we agree with *amicus* or the dissent that our holding will "substantially limit the states' ability" to impose probation, or encumber them with a "large, new burden." Most jurisdictions already provide a state-law right to appointed counsel more generous than that afforded by the Federal Constitution. All but 16 States, for example, would provide counsel to a defendant in Shelton's circumstances, either because he received a substantial fine or because state law authorized incarceration for the charged offense or provided for a maximum prison term of one year. There is thus scant reason to believe that a rule conditioning imposition of a suspended sentence on provision of appointed counsel would affect existing practice in the large majority of the States. And given the current commitment of most jurisdictions to affording court-appointed counsel to indigent misdemeanants while simultaneously preserving the option of probationary punishment, we do not share *amicus'* concern that other States may lack the capacity and resources to do the same.

Moreover, even if *amicus* is correct that "some courts and jurisdictions at least [can]not bear" the costs of the rule we confirm today, those States need not abandon probation or equivalent measures as viable forms of punishment. Although they may not attach proba-

tion to an imposed and suspended prison sentence, States unable or unwilling routinely to provide appointed counsel to misdemeanants in Shelton's situation are not without recourse to another option capable of yielding a similar result.

That option is pretrial probation, employed in some form by at least 23 States. Under such an arrangement, the prosecutor and defendant agree to the defendant's participation in a pretrial rehabilitation program, which includes conditions typical of post-trial probation. The adjudication of guilt and imposition of sentence for the underlying offense then occur only if and when the defendant breaches those conditions.

Like the regime urged by *amicus,* this system reserves the appointed-counsel requirement for the "small percentage" of cases in which incarceration proves necessary, thus allowing a State to "supervise a course of rehabilitation" without providing a lawyer every time it wishes to pursue such a course. Unlike *amicus'* position, however, pretrial probation also respects the constitutional imperative that "no person may be imprisoned for any offense ... unless he was represented by counsel at his trial.".

C

Alabama concedes that activation of a suspended sentence results in the imprisonment of an uncounseled defendant "for a term that relates to the original offense" and therefore "crosses the line of 'actual imprisonment'" established in *Argersinger* and *Scott.* * * *. Alabama maintains, however, that there is no constitutional barrier to *imposition* of a suspended sentence that can never be enforced; the State therefore urges reversal of the Alabama Supreme Court's judgment insofar as it vacated the term of probation Shelton was ordered to serve.

In effect, Alabama invites us to regard two years' probation for Shelton as a separate and independent sentence, which "the State would have the same power to enforce [as] a judgment of a mere fine." *Scott,* Alabama emphasizes, squarely held that a fine-only sentence does not trigger a right to court-appointed counsel.; similarly, Alabama maintains, probation uncoupled from a prison sentence should trigger no immediate right to appointed counsel. Seen as a freestanding sentence, Alabama further asserts, probation could be enforced, as a criminal fine or restitution order could, in a contempt proceeding.

Alabama describes the contempt proceeding it envisions as one in which Shelton would receive "the full panoply of due process," including the assistance of counsel. Any sanction imposed would be for "post-conviction wrongdoing," not for the offense of conviction. "The maximum penalty faced would be a $100 fine and five days' imprisonment," not the 30 days ordered and suspended by the Alabama Circuit Court. There is not so much as a hint, however, in the decision of the Supreme Court of Alabama, that Shelton's probation term is separable from the prison term to which it was tethered. Absent any prior presentation of the position the State now takes, we resist passing on it in the first instance. Our resistance to acting as a court of first view instead of one of review is heightened

by the Alabama Attorney General's acknowledgment at oral argument that he did not know of any State that imposes, postconviction, on a par with a fine, a term of probation unattached to a suspended sentence. * * *

In short, Alabama has developed its position late in this litigation and before the wrong forum. It is for the Alabama Supreme Court to consider before this Court does whether the suspended sentence alone is invalid, leaving Shelton's probation term freestanding and independently effective. We confine our review to the ruling the Alabama Supreme Court made in the case as presented to it: "[A] defendant who receives a suspended or probated sentence *to imprisonment* has a constitutional right to counsel." We find no infirmity in that holding.

Satisfied that Shelton is entitled to appointed counsel at the critical stage when his guilt or innocence of the charged crime is decided and his vulnerability to imprisonment is determined, we affirm the judgment of the Supreme Court of Alabama.

It is so ordered.

JUSTICE SCALIA, **joined by the** CHIEF JUSTICE, JUSTICE KENNEDY, **and** JUSTICE THOMAS, **dissenting.**

* * *

Today's decision ignores * * * long and consistent jurisprudence, extending the misdemeanor right to counsel to cases bearing the mere threat of imprisonment. Respondent's 30–day suspended sentence, and the accompanying 2–year term of probation, are invalidated for lack of appointed counsel even though respondent has not suffered, and may never suffer, a deprivation of liberty. The Court holds that the suspended sentence violates respondent's Sixth Amendment right to counsel because it "*may* 'end up in the actual deprivation of [respondent's] liberty,' " *if* he someday violates the terms of probation, *if* a court determines that the violation merits revocation of probation, and *if* the court determines that no other punishment will "adequately protect the community from further criminal activity" or "avoid depreciating the seriousness of the violation." And to all of these contingencies there must yet be added, before the Court's decision makes sense, an element of rank speculation. Should all these contingencies occur, the Court speculates, the Alabama Supreme Court would mechanically apply its decisional law applicable to routine probation revocation (which establishes procedures that the Court finds inadequate) rather than adopt special procedures for situations that raise constitutional questions in light of *Argersinger* and *Scott.* * * *

Surely the procedures attending reimposition of a suspended sentence would be adequate if they required, upon the defendant's request, complete retrial of the misdemeanor violation with assistance of counsel. By what right does the Court deprive the State of that option? It may well be a sensible option, since most defendants will be induced to comply with the terms of their probation by the mere threat of a retrial that could send them to jail, and since the expense of those rare, counseled retrials may be much less than the expense of providing counsel initially in all misdemeanor cases that bear a possible sentence of imprisonment. And it may well be that, in some

cases, even procedures short of complete retrial will suffice

* * *

Our prior opinions placed considerable weight on the practical consequences of expanding the right to appointed counsel beyond cases of actual imprisonment. Today, the Court gives this consideration the back of its hand. Its observation that "[a]ll but 16 States" already appoint counsel for defendants like respondent, is interesting but quite irrelevant, since today's holding is not confined to *defendants like respondent.* Appointed counsel must henceforth be offered before *any* defendant can be awarded a suspended sentence, no matter how short. Only 24 States have announced a rule of this scope. Thus, the Court's decision imposes a large, new burden on a majority of the States, including some of the poorest (*e.g.,* Alabama, Arkansas, and Mississippi, see U.S. Census Bureau, Statistical Abstract of the United States 426 (2001)). That burden consists not only of the cost of providing state-paid counsel in cases of such insignificance that even financially prosperous defendants sometimes forgo the expense of hired counsel; but also the cost of enabling courts and prosecutors to respond to the "over-lawyering" of minor cases. Nor should we discount the burden placed on the minority 24 States that currently provide counsel: that they keep their current disposition forever in place, however imprudent experience proves it to be.

Today's imposition upon the States finds justification neither in the text of the Constitution, nor in the settled practices of our people, nor in the prior jurisprudence of this Court. I respectfully dissent

Chapter Six

THE SCREENING AND CHARGING PROCESS

V. THE GRAND JURY

C. THE PROCEDURES OF THE GRAND JURY

Page 838. Add the following Editor's Note:

The USA PATRIOT Act, enacted in response to the terrorist attacks of September 11, 2001, adds an additional exception to subdivision (e) of Fed.R.Crim.P.6. This new exception to grand jury secrecy allows an attorney for the government to disclose any grand jury matter involving foreign intelligence to any law enforcement official to assist that official in performing his or her duties. Certain procedural protections are provided to prevent widespread dissemination of the grand jury information subject to this exception. The pertinent provision of the USA PATRIOT Act is set forth in Part IV of this Supplement, *infra*. An amendment to Federal Rule 6, effective December 1, 2002, incorporates the pertinent provisions of the USA PATRIOT Act. That amendment also restylizes the entirety of Rule 6. The amended Rule 6 is found in Part III of this Supplement.

VII. THE PROBLEM OF CONSTRUCTIVE AMENDMENT, VARIANCE, AND ADEQUATE NOTICE

Page 867. At the end of the Chapter, add the following:

The Failure to Include All Elements of the Crime in the Indictment: United States v. Cotton

In the following case, the Court considered the consequences of an indictment that does not include an element of the crime, and specifically whether such a failure deprives a court of jurisdiction to hear the criminal case.

UNITED STATES v. COTTON

Supreme Court of the United States, 2002.
535 U.S. 625.

CHIEF JUSTICE REHNQUIST **delivered the opinion of the Court.**

In Apprendi v. New Jersey, 530 U.S. 466 (2000), we held that "[o]ther than the fact of a prior conviction, any fact that increases the penalty for a crime beyond the prescribed statutory maximum must be submitted to a jury, and proved beyond a reasonable doubt." [*Apprendi* is set forth in this Supplement, Chapter 10]. In federal prosecutions, such facts must also be charged in the indictment. Id. at 476. In this case, we address whether the omission from a federal indictment of a fact that enhances the statutory maximum sentence justifies a court of appeals' vacating the enhanced sentence, even though the defendant did not object in the trial court.

Respondent Stanley Hall, Jr., led a "vast drug organization" in Baltimore. The six other respondents helped run the operation. In October 1997, a federal grand jury returned an indictment charging respondents with conspiring to distribute and to possess with intent to distribute 5 kilograms or more of cocaine and 50 grams or more of cocaine base, in violation of 21 U.S.C. §§ 846 and 841(a)(1). A superseding indictment returned in March 1998, which extended the time period of the conspiracy and added five more defendants, charged a conspiracy to distribute and to possess with intent to distribute a "detectable amount" of cocaine and cocaine base. The superseding indictment did not allege any of the threshold levels of drug quantity that lead to enhanced penalties under § 841(b).

In accord with the superseding indictment, the District Court instructed the jury that "as long as you find that a defendant conspired to distribute or posses[s] with intent to distribute these controlled substances, the amounts involved are not important." The jury found respondents guilty.

Congress established "a term of imprisonment of not more than 20 years" for drug offenses involving a detectable quantity of cocaine or cocaine base. § 841(b)(1)(C). But the District Court did not sentence respondents under this provision. Consistent with the practice in federal courts at the time, at sentencing the District Court made a finding of drug quantity that implicated the enhanced penalties of § 841(b)(1)(A), which prescribes "a term of imprisonment which may not be ... more than life" for drug offenses involving at least 50 grams of cocaine base. The District Court found, based on the trial testimony, respondent Hall responsible for at least 500 grams of cocaine base, and the other respondents responsible for at least 1.5 kilograms of cocaine base. The court sentenced respondents Hall and Powell to 30 years' imprisonment and the other respondents to life imprisonment. Respondents did not object in the District Court to the fact that these sentences were based on an amount of drug quantity not alleged in the indictment.

While respondents' appeal was pending in the United States Court of Appeals for the Fourth Circuit, we decided Apprendi v. New Jersey, *supra.* Respondents then argued in the Court of Appeals that their sentences were invalid under *Apprendi,* because the issue of drug quantity was neither alleged in the indictment nor submitted to the petit jury. The Court of Appeals noted that respondents "failed to raise this argument before the district court" and thus reviewed the argument for plain error. 261 F.3d, at 403 (citing Fed. Rule Crim. Proc. 52(b)). A divided court nonetheless vacated respondents' sentences on the ground that "because an indictment setting forth all the essential elements of an offense is both mandatory and jurisdictional, ... a court is without jurisdiction to ... *impose a sentence* for an offense not charged in the indictment." Such an error, the Court of Appeals concluded, "seriously affects the fairness, integrity or public reputation of judicial proceedings." We granted certiorari, and now reverse.

We first address the Court of Appeals' conclusion that the omission from the indictment was a "jurisdictional" defect and thus required vacating respondents' sentences. Ex parte Bain, 121 U.S. 1 (1887), is the progenitor of this view. In *Bain,* the indictment charged that Bain, the cashier and director of a bank, made false statements "with intent to deceive the Comptroller of the Currency and the agent appointed to examine the affairs" of the bank. Before trial, the court struck the words "the Comptroller of the Currency and," on the ground that they were superfluous. The jury found Bain guilty. Bain challenged the amendment to the indictment in a petition for a writ of habeas corpus. The Court concluded that the amendment was improper and that therefore "the jurisdiction of the offence [was] gone, and the court [had] no right to proceed any further in the progress of the case for want of an indictment."

Bain, however, is a product of an era in which this Court's authority to review criminal convictions was greatly circumscribed. At the time it was decided, a defendant could not obtain direct review of his criminal conviction in the Supreme Court. The Court's authority to issue a writ of habeas corpus was limited to cases in which the convicting "court had no jurisdiction to render the judgment which it gave." *Bain, supra,* at 3. In 1887, therefore, this Court could examine constitutional errors in a criminal trial only on a writ of habeas corpus, and only then if it deemed the error "jurisdictional." The Court's desire to correct obvious constitutional violations led to a "somewhat expansive notion of 'jurisdiction,'" Custis v. United States, 511 U.S. 485 (1994), which was "more a fiction than anything else," Wainwright v. Sykes, 433 U.S. 72, 79 (1977).

Bain's elastic concept of jurisdiction is not what the term "jurisdiction" means today, *i.e.,* "the courts' statutory or constitutional *power* to adjudicate the case." Steel Co. v. Citizens for Better Environment, 523 U.S. 83, 89 (1998). This latter concept of subject-matter jurisdiction, because it involves a court's power to hear a case, can never be forfeited or waived. Consequently, defects in subject-matter jurisdiction require correction regardless of whether the error was raised in district court. In contrast, the grand jury right can be waived. See Fed. Rule Crim. Proc. 7(b).

Post-*Bain* cases confirm that defects in an indictment do not deprive a court of its power to adjudicate a case. In Lamar v. United States, 240 U.S. 60 (1916), the Court rejected the claim that "the court had no jurisdiction because the indictment does not charge a crime against the United States." Justice Holmes explained that a district court "has jurisdiction of all crimes cognizable under the authority of the United States ... [and][t]he objection that the indictment does not charge a crime against the United States goes only to the merits of the case." *Id.,* at 65. Similarly, United States v. Williams, 341 U.S. 58, 66 (1951), held that a ruling "that the indictment is defective does not affect the jurisdiction of the trial court to determine the case presented by the indictment."

Thus, this Court some time ago departed from *Bain's* view that indictment defects are "jurisdictional." *Bain* has been cited in later cases such as Stirone v. United States, *361 U.S. 212 (1960), and* Russell v. United States, 369 U.S. 749 (1962), for the proposition that "an indictment may not be amended except by resubmission to the grand jury, unless the change is merely a matter of form." But in each of these cases proper objection had been made in the District Court to the sufficiency of the indictment. We need not retreat from this settled proposition of law decided in *Bain* to say that the analysis of that issue in terms of "jurisdiction" was mistaken in the light of later cases such as *Lamar* and *Williams.* Insofar as it held that a defective indictment deprives a court of jurisdiction, *Bain* is overruled.

Freed from the view that indictment omissions deprive a court of jurisdiction, we proceed to apply the plain-error test of Federal Rule of Criminal Procedure 52(b) to respondents' forfeited claim

[The Court found that the failure to include the amount of drugs in the indictment was not plain error because there was substantial evidence of the amount of drugs presented at trial. For a discussion of the "plain error" analysis in *Cotton*, see Chapter 13 of this Supplement.]

Chapter Seven

BAIL AND PRETRIAL DETENTION

IV. BAIL REFORM AND PREVENTIVE DETENTION

B. THE CONSTITUTIONALITY OF PREVENTIVE DETENTION

Page 900.   At the end of the section, add the following:

Constitutionality of Other Forms of Preventive Detention–
Persons Subject To Deportation: Zadvydas v. Davis

In Zadvydas v. Davis, 533 U.S. 678 (2001), the Court considered the plight of an alien ordered removed from the United States but who could not be deported to a receiving country. A statute, 8 U.S.C. § 1231(a)(6), provides for detention for certain categories of aliens who have been ordered removed but who cannot be removed within 90 days of the deportation order. Those aliens subject to continued detention are: inadmissible aliens, criminal aliens, aliens who have violated their non-immigrant status conditions, and aliens removable for certain national security or foreign relations reasons, as well as any alien "who has been determined by the Attorney General to be a risk to the community or unlikely to comply with the order of removal." The statute states that an alien who falls into one of these categories "may be detained beyond the removal period and, if released, shall be subject to [certain] terms of supervision."

The Government in *Zadvydas* argued that the statute means literally what it says, setting no limit on the length of time that an alien subject to the statute may be detained if they cannot be removed within 90 days. Justice Stevens, writing for five members of the Court, refused to read the statute to provide for indefinite detention, reasoning that to so read the statute would result in a serious constitutional question under the Due Process Clause. Justice Stevens discussed the constitutional concerns in the following passage:

> Freedom from imprisonment—from government custody, detention, or other forms of physical restraint—lies at the heart of the liberty that Clause protects. See Foucha v. Louisiana, 504 U.S.

71, 80 (1992). And this Court has said that government detention violates that Clause unless the detention is ordered in a criminal proceeding with adequate procedural protections, see United States v. Salerno, 481 U.S. 739, 746 (1987), or, in certain special and "narrow" non-punitive "circumstances," where a special justification, such as harm-threatening mental illness, outweighs the "individual's constitutionally protected interest in avoiding physical restraint." Kansas v. Hendricks, 521 U.S. 346, 356 (1997). The proceedings at issue here are civil, not criminal, and we assume that they are nonpunitive in purpose and effect. There is no sufficiently strong special justification here for indefinite civil detention—at least as administered under this statute. The statute, says the Government, has two regulatory goals: "ensuring the appearance of aliens at future immigration proceedings" and "preventing danger to the community." But by definition the first justification—preventing flight—is weak or nonexistent where removal seems a remote possibility at best. * * * The second justification—protecting the community—does not necessarily diminish in force over time. But we have upheld preventive detention based on dangerousness only when limited to specially dangerous individuals and subject to strong procedural protections. Compare *Hendricks,* (upholding scheme that imposes detention upon "a small segment of particularly dangerous individuals" and provides "strict procedural safeguards") and *Salerno* (in upholding pretrial detention, stressing "stringent time limitations," the fact that detention is reserved for the "most serious of crimes," the requirement of proof of dangerousness by clear and convincing evidence, and the presence of judicial safeguards), with *Foucha,* (striking down insanity-related detention system that placed burden on detainee to prove nondangerousness). In cases in which preventive detention is of potentially indefinite duration, we have also demanded that the dangerousness rationale be accompanied by some other special circumstance, such as mental illness, that helps to create the danger. See *Hendricks.*

The civil confinement here at issue is not limited, but potentially permanent. Cf. *Salerno* (noting that "maximum length of pretrial detention is limited" by "stringent" requirements); Carlson v. Landon, 342 U.S. 524, 545–546 (1952) (upholding temporary detention of alien during deportation proceeding while noting that "problem of . . . unusual delay" was not present). The provision authorizing detention does not apply narrowly to "a small segment of particularly dangerous individuals," *Hendricks,* say suspected terrorists, but broadly to aliens ordered removed for many and various reasons, including tourist visa violations. Cf. *Hendricks,* (only individuals with "past sexually violent behavior and a present mental condition that creates a likelihood of such conduct in the future" may be detained). And, once the flight risk justification evaporates, the only special circumstance present is the alien's removable status itself, which bears no relation to a detainee's dangerousness. * * * The serious constitutional problem arising out of a statute that, in these circumstances, permits an indefinite, perhaps permanent, deprivation of human liberty without any such protection is obvious.

The majority in *Zadvydas* construed the statute to avoid the constitutional problem that it perceived. It held that an alien who is not removed within the 90–day period can bring a habeas corpus action to challenge his continued detention as unreasonable. In that action,

> the habeas court must ask whether the detention in question exceeds a period reasonably necessary to secure removal. It should measure reasonableness primarily in terms of the statute's basic purpose, namely assuring the alien's presence at the moment of removal. Thus, if removal is not reasonably foreseeable, the court should hold continued detention unreasonable and no longer authorized by statute. In that case, of course, the alien's release may and should be conditioned on any of the various forms of supervised release that are appropriate in the circumstances, and the alien may no doubt be returned to custody upon a violation of those conditions. And if removal is reasonably foreseeable, the habeas court should consider the risk of the alien's committing further crimes as a factor potentially justifying confinement within that reasonable removal period.

The Court emphasized that it did not deny "the right of Congress to remove aliens, to subject them to supervision with conditions when released from detention, or to incarcerate them where appropriate for violation of those conditions."

Justice Kennedy wrote a dissenting opinion joined by Chief Justice Rehnquist and joined in part by Justices Scalia and Thomas.

Constitutionality of Other Forms of Preventive Detention–Detention of Aliens During Removal Proceedings: Demore v. Kim

In the following case, the Court considered the constitutionality of detaining a deportable alien during the pendency of removal proceedings. In doing so, the Court distinguishes *Zadvydas, supra,* much to the chagrin of the dissenters.

DEMORE v. HYUNG JOON KIM

Supreme Court of the United States, 2003.
123 S.Ct. 1708.

CHIEF JUSTICE REHNQUIST **delivered the opinion of the Court**

Section 236(c) of the Immigration and Nationality Act, 66 Stat. 200, as amended, 110 Stat. 3009–585, 8 U.S.C. § 1226(c), provides that "the Attorney General shall take into custody any alien who" is removable from this country because he has been convicted of one of a specified set of crimes. Respondent is a citizen of the Republic of South Korea. He entered the United States in 1984, at the age of six, and became a lawful permanent resident of the United States two years later. In July 1996, he was convicted of first-degree burglary in state court in California and, in April 1997, he was convicted of a second crime, "petty theft with priors." The Immigration and Naturalization Service (INS) charged respondent with being deportable from the United States in light of these convictions, and detained him pending his removal hearing. We hold that Congress, justifiably concerned that deportable criminal aliens who are not detained continue to engage in crime and fail to appear for their removal hearings in large numbers, may require that persons such as respondent be detained for the brief period necessary for their removal proceedings.

Respondent does not dispute the validity of his prior convictions, which were obtained following the full procedural protections our criminal justice system offers. Respondent also did not dispute the INS' conclusion that he is subject to mandatory detention under § 1226(c). In conceding that he was deportable, respondent forwent a hearing at which he would have been entitled to raise any nonfrivolous argument available to demonstrate that he was not properly included in a mandatory detention category. Respondent instead filed a habeas corpus action pursuant to 28 U.S.C. § 2241 in the United States District Court for the Northern District of California challenging the constitutionality of § 1226(c) itself. He argued that his detention

under § 1226(c) violated due process because the INS had made no determination that he posed either a danger to society or a flight risk.

The District Court agreed with respondent that § 1226(c)'s requirement of mandatory detention for certain criminal aliens was unconstitutional. The District Court therefore granted respondent's petition subject to the INS' prompt undertaking of an individualized bond hearing to determine whether respondent posed either a flight risk or a danger to the community. Following that decision, the District Director of the INS released respondent on $5,000 bond.

The Court of Appeals for the Ninth Circuit affirmed. That court held that § 1226(c) violates substantive due process as applied to respondent because he is a permanent resident alien. It noted that permanent resident aliens constitute the most favored category of aliens and that they have the right to reside permanently in the United States, to work here, and to apply for citizenship. The court recognized and rejected the Government's two principal justifications for mandatory detention under § 1226(c): (1) ensuring the presence of criminal aliens at their removal proceedings; and (2) protecting the public from dangerous criminal aliens. The Court of Appeals discounted the first justification because it found that not all aliens detained pursuant to § 1226(c) would ultimately be deported. And it discounted the second justification on the grounds that the aggravated felony classification triggering respondent's detention included crimes that the court did not consider "egregious" or otherwise sufficiently dangerous to the public to necessitate mandatory detention. Respondent's crimes of first-degree burglary (burglary of an inhabited dwelling) and petty theft, for instance, the Ninth Circuit dismissed as "rather ordinary crimes." Relying upon our recent decision in Zadvydas v. Davis, 533 U.S. 678 (2001), the Court of Appeals concluded that the INS had not provided a justification "for no-bail civil detention sufficient to overcome a lawful permanent resident alien's liberty interest."

Three other Courts of Appeals have reached the same conclusion. The Seventh Circuit, however, rejected a constitutional challenge to § 1226(c) by a permanent resident alien. We granted certiorari to resolve this conflict, see 536 U.S. 956 (2002), and now reverse.

I

[The Court determined that it had jurisdiction to review a constitutional challenge to the detention statute.]

II

Having determined that the federal courts have jurisdiction to review a constitutional challenge to § 1226(c), we proceed to review respondent's claim. Section 1226(c) mandates detention during removal proceedings for a limited class of deportable aliens—including those convicted of an aggravated felony. Congress adopted this provision against a backdrop of wholesale failure by the INS to deal with increasing rates of criminal activity by aliens. Criminal aliens were the fastest growing segment of the federal prison population, already constituting roughly 25% of all federal

prisoners, and they formed a rapidly rising share of state prison populations as well. Congress' investigations showed, however, that the INS could not even *identify* most deportable aliens, much less locate them and remove them from the country. One study showed that, at the then-current rate of deportation, it would take 23 years to remove every criminal alien already subject to deportation. Making matters worse, criminal aliens who were deported swiftly reentered the country illegally in great numbers.

The agency's near-total inability to remove deportable criminal aliens imposed more than a monetary cost on the Nation. First, as Congress explained, "aliens who enter or remain in the United States in violation of our law are effectively taking immigration opportunities that might otherwise be extended to others." S. Rep. No. 104–249, p. 7 (1996). Second, deportable criminal aliens who remained in the United States often committed more crimes before being removed. One 1986 study showed that, after criminal aliens were identified as deportable, 77% were arrested at least once more and 45%—nearly half—were arrested multiple times before their deportation proceedings even began.

Congress also had before it evidence that one of the major causes of the INS' failure to remove deportable criminal aliens was the agency's failure to detain those aliens during their deportation proceedings. The Attorney General at the time had broad discretion to conduct individualized bond hearings and to release criminal aliens from custody during their removal proceedings when those aliens were determined not to present an excessive flight risk or threat to society. Despite this discretion to conduct bond hearings, however, in practice the INS faced severe limitations on funding and detention space, which considerations affected its release determinations.

Once released, more than 20% of deportable criminal aliens failed to appear for their removal hearings. * * * [The information before Congress] strongly supports Congress' concern that, even with individualized screening, releasing deportable criminal aliens on bond would lead to an unacceptable rate of flight.

* * *

During the same period in which Congress was making incremental changes to the immigration laws, it was also considering wholesale reform of those laws. Some studies presented to Congress suggested that detention of criminal aliens during their removal proceedings might be the best way to ensure their successful removal from this country. See, *e.g.,* 1989 House Hearing 75; Inspection Report, App. 46; S. Rep. 104–48, at 32 ("Congress should consider requiring that all aggravated felons be detained pending deportation. Such a step may be necessary because of the high rate of no-shows for those criminal aliens released on bond"). It was following those Reports that Congress enacted 8 U.S.C. § 1226, requiring the Attorney General to detain a subset of deportable criminal aliens pending a determination of their removability.

"In the exercise of its broad power over naturalization and immigration, Congress regularly makes rules that would be unacceptable if applied to citizens." Mathews v. Diaz, 426 U.S. 67, 79–80 (1976). The dissent seeks to avoid this fundamental premise of immigration law by repeatedly referring to it as "dictum." The Court in *Mathews,* however, made the statement the dissent now seeks to avoid in reliance on clear precedent establishing that " 'any policy toward aliens is vitally and intricately interwoven with contemporaneous policies in regard to the conduct of foreign relations, the war power, and the maintenance of a republican form of government.' " And, since *Mathews,* this Court has firmly and repeatedly endorsed the proposition that Congress may make rules as to aliens that would be unacceptable if applied to citizens.

* * *

It is well established that the Fifth Amendment entitles aliens to due process of law in deportation proceedings. At the same time, however, this Court has recognized detention during deportation proceedings as a constitutionally valid aspect of the deportation process. As we said more than a century ago, deportation proceedings "would be vain if those accused could not be held in custody pending the inquiry into their true character." Wong Wing v. United States, 163 U.S. 228, 235 (1896).

In *Carlson v. Landon,* 342 U.S. 524 (1952), the Court considered a challenge to the detention of aliens who were deportable because of their participation in Communist activities. The detained aliens did not deny that they were members of the Communist Party or that they were therefore deportable. Instead, like respondent in the present case, they challenged their detention on the grounds that there had been no finding that they were unlikely to appear for their deportation proceedings when ordered to do so. Although the Attorney General ostensibly had discretion to release detained Communist aliens on bond, the INS had adopted a policy of refusing to grant bail to those aliens in light of what Justice Frankfurter viewed as the mistaken "conception that Congress had made [alien Communists] in effect unbailable." 342 U.S., at 559, 568 (dissenting opinion).

The Court rejected the aliens' claims that they were entitled to be released from detention if they did not pose a flight risk, explaining "detention is necessarily a part of this deportation procedure." The Court noted that Congress had chosen to make such aliens deportable based on its "understanding of [Communists'] attitude toward the use of force and violence . . . to accomplish their political aims." And it concluded that the INS could deny bail to the detainees "by reference to the legislative scheme" even without any finding of flight risk.

The dissent argues that, even though the aliens in *Carlson* were not flight risks, "individualized findings of dangerousness were made" as to each of the aliens. The dissent, again, is mistaken. The aliens in *Carlson* had *not* been found individually dangerous. The only evidence against them was their membership in the Communist Party and "a degree . . . of participation in Communist activities." 342 U.S., at 541. There was no "individualized finding" of likely future dangerousness as to any of the aliens and, in

at least one case, there was a specific finding of nondangerousness. The Court nonetheless concluded that the denial of bail was permissible "by reference to the legislative scheme to eradicate the evils of Communist activity."

In Reno v. Flores, 507 U.S. 292 (1993) the Court considered another due process challenge to detention during deportation proceedings. The due process challenge there was brought by a class of alien juveniles. The INS had arrested them and was holding them in custody pending their deportation hearings. The aliens challenged the agency's policy of releasing detained alien juveniles only into the care of their parents, legal guardians, or certain other adult relatives. The aliens argued that the policy improperly relied "upon a 'blanket' presumption of the unsuitability of custodians other than parents, close relatives, and guardians" to care for the detained juvenile aliens. In rejecting this argument, the Court emphasized that "reasonable presumptions and generic rules," even when made by the INS rather than Congress, are not necessarily impermissible exercises of Congress' traditional power to legislate with respect to aliens. Thus, as with the prior challenges to detention during deportation proceedings, the Court in *Flores* rejected the due process challenge and upheld the constitutionality of the detention.

Despite this Court's longstanding view that the Government may constitutionally detain deportable aliens during the limited period necessary for their removal proceedings, respondent argues that the narrow detention policy reflected in 8 U.S.C. § 1226(c) violates due process. Respondent, like the four Courts of Appeals that have held § 1226(c) to be unconstitutional, relies heavily upon our recent opinion in *Zadvydas v. Davis,* 533 U.S. 678 (2001).

In *Zadvydas*, the Court considered a due process challenge to detention of aliens under 8 U.S.C. § 1231, which governs detention following a final order of removal. Section 1231(a)(b) provides, among other things, that when an alien who has been ordered removed is not in fact removed during the 90–day statutory "removal period," that alien "may be detained beyond the removal period" in the discretion of the Attorney General. The Court in *Zadvydas* read § 1231 to authorize continued detention of an alien following the 90–day removal period for only such time as is reasonably necessary to secure the alien's removal.

But *Zadvydas* is materially different from the present case in two respects.

First, in *Zadvydas*, the aliens challenging their detention following final orders of deportation were ones for whom removal was "no longer practically attainable." The Court thus held that the detention there did not serve its purported immigration purpose. In so holding, the Court rejected the Government's claim that, by detaining the aliens involved, it could prevent them from fleeing prior to their removal. The Court observed that where, as there, "detention's goal is no longer practically attainable, detention no longer bears a reasonable relation to the purpose for which the individual was committed."

In the present case, the statutory provision at issue governs detention of deportable criminal aliens *pending their removal proceedings*. Such detention necessarily serves the purpose of preventing deportable criminal aliens from fleeing prior to or during their removal proceedings, thus increasing the chance that, if ordered removed, the aliens will be successfully removed. Respondent disagrees, arguing that there is no evidence that mandatory detention is necessary because the Government has never shown that individualized bond hearings would be ineffective. But as discussed above, in adopting § 1226(c), Congress had before it evidence suggesting that permitting discretionary release of aliens pending their removal hearings would lead to large numbers of deportable criminal aliens skipping their hearings and remaining at large in the United States unlawfully.

Respondent argues that these statistics are irrelevant and do not demonstrate that individualized bond hearings "are ineffective or burdensome." It is of course true that when Congress enacted § 1226, individualized bail determinations had not been tested under optimal conditions, or tested in all their possible permutations. But when the Government deals with deportable aliens, the Due Process Clause does not require it to employ the least burdensome means to accomplish its goal. The evidence Congress had before it certainly supports the approach it selected even if other, hypothetical studies might have suggested different courses of action. Cf. *Flores*, 507 U.S., at 315 ("It may well be that other policies would be even better, but we are not a legislature charged with formulating public policy").

Zadvydas is materially different from the present case in a second respect as well. While the period of detention at issue in *Zadvydas* was "indefinite" and "potentially permanent," the detention here is of a much shorter duration.

Zadvydas distinguished the statutory provision it was there considering from § 1226 on these very grounds, noting that "post-removal-period detention, *unlike detention pending a determination of removability* . . . , has no obvious termination point." (emphasis added). Under 1226(c), not only does detention have a definite termination point, in the majority of cases it lasts for less than the 90 days we considered presumptively valid in *Zadvydas*. The Executive Office for Immigration Review has calculated that, in 85% of the cases in which aliens are detained pursuant to § 1226(c), removal proceedings are completed in an average time of 47 days and a median of 30 days. Brief for Petitioners 39–40. In the remaining 15% of cases, in which the alien appeals the decision of the Immigration Judge to the Board of Immigration Appeals, appeal takes an average of four months, with a median time that is slightly shorter.

These statistics do not include the many cases in which removal proceedings are completed while the alien is still serving time for the underlying conviction. In those cases, the aliens involved are never subjected to mandatory detention at all. In sum, the detention at stake under § 1226(c) lasts roughly a month and a half in the vast majority of cases in which it is invoked, and about five months in the minority of cases in which the alien chooses to appeal. Respondent was detained for somewhat longer than the average—spending six months in INS custody prior to the District Court's order granting habeas relief, but respondent himself had requested a continuance of his removal hearing.

For the reasons set forth above, respondent's claim must fail. Detention during removal proceedings is a constitutionally permissible part of that process. See, *e.g.*, *Wong Wing*, 163 U.S., at 235 ("We think it clear that detention, or temporary confinement, as part of the means necessary to give effect to the provisions for the exclusion or expulsion of aliens would be valid"). The INS detention of respondent, a criminal alien who has conceded that he is deportable, for the limited period of his removal proceedings, is governed by these cases. The judgment of the Court of Appeals is

Reversed.

JUSTICE KENNEDY, concurring

While the justification for 8 U.S.C. § 1226(c) is based upon the Government's concerns over the risks of flight and danger to the community, the ultimate purpose behind the detention is premised upon the alien's deportability. As a consequence, due process requires individualized procedures to ensure there is at least some merit to the Immigration and Naturalization Service's (INS) charge and, therefore, sufficient justification to detain a lawful permanent resident alien pending a more formal hearing. If the Government cannot satisfy this minimal, threshold burden, then the permissibility of continued detention pending deportation proceedings turns solely upon the alien's ability to satisfy the ordinary bond procedures—namely, whether if released the alien would pose a risk of flight or a danger to the community.

As the Court notes, these procedures were apparently available to respondent in this case. Respondent was entitled to a hearing in which he could have "raised any nonfrivolous argument available to demonstrate that he was not properly included in a mandatory detention category." Had he prevailed in such a proceeding, the Immigration Judge then would have had to determine if respondent "could be considered ... for release under the general bond provisions" of § 1226(a). Respondent, however, did not seek relief under these procedures, and the Court had no occasion here to determine their adequacy.

For similar reasons, since the Due Process Clause prohibits arbitrary deprivations of liberty, a lawful permanent resident alien such as respondent could be entitled to an individualized determination as to his risk of flight and dangerousness if the continued detention became unreasonable or unjustified. *Zadvydas*, 533 U.S., at 684–686. Were there to be an unreasonable delay by the INS in pursuing and completing deportation proceedings, it could become necessary then to inquire whether the detention is not to facilitate deportation, or to protect against risk of flight or dangerousness, but to incarcerate for other reasons. That is not a proper inference, however, either from the statutory scheme itself or from the circumstances of this case. The Court's careful opinion is consistent with these premises, and I join it in full.

[Justice O'Connor, joined by Justices Scalia and Thomas, wrote a separate opinion contending that the Court had no jurisdiction over the case. She agreed, however, with the Court's resolution of the challenge on the merits.]

JUSTICE SOUTER, **with whom JUSTICE STEVENS and JUSTICE GINSBURG join, concurring in part and dissenting in part.**

Respondent Kim is an alien lawfully admitted to permanent residence in the United States. He claims that the Constitution forbids the Immigration and Naturalization Service (INS) from detaining him under 8 U.S.C. § 1226(c) unless his detention serves a government interest, such as preventing flight or danger to the community. He contends that due process affords him a right to a hearing before an impartial official, giving him a chance to show that he poses no risk that would justify confining him between the moment the Government claims he is removable and the adjudication of the Government's claim.

I join Part I of the Court's opinion, which upholds federal jurisdiction in this case, but I dissent from the Court's disposition on the merits. The Court's holding that the Constitution permits the Government to lock up a lawful permanent resident of this country when there is concededly no reason to do so forgets over a century of precedent acknowledging the rights of permanent residents, including the basic liberty from physical confinement lying at the heart of due process.

The INS has never argued that detaining Kim is necessary to guarantee his appearance for removal proceedings or to protect anyone from danger in the meantime. Instead, shortly after the District Court issued its order in this case, the INS, *sua sponte* and without even holding a custody hearing, concluded that Kim "would not be considered a threat" and that any risk of flight could be met by a bond of $5,000. He was released soon thereafter, and there is no indication that he is not complying with the terms of his release.

The Court's approval of lengthy mandatory detention can therefore claim no justification in national emergency or any risk posed by Kim particularly. The Court's judgment is unjustified by past cases or current facts, and I respectfully dissent.

I

* * *

[Justice Souter contests the majority's assertion that Kim had conceded his removability.]

II

A

It has been settled for over a century that all aliens within our territory are "persons" entitled to the protection of the Due Process Clause. Aliens "residing in the United States for a shorter or longer time, are entitled, so long as they are permitted by the government of the United States to remain in the country, to the safeguards of the Constitution, and to the protection of the laws, in regard to their rights of person and of property, and to their civil and criminal responsibili-

ty." Fong Yue Ting v. United States, 149 U.S. 698, 724 (1893). * * *

The constitutional protection of an alien's person and property is particularly strong in the case of aliens lawfully admitted to permanent residence (LPRs). The immigration laws give LPRs the opportunity to establish a life permanently in this country by developing economic, familial, and social ties indistinguishable from those of a citizen. In fact, the law of the United States goes out of its way to encourage just such attachments by creating immigration preferences for those with a citizen as a close relation, and those with valuable professional skills or other assets promising benefits to the United States.

Once they are admitted to permanent residence, LPRs share in the economic freedom enjoyed by citizens: they may compete for most jobs in the private and public sectors without obtaining job-specific authorization, and apart from the franchise, jury duty, and certain forms of public assistance, their lives are generally indistinguishable from those of United States citizens. That goes for obligations as well as opportunities. Unlike temporary, nonimmigrant aliens, who are generally taxed only on income from domestic sources or connected with a domestic business, LPRs, like citizens, are taxed on their worldwide income. Male LPRs between the ages of 18 and 26 must register under the Selective Service Act of 1948. "Resident aliens, like citizens, pay taxes, support the economy, serve in the Armed Forces, and contribute in myriad other ways to our society." In re Griffiths, 413 U.S. 717, 722 (1973). And if they choose, they may apply for full membership in the national polity through naturalization . . * * *

The law therefore considers an LPR to be at home in the United States, and even when the Government seeks removal, we have accorded LPRs greater protections than other aliens under the Due Process Clause. In *Landon v. Plasencia,* 459 U.S. 21 (1982), we held that a long-term resident who left the country for a brief period and was placed in exclusion proceedings upon return was entitled to claim greater procedural protections under that Clause than aliens seeking initial entry. The LPR's interest in remaining in the United States is, we said, "without question, a weighty one." *Id.*, at 34.

Although LPRs remain subject to the federal removal power, that power may not be exercised without due process, and any decision about the requirements of due process for an LPR must account for the difficulty of distinguishing in practical as well as doctrinal terms between the liberty interest of an LPR and that of a citizen. (This case provides no occasion to determine the constitutionality of mandatory detention of aliens other than LPRs.) In evaluating Kim's challenge to his mandatory detention under 8 U.S.C. § 1226(c), the only reasonable starting point is the traditional doctrine concerning the Government's physical confinement of individuals.

B

Kim's claim is a limited one: not that the Government may not detain LPRs to ensure their appearance at removal hearings, but that due process under the Fifth Amendment conditions a potentially lengthy detention on a hearing and an impartial decisionmaker's finding that detention is necessary to a governmental purpose. He thus invokes our repeated decisions that the claim of liberty protected by the Fifth Amendment is at its strongest when government seeks to detain an individual. THE CHIEF JUSTICE wrote in 1987 that "in our society liberty is the norm, and detention prior to trial or without trial is the carefully limited exception." United States v. Salerno, 481 U.S. 739, 755. See also Foucha v. Louisiana, 504 U.S. 71, 80 (1992) ("Freedom from bodily restraint has always been at the core of the liberty protected by the Due Process Clause from arbitrary governmental action").

* * * In deciding in *Salerno* that this principle did not categorically bar pretrial detention of criminal defendants without bail under the Bail Reform Act of 1984, it was crucial that the statute provided that, "in a full-blown adversary hearing, the Government must convince a neutral decisionmaker by clear and convincing evidence that no conditions of release can reasonably assure the safety of the community or any person." We stressed that the Act was not a "scattershot attempt to incapacitate those who are merely suspected of" serious offenses, and held that due process allowed some pretrial detention because the Act confined it to a sphere of real need: "when the Government proves by clear and convincing evidence that an arrestee presents an identified and articulable threat to an individual or the community."

We have reviewed involuntary civil commitment statutes the same way. In Addington v. Texas, 441

U.S. 418 (1979), we held that a State could not civilly commit the mentally ill without showing by "clear and convincing evidence" that the person was dangerous to others. The elevated burden of proof was demanded because "loss of liberty calls for a showing that the individual suffers from something more serious than is demonstrated by idiosyncratic behavior." The statutory deficiency was the same in *Foucha*, where we held that Louisiana's civil commitment statute failed due process because the individual was denied an "adversary hearing at which the State must prove by clear and convincing evidence that he is demonstrably dangerous to the community." 504 U.S., at 81.

In addition to requiring a compelling reason for detention, we held that the class of persons affected must be narrow and, in pretrial-type lockup, the time must be no more than what is reasonably necessary before the merits can be resolved. In the case of the Bail Reform Act, we placed weight on the fact that the statute applied only to defendants suspected of "the most serious of crimes," *Salerno, supra*, at 747, while the statute in Kansas v. Hendricks, 521 U.S. 346 (1997), likewise provided only for confinement of "a limited subclass of dangerous persons" who had committed " 'a sexually violent offense' " and who suffered from "a mental abnormality or personality disorder" portending "predatory acts of sexual violence." *Salerno* relied on the restriction of detention "by the stringent time limitations of the Speedy Trial Act," 481 U.S., at 747, whereas in *Foucha*, it was a fault that the statute did not impose any

comparable limitation, 504 U.S., at 82 (citing *Salerno*).

The substantive demands of due process necessarily go hand in hand with the procedural, and the cases insist at the least on an opportunity for a detainee to challenge the reason claimed for committing him. *E. g.*, *Hendricks, supra*, at 357 (stating that civil commitment was permitted where "the confinement takes place pursuant to proper procedures and evidentiary standards"); *Foucha, supra*, at 81–82 (invalidating a statute under which "the State need prove nothing to justify continued detention"); *Salerno, supra*, at 751 ("The procedures by which a judicial officer evaluates the likelihood of future dangerousness are specifically designed to further the accuracy of that determination").

These cases yield a simple distillate that should govern the result here. Due process calls for an individual determination before someone is locked away. In none of the cases cited did we ever suggest that the government could avoid the Due Process Clause by doing what § 1226(c) does, by selecting a class of people for confinement on a categorical basis and denying members of that class any chance to dispute the necessity of putting them away. The cases, of course, would mean nothing if citizens and comparable residents could be shorn of due process by this sort of categorical sleight of hand. Without any "full-blown adversary hearing" before detention, *Salerno, supra*, at 750, or heightened burden of proof, *Addington, supra*, or other procedures to show the government's interest in committing an individual, *Foucha, supra*, procedural rights would amount to nothing but mechanisms for testing group membership. And if procedure could be dispensed with so expediently, so presumably could the substantive requirements that the class of detainees be narrow and the detention period strictly limited.

C

We held as much just two Terms ago in Zadvydas v. Davis, 533 U.S. 678 (2001), which stands for the proposition that detaining an alien requires more than the rationality of a general detention statute; any justification must go to the alien himself. *Zadvydas* considered detention of two aliens, Zadvydas and Ma, who had already been ordered removed and therefore enjoyed no lawful immigration status. Their cases arose because actual removal appeared unlikely owing to the refusal of their native countries to accept them, with the result that they had been detained not only for the standard 90–day removal period, during which time most removal orders are executed, but beyond that period because the INS considered them to be a " 'risk to the community' " and " 'unlikely to comply with the order of removal.' " Zadvydas and Ma challenged their continued and potentially indefinite detention under the Due Process Clause of the Fifth Amendment.

* * *

* * * [W]e began by positing commonly accepted substantive standards and proceeded to enquire into any "special justification" that might outweigh the aliens' powerful interest in avoiding physical confinement "under [individually ordered] release conditions that may

not be violated." We found nothing to justify the Government's position. The statute was not narrowed to a particularly dangerous class of aliens, but rather affected "aliens ordered removed for many and various reasons, including tourist visa violations." The detention itself was not subject to "stringent time limitations," *Salerno*, 481 U.S., at 747, but was potentially indefinite or even permanent, *Zadvydas*, 533 U.S., at 691. Finally, although both Zadvydas and Ma appeared to be dangerous, this conclusion was undermined by defects in the procedures resulting in the finding of dangerousness. The upshot was such serious doubt about the constitutionality of the detention statute that we construed it as authorizing continuing detention only when an alien's removal was "reasonably foreseeable." In the cases of Zadvydas and Ma, the fact that their countries of citizenship were not willing to accept their return weighed against the Government's interest in keeping them at hand for instant removal, * * * and we remanded the cases to the Courts of Appeals for a determination of the sufficiency of the Government's interests in Zadvydas's and Ma's individual detention.

Our individualized analysis and disposition in *Zadvydas* support Kim's claim for an individualized review of his challenge to the reasons that are supposed to justify confining him prior to any determination of removability. In fact, aliens in removal proceedings have an additional interest in avoiding confinement, beyond anything considered in *Zadvydas:* detention prior to entry of a removal order may well impede the alien's ability to develop and present his case on the very issue of removability. After all, our recognition that the serious penalty of removal must be justified on a heightened standard of proof, Woodby v. INS, 385 U.S. 276 (1966), will not mean all that much when the INS can detain, transfer, and isolate aliens away from their lawyers, witnesses, and evidence. Kim's right to defend against removal gives him an even stronger claim than the aliens in *Zadvydas* could raise.

* * *

D

In sum, due process requires a "special justification" for physical detention that "outweighs the individual's constitutionally protected interest in avoiding physical restraint" as well as "adequate procedural protections." *Zadvydas*, 533 U.S., at 690–691. There must be a sufficiently compelling governmental interest to justify such an action, usually a punitive interest in imprisoning the convicted criminal or a regulatory interest in forestalling danger to the community. The class of persons subject to confinement must be commensurately narrow and the duration of confinement limited accordingly. * * * Finally, procedural due process requires, at a minimum, that a detainee have the benefit of an impartial decisionmaker able to consider particular circumstances on the issue of necessity.

By these standards, Kim's case is an easy one. Heightened, substantive due process scrutiny uncovers serious infirmities in § 1226(c). Detention is not limited to dangerous criminal aliens or those found likely to flee, but applies to all aliens claimed to be deportable for criminal convictions, even where the underlying offenses are minor. *E. g.*, Michel v. INS, 206 F.3d 253, 256 (C.A.2 2000) (possession of stolen bus transfers); Matter of Bart, 20 I. & N. Dec. 436 (BIA 1992) (issuance of a bad check). Detention under § 1226(c) is not limited by the kind of time limit imposed by the Speedy Trial Act, and while it lasts only as long as the removal proceedings, those proceedings have no deadline and may last over a year. Section 1226(c) neither requires nor permits an official to determine whether Kim's detention was necessary to prevent flight or danger.

Kim's detention without particular justification in these respects, or the opportunity to enquire into it, violates both components of due process, and I would accordingly affirm the judgment of the Court of Appeals requiring the INS to hold a bail hearing to see whether detention is needed to avoid a risk of flight or a danger to the community. This is surely little enough, given the fact that 8 U.S.C. § 1536 gives an LPR charged with being a foreign terrorist the right to a release hearing pending a determination that he be removed.

III

[Part III of Justice Souter's lengthy dissent attacks the majority's distinguishing of *Zadvydas* and reliance upon Carlson v. Landon and Reno v. Flores, among other things.]

IV

This case is not about the National Government's undisputed power to detain aliens in order to avoid flight or prevent danger to the community. The issue is whether that power may be exercised by detaining a still lawful permanent resident alien when there is no reason for it and no way to challenge it. The Court's holding that the Due Process Clause allows this under a blanket rule is devoid of even ostensible justification in fact and at odds with the settled standard of liberty. I respectfully dissent.

JUSTICE BREYER, concurring in part and dissenting in part.

I agree with the majority that the courts have jurisdiction, and I join Part I of its opinion. If I believed (as the majority apparently believes) that Kim had conceded that he is deportable, then I would conclude that the Government could detain him without bail for the few weeks ordinarily necessary for formal entry of a removal order. Time limits of the kind set forth in Zadvydas v. Davis, 533 U.S. 678 (2001), should govern these and longer periods of detention, for an alien's concession that he is deportable seems to me the rough equivalent of the entry of an order of removal.

This case, however, is not one in which an alien concedes deportability.* * * That being so—as long as Kim's legal arguments are neither insubstantial nor interposed solely for purposes of delay—then the immigration statutes, interpreted in light of the Constitution, permit Kim (if neither dangerous nor a flight risk) to obtain bail. For one thing, Kim's constitutional claims to bail in these circumstances are strong. * * *For another, the relevant statutes literally say nothing about an individual who, armed with a strong argument against deportability, might, or might not, fall within their terms. * * * Finally, bail standards drawn from the criminal justice system are available to fill this statutory gap. Federal law makes bail available to a criminal defendant after conviction and pending appeal provided (1) the appeal is "not for the purpose of delay," (2) the appeal "raises a substantial question of law or fact," and (3) the defendant shows by "clear and convincing evidence" that, if released, he "is not likely to flee or pose a danger to the safety" of the community. 18 U.S.C. § 3143(b). These standards give considerable weight to any special governmental interest in detention (*e.g.*, process-related concerns or class-related flight risks). * * * Nothing in the statute forbids their use when § 1226(c) deportability is in doubt.

I would interpret the (silent) statute as imposing these bail standards. So interpreted, the statute would require the Government to permit a detained alien to seek an individualized assessment of flight risk and dangerousness as long as the alien's claim that he is not deportable is (1) not interposed solely for purposes of delay and (2) raises a question of "law or fact" that is not insubstantial. And that interpretation, in my view, is consistent with what the Constitution demands. I would remand this case to the Ninth Circuit to determine whether Kim has raised such a claim.

With respect, I dissent from the Court's contrary disposition.

Chapter Eight

DISCOVERY

IV. THE PROSECUTOR'S CONSTITUTIONAL DUTY TO DISCLOSE

B. APPLYING THE *BRADY* RULE

Page 945. In the section entitled *Brady and Guilty Pleas,* add the following:

In United States v. Ruiz, 536 U.S. 622 (2002), the Court held that during guilty plea negotiations the government is not required to disclose information that could impeach government witnesses, or information that could be used by the defendant on an affirmative defense. Ruiz was offered a deal whereby she would waive the right to disclosure of any information that could be used to impeach government witnesses or for any affirmative defenses she might have; however, the agreement acknowledged the government's continuing obligation to disclose "information establishing the factual innocence of the defendant." The lower court had held that a defendant pleading guilty has a constitutional right to disclosure of materially exculpatory impeachment information as well as information the defendant could use to prove affirmative defenses, and that a plea agreement requiring waiver of these rights could not be voluntary. But the Court, in an opinion by Justice Breyer, unanimously rejected the lower court's reasoning.

Justice Breyer noted that "impeachment information is special in relation to the *fairness of a trial,* not in respect to whether a plea is *voluntary.*" He stated that the Constitution "permits a court to accept a guilty plea, with its accompanying waiver of various constitutional rights, despite various forms of misapprehension under which a defendant might labor." [See Chapter Nine for the cases discussing knowing and voluntary waiver of guilty pleas.] Justice Breyer expressed concern that requiring disclosure of impeachment information during guilty plea negotiations "could seriously interfere with the Government's interest in securing those guilty pleas that are factually justified, desired by defendants, and help to secure the efficient administration of justice." Specifically, early disclosure of impeachment evidence "could disrupt ongoing investigations and expose prospective witnesses to serious harm."

As to required disclosure of impeachment evidence, Justice Breyer concluded that it

> could force the Government to abandon its general practice of not disclosing to a defendant pleading guilty information that would reveal the identities of cooperating informants, undercover investigators, or other prospective witnesses. It could require the Government to devote substantially more resources to trial preparation prior to plea bargaining, thereby depriving the plea-bargaining process of its main resource-saving advantages. Or it could lead the Government instead to abandon its heavy reliance upon plea bargaining in a vast number—90% or more—of federal criminal cases. We cannot say that the Constitution's due process requirement demands so radical a change in the criminal justice process in order to achieve so comparatively small a constitutional benefit.

As to required disclosure of information bearing on an affirmative defense, the Court concluded as follows:

> We do not believe the Constitution here requires provision of this information to the defendant prior to plea bargaining—for most (though not all) of the reasons previously stated. That is to say, in the context of this agreement, the need for this information is more closely related to the *fairness* of a trial than to the *voluntariness* of the plea; the value in terms of the defendant's added awareness of relevant circumstances is ordinarily limited; yet the added burden imposed upon the Government by requiring its provision well in advance of trial (often before trial preparation begins) can be serious, thereby significantly interfering with the administration of the plea bargaining process.

It should be noted that *Ruiz* could be read narrowly as dealing only with the enforceability of a provision under which the defendant waives his right to disclosure of information bearing on impeachment of government witnesses and affirmative defenses. In other words, the case could be looked at as holding that there is a right to this information, but that the right can be waived by the defendant. Thus, a guilty plea might still be invalid, *in the absence of a waiver clause*, if the government has failed to disclose information concerning impeachment or affirmative defenses. Obviously, the government now has an incentive to include such waiver provisions as boilerplate in its plea agreements.

Another point of limitation on the *Ruiz* holding is that the Court recognized the government's duty to disclose information bearing on the defendant's "factual innocence" during guilty plea negotiations, as well as a continuing duty to disclose such information throughout the plea proceedings. Indeed, the government recognized this obligation by including it in the plea agreement in *Ruiz*.

Chapter Nine

GUILTY PLEAS AND PLEA BARGAINING

C. VOLUNTARY AND INTELLIGENT PLEAS AND THE ADVANTAGES OF A COMPLETE RECORD

1. A Voluntary Plea

Page 977. At the end of the section, add the following:

Can the Defendant Voluntarily Waive the Right to Disclosure of Information That Could Be Used To Impeach Government Witnesses or for Affirmative Defenses? United States v. Ruiz

In the following case, the Court adhered to its position that the free market principles behind plea bargaining generally permit criminal defendants to knowingly and voluntarily waive rights that could be invoked at trial.

UNITED STATES v. RUIZ

Supreme Court of the United States, 2002.
536 U.S. 622.

JUSTICE BREYER delivered the opinion of the Court.

In this case we primarily consider whether the Fifth and Sixth Amendments require federal prosecutors, before entering into a binding plea agreement with a criminal defendant, to disclose "impeachment information relating to any informants or other witnesses." We hold that the Constitution does not require that disclosure.

I

After immigration agents found 30 kilograms of marijuana in Angela Ruiz's luggage, federal prosecutors offered her what is known in the Southern District of California as a "fast track" plea bargain. That bargain—standard in that district—asks a defendant to waive indictment, trial, and an appeal. In return, the Government agrees to recommend to the sentencing judge a two-level departure downward from the otherwise applicable United States Sen-

201

tencing Guidelines sentence. In Ruiz's case, a two-level departure downward would have shortened the ordinary Guidelines-specified 18–to–24–month sentencing range by 6 months, to 12–to–18 months.

The prosecutors' proposed plea agreement contains a set of detailed terms. Among other things, it specifies that "any [known] information establishing the factual innocence of the defendant" "has been turned over to the defendant," and it acknowledges the Government's "continuing duty to provide such information." At the same time it requires that the defendant "waiv[e] the right" to receive "impeachment information relating to any informants or other witnesses" as well as the right to receive information supporting any affirmative defense the defendant raises if the case goes to trial. Because Ruiz would not agree to this last-mentioned waiver, the prosecutors withdrew their bargaining offer. The Government then indicted Ruiz for unlawful drug possession. And despite the absence of any agreement, Ruiz ultimately pleaded guilty.

At sentencing, Ruiz asked the judge to grant her the same two-level downward departure that the Government would have recommended had she accepted the "fast track" agreement. The Government opposed her request, and the District Court denied it, imposing a standard Guideline sentence instead.

* * * Ruiz appealed her sentence to the United States Court of Appeals for the Ninth Circuit. The Ninth Circuit vacated the District Court's sentencing determination. The Ninth Circuit pointed out that the Constitution requires prosecu-

tors to make certain impeachment information available to a defendant before trial. It decided that this obligation entitles defendants to receive that same information before they enter into a plea agreement. The Ninth Circuit also decided that the Constitution prohibits defendants from waiving their right to that information. And it held that the prosecutors' standard "fast track" plea agreement was unlawful because it insisted upon that waiver. The Ninth Circuit remanded the case so that the District Court could decide any related factual disputes and determine an appropriate remedy.

The Government sought certiorari. It stressed what it considered serious adverse practical implications of the Ninth Circuit's constitutional holding. And it added that the holding is unique among courts of appeals. We granted the Government's petition.

II

* * *

III

The constitutional question concerns a federal criminal defendant's waiver of the right to receive from prosecutors exculpatory impeachment material—a right that the Constitution provides as part of its basic "fair trial" guarantee. See * * * Brady v. Maryland, 373 U.S. 83, 87 (1963) * * * Giglio v. United States, 405 U.S. 150, 154 (1972) (exculpatory evidence includes "evidence affecting" witness "credibility," where the witness' "reliability" is likely "determinative of guilt or innocence").

When a defendant pleads guilty he or she, of course, forgoes not only a fair trial, but also other accompanying constitutional guarantees. Boykin v. Alabama, 395 U.S. 238, 243 (1969) (pleading guilty implicates the Fifth Amendment privilege against self-incrimination, the Sixth Amendment right to confront one's accusers, and the Sixth Amendment right to trial by jury). Given the seriousness of the matter, the Constitution insists, among other things, that the defendant enter a guilty plea that is "voluntary" and that the defendant must make related waivers "knowing[ly], intelligent[ly], [and] with sufficient awareness of the relevant circumstances and likely consequences." Brady v. United States, 397 U.S. 742, 748 (1970); see also *Boykin, supra,* at 242.

In this case, the Ninth Circuit in effect held that a guilty plea is not "voluntary" (and that the defendant could not, by pleading guilty, waive his right to a fair trial) unless the prosecutors first made the same disclosure of material impeachment information that the prosecutors would have had to make had the defendant insisted upon a trial. We must decide whether the Constitution requires that preguilty plea disclosure of impeachment information. We conclude that it does not.

First, impeachment information is special in relation to the *fairness of a trial,* not in respect to whether a plea is *voluntary* ("knowing," "intelligent," and "sufficient[ly] aware"). Of course, the more information the defendant has, the more aware he is of the likely consequences of a plea, waiver, or decision, and the wiser that decision will likely be. But the Constitution does not require the prosecutor to share all useful information with the defendant. Weatherford v. Bursey, 429 U.S. 545, 559 (1977) ("There is no general constitutional right to discovery in a criminal case"). And the law ordinarily considers a waiver knowing, intelligent, and sufficiently aware if the defendant fully understands the nature of the right and how it would likely apply *in general* in the circumstances—even though the defendant may not know the *specific detailed* consequences of invoking it. A defendant, for example, may waive his right to remain silent, his right to a jury trial, or his right to counsel even if the defendant does not know the specific questions the authorities intend to ask, who will likely serve on the jury, or the particular lawyer the State might otherwise provide. Cf. Colorado v. Spring, 479 U.S. 564, 573–575 (1987) (Fifth Amendment privilege against self-incrimination waived when defendant received standard *Miranda* warnings regarding the nature of the right but not told the specific interrogation questions to be asked).

It is particularly difficult to characterize impeachment information as critical information of which the defendant must always be aware prior to pleading guilty given the random way in which such information may, or may not, help a particular defendant. The degree of help that impeachment information can provide will depend upon the defendant's own independent knowledge of the prosecution's potential case—a matter that the Constitution does not require prosecutors to disclose.

Second, we have found no legal authority embodied either in this Court's past cases or in cases from other circuits that provide significant support for the Ninth Circuit's decision. To the contrary, this Court has found that the Constitution, in respect to a defendant's awareness of relevant circumstances, does not require complete knowledge of the relevant circumstances, but permits a court to accept a guilty plea, with its accompanying waiver of various constitutional rights, despite various forms of misapprehension under which a defendant might labor. See Brady v. United States, 397 U.S., at 757 (defendant "misapprehended the quality of the State's case"); *ibid.* (defendant misapprehended "the likely penalties"); *ibid.* (defendant failed to "anticipate a change in the law regarding" relevant "punishments"); McMann v. Richardson, 397 U.S. 759, 770 (1970) (counsel "misjudged the admissibility" of a "confession"); United States v. Broce, 488 U.S. 563, 573 (1989) (counsel failed to point out a potential defense); Tollett v. Henderson, 411 U.S. 258, 267 (1973) (counsel failed to find a potential constitutional infirmity in grand jury proceedings). It is difficult to distinguish, in terms of importance, (1) a defendant's ignorance of grounds for impeachment of potential witnesses at a possible future trial from (2) the varying forms of ignorance at issue in these cases.

Third, due process considerations, the very considerations that led this Court to find trial-related rights to exculpatory and impeachment information in *Brady* and *Giglio*, argue against the existence of the "right" that the Ninth Circuit found here. This Court has said that due process considerations include not only (1) the nature of the private interest at stake, but also (2) the value of the additional safeguard, and (3) the adverse impact of the requirement upon the Government's interests. Ake v. Oklahoma, 470 U.S. 68, 77 (1985). Here, as we have just pointed out, the added value of the Ninth Circuit's "right" to a defendant is often limited, for it depends upon the defendant's independent awareness of the details of the Government's case. And in any case, as the proposed plea agreement at issue here specifies, the Government will provide "any information establishing the factual innocence of the defendant" regardless. That fact, along with other guilty-plea safeguards, see Fed. Rule Crim. Proc. 11, diminishes the force of Ruiz's concern that, in the absence of impeachment information, innocent individuals, accused of crimes, will plead guilty. Cf. McCarthy v. United States, 394 U.S. 459, 465–467 (1969) (discussing Rule 11's role in protecting a defendant's constitutional rights).

At the same time, a constitutional obligation to provide impeachment information during plea bargaining, prior to entry of a guilty plea, could seriously interfere with the Government's interest in securing those guilty pleas that are factually justified, desired by defendants, and help to secure the efficient administration of justice. The Ninth Circuit's rule risks premature disclosure of Government witness information, which, the Government tells us, could "disrupt ongoing investigations" and expose prospective witnesses to serious harm. Cf. Amendments to Federal Rules of Criminal Procedure: Hearings before the Subcommittee on Criminal Justice of the House Committee on the Judiciary, 94th Cong., 1st Sess., 92 (1975) (statement of John C. Keney, Acting Assistant Attorney General, Criminal Div., Dept. of Justice) (opposing mandated witness disclosure three days before trial because of documented instances of witness intimidation). And the careful tailoring that characterizes most legal Government witness disclosure requirements suggests recognition by both Congress and the Federal Rules Committees that such concerns are valid. See, *e.g.*, 18 U.S.C. § 3432 (witness list disclosure required in capital cases three days before trial with exceptions); § 3500 (Government witness statements ordinarily subject to discovery only after testimony given); Fed. Rule Crim. Proc. 16(a)(2) (embodies limitations of 18 U.S.C. § 3500).

Consequently, the Ninth Circuit's requirement could force the Government to abandon its "general practice" of not "disclos[ing] to a defendant pleading guilty information that would reveal the identities of cooperating informants, undercover investigators, or other prospective witnesses." It could require the Government to devote substantially more resources to trial preparation prior to plea bargaining, thereby depriving the plea-bargaining process of its main resource-saving advantages. Or it could lead the Government instead to abandon its heavy reliance upon plea bargaining in a vast number—90% or more—of federal criminal cases. We cannot say that the Constitution's

due process requirement demands so radical a change in the criminal justice process in order to achieve so comparatively small a constitutional benefit.

These considerations, taken together, lead us to conclude that the Constitution does not require the Government to disclose material impeachment evidence prior to entering a plea agreement with a criminal defendant.

In addition, we note that the "fast track" plea agreement requires a defendant to waive her right to receive information the Government has regarding any "affirmative defense" she raises at trial. We do not believe the Constitution here requires provision of this information to the defendant prior to plea bargaining—for most (though not all) of the reasons previously stated. That is to say, in the context of this agreement, the need for this information is more closely related to the *fairness* of a trial than to the *voluntariness* of the plea; the value in terms of the defendant's added awareness of relevant circumstances is ordinarily limited; yet the added burden imposed upon the Government by requiring its provision well in advance of trial (often before trial preparation begins) can be serious, thereby significantly interfering with the administration of the plea bargaining process.

For these reasons the decision of the Court of Appeals for the Ninth Circuit is

Reversed.

JUSTICE THOMAS, concurring in the judgment.

I agree with the Court that the Constitution does not require the

Government to disclose either affirmative defense information or impeachment information relating to informants or other witnesses before entering into a binding plea agreement with a criminal defendant. The Court, however, suggests that the constitutional analysis turns in some part on the "degree of help" such information would provide to the defendant at the plea stage, a distinction that is neither necessary nor accurate. To the extent that the Court is implicitly drawing a line based on a flawed characterization about the usefulness of certain types of information, I can only concur in the judgment. The principle supporting *Brady* was "avoidance of an unfair trial to the accused." *Brady v. Maryland,* 373 U.S. 83, 87 (1963). That concern is not implicated at the plea stage regardless.

II. THE REQUIREMENTS FOR A VALID GUILTY PLEA

D. REGULATING GUILTY PLEAS UNDER FEDERAL RULE 11

Page 986.   **Add the following at the end of the section:**

3. *Harmless Error and Plain Error*

Fed.R.Crim.P. 11(h) provides that any error under Rule 11 "that does not affect substantial rights shall be disregarded." This is the classic definition of harmless error that is also found in Fed.R.Crim.P. 52(a). But what if the defendant does not object to an error under Rule 11? Should the same harmless error standard apply as if he did? With respect to trial errors, Rule 52(b) provides that a defendant who fails to object has the burden of showing "plain error" that affected substantial rights. [See the discussion of plain error in Chapter 13 of the Casebook]. But Rule 11(h) does not include a plain-error provision comparable to Rule 52(b).

The Court in United States v. Vonn, 535 U.S. 55 (2002), held that a defendant who does not object to an error under Rule 11 has the burden of showing "plain error." Justice Souter wrote for eight Justices. Justice Souter was not persuaded that there was any intent in including a plain error provision in Rule 52 but not in Rule 11. He found that the contrary view would create an anomalous result, in that a defendant would be able to stand by and do nothing to correct an obvious Rule 11 error, and would lose nothing in doing so. The Court reasoned that Rule 52(b) implicitly applied to Rule 11 errors, and declared that the policy of the plain error rule is sound: "the value of finality requires defense counsel to be on his toes, not just the judge, and the defendant who just sits there when a mistake can be fixed cannot just sit there when he speaks up later on." Justice Stevens dissented from the Court's holding on plain error.

The *Vonn* Court also held, unanimously, that in assessing whether a Rule 11 error affected the defendant's substantial rights, a reviewing court may look at information outside the record of the plea proceeding.

In this case, the defendant was not told at his plea hearing that by pleading guilty, he would be giving up the right to assistance of counsel at trial. He did not raise this Rule 11 error until he appealed the conviction resulting from his guilty plea. Transcripts indicated that Vonn was informed of his right to trial counsel at his initial appearance before the magistrate and at his first arraignment. The Court remanded for the lower court to determine whether, in light of this extra information, Vonn could meet his burden of showing plain error in the failure to inform him of his right to trial counsel at the plea hearing.

Chapter Ten

TRIAL AND TRIAL–RELATED RIGHTS

I. THE RIGHT TO A SPEEDY TRIAL

E. BEYOND THE CONSTITUTION: STATUTORY AND JUDICIAL TIME LIMITS

Page 1025. Add immediately before F:

Ex Post Facto Limitations

In Stogner v. California, 123 S.Ct. 2446 (2003), Justice Breyer wrote for a 5–4 majority as it held that a law enacted after expiration of a previously applicable limitations period violates the Ex Post Facto Clause, Art I, § 10, cl. 1, of the Constitution. The Court invalidated a 1993 California statute permitting prosecution of child abuse crimes where the limitations period had expired provided that (1) a victim reported an allegation of abuse to the police, (2) there is clear and convincing independent evidence, and (3) the prosecution is begun within one year of the report. The majority relied upon Calder v. Bull, 3 U.S. (3 Dall.) 386 (1798), reasoning that the statute of limitations is an amnesty which may not be arbitrarily disregarded by a legislature. The majority concluded that the statute "aggravated" Stogner's alleged crime "in the sense that, and to the extent that, it 'inflicted punishment' for past criminal conduct that (when the new law was enacted) did not trigger any such liability." Moreover, "to resurrect a prosecution after the relevant statute of limitations has expired is to eliminate a currently existing conclusive presumption forbidding prosecution, and thereby to permit conviction on a quantum of evidence where that quantum, at the time the new law is enacted, would have been legally insufficient." The majority noted that its decision did not effect extensions of unexpired statutes of limitations which some courts have upheld.

Justice Kennedy wrote a dissenting opinion, joined by the Chief Justice, Justice Scalia and Justice Thomas. The dissenters argued that there is no satisfactory rationale for distinguishing between reviving an expired statute of limitations and extending an unexpired statute, since in neither case does a crime become more serious and it is doubtful that "criminals keep calendars so they can mark they day to discard their records or to place a gloating phone call to the victim."

III. CONSTITUTIONALLY BASED PROOF REQUIREMENTS

C. THE SCOPE OF THE REASONABLE DOUBT REQUIREMENT

Page 1061. After *Jones*, add the following:

In the following case, the Court extended *Jones*, limited *McMillan* to its facts, and established a broad principle that prohibits the state and federal governments from using sentence enhancements to increase a sentence beyond the statutory maximum.

APPRENDI v. NEW JERSEY

Supreme Court of the United States, 2000.
530 U.S. 466.

JUSTICE STEVENS **delivered the opinion of the Court.**

A New Jersey statute classifies the possession of a firearm for an unlawful purpose as a "second-degree" offense. N. J. Stat. Ann. § 2C:39–4(a) (West 1995). Such an offense is punishable by imprisonment for "between five years and 10 years." § 2C:43–6(a)(2). A separate statute, described by that State's Supreme Court as a "hate crime" law, provides for an "extended term" of imprisonment if the trial judge finds, by a preponderance of the evidence, that "[t]he defendant in committing the crime acted with a purpose to intimidate an individual or group of individuals because of race, color, gender, handicap, religion, sexual orientation or ethnicity." N. J. Stat. Ann. § 2C:44–3(e) (West Supp. 2000). The extended term authorized by the hate crime law for second-degree offenses is imprisonment for "between 10 and 20 years." § 2C:43–7(a)(3).

The question presented is whether the Due Process Clause of the Fourteenth Amendment requires that a factual determination authorizing an increase in the maximum prison sentence for an offense from 10 to 20 years be made by a jury on the basis of proof beyond a reasonable doubt.

I

At 2:04 a.m. on December 22, 1994, petitioner Charles C. Apprendi, Jr., fired several .22–caliber bullets into the home of an African–American family that had recently moved into a previously all-white neighborhood in Vineland, New Jersey. Apprendi was promptly arrested and, at 3:05 a.m., admitted that he was the shooter. After further questioning, at 6:04 a.m., he made a statement—which he later retracted—that even though he did not know the occupants of the house personally, "because they are black in color he does not want them in the neighborhood."

A New Jersey grand jury returned a 23–count indictment charging Apprendi with four first-degree, eight second-degree, six third-degree, and five fourth-degree offenses. The charges alleged shootings on four different dates, as well as the unlawful possession of various weapons. None of the counts referred to the hate crime statute, and none alleged that Apprendi acted with a racially biased purpose.

The parties entered into a plea agreement, pursuant to which Apprendi pleaded guilty to two counts (3 and 18) of second-degree possession of a firearm for an unlawful purpose, N. J. Stat. Ann. § 2C:39–4a (West 1995), and one count (22) of the third-degree offense of unlawful possession of an antipersonnel bomb, § 2C:39–3a; the prosecutor dismissed the other 20 counts. Under state law, a second-degree offense carries a penalty range of 5 to 10 years, § 2C:43–6(a)(2); a third-degree offense carries a penalty range of between 3 and 5 years, § 2C:43–6(a)(3). As part of the plea agreement, however, the State reserved the right to request the court to impose a higher "enhanced" sentence on count 18 (which was based on the December 22 shooting) on the ground that that offense was committed with a biased purpose, as described in § 2C:44–3(e). Apprendi, correspondingly, reserved the right to challenge the hate crime sentence enhancement on the ground that it violates the United States Constitution.

At the plea hearing, the trial judge heard sufficient evidence to establish Apprendi's guilt on counts 3, 18, and 22; the judge then confirmed that Apprendi understood the maximum sentences that could be imposed on those counts. Because the plea agreement provided that the sentence on the sole third-degree offense (count 22) would run concurrently with the other sentences, the potential sentences on the two second-degree counts were critical. If the judge found no basis for the biased purpose enhancement, the maximum consecutive sentences on those counts would amount to 20 years in aggregate; if, however, the judge enhanced the sentence on count 18, the maximum on that count alone would be 20 years and the maximum for the two counts in aggregate would be 30 years, with a 15–year period of parole ineligibility.

After the trial judge accepted the three guilty pleas, the prosecutor filed a formal motion for an extended term. The trial judge thereafter held an evidentiary hearing on the issue of Apprendi's "purpose" for the shooting on December 22. Apprendi adduced evidence from a psychologist and from seven character witnesses who testified that he did not have a reputation for racial bias. He also took the stand himself, explaining that the incident was an unintended consequence of overindulgence in alcohol, denying that he was in any way biased against African–Americans, and denying that his statement to the police had been accurately described. The judge, however, found the police officer's testimony credible, and concluded that the evidence supported a finding "that the crime was motivated by racial bias.". Having found "by a preponderance of the evidence" that Apprendi's actions were taken "with a purpose to intimidate" as provided by the statute, the trial judge held that the hate crime enhancement applied. Rejecting Apprendi's constitutional challenge to the statute, the judge sentenced him to a 12–year term of imprisonment on count 18, and to shorter concurrent sentences on the other two counts.

Apprendi appealed, arguing, inter alia, that the Due Process Clause of the United States Constitution requires that the finding of bias upon which his hate crime sentence was based must be proved to a jury beyond a reasonable doubt, In re Winship, 397 U.S. 358 (1970). Over dissent, the Appellate Division of the Superior Court of New Jersey upheld the enhanced sentence. Relying on our decision in McMillan v. Pennsylvania, 477 U.S. 79 (1986), the appeals court found that the state legislature decided to make the hate crime enhancement a"sentencing factor," rather than an element of an underlying offense—and that decision was within the State's established power to define the elements of its crimes. The hate crime statute did not create a presumption of guilt, the court determined, and did not appear "tailored to permit the . . . finding to be a tail which wags the dog of the substantive offense." Characterizing the required finding as one of "motive," the court described it as a traditional"sentencing factor," one not considered an "essential element" of any crime unless the legislature so provides.

A divided New Jersey Supreme Court affirmed. The court began by explaining that while due process only requires the State to prove the "elements" of an offense beyond a reasonable doubt, the mere fact that a state legislature has placed a criminal component

"within the sentencing provisions" of the criminal code "does not mean that the finding of a biased purpose to intimidate is not an essential element of the offense." "Were that the case," the court continued, "the Legislature could just as easily allow judges, not juries, to determine if a kidnapping victim has been released unharmed." Neither could the constitutional question be settled simply by defining the hate crime statute's "purpose to intimidate" as "motive" and thereby excluding the provision from any traditional conception of an "element" of a crime. Even if one could characterize the language this way—and the court doubted that such a characterization was accurate—proof of motive did not ordinarily "increase the penal consequences to an actor." Such "[l]abels," the court concluded, would not yield an answer to Apprendi's constitutional question.

While noting that we had just last year expressed serious doubt concerning the constitutionality of allowing penalty-enhancing findings to be determined by a judge by a preponderance of the evidence, Jones v. United States, 526 U.S. 227 (1999), the court concluded that those doubts were not essential to our holding. Turning then, as the appeals court had, to *McMillan*, as well as to Almendarez–Torres v. United States, 523 U.S. 224 (1998), the court undertook a multifactor inquiry and then held that the hate crime provision was valid. In the majority's view, the statute did not allow impermissible burden shifting, and did not "create a separate offense calling for a separate penalty." Rather, "the Legislature simply took one factor that has always been considered by sentencing courts to bear on punishment and dictated the weight to be given that factor.'' As had the appeals court, the majority recognized that the state statute was unlike that in *McMillan* inasmuch as it increased the maximum penalty to which a defendant could be subject. But it was not clear that this difference alone would "change the constitutional calculus," especially where, as here, "there is rarely any doubt whether the defendants committed the crimes with the purpose of intimidating the victim on the basis of race or ethnicity."

The dissent rejected this conclusion, believing instead that the case turned on two critical characteristics: (1) "a defendant's mental state in committing the subject offense . . . necessarily involves a finding so integral to the charged offense that it must be characterized as an element thereof"; and (2) "the significantly increased sentencing range triggered by . . . the finding of a purpose to intimidate" means that the purpose "must be treated as a material element [that] must be found by a jury beyond a reasonable doubt." In the dissent's view, the facts increasing sentences in both *Almendarez-Torres* (recidivism) and *Jones* (serious bodily injury) were quite distinct from New Jersey's required finding of purpose here; the latter finding turns directly on the conduct of the defendant during the crime and defines a level of culpability necessary to form the hate crime offense. While acknowledging "analytical tensions" in this Court's post-*Winship* jurisprudence, the dissenters concluded that "there can be little doubt that the

sentencing factor applied to this defendant—the purpose to intimidate a victim because of race—must fairly be regarded as an element of the crime requiring inclusion in the indictment and proof beyond a reasonable doubt."

We granted certiorari, and now reverse.

II

It is appropriate to begin by explaining why certain aspects of the case are not relevant to the narrow issue that we must resolve. First, the State has argued that even without the trial judge's finding of racial bias, the judge could have imposed consecutive sentences on counts 3 and 18 that would have produced the 12–year term of imprisonment that Apprendi received; Apprendi's actual sentence was thus within the range authorized by statute for the three offenses to which he pleaded guilty. The constitutional question, however, is whether the 12–year sentence imposed on count 18 was permissible, given that it was above the 10–year maximum for the offense charged in that count. The finding is legally significant because it increased—indeed, it doubled—the maximum range within which the judge could exercise his discretion, converting what otherwise was a maximum 10–year sentence on that count into a minimum sentence. The sentences on counts 3 and 22 have no more relevance to our disposition than the dismissal of the remaining 18 counts.

Second, although the constitutionality of basing an enhanced sentence on racial bias was argued in the New Jersey courts, that issue was not raised here. The substantive basis for New Jersey's enhancement is thus not at issue; the adequacy of New Jersey's procedure is. The strength of the state interests that are served by the hate crime legislation has no more bearing on this procedural question than the strength of the interests served by other provisions of the criminal code.

Third, we reject the suggestion by the State Supreme Court that "there is rarely any doubt" concerning the existence of the biased purpose that will support an enhanced sentence. In this very case, that issue was the subject of the full evidentiary hearing we described. We assume that both the purpose of the offender, and even the known identity of the victim, will sometimes be hotly disputed, and that the outcome may well depend in some cases on the standard of proof and the identity of the factfinder.

Fourth, because there is no ambiguity in New Jersey's statutory scheme, this case does not raise any question concerning the State's power to manipulate the prosecutor's burden of proof by, for example, relying on a presumption rather than evidence to establish an element of an offense, cf. Mullaney v. Wilbur, 421 U.S. 684 (1975); or by placing the affirmative defense label on "at least some elements" of traditional crimes, Patterson v. New York, 432 U.S. 197, 210 (1977). The prosecutor did not invoke any presumption to buttress the evidence of racial bias and did not claim that Apprendi had the burden of disproving an improper motive. The question whether Apprendi had a constitutional right to have a jury find such bias on the basis of proof beyond a reasonable doubt is starkly presented.

Our answer to that question was foreshadowed by our opinion in Jones v. United States, 526 U.S. 227 (1999), construing a federal statute. We there noted that "under the Due Process Clause of the Fifth Amendment and the notice and jury trial guarantees of the Sixth Amendment, any fact (other than prior conviction) that increases the maximum penalty for a crime must be charged in an indictment, submitted to a jury, and proven beyond a reasonable doubt." The Fourteenth Amendment commands the same answer in this case involving a state statute.

III

In his 1881 lecture on the criminal law, Oliver Wendell Holmes, Jr., observed: "The law threatens certain pains if you do certain things, intending thereby to give you a new motive for not doing them. If you persist in doing them, it has to inflict the pains in order that its threats may continue to be believed." New Jersey threatened Apprendi with certain pains if he unlawfully possessed a weapon and with additional pains if he selected his victims with a purpose to intimidate them because of their race. As a matter of simple justice, it seems obvious that the procedural safeguards designed to protect Apprendi from unwarranted pains should apply equally to the two acts that New Jersey has singled out for punishment. Merely using the label "sentence enhancement" to describe the latter surely does not provide a principled basis for treating them differently.

At stake in this case are constitutional protections of surpassing importance: the proscription of any deprivation of liberty without "due process of law," Amdt. 14, and the guarantee that "[i]n all criminal prosecutions, the accused shall enjoy the right to a speedy and public trial, by an impartial jury," Amdt. 6. Taken together, these rights indisputably entitle a criminal defendant to "a jury determination that [he] is guilty of every element of the crime with which he is charged, beyond a reasonable doubt." United States v. Gaudin, 515 U.S. 506, 510 (1995); see also Sullivan v. Louisiana, 508 U.S. 275, 278 (1993); *Winship*, 397 U.S., at 364 ("[T]he Due Process Clause protects the accused against conviction except upon proof beyond a reasonable doubt of every fact necessary to constitute the crime with which he is charged").

As we have, unanimously, explained, *Gaudin,* 515 U.S., at 510–511, the historical foundation for our recognition of these principles extends down centuries into the common law. "[T]o guard against a spirit of oppression and tyranny on the part of rulers," and "as the great bulwark of [our] civil and political liberties," 2 J. Story, Commentaries on the Constitution of the United States 540–541 (4th ed. 1873), trial by jury has been understood to require that "the truth of every accusation, whether preferred in the shape of indictment, information, or appeal, should afterwards be confirmed by the unanimous suffrage of twelve of [the defendant's] equals and neighbours...." 4 W. Blackstone, Commentaries on the Laws of England 343 (1769) (hereinafter Blackstone) (emphasis add-

ed). See also Duncan v. Louisiana, 391 U.S. 145 (1968).

Equally well founded is the companion right to have the jury verdict based on proof beyond a reasonable doubt. "The demand for a higher degree of persuasion in criminal cases was recurrently expressed from ancient times, [though] its crystallization into the formula 'beyond a reasonable doubt' seems to have occurred as late as 1798. It is now accepted in common law jurisdictions as the measure of persuasion by which the prosecution must convince the trier of all the essential elements of guilt." C. McCormick, Evidence § 321, pp. 681–682 (1954).

Any possible distinction between an "element" of a felony offense and a "sentencing factor" was unknown to the practice of criminal indictment, trial by jury, and judgment by court as it existed during the years surrounding our Nation's founding. As a general rule, criminal proceedings were submitted to a jury after being initiated by an indictment containing "all the facts and circumstances which constitute the offence, ... stated with such certainty and precision, that the defendant ... may be enabled to determine the species of offence they constitute, in order that he may prepare his defence accordingly ... and that there may be no doubt as to the judgment which should be given, if the defendant be convicted." J. Archbold, Pleading and Evidence in Criminal Cases 44 (15th ed. 1862). The defendant's ability to predict with certainty the judgment from the face of the felony indictment flowed from the invariable linkage of punishment with crime.

Thus, with respect to the criminal law of felonious conduct, "the English trial judge of the later eighteenth century had very little explicit discretion in sentencing. The substantive criminal law tended to be sanction-specific; it prescribed a particular sentence for each offense. The judge was meant simply to impose that sentence (unless he thought in the circumstances that the sentence was so inappropriate that he should invoke the pardon process to commute it)." As Blackstone, among many others, has made clear, "[t]he judgment, though pronounced or awarded by the judges, is not their determination or sentence, but the determination and sentence of the law." 3 Blackstone 396.

* * *

We should be clear that nothing in this history suggests that it is impermissible for judges to exercise discretion—taking into consideration various factors relating both to offense and offender—in imposing a judgment within the range prescribed by statute. We have often noted that judges in this country have long exercised discretion of this nature in imposing sentence within statutory limits in the individual case. See, e.g., Williams v. New York, 337 U.S. 241, 246 (1949) ("[B]oth before and since the American colonies became a nation, courts in this country and in England practiced a policy under which a sentencing judge could exercise a wide discretion in the sources and types of evidence used to assist him in determining the kind and extent of punishment to be imposed within limits fixed by law"). As in *Williams*, our periodic recognition of judges' broad discretion in sen-

tencing—since the 19th-century shift in this country from statutes providing fixed-term sentences to those providing judges discretion within a permissible range, has been regularly accompanied by the qualification that that discretion was bound by the range of sentencing options prescribed by the legislature.

The historic link between verdict and judgment and the consistent limitation on judges' discretion to operate within the limits of the legal penalties provided highlight the novelty of a legislative scheme that removes the jury from the determination of a fact that, if found, exposes the criminal defendant to a penalty exceeding the maximum he would receive if punished according to the facts reflected in the jury verdict alone.

We do not suggest that trial practices cannot change in the course of centuries and still remain true to the principles that emerged from the Framers' fears "that the jury right could be lost not only by gross denial, but by erosion." But practice must at least adhere to the basic principles undergirding the requirements of trying to a jury all facts necessary to constitute a statutory offense, and proving those facts beyond reasonable doubt. As we made clear in *Winship*, the "reasonable doubt" requirement "has a vital role in our criminal procedure for cogent reasons." 397 U.S., at 363. Prosecution subjects the criminal defendant both to "the possibility that he may lose his liberty upon conviction and . . . the certainty that he would be stigmatized by the conviction." We thus require this, among other, procedural protections in order to "provid[e] concrete substance for the presumption of innocence," and to reduce the risk of imposing such deprivations erroneously. If a defendant faces punishment beyond that provided by statute when an offense is committed under certain circumstances but not others, it is obvious that both the loss of liberty and the stigma attaching to the offense are heightened; it necessarily follows that the defendant should not—at the moment the State is put to proof of those circumstances—be deprived of protections that have, until that point, unquestionably attached.

Since *Winship*, we have made clear beyond peradventure that *Winship's* due process and associated jury protections extend, to some degree, "to determinations that [go] not to a defendant's guilt or innocence, but simply to the length of his sentence." This was a primary lesson of Mullaney v. Wilbur, 421 U.S. 684 (1975), in which we invalidated a Maine statute that presumed that a defendant who acted with an intent to kill possessed the "malice aforethought" necessary to constitute the State's murder offense (and therefore, was subject to that crime's associated punishment of life imprisonment). The statute placed the burden on the defendant of proving, in rebutting the statutory presumption, that he acted with a lesser degree of culpability, such as in the heat of passion, to win a reduction in the offense from murder to manslaughter (and thus a reduction of the maximum punishment of 20 years).

The State had posited in *Mullaney* that requiring a defendant to prove heat-of-passion intent to overcome a presumption of murderous intent did not implicate *Winship* protections because, upon conviction of either offense, the defendant would lose his liberty and face societal stigma just the same. Rejecting this argument, we acknowledged that criminal law "is concerned not only with guilt or innocence in the abstract, but also with the degree of criminal culpability" assessed. Because the "consequences" of a guilty verdict for murder and for manslaughter differed substantially, we dismissed the possibility that a State could circumvent the protections of *Winship* merely by "redefin[ing] the elements that constitute different crimes, characterizing them as factors that bear solely on the extent of punishment."

IV

It was in McMillan v. Pennsylvania, 477 U.S. 79 (1986), that this Court, for the first time, coined the term "sentencing factor" to refer to a fact that was not found by a jury but that could affect the sentence imposed by the judge. That case involved a challenge to the State's Mandatory Minimum Sentencing Act. According to its provisions, anyone convicted of certain felonies would be subject to a mandatory minimum penalty of five years imprisonment if the judge found, by a preponderance of the evidence, that the person "visibly possessed a firearm" in the course of committing one of the specified felonies. Articulating for the first time, and then applying, a multifactor set of criteria for determining whether the *Winship* protections applied to bar such a system, we concluded that the Pennsylvania statute did not run afoul of our previous admonitions against relieving the State of its burden of proving guilt, or tailoring the mere form of a criminal statute solely to avoid *Winship's* strictures.

We did not, however, there budge from the position that (1) constitutional limits exist to States' authority to define away facts necessary to constitute a criminal offense, and (2) that a state scheme that keeps from the jury facts that "expos[e] [defendants] to greater or additional punishment," may raise serious constitutional concern. As we explained:

> Section 9712 neither alters the maximum penalty for the crime committed nor creates a separate offense calling for a separate penalty; it operates solely to limit the sentencing Court's discretion in selecting a penalty within the range already available to it without the special finding of visible possession of a firearm.... The statute gives no impression of having been tailored to permit the visible possession finding to be a tail which wags the dog of the substantive offense. Petitioners' claim that visible possession under the Pennsylvania statute is "really" an element of the offenses for which they are being punished—that Pennsylvania has in effect defined a new set of upgraded felonies—would have at least more superficial appeal if a finding of visible possession exposed them to greater or additional punishment, cf. 18 U.S.C.

§ 2113(d) (providing separate and greater punishment for bank robberies accomplished through "use of a dangerous weapon or device"), but it does not.[1]

Finally, as we made plain in *Jones* last Term, Almendarez–Torres v. United States, 523 U.S. 224 (1998), represents at best an exceptional departure from the historic practice that we have described. In that case, we considered a federal grand jury indictment, which charged the petitioner with "having been found in the United States ... after being deported," "in violation of 8 U.S.C. § 1326(a)—an offense carrying a maximum sentence of two years." Almendarez–Torres pleaded guilty to the indictment, admitting at the plea hearing that he had been deported, that he had unlawfully reentered this country, and that "the earlier deportation had taken place pursuant to three earlier convictions for aggravated felonies." The Government then filed a presentence report indicating that Almendarez–Torres' offense fell within the bounds of § 1326(b) because, as specified in that provision, his original deportation had been subsequent to an aggravated felony conviction; accordingly, Almendarez–Torres could be subject to a sentence of up to 20 years. Almendarez–Torres objected, contending that because the indictment "had not mentioned his earlier aggravated felony convictions," he could be sentenced to no more than two years in prison.

---

1. The principal dissent accuses us of today "overruling *McMillan*." We do not overrule *McMillan*. We limit its holding to cases that do not involve the imposition of a sentence more severe than the statutory maximum for the offense established by the jury's verdict—a limitation identified in the

McMillan opinion itself. Conscious of the likelihood that legislative decisions may have been made in reliance on *McMillan*, we reserve for another day the question whether *stare decisis* considerations preclude reconsideration of its narrower holding.

Rejecting Almendarez–Torres' objection, we concluded that sentencing him to a term higher than that attached to the offense alleged in the indictment did not violate the strictures of *Winship* in that case. Because Almendarez–Torres had admitted the three earlier convictions for aggravated felonies—all of which had been entered pursuant to proceedings with substantial procedural safeguards of their own—no question concerning the right to a jury trial or the standard of proof that would apply to a contested issue of fact was before the Court. Although our conclusion in that case was based in part on our application of the criteria we had invoked in *McMillan*, the specific question decided concerned the sufficiency of the indictment. More important, as *Jones* made crystal clear, our conclusion in *Almendarez-Torres* turned heavily upon the fact that the additional sentence to which the defendant was subject was "the prior commission of a serious crime." 523 U.S., at 243 (explaining that "recidivism ... is a traditional, if not the most traditional, basis for a sentencing Court's increasing an offender's sentence"). Both the certainty that procedural safeguards attached to any "fact" of prior conviction, and the reality that Almendarez–Torres did not challenge the accuracy of that "fact" in his case, mitigated the due process and Sixth Amendment concerns otherwise implicated in allowing a judge to determine a "fact" increasing punishment beyond the maximum of the statutory range.

Even though it is arguable that *Almendarez-Torres* was incorrectly decided, and that a logical application of our reasoning today should apply if the recidivist issue were contested, Apprendi does not contest the decision's validity and we need not revisit it for purposes of our decision today to treat the case as a narrow exception to the general rule we recalled at the outset. Given its unique facts, it surely does not warrant rejection of the otherwise uniform course of decision during the entire history of our jurisprudence.

In sum, our reexamination of our cases in this area, and of the history upon which they rely, confirms the opinion that we expressed in *Jones*. Other than the fact of a prior conviction, any fact that increases the penalty for a crime beyond the prescribed statutory maximum must be submitted to a jury, and proved beyond a reasonable doubt. With that exception, we endorse the statement of the rule set forth in the concurring opinions in that case: "[I]t is unconstitutional for a legislature to remove from the jury the assessment of facts that increase the prescribed range of penalties to which a criminal defendant is exposed. It is equally clear that such facts must be established by proof beyond a reasonable doubt." 526 U.S., at 252–253 (opinion of Stevens, J.); see also id., at 253 (opinion of Scalia, J.).[2]

2. The principal dissent would reject the Court's rule as a "meaningless formalism," because it can conceive of hypothetical statutes that would comply with the rule and achieve the same result as the New Jersey statute. While a State could, hypothetically, undertake to revise its entire criminal code in the manner the dissent suggests—extending all statutory maximum sentences to, for example, 50 years and giving judges guided discretion as to a few specially selected factors within that range—this possibility seems remote. Among other reasons, structural democratic constraints exist to

V

The New Jersey statutory scheme that Apprendi asks us to invalidate allows a jury to convict a defendant of a second-degree offense based on its finding beyond a reasonable doubt that he unlawfully possessed a prohibited weapon; after a subsequent and separate proceeding, it then allows a judge to impose punishment identical to that New Jersey provides for crimes of the first degree, N. J. Stat. Ann. § 2C:43–6(a)(1) (West 1999), based upon the judge's finding, by a preponderance of the evidence, that the defendant's "purpose" for unlawfully possessing the weapon was "to intimidate" his victim on the basis of a particular characteristic the victim possessed. In light of the constitutional rule explained above, and all of the cases supporting it, this practice cannot stand.

New Jersey's defense of its hate crime enhancement statute has three primary components: (1) the required finding of biased purpose is not an "element" of a distinct hate crime offense, but rather the traditional "sentencing factor" of motive; (2) *McMillan* holds that the legislature can authorize a judge to find a traditional sentencing factor on the basis of a preponderance of the evidence; and (3) *Almendarez-Torres* extended *McMillan's* holding to encompass factors that authorize a judge to impose a sentence beyond the maximum provided by the substantive statute under which a defendant is charged. None of these persuades us that the constitutional rule that emerges from our history and case law should incorporate an exception for this New Jersey statute.

New Jersey's first point is nothing more than a disagreement with the rule we apply today. Beyond this, we do not see how the argument can succeed on its own terms. The state high court evinced substantial skepticism at the suggestion that the hate crime statute's "purpose to intimidate" was simply an inquiry

---

discourage legislatures from enacting penal statutes that expose every defendant convicted of, for example, weapons possession, to a maximum sentence exceeding that which is, in the legislature's judgment, generally proportional to the crime. This is as it should be. Our rule ensures that a State is obliged "to make its choices concerning the substantive content of its criminal laws with full awareness of the consequence, unable to mask substantive policy choices" of exposing all who are convicted to the maximum sentence it provides. Patterson v. New York, 432 U.S., at 228–229, n. 13 (Powell, J., dissenting). So exposed, "[t]he political check on potentially harsh legislative action is then more likely to operate." Ibid.

In all events, if such an extensive revision of the State's entire criminal code were enacted for the purpose the dissent suggests, or if New Jersey simply reversed the burden of the hate crime finding (effectively assuming a crime was performed with a purpose to intimidate and then requiring a defendant to prove that it was not), we would be required to question whether the revision was constitutional under this Court's prior decisions. See *Patterson*, 432 U.S., at 210; Mullaney v. Wilbur, 421 U.S. 684, 698–702. Finally, the principal dissent ignores the distinction the Court has often recognized, between facts in aggravation of punishment and facts in mitigation. If facts found by a jury support a guilty verdict of murder, the judge is authorized by that jury verdict to sentence the defendant to the maximum sentence provided by the murder statute. If the defendant can escape the statutory maximum by showing, for example, that he is a war veteran, then a judge that finds the fact of veteran status is neither exposing the defendant to a deprivation of liberty greater than that authorized by the verdict according to statute, nor is the Judge imposing upon the defendant a greater stigma than that accompanying the jury verdict alone. Core concerns animating the jury and burden-of-proof requirements are thus absent from such a scheme.

into "motive." We share that skepticism. The text of the statute requires the factfinder to determine whether the defendant possessed, at the time he committed the subject act, a "purpose to intimidate" on account of, inter alia, race. By its very terms, this statute mandates an examination of the defendant's state of mind—a concept known well to the criminal law as the defendant's mens rea. * * * The defendant's intent in committing a crime is perhaps as close as one might hope to come to a core criminal offense "element."

The foregoing notwithstanding, however, the New Jersey Supreme Court correctly recognized that it does not matter whether the required finding is characterized as one of intent or of motive, because "[l]abels do not afford an acceptable answer." That point applies as well to the constitutionally novel and elusive distinction between "elements" and "sentencing factors." Despite what appears to us the clear "elemental" nature of the factor here, the relevant inquiry is one not of form, but of effect—does the required finding expose the defendant to a greater punishment than that authorized by the jury's guilty verdict?[3]

* * *

The preceding discussion should make clear why the State's reliance on *McMillan* is likewise misplaced. * * * When a judge's finding based on a mere preponderance of the evidence authorizes an increase in the maximum punishment, it is appropriately characterized as "a tail which wags the dog of the substantive offense." *McMillan*, 477 U.S., at 88.

New Jersey would also point to the fact that the State did not, in placing the required biased purpose finding in a sentencing enhancement provision, create a "separate offense calling for a separate penalty." As for this, we agree wholeheartedly with the New Jersey Supreme Court that merely because the state legislature placed its hate crime sentence "enhancer" "within the sentencing provisions" of the criminal code "does not mean that the finding of a biased purpose to intimidate is not an essential element of the offense." Indeed, the fact that New Jersey, along with numerous other States, has also made precisely the same conduct the subject of an independent substantive offense makes it clear that the mere presence of this "enhancement" in a sentencing statute does not define its character.

New Jersey's reliance on *Almendarez-Torres* is also unavailing. The reasons supporting an exception from the general rule for the statute construed in that case do not apply to the New Jersey statute. Whereas recidivism "does not relate to the commission of the offense" itself,

---

3. This is not to suggest that the term "sentencing factor" is devoid of meaning. The term appropriately describes a circumstance, which may be either aggravating or mitigating in character, that supports a specific sentence within the range authorized by the jury's finding that the defendant is guilty of a particular offense. On the other hand, when the term "sentence enhancement" is used to describe an increase beyond the maximum authorized statutory sentence, it is the functional equivalent of an element of a greater offense than the one covered by the jury's guilty verdict. Indeed, it fits squarely within the usual definition of an "element" of the offense.

New Jersey's biased purpose inquiry goes precisely to what happened in the "commission of the offense." Moreover, there is a vast difference between accepting the validity of a prior judgment of conviction entered in a proceeding in which the defendant had the right to a jury trial and the right to require the prosecutor to prove guilt beyond a reasonable doubt, and allowing the judge to find the required fact under a lesser standard of proof.

* * *

The New Jersey procedure challenged in this case is an unacceptable departure from the jury tradition that is an indispensable part of our criminal justice system. Accordingly, the judgment of the Supreme Court of New Jersey is reversed, and the case is remanded for further proceedings not inconsistent with this opinion.

JUSTICE SCALIA, concurring.

I feel the need to say a few words in response to Justice Breyer's dissent. It sketches an admirably fair and efficient scheme of criminal justice designed for a society that is prepared to leave criminal justice to the State. (Judges, it is sometimes necessary to remind ourselves, are part of the State—and an increasingly bureaucratic part of it, at that.) The founders of the American Republic were not prepared to leave it to the State, which is why the jury-trial guarantee was one of the least controversial provisions of the Bill of Rights. It has never been efficient; but it has always been free.

As for fairness, which Justice Breyer believes "[i]n modern times," the jury cannot provide: I think it not unfair to tell a prospective felon that if he commits his contemplated crime he is exposing himself to a jail sentence of 30 years—and that if, upon conviction, he gets anything less than that he may thank the mercy of a tender-hearted judge (just as he may thank the mercy of a tenderhearted parole commission if he is let out inordinately early, or the mercy of a tenderhearted governor if his sentence is commuted). Will there be disparities? Of course. But the criminal will never get more punishment than he bargained for when he did the crime, and his guilt of the crime (and hence the length of the sentence to which he is exposed) will be determined beyond a reasonable doubt by the unanimous vote of 12 of his fellow citizens.

In Justice Breyer's bureaucratic realm of perfect equity, by contrast, the facts that determine the length of sentence to which the defendant is exposed will be determined to exist (on a more-likely-than-not basis) by a single employee of the State. It is certainly arguable (Justice Breyer argues it) that this sacrifice of prior protections is worth it. But it is not arguable that, just because one thinks it is a better system, it must be, or is even more likely to be, the system envisioned by a Constitution that guarantees trial by jury. What ultimately demolishes the case for the dissenters is that they are unable to say what the right to trial by jury does guarantee if, as they assert, it does not guarantee—what it has been assumed to guarantee throughout our history—the right to have a jury determine those facts that determine the maximum sentence the law allows. They provide no coherent alternative.

Justice Breyer proceeds on the erroneous and all-too-common assumption that the Constitution means what we think it ought to mean. It does not; it means what it says. And the guarantee that "[i]n all criminal prosecutions, the accused shall enjoy the right to ... trial, by an impartial jury" has no intelligible content unless it means that all the facts which must exist in order to subject the defendant to a legally prescribed punishment must be found by the jury.

JUSTICE THOMAS, **with whom JUS-TICE SCALIA joins as to Parts I and II, concurring.**

I join the opinion of the Court in full. I write separately to explain my view that the Constitution requires a broader rule than the Court adopts.

I

This case turns on the seemingly simple question of what constitutes a "crime." Under the Federal Constitution, "the accused" has the right (1) "to be informed of the nature and cause of the accusation" (that is, the basis on which he is accused of a crime), (2) to be "held to answer for a capital, or otherwise infamous crime" only on an indictment or presentment of a grand jury, and (3) to be tried by "an impartial jury of the State and district wherein the crime shall have been committed." Amdts. 5 and 6. See also Art. III, § 2, cl. 3 ("The Trial of all Crimes ... shall be by Jury"). With the exception of the Grand Jury Clause, see Hurtado v. California, 110 U.S. 516, 538 (1884), the Court has held that these protections apply in state prosecutions, Herring v. New York, 422 U.S. 853 (1975). Further, the Court has held that due process requires that the jury find beyond a reasonable doubt every fact necessary to constitute the crime. In re Winship, 397 U.S. 358, 364 (1970).

All of these constitutional protections turn on determining which facts constitute the "crime"—that is, which facts are the "elements" or "ingredients" of a crime. In order for an accusation of a crime (whether by indictment or some other form) to be proper under the common law, and thus proper under the codification of the common-law rights in the Fifth and Sixth Amendments, it must allege all elements of that crime; likewise, in order for a jury trial of a crime to be proper, all elements of the crime must be proved to the jury (and, under *Winship*, proved beyond a reasonable doubt).

Thus, it is critical to know which facts are elements. This question became more complicated following the Court's decision in McMillan v. Pennsylvania, 477 U.S. 79 (1986), which spawned a special sort of fact known as a sentencing enhancement. Such a fact increases a defendant's punishment but is not subject to the constitutional protections to which elements are subject. Justice O'Connor's dissent, in agreement with *McMillan* and Almendarez–Torres v. United States, 523 U.S. 224 (1998), takes the view that a legislature is free (within unspecified outer limits) to decree which facts are elements and which are sentencing enhancements.

Sentencing enhancements may be new creatures, but the question that they create for courts is not. Courts have long had to consider which facts are elements in order to determine the sufficiency of an accusation (usually an indictment). The answer that courts have provided regarding the accusation tells us what an element is, and it is then a simple matter to apply that answer to whatever constitutional right may be at issue in a case—here, *Winship* and the right to trial by jury. A long line of essentially uniform authority addressing accusations, and stretching from the earliest reported cases after the founding until well into the 20th century, establishes that the original understanding of which facts are elements was even broader than the rule that the Court adopts today.

This authority establishes that a "crime" includes every fact that is by law a basis for imposing or increasing punishment (in contrast with a fact that mitigates punishment). Thus, if the legislature defines some core crime and then provides for increasing the punishment of that crime upon a finding of some aggravating fact—of whatever sort, including the fact of a prior conviction—the core crime and the aggravating fact together constitute an aggravated crime, just as much as grand larceny is an aggravated form of petit larceny. The aggravating fact is an element of the aggravated crime. Similarly, if the legislature, rather than creating grades of crimes, has provided for setting the punishment of a crime based on some fact—such as a fine that is proportional to the value of stolen goods—that fact is also an element. No multi-factor parsing of statutes, of the sort that we have attempted since *McMillan*, is necessary. One need only look to the kind, degree, or range of punishment to which the prosecution is by law entitled

for a given set of facts. Each fact necessary for that entitlement is an element.

II

[Justice Thomas undertakes a long disquisition into the common-law cases interpreting the elements of a crime.]

Without belaboring the point any further, I simply note that this traditional understanding—that a "crime" includes every fact that is by law a basis for imposing or increasing punishment—continued well into the 20th century, at least until the middle of the century. In fact, it is fair to say that *McMillan* began a revolution in the law regarding the definition of "crime." Today's decision, far from being a sharp break with the past, marks nothing more than a return to the status quo ante—the status quo that reflected the original meaning of the Fifth and Sixth Amendments.

III

The consequence of the above discussion for our decisions in *Almendarez-Torres* and *McMillan* should be plain enough, but a few points merit special mention.

First, it is irrelevant to the question of which facts are elements that legislatures have allowed sentencing judges discretion in determining punishment (often within extremely broad ranges). * * * In other words, establishing what punishment is available by law and setting a specific punishment within the bounds that the law has prescribed are two different things. * * * Thus, it is one thing to consider what the Constitution requires the prosecution to do in order to entitle itself to a particular kind, degree, or range of punishment of the accused, and quite another to consider what constitutional constraints apply either to the imposition of punishment within the limits of that entitlement or to a legislature's ability to set broad ranges of punishment. In answering the former constitutional question, I need not, and do not, address the latter.

Second, and related, one of the chief errors of *Almendarez-Torres*— an error to which I succumbed— was to attempt to discern whether a particular fact is traditionally (or typically) a basis for a sentencing court to increase an offender's sentence. For the reasons I have given, it should be clear that this approach just defines away the real issue. What matters is the way by which a fact enters into the sentence. If a fact is by law the basis for imposing or increasing punishment—for establishing or increasing the prosecution's entitlement—it is an element. (To put the point differently, I am aware of no historical basis for treating as a nonelement a fact that by law sets or increases punishment.) When one considers the question from this perspective, it is evident why the fact of a prior conviction is an element under a recidivism statute. Indeed, cases addressing such statutes provide some of the best discussions of what constitutes an element of a crime. One reason frequently offered for treating recidivism differently, a reason on which we relied in *Almendarez-Torres*, is a concern for prejudicing the jury by informing it of the prior conviction. But this concern, of which earlier courts were well aware, does not make the traditional understanding of what an ele-

ment is any less applicable to the fact of a prior conviction.

Third, I think it clear that the common-law rule would cover the *McMillan* situation of a mandatory minimum sentence (in that case, for visible possession of a firearm during the commission of certain crimes). No doubt a defendant could, under such a scheme, find himself sentenced to the same term to which he could have been sentenced absent the mandatory minimum. The range for his underlying crime could be 0 to 10 years, with the mandatory minimum of 5 years, and he could be sentenced to 7. * * * But it is equally true that his expected punishment has increased as a result of the narrowed range and that the prosecution is empowered, by invoking the mandatory minimum, to require the judge to impose a higher punishment than he might wish. * * * Thus, the fact triggering the mandatory minimum is part of the punishment sought to be inflicted; it undoubtedly "enters into the punishment" so as to aggravate it, "ac[t] to which the law affixes . . . punishment."

* * *

For the foregoing reasons, as well as those given in the Court's opinion, I agree that the New Jersey procedure at issue is unconstitutional.

JUSTICE O'CONNOR, **with whom** THE CHIEF JUSTICE, JUSTICE KENNEDY, **and** JUSTICE BREYER **join, dissenting.**

Last Term, in Jones v. United States, 526 U.S. 227 (1999), this Court found that our prior cases suggested the following principle: "[U]nder the Due Process Clause of the Fifth Amendment and the notice and jury trial guarantees of the Sixth Amendment, any fact (other than prior conviction) that increases the maximum penalty for a crime must be charged in an indictment, submitted to a jury, and proven beyond a reasonable doubt.'' At the time, Justice Kennedy rightly criticized the Court for its failure to explain the origins, contours, or consequences of its purported constitutional principle; for the inconsistency of that principle with our prior cases; and for the serious doubt that the holding cast on sentencing systems employed by the Federal Government and States alike. Today, in what will surely be remembered as a watershed change in constitutional law, the Court imposes as a constitutional rule the principle it first identified in *Jones*.

I

Our Court has long recognized that not every fact that bears on a defendant's punishment need be charged in an indictment, submitted to a jury, and proved by the government beyond a reasonable doubt. Rather, we have held that the ''legislature's definition of the elements of the offense is usually dispositive.'' McMillan v. Pennsylvania, 477 U.S. 79, 85 (1986); see also Almendarez–Torres v. United States, 523 U.S. 224, 228 (1998); Patterson v. New York, 432 U.S. 197, 210, 211, n. 12 (1977). Although we have recognized that ''there are obviously constitutional limits beyond which the States may not go in this regard,'' and that ''in certain limited circumstances *Winship's* reasonable-doubt requirement applies to facts not formally identified as elements of the offense charged,'' we have proceeded with caution before deciding that a certain fact must be treated as an offense element despite the legislature's choice not to characterize it as such. We have therefore declined to establish any bright-line rule for making such judgments and have instead approached each case individually, sifting through the considerations most relevant to determining whether the legislature has acted properly within its broad power to define crimes and their punishments or instead has sought to evade the constitutional requirements associated with the characterization of a fact as an offense element.

In one bold stroke the Court today casts aside our traditional cautious approach and instead embraces a universal and seemingly bright-line rule limiting the power of Congress and state legislatures to define criminal offenses and the sentences that follow from convictions thereunder. The Court states: ''Other than the fact of a prior conviction, any fact that increases the penalty for a crime beyond the prescribed statutory maximum must be submitted to a jury, and proved beyond a reasonable doubt.'' In its opinion, the Court marshals virtually no authority to support its extraordinary rule. Indeed, it is remarkable that the Court cannot identify a single instance, in the over 200 years since the ratification of the Bill of Rights, that our Court has applied, as a constitutional requirement, the rule it announces today.

* * *

* * * That the Court begins its review of our precedent with a quotation from a dissenting opinion speaks volumes about the support that actually can be drawn from our cases for the "increase in the maximum penalty" rule announced today. See ante (quoting Almendarez–Torres, 523 U.S., at 251 (Scalia, J., dissenting)). The Court then cites our decision in Mullaney v. Wilbur, 421 U.S. 684 (1975), to demonstrate the "lesson" that due process and jury protections extend beyond those factual determinations that affect a defendant's guilt or innocence. The Court explains *Mullaney* as having held that the due process proof-beyond-a-reasonable-doubt requirement applies to those factual determinations that, under a State's criminal law, make a difference in the degree of punishment the defendant receives. The Court chooses to ignore, however, the decision we issued two years later, Patterson v. New York, 432 U.S. 197 (1977), which clearly rejected the Court's broad reading of *Mullaney*.

In *Patterson*, the jury found the defendant guilty of second-degree murder. Under New York law, the fact that a person intentionally killed another while under the influence of extreme emotional disturbance distinguished the reduced offense of first-degree manslaughter from the more serious offense of second-degree murder. Thus, the presence or absence of this one fact was the defining factor separating a greater from a lesser punishment. Under New York law, however, the State did not need to prove the absence of extreme emotional disturbance beyond a reasonable doubt. Rather, state law imposed the burden of proving the presence of extreme emotional disturbance on the defendant, and required that the fact be proved by a preponder-

ance of the evidence. We rejected Patterson's due process challenge to his conviction * * *.

Although we characterized the factual determination under New York law as one going to the mitigation of culpability, as opposed to the aggravation of the punishment, it is difficult to understand why the rule adopted by the Court in today's case (or the broader rule advocated by Justice Thomas) would not require the overruling of *Patterson*. Unless the Court is willing to defer to a legislature's formal definition of the elements of an offense, it is clear that the fact that Patterson did not act under the influence of extreme emotional disturbance, in substance, "increase[d] the penalty for [his] crime beyond the prescribed statutory maximum" for first-degree manslaughter. Nonetheless, we held that New York's requirement that the defendant, rather than the State, bear the burden of proof on this factual determination comported with the Fourteenth Amendment's Due Process Clause.

Patterson is important because it plainly refutes the Court's expansive reading of *Mullaney*. Indeed, the defendant in *Patterson* characterized *Mullaney* exactly as the Court has today and we rejected that interpretation * * *. We explained *Mullaney* instead as holding only "that a State must prove every ingredient of an offense beyond a reasonable doubt, and that it may not shift the burden of proof to the defendant by presuming that ingredient upon proof of the other elements of the offense." Because nothing had been presumed against Patterson under New York law, we found no due process violation. Ever since our decision in *Patter-*

son, we have consistently explained the holding in *Mullaney* in these limited terms and have rejected the broad interpretation the Court gives *Mullaney* today.

The case law from which the Court claims that its rule emerges consists of only one other decision—McMillan v. Pennsylvania. The Court's reliance on *McMillan* is also puzzling, given that our holding in that case points to the rejection of the Court's rule. There, we considered a Pennsylvania statute that subjected a defendant to a mandatory minimum sentence of five years' imprisonment if a judge found, by a preponderance of the evidence, that the defendant had visibly possessed a firearm during the commission of the offense for which he had been convicted. The petitioners claimed that the Fourteenth Amendment's Due Process Clause and the Sixth Amendment's jury trial guarantee (as incorporated by the Fourteenth Amendment) required the State to prove to the jury beyond a reasonable doubt that they had visibly possessed firearms. We rejected both constitutional claims.

The essential holding of *McMillan* conflicts with at least two of the several formulations the Court gives to the rule it announces today. First, the Court endorses the following principle: "[I]t is unconstitutional for a legislature to remove from the jury the assessment of facts that increase the prescribed range of penalties to which a criminal defendant is exposed. It is equally clear that such facts must be established by proof beyond a reasonable doubt." Second, the Court endorses the rule as restated in Justice Scalia's concurring opinion in *Jones*. See ante, at 24. There, Justice

Scalia wrote: "[I]t is unconstitutional to remove from the jury the assessment of facts that alter the congressionally prescribed range of penalties to which a criminal defendant is exposed." Thus, the Court appears to hold that any fact that increases or alters the range of penalties to which a defendant is exposed—which, by definition, must include increases or alterations to either the minimum or maximum penalties—must be proved to a jury beyond a reasonable doubt. In *McMillan*, however, we rejected such a rule to the extent it concerned those facts that increase or alter the minimum penalty to which a defendant is exposed. Accordingly, it is incumbent on the Court not only to admit that it is overruling *McMillan*, but also to explain why such a course of action is appropriate under normal principles of stare decisis.

* * * If any single rule can be derived from *McMillan*, it is not the Court's "increase in the maximum penalty" principle, but rather the following: When a State takes a fact that has always been considered by sentencing courts to bear on punishment, and dictates the precise weight that a court should give that fact in setting a defendant's sentence, the relevant fact need not be proved to a jury beyond a reasonable doubt as would an element of the offense.

* * *

II

That the Court's rule is unsupported by the history and case law it cites is reason enough to reject such a substantial departure from our settled jurisprudence.

Significantly, the Court also fails to explain adequately why the Due Process Clauses of the Fifth and Fourteenth Amendments and the jury trial guarantee of the Sixth Amendment require application of its rule. Upon closer examination, it is possible that the Court's "increase in the maximum penalty" rule rests on a meaningless formalism that accords, at best, marginal protection for the constitutional rights that it seeks to effectuate.

Any discussion of either the constitutional necessity or the likely effect of the Court's rule must begin, of course, with an understanding of what exactly that rule is. As was the case in *Jones*, however, that discussion is complicated here by the Court's failure to clarify the contours of the constitutional principle underlying its decision. In fact, there appear to be several plausible interpretations of the constitutional principle on which the Court's decision rests.

For example, under one reading, the Court appears to hold that the Constitution requires that a fact be submitted to a jury and proved beyond a reasonable doubt only if that fact, as a formal matter, extends the range of punishment beyond the prescribed statutory maximum. A State could, however, remove from the jury (and subject to a standard of proof below "beyond a reasonable doubt") the assessment of those facts that define narrower ranges of punishment, within the overall statutory range, to which the defendant may be sentenced. Thus, apparently New Jersey could cure its sentencing scheme, and achieve virtually the same results, by drafting its weapons possession statute in the following manner: First, New Jersey could prescribe, in the weapons possession statute itself, a range of 5 to 20 years' imprisonment for one who commits that criminal offense. Second, New Jersey could provide that only those defendants convicted under the statute who are found by a judge, by a preponderance of the evidence, to have acted with a purpose to intimidate an individual on the basis of race may receive a sentence greater than 10 years' imprisonment. * * * It is difficult to understand, and the Court does not explain, why the Constitution would require a state legislature to follow such a meaningless and formalistic difference in drafting its criminal statutes.

Under another reading of the Court's decision, it may mean only that the Constitution requires that a fact be submitted to a jury and proved beyond a reasonable doubt if it, as a formal matter, increases the range of punishment beyond that which could legally be imposed absent that fact. A State could, however, remove from the jury (and subject to a standard of proof below "beyond a reasonable doubt") the assessment of those facts that, as a formal matter, decrease the range of punishment below that which could legally be imposed absent that fact. Thus, consistent with our decision in *Patterson*, New Jersey could cure its sentencing scheme, and achieve virtually the same results, by drafting its weapons possession statute in the following manner: First, New Jersey could prescribe, in the weapons possession statute itself, a range of 5 to 20 years' imprisonment for one who commits that criminal offense. Second, New Jersey could provide that a defendant convicted under the statute whom a judge finds, by a preponderance of the evidence, not to have acted with a purpose to intimidate an individual on the basis of race may receive a sentence no greater than 10 years' imprisonment. * * * Again, it is difficult to understand, and neither the Court nor Justice Thomas explains, why the Constitution would require a state legislature to follow such a meaningless and formalistic difference in drafting its criminal statutes.

If either of the above readings is all that the Court's decision means, the Court's principle amounts to nothing more than chastising the New Jersey Legislature for failing to use the approved phrasing in expressing its intent as to how unlawful weapons possession should be punished. If New Jersey can, consistent with the Constitution, make precisely the same differences in punishment turn on precisely the same facts, and can remove the assessment of those facts from the jury and subject them to a standard of proof below "beyond a reasonable doubt," it is impossible to say that the Fifth, Sixth, and Fourteenth Amendments require the Court's rule. For the same reason, the "structural democratic constraints" that might discourage a legislature from enacting either of the above hypothetical statutes would be no more significant than those that would discourage the enactment of New Jersey's present sentence-enhancement statute. In all three cases, the legislature is able to calibrate punishment perfectly, and subject to a maximum penalty only those defendants whose cases satisfy the sentence-enhancement criterion. * * *

Given the pure formalism of the above readings of the Court's opinion, one suspects that the constitutional principle underlying its decision is more far reaching. The actual principle underlying the Court's decision may be that any fact (other than prior conviction) that has the effect, in real terms, of increasing the maximum punishment beyond an otherwise applicable range must be submitted to a jury and proved beyond a reasonable doubt. The principle thus would apply not only to schemes like New Jersey's, under which a factual determination exposes the defendant to a sentence beyond the prescribed statutory maximum, but also to all determinate-sentencing schemes in which the length of a defendant's sentence within the statutory range turns on specific factual determinations (e.g., the federal Sentencing Guidelines). * * *

I would reject any such principle. * * * [G]iven our approval of—and the significant history in this country of—discretionary sentencing by judges, it is difficult to understand how the Fifth, Sixth, and Fourteenth Amendments could possibly require the Court's or Justice Thomas' rule. Finally, in light of the adoption of determinate-sentencing schemes by many States and the Federal Government, the consequences of the Court's and Justice Thomas' rules in terms of sentencing schemes invalidated by today's decision will likely be severe.

* * *

* * * Under the Court's decision today, * * * it appears that once a legislature constrains judges' sentencing discretion by prescribing

certain sentences that may only be imposed (or must be imposed) in connection with the same determinations of the same contested facts, the Constitution requires that the facts instead be proved to a jury beyond a reasonable doubt. I see no reason to treat the two schemes differently. See, e.g., *McMillan*, 477 U.S., at 92 ("We have some difficulty fathoming why the due process calculus would change simply because the legislature has seen fit to provide sentencing courts with additional guidance"). In this respect, I agree with the Solicitor General that "[a] sentence that is constitutionally permissible when selected by a court on the basis of whatever factors it deems appropriate does not become impermissible simply because the court is permitted to select that sentence only after making a finding prescribed by the legislature." Although the Court acknowledges the legitimacy of discretionary sentencing by judges, it never provides a sound reason for treating judicial factfinding under determinate-sentencing schemes differently under the Constitution.

Consideration of the purposes underlying the Sixth Amendment's jury trial guarantee further demonstrates why our acceptance of judge-made findings in the context of discretionary sentencing suggests the approval of the same judge-made findings in the context of determinate sentencing as well. One important purpose of the Sixth Amendment's jury trial guarantee is to protect the criminal defendant against potentially arbitrary judges. It effectuates this promise by preserving, as a constitutional matter, certain fundamental decisions for a jury of one's peers, as opposed to a judge. * * * Clearly, the concerns animating the Sixth Amendment's jury trial guarantee, if they were to extend to the sentencing context at all, would apply with greater strength to a discretionary-sentencing scheme than to determinate sentencing. In the former scheme, the potential for mischief by an arbitrary judge is much greater, given that the judge's decision of where to set the defendant's sentence within the prescribed statutory range is left almost entirely to discretion. In contrast, under a determinate-sentencing system, the discretion the judge wields within the statutory range is tightly constrained. Accordingly, our approval of discretionary-sentencing schemes, in which a defendant is not entitled to have a jury make factual findings relevant to sentencing despite the effect those findings have on the severity of the defendant's sentence, demonstrates that the defendant should have no right to demand that a jury make the equivalent factual determinations under a determinate-sentencing scheme.

The Court appears to hold today, however, that a defendant is entitled to have a jury decide, by proof beyond a reasonable doubt, every fact relevant to the determination of sentence under a determinate-sentencing scheme. If this is an accurate description of the constitutional principle underlying the Court's opinion, its decision will have the effect of invalidating significant sentencing reform accomplished at the federal and state levels over the past three decades. * * *

Prior to the most recent wave of sentencing reform, the Federal Government and the States employed indeterminate-sentencing schemes in which judges and executive branch officials (e.g., parole board officials) had substantial discretion to determine the actual length of a defendant's sentence. Studies of indeterminate-sentencing schemes found that similarly situated defendants often received widely disparate sentences. Although indeterminate sentencing was intended to soften the harsh and uniform sentences formerly imposed under mandatory-sentencing systems, some studies revealed that indeterminate sentencing actually had the opposite effect.

In response, Congress and the state legislatures shifted to determinate-sentencing schemes that aimed to limit judges' sentencing discretion and, thereby, afford similarly situated offenders equivalent treatment. The most well known of these reforms was the federal Sentencing Reform Act of 1984, 18 U.S.C. § 3551 et seq. In the Act, Congress created the United States Sentencing Commission, which in turn promulgated the Sentencing Guidelines that now govern sentencing by federal judges. Whether one believes the determinate-sentencing reforms have proved successful or not—and the subject is one of extensive debate among commentators—the apparent effect of the Court's opinion today is to halt the current debate on sentencing reform in its tracks and to invalidate with the stroke of a pen three decades' worth of nationwide reform, all in the name of a principle with a questionable constitutional pedigree. Indeed, it is ironic that the Court, in the name of constitutional rights meant to protect crimi-

nal defendants from the potentially arbitrary exercise of power by prosecutors and judges, appears to rest its decision on a principle that would render unconstitutional efforts by Congress and the state legislatures to place constraints on that very power in the sentencing context.

Finally, perhaps the most significant impact of the Court's decision will be a practical one—its unsettling effect on sentencing conducted under current federal and state determinate-sentencing schemes. As I have explained, the Court does not say whether these schemes are constitutional, but its reasoning strongly suggests that they are not. Thus, with respect to past sentences handed down by judges under determinate-sentencing schemes, the Court's decision threatens to unleash a flood of petitions by convicted defendants seeking to invalidate their sentences in whole or in part on the authority of the Court's decision today. Statistics compiled by the United States Sentencing Commission reveal that almost a half-million cases have been sentenced under the Sentencing Guidelines since 1989. Federal cases constitute only the tip of the iceberg. * * * Because many States, like New Jersey, have determinate-sentencing schemes, the number of individual sentences drawn into question by the Court's decision could be colossal.

The decision will likely have an even more damaging effect on sentencing conducted in the immediate future under current determinate-sentencing schemes. Because the Court fails to clarify the precise contours of the constitutional principle underlying its decision, federal and state judges are left in a state of limbo. Should they continue to assume the constitutionality of the determinate-sentencing schemes under which they have operated for so long, and proceed to sentence convicted defendants in accord with those governing statutes and guidelines? The Court provides no answer, yet its reasoning suggests that each new sentence will rest on shaky ground. The most unfortunate aspect of today's decision is that our precedents did not foreordain this disruption in the world of sentencing. Rather, our cases traditionally took a cautious approach to questions like the one presented in this case. The Court throws that caution to the wind and, in the process, threatens to cast sentencing in the United States into what will likely prove to be a lengthy period of considerable confusion.

III

Because I do not believe that the Court's "increase in the maximum penalty" rule is required by the Constitution, I would evaluate New Jersey's sentence-enhancement statute, N. J. Stat. Ann. § 2C:44–3 (West Supp. 2000), by analyzing the factors we have examined in past cases. First, the New Jersey statute does not shift the burden of proof on an essential ingredient of the offense by presuming that ingredient upon proof of other elements of the offense. Second, the magnitude of the New Jersey sentence enhancement, as applied in petitioner's case, is constitutionally permissible. Under New Jersey law, the weapons possession offense to which petitioner pleaded guilty carries a sentence range of 5 to 10 years' imprisonment. The fact that

petitioner, in committing that offense, acted with a purpose to intimidate because of race exposed him to a higher sentence range of 10 to 20 years' imprisonment. The 10–year increase in the maximum penalty to which petitioner was exposed falls well within the range we have found permissible. Third, the New Jersey statute gives no impression of having been enacted to evade the constitutional requirements that attach when a State makes a fact an element of the charged offense. For example, New Jersey did not take what had previously been an element of the weapons possession offense and transform it into a sentencing factor.

In sum, New Jersey "simply took one factor that has always been considered by sentencing courts to bear on punishment"—a defendant's motive for committing the criminal offense—"and dictated the precise weight to be given that factor" when the motive is to intimidate a person because of race. * * * New Jersey, therefore, has done no more than what we held permissible in *McMillan*; it has taken a traditional sentencing factor and dictated the precise weight judges should attach to that factor when the specific motive is to intimidate on the basis of race.

The New Jersey statute resembles the Pennsylvania statute we upheld in *McMillan* in every respect but one. That difference—that the New Jersey statute increases the maximum punishment to which petitioner was exposed—does not persuade me that New Jersey "sought to evade the constitutional requirements associated with the characterization of a fact as an offense element." There is no question that

New Jersey could prescribe a range of 5 to 20 years' imprisonment as punishment for its weapons possession offense. Thus, as explained above, the specific means by which the State chooses to control judges' discretion within that permissible range is of no moment. The New Jersey statute also resembles in virtually every respect the federal statute we considered in *Almendarez-Torres*. That the New Jersey statute provides an enhancement based on the defendant's motive while the statute in *Almendarez-Torres* provided an enhancement based on the defendant's commission of a prior felony is a difference without constitutional importance. Both factors are traditional bases for increasing an offender's sentence and, therefore, may serve as the grounds for a sentence enhancement.

On the basis of our prior precedent, then, I would hold that the New Jersey sentence-enhancement statute is constitutional, and affirm the judgment of the Supreme Court of New Jersey.

JUSTICE BREYER, with whom CHIEF JUSTICE REHNQUIST joins, dissenting.

The majority holds that the Constitution contains the following requirement: "any fact [other than recidivism] that increases the penalty for a crime beyond the prescribed statutory maximum must be submitted to a jury, and proved beyond a reasonable doubt." This rule would seem to promote a procedural ideal—that of juries, not judges, determining the existence of those facts upon which increased punishment turns. But the real world of criminal justice cannot hope to meet any such ideal. It can function only with the help of procedural compromises, particularly in respect to sentencing. And those compromises, which are themselves necessary for the fair functioning of the criminal justice system, preclude implementation of the procedural model that today's decision reflects. At the very least, the impractical nature of the requirement that the majority now recognizes supports the proposition that the Constitution was not intended to embody it.

I

* * * There are, to put it simply, far too many potentially relevant sentencing factors to permit submission of all (or even many) of them to a jury. As the Sentencing Guidelines state the matter, "[a] bank robber with (or without) a gun, which the robber kept hidden (or brandished), might have frightened (or merely warned), injured seriously (or less seriously), tied up (or simply pushed) a guard, a teller or a customer, at night (or at noon), for a bad (or arguably less bad) motive, in an effort to obtain money for other crimes (or for other purposes), in the company of a few (or many) other robbers, for the first (or fourth) time that day, while sober (or under the influence of drugs or alcohol), and so forth." Sentencing Guidelines, Part A, at 1.2.

The Guidelines note that "a sentencing system tailored to fit every conceivable wrinkle of each case can become unworkable and seriously compromise the certainty of punishment and its deterrent effect." To ask a jury to consider all, or many, such matters would do the same.

At the same time, to require jury consideration of all such factors—say, during trial where the issue is guilt or innocence—could easily place the defendant in the awkward (and conceivably unfair) position of having to deny he committed the crime yet offer proof about how he committed it, e.g., "I did not sell drugs, but I sold no more than 500 grams." And while special postverdict sentencing juries could cure this problem, they have seemed (but for capital cases) not worth their administrative costs. * * *

* * * A sentencing system in which judges have discretion to find sentencing-related factors is a workable system and one that has long been thought consistent with the Constitution; why, then, would the Constitution treat sentencing statutes any differently?

II

* * *

III

* * * The majority raises no objection to traditional pre-Guidelines sentencing procedures under which judges, not juries, made the factual findings that would lead to an increase in an individual offender's sentence. How does a legislative determination differ in any significant way? For example, if a judge may on his or her own decide that victim injury or bad motive should increase a bank robber's sentence from 5 years to 10, why does it matter that a legislature instead enacts a statute that increases a bank robber's sentence from 5 years to 10 based on this same judicial finding?

* * *

IV

I certainly do not believe that the present sentencing system is one of "perfect equity," and I am willing, consequently, to assume that the majority's rule would provide a degree of increased procedural protection in respect to those particular sentencing factors currently embodied in statutes. I nonetheless believe that any such increased protection provides little practical help and comes at too high a price. For one thing, by leaving mandatory minimum sentences untouched, the majority's rule simply encourages any legislature interested in asserting control over the sentencing process to do so by creating those minimums. That result would mean significantly less procedural fairness, not more.

For another thing, this Court's case law, prior to Jones v. United States, led legislatures to believe that they were permitted to increase a statutory maximum sentence on the basis of a sentencing factor. And legislatures may well have relied upon that belief. See, e.g., 21 U.S.C. § 841(b) (1994 ed. and Supp. III) (providing penalties for, among other things, possessing a "controlled substance" with intent to distribute it, which sentences vary dramatically depending upon the amount of the drug possessed, without requiring jury determination of the amount); N. J. Stat. Ann. §§ 2C:43–6, 2C:43–7, 2C:44–1a-f, 2C:44–3 (West 1995 and Supp. 1999–2000) (setting sentencing ranges for crimes, while providing for lesser or greater punishments depending upon judicial findings regarding certain "aggravating" or "mitigating" factors); Cal. Penal Code Ann. § 1170 (West Supp. 2000) (similar); see also Cal. Court Rule 420(b) (1996) (providing that "[c]ircumstances in aggravation and mitigation" are to be established by the sentencing judge based on "the case record, the probation officer's report, [and] other reports and statements properly received").

As Justice O'Connor points out, the majority's rule creates serious uncertainty about the constitutionality of such statutes and about the constitutionality of the confinement of those punished under them. * * * Moreover, the rationale that underlies the Court's rule suggests a principle—jury determination of all sentencing-related facts—that, unless restricted, threatens the workability of every criminal justice system (if applied to judges) or threatens efforts to make those systems more uniform, hence more fair (if applied to commissions).

Finally, the Court's new rule will likely impede legislative attempts to provide authoritative guidance as to how courts should respond to the presence of traditional sentencing factors. The factor at issue here—motive—is such a factor. Whether a robber takes money to finance other crimes or to feed a starving family can matter, and long has mattered, when the length of a sentence is at issue. The State of New Jersey has determined that one motive—racial hatred—is particularly bad and ought to make a difference in respect to punishment for a crime. That determination is reasonable. The procedures mandated are consistent with traditional sentencing practice. Though additional procedural protections might well be desirable, for the reasons Justice O'Connor discusses and those I have discussed, I do not believe the Constitution requires them where ordinary sentencing factors are at issue. Consequently, in my view, New Jersey's statute is constitutional.

I respectfully dissent.

Apprendi and Statutory Minimums: Harris v. United States

In the following case, the Court considered the implications of its decision in *Apprendi*.

HARRIS v. UNITED STATES

United States Supreme Court, 2002.
536 U.S. 545.

Justice Kennedy announced the judgment of the Court and delivered the opinion of the Court with respect to Parts I, II, and IV, and an opinion with respect to Part III, in which the Chief Justice, Justice O'Connor, and Justice Scalia join.

Once more we consider the distinction the law has drawn between the elements of a crime and factors that influence a criminal sentence. Legislatures define crimes in terms of the facts that are their essential elements, and constitutional guarantees attach to these facts. In federal prosecutions, "[n]o person shall be held to answer for a capital, or otherwise infamous crime, unless on a presentment or indictment of a Grand Jury" alleging all the elements of the crime. U.S. Const., Amdt. 5. "In all criminal prosecutions," state and federal, "the accused shall enjoy the right to ... trial ... by an impartial jury," U.S. Const., Amdt. 6; see Duncan v. Louisiana, 391 U.S. 145, 149 (1968), at which the government must prove each element beyond a reasonable doubt, see In re Winship, 397 U.S. 358, 364 (1970).

Yet not all facts affecting the defendant's punishment are elements. After the accused is convicted, the judge may impose a sentence within a range provided by statute, basing it on various facts relating to the defendant and the manner in which the offense was committed. Though these facts may have a substantial impact on the sentence, they are not elements, and are thus not subject to the Constitution's indictment, jury, and proof requirements. Some statutes also direct judges to give specific weight to certain facts when choosing the sentence. The statutes do not require these facts, sometimes referred to as sentencing factors, to be alleged in the indictment, submitted to the jury, or established beyond a reasonable doubt.

The Constitution permits legislatures to make the distinction between elements and sentencing factors, but it imposes some limitations as well. For if it did not, legislatures could evade the indictment, jury, and proof requirements by labeling almost every relevant fact a sentencing factor. The Court described one limitation in this respect two Terms ago in Apprendi v. New Jersey, 530 U.S. 466, 490 (2000): "Other than the fact of a prior conviction, any fact that increases the penalty for a crime beyond the prescribed statutory maximum," whether the statute calls it an element or a sentencing factor,

"must be submitted to a jury, and proved beyond a reasonable doubt." Fourteen years before, in McMillan v. Pennsylvania, 477 U.S. 79 (1986), the Court had declined to adopt a more restrictive constitutional rule. *McMillan* sustained a statute that increased the minimum penalty for a crime, though not beyond the statutory maximum, when the sentencing judge found, by a preponderance of the evidence, that the defendant had possessed a firearm.

The principal question before us is whether *McMillan* stands after *Apprendi*.

I

Petitioner William Joseph Harris sold illegal narcotics out of his pawnshop with an unconcealed semiautomatic pistol at his side. He was later arrested for violating federal drug and firearms laws, including 18 U.S.C. § 924(c)(1)(A). That statute provides in relevant part:

[A]ny person who, during and in relation to any crime of violence or drug trafficking crime ... uses or carries a firearm, or who, in furtherance of any such crime, possesses a firearm, shall, in addition to the punishment provided for such crime of violence or drug trafficking crime—

(i) be sentenced to a term of imprisonment of not less than 5 years;

(ii) if the firearm is brandished, be sentenced to a term of imprisonment of not less than 7 years; and

(iii) if the firearm is discharged, be sentenced to a

term of imprisonment of not less than 10 years.

The Government proceeded on the assumption that § 924(c)(1)(A) defines a single crime and that brandishing is a sentencing factor to be considered by the judge after the trial. For this reason the indictment said nothing of brandishing and made no reference to subsection (ii). Instead, it simply alleged the elements from the statute's principal paragraph: that "during and in relation to a drug trafficking crime," petitioner had "knowingly carr[ied] a firearm." At a bench trial the United States District Court for the Middle District of North Carolina found petitioner guilty as charged.

Following his conviction, the presentence report recommended that petitioner be given the 7–year minimum because he had brandished the gun. Petitioner objected, citing this Court's decision in Jones v. United States, 526 U.S. 227 (1999), and arguing that, as a matter of statutory interpretation, brandishing is an element of a separate offense, an offense for which he had not been indicted or tried. At the sentencing hearing the District Court overruled the objection, found by a preponderance of the evidence that petitioner had brandished the gun, and sentenced him to seven years in prison.

In the Court of Appeals for the Fourth Circuit petitioner again pressed his statutory argument. He added that if brandishing is a sentencing factor as a statutory matter, the statute is unconstitutional in light of *Apprendi*—even though, as petitioner acknowledged, the judge's finding did not alter the maximum penalty to which he was exposed. Rejecting these argu-

ments, the Court of Appeals affirmed. Like every other Court of Appeals to have addressed the question, it held that the statute makes brandishing a sentencing factor. The court also held that the constitutional argument was foreclosed by *McMillan*.

We granted certiorari, and now affirm.

II

We must first answer a threshold question of statutory construction: Did Congress make brandishing an element or a sentencing factor in § 924(c)(1)(A)? In the Government's view the text in question defines a single crime, and the facts in subsections (ii) and (iii) are considerations for the sentencing judge. Petitioner, on the other hand, contends that Congress meant the statute to define three different crimes. Subsection (ii), he says, creates a separate offense of which brandishing is an element. If petitioner is correct, he was neither indicted nor tried for that offense, and the 7–year minimum did not apply.

So we begin our analysis by asking what § 924(c)(1)(A) means. The statute does not say in so many words whether brandishing is an element or a sentencing factor, but the structure of the prohibition suggests it is the latter. Federal laws usually list all offense elements "in a single sentence" and separate the sentencing factors "into subsections." Castillo v. United States, 530 U.S. 120, 125 (2000). Here, § 924(c)(1)(A) begins with a lengthy principal paragraph listing the elements of a complete crime— the basic federal offense of using or carrying a gun during and in relation to a violent crime or drug offense. Toward the end of the paragraph is "the word 'shall,' which often divides offense-defining provisions from those that specify sentences." *Jones,* 526 U.S., at 233. And following "shall" are the separate subsections, which explain how defendants are to "be sentenced." Subsection (i) sets a catchall minimum and certainly adds no further element. Subsections (ii) and (iii), in turn, increase the minimum penalty if certain facts are present, and those subsections do not repeat the elements from the principal paragraph.

When a statute has this sort of structure, we can presume that its principal paragraph defines a single crime and its subsections identify sentencing factors. But even if a statute "has a look to it suggesting that the numbered subsections are only sentencing provisions," *id.,* at 232, the text might provide compelling evidence to the contrary. This was illustrated by the Court's decision in *Jones,* in which the federal carjacking statute, which had a similar structure, was interpreted as setting out the elements of multiple offenses.

The critical textual clues in this case, however, reinforce the single-offense interpretation implied by the statute's structure. Tradition and past congressional practice, for example, were perhaps the most important guideposts in *Jones.* The fact at issue there—serious bodily injury—is an element in numerous federal statutes, including two on which the carjacking statute was modeled; and the *Jones* Court doubted that Congress would have made this fact a sentencing factor in

one isolated instance. In contrast, there is no similar federal tradition of treating brandishing and discharging as offense elements. In Castillo v. United States, *supra,* the Court singled out brandishing as a paradigmatic sentencing factor: "Traditional sentencing factors often involve . . . special features of the manner in which a basic crime was carried out (*e.g.,* that the defendant . . . brandished a gun)." Under the Sentencing Guidelines, moreover, brandishing and discharging affect the sentences for numerous federal crimes. Indeed, the Guidelines appear to have been the only antecedents for the statute's brandishing provision. * * * It thus seems likely that brandishing and discharging were meant to serve the same function under the statute as they do under the Guidelines.

We might have had reason to question that inference if brandishing or discharging altered the defendant's punishment in a manner not usually associated with sentencing factors. *Jones* is again instructive. There the Court accorded great significance to the "steeply higher penalties" authorized by the carjacking statute's three subsections, which enhanced the defendant's maximum sentence from 15 years, to 25 years, to life—enhancements the Court doubted Congress would have made contingent upon judicial factfinding. The provisions before us now, however, have an effect on the defendant's sentence that is more consistent with traditional understandings about how sentencing factors operate; the required findings constrain, rather than extend, the sentencing judge's discretion. Section 924(c)(1)(A) does not authorize the judge to impose "steeply higher penalties"—or higher penalties at all—once the facts in question are found. Since the subsections alter only the minimum, the judge may impose a sentence well in excess of seven years, whether or not the defendant brandished the firearm. The incremental changes in the minimum—from 5 years, to 7, to 10—are precisely what one would expect to see in provisions meant to identify matters for the sentencing judge's consideration.

Nothing about the text or history of the statute rebuts the presumption drawn from its structure. Against the single-offense interpretation to which these considerations point, however, petitioner invokes the canon of constitutional avoidance. Under that doctrine, when "a statute is susceptible of two constructions, by one of which grave and doubtful constitutional questions arise and by the other of which such questions are avoided, our duty is to adopt the latter." United States ex rel. Attorney General v. Delaware & Hudson Co., 213 U.S. 366, 408 (1909). It is at least an open question, petitioner contends, whether the Fifth and Sixth Amendments require every fact increasing a federal defendant's minimum sentence to be alleged in the indictment, submitted to the jury, and proved beyond a reasonable doubt. To avoid resolving that question (and possibly invalidating the statute), petitioner urges, we should read § 924(c)(1)(A) as making brandishing an element of an aggravated federal crime.

The avoidance canon played a role in *Jones,* for the subsections of the carjacking statute enhanced the maximum sentence, and a single-offense interpretation would have implicated constitutional questions later addressed—and resolved in the defendant's favor—by *Apprendi.* Yet the canon has no role to play here. It applies only when there are serious concerns about the statute's constitutionality, and petitioner's proposed rule—that the Constitution requires any fact increasing the statutory minimum sentence to be accorded the safeguards assigned to elements—was rejected 16 years ago in *McMillan.* Petitioner acknowledges as much but argues that recent developments cast doubt on *McMillan*'s viability. To avoid deciding whether *McMillan* must be overruled, he says, we should construe the problem out of the statute.

Petitioner's suggestion that we use the canon to avoid overruling one of our own precedents is novel and, given that *McMillan* was in place when § 924(c)(1)(A) was enacted, unsound. The avoidance canon rests upon our respect for Congress, which we assume legislates in the light of constitutional limitations. The statute at issue in this case was passed when *McMillan* provided the controlling instruction, and Congress would have had no reason to believe that it was approaching the constitutional line by following that instruction. We would not further the canon's goal of eliminating friction with our coordinate branch, moreover, if we alleviated our doubt about a constitutional premise we had supplied by adopting a strained reading of a statute that Congress had enacted in reliance on the premise. And if we stretched the text to avoid the question of *McMillan*'s continuing vitality, the canon would embrace a dynamic view of statutory interpretation, under which the text might mean one thing when enacted yet another if the prevailing view of the Constitution later changed. We decline to adopt that approach.

As the avoidance canon poses no obstacle and the interpretive circumstances point in a common direction, we conclude that, as a matter of statutory interpretation, § 924(c)(1)(A) defines a single offense. The statute regards brandishing and discharging as sentencing factors to be found by the judge, not offense elements to be found by the jury.

III

Confident that the statute does just what *McMillan* said it could, we consider petitioner's argument that § 924(c)(1)(A)(ii) is unconstitutional because *McMillan* is no longer sound authority. *Stare decisis* is not an inexorable command, but the doctrine is of fundamental importance to the rule of law. Even in constitutional cases, in which *stare decisis* concerns are less pronounced, we will not overrule a precedent absent a "special justification." Arizona v. Rumsey, 467 U.S. 203, 212 (1984).

The special justification petitioner offers is our decision in *Apprendi*, which, he says, cannot be reconciled with *McMillan*. We do not find the argument convincing. As we shall explain, *McMillan* and *Apprendi* are consistent because there is a fundamental distinction between the factual findings that were at issue in those two cases. *Apprendi* said that any fact extending the defendant's sentence beyond the maximum authorized by the jury's verdict would have been considered an element of an aggravated crime—and thus the domain of the jury—by those who framed the Bill of Rights. The same cannot be said of a fact increasing the mandatory minimum (but not extending the sentence beyond the statutory maximum), for the jury's verdict has authorized the judge to impose the minimum with or without the finding As *McMillan* recognized, a statute may reserve this type of factual finding for the judge without violating the Constitution.

Though defining criminal conduct is a task generally "left to the legislative branch," Patterson v. New York, 432 U.S. 197, 210 (1977), Congress may not manipulate the definition of a crime in a way that relieves the Government of its constitutional obligations to charge each element in the indictment, submit each element to the jury, and prove each element beyond a reasonable doubt, *Jones, supra,* at 240–241; Mullaney v. Wilbur, 421 U.S. 684, 699 (1975). *McMillan* and *Apprendi* asked whether certain types of facts, though labeled sentencing factors by the legislature, were nevertheless "traditional elements" to which these constitutional safeguards were intended to apply.

McMillan's answer stemmed from certain historical and doctrinal understandings about the role of the judge at sentencing. The mid–19th century produced a general shift in this country from criminal statutes "providing fixed-term sentences to those providing judges discretion within a permissible range." *Apprendi*, 530 U.S., at 481. Under these statutes, judges exercise their sentencing discretion through "an inquiry broad in scope, largely unlimited either as to the kind of information [they] may consider, or the source from which it may come." United States v. Tucker, 404 U.S. 443, 446 (1972). The Court has recognized that this process is constitutional—and that the facts taken into consideration need not be alleged in the indictment, submitted to the jury, or proved beyond a reasonable doubt. As the Court reiterated in *Jones:* "It is not, of course, that anyone today would claim that every fact with a bearing on sentencing must be found by a jury; we have resolved that general issue and have no intention of questioning its resolution." Judicial factfinding in the course of selecting a sentence within the authorized range does not implicate the indictment, jurytrial, and reasonable-doubt components of the Fifth and Sixth Amendments.

That proposition, coupled with another shift in prevailing sentencing practices, explains *McMillan.* In the latter part of the 20th century, many legislatures, dissatisfied with sentencing disparities among like offenders, implemented measures regulating judicial discretion. These systems maintained the statutory ranges and the judge's factfinding role but assigned a uniform weight to factors judges often relied upon when choosing a sentence. One example of reform, the kind addressed in *McMillan,* was mandatory minimum sentencing. The Pennsylvania Mandatory Minimum Sentencing Act imposed a minimum prison term of five years when the sentencing judge found, by a preponderance of the evidence, that the defendant had possessed a firearm while committing the crime of conviction.

In sustaining the statute the *McMillan* Court placed considerable reliance on the similarity between the sentencing factor at issue and the facts judges contemplate when exercising their discretion within the statutory range. Given that the latter are not elements of the crime, the Court explained, neither was the former:

> Section 9712 neither alters the maximum penalty for the crime committed nor creates a separate offense calling for a separate penalty; it operates solely to limit the sentencing court's discretion in selecting a penalty within the range already available to it without the special finding of visible possession of a firearm. Section 9712 "ups the ante" for the defendant only by raising to five years the minimum sentence which may be imposed within the statutory plan. . . . Petitioners' claim that visible possession under the Pennsylvania statute is "really" an element of the offenses for which they are being punished . . . would have at least more superficial appeal if a finding of visible possession exposed them to greater or additional punishment, . . . but it does not. 477 U.S., at 87–88 (footnote omitted).

In response to the argument that the Act evaded the Constitution's procedural guarantees, the Court noted that the statute "simply took one factor that has always been considered by sentencing courts to bear on punishment . . . and dictated the precise weight to be given that factor.

That reasoning still controls. If the facts judges consider when exercising their discretion within the statutory range are not elements, they do not become as much merely because legislatures require the judge to impose a minimum sentence when those facts are found— a sentence the judge could have imposed absent the finding. It does not matter, for the purposes of the constitutional analysis, that in statutes like the Pennsylvania Act the State provides that a fact shall give rise both to a special stigma and to a special punishment. Judges choosing a sentence within the range do the same, and "[j]udges, it is sometimes necessary to remind ourselves, are part of the State." *Apprendi, supra,* at 498 (SCALIA, J., concurring). These facts, though stigmatizing and punitive, have been the traditional domain of judges; they have not been alleged in the indictment or proved beyond a reasonable doubt. There is no reason to believe that those who framed the Fifth and Sixth Amendments would have thought of them as the elements of the crime.

This conclusion might be questioned if there were extensive historical evidence showing that facts increasing the defendant's minimum sentence (but not affecting the maximum) have, as a matter of course, been treated as elements. The evidence on this score, however, is lacking. Statutes like the Pennsylvania Act, which alter the minimum sentence without changing the maximum, were for the most part the product of the 20th century, when legislatures first asserted control over the sentencing judge's discretion. Courts at the founding (whose views might be relevant, giv-

en the contemporaneous adoption of the Bill of Rights, see *Apprendi,* 530 U.S., at 478–484) and in the mid–19th century (whose views might be relevant, given that sentencing ranges first arose then) were not as a general matter required to decide whether a fact giving rise to a mandatory minimum sentence within the available range was to be alleged in the indictment and proved to the jury. Indeed, though there is no clear record of how history treated these facts, it is clear that they did not fall within the principle by which history determined what facts were elements. That principle defined elements as "fact[s] . . . legally essential to the punishment to be inflicted." United States v. Reese, 92 U.S. 214, 232 (1876) (Clifford, J., dissenting) (citing 1 J. Bishop, Law of Criminal Procedure § 81, p. 51 (2d ed. 1872)). This formulation includes facts that, as *McMillan* put it, "alte[r] the maximum penalty," but it does not include facts triggering a mandatory minimum. The minimum may be imposed with or without the factual finding; the finding is by definition not "essential" to the defendant's punishment.

McMillan was on firm historical ground, then, when it held that a legislature may specify the condition for a mandatory minimum without making the condition an element of the crime. The fact of visible firearm possession was more like the facts considered by judges when selecting a sentence within the statutory range—facts that, as the authorities from the 19th century confirm, have never been charged in the indictment, submitted to the jury, or proved beyond a reasonable doubt:

* * *

Since sentencing ranges came into use, defendants have not been able to predict from the face of the indictment precisely what their sentence will be; the charged facts have simply made them aware of the heaviest punishment they face if convicted. Judges, in turn, have always considered uncharged aggravating circumstances that, while increasing the defendant's punishment, have not "swell[ed] the penalty above what the law has provided for the acts charged." Because facts supporting a mandatory minimum fit squarely within that description, the legislature's choice to entrust them to the judge does not implicate the "competition . . . between judge and jury over . . . their respective roles," *Jones,* 526 U.S., at 245, that is the central concern of the Fifth and Sixth Amendments.

At issue in *Apprendi,* by contrast, was a sentencing factor that did "swell the penalty above what the law has provided," and thus functioned more like a "traditional elemen[t]." *Patterson v. New York,* 432 U.S., at 211, n. 12. * * *

Apprendi's conclusions do not undermine *McMillan*'s. There was no comparable historical practice of submitting facts increasing the mandatory minimum to the jury, so the *Apprendi* rule did not extend to those facts. Indeed, the Court made clear that its holding did not affect *McMillan* at all:

> We do not overrule *McMillan*. We limit its holding to cases that do not involve the imposition of a sentence more severe than the

statutory maximum for the offense established by the jury's verdict—a limitation identified in the *McMillan* opinion itself. 530 U.S., at 487, n. 13.

The sentencing factor in *McMillan* did not increase "the penalty for a crime beyond the prescribed statutory maximum," *Apprendi,* 530 U.S., at 490; nor did it, as the concurring opinions in *Jones* put it, "alter the congressionally prescribed range of penalties to which a criminal defendant is exposed," 526 U.S., at 253 (SCALIA, J., concurring)). As the *Apprendi* Court observed, the *McMillan* finding merely required the judge to impose "a specific sentence *within the range* authorized by the jury's finding that the defendant [was] guilty." 530 U.S., at 494, n. 19.

As its holding and the history on which it was based would suggest, the *Apprendi* Court's understanding of the Constitution is consistent with the holding in *McMillan*. Facts extending the sentence beyond the statutory maximum had traditionally been charged in the indictment and submitted to the jury, *Apprendi* said, because the function of the indictment and jury had been to authorize the State to impose punishment:

> The evidence . . . that punishment was, by law, tied to the offense . . . and the evidence that American judges have exercised sentencing discretion within a legally prescribed range . . . point to a single, consistent conclusion: The judge's role in sentencing is constrained at its outer limits by the facts alleged in the indictment and found by the jury. Put simply, facts that expose a defendant to a

punishment greater than that otherwise legally prescribed were by definition 'elements' of a separate legal offense. 530 U.S., at 483, n. 10.

The grand and petit juries thus form a "strong and two-fold barrier ... between the liberties of the people and the prerogative of the [government]." *Duncan v. Louisiana,* 391 U.S., at 151. Absent authorization from the trial jury—in the form of a finding, by proof beyond a reasonable doubt, of the facts warranting the extended sentence under the New Jersey statute—the State had no power to sentence the defendant to more than 10 years, the maximum "authorized by the jury's guilty verdict." *Apprendi,* 530 U.S., at 494. "[T]hose facts that determine the maximum sentence the law allows, then, are necessarily elements of the crime." *Id.,* at 499 (SCALIA, J., concurring).

Yet once the jury finds all those facts, *Apprendi* says that the defendant has been convicted of the crime; the Fifth and Sixth Amendments have been observed; and the Government has been authorized to impose any sentence below the maximum. That is why, as *Apprendi* noted, "nothing in this history suggests that it is impermissible for judges to exercise discretion—taking into consideration various factors relating both to offense and offender—in imposing a judgment *within the range.*" *Id.,* at 481. That is also why, as *McMillan* noted, nothing in this history suggests that it is impermissible for judges to find facts that give rise to a mandatory minimum sentence below "the maximum penalty for the crime committed." 477 U.S., at 87–88. In both instances the judicial factfind-

ing does not "expose a defendant to a punishment greater than that otherwise legally prescribed." *Apprendi, supra,* at 483, n. 10. Whether chosen by the judge or the legislature, the facts guiding judicial discretion below the statutory maximum need not be alleged in the indictment, submitted to the jury, or proved beyond a reasonable doubt. When a judge sentences the defendant to a mandatory minimum, no less than when the judge chooses a sentence within the range, the grand and petit juries already have found all the facts necessary to authorize the Government to impose the sentence. The judge may impose the minimum, the maximum, or any other sentence within the range without seeking further authorization from those juries—and without contradicting *Apprendi.*

Petitioner argues, however, that the concerns underlying *Apprendi* apply with equal or more force to facts increasing the defendant's minimum sentence. Those factual findings, he contends, often have a greater impact on the defendant than the findings at issue in *Apprendi.* This is so because when a fact increasing the statutory maximum is found, the judge may still impose a sentence far below that maximum; but when a fact increasing the minimum is found, the judge has no choice but to impose that minimum, even if he or she otherwise would have chosen a lower sentence. Why, petitioner asks, would fairness not also require the latter sort of fact to be alleged in the indictment and found by the jury under a reasonable-doubt standard? The answer is that because it is beyond dispute that the judge's choice of sentences within the authorized range may be influenced by facts not considered by the jury, a factual finding's practical effect cannot by itself control the constitutional analysis. The Fifth and Sixth Amendments ensure that the defendant "will never get *more* punishment than he bargained for when he did the crime," but they do not promise that he will receive "anything less" than that. *Apprendi, supra*, at 498 (SCALIA, J., concurring). If the grand jury has alleged, and the trial jury has found, all the facts necessary to impose the maximum, the barriers between government and defendant fall. The judge may select any sentence within the range, based on facts not alleged in the indictment or proved to the jury—even if those facts are specified by the legislature, and even if they persuade the judge to choose a much higher sentence than he or she otherwise would have imposed. That a fact affects the defendant's sentence, even dramatically so, does not by itself make it an element.

* * * The factual finding in *Apprendi* extended the power of the judge, allowing him or her to impose a punishment exceeding what was authorized by the jury. The finding in *McMillan* restrained the judge's power, limiting his or her choices within the authorized range. It is quite consistent to maintain that the former type of fact must be submitted to the jury while the latter need not be.

Read together, *McMillan* and *Apprendi* mean that those facts setting the outer limits of a sentence, and of the judicial power to impose it, are the elements of the crime for the purposes of the constitutional analysis. Within the range authorized by the jury's verdict, however, the political system may channel judicial discretion—and rely upon judicial expertise—by requiring defendants to serve minimum terms after judges make certain factual findings. It is critical not to abandon that understanding at this late date. Legislatures and their constituents have relied upon *McMillan* to exercise control over sentencing through dozens of statutes like the one the Court approved in that case. Congress and the States have conditioned mandatory minimum sentences upon judicial findings that, as here, a firearm was possessed, brandished, or discharged, * * * or among other examples, that the victim was over 60 years of age, that the defendant possessed a certain quantity of drugs, that the victim was related to the defendant, and that the defendant was a repeat offender. We see no reason to overturn those statutes or cast uncertainty upon the sentences imposed under them.

IV

Reaffirming *McMillan* and employing the approach outlined in that case, we conclude that the federal provision at issue, 18 U.S.C. § 924(c)(1)(A)(ii), is constitutional. Basing a 2–year increase in the defendant's minimum sentence on a judicial finding of brandishing does not evade the requirements of the Fifth and Sixth Amendments. Congress "simply took one factor that has always been considered by sentencing courts to bear on punishment . . . and dictated the precise weight to be given that factor." *McMillan,* 477 U.S., at 89–90. That factor need not be alleged in the indictment, submitted to the jury, or proved beyond a reasonable doubt.

The Court is well aware that many question the wisdom of mandatory minimum sentencing. Mandatory minimums, it is often said, fail to account for the unique circumstances of offenders who warrant a lesser penalty. See, *e.g.,* Brief for Families Against Mandatory Minimums Foundation as *Amicus Curiae* 25, n. 16; cf. *Almendarez-Torres, supra,* at 245 (citing United States Sentencing Commission, Mandatory Minimum Penalties in the Federal Criminal Justice System 26–34 (Aug. 1991)). These criticisms may be sound, but they would persist whether the judge or the jury found the facts giving rise to the minimum. We hold only that the Constitution permits the judge to do so, and we leave the other questions to Congress, the States, and the democratic processes.

The judgment of the Court of Appeals is affirmed.

It is so ordered.

JUSTICE O'CONNOR, **concurring**.

Petitioner bases his statutory argument that brandishing must be interpreted as an offense element on *Jones v. United States,* 526 U.S. 227 (1999). He bases his constitutional argument that regardless of how the statute is interpreted, brandishing must be charged in the indictment and found by the jury beyond a reasonable doubt on *Apprendi v. New Jersey,* 530 U.S. 466 (2000). As I dissented in *Jones* and *Apprendi* and still believe both were wrongly decided, I find it easy to reject petitioner's arguments. Even assuming the validity of *Jones* and *Apprendi,* however, I agree that petitioner's arguments that brandish-

ing must be charged in the indictment and found by the jury beyond a reasonable doubt are unavailing. I therefore join JUSTICE KENNEDY's opinion in its entirety.

JUSTICE BREYER, **concurring in part and concurring in the judgment.**

I cannot easily distinguish Apprendi v. New Jersey, 530 U.S. 466 (2000), from this case in terms of logic. For that reason, I cannot agree with the plurality's opinion insofar as it finds such a distinction. At the same time, I continue to believe that the Sixth Amendment permits judges to apply sentencing factors—whether those factors lead to a sentence beyond the statutory maximum (as in *Apprendi*) or the application of a mandatory minimum (as here). And because I believe that extending *Apprendi* to mandatory minimums would have adverse practical, as well as legal, consequences, I cannot yet accept its rule. I therefore join the Court's judgment, and I join its opinion to the extent that it holds that *Apprendi* does not apply to mandatory minimums.

In saying this, I do not mean to suggest my approval of mandatory minimum sentences as a matter of policy. During the past two decades, as mandatory minimum sentencing statutes have proliferated in number and importance, judges, legislators, lawyers, and commentators have criticized those statutes, arguing that they negatively affect the fair administration of the criminal law, a matter of concern to judges and to legislators alike.

Mandatory minimum statutes are fundamentally inconsistent with Congress' simultaneous effort to create a fair, honest, and rational sentencing system through the use of Sentencing Guidelines. Unlike Guideline sentences, statutory mandatory minimums generally deny the judge the legal power to depart downward, no matter how unusual the special circumstances that call for leniency. They rarely reflect an effort to achieve sentencing proportionality—a key element of sentencing fairness that demands that the law punish a drug "kingpin" and a "mule" differently. They transfer sentencing power to prosecutors, who can determine sentences through the charges they decide to bring, and who thereby have reintroduced much of the sentencing disparity that Congress created Guidelines to eliminate. They rarely are based upon empirical study. And there is evidence that they encourage subterfuge, leading to more frequent downward departures (on a random basis), thereby making them a comparatively ineffective means of guaranteeing tough sentences.

Applying *Apprendi* in this case would not, however, lead Congress to abolish, or to modify, mandatory minimum sentencing statutes. Rather, it would simply require the prosecutor to charge, and the jury to find beyond a reasonable doubt, the existence of the "factor," say, the amount of unlawful drugs, that triggers the mandatory minimum. In many cases, a defendant, claiming innocence and arguing, say, mistaken identity, will find it impossible simultaneously to argue to the jury that the prosecutor has overstated the drug amount. How, the jury might ask, could this "innocent" defendant know anything about that matter? The upshot is that in many such cases defendant and prosecutor will enter into a stipulation before trial as to drug amounts to be used at sentencing (if the jury finds the defendant guilty). To that extent, application of *Apprendi* would take from the judge the power to make a factual determination, while giving that power not to juries, but to prosecutors. And such consequences, when viewed through the prism of an open, fair sentencing system, are seriously adverse.

The legal consequences of extending *Apprendi* to the mandatory minimum sentencing context are also seriously adverse. Doing so would diminish further Congress' otherwise broad constitutional authority to define crimes through the specification of elements, to shape criminal sentences through the specification of sentencing factors, and to limit judicial discretion in applying those factors in particular cases. I have discussed these matters fully in my *Apprendi* dissent. For the reasons set forth there * * * I would not apply *Apprendi* in this case.

I consequently join Parts I, II, and IV of the Court's opinion and concur in its judgment.

Justice Thomas, with whom Justice Stevens, Justice Souter, and Justice Ginsburg join, dissenting.

The range of punishment to which petitioner William J. Harris was exposed turned on the fact that he brandished a firearm, a fact that was neither charged in his indictment nor proved at trial beyond a reasonable doubt. The United States Court of Appeals for the Fourth Circuit nonetheless held, in reliance on McMillan v. Pennsylvania, 477

U.S. 79 (1986), that the fact that Harris brandished a firearm was a mere sentencing factor to which no constitutional protections attach.

McMillan, however, conflicts with the Court's later decision in Apprendi v. New Jersey, 530 U.S. 466 (2000), as the dissenting opinion in *Apprendi* recognized. See *id.*, at 533 (O'CONNOR, J., dissenting). The Court's holding today therefore rests on either a misunderstanding or a rejection of the very principles that animated *Apprendi* just two years ago. Given that considerations of *stare decisis* are at their nadir in cases involving procedural rules implicating fundamental constitutional protections afforded criminal defendants, I would reaffirm *Apprendi*, overrule *McMillan*, and reverse the Court of Appeals.

I

* * *

II

* * *

A

The Federal Constitution provides those "accused" in federal courts with specific rights, such as the right "to be informed of the nature and cause of the accusation," the right to be "held to answer for a capital, or otherwise infamous crime" only on an indictment or presentment of a grand jury, and the right to be tried by "an impartial jury of the State and district wherein the crime shall have been committed." Amdts. 5 and 6. Also, no Member of this Court disputes that due process requires that every fact necessary to constitute a crime must be found beyond a reasonable

doubt by a jury if that right is not waived. See In re Winship, 397 U.S. 358, 364 (1970). As with *Apprendi*, this case thus turns on the seemingly simple question of what constitutes a "crime."

This question cannot be answered by reference to statutory construction alone solely because the sentence does not exceed the statutory maximum. * * * The fact that a defendant brandished a firearm indisputably alters the prescribed range of penalties to which he is exposed under 18 U.S.C. § 924(c)(1)(A). Without a finding that a defendant brandished or discharged a firearm, the penalty range for a conviction under § 924(c)(1)(A)(i) is five years to life in prison. But with a finding that a defendant brandished a firearm, the penalty range becomes harsher, seven years to life imprisonment. § 924(c)(1)(A)(ii). And if the court finds that a defendant discharged a firearm, the range becomes even more severe, 10 years to life. § 924(c)(1)(A)(iii). Thus, it is ultimately beside the point whether as a matter of statutory interpretation brandishing is a sentencing factor, because as a constitutional matter brandishing must be deemed an element of an aggravated offense.

I agree with the Court that a legislature is free to decree, within constitutional limits, which facts are elements that constitute a crime. But when the legislature provides that a particular fact shall give rise both to a special stigma and to a special punishment, the constitutional consequences are clear. * * * We made clear in *Apprendi* that if a statute "annexes a higher degree of punishment based on certain circumstances, exposing a defendant to that higher degree of punishment requires that those circumstances be charged in the indictment and proved beyond a reasonable doubt."

This constitutional limitation neither interferes with the legislature's ability to define statutory ranges of punishment nor calls into question judicial discretion to impose "judgment *within the range* prescribed by statute." *Apprendi*, 530 U.S., at 481. But it does protect the criminal defendant's constitutional right to know, *ex ante*, those circumstances that will determine the applicable range of punishment and to have those circumstances proved beyond a reasonable doubt * * *.

B

The Court truncates this protection and holds that "facts, sometimes referred to as sentencing factors," do not need to be "alleged in the indictment, submitted to the jury, or established beyond a reasonable doubt," so long as they do not increase the penalty for the crime beyond the statutory maximum. This is so even if the fact alters the statutorily mandated sentencing range, by increasing the mandatory minimum sentence. But to say that is in effect to claim that the imposition of a 7–year, rather than a 5–year, mandatory minimum does not change the constitutionally relevant sentence range because, regardless, either sentence falls between five years and the statutory maximum of life, the longest sentence range available under the statute. This analysis is flawed precisely because the statute provides incremental sentencing ranges, in which the mandatory minimum sentence varies upward if a defen-

dant "brandished" or "discharged" a weapon. As a matter of common sense, an increased mandatory minimum heightens the loss of liberty and represents the increased stigma society attaches to the offense. Consequently, facts that trigger an increased mandatory minimum sentence warrant constitutional safeguards.

Actual sentencing practices appear to bolster this conclusion. The suggestion that a 7–year sentence could be imposed even without a finding that a defendant brandished a firearm ignores the fact that the sentence imposed when a defendant is found only to have "carried" a firearm "in relation to" a drug trafficking offense appears to be, almost uniformly, if not invariably, five years. Similarly, those found to have brandished a firearm typically, if not always, are sentenced only to 7 years in prison while those found to have discharged a firearm are sentenced only to 10 years. * * * Yet under the decision today, those key facts actually responsible for fixing a defendant's punishment need not be charged in an indictment or proved beyond a reasonable doubt.

The incremental increase between five and seven years in prison may not seem so great in the abstract (of course it must seem quite different to a defendant actually being incarcerated). However, the constitutional analysis adopted by the plurality would hold equally true if the mandatory minimum for a violation of § 924(c)(1) without brandishing was five years, but the mandatory minimum with brandishing was life imprisonment. The result must be the same because surely our fundamental constitutional principles cannot alter depending on degrees of sentencing severity. So long as it was clear that Congress intended for "brandishing" to be a sentencing factor, that fact would still neither have to be charged in the indictment nor proved beyond a reasonable doubt. But if this is the case, then *Apprendi* can easily be avoided by clever statutory drafting.

It is true that *Apprendi* concerned a fact that increased the penalty for a crime beyond the prescribed statutory maximum, but the principles upon which it relied apply with equal force to those facts that expose the defendant to a higher mandatory minimum * * * . Whether one raises the floor or raises the ceiling it is impossible to dispute that the defendant is exposed to greater punishment than is otherwise prescribed.

* * *

III

* * *

* * * [B]efore today, no one seriously believed that the Court's earlier decision in *McMillan* could coexist with the logical implications of the Court's later decisions in *Apprendi* and *Jones*. In both cases, the dissent said as much:

The essential holding of *McMillan* conflicts with at least two of the several formulations the Court gives to the rule it announces today. First, the Court endorses the following principle: "[I]t is unconstitutional for a legislature to remove from the jury the assessment of facts *that increase the prescribed range of penalties* to which a criminal defendant is exposed. It is equally clear that such facts must be established by proof beyond a reasonable doubt." Second, the Court endorses the rule as restated in JUSTICE SCALIA's concurring opinion in *Jones*. There, JUSTICE SCALIA wrote: "[I]t is unconstitutional to remove from the jury the assessment of facts *that alter the congressionally prescribed range of penalties* to which a criminal defendant is exposed." Thus, the Court appears to hold that any fact that increases or alters *the range* of penalties to which a defendant is exposed—which, by definition, must include increases or alterations to either the minimum or maximum penalties—must be proved to a jury beyond a reasonable doubt. In *McMillan*, however, we rejected such a rule to the extent it concerned those facts that increase or alter the minimum penalty to which a defendant is exposed. Accordingly, it is incumbent on the Court not only to admit that it is overruling *McMillan*, but also to explain why such a course of action is appropriate under normal principles of stare decisis.' *Apprendi*, 530 U.S., at 533 (O'CONNOR, J., dissenting).

See also *Jones*, 526 U.S., at 268 (KENNEDY, J., dissenting) ("[B]y its terms, JUSTICE SCALIA's view ... would call into question the validity of judge-administered mandatory minimum sentencing provisions, contrary to our holding in *McMillan*. Once the facts triggering application of the mandatory minimum are found by the judge, the sentencing range to which the defendant is exposed is altered"). There is no question but that *stare decisis* may yield where a prior decision's "underpinnings [have been] eroded, by subsequent decisions of this Court." United States v. Gaudin, 515 U.S. 506, 521 (1995).

Further supporting the essential incompatibility of *Apprendi* and *McMillan*, JUSTICE BREYER concurs in the judgment but not the entire opinion of the Court, recognizing that he "cannot easily distinguish *Apprendi* . . . from this case in terms of logic. For that reason, I cannot agree with the plurality's opinion insofar as it finds such a distinction." This leaves only a minority of the Court embracing the distinction between *McMillan* and *Apprendi* that forms the basis of today's holding, and at least one Member explicitly continues to reject both *Apprendi* and *Jones*. *Ante*, at 1 (O'CONNOR, J., concurring).

* * *

"Conscious of the likelihood that legislative decisions may have been made in reliance on *McMillan*," in *Apprendi*, "we reserve[d] for another day the question whether *stare decisis* considerations preclude reconsideration of its narrower holding." 530 U.S., at 487, n. 13. But that day has come, and adherence to *stare decisis* in this case would require infidelity to our constitutional values. Because, like most Members of this Court, I cannot logically distinguish the issue here from the principles underlying the Court's decision in *Apprendi*, I respectfully dissent.

Apprendi and the Death Penalty: Ring v. Arizona

In the following case, the Court determines that the logic of *Apprendi* extends to the death penalty.

RING v. ARIZONA

United States Supreme Court, 2002.
536 U.S. 584.

JUSTICE GINSBURG **delivered the opinion of the Court.**

This case concerns the Sixth Amendment right to a jury trial in capital prosecutions. In Arizona, following a jury adjudication of a defendant's guilt of first-degree murder, the trial judge, sitting alone, determines the presence or absence of the aggravating factors required by Arizona law for imposition of the death penalty.

In Walton v. Arizona, 497 U.S. 639 (1990), this Court held that Arizona's sentencing scheme was compatible with the Sixth Amendment because the additional facts found by the judge qualified as sentencing considerations, not as "element[s] of the offense of capital murder." Ten years later, however, we decided Apprendi v. New Jersey, 530 U.S. 466 (2000), which held that the Sixth Amendment does not permit a defendant to be "expose[d] . . . to a penalty *exceeding* the maximum he would receive if punished according to the facts reflected in the jury verdict alone." This prescription governs, *Apprendi* determined, even if the State characterizes the additional findings made by the judge as "sentencing factor[s]."

Apprendi's reasoning is irreconcilable with *Walton*'s holding in this regard, and today we overrule *Walton* in relevant part. Capital defendants, no less than non-capital defendants, we conclude, are entitled to a jury determination of any fact on which the legislature conditions an increase in their maximum punishment.

I

[Ring was tried for murder, armed robbery, and related charges. An armored van was hijacked and Magoch, the driver, was shot to death. The perpetrators took more than $800,000 in cash and checks from the van. Evidence, including wiretapped conversations, pointed to the involvement of Ring and his friends Greenham and Ferguson. Eventually Ring's house was searched, and police found $271,000 in cash, and a note appearing to indicate arrangements for splitting a large sum of money with Greenham and Ferguson.]

Testifying in his own defense, Ring said the money seized at his house was startup capital for a construction company he and Greenham were planning to form. Ring testified that he made his share of the money as a confidential informant for the Federal Bureau of Investigation and as a bail bondsman and gunsmith. But an FBI agent testified that Ring had been paid only $458, and other evidence showed that Ring had made no more than $8,800 as a bail bondsman.

The trial judge instructed the jury on alternative charges of premeditated murder and felony murder. The jury deadlocked on premeditated murder, with 6 of 12 jurors voting to acquit, but convicted Ring of felony murder occurring in the course of armed robbery.

As later summed up by the Arizona Supreme Court, "the evidence admitted at trial failed to prove, beyond a reasonable doubt, that [Ring] was a major participant in the armed robbery or that he actually murdered Magoch." Although clear evidence connected Ring to the robbery's proceeds, nothing submitted at trial put him at the scene of the robbery. Furthermore, "[f]or all we know from the trial evidence," the Arizona court stated, "[Ring] did not participate in, plan, or even expect the killing. This lack of evidence no doubt explains why the jury found [Ring] guilty of felony, but not premeditated, murder"

Under Arizona law, Ring could not be sentenced to death, the statutory maximum penalty for first-degree murder, unless further findings were made. [The relevant Arizona statute] directs the judge who presided at trial to "conduct a separate sentencing hearing to determine the existence or nonexistence of [certain enumerated] circumstances . . . for the purpose of determining the sentence to be imposed." The statute further instructs: "The hearing shall be conducted before the court alone. The court alone shall make all factual determinations required by this section or the constitution of the United States or this state."

At the conclusion of the sentencing hearing, the judge is to determine the presence or absence of the enumerated "aggravating circumstances" and any "mitigating circumstances." The State's law authorizes the judge to sentence the defendant to death only if there is at least one aggravating circumstance and "there are no mitigating circumstances sufficiently substantial to call for leniency."

Between Ring's trial and sentencing hearing, Greenham pleaded guilty to second-degree murder and armed robbery. He stipulated to a 27 1/2 year sentence and agreed to cooperate with the prosecution in the cases against Ring and Ferguson.

Called by the prosecution at Ring's sentencing hearing, Greenham testified that he, Ring, and Ferguson had been planning the robbery for several weeks before it occurred. According to Greenham, Ring "had I guess taken the role as leader because he laid out all the tactics." On the day of the robbery, Greenham said, the three watched the armored van pull up [and when] Magoch opened the door to smoke a cigarette, Ring shot him with a rifle equipped with a homemade silencer. Greenham then pushed Magoch's body aside and drove the van away. * * * Later, Greenham recalled, as the three robbers were dividing up the money, Ring upbraided him and Ferguson for "forgetting to congratulate [Ring] on [his] shot."

On cross-examination, Greenham acknowledged having previously told Ring's counsel that Ring had nothing to do with the planning or execution of the robbery. Greenham explained that he had made that prior statement only because Ring had threatened his life. Greenham also acknowledged that he was now testifying against Ring as "pay back" for the threats and for Ring's interference in Greenham's relationship with Greenham's ex-wife.

On October 29, 1997, the trial judge entered his "Special Verdict"

sentencing Ring to death. Because Ring was convicted of felony murder, not premeditated murder, the judge recognized that Ring was eligible for the death penalty only if he was Magoch's actual killer or if he was "a major participant in the armed robbery that led to the killing and exhibited a reckless disregard or indifference for human life." Citing Greenham's testimony at the sentencing hearing, the judge concluded that Ring "is the one who shot and killed Mr. Magoch." The judge also found that Ring was a major participant in the robbery and that armed robbery "is unquestionably a crime which carries with it a grave risk of death."

The judge then turned to the determination of aggravating and mitigating circumstances. He found two aggravating factors. First, the judge determined that Ring committed the offense in expectation of receiving something of "pecuniary value," as described in [the Arizona statute]; "[t]aking the cash from the armored car was the motive and reason for Mr. Magoch's murder and not just the result." Second, the judge found that the offense was committed "in an especially heinous, cruel or depraved manner." In support of this finding, he cited Ring's comment, as reported by Greenham at the sentencing hearing, expressing pride in his marksmanship. The judge found one nonstatutory mitigating factor: Ring's "minimal" criminal record. In his judgment, that mitigating circumstance did not "call for leniency"; he therefore sentenced Ring to death.

On appeal, Ring argued that Arizona's capital sentencing scheme violates the Sixth and Fourteenth

Amendments to the U.S. Constitution because it entrusts to a judge the finding of a fact raising the defendant's maximum penalty. See Jones v. United States, 526 U.S. 227 (1999); Apprendi v. New Jersey, 530 U.S. 466 (2000). The State, in response, noted that this Court had upheld Arizona's system in Walton v. Arizona, 497 U.S. 639 (1990), and had stated in *Apprendi* that *Walton* remained good law.

Reviewing the death sentence, the Arizona Supreme Court made two preliminary observations. *Apprendi* and *Jones*, the Arizona high court said, "raise some question about the continued viability of *Walton*." The court then examined the *Apprendi* majority's interpretation of Arizona law and found it wanting. *Apprendi*, the Arizona court noted, described Arizona's sentencing system as one that "requir[es] judges, after a jury verdict holding a defendant guilty of a capital crime, to find specific aggravating factors before imposing a sentence of death," and not as a system that "permits a judge to determine the existence of a factor which makes a crime a capital offense." JUSTICE O'CONNOR's *Apprendi* dissent, the Arizona court noted, squarely rejected the *Apprendi* majority's characterization of the Arizona sentencing scheme: "A defendant convicted of first-degree murder in Arizona cannot receive a death sentence unless a judge makes the factual determination that a statutory aggravating factor exists. Without that critical finding, the maximum sentence to which the defendant is exposed is life imprisonment, and not the death penalty."

After reciting this Court's divergent constructions of Arizona law in *Apprendi*, the Arizona Supreme Court described how capital sentencing in fact works in the State. The Arizona high court concluded that "the present case is precisely as described in Justice O'Connor's dissent [in *Apprendi*]—Defendant's death sentence required the judge's factual findings." Although it agreed with the *Apprendi* dissent's reading of Arizona law, the Arizona court understood that it was bound by the Supremacy Clause to apply *Walton*, which this Court had not overruled. It therefore rejected Ring's constitutional attack on the State's capital murder judicial sentencing system.

The court agreed with Ring that the evidence was insufficient to support the aggravating circumstance of depravity, but it upheld the trial court's finding on the aggravating factor of pecuniary gain. The Arizona Supreme Court then reweighed that remaining factor against the sole mitigating circumstance (Ring's lack of a serious criminal record), and affirmed the death sentence.

We granted Ring's petition for a writ of certiorari, to allay uncertainty in the lower courts caused by the manifest tension between *Walton* and the reasoning of *Apprendi*. We now reverse the judgment of the Arizona Supreme Court.

II

Based solely on the jury's verdict finding Ring guilty of first-degree felony murder, the maximum punishment he could have received was life imprisonment. This was so because, in Arizona, a "death sentence may not legally be imposed . . . unless at least one aggravating factor is found to exist beyond a reasonable doubt." The question presented is whether that aggravating factor may be found by the judge, as Arizona law specifies, or whether the Sixth Amendment's jury trial guarantee, made applicable to the States by the Fourteenth Amendment, requires that the aggravating factor determination be entrusted to the jury.

As earlier indicated, this is not the first time we have considered the constitutionality of Arizona's capital sentencing system. In Walton v. Arizona, 497 U.S. 639 (1990), we upheld Arizona's scheme against a charge that it violated the Sixth Amendment. The Court had previously denied a Sixth Amendment challenge to Florida's capital sentencing system, in which the jury recommends a sentence but makes no explicit findings on aggravating circumstances; we so ruled, *Walton* noted, on the ground that "the Sixth Amendment does not require that the specific findings authorizing the imposition of the sentence of death be made by the jury." *Walton* found unavailing the attempts by the defendant-petitioner in that case to distinguish Florida's capital sentencing system from Arizona's. In neither State, according to *Walton*, were the aggravating factors "elements of the offense"; in both States, they ranked as "sentencing considerations" guiding the choice between life and death.

* * *

In dissent in *Walton*, JUSTICE STEVENS urged that the Sixth Amendment requires "a jury determination of facts that must be established before the death penalty may be imposed." Aggravators "operate as statutory elements of capital mur-

der under Arizona law," he reasoned, "because in their absence, [the death] sentence is unavailable." * * *

[Justice Ginsburg discusses cases leading up to Apprendi v. New Jersey, 530 U.S. 466 (2000).]

The defendant-petitioner in [*Apprendi*] was convicted of, *inter alia*, second-degree possession of a firearm, an offense carrying a maximum penalty of ten years under New Jersey law. On the prosecutor's motion, the sentencing judge found by a preponderance of the evidence that Apprendi's crime had been motivated by racial animus. That finding triggered application of New Jersey's 'hate crime enhancement,' which doubled Apprendi's maximum authorized sentence. The judge sentenced Apprendi to 12 years in prison, 2 years over the maximum that would have applied but for the enhancement.

We held that Apprendi's sentence violated his right to "a jury determination that [he] is guilty of every element of the crime with which he is charged, beyond a reasonable doubt." That right attached not only to Apprendi's weapons offense but also to the "hate crime" aggravating circumstance. New Jersey, the Court observed, "threatened Apprendi with certain pains if he unlawfully possessed a weapon and with additional pains if he selected his victims with a purpose to intimidate them because of their race." "Merely using the label 'sentence enhancement' to describe the [second act] surely does not provide a principled basis for treating [the two acts] differently."

The dispositive question, we said, "is one not of form, but of effect."

If a State makes an increase in a defendant's authorized punishment contingent on the finding of a fact, that fact—no matter how the State labels it—must be found by a jury beyond a reasonable doubt. A defendant may not be "expose[d] . . . to a penalty *exceeding* the maximum he would receive if punished according to the facts reflected in the jury verdict alone."

Walton could be reconciled with *Apprendi*, the Court finally asserted. The key distinction, according to the *Apprendi* Court, was that a conviction of first-degree murder in Arizona carried a maximum sentence of death. "[O]nce a jury has found the defendant guilty of all the elements of an offense which carries as its maximum penalty the sentence of death, it may be left to the judge to decide whether that maximum penalty, rather than a lesser one, ought to be imposed."

The *Apprendi* dissenters called the Court's distinction of *Walton* "baffling." 530 U.S., at 538 (opinion of O'CONNOR, J.). * * * "If a State can remove from the jury a factual determination that makes the difference between life and death, as *Walton* holds that it can, it is inconceivable why a State cannot do the same with respect to a factual determination that results in only a 10–year increase in the maximum sentence to which a defendant is exposed."

The Arizona Supreme Court, as we earlier recounted, found the *Apprendi* majority's portrayal of Arizona's capital sentencing law incorrect, and the description in JUSTICE O'CONNOR's dissent precisely right: "Defendant's death sentence required the judge's factual findings." Recognizing that the Arizona

court's construction of the State's own law is authoritative, we are persuaded that *Walton*, in relevant part, cannot survive the reasoning of *Apprendi*.

In an effort to reconcile its capital sentencing system with the Sixth Amendment as interpreted by *Apprendi*, Arizona first restates the *Apprendi* majority's portrayal of Arizona's system: Ring was convicted of first-degree murder, for which Arizona law specifies "death or life imprisonment" as the only sentencing options; Ring was therefore sentenced within the range of punishment authorized by the jury verdict. This argument overlooks *Apprendi*'s instruction that "the relevant inquiry is one not of form, but of effect." In effect, "the required finding [of an aggravated circumstance] expose[d] [Ring] to a greater punishment than that authorized by the jury's guilty verdict." The Arizona first-degree murder statute "authorizes a maximum penalty of death only in a formal sense," *Apprendi*, 530 U.S., at 541 (O'CONNOR, J., dissenting), for it explicitly cross-references the statutory provision requiring the finding of an aggravating circumstance before imposition of the death penalty. See Ariz. Stat. § 13–1105(C) ('First degree murder is a class 1 felony and is punishable by death or life imprisonment *as provided by § 13–703.*' (emphasis added)). If Arizona prevailed on its opening argument, *Apprendi* would be reduced to a "meaningless and formalistic" rule of statutory drafting. See 530 U.S., at 541 (O'CONNOR, J., dissenting).

Arizona also supports the distinction relied upon in *Walton* between elements of an offense and sentencing factors. As to elevation of the maximum punishment, however, *Apprendi* renders the argument untenable; *Apprendi* repeatedly instructs in that context that the characterization of a fact or circumstance as an "element" or a "sentencing factor" is not determinative of the question "who decides," judge or jury.

Even if facts increasing punishment beyond the maximum authorized by a guilty verdict standing alone ordinarily must be found by a jury, Arizona further urges, aggravating circumstances necessary to trigger a death sentence may nonetheless be reserved for judicial determination. As Arizona's counsel maintained at oral argument, there is no doubt that "[d]eath is different." States have constructed elaborate sentencing procedures in death cases, Arizona emphasizes, because of constraints we have said the Eighth Amendment places on capital sentencing. Brief for Respondent 21–25 (citing Furman v. Georgia, 408 U.S. 238 (1972) *(per curiam)*); see also Maynard v. Cartwright, 486 U.S. 356, 362 (1988) ("Since *Furman*, our cases have insisted that the channeling and limiting of the sentencer's discretion in imposing the death penalty is a fundamental constitutional requirement for sufficiently minimizing the risk of wholly arbitrary and capricious action."); *Apprendi*, 530 U.S., at 522–523 (THOMAS, J., concurring) ("[I]n the area of capital punishment, unlike any other area, we have imposed special constraints on a legislature's ability to determine what facts shall lead to what punishment—we have restricted the legislature's ability to define crimes.").

Apart from the Eighth Amendment provenance of aggravating factors, Arizona presents "no specific reason for excepting capital defendants from the constitutional protections ... extend[ed] to defendants generally, and none is readily apparent." *Id.*, at 539 (O'CONNOR, J., dissenting). The notion "that the Eighth Amendment's restriction on a state legislature's ability to define capital crimes should be compensated for by permitting States more leeway under the Fifth and Sixth Amendments in proving an aggravating fact necessary to a capital sentence ... is without precedent in our constitutional jurisprudence." *Ibid.*

In various settings, we have interpreted the Constitution to require the addition of an element or elements to the definition of a criminal offense in order to narrow its scope. See, *e.g.*, United States v. Lopez, 514 U.S. 549, 561–562 (1995) (suggesting that addition to federal gun possession statute of "express jurisdictional element" requiring connection between weapon and interstate commerce would render statute constitutional under Commerce Clause); Brandenburg v. Ohio, 395 U.S. 444, 447 (1969) *(per curiam)* (First Amendment prohibits States from "proscrib[ing] advocacy of the use of force or of law violation except where such advocacy is directed to inciting or producing imminent lawless action and is likely to incite or produce such action"); Lambert v. California, 355 U.S. 225, 229 (1957) (Due Process Clause of Fourteenth Amendment requires "actual knowledge of the duty to register or proof of the probability of such knowledge" before ex-felon may be convicted of failing to register presence in municipality). If a legislature responded to one of these decisions by adding the element we held constitutionally required, surely the Sixth Amendment guarantee would apply to that element. We see no reason to differentiate capital crimes from all others in this regard.

Arizona suggests that judicial authority over the finding of aggravating factors "may ... be a better way to guarantee against the arbitrary imposition of the death penalty." The Sixth Amendment jury trial right, however, does not turn on the relative rationality, fairness, or efficiency of potential factfinders. Entrusting to a judge the finding of facts necessary to support a death sentence might be

> "an admirably fair and efficient scheme of criminal justice designed for a society that is prepared to leave criminal justice to the State. ... The founders of the American Republic were not prepared to leave it to the State, which is why the jury-trial guarantee was one of the least controversial provisions of the Bill of Rights. It has never been efficient; but it has always been free." *Apprendi*, 530 U.S., at 498 (SCALIA, J., concurring).

In any event, the superiority of judicial factfinding in capital cases is far from evident. Unlike Arizona, the great majority of States responded to this Court's Eighth Amendment decisions requiring the presence of aggravating circumstances in capital cases by entrusting those determinations to the jury.

Although the doctrine of *stare decisis* is of fundamental importance to the rule of law, our precedents are not sacrosanct. We have overruled prior decisions where the necessity and propriety of doing so has been established. We are satisfied that this is such a case.

For the reasons stated, we hold that *Walton* and *Apprendi* are irreconcilable; our Sixth Amendment jurisprudence cannot be home to both. Accordingly, we overrule *Walton* to the extent that it allows a sentencing judge, sitting without a jury, to find an aggravating circumstance necessary for imposition of the death penalty. Because Arizona's enumerated aggravating factors operate as "the functional equivalent of an element of a greater offense," *Apprendi*, 530 U.S., at 494, n. 19, the Sixth Amendment requires that they be found by a jury.

* * *

The right to trial by jury guaranteed by the Sixth Amendment would be senselessly diminished if it encompassed the factfinding necessary to increase a defendant's sentence by two years, but not the factfinding necessary to put him to death. We hold that the Sixth Amendment applies to both. The judgment of the Arizona Supreme Court is therefore reversed, and the case is remanded for further proceedings not inconsistent with this opinion.

It is so ordered.

JUSTICE SCALIA, with whom JUSTICE THOMAS joins, concurring.

The question whether Walton v. Arizona, 497 U.S. 639 (1990), survives our decision in Apprendi v. New Jersey, 530 U.S. 466 (2000), confronts me with a difficult choice. What compelled Arizona (and many other States) to specify particular "aggravating factors" that must be found before the death penalty can be imposed, was the line of this Court's cases beginning with Furman v. Georgia, 408 U.S. 238 (1972) *(per curiam)*. In my view, that line of decisions had no proper foundation in the Constitution. I am therefore reluctant to magnify the burdens that our *Furman* jurisprudence imposes on the States. Better for the Court to have invented an evidentiary requirement that a judge can find by a preponderance of the evidence, than to invent one that a unanimous jury must find beyond a reasonable doubt.

On the other hand, as I wrote in my dissent in Almendarez–Torres v. United States, 523 U.S. 224, 248 (1998), and as I reaffirmed by joining the opinion for the Court in *Apprendi*, I believe that the fundamental meaning of the jury-trial guarantee of the Sixth Amendment is that all facts essential to imposition of the level of punishment that the defendant receives—whether the statute calls them elements of the offense, sentencing factors, or Mary Jane—must be found by the jury beyond a reasonable doubt.

The quandary is apparent: Should I continue to apply the last-stated principle when I know that the only reason the fact *is* essential is that this Court has mistakenly said that the Constitution *requires* state law to impose such "aggravating factors"? In *Walton*, to tell the truth, the Sixth Amendment claim was not put with the clarity it obtained in *Almendarez-Torres* and *Apprendi*. There what the appellant argued had to be found by the jury was not all facts essential to imposition of the death penalty, but rather "*every*

finding of fact underlying the sentencing decision," including not only the aggravating factors without which the penalty could not be imposed, but also the *mitigating* factors that might induce a sentencer to give a lesser punishment. But even if the point had been put with greater clarity in *Walton*, I think I still would have approved the Arizona scheme—I would have favored the States' freedom to develop their own capital sentencing procedures (already erroneously abridged by *Furman*) over the logic of the *Apprendi* principle.

Since *Walton*, I have acquired new wisdom that consists of two realizations—or, to put it more critically, have discarded old ignorance that consisted of the failure to realize two things: First, that it is impossible to identify with certainty those aggravating factors whose adoption has been wrongfully coerced by *Furman*, as opposed to those that the State would have adopted in any event. Some States, for example, already had aggravating-factor requirements for capital murder (*e.g.*, murder of a peace officer, see 1965 N. Y. Laws p. 1022 (originally codified at N. Y. Penal Law § 1045)) when *Furman* was decided. When such a State has added aggravating factors, are the new ones the *Apprendi*-exempt product of *Furman*, and the old ones not? And even as to those States that did not previously have aggravating-factor requirements, who is to say that their adoption of a new one today—or, for that matter, even their retention of old ones adopted immediately post-*Furman*—is still the product of that case, and not of a changed social belief that murder *simpliciter* does not deserve death?

Second, and more important, my observing over the past 12 years the accelerating propensity of both state and federal legislatures to adopt "sentencing factors" determined by judges that increase punishment beyond what is authorized by the jury's verdict, and my witnessing the belief of a near majority of my colleagues that this novel practice is perfectly OK, see *Apprendi, supra,* at 523 (O'CONNOR, J., dissenting), cause me to believe that our people's traditional belief in the right of trial by jury is in perilous decline. That decline is bound to be confirmed, and indeed accelerated, by the repeated spectacle of a man's going to his death because *a judge* found that an aggravating factor existed. We cannot preserve our veneration for the protection of the jury in criminal cases if we render ourselves callous to the need for that protection by regularly imposing the death penalty without it.

Accordingly, *whether or not* the States have been erroneously coerced into the adoption of "aggravating factors," wherever those factors exist they must be subject to the usual requirements of the common law, and to the requirement enshrined in our Constitution, in criminal cases: they must be found by the jury beyond a reasonable doubt.

I add one further point, lest the holding of today's decision be confused by the separate concurrence. JUSTICE BREYER, who refuses to accept *Apprendi*, nonetheless concurs in today's judgment because he "believe[s] that jury sentencing in capital cases is mandated by the Eighth Amendment." While I am, as

always, pleased to travel in JUSTICE BREYER's company, the unfortunate fact is that today's judgment has nothing to do with jury sentencing. What today's decision says is that the jury must find the existence of the *fact* that an aggravating factor existed. Those States that leave the ultimate life-or-death decision to the judge may continue to do so— by requiring a prior jury finding of aggravating factor in the sentencing phase or, more simply, by placing the aggravating-factor determination (where it logically belongs anyway) in the guilt phase. There is really no way in which JUSTICE BREYER can travel with the happy band that reaches today's result unless he says yes to *Apprendi*. Concisely put, JUSTICE BREYER is on the wrong flight; he should either get off before the doors close, or buy a ticket to *Apprendi*-land.

JUSTICE KENNEDY, concurring.

Though it is still my view that Apprendi v. New Jersey, 530 U.S. 466 (2000), was wrongly decided, *Apprendi* is now the law, and its holding must be implemented in a principled way. As the Court suggests, no principled reading of *Apprendi* would allow Walton v. Arizona, 497 U.S. 639 (1990), to stand. It is beyond question that during the penalty phase of a first-degree murder prosecution in Arizona, the finding of an aggravating circumstance exposes "the defendant to a greater punishment than that authorized by the jury's guilty verdict." When a finding has this effect, *Apprendi* makes clear, it cannot be reserved for the judge.

This is not to say *Apprendi* should be extended without caution, for the States' settled expectations deserve our respect. A sound understanding of the Sixth Amendment will allow States to respond to the needs and realities of criminal justice administration, and *Apprendi* can be read as leaving in place many reforms designed to reduce unfairness in sentencing. I agree with the Court, however, that *Apprendi* and *Walton* cannot stand together as the law.

With these observations I join the opinion of the Court.

JUSTICE BREYER, concurring in the judgment.

I

Given my views in Apprendi v. New Jersey, 530 U.S. 466, 555 (2000) (dissenting opinion) * * * I cannot join the Court's opinion. I concur in the judgment, however, because I believe that jury sentencing in capital cases is mandated by the Eighth Amendment.

II

This Court has held that the Eighth Amendment requires States to apply special procedural safeguards when they seek the death penalty. Otherwise, the constitutional prohibition against 'cruel and unusual punishments' would forbid its use. Furman v. Georgia, 408 U.S. 238 (1972) *(per curiam)*. JUSTICE STEVENS has written that those safeguards include a requirement that a *jury* impose any sentence of death. Harris v. Alabama, 513 U.S. 504, 515–526 (1995) (dissenting opinion); Spaziano v. Florida, 468 U.S. 447, 467–490 (1984) (STEVENS, J., joined by Brennan and Marshall, JJ., concurring in part and dissenting in part). Although I joined the majority in Harris v. Alabama, I have come to agree with the

dissenting view, and with the related views of others upon which it in part relies. I therefore conclude that the Eighth Amendment requires that a jury, not a judge, make the decision to sentence a defendant to death.

I am convinced by the reasons that JUSTICE STEVENS has given. These include (1) his belief that retribution provides the main justification for capital punishment, and (2) his assessment of the jury's comparative advantage in determining, in a particular case, whether capital punishment will serve that end.

As to the first, I note the continued difficulty of justifying capital punishment in terms of its ability to deter crime, to incapacitate offenders, or to rehabilitate criminals. Studies of deterrence are, at most, inconclusive. See, *e.g.*, Sorenson, Wrinkle, Brewer, & Marquart, Capital Punishment and Deterrence: Examining the Effect of Executions on Murder in Texas, 45 Crime & Delinquency 481 (1999) (no evidence of a deterrent effect); Bonner & Fessenden, Absence of Executions: A special report, States With No Death Penalty Share Lower Homicide Rates, N. Y. Times, Sept. 22, 2000, p. A1 (during last 20 years, homicide rate in death penalty States has been 48% to 101% higher than in non-death-penalty States); see also Radelet & Akers, Deterrence and the Death Penalty: The Views of the Experts, 87 J. Crim. L. & C. 1, 8 (1996) (over 80% of criminologists believe existing research fails to support deterrence justification).

As to incapacitation, few offenders sentenced to life without parole (as an alternative to death) commit further crimes. See, *e.g.*, Sorensen &

Pilgrim, An Actuarial Risk Assessment of Violence Posed by Capital Murder Defendants, 90 J. Crim. L. & C. 1251, 1256 (2000) (studies find average repeat murder rate of .002% among murderers whose death sentences were commuted); Marquart & Sorensen, A National Study of the *Furman*-Commuted Inmates: Assessing the Threat to Society from Capital Offenders, 23 Loyola (LA) L. Rev. 5, 26 (1989) (98% did not kill again either in prison or in free society). And rehabilitation, obviously, is beside the point.

In respect to retribution, jurors possess an important comparative advantage over judges. In principle, they are more attuned to "the community's moral sensibility," *Spaziano*, 468 U.S., at 481 (STEVENS, J., concurring in part and dissenting in part), because they "reflect more accurately the composition and experiences of the community as a whole," *id.*, at 486. Hence they are more likely to "express the conscience of the community on the ultimate question of life or death," Witherspoon v. Illinois, 391 U.S. 510, 519 (1968), and better able to determine in the particular case the need for retribution * * *.

* * *

The importance of trying to translate a community's sense of capital punishment's appropriateness in a particular case is underscored by the continued division of opinion as to whether capital punishment is in all circumstances, as currently administered, 'cruel and unusual.' Those who make this claim point, among other things, to the fact that death is not reversible, and to death sentences imposed upon those whose convictions proved un-

reliable. * * * They point to the potentially arbitrary application of the death penalty, adding that the race of the victim and socio-economic factors seem to matter. * * * They argue that the delays that increasingly accompany sentences of death make those sentences unconstitutional because of the suffering inherent in a prolonged wait for execution. * * * They point to the inadequacy of representation in capital cases, a fact that aggravates the other failings. * * * And they note that other nations have increasingly abandoned capital punishment. * * *

Many communities may have accepted some or all of these claims, for they do not impose capital sentences. See A Broken System, App. B, Table 11A (more than two-thirds of American counties have never imposed the death penalty * * * (2,064 out of 3,066), and only 3% of the Nation's counties account for 50% of the Nation's death sentences (92 out of 3,066)). Leaving questions of arbitrariness aside, this diversity argues strongly for procedures that will help assure that, in a particular case, the community indeed believes application of the death penalty is appropriate, not "cruel," "unusual," or otherwise unwarranted.

For these reasons, the danger of unwarranted imposition of the penalty cannot be avoided unless the decision to impose the death penalty is made by a jury rather than by a single governmental official. And I conclude that the Eighth Amendment requires individual jurors to make, and to take responsibility for, a decision to sentence a person to death.

JUSTICE O'CONNOR, with whom the CHIEF JUSTICE joins, dissenting.

I understand why the Court holds that the reasoning of Apprendi v. New Jersey, 530 U.S. 466 (2000), is irreconcilable with Walton v. Arizona, 497 U.S. 639 (1990). Yet in choosing which to overrule, I would choose *Apprendi*, not *Walton*.

I continue to believe, for the reasons I articulated in my dissent in *Apprendi*, that the decision in *Apprendi* was a serious mistake. As I argued in that dissent, *Apprendi*'s rule that any fact that increases the maximum penalty must be treated as an element of the crime is not required by the Constitution, by history, or by our prior cases. Indeed, the rule directly contradicts several of our prior cases. See *id.*, at 531–539 (explaining that the rule conflicts with Patterson v. New York, 432 U.S. 197 (1977), Almendarez–Torres v. United States, 523 U.S. 224 (1998), and *Walton, supra*). And it ignores the "significant history in this country of . . . discretionary sentencing by judges." The Court has failed, both in *Apprendi* and in the decision announced today, to "offer any meaningful justification for deviating from years of cases both suggesting and holding that application of the 'increase in the maximum penalty' rule is not required by the Constitution."

Not only was the decision in *Apprendi* unjustified in my view, but it has also had a severely destabilizing effect on our criminal justice system. I predicted in my dissent that the decision would "unleash a flood of petitions by convicted defendants seeking to invalidate their sentences in whole or in part on the authority of [*Apprendi*]." As of May 31, 2002, less than two years

after *Apprendi* was announced, the United States Courts of Appeals had decided approximately 1,802 criminal appeals in which defendants challenged their sentences, and in some cases even their convictions, under *Apprendi*. These federal appeals are likely only the tip of the iceberg, as federal criminal prosecutions represent a tiny fraction of the total number of criminal prosecutions nationwide. The number of second or successive habeas corpus petitions filed in the federal courts also increased by 77% in 2001, a phenomenon the Administrative Office of the United States Courts attributes to prisoners bringing *Apprendi* claims. This Court has been similarly overwhelmed by the aftershocks of *Apprendi*. A survey of the petitions for certiorari we received in the past year indicates that 18% raised *Apprendi*-related claims. It is simply beyond dispute that *Apprendi* threw countless criminal sentences into doubt and thereby caused an enormous increase in the workload of an already overburdened judiciary.

The decision today is only going to add to these already serious effects. The Court effectively declares five States' capital sentencing schemes unconstitutional. [Colorado, Idaho, Montana and Nebraska have capital sentencing schemes similar to Arizona.] There are 168 prisoners on death row in these States * * * each of whom is now likely to challenge his or her death sentence. I believe many of these challenges will ultimately be unsuccessful, either because the prisoners will be unable to satisfy the standards of harmless error or plain error review, or because, having completed their direct appeals, they will be barred from taking advantage of today's holding on federal collateral review. Nonetheless, the need to evaluate these claims will greatly burden the courts in these five States. In addition, I fear that the prisoners on death row in Alabama, Delaware, Florida, and Indiana, which [have] hybrid sentencing schemes in which the jury renders an advisory verdict but the judge makes the ultimate sentencing determination may also seize on today's decision to challenge their sentences. There are 529 prisoners on death row in these States.

By expanding on *Apprendi*, the Court today exacerbates the harm done in that case. Consistent with my dissent, I would overrule *Apprendi* rather than *Walton*.

IV. TRIAL BY JURY

B. WHAT THE JURY DECIDES

Page 1080. After the paragraph on *Jones* at the bottom of the page, add the following:

In Apprendi v. New Jersey, 530 U.S. 466 (2000), the Court relied heavily on *Jones* and held that "it is unconstitutional for a legislature to remove from the jury the assessment of facts that increase the prescribed range of penalties to which a criminal defendant is exposed." The Court invalidated a statute that allowed the judge to increase a sentence for a weapons crime, beyond the statutory maximum, if the judge found at sentencing that the crime was committed with a racial bias. The question of racial bias had to be submitted to a jury; to increase the punishment beyond the statutory maximum deprived the defendant of his constitutional right to a jury trial on the question of racial bias. *Apprendi* is set forth in detail in this Supplement, *supra*, in the section on constitutionally-based proof requirements.

In Harris v. United States, 536 U.S. 545 (2002), the Court held that *Apprendi* does not prevent the judge from finding a fact that forms the basis of a mandatory minimum sentence, so long as the sentence imposed does not exceed the statutory maximum. The Court reasoned that so long as the sentence was within the prescribed sentencing range, the protection of a jury determination was not required by the Constitution. *Harris* is set forth in detail in this Supplement, *supra*, in the section on constitutionally-based proof requirements.

G. THE JURY VERDICT

Page 1168. At the end of the Note on *Schmuck*, add the following:

The Court applied the *Schmuck* "elements" test in Carter v. United States, 530 U.S. 255 (2000). Carter entered a bank, confronted an exiting customer, and pushed her back inside. She screamed, startling others in the bank. Undeterred, Carter ran inside and leaped over a counter and through one of the teller windows. A teller rushed into the manager's office. Meanwhile, Carter opened several teller drawers and emptied the money into a bag. After removing almost $16,000, he jumped back over the counter and fled. He was charged with violating 18 U.S.C. § 2113(a), which punishes "[w]hoever, by force and violence, or by intimidation, takes ... any ... thing of value [from a] bank." While not contesting the basic facts, Carter pleaded not guilty on the theory that he had not taken the bank's money "by force and violence, or by intimidation," as § 2113(a) requires. Before trial, he moved for a jury instruction on the offense described by § 2113(b) as a lesser included offense of the offense described by § 2113(a). Section 2113(b) entails less severe penalties than § 2113(a), punishing "[w]hoever takes and carries away, with intent to steal or purloin, any ... thing of value exceeding $1,000 [from a] ... bank." The District Court denied the motion. The jury, instructed on § 2113(a) alone, returned a guilty verdict.

The Supreme Court, in an opinion by Justice Thomas for five members of the Court, held that subsection (b) was not a lesser included offense of subsection (a), because it contains three elements that are not required by subsection (a). Those three elements are: (1) specific intent to steal; (2) asportation; and (3) valuation exceeding $1,000. Justice Thomas applied a "textual comparison" of the elements of the two offenses and concluded as follows:

> First, whereas subsection (b) requires that the defendant act "with intent to steal or purloin," subsection (a) contains no similar requirement. Second, whereas subsection (b) requires that the defendant "tak[e] and carr[y] away" the property, subsection (a) only requires that the defendant "tak[e]" the property. Third, whereas the first paragraph of subsection (b) requires that the property have a "value exceeding $1,000," subsection (a) contains no valuation requirement. These extra clauses in subsection (b) cannot be regarded as mere surplusage; they mean something.

Justice Ginsburg, joined by Justices Stevens, Souter and Breyer, dissented in *Carter*. She relied on common law traditions rather than strict textual comparison. She explained as follows:

> At common law, robbery meant larceny plus force, violence, or putting in fear. Because robbery was an aggravated form of larceny at common law, larceny was a lesser included offense of robbery. Congress, I conclude, did not depart from that traditional understanding when it rendered "Bank robbery and incidental crimes" federal offenses. Accordingly, I would hold that petitioner Carter is not prohibited as a matter of law from obtaining an instruction on bank larceny as a lesser included offense. The Court holds that Congress, in 18 U.S.C. § 2113, has dislodged bank robbery and bank larceny from their common-law mooring. I dissent from that determination.

VI. THE DEFENDANT'S RIGHT TO PARTICIPATE IN THE TRIAL

A. THE RIGHT OF THE DEFENDANT TO BE PRESENT

Page 1209.   Add the following at the end of the section:

Commenting on the Defendant's Presence at Trial: Portuondo v. Agard

Witnesses are ordinarily sequestered before they testify in a criminal trial. See Federal Rule of Evidence 615. Sequestration addresses the concern that if a witness knows the evidence already presented, he may tailor his testimony to fit the evidence. But a criminal defendant who chooses to testify cannot be sequestered, because he has a constitutional right to attend the trial. In Portuondo v. Agard, 529 U.S. 61 (2000), the prosecutor in summation sought to draw this fact to the jury's attention. The case presented a credibility determination between the defendant Agard and the victims. The prosecutor argued as follows:

> You know, ladies and gentlemen, unlike all the other witnesses in this case the defendant has a benefit and the benefit that he has, unlike all the other witnesses, is he gets to sit here and listen to the testimony of all the other witnesses before he testifies. * * * That gives you a big advantage, doesn't it. You get to sit here and think what am I going to say and how am I going to say it? How am I going to fit it into the evidence? * * * He's a smart man. I never said he was stupid.... He used everything to his advantage.

Agard contended that the prosecutor's argument placed an impermissible burden on his right to be present at trial. The trial court rejected this claim, reasoning that Agard's status as the last witness in the case was simply a matter of fact, and held that his presence during the entire trial, and the advantage that this afforded him, "may fairly be commented on." The Supreme Court, in an opinion by Justice Scalia for five Justices, agreed with the trial court. Justice Scalia analyzed, and rejected, Agard's argument in the following passage:

> Respondent's argument boils down to a request that we extend to comments of the type the prosecutor made here the rationale of Griffin v. California, 380 U.S. 609 (1965), which involved comments upon a defendant's refusal to testify. In that case, the trial court instructed the jury that it was free to take the defendant's failure to deny or explain facts within his knowledge as tending to indicate the truth of the prosecution's case. This Court held that such a comment, by "solemniz[ing] the silence of the accused into evidence against him," unconstitutionally "cuts down on the privilege [against self-incrimination] by making its assertion costly." We decline to extend *Griffin* to the present context. * * *
>
> That case is a poor analogue * * * for several reasons. What we prohibited the prosecutor from urging the jury to do in *Griffin* was

something the jury is not permitted to do. The defendant's right to hold the prosecution to proving its case without his assistance is not to be impaired by the jury's counting the defendant's silence at trial against him—and upon request the court must instruct the jury to that effect. It is reasonable enough to expect a jury to comply with that instruction since, as we observed in *Griffin*, the inference of guilt from silence is not always "natural or irresistible." A defendant might refuse to testify simply out of fear that he will be made to look bad by clever counsel, or fear "that his prior convictions will prejudice the jury." By contrast, it is natural and irresistible for a jury, in evaluating the relative credibility of a defendant who testifies last, to have in mind and weigh in the balance the fact that he heard the testimony of all those who preceded him. It is one thing (as *Griffin* requires) for the jury to evaluate all the other evidence in the case without giving any effect to the defendant's refusal to testify; it is something else (and quite impossible) for the jury to evaluate the credibility of the defendant's testimony while blotting out from its mind the fact that before giving the testimony the defendant had been sitting there listening to the other witnesses. Thus, the principle respondent asks us to adopt here differs from what we adopted in *Griffin* in one or the other of the following respects: It either prohibits inviting the jury to do what the jury is perfectly entitled to do; or it requires the jury to do what is practically impossible.

Second, *Griffin* prohibited comments that suggest a defendant's silence is "evidence of guilt." The prosecutor's comments in this case, by contrast, concerned respondent's credibility as a witness, and were therefore in accord with our longstanding rule that when a defendant takes the stand, his credibility may be impeached and his testimony assailed like that of any other witness. When a defendant assumes the role of a witness, the rules that generally apply to other witnesses—rules that serve the truth-seeking function of the trial—are generally applicable to him as well.

Justice Scalia was not troubled by the fact that the prosecutor's comments were made in summation, leaving the defendant no opportunity to reply. Justice Scalia stated that "[o]ur trial structure, which requires the defense to close before the prosecution, regularly forces the defense to predict what the prosecution will say." Justice Scalia concluded as follows:

In sum, we see no reason to depart from the practice of treating testifying defendants the same as other witnesses. A witness's ability to hear prior testimony and to tailor his account accordingly, and the threat that ability presents to the integrity of the trial, are no different when it is the defendant doing the listening. Allowing comment upon the fact that a defendant's presence in the courtroom provides him a unique opportunity to tailor his testimony is appropriate—and indeed, given the inability to sequester the defendant, sometimes essential—to the central function of the trial, which is to discover the truth.

Justice Stevens, joined by Justice Breyer, concurred in the judgment in *Agard*. Justice Stevens found no constitutional violation in the prosecutor's tailoring argument. He wrote, however, to express his "disagreement with the Court's implicit endorsement of her summation" and concluded that such arguments should be discouraged as a matter of fair trial practice.

Justice Ginsburg, joined by Justice Souter, dissented in *Agard*. She focused on the fact that the prosecutor's tailoring argument was "generic", i.e., it could be applied in any case in which the defendant testified. Such an "automatic burden" on the defendant's credibility resulted, in her view, in an unfair penalty for the defendant's exercise of his constitutional right to be present.

VII. THE RIGHT TO EFFECTIVE ASSISTANCE OF COUNSEL

A. INEFFECTIVENESS AND PREJUDICE

1. *The Two–Pronged Test*

Page 1227.   After the section on Evitts v. Lucey, add the following section:

Failing to File a Notice of Appeal

What if a defendant's right to bring a first appeal is lost because defense counsel failed to file a notice of appeal? Does this failure necessarily constitute ineffective assistance of appellate counsel? Is it necessarily prejudicial? These are the questions discussed in the next case.

Page 1238.   Add after the Headnote on the duty to investigate:

The Duty to Investigated Mitigating Evidence in a Capital Trial: Wiggins v. Smith

WIGGINS v. SMITH
Supreme Court of the United States, 2003.
123 S.Ct. 2527.

JUSTICE O'CONNOR delivered the opinion of the Court.

Petitioner, Kevin Wiggins, argues that his attorneys' failure to investigate his background and present mitigating evidence of his unfortunate life history at his capital sentencing proceedings violated his Sixth Amendment right to counsel. In this case, we consider whether the United States Court of Appeals for the Fourth Circuit erred in upholding the Maryland Court of Appeals' rejection of this claim.

I

A

On September 17, 1988, police discovered 77–year-old Florence

Lacs drowned in the bathtub of her ransacked apartment in Woodlawn, Maryland. The State indicted petitioner for the crime on October 20, 1988, and later filed a notice of intention to seek the death penalty. Two Baltimore County public defenders, Carl Schlaich and Michelle Nethercott, assumed responsibility for Wiggins' case. In July 1989, petitioner elected to be tried before a judge in Baltimore County Circuit Court. On August 4, after a 4–day trial, the court found petitioner guilty of first-degree murder, robbery, and two counts of theft.

After his conviction, Wiggins elected to be sentenced by a jury, and the trial court scheduled the proceedings to begin on October 11, 1989. On September 11, counsel filed a motion for bifurcation of sentencing in hopes of presenting Wiggins' case in two phases. Counsel intended first to prove that Wiggins did not act as a "principal in the first degree,"—i.e., that he did not kill the victim by his own hand. See Md. Ann. Code, Art. 27, § 413 (1996) (requiring proof of direct responsibility for death eligibility). Counsel then intended, if necessary, to present a mitigation case. In the memorandum in support of their motion, counsel argued that bifurcation would enable them to present each case in its best light; separating the two cases would prevent the introduction of mitigating evidence from diluting their claim that Wiggins was not directly responsible for the murder.

On October 12, the court denied the bifurcation motion, and sentencing proceedings commenced immediately thereafter. In her opening statement, Nethercott told the jurors they would hear evidence suggesting that someone other than Wiggins actually killed Lacs. Counsel then explained that the judge would instruct them to weigh Wiggins' clean record as a factor against a death sentence. She concluded: "You're going to hear that Kevin Wiggins has had a difficult life. It has not been easy for him. But he's worked. He's tried to be a productive citizen, and he's reached the age of 27 with no convictions for prior crimes of violence and no convictions, period.... I think that's an important thing for you to consider." During the proceedings themselves, however, counsel introduced no evidence of Wiggins' life history.

Before closing arguments, Schlaich made a proffer to the court, outside the presence of the jury, to preserve bifurcation as an issue for appeal. He detailed the mitigation case counsel would have presented had the court granted their bifurcation motion. He explained that they would have introduced psychological reports and expert testimony demonstrating Wiggins' limited intellectual capacities and childlike emotional state on the one hand, and the absence of aggressive patterns in his behavior, his capacity for empathy, and his desire to function in the world on the other. At no point did Schlaich proffer any evidence of petitioner's life history or family background. On October 18, the court instructed the jury on the sentencing task before it, and later that afternoon, the jury returned with a sentence of death. A divided Maryland Court of Appeals affirmed.

B

In 1993, Wiggins sought postconviction relief in Baltimore County

Circuit Court. With new counsel, he challenged the adequacy of his representation at sentencing, arguing that his attorneys had rendered constitutionally defective assistance by failing to investigate and present mitigating evidence of his dysfunctional background. To support his claim, petitioner presented testimony by Hans Selvog, a licensed social worker certified as an expert by the court. Selvog testified concerning an elaborate social history report he had prepared containing evidence of the severe physical and sexual abuse petitioner suffered at the hands of his mother and while in the care of a series of foster parents. Relying on state social services, medical, and school records, as well as interviews with petitioner and numerous family members, Selvog chronicled petitioner's bleak life history.

According to Selvog's report, petitioner's mother, a chronic alcoholic, frequently left Wiggins and his siblings home alone for days, forcing them to beg for food and to eat paint chips and garbage. Mrs. Wiggins' abusive behavior included beating the children for breaking into the kitchen, which she often kept locked. She had sex with men while her children slept in the same bed and, on one occasion, forced petitioner's hand against a hot stove burner—an incident that led to petitioner's hospitalization. At the age of six, the State placed Wiggins in foster care. Petitioner's first and second foster mothers abused him physically, and, as petitioner explained to Selvog, the father in his second foster home repeatedly molested and raped him. At age 16, petitioner ran away from his foster home and began living on the streets. He returned intermittently to additional foster homes, including one in which the foster mother's sons allegedly gang-raped him on more than one occasion. After leaving the foster care system, Wiggins entered a Job Corps program and was allegedly sexually abused by his supervisor.

During the postconviction proceedings, Schlaich testified that he did not remember retaining a forensic social worker to prepare a social history, even though the State made funds available for that purpose. He explained that he and Nethercott, well in advance of trial, decided to focus their efforts on "retry[ing] the factual case" and disputing Wiggins' direct responsibility for the murder. In April 1994, at the close of the proceedings, the judge observed from the bench that he could not remember a capital case in which counsel had not compiled a social history of the defendant, explaining, "[n]ot to do a social history, at least to see what you have got, to me is absolute error. I just—I would be flabbergasted if the Court of Appeals said anything else." In October 1997, however, the trial court denied Wiggins' petition for postconviction relief. The court concluded that "when the decision not to investigate . . . is a matter of trial tactics, there is no ineffective assistance of counsel."

The Maryland Court of Appeals affirmed the denial of relief, concluding that trial counsel had made "a deliberate, tactical decision to concentrate their effort at convincing the jury" that appellant was not directly responsible for the murder. The court observed that counsel knew of Wiggins' unfortunate childhood. They had available to them both the presentence investigation (PSI) report prepared by the Division of Parole and Probation, as required by Maryland law, as well as "more detailed social service records that recorded incidences of physical and sexual abuse, an alcoholic mother, placements in foster care, and borderline retardation." The court acknowledged that this evidence was neither as detailed nor as graphic as the history elaborated in the Selvog report but emphasized that counsel did investigate and were aware of appellant's background. Counsel knew that at least one uncontested mitigating factor—Wiggins' lack of prior convictions—would be before the jury should their attempt to disprove Wiggins' direct responsibility for the murder fail. As a result, the court concluded, Schlaich and Nethercott "made a reasoned choice to proceed with what they thought was their best defense."

C

In September 2001, Wiggins filed a petition for writ of habeas corpus in Federal District Court. The trial court granted him relief, holding that the Maryland courts' rejection of his ineffective assistance claim "involved an unreasonable application of clearly established federal law." Wiggins v. Corcoran, 164 F.Supp.2d 538, 557 (2001) (citing Williams v. Taylor, 529 U.S. 362 (2000)). The court rejected the State's defense of counsel's "tactical" decision to retry guilt, concluding that for a strategic decision to be reasonable, it must be "based upon information the attorney has made after conducting a reasonable investigation." The court found that though counsel were aware of some

aspects of Wiggins' background, that knowledge did not excuse them from their duty to make a "fully informed and deliberate decision" about whether to present a mitigation case. In fact, the court concluded, their knowledge triggered an obligation to look further.

Reviewing the District Court's decision de novo, the Fourth Circuit reversed, holding that counsel had made a reasonable strategic decision to focus on petitioner's direct responsibility. The court contrasted counsel's complete failure to investigate potential mitigating evidence in *Williams* with the fact that Schlaich and Nethercott knew at least some details of Wiggins' childhood from the PSI and social services records. The court acknowledged that counsel likely knew further investigation "would have resulted in more sordid details surfacing," but agreed with the Maryland Court of Appeals that counsel's knowledge of the avenues of mitigation available to them "was sufficient to make an informed strategic choice" to challenge petitioner's direct responsibility for the murder. The court emphasized that conflicting medical testimony with respect to the time of death, the absence of direct evidence against Wiggins, and unexplained forensic evidence at the crime scene supported counsel's strategy.

We granted certiorari, and now reverse.

II

A

Petitioner renews his contention that his attorneys' performance at sentencing violated his Sixth

Amendment right to effective assistance of counsel. The amendments to 28 U.S.C. § 2254, enacted as part of the Antiterrorism and Effective Death Penalty Act of 1996 (AEDPA), circumscribe our consideration of Wiggins' claim and require us to limit our analysis to the law as it was 'clearly established' by our precedents at the time of the state court's decision. Section 2254 provides:

(d) An application for a writ of habeas corpus on behalf of a person in custody pursuant to the judgment of a State court shall not be granted with respect to any claim that was adjudicated on the merits in State court proceedings unless the adjudication of the claim—

(1) resulted in a decision that was contrary to, or involved an unreasonable application of, clearly established Federal law, as determined by the Supreme Court of the United States; or

(2) resulted in a decision that was based on an unreasonable determination of the facts in light of the evidence presented at the State court proceeding.

We have made clear that the "unreasonable application" prong of § 2254(d)(1) permits a federal habeas court to "grant the writ if the state court identifies the correct governing legal principle from this Court's decisions but unreasonably applies that principle to the facts" of petitioner's case. Williams v. Taylor, *supra*, at 413; see also Bell v. Cone, 535 U.S. 685, 694 (2002). In other words, a federal court may grant relief when a state court has misapplied a "governing legal principle" to "a set of facts different

from those of the case in which the principle was announced." Lockyer v. Andrade, 538 U.S. __, __ (2003) citing Williams v. Taylor, supra, at 407. In order for a federal court to find a state court's application of our precedent "unreasonable," the state court's decision must have been more than incorrect or erroneous. See Lockyer, supra, at __ (slip op., at 11). The state court's application must have been "objectively unreasonable." See Williams v. Taylor, supra, at 409.

We established the legal principles that govern claims of ineffective assistance of counsel in Strickland v. Washington, 466 U.S. 668 (1984). An ineffective assistance claim has two components: A petitioner must show that counsel's performance was deficient, and that the deficiency prejudiced the defense. To establish deficient performance, a petitioner must demonstrate that counsel's representation "fell below an objective standard of reasonableness." We have declined to articulate specific guidelines for appropriate attorney conduct and instead have emphasized that "[t]he proper measure of attorney performance remains simply reasonableness under prevailing professional norms."

In this case, as in *Strickland*, petitioner's claim stems from counsel's decision to limit the scope of their investigation into potential mitigating evidence. Here, as in *Strickland*, counsel attempt to justify their limited investigation as reflecting a tactical judgment not to present mitigating evidence at sentencing and to pursue an alternate strategy instead. In rejecting Strickland's claim, we defined the deference owed such strategic judgments in terms of the adequacy of the investigations supporting those judgments:

> [S]trategic choices made after thorough investigation of law and facts relevant to plausible options are virtually unchallengeable; and strategic choices made after less than complete investigation are reasonable precisely to the extent that reasonable professional judgments support the limitations on investigation. In other words, counsel has a duty to make reasonable investigations or to make a reasonable decision that makes particular investigations unnecessary. In any ineffectiveness case, a particular decision not to investigate must be directly assessed for reasonableness in all the circumstances, applying a heavy measure of deference to counsel's judgments.

Our opinion in Williams v. Taylor is illustrative of the proper application of these standards. In finding Williams' ineffectiveness claim meritorious, we applied Strickland and concluded that counsel's failure to uncover and present voluminous mitigating evidence at sentencing could not be justified as a tactical decision to focus on Williams' voluntary confessions, because counsel had not "fulfill[ed] their obligation to conduct a thorough investigation of the defendant's background." While *Williams* had not yet been decided at the time the Maryland Court of Appeals rendered the decision at issue in this case, Williams' case was before us on habeas review. Contrary to the dissent's contention, we therefore made no new law in resolving Williams' ineffectiveness claim. In highlighting counsel's duty to investigate, and in referring to the ABA Standards for

Criminal Justice as guides, we applied the same "clearly established" precedent of Strickland we apply today. Cf. *Strickland*, 466 U.S., at 690–691 (establishing that 'thorough investigation[s]' are "virtually unchallengeable" and underscoring that "counsel has a duty to make reasonable investigation' "); see also id., at 688–689 ("Prevailing norms of practice as reflected in American Bar Association standards and the like ... are guides to determining what is reasonable").

In light of these standards, our principal concern in deciding whether Schlaich and Nethercott exercised "reasonable professional judgmen[t]" is not whether counsel should have presented a mitigation case. Rather, we focus on whether the investigation supporting counsel's decision not to introduce mitigating evidence of Wiggins' background was itself reasonable. In assessing counsel's investigation, we must conduct an objective review of their performance, measured for "reasonableness under prevailing professional norms" which includes a context-dependent consideration of the challenged conduct as seen "from counsel's perspective at the time."

B

1

The record demonstrates that counsel's investigation drew from three sources. App. 490–491. Counsel arranged for William Stejskal, a psychologist, to conduct a number of tests on petitioner. Stejskal concluded that petitioner had an IQ of 79, had difficulty coping with demanding situations, and exhibited features of a personality disorder.

These reports revealed nothing, however, of petitioner's life history.

With respect to that history, counsel had available to them the written PSI, which included a one-page account of Wiggins' personal history noting his "misery as a youth," quoting his description of his own background as "disgusting," and observing that he spent most of his life in foster care. Counsel also tracked down records kept by the Baltimore City Department of Social Services (DSS) documenting petitioner's various placements in the State's foster care system. In describing the scope of counsel's investigation into petitioner's life history, both the Fourth Circuit and the Maryland Court of Appeals referred only to these two sources of information.

Counsel's decision not to expand their investigation beyond the PSI and the DSS records fell short of the professional standards that prevailed in Maryland in 1989. As Schlaich acknowledged, standard practice in Maryland in capital cases at the time of Wiggins' trial included the preparation of a social history report. Despite the fact that the Public Defender's office made funds available for the retention of a forensic social worker, counsel chose not to commission such a report. Counsel's conduct similarly fell short of the standards for capital defense work articulated by the American Bar Association (ABA)— standards to which we long have referred as "guides to determining what is reasonable." *Strickland*, supra, at 688; Williams v. Taylor, supra, at 396. The ABA Guidelines provide that investigations into mitigating evidence "should comprise efforts to discover all reasonably available mitigating evidence and evidence to rebut any aggravating evidence that may be introduced by the prosecutor." ABA Guidelines for the Appointment and Performance of Counsel in Death Penalty Cases 11.4.1(C), p. 93 (1989).

The scope of their investigation was also unreasonable in light of what counsel actually discovered in the DSS records. The records revealed several facts: Petitioner's mother was a chronic alcoholic; Wiggins was shuttled from foster home to foster home and displayed some emotional difficulties while there; he had frequent, lengthy absences from school; and, on at least one occasion, his mother left him and his siblings alone for days without food. As the Federal District Court emphasized, any reasonably competent attorney would have realized that pursuing these leads was necessary to making an informed choice among possible defenses, particularly given the apparent absence of any aggravating factors in petitioner's background. Indeed, counsel uncovered no evidence in their investigation to suggest that a mitigation case, in its own right, would have been counterproductive, or that further investigation would have been fruitless; this case is therefore distinguishable from our precedents in which we have found limited investigations into mitigating evidence to be reasonable. See, e.g., Burger v. Kemp, 483 U.S. 776, 794 (1987) (concluding counsel's limited investigation was reasonable because he interviewed all witnesses brought to his attention, discovering little that was helpful and much that was harmful); Darden v. Wainwright, 477 U.S. 168, 186 (1986) (concluding that counsel engaged in extensive preparation and that the decision to present a mitigation case would have resulted in the jury hearing evidence that petitioner had been convicted of violent crimes and spent much of his life in jail). Had counsel investigated further, they may well have discovered the sexual abuse later revealed during state postconviction proceedings.

The record of the actual sentencing proceedings underscores the unreasonableness of counsel's conduct by suggesting that their failure to investigate thoroughly resulted from inattention, not reasoned strategic judgment. Counsel sought, until the day before sentencing, to have the proceedings bifurcated into a retrial of guilt and a mitigation stage. On the eve of sentencing, counsel represented to the court that they were prepared to come forward with mitigating evidence, and that they intended to present such evidence in the event the court granted their motion to bifurcate. In other words, prior to sentencing, counsel never actually abandoned the possibility that they would present a mitigation defense. Until the court denied their motion, then, they had every reason to develop the most powerful mitigation case possible.

What is more, during the sentencing proceeding itself, counsel did not focus exclusively on Wiggins' direct responsibility for the murder. After introducing that issue in her opening statement, Nethercott entreated the jury to consider not just what Wiggins "is found to have done," but also "who [he] is." Though she told the jury it would "hear that Kevin Wiggins has had a difficult life," counsel never fol-

lowed up on that suggestion with details of Wiggins' history. At the same time, counsel called a criminologist to testify that inmates serving life sentences tend to adjust well and refrain from further violence in prison—testimony with no bearing on whether petitioner committed the murder by his own hand. Far from focusing exclusively on petitioner's direct responsibility, then, counsel put on a halfhearted mitigation case, taking precisely the type of "shotgun" approach the Maryland Court of Appeals concluded counsel sought to avoid. When viewed in this light, the "strategic decision" the state courts and respondents all invoke to justify counsel's limited pursuit of mitigating evidence resembles more a post-hoc rationalization of counsel's conduct than an accurate description of their deliberations prior to sentencing.

In rejecting petitioner's ineffective assistance claim, the Maryland Court of Appeals appears to have assumed that because counsel had some information with respect to petitioner's background—the information in the PSI and the DSS records—they were in a position to make a tactical choice not to present a mitigation defense. In assessing the reasonableness of an attorney's investigation, however, a court must consider not only the quantum of evidence already known to counsel, but also whether the known evidence would lead a reasonable attorney to investigate further. Even assuming Schlaich and Nethercott limited the scope of their investigation for strategic reasons, Strickland does not establish that a cursory investigation automatically justifies a tactical decision with respect to sentencing strategy. Rather, a reviewing court must consider the reasonableness of the investigation said to support that strategy.

The Maryland Court of Appeals' application of *Strickland's* governing legal principles was objectively unreasonable. Though the state court acknowledged petitioner's claim that counsel's failure to prepare a social history "did not meet the minimum standards of the profession," the court did not conduct an assessment of whether the decision to cease all investigation upon obtaining the PSI and the DSS records actually demonstrated reasonable professional judgment. The state court merely assumed that the investigation was adequate. In light of what the PSI and the DSS records actually revealed, however, counsel chose to abandon their investigation at an unreasonable juncture, making a fully informed decision with respect to sentencing strategy impossible. The Court of Appeals' assumption that the investigation was adequate, ibid., thus reflected an unreasonable application of *Strickland*. As a result, the court's subsequent deference to counsel's strategic decision not "to present every conceivable mitigation defense," despite the fact that counsel based this alleged choice on what we have made clear was an unreasonable investigation, was also objectively unreasonable. As we established in *Strickland*, "strategic choices made after less than complete investigation are reasonable precisely to the extent that reasonable professional judgments support the limitations on investigation."

Additionally, the court based its conclusion, in part, on a clear factual error—that the "social service records . . . recorded incidences of . . . sexual abuse." As the State and the United States now concede, the records contain no mention of sexual abuse, much less of the repeated molestations and rapes of petitioner detailed in the Selvog The state court's assumption that the records documented instances of this abuse has been shown to be incorrect by "clear and convincing evidence," 28 U.S.C. § 2254(e)(1), and reflects "an unreasonable determination of the facts in light of the evidence presented in the State court proceeding," § 2254(d)(2). This partial reliance on an erroneous factual finding further highlights the unreasonableness of the state court's decision.

The dissent insists that this Court's hands are tied, under § 2254(d), by the state court's factual determinations that Wiggins' trial counsel "did investigate and were aware of [Wiggins'] background." But as we have made clear, the Maryland Court of Appeals' conclusion that the scope of counsel's investigation into petitioner's background met the legal standards set in *Strickland* represented an objectively unreasonable application of our precedent. Moreover, the court's assumption that counsel learned of a major aspect of Wiggins' background, i.e., the sexual abuse, from the DSS records was clearly erroneous. The requirements of § 2254(d) thus pose no bar to granting petitioner habeas relief.

2

In their briefs to this Court, the State and the United States contend that counsel, in fact, conducted a more thorough investigation than the one we have just described. This conclusion, they explain, follows from Schlaich's postconviction testimony that he knew of the sexual abuse Wiggins suffered, as well as of the hand-burning incident. According to the State and its amicus, the fact that counsel claimed to be aware of this evidence, which was not in the social services records, coupled with Schlaich's statement that he knew what was in "other people's reports," suggests that counsel's investigation must have extended beyond the social services records. Schlaich simply "was not asked to and did not reveal the source of his knowledge" of the abuse.

In considering this reading of the state postconviction record, we note preliminarily that the Maryland Court of Appeals clearly assumed both that counsel's investigation began and ended with the PSI and the DSS records and that this investigation was sufficient in scope to satisfy *Strickland's* reasonableness requirement. The court also assumed, erroneously, that the social services records cited incidences of sexual abuse. Respondents' interpretation of Schlaich's postconviction testimony therefore has no bearing on whether the Maryland Court of Appeals' decision reflected an objectively unreasonable application of *Strickland.*

In its assessment of the Maryland Court of Appeals' opinion, the dissent apparently does not dispute that if counsel's investigation in this case had consisted exclusively of the PSI and the DSS records, the court's decision would have constituted an unreasonable application of *Strick-*

land. Of necessity, then, the dissent's primary contention is that the Maryland Court of Appeals did decide that Wiggins' counsel looked beyond the PSI and the DSS records and that we must therefore defer to that finding under § 2254(e)(1). Had the court found that counsel's investigation extended beyond the PSI and the DSS records, the dissent, of course, would be correct that § 2254(e) would require that we defer to that finding. But the state court made no such finding.

The dissent bases its conclusion on the Maryland Court of Appeals' statements that "[c]ounsel were aware that appellant had a most unfortunate childhood," and that "counsel did investigate and were aware of appellant's background." But the state court's description of how counsel learned of petitioner's childhood speaks for itself. The court explained: "Counsel were aware that appellant had a most unfortunate childhood. Mr. Schlaich had available to him not only the pre-sentence investigation report ... but also more detailed social service records." This construction reflects the state court's understanding that the investigation consisted of the two sources the court mentions. Indeed, when describing counsel's investigation into petitioner's background, the court never so much as implies that counsel uncovered any source other than the PSI and the DSS records. The court's conclusion that counsel were aware of "incidences ... of sexual abuse" does not suggest otherwise, because the court assumed that counsel learned of such incidents from the social services records.

* * *

We therefore must determine, de novo, whether counsel reached beyond the PSI and the DSS records in their investigation of petitioner's background. The record as a whole does not support the conclusion that counsel conducted a more thorough investigation than the one we have described. The dissent, like the State and the United States, relies primarily on Schlaich's postconviction testimony to establish that counsel investigated more extensively. But the questions put to Schlaich during his postconviction testimony all referred to what he knew from the social services records; the line of questioning, after all, first directed him to his discovery of those documents. His subsequent reference to "other people's reports," made in direct response to a question concerning petitioner's mental retardation, appears to be an acknowledgement of the psychologist's reports we know counsel commissioned—reports that also revealed nothing of the sexual abuse Wiggins experienced. * * *

* * *

Contrary to the dissent's claim, we are not accusing Schlaich of lying. His statements at the postconviction proceedings that he knew of this abuse, as well as of the hand-burning incident, may simply reflect a mistaken memory shaped by the passage of time. After all, the state postconviction proceedings took place over four years after Wiggins' sentencing. Ultimately, given counsel's likely ignorance of the history of sexual abuse at the time of sentencing, we cannot infer from Schlaich's postconviction testimony that counsel looked further than the PSI and the DSS records in investigating petitioner's background. Indeed, the record contains no mention of sources other than those it is undisputed counsel possessed. We therefore conclude that counsel's investigation of petitioner's background was limited to the PSI and the DSS records.

3

In finding that Schlaich and Nethercott's investigation did not meet *Strickland's* performance standards, we emphasize that *Strickland* does not require counsel to investigate every conceivable line of mitigating evidence no matter how unlikely the effort would be to assist the defendant at sentencing. Nor does *Strickland* require defense counsel to present mitigating evidence at sentencing in every case. Both conclusions would interfere with the constitutionally protected independence of counsel at the heart of *Strickland.* We base our conclusion on the much more limited principle that "strategic choices made after less than complete investigation are reasonable" only to the extent that "reasonable professional judgments support the limitations on investigation." A decision not to investigate thus "must be directly assessed for reasonableness in all the circumstances."

Counsel's investigation into Wiggins' background did not reflect reasonable professional judgment. Their decision to end their investigation when they did was neither consistent with the professional standards that prevailed in 1989, nor reasonable in light of the evidence counsel uncovered in the social services records—evidence that would have led a reasonably competent attorney to investigate further. Counsel's pursuit of bifurcation until the eve of sentencing and their partial presentation of a mitigation case suggest that their incomplete investigation was the result of inattention, not reasoned strategic judgment. In deferring to counsel's decision not to pursue a mitigation case despite their unreasonable investigation, the Maryland Court of Appeals unreasonably applied *Strickland.* Furthermore, the court partially relied on an erroneous factual assumption. The requirements for habeas relief established by 28 U.S.C. § 2254(d) are thus satisfied.

III

In order for counsel's inadequate performance to constitute a Sixth Amendment violation, petitioner must show that counsel's failures prejudiced his defense. In *Strickland,* we made clear that, to establish prejudice, a "defendant must show that there is a reasonable probability that, but for counsel's unprofessional errors, the result of the proceeding would have been different. A reasonable probability is a probability sufficient to undermine confidence in the outcome." In assessing prejudice, we reweigh the evidence in aggravation against the totality of available mitigating evidence. In this case, our review is not circumscribed by a state court conclusion with respect to prejudice, as neither of the state courts below reached this prong of the *Strickland* analysis.

The mitigating evidence counsel failed to discover and present in this case is powerful. As Selvog reported based on his conversations with Wiggins and members of his family, Wiggins experienced severe privation and abuse in the first six years of his life while in the custody of his alcoholic, absentee mother. He suffered physical torment, sexual molestation, and repeated rape during his subsequent years in foster care. The time Wiggins spent homeless, along with his diminished mental capacities, further augment his mitigation case. Petitioner thus has the kind of troubled history we have declared relevant to assessing a defendant's moral culpability. Penry v. Lynaugh, 492 U.S. 302, 319 (1989) ("[E]vidence about the defendant's background and character is relevant because of the belief, long held by this society, that defendants who commit criminal acts that are attributable to a disadvantaged background ... may be less culpable than defendants who have no such excuse"); see also Eddings v. Oklahoma, 455 U.S. 104, 112 (1982) (noting that consideration of the offender's life history is a "part of the process of inflicting the penalty of death").

Given both the nature and the extent of the abuse petitioner suffered, we find there to be a reasonable probability that a competent attorney, aware of this history, would have introduced it at sentencing in an admissible form. While it may well have been strategically defensible upon a reasonably thorough investigation to focus on Wiggins' direct responsibility for the murder, the two sentencing strategies are not necessarily mutually exclusive. Moreover, given the strength of the available evidence, a reasonable attorney may well have chosen to prioritize the mitigation case over the direct responsibility challenge, particularly given that

Wiggins' history contained little of the double edge we have found to justify limited investigations in other cases.

* * *

We further find that had the jury been confronted with this considerable mitigating evidence, there is a reasonable probability that it would have returned with a different sentence. * * *

Wiggins' sentencing jury heard only one significant mitigating factor—that Wiggins had no prior convictions. Had the jury been able to place petitioner's excruciating life history on the mitigating side of the scale, there is a reasonable probability that at least one juror would have struck a different balance. Cf. Borchardt v. Maryland, 367 Md. 91, 139–140, 786 A.2d 631, 660 (2001) (noting that as long as a single juror concludes that mitigating evidence outweighs aggravating evidence, the death penalty cannot be imposed).

Moreover, in contrast to the petitioner in Williams v. Taylor, *supra*, Wiggins does not have a record of violent conduct that could have been introduced by the State to offset this powerful mitigating narrative. As the Federal District Court found, the mitigating evidence in this case is stronger, and the State's evidence in support of the death penalty far weaker, than in *Williams*, where we found prejudice as the result of counsel's failure to investigate and present mitigating evidence. We thus conclude that the available mitigating evidence, taken as a whole, "might

well have influenced the jury's appraisal" of Wiggins' moral culpability. Accordingly, the judgment of the United States Court of Appeals for the Fourth Circuit is reversed, and the case is remanded for further proceedings consistent with this opinion.

JUSTICE SCALIA, with whom JUSTICE THOMAS joins, dissenting.

The Court today vacates Kevin Wiggins' death sentence on the ground that his trial counsel's investigation of potential mitigating evidence was "incomplete." Wiggins' trial counsel testified under oath, however, that he was aware of the basic features of Wiggins' troubled childhood that the Court claims he overlooked. The Court chooses to disbelieve this testimony for reasons that do not withstand analysis. Moreover, even if this disbelief could plausibly be entertained, that would certainly not establish (as 28 U.S.C. § 2254(d) requires) that the Maryland Court of Appeals was unreasonable in believing it, and in therefore concluding that counsel adequately investigated Wiggins' background. The Court also fails to observe § 2254(e)(1)'s requirement that federal habeas courts respect state-court factual determinations not rebutted by "clear and convincing evidence." The decision sets at naught the statutory scheme we once described as a "highly deferential standard for evaluating state-court rulings," Lindh v. Murphy, 521 U.S. 320, 333, n. 7 (1997). I respectfully dissent.

* * *

ROE v. FLORES–ORTEGA

Supreme Court of the United States, 2000.
528 U.S. 470.

JUSTICE O'CONNOR **delivered the opinion of the Court.**

In this case we must decide the proper framework for evaluating an ineffective assistance of counsel claim, based on counsel's failure to file a notice of appeal without respondent's consent.

I

The State of California charged respondent, Lucio Flores–Ortega, with one count of murder, two counts of assault, and a personal use of a deadly weapon enhancement allegation. In October 1993, respondent appeared in Superior Court with his court-appointed public defender, Nancy Kops, and a Spanish language interpreter, and pleaded guilty to second-degree murder. The plea was entered pursuant to a California rule permitting a defendant both to deny committing a crime and to admit that there is sufficient evidence to convict him. In exchange for the guilty plea, the state prosecutor moved to strike the allegation of personal use of a deadly weapon and to dismiss both assault charges. On November 10, 1993, respondent was sentenced to 15 years to life in state prison. After pronouncing sentence, the trial judge informed respondent, "You may file an appeal within 60 days from today's date with this Court. If you do not have money for Counsel, Counsel will be appointed for you to represent you on your appeal."

Although Ms. Kops wrote "bring appeal papers" in her file, no notice of appeal was filed within the 60

days allowed by state law. (A notice of appeal is generally a one-sentence document stating that the defendant wishes to appeal from the judgment.) Filing such a notice is a purely ministerial task that imposes no great burden on counsel. During the first 90 days after sentencing, respondent was apparently in lock-up, undergoing evaluation, and unable to communicate with counsel. About four months after sentencing, on March 24, 1994, respondent tried to file a notice of appeal, which the Superior Court Clerk rejected as untimely. Respondent sought habeas relief from California's appellate courts, challenging the validity of both his plea and conviction, and (before the California Supreme Court) alleging that Ms. Kops had not filed a notice of appeal as she had promised. These efforts were uniformly unsuccessful.

Respondent then filed a federal habeas petition pursuant to 28 U.S.C. § 2254, alleging constitutionally ineffective assistance of counsel based on Ms. Kops' failure to file a notice of appeal on his behalf after promising to do so. The United States District Court for the Eastern District of California referred the matter to a Magistrate Judge, who in turn ordered an evidentiary hearing on the limited issue of whether Ms. Kops promised to file a notice of appeal on respondent's behalf. At the conclusion of the hearing, the Magistrate Judge found:

"The evidence in this case is, I think, quite clear that there was no consent to a failure to file [a notice of appeal]. It's clear to me that Mr. Ortega had little or no understanding of what the process was, what the appeal process was, or what appeal meant at that stage of the game.

"I think there was a conversation [between Ortega and Kops] in the jail. Mr. Ortega testified, and I'm sure he's testifying as to the best of his belief, that there was a conversation after the pronouncement of judgment at the sentencing hearing where it's his understanding that Ms. Kops was going to file a notice of appeal. She has no specific recollection of that. However, she is obviously an extremely experienced defense counsel. She's obviously a very meticulous person. And I think had Mr. Ortega requested that she file a notice of appeal, she would have done so.

"But, I cannot find that he has carried his burden of showing by a preponderance of the evidence that she made that promise."

The Magistrate Judge acknowledged that under precedent from the Court of Appeals for the Ninth Circuit, United States v. Stearns, 68 F.3d 328 (C.A.9 1995), a defendant need only show that he did not consent to counsel's failure to file a notice of appeal to be entitled to relief. * * * The Court of Appeals for the Ninth Circuit reversed * * *. Because respondent did not consent to the failure to file a notice of appeal—and thus qualified for relief under *Stearns*—the court remanded the case to the District Court with instructions to issue a conditional habeas writ unless the state court allowed respondent a new appeal. We granted certiorari

to resolve a conflict in the lower courts regarding counsel's obligations to file a notice of appeal. Compare United States v. Tajeddini, 945 F.2d 458, 468 (C.A.1 1991) (per curiam) (counsel's failure to file a notice of appeal, allegedly without the defendant's knowledge or consent, constitutes deficient performance); Morales v. United States, 143 F.3d 94, 97 (C.A.2 1998) (counsel has no duty to file a notice of appeal unless requested by the defendant); Romero v. Tansy, 46 F.3d 1024, 1030–1031 (C.A.10 1995) (defendant does not need to express to counsel his intent to appeal for counsel to be constitutionally obligated to perfect defendant's appeal; unless defendant waived right, counsel was deficient for failing to advise defendant about appeal right); United States v. Stearns, supra, (counsel's failure to file a notice of appeal is deficient unless the defendant consents to the abandonment of his appeal).

II

In Strickland v. Washington, 466 U.S. 668 (1984), we held that criminal defendants have a Sixth Amendment right to "reasonably effective" legal assistance, and announced a now-familiar test: A defendant claiming ineffective assistance of counsel must show (1) that counsel's representation "fell below an objective standard of reasonableness," and (2) that counsel's deficient performance prejudiced the defendant. Today we hold that this test applies to claims, like respondent's, that counsel was constitutionally ineffective for failing to file a notice of appeal.

A

As we have previously noted, "[n]o particular set of detailed rules for counsel's conduct can satisfactorily take account of the variety of circumstances faced by defense counsel." . Rather, courts must "judge the reasonableness of counsel's conduct on the facts of the particular case, viewed as of the time of counsel's conduct," and "[j]udicial scrutiny of counsel's performance must be highly deferential."

We have long held that a lawyer who disregards specific instructions from the defendant to file a notice of appeal acts in a manner that is professionally unreasonable. This is so because a defendant who instructs counsel to initiate an appeal reasonably relies upon counsel to file the necessary notice. Counsel's failure to do so cannot be considered a strategic decision; filing a notice of appeal is a purely ministerial task, and the failure to file reflects inattention to the defendant's wishes. At the other end of the spectrum, a defendant who explicitly tells his attorney not to file an appeal plainly cannot later complain that, by following his instructions, his counsel performed deficiently. See Jones v. Barnes, 463 U.S. 745 (1983) (accused has ultimate authority to make fundamental decision whether to take an appeal). The question presented in this case lies between those poles: Is counsel deficient for not filing a notice of appeal when the defendant has not clearly conveyed his wishes one way or the other?

The Courts of Appeals for the First and Ninth Circuits have answered that question with a bright-line rule: Counsel must file a notice of appeal unless the defendant specifically instructs otherwise; failing to do so is per se deficient. Such a rule effectively imposes an obligation on counsel in all cases either (1) to file a notice of appeal, or (2) to discuss the possibility of an appeal with the defendant, ascertain his wishes, and act accordingly. We reject this per se rule as inconsistent with *Strickland's* holding that "the performance inquiry must be whether counsel's assistance was reasonable considering all the circumstances." The Court of Appeals failed to engage in the circumstance-specific reasonableness inquiry required by *Strickland*, and that alone mandates vacatur and remand.

In those cases where the defendant neither instructs counsel to file an appeal nor asks that an appeal not be taken, we believe the question whether counsel has performed deficiently by not filing a notice of appeal is best answered by first asking a separate, but antecedent, question: whether counsel in fact consulted with the defendant about an appeal. We employ the term "consult" to convey a specific meaning—advising the defendant about the advantages and disadvantages of taking an appeal, and making a reasonable effort to discover the defendant's wishes. If counsel has consulted with the defendant, the question of deficient performance is easily answered: Counsel performs in a professionally unreasonable manner only by failing to follow the defendant's express instructions with respect to an appeal. If counsel has not consulted with the defendant, the court must in turn ask a second, and subsidiary, question: whether counsel's failure to consult with the defendant itself constitutes deficient performance. That question lies at the heart of this case: Under what circumstances does counsel have an obligation to consult with the defendant about an appeal?

Because the decision to appeal rests with the defendant, we agree * * * that the better practice is for counsel routinely to consult with the defendant regarding the possibility of an appeal. See ABA Standards for Criminal Justice, Defense Function § 4–8.2(a) (3d. ed.1993). In fact, California imposes on trial counsel a per se duty to consult with defendants about the possibility of an appeal. See Cal.Penal Code Ann. § 1240.1(a) (West Supp.2000). Nonetheless, "[p]revailing norms of practice as reflected in American Bar Association standards and the like ... are only guides," and imposing "specific guidelines" on counsel is "not appropriate." *Strickland*, supra, at 688. And, while States are free to impose whatever specific rules they see fit to ensure that criminal defendants are well represented, we have held that the Federal Constitution imposes one general requirement: that counsel make objectively reasonable choices. We cannot say, as a constitutional matter, that in every case counsel's failure to consult with the defendant about an appeal is necessarily unreasonable, and therefore deficient. Such a holding would be inconsistent with both our decision in *Strickland* and common sense. For example, suppose that a defendant consults with counsel; counsel advises the defendant that a guilty plea probably will lead to a 2 year sentence; the defendant expresses satisfaction and pleads guilty; the court sentences the defendant to 2 years' imprisonment as expected and informs the defendant of his appeal rights; the defendant does not express any interest in appealing, and counsel concludes that there are no nonfrivolous grounds for appeal. Under these circumstances, it would be difficult to say that counsel is "professionally unreasonable," as a constitutional matter, in not consulting with such a defendant regarding an appeal. Or, for example, suppose a sentencing court's instructions to a defendant about his appeal rights in a particular case are so clear and informative as to substitute for counsel's duty to consult. In some cases, counsel might then reasonably decide that he need not repeat that information. We therefore reject a bright-line rule that counsel must always consult with the defendant regarding an appeal.

We instead hold that counsel has a constitutionally-imposed duty to consult with the defendant about an appeal when there is reason to think either (1) that a rational defendant would want to appeal (for example, because there are nonfrivolous grounds for appeal), or (2) that this particular defendant reasonably demonstrated to counsel that he was interested in appealing. In making this determination, courts must take into account all the information counsel knew or should have known. Although not determinative, a highly relevant factor in this inquiry will be whether the conviction follows a trial or a guilty plea, both because a guilty plea reduces the scope of potentially appealable issues and because such a plea may indicate that the defendant seeks an end to judicial proceedings. Even in cases when the defendant pleads guilty, the court must consider such factors as whether the defendant received the sentence bargained for as part of the plea and whether the plea expressly reserved or waived some or all appeal rights. Only by considering all relevant factors in a given case can a court properly determine whether a rational defendant would have desired an appeal or that the particular defendant sufficiently demonstrated to counsel an interest in an appeal.

Rather than the standard we announce today, Justice SOUTER would have us impose an "almost" bright-line rule and hold that counsel "almost always" has a duty to consult with a defendant about an appeal .. Although he recognizes that "detailed rules for counsel's conduct" have no place in a *Strickland* inquiry, he argues that this "qualification" has no application here. According to Justice SOUTER, in *Strickland* we only rejected per se rules in order to respect the reasonable strategic choices made by lawyers, and that failing to consult about an appeal cannot be a strategic choice .. But we have consistently declined to impose mechanical rules on counsel—even when those rules might lead to better representation—not simply out of deference to counsel's strategic choices, but because "the purpose of the effective assistance guarantee of the Sixth Amendment is not to improve the quality of legal representation.... [but rather] simply to ensure that criminal defendants receive a fair trial." The relevant question is not whether counsel's choices were strategic, but whether

they were reasonable. We expect that courts evaluating the reasonableness of counsel's performance using the inquiry we have described will find, in the vast majority of cases, that counsel had a duty to consult with the defendant about an appeal. We differ from Justice Souter only in that we refuse to make this determination as a per se (or "almost" per se) matter.

B

The second part of the *Strickland* test requires the defendant to show prejudice from counsel's deficient performance.

1

In most cases, a defendant's claim of ineffective assistance of counsel involves counsel's performance during the course of a legal proceeding, either at trial or on appeal. In such circumstances, whether we require the defendant to show actual prejudice—"a reasonable probability that, but for counsel's unprofessional errors, the result of the proceeding would have been different"—or whether we instead presume prejudice turns on the magnitude of the deprivation of the right to effective assistance of counsel. That is because "the right to the effective assistance of counsel is recognized not for its own sake, but because of the effect it has on the ability of the accused to receive a fair trial," or a fair appeal. Absent some effect of challenged conduct on the reliability of the process, the effective counsel guarantee is generally not implicated.

We normally apply a strong presumption of reliability to judicial proceedings and require a defendant to overcome that presumption, by showing how specific errors of counsel undermined the reliability of the finding of guilt. Thus, in cases involving mere "attorney error," we require the defendant to demonstrate that the errors "actually had an adverse effect on the defense."

2

In some cases, however, the defendant alleges not that counsel made specific errors in the course of representation, but rather that during the judicial proceeding he was—either actually or constructively—denied the assistance of counsel altogether. "The presumption that counsel's assistance is essential requires us to conclude that a trial is unfair if the accused is denied counsel at a critical stage." United States v. Cronic [Casebook, page 1243]. The same is true on appeal. Under such circumstances, "[n]o specific showing of prejudice [is] required," because "the adversary process itself [is] presumptively unreliable." *Cronic*; Penson v. Ohio [Casebook, page 1227] (complete denial of counsel on appeal requires a presumption of prejudice).

Today's case is unusual in that counsel's alleged deficient performance arguably led not to a judicial proceeding of disputed reliability, but rather to the forfeiture of a proceeding itself. According to respondent, counsel's deficient performance deprived him of a notice of appeal and, hence, an appeal altogether. Assuming those allegations are true, counsel's deficient performance has deprived respondent of more than a fair judicial proceeding; that deficiency deprived respondent of the appellate proceeding altogether. In *Cronic*

[and] *Penson*, * * * we held that the complete denial of counsel during a critical stage of a judicial proceeding mandates a presumption of prejudice because "the adversary process itself" has been rendered "presumptively unreliable." The even more serious denial of the entire judicial proceeding itself, which a defendant wanted at the time and to which he had a right, similarly demands a presumption of prejudice. Put simply, we cannot accord any presumption of reliability, to judicial proceedings that never took place.

3

The Court of Appeals below applied a per se prejudice rule, and granted habeas relief based solely upon a showing that counsel had performed deficiently under its standard. Unfortunately, this per se prejudice rule ignores the critical requirement that counsel's deficient performance must actually cause the forfeiture of the defendant's appeal. If the defendant cannot demonstrate that, but for counsel's deficient performance, he would have appealed, counsel's deficient performance has not deprived him of anything, and he is not entitled to relief. Accordingly, we hold that, to show prejudice in these circumstances, a defendant must demonstrate that there is a reasonable probability that, but for counsel's deficient failure to consult with him about an appeal, he would have timely appealed.

In adopting this standard, we follow the pattern established in *Strickland* and *Cronic*, * * * requiring a showing of actual prejudice (i.e., that, but for counsel's errors, the defendant might have prevailed) when the proceeding in question was presumptively reliable, but presuming prejudice with no further showing from the defendant of the merits of his underlying claims when the violation of the right to counsel rendered the proceeding presumptively unreliable or entirely nonexistent. Today, drawing on that line of cases and following the suggestion of the Solicitor General, we hold that when counsel's constitutionally deficient performance deprives a defendant of an appeal that he otherwise would have taken, the defendant has made out a successful ineffective assistance of counsel claim entitling him to an appeal.

* * *

As with all applications of the *Strickland* test, the question whether a given defendant has made the requisite showing will turn on the facts of a particular case. Nonetheless, evidence that there were nonfrivolous grounds for appeal or that the defendant in question promptly expressed a desire to appeal will often be highly relevant in making this determination. We recognize that the prejudice inquiry we have described is not wholly dissimilar from the inquiry used to determine whether counsel performed deficiently in the first place; specifically, both may be satisfied if the defendant shows nonfrivolous grounds for appeal. But, while the performance and prejudice prongs may overlap, they are not in all cases coextensive. To prove deficient performance, a defendant can rely on evidence that he sufficiently demonstrated to counsel his interest in an appeal. But such evidence alone is insufficient to establish that, had the defendant received reasonable ad-

vice from counsel about the appeal, he would have instructed his counsel to file an appeal.

By the same token, although showing nonfrivolous grounds for appeal may give weight to the contention that the defendant would have appealed, a defendant's inability to specify the points he would raise were his right to appeal reinstated will not foreclose the possibility that he can satisfy the prejudice requirement where there are other substantial reasons to believe that he would have appealed. We similarly conclude here that it is unfair to require an indigent, perhaps pro se, defendant to demonstrate that his hypothetical appeal might have had merit before any advocate has ever reviewed the record in his case in search of potentially meritorious grounds for appeal. Rather, we require the defendant to demonstrate that, but for counsel's deficient conduct, he would have appealed.

III

The court below undertook neither part of the *Strickland* inquiry we have described, but instead presumed both that Ms. Kops was deficient for failing to file a notice of appeal without respondent's consent and that her deficient performance prejudiced respondent. Justice Souter finds Ms. Kops' performance in this case to have been "derelict," presumably because he believes that she did not consult with respondent about an appeal. But the Magistrate Judge's findings do not provide us with sufficient information to determine whether Ms. Kops rendered constitutionally inadequate assistance. Specifically, the findings below suggest that there may have been some conversation between Ms. Kops and respondent about an appeal, (Ms. Kops wrote "bring appeal papers" in her file), but do not indicate what was actually said. Assuming, arguendo, that there was a duty to consult in this case, it is impossible to determine whether that duty was satisfied without knowing whether Ms. Kops advised respondent about the advantages and disadvantages of taking an appeal and made a reasonable effort to discover his wishes. Based on the record before us, we are unable to determine whether Ms. Kops had a duty to consult with respondent (either because there were potential grounds for appeal or because respondent expressed interest in appealing), whether she satisfied her obligations, and, if she did not, whether respondent was prejudiced thereby. Accordingly, the judgment of the Court of Appeals is vacated, and the case is remanded for further proceedings consistent with this opinion.

JUSTICE BREYER concurring.

I write to emphasize that the question presented concerned the filing of a notice of appeal following a guilty plea. In that context I agree with the Court. I also join its opinion, which, in my view, makes clear that counsel does "almost always" have a constitutional duty to consult with a defendant about an appeal after a trial.

JUSTICE SOUTER, with whom JUSTICE STEVENS and JUSTICE GINSBURG join, concurring in part and dissenting in part.

I join Part II–B of the Court's opinion, but I respectfully dissent from Part II–A. As the opinion says, the crucial question in this case is whether, after a criminal conviction, a lawyer has a duty to consult with her client about the choice to appeal. The majority's conclusion is sometimes; mine is, almost always in those cases in which a plea of guilty has not obviously waived any claims of error. It is unreasonable for a lawyer with a client like respondent Flores–Ortega to walk away from her representation after trial or after sentencing without at the very least acting affirmatively to ensure that the client understands the right to appeal.

* * *

While *Strickland's* disclaimer that no particular set of rules should be treated as dispositive respects the need to defer to reasonable "strategic choices" by lawyers, no such strategic concerns arise in this case. Strategic choices are made about the extent of investigation, the risks of a defense requiring defendant's testimony and exposure to cross-examination, the possibility that placing personal background information before a jury will backfire, and so on. It is not, however, an issue of "strategy" to decide whether or not to give a defendant any advice before he loses the chance to appeal a conviction or sentence. The concern about too much judicial second-guessing after the fact is simply not raised by a claim that a lawyer should have counseled her client to make an intelligent decision to invoke or forgo the right of appeal or the opportunity to seek an appeal.

The Court's position is even less explicable when one considers the condition of the particular defendant claiming Strickland relief here. Flores–Ortega spoke no English and had no sophistication in the ways of the legal system. * * * To condition the duty of a lawyer to such a client on whether, inter alia, "a rational defendant would want to appeal (for example, because there are nonfrivolous grounds for appeal)," is not only to substitute a harmless-error rule for a showing of reasonable professional conduct, but to employ a rule that simply ignores the reality that the constitutional norm must address. Most criminal defendants, and certainly this one, will be utterly incapable of making rational judgments about appeal without guidance. They cannot possibly know what a rational decision-maker must know unless they are given the benefit of a professional assessment of chances of success and risks of trying. And they will often (indeed, usually) be just as bad off if they seek relief on habeas after failing to take a direct appeal, having no right to counsel in state postconviction proceedings. * * *

In effect, today's decision erodes the principle that a decision about appeal is validly made only by a defendant with a fair sense of what he is doing. Now the decision may be made inadvertently by a lawyer who never utters the word "appeal" in his client's hearing, so long as that client cannot later demonstrate

(probably without counsel) that he unwittingly had "nonfrivolous grounds" for seeking review. This state of the law amounts to just such a breakdown of the adversary system that Strickland warned against. * * *

I would hold that in the aftermath of the hearing at which Flores–Ortega was sentenced, his lawyer was obliged to consult with her client about the availability and prudence of an appeal, and that failure to do that violated Strickland's standard of objective reasonableness. I therefore respectfully dissent from Part II–A of the majority's opinion.

JUSTICE GINSBURG, concurring in part and dissenting in part.

This case presents the question whether, after a defendant pleads guilty or is convicted, the Sixth Amendment permits defense counsel simply to walk away, leaving the defendant uncounseled about his appeal rights. The Court is not deeply divided on this question. Both the Court and Justice Souter effectively respond: hardly ever. Because the test articulated by Justice Souter provides clearer guidance to lower courts and to counsel, and because I think it plain that the duty to consult was not satisfied in this case, I join Justice Souter's opinion.

3. Assessing Prejudice

Page 1241.   Add after the runover paragraph:

Prejudice From an Increased Sentence: Glover v. United States

In Glover v. United States, 531 U.S. 198 (2001), Glover argued that his trial counsel was ineffective for failing to challenge a sentence that was allegedly set in violation of the Federal Sentencing Guidelines. The Court of Appeals assumed that counsel was ineffective, but denied relief on the ground that any ineffectiveness did not prejudice Glover within the meaning of *Strickland*. The Court of Appeals read Lockhart v. Fretwell (Text, page 1239) to require a finding of "significant" prejudice. In this case, counsel's ineffectiveness resulted in an increased sentence somewhere between 6 and 21 months; the Court of Appeals did not view this increase as "significant".

The Supreme Court unanimously reversed in an opinion by Justice Kennedy. The Court assumed, as did the lower court, that counsel had been ineffective. Justice Kennedy criticized the lower court's analysis of prejudice in the following passage:

> The Seventh Circuit was incorrect to rely on *Lockhart* to deny relief to persons attacking their sentence who might show deficient performance in counsel's failure to object to an error of law affecting the calculation of a sentence because the sentence increase does not meet some baseline standard of prejudice. Authority does not suggest that a minimal amount of additional time in prison cannot constitute prejudice. Quite to the contrary, our jurisprudence suggests that any amount of actual jail time has Sixth Amendment significance. Compare Argersinger v. Hamlin, 407 U.S. 25 (1972) (holding that the assistance of counsel must be provided when a defendant is tried for a crime that results in a sentence of imprisonment), with Scott v. Illinois, 440 U.S. 367 (1979) (holding that a criminal defendant has no Sixth Amendment right to counsel when his trial does not result in a sentence of imprisonment). Our decisions on the right to jury trial in a criminal case do not suggest that there is no prejudice in the circumstances here. Those cases have limited the right to jury trial to offenses where the potential punishment was imprisonment for six months or more. But they do not control the question whether a showing of prejudice, in the context of a claim for ineffective assistance of counsel, requires a significant increase in a term of imprisonment.

> The Seventh Circuit's rule is not well considered in any event, because there is no obvious dividing line by which to measure how much longer a sentence must be for the increase to constitute substantial prejudice. Indeed, it is not even clear if the relevant increase is to be measured in absolute terms or by some fraction of the total authorized sentence. Although the amount by which a defendant's sentence is increased by a particular decision may be a factor to consider in determining whether counsel's performance in failing to argue the point constitutes ineffective assistance, under a determinate system of constrained discretion such as the Sentencing Guidelines it cannot serve as a bar to a showing of prejudice. We hold that the Seventh Circuit erred in engrafting this additional requirement onto the prejudice branch of the *Strickland* test. This is not a case where trial strategies, in retrospect, might be criticized for leading to a harsher sentence. Here we consider the sentencing calculation itself, a calculation resulting from a ruling which, if it had been error, would have been correctable on appeal. We express no opinion on the ultimate merits of Glover's claim because the

question of deficient performance is not before us, but it is clear that prejudice flowed from the asserted error in sentencing.

Prejudice Due to Ineffectiveness on Appeal

Page 1243. Add after the runover paragraph:

In Roe v. Flores–Ortega, 528 U.S. 470 (2000), the Court considered the circumstances under which defense counsel's failure to file a notice of appeal would be prejudicial within the meaning of *Strickland*. The Court declared that "to show prejudice in these circumstances, a defendant must demonstrate that there is a reasonable probability that, but for counsel's deficient failure to consult with him about an appeal, he would have timely appealed." The opinion in *Flores-Ortega* is set forth in this Supplement, *supra*.

4. Per Se Ineffectiveness and Prejudice

Page 1248. At the end of the section, add the following:

Application of Per Se Prejudice Standard
Not Warranted: Bell v. Cone

In the following case, the Court found that defense counsel in a capital case did not perform so poorly as to justify a ruling of *per se* prejudice under *Cronic*.

BELL v. CONE

Supreme Court of the United States, 2002.
535 U.S. 685.

CHIEF JUSTICE REHNQUIST **delivered the opinion of the Court**

The Tennessee Court of Appeals rejected respondent's claim that his counsel rendered ineffective assistance during his sentencing hearing under principles announced in Strickland v. Washington, 466 U.S. 668 (1984). The Court of Appeals for the Sixth Circuit concluded that United States v. Cronic, 466 U.S. 648 (1984), should have controlled the state court's analysis and granted him a conditional writ of habeas corpus. We hold that respondent's claim was governed by *Strickland*, and that the state court's decision neither was "contrary to" nor involved "an unreasonable application of clearly established Federal law" under the provisions of 28 U.S.C. § 2254(d)(1).

In 1982, respondent was convicted of, and sentenced to death for, the murder of an elderly couple in Memphis, Tennessee. The killings culminated a 2–day crime rampage that began when respondent robbed a Memphis jewelry store of approximately $112,000 in merchandise on a Saturday in August 1980. Shortly after the 12:45 p.m. robbery, a police officer in an unmarked vehicle spotted respondent driving at a normal speed and began to follow him. After a few blocks, respondent accelerated, prompting a high-speed chase through midtown Memphis and into a residential neighborhood where respondent abandoned his vehicle. Attempting to flee, respondent shot an officer who tried to apprehend him, shot a citizen who confronted him, and, at gunpoint, demanded that another hand over his car keys. As a police helicopter hovered overhead, respondent tried to shoot the fleeing car owner, but was frustrated because his gun was out of ammunition.

Throughout the afternoon and into the next morning, respondent managed to elude detection as police combed the surrounding area. In the meantime, officers inventorying his car found an array of illegal and prescription drugs, the stolen merchandise, and more than $2,400 in cash. Respondent reappeared early Sunday morning when he drew a gun on an elderly resident who refused to let him in to use her telephone. Later that afternoon, respondent broke into the home of Shipley and Cleopatra Todd, aged 93 and 79 years old, and killed them by repeatedly beating them about the head with a blunt instrument. He moved their bodies so that they would not be visible from the front and rear doors and ransacked the first floor of their home. After shaving his beard, respondent traveled to Florida. He was arrested there for robbing a drugstore in Pompano Beach. He admitted killing the Todds and shooting the police officer.

A Tennessee grand jury charged respondent with two counts of first-degree murder in the perpetration of a burglary in connection with the Todds' deaths, three counts of assault with intent to murder in connection with the shootings and attempted shooting of the car owner, and one count of robbery with a deadly weapon for the jewelry store theft. At a jury trial in the Criminal Court of Shelby County, the prosecution adduced overwhelming physical and testimonial evidence showing that respondent perpetrated the crimes and that he killed the Todds in a brutal and callous fashion.

The defense conceded that respondent committed most of the acts in question, but sought to prove that he was not guilty by reason of insanity. A clinical psychologist testified that respondent suffered from substance abuse and posttraumatic stress disorders related to his military service in Vietnam. A neuropharmacologist recounted at length respondent's history of illicit drug use, which began after he joined the Army and escalated to the point where he was daily consuming "rather horrific" quantities. That drug use, according to the expert, caused chronic amphetamine psychosis, hallucinations, and ongoing paranoia, which affected respondent's mental capacity and ability to obey the law. Defense counsel also called respondent's mother, who spoke of her son coming back from Vietnam in 1969 a changed person, his honorable discharge from service, his graduation with honors from college, and the deaths of his father and fiancee while he was in prison from 1972–1979 for robbery. Although respondent did not take the stand, defense counsel was able to elicit through other testimony that he had expressed remorse for the killings. Rejecting his insanity defense, the jury found him guilty on all charges.

Punishment for the first-degree murder counts was fixed in a separate sentencing hearing that took place the next day and lasted about three hours. Under then-applicable Tennessee law, a death sentence was required if the jury found unanimously that the State proved beyond a reasonable doubt the existence of at least one statutory aggravating circumstance that was not outweighed by any mitigating circumstance. In making these determinations, the jury could (and was instructed that it could) consider evidence from both the guilt and punishment phases.

During its opening statement, the State said it would prove four aggravating factors: that (1) respondent had previously been convicted of one or more felonies involving the use or threat of violence to a person; (2) he knowingly created a great risk of death to two or more persons other than the victim during the act of murder; (3) the murder was especially heinous, atrocious, or cruel; and (4) the murder was committed for the purpose of avoiding unlawful arrest. In his opening statement, defense counsel called the jury's attention to the mitigating evidence already before them. He suggested that respondent was under the influence of extreme mental disturbance or duress, that he was an addict whose drug and other problems stemmed from the stress of his military service, and that he felt remorse. Counsel urged the jury that there was a good reason for preserving his client's life if one looked at "the whole man." He asked for mercy, calling it a blessing that would raise them above the State to the level of God.

The prosecution then called a records custodian and fingerprint examiner to establish that respondent had three armed robbery convictions and two officers who said they tried unsuccessfully to arrest respondent for armed robbery after the jewelry store heist. Through cross-examination of the records custodian, respondent's attorney brought out that his client had been awarded the Bronze Star in Vietnam. After defense counsel successfully objected to the State's proffer of photos of the Todds' decomposing bodies, both sides rested. The junior prosecuting attorney on the case gave what the state courts described as a "low-key" closing. Defense counsel waived final argument, preventing the lead prosecutor, who by all accounts was an extremely effective advocate, from arguing in rebuttal. The jury found in both murder cases four aggravating factors and no mitigating circumstances substantial enough to outweigh them. The Tennessee Supreme Court affirmed respondent's convictions and sentence on appeal, and we denied certiorari.

Respondent then petitioned for state postconviction relief, contending that his counsel rendered ineffective assistance during the sentencing phase by failing to present mitigating evidence and by waiving final argument. After a hearing in which respondent's trial counsel testified, a division of the Tennessee Criminal Court rejected this contention. The Tennessee Court of Criminal Appeals affirmed .. The appellate court reviewed counsel's explanations for his decisions concerning the calling of witnesses and the waiving of final argument. Describing counsel's representation as "very conscientious," the court concluded that his performance was within the permissible range of competency * * *. The court also expressed its view that respondent received the death penalty based on the law and facts, not on the shortcomings of counsel. The Tennessee Supreme Court denied respondent permission to appeal, and we denied further review.

In 1997, after his second application for state postconviction relief was dismissed, respondent sought a federal writ of habeas corpus under 28 U.S.C. § 2254 as amended by the Antiterrorism and Effective Death Penalty Act of 1996. His petition alleged numerous grounds for relief including ineffective assistance at the sentencing phase. The District Court ruled that respondent did not meet § 2254(d)'s requirements and denied the petition.

The Court of Appeals affirmed the refusal to issue a writ with respect to respondent's conviction, but reversed with respect to his sentence. It held that respondent suffered a Sixth Amendment violation for which prejudice should be presumed under United States v. Cronic, because his counsel, by not asking for mercy after the prosecutor's final argument, did not subject the State's call for the death penalty to meaningful adversarial testing. The state court's adjudication of respondent's Sixth Amendment claim, in the Court of Appeals' analysis, was therefore an unreasonable application of the clearly established law * * * . We granted certiorari, and now reverse the Court of Appeals.

II

The Antiterrorism and Effective Death Penalty Act of 1996 [dis-cussed in Chapter Thirteen of the Casebook] modified a federal habeas court's role in reviewing state prisoner applications in order to prevent federal habeas "retrials" and to ensure that state-court convictions are given effect to the extent possible under law. To these ends, § 2254(d)(1) provides:

"(d) An application for a writ of habeas corpus on behalf of a person in custody pursuant to the judgment of a State court shall not be granted with respect to any claim that was adjudicated on the merits in State court proceedings unless the adjudication of the claim—

"(1) resulted in a decision that was contrary to, or involved an unreasonable application of, clearly established Federal law, as determined by the Supreme Court of the United States."

* * * A federal habeas court may issue the writ under the "contrary to" clause if the state court applies a rule different from the governing law set forth in our cases, or if it decides a case differently than we have done on a set of materially indistinguishable facts. The court may grant relief under the "unreasonable application" clause if the state court correctly identifies the governing legal principle from our decisions but unreasonably applies it to the facts of the particular case. The focus of the latter inquiry is on whether the state court's application of clearly established federal law is objectively unreasonable, and * * * an unreasonable application is different from an incorrect one.

Petitioner contends that the Court of Appeals exceeded its statutory authority to grant relief under § 2254(d)(1) because the decision of the Tennessee courts was neither contrary to nor an unreasonable application of the clearly established law of *Strickland*. Respondent counters that he is entitled to relief under § 2254(d)(1)'s "contrary to" clause because the state court applied the wrong legal rule. In his view, *Cronic,* not *Strickland,* governs the analysis of his claim that his counsel rendered ineffective assistance at the sentencing hearing. We address this issue first.

In *Strickland * * * we announced a two-part test for evaluating claims that a defendant's counsel performed so incompetently in his or her representation of a defendant that the defendant's sentence or conviction should be reversed. We reasoned that there would be a sufficient indication that counsel's assistance was defective enough to undermine confidence in a proceeding's result if the defendant proved two things: first, that counsel's "representation fell below an objective standard of reasonableness"; and second, that "there is a reasonable probability that, but for counsel's unprofessional errors, the result of the proceeding would have been different." Without proof of both deficient performance and prejudice to the defense, we concluded, it could not be said that the sentence or conviction "resulted from a breakdown in the adversary process that rendered the result of the proceeding unreliable," and the sentence or conviction should stand.

In *Cronic,* we considered whether the Court of Appeals was correct in reversing a defendant's conviction under the Sixth Amendment without inquiring into counsel's actual performance or requiring the defendant to show the effect it had on the trial. * * * In the course of deciding this question, we identified three situations implicating the right to counsel that involved circumstances "so likely to prejudice the accused that the cost of litigating their effect in a particular case is unjustified."

First and "[m]ost obvious" was the "complete denial of counsel." A trial would be presumptively unfair, we said, where the accused is denied the presence of counsel at "a critical stage," a phrase we used * * * to denote a step of a criminal proceeding, such as arraignment, that held significant consequences for the accused. Second, we posited that a similar presumption was warranted if "counsel entirely fails to subject the prosecution's case to meaningful adversarial testing." Finally, we said that in cases like Powell v. Alabama, 287 U.S. 45 (1932), where counsel is called upon to render assistance under circumstances where competent counsel very likely could not, the defendant need not show that the proceedings were affected.

The aspects of counsel's performance challenged by respondent— the failure to adduce mitigating evidence and the waiver of closing argument—are plainly of the same ilk as other specific attorney errors we have held subject to *Strickland's* performance and prejudice components. In Darden v. Wainwright, 477 U.S. 168, 184 (1986), for example, we evaluated under *Strickland* a claim that counsel was ineffective for failing to put on any mitigating evidence at a capital sentencing hearing. In Burger v. Kemp, 483 U.S. 776, 788 (1987), we did the same when presented with a challenge to counsel's decision at a capital sentencing hearing not to offer any mitigating evidence at all.

We hold, therefore, that the state court correctly identified the principles announced in *Strickland* as those governing the analysis of respondent's claim. Consequently, we find no merit in respondent's contention that the state court's adjudication was contrary to our clearly established law.

III

The remaining issue, then, is whether respondent can obtain relief on the ground that the state court's adjudication of his claim involved an "unreasonable application" of *Strickland*. In *Strickland* we said that "[j]udicial scrutiny of a counsel's performance must be highly deferential" and that "every effort [must] be made to eliminate the distorting effects of hindsight, to reconstruct the circumstances of counsel's challenged conduct, and to evaluate the conduct from counsel's perspective at the time." Thus, even when a court is presented with an ineffective-assistance claim not subject to § 2254(d)(1) deference, a defendant must overcome the "presumption that, under the circumstances, the challenged action 'might be considered sound trial strategy.' "

For respondent to succeed, however, he must do more than show that he would have satisfied *Strickland's* test if his claim were being analyzed in the first instance, because under § 2254(d)(1), it is not enough to convince a federal habeas court that, in its independent judgment, the state-court decision applied *Strickland* incorrectly. Rather, he must show that the Tennessee Court of Appeals applied *Strickland* to the facts of his case in an objectively unreasonable manner. This, we conclude, he cannot do.

Respondent's counsel was faced with the formidable task of defending a client who had committed a horribly brutal and senseless crime against two elderly persons in their home. He had just the day before shot a police officer and an unarmed civilian, attempted to shoot another person, and committed a robbery. The State had near conclusive proof of guilt on the murder charges as well as extensive evidence demonstrating the cruelty of the killings. Making the situation more onerous were the facts that respondent, despite his high intelligence and relatively normal upbringing, had turned into a drug addict and had a history of robbery convictions.

Because the defense's theory at the guilt phase was not guilty by reason of insanity, counsel was able to put before the jury extensive testimony about what he believed to be the most compelling mitigating evidence in the case— evidence regarding the change his client underwent after serving in Vietnam; his drug dependency, which apparently drove him to commit the robbery in the first place; and its effects. Before the state courts, respondent faulted his counsel for not recalling his medical experts during the sentencing hearing. But we think counsel reasonably could have concluded that the substance of their testimony was still fresh to the jury. Each had taken the stand not long before, and counsel focused on their testimony in his guilt phase closing argument, which took place the day before the sentencing hearing was held. Respondent's suggestion that the jury could not fully consider the mental health proof as potentially mitigating because it was adduced during the guilt phase finds no support in the record. Defense counsel advised the jury that the testimony of the experts established the existence of mitigating circumstances, and the trial court specifically instructed the jury that evidence of a mental disease or defect insufficient to establish a criminal defense could be considered in mitigation.

Respondent also assigned error in his counsel's decision not to recall his mother. While counsel recognized that respondent's mother could have provided further information about respondent's childhood and spoken of her love for him, he concluded that she had not made a good witness at the guilt stage, and he did not wish to subject her to further cross-examination. Respondent advances no argument that would call his attorney's assessment into question.

In his trial preparations, counsel investigated the possibility of calling other witnesses. He thought respondent's sister, who was closest to him, might make a good witness, but she did not want to testify. And even if she had agreed, putting her on the stand would have allowed the prosecutor to question her about the fact that respondent called her from the Todds' house just after the killings. After consulting with his client, counsel opted not to call respondent himself as a

witness. And we think counsel had sound tactical reasons for deciding against it. Respondent said he was very angry with the prosecutor and thought he might lash out if pressed on cross-examination, which could have only alienated him in the eyes of the jury. There was also the possibility of calling other witnesses from his childhood or days in the Army. But counsel feared that the prosecution might elicit information about respondent's criminal history. He further feared that testimony about respondent's normal youth might, in the jury's eyes, cut the other way.

Respondent also focuses on counsel's decision to waive final argument. He points out that counsel could have explained the significance of his Bronze Star decoration and argues that his counsel's failure to advocate for life in closing necessarily left the jury with the impression that he deserved to die. The Court of Appeals "reject[ed] out of hand" the idea that waiving summation could ever be considered sound trial strategy. In this case, we think at the very least that the state court's contrary assessment was not "unreasonable." After respondent's counsel gave his opening statement discussing the mitigating evidence before them and urging that they choose life for his client, the prosecution did not put on any particularly dramatic or impressive testimony. The State's witnesses testified rather briefly about the undisputed facts that respondent had prior convictions and was evading arrest.

When the junior prosecutor delivered a very matter-of-fact closing that did not dwell on any of the brutal aspects of the crime, counsel was faced with a choice. He could make a closing argument and reprise for the jury, perhaps in greater detail than his opening, the primary mitigating evidence concerning his client's drug dependency and post-traumatic stress from Vietnam. And he could plead again for life for his client and impress upon the jurors the importance of what he believed were less significant facts, such as the Bronze Star decoration or his client's expression of remorse. But he knew that if he took this opportunity, he would give the lead prosecutor, who all agreed was very persuasive, the chance to depict his client as a heartless killer just before the jurors began deliberation. Alternatively, counsel could prevent the lead prosecutor from arguing by waiving his own summation and relying on the jurors' familiarity with the case and his opening plea for life made just a few hours before. Neither option, it seems to us, so clearly outweighs the other that it was objectively unreasonable for the Tennessee Court of Appeals to deem counsel's choice to waive argument a tactical decision about which competent lawyers might disagree.

We cautioned in *Strickland* that a court must indulge a "strong presumption" that counsel's conduct falls within the wide range of reasonable professional assistance because it is all too easy to conclude that a particular act or omission of counsel was unreasonable in the harsh light of hindsight .. Given the choices available to respondent's counsel and the reasons we have identified, we cannot say that the state court's application of *Strickland's* attorney-performance standard was objectively unreason-

able. The judgment of the Court of Appeals is therefore reversed, and the case is remanded for further proceedings consistent with this opinion.

JUSTICE STEVENS, dissenting

In my judgment, the Court of Appeals correctly concluded that during the penalty phase of respondent's capital murder trial, his counsel "entirely fail [ed] to subject the prosecution's case to meaningful adversarial testing." United States v. Cronic, 466 U.S. 648, 659 (1984). Counsel's shortcomings included a failure to interview witnesses who could have provided mitigating evidence; a failure to introduce available mitigating evidence; and the failure to make any closing argument or plea for his client's life at the conclusion of the penalty phase. Furthermore, respondent's counsel was, subsequent to trial, diagnosed with a mental illness that rendered him unqualified to practice law, and that apparently led to his suicide. These circumstances "justify a presumption that respondent's conviction was insufficiently reliable to satisfy the Constitution."

I.

* * *

Dice's [the defense lawyer's] stated attitude toward the penalty phase must frame our consideration of the constitutional standard applicable to this case. Once his "Vietnam Veterans Syndrome" defense was rejected in the guilt phase, it appears that Dice approached the penalty phase with a sense of hopelessness because his "basic tactic was to try to convince the jury that Gary Cone was insane at the time of the commission of these acts, and the jury rejected that." Dice perceived that the guilt phase evidence concerning Cone's mental health "made absolutely no difference to the jury," and that the jurors "weren't buying any of it," even though that evidence had been introduced to the jury through the lens of the insanity defense, not as mitigation for the death penalty. Dice's co-counsel echoed the sentiment that death was a foregone conclusion: * * * Dice expressed this hopelessness even before the trial began; he testified that he told Cone's mother "the first day I met her, that if [the prosecutor] does not elect to offer life in this case, your boy is going to the chair and there's not going to be a darn thing ... I'm going to be able to do to stop it except to maybe screw up the prosecution." * * *

The parties agree that Dice did four things in the penalty phase. First, he made a brief opening argument in the penalty phase asking for mercy. Second, in this opening, he referenced the evidence concerning Vietnam Veterans Syndrome that had been presented in the guilt phase. Third, he brought out on cross-examination of the State's witness who presented court records of respondent's prior convictions that Cone had been awarded the Bronze Star in Vietnam, though he did not explain the significance of that decoration to the jury because he made no closing remarks after the cross-examination. And, fourth, outside of the jury's presence, he successfully objected to the State's introduction of two photographs of the murder victims. Aside from doing these things, however, Dice did nothing before or during the penal-

ty phase—he did not interview witnesses aside from those relevant to the guilt phase; he did not present testimony relevant to mitigation from the witnesses who were available; and he made no plea for Cone's life or closing remarks after the State's case.

Dice conceded that he did not interview various people from Cone's past, such as his high school teachers and classmates, who could have testified that Cone was a good person who did not engage in criminal behavior pre-Vietnam. Dice agreed that such witnesses would likely have been available if Dice had, in his words, "been stupid enough to put them on." Apparently, Dice did not interview these individuals in preparation for the penalty phase, because he assumed that the State's cross-examination of those witnesses would emphasize the seriousness of Cone's post-Vietnam criminal behavior. Dice's reasoning is doubtful to say the least because * * * these post-Vietnam crimes were already known to the jury through the State's penalty phase evidence of respondent's prior convictions. Further, it is hard to imagine how evidence of Cone's post-Vietnam behavior would change their assessments—indeed, Dice's whole case was that Cone had changed.

Dice also failed to present to the jury mitigation evidence that he did have on hand. He admitted that other witnesses—including those whose testimony he promised to the jury in the guilt phase opening, such as Cone's mother, sister, and aunts—had been interviewed and were available to testify at the penalty phase. Dice had ready access to other mitigation evidence as well:

testimony from Cone himself (in which he could have, among other things, expressed remorse and discussed his brother's drowning and his fiancee's murder), the letter of forgiveness from the victim's sister, the Bronze Star, and the medical experts. Dice's post hoc reasons for not putting on these additional witnesses and evidence are puzzling, but appear to rest largely on his incorrect assumption that the guilt phase record already included "what little mitigating circumstances we had," and his fear of the prosecutor, "who by all accounts was an extremely effective advocate."

Although the guilt phase evidence included information about Cone's post-Vietnam behavior, it told the jury little about Cone's earlier life. During the guilt phase, Dice had a difficult enough time convincing the court to allow him to present evidence of respondent's post-Vietnam behavior and drug addiction as an insanity defense, that he did not seriously attempt to introduce evidence of respondent's childhood. However, such evidence would have been permissible mitigation in the penalty phase. This evidence would have revealed Cone to be "a quiet, studious child," with "absolutely no suggestion of any behavioral disturbance, even in adolescence." Indeed, his mother could have described him as a "perfect" child, and she "absolutely" wanted to testify at the penalty hearing to make a plea for Cone's life, but Dice "wouldn't put her on even if she'd wanted to," because he "did not feel that she did well on the stand," and because of "the cross-examination skills of the District Attorney involved." Dice's claim that

she had not made a good witness at the guilt phase, is contradicted by the transcript of her straightforward trial testimony, and his desire not to subject her to cross-examination is surely an insufficient reason, absent more, to prevent her from asking the jury to spare her son's life.

Dice also did not call as witnesses in mitigation either of Cone's sisters or his aunt, all of whom were promised in Dice's opening statement. Dice's statement that Cone's sister Sue "did not want to testify," is contradicted by his opening statement. And his fear that she might have been questioned "about the fact that [Cone] called her from the [victims'] house just after the killings," is unfounded: Evidence of this call was already in the record, and further reference to the call could do no conceivable additional harm to Cone's case. Indeed, Dice's justification for not calling Sue merely illustrates Dice's extraordinary fear of his adversaries. Dice's explanation for his failure to call Cone's other sister, Rita, is even more unsatisfying: "I think that we had a letter exchange or a phone call. My tactics do not necessarily involve putting the family on down here because, again, ... I thought that we were in a position which we should say was tenuous from the outset." His failure to call Cone's aunt is unexplained. His failure to offer into evidence the letter written by the victim's sister, offering her prayers for Cone, is also unexplained.

Dice did not put Cone on the stand during the penalty phase, forfeiting the opportunity for him to express the remorse he apparently felt. Dice testified that he discussed with Cone the possibility of testifying, but opted not to call him at the penalty phase because of fear that respondent might "lash out if pressed on cross-examination." He also claimed that Cone made the decision not to testify at the penalty phase because Cone feared the prosecutor. In Dice's words, Cone "realized that [the prosecutor] was a very intelligent and skilled cross-examiner and [Cone] felt that he would go off if he took the stand." However, this explanation conspicuously echoes Dice's own fears about the prosecutor's prowess. Furthermore, respondent testified that Dice never "urged [him] as to the importance of testifying at the penalty stage," and Dice testified that his duties did not include urging Cone to testify. Given the undisputed evidence of Cone's intelligence and no indication that his behavior in the courtroom was anything but exemplary, it is difficult to imagine why any competent lawyer would so readily abandon any effort to persuade his client to take the stand when his life was at stake. Dice's claim that he did no more than permit Cone to reach his own decision about testifying in the penalty phase is simply not credible. Rather, it appears that Dice, fearful of the prosecutor, did not specifically discuss testifying in the penalty phase with Cone, but rather discussed with him the possibility of taking the stand on only one occasion—during the guilt phase of the trial.

* * *

In addition to performing no penalty phase investigation and failing to introduce available mitigation, Dice made no closing statement after the State's affirmative case for death. Rather, Dice's "strategy" was to rely on his brief penalty phase opening statement. * * * Dice's decision not to make a closing argument was most strongly motivated by his fear that his adversary would make a persuasive argument depicting Cone as a heartless killer. At all costs, Dice wanted to avoid the prosecutor "slash [ing] me to pieces on rebuttal," as "[h]e's done . . . a hundred times." Dice hoped that by not making a closing statement, the prosecutor would "kind of follo[w] me right down the primrose path." Of course, at the time Dice waived closing argument, the aggravating circumstances had already been proved, and Dice knew that the judge would instruct the jury to return a verdict of death unless the jurors were persuaded that the aggravating circumstances were outweighed by mitigating evidence. Perhaps that burden was insurmountable, but the jury must have viewed the absence of any argument in response to the State's case for death as Dice's concession that no case for life could be made. A closing argument provided the only chance to avoid the inevitable outcome of the "primrose path"—a death sentence.

Both of the experienced criminal lawyers who testified as expert witnesses in the state postconviction proceedings refused to state categorically that it would never be appropriate to waive closing argument, to fail to put the defendant on the stand during the penalty phase of the trial, or to offer no mitigating evidence in the penalty phase. Both witnesses agreed, however, that Dice's tactical decisions were highly abnormal, and perhaps unprecedented in a capital case.

II.

On these facts, and as a result of Dice's overwhelming failure at the penalty phase, the Court of Appeals properly concluded that *Cronic* controls the Sixth Amendment claim in this case, and that prejudice to respondent should be presumed. Given Dice's repeated and unequivocal testimony about Cone's truthfulness, together with Cone's apparent feelings of remorse, Dice's decision not to offer Cone's testimony in the penalty phase is simply bewildering. And his decisions to present no mitigation case in the penalty phase, and to offer no closing argument in the face of the prosecution's request for death, are nothing short of incredible. Moreover, Dice's explanations for his decisions were not only uncorroborated, but were, in my judgment, patently unsatisfactory. Indeed, his rambling and often incoherent descriptions of his unusual trial strategy lend strong support to the Court of Appeals' evaluation of this case and its decision not to defer to Dice's lack of meaningful participation in the penalty phase as "strategy."

Although the state courts did not have the benefit of evidence concerning Dice's mental health, it appears from Dice's medical records that he suffered from a severe mental impairment. He began treatment for this illness a couple of years after trial, and he committed suicide approximately six months after the postconviction hearing in this case. The symptoms of his disorder included "confused thinking, impaired memory, inability to concen-

trate for more than a short period of time, paranoia, grandiosity, [and] inappropriate behavior." While these mental health problems may have onset after Cone's trial, a complete reading of the trial transcript and an assessment of Dice's actions at trial suggest this not to be the case.

A theme of fear of possible counterthrusts by his adversaries permeates Dice's loquacious explanations of his tactical decisions. But fear of the opponent cannot justify such absolute dereliction of a lawyer's duty to the client—especially a client facing death. * * * There may be cases in which such timidity is consistent with a "meaningful adversarial testing" of the prosecution's case, but my examination of the record has produced a firm conviction that this is not such a case.

* * *

* * * [P]resuming prejudice when counsel has entirely failed to function as an adversary makes sense, for three reasons. First, counsel's complete failure to advocate, coupled here with his likely mental illness, undermines *Strickland's* basic assumption: that counsel has "made all significant decisions in the exercise of reasonable professional judgment." Second, a proper *Strickland* inquiry is difficult, if not impossible, to conduct when counsel has completely abdicated his role as advocate, because the abdication results in an incomplete trial record from which a court cannot properly evaluate whether a defendant has or has not suffered prejudice from the attorney's conduct. Finally, counsel's total failure as an adversary renders "the likelihood that the verdict is unreliable" to be "so high that a case-by-case inquiry is unnecessary."

* * * Effective representation provides "the means through which the other rights of the person on trial are secured." For that reason, there is "a denial of Sixth Amendment rights that makes the adver-sary process itself presumptively un-reliable" whenever defense counsel "entirely fails to subject the prose-cution's case to meaningful adver-sary testing." That is exactly what happened in the penalty phase of Gary Cone's trial.

I respectfully dissent.

B. THE RIGHT TO CONFLICT–FREE REPRESENTATION

2. *Active Conflict Impairing the Representation*

Page 1258. At the end of the section, add the following:

Interface Between Holloway Automatic Reversal Rule and Cuyler Rule Regulating Active Representation of Conflicting Interests: Mickens v. Taylor

In the following case, the Court divided over whether the *Holloway* rule–requiring automatic reversal when the trial court fails to inquire into a multiple representation conflict raised by defense counsel–applies when the trial court becomes aware of a conflict that is *not* raised by defense counsel.

MICKENS v. TAYLOR

Supreme Court of the United States, 2002.
535 U.S. 162.

JUSTICE SCALIA delivered the opin-ion of the Court.

The question presented in this case is what a defendant must show in order to demonstrate a Sixth Amendment violation where the tri-al court fails to inquire into a po-tential conflict of interest about which it knew or reasonably should have known.

I

In 1993, a Virginia jury convicted petitioner Mickens of the premedi-tated murder of Timothy Hall dur-ing or following the commission of an attempted forcible sodomy. Finding the murder outrageously and wantonly vile, it sentenced pe-titioner to death. In June 1998, Mickens filed a petition for writ of habeas corpus, * * * alleging, inter alia, that he was denied effective as-sistance of counsel because one of his court-appointed attorneys had a conflict of interest at trial. Federal habeas counsel had discovered that petitioner's lead trial attorney, Bryan Saunders, was representing Hall (the victim) on assault and concealed-weapons charges at the time of the murder. Saunders had been appointed to represent Hall, a juvenile, on March 20, 1992, and had met with him once for 15 to 30 minutes some time the following week. Hall's body was discovered on March 30, 1992, and four days later a juvenile court judge dis-missed the charges against him, noting on the docket sheet that

Hall was deceased. The one-page docket sheet also listed Saunders as Hall's counsel. On April 6, 1992, the same judge appointed Saunders to represent petitioner. Saunders did not disclose to the court, his co-counsel, or petitioner that he had previously represented Hall. Under Virginia law, juvenile case files are confidential and may not generally be disclosed without a court order, but petitioner learned about Saunders' prior representation when a clerk mistakenly produced Hall's file to federal habeas counsel.

The District Court held an evidentiary hearing and denied petitioner's habeas petition.* * * On the merits, the Court of Appeals assumed that the juvenile court judge had neglected a duty to inquire into a potential conflict, but rejected petitioner's argument that this failure either mandated automatic reversal of his conviction or relieved him of the burden of showing that a conflict of interest adversely affected his representation. Relying on Cuyler v. Sullivan, 446 U.S. 335 (1980), the court held that a defendant must show "both an actual conflict of interest and an adverse effect even if the trial court failed to inquire into a potential conflict about which it reasonably should have known." Concluding that petitioner had not demonstrated adverse effect, it affirmed the District Court's denial of habeas relief. We granted a stay of execution of petitioner's sentence and granted certiorari.

II

The Sixth Amendment provides that a criminal defendant shall have the right to "the assistance of counsel for his defence." This right has been accorded, we have said, "not for its own sake, but because of the effect it has on the ability of the accused to receive a fair trial." United States v. Cronic, 466 U.S. 648, 658 (1984). It follows from this that assistance which is ineffective in preserving fairness does not meet the constitutional mandate, see Strickland v. Washington, 466 U.S. 668, 685–686 (1984); and it also follows that defects in assistance that have no probable effect upon the trial's outcome do not establish a constitutional violation. As a general matter, a defendant alleging a Sixth Amendment violation must demonstrate "a reasonable probability that, but for counsel's unprofessional errors, the result of the proceeding would have been different."

There is an exception to this general rule. We have spared the defendant the need of showing probable effect upon the outcome, and have simply presumed such effect, where assistance of counsel has been denied entirely or during a critical stage of the proceeding. When that has occurred, the likelihood that the verdict is unreliable is so high that a case-by-case inquiry is unnecessary. See *Cronic, supra*, at 658–659. But only in "circumstances of that magnitude" do we forgo individual inquiry into whether counsel's inadequate performance undermined the reliability of the verdict.

We have held in several cases that "circumstances of that magnitude" may also arise when the defendant's attorney actively represented conflicting interests. The nub of the question before us is whether the principle established by these cases provides an exception to the general rule of *Strickland* under the circumstances of the present case. To answer that question, we must examine those cases in some detail.

In Holloway v. Arkansas, 435 U.S. 475 (1978), defense counsel had objected that he could not adequately represent the divergent interests of three codefendants. Without inquiry, the trial court had denied counsel's motions for the appointment of separate counsel and had refused to allow counsel to cross-examine any of the defendants on behalf of the other two. The *Holloway* Court deferred to the judgment of counsel regarding the existence of a disabling conflict, recognizing that a defense attorney is in the best position to determine when a conflict exists, that he has an ethical obligation to advise the court of any problem, and that his declarations to the court are "virtually made under oath." *Holloway* presumed, moreover, that the conflict, "which [the defendant] and his counsel tried to avoid by timely objections to the joint representation," undermined the adversarial process. The presumption was justified because joint representation of conflicting interests is inherently suspect, and because counsel's conflicting obligations to multiple defendants "effectively sea[l] his lips on crucial matters" and make it difficult to measure the precise harm arising from counsel's errors. *Holloway* thus creates an automatic reversal rule only where defense counsel is forced to represent codefendants over his timely objection, unless the trial court has determined that there is no conflict. ("[W]henever a trial court improperly requires joint representation over timely objection reversal is automatic").

In Cuyler v. Sullivan, 446 U.S. 335 (1980), the respondent was one of three defendants accused of murder who were tried separately, represented by the same counsel. Neither counsel nor anyone else objected to the multiple representation, and counsel's opening argument at Sullivan's trial suggested that the interests of the defendants were aligned. We declined to extend *Holloway's* automatic reversal rule to this situation and held that, absent objection, a defendant must demonstrate that "a conflict of interest actually affected the adequacy of his representation." In addition to describing the defendant's burden of proof, *Sullivan* addressed separately a trial court's duty to inquire into the propriety of a multiple representation, construing *Holloway* to require inquiry only when "the trial court knows or reasonably should know that a particular conflict exists"—which is not to be confused with when the trial court is aware of a vague, unspecified possibility of conflict, such as that which "inheres in almost every instance of multiple representation." In *Sullivan*, no "special circumstances" triggered the trial court's duty to inquire.

* * *

Petitioner's proposed rule of automatic reversal when there existed a conflict that did not affect counsel's performance, but the trial judge failed to make the *Sullivan*-mandated inquiry, makes little policy sense. As discussed, the rule applied when the trial judge is not aware of the conflict (and thus not obligated to inquire) is that prejudice will be presumed only if the conflict has significantly affected counsel's performance—thereby rendering the verdict unreliable, even though *Strickland* prejudice cannot be shown. The trial court's awareness of a potential conflict neither renders it more likely that counsel's performance was significantly affected nor in any other way renders the verdict unreliable. Nor does the trial judge's failure to make the *Sullivan*-mandated inquiry often make it harder for reviewing courts to determine conflict and effect, particularly since those courts may rely on evidence and testimony whose importance only becomes established at the trial.

Nor, finally, is automatic reversal simply an appropriate means of enforcing *Sullivan's* mandate of inquiry. Despite Justice SOUTER's belief that there must be a threat of sanction (to-wit, the risk of conferring a windfall upon the defendant) in order to induce "resolutely obdurate" trial judges to follow the law we do not presume that judges are as careless or as partial as those police officers who need the incentive of the exclusionary rule, see United States v. Leon, 468 U.S. 897, 916–917 (1984). And in any event, the *Sullivan* standard, which requires proof of effect upon representation but (once such effect is shown) presumes prejudice, already creates an "incentive" to inquire into a potential conflict. In those cases where the potential conflict is in fact an actual one, only inquiry will enable the judge to avoid all possibility of reversal by either seeking waiver or replacing a conflicted attorney. We doubt that the deterrence of "judicial dereliction" that would be achieved by an automatic reversal rule is significantly greater.

Since this was not a case in which (as in *Holloway*) counsel protested his inability simultaneously to represent multiple defendants; and since the trial court's failure to make the *Sullivan*-mandated inquiry does not reduce the petitioner's burden of proof; it was at least necessary, to void the conviction, for petitioner to establish that the conflict of interest adversely affected his counsel's performance. The Court of Appeals having found no such effect, the denial of habeas relief must be affirmed.

III

Lest today's holding be misconstrued, we note that the only question presented was the effect of a trial court's failure to inquire into a potential conflict upon the *Sullivan* rule that deficient performance of counsel must be shown. The case was presented and argued on the assumption that (absent some exception for failure to inquire) *Sullivan* would be applicable—requiring a showing of defective performance, but not requiring in addition (as *Strickland* does in other ineffectiveness-of-counsel cases), a showing of probable effect upon the outcome of trial. That assumption was not unreasonable in light of the holdings of Courts of Appeals, which have applied *Sullivan* "unblinkingly" to "all kinds of alleged attorney ethical conflicts," Beets v. Scott, 65 F.3d 1258, 1266 (C.A.5 1995) (en banc). They have invoked the *Sullivan* standard not only when (as here) there is a conflict rooted in counsel's obligations to former clients, but even when representation of the defendant somehow implicates counsel's personal or financial interests, including a book deal,

United States v. Hearst, 638 F.2d 1190, 1193 (C.A.9 1980), a job with the prosecutor's office, Garcia v. Bunnell, 33 F.3d 1193, 1194–1195, 1198, n. 4 (C.A.9 1994), the teaching of classes to Internal Revenue Service agents, United States v. Michaud, 925 F.2d 37, 40–42 (C.A.1 1991), a romantic "entanglement" with the prosecutor, Summerlin v. Stewart, 267 F.3d 926, 935–941 (C.A.9 2001), or fear of antagonizing the trial judge, United States v. Sayan, 968 F.2d 55, 64–65 (C.A.D.C. 1992).

It must be said, however, that the language of *Sullivan* itself does not clearly establish, or indeed even support, such expansive application. "[U]ntil," it said, "a defendant shows that his counsel actively represented conflicting interests, he has not established the constitutional predicate for his claim of ineffective assistance." Both *Sullivan* itself, and *Holloway*, stressed the high probability of prejudice arising from multiple concurrent representation, and the difficulty of proving that prejudice. Not all attorney conflicts present comparable difficulties. Thus, the Federal Rules of Criminal Procedure treat concurrent representation and prior representation differently, requiring a trial court to inquire into the likelihood of conflict whenever jointly charged defendants are represented by a single attorney (Rule 44(c)), but not when counsel previously represented another defendant in a substantially related matter, even where the trial court is aware of the prior representation.

This is not to suggest that one ethical duty is more or less important than another. The purpose of our *Holloway* and *Sullivan* excep-tions from the ordinary requirements of *Strickland*, however, is not to enforce the Canons of Legal Ethics, but to apply needed prophylaxis in situations where *Strickland* itself is evidently inadequate to assure vindication of the defendant's Sixth Amendment right to counsel. See Nix v. Whiteside, 475 U.S. 157, 165 (1986) ("[B]reach of an ethical standard does not necessarily make out a denial of the Sixth Amendment guarantee of assistance of counsel"). In resolving this case on the grounds on which it was presented to us, we do not rule upon the need for the *Sullivan* prophylaxis in cases of successive representation. Whether *Sullivan* should be extended to such cases remains, as far as the jurisprudence of this Court is concerned, an open question.

* * *

For the reasons stated, the judgment of the Court of Appeals is

Affirmed.

JUSTICE KENNEDY, with whom JUSTICE O'CONNOR joins, concurring.

In its comprehensive analysis the Court has said all that is necessary to address the issues raised by the question presented, and I join the opinion in full. The trial judge's failure to inquire into a suspected conflict is not the kind of error requiring a presumption of prejudice. We did not grant certiorari on a second question presented by petitioner: whether, if we rejected his proposed presumption, he had nonetheless established that a conflict of interest adversely affected his representation. I write separately to emphasize that the facts of this case well illustrate why a wooden rule requiring reversal is inappropriate for cases like this one.

At petitioner's request, the District Court conducted an evidentiary hearing on the conflict claim and issued a thorough opinion, which found that counsel's brief representation of the victim had no effect whatsoever on the course of petitioner's trial. * * * The District Court found that Saunders did not believe he had any obligation to his former client, Timothy Hall, that would interfere with the litigation. Although the District Court concluded that Saunders probably did learn some matters that were confidential, it found that nothing the attorney learned was relevant to the subsequent murder case. Indeed, even if Saunders had learned relevant information, the District Court found that he labored under the impression he had no continuing duty at all to his deceased client. ("[T]he record here reflects that, as far as Saunders was concerned, his allegiance to Hall, '[e]nded when I walked into the courtroom and they told me he was dead and the case was gone' "). While Saunders' belief may have been mistaken, it establishes that the prior representation did not influence the choices he made during the course of the trial. This conclusion is a good example of why a case-by-case inquiry is required, rather than simply adopting an automatic rule of reversal.

Petitioner's description of roads not taken would entail two degrees of speculation. We would be required to assume that Saunders believed he had a continuing duty to the victim, and we then would be required to consider whether in this hypothetical case, the counsel would have been blocked from pursuing an alternative defense strategy. The District Court concluded that the prosecution's case, coupled with the defendant's insistence on testifying, foreclosed the strategies suggested by petitioner after the fact. According to the District Court, there was no plausible argument that the victim consented to sexual relations with his murderer, given the bruises on the victim's neck, blood marks showing the victim was stabbed before or during sexual intercourse, and, most important, petitioner's insistence on testifying at trial that he had never met the victim. The basic defense at the guilt phase was that petitioner was not at the scene; this is hardly consistent with the theory that there was a consensual encounter.

The District Court said the same for counsel's alleged dereliction at the sentencing phase. Saunders' failure to attack the character of the 17–year-old victim and his mother had nothing to do with the putative conflict of interest. This strategy was rejected as likely to backfire, not only by Saunders, but also by his co-counsel, who owed no duty to Hall. These facts, and others relied upon by the District Court, provide compelling evidence that a theoretical conflict does not establish a constitutional violation, even when the conflict is one about which the trial judge should have known.

The constitutional question must turn on whether trial counsel had a conflict of interest that hampered the representation, not on whether the trial judge should have been more assiduous in taking prophylactic measures. If it were otherwise, the judge's duty would not be limited to cases where the attorney is suspected of harboring a conflict of interest. The Sixth Amendment protects the defendant against an ineffective attorney, as well as a conflicted one. It would be a major departure to say that the trial judge must step in every time defense counsel appears to be providing ineffective assistance, and indeed, there is no precedent to support this proposition. As the Sixth Amendment guarantees the defendant the assistance of counsel, the infringement of that right must depend on a deficiency of the lawyer, not of the trial judge. There is no reason to presume this guarantee unfulfilled when the purported conflict has had no effect on the representation.

With these observations, I join the opinion of the Court.

JUSTICE STEVENS, **dissenting**.

* * *

Mickens had a constitutional right to the services of an attorney devoted solely to his interests. That right was violated. The lawyer who did represent him had a duty to disclose his prior representation of the victim to Mickens and to the trial judge. That duty was violated. When Mickens had no counsel, the trial judge had a duty to "make a thorough inquiry and to take all steps necessary to insure the fullest protection of" his right to counsel. Despite knowledge of the lawyer's prior representation, she violated that duty.

We will never know whether Mickens would have received the death penalty if those violations had not occurred nor precisely what effect they had on Saunders' representation of Mickens. We do know

that he did not receive the kind of representation that the Constitution guarantees. If Mickens had been represented by an attorney-impostor who never passed a bar examination, we might also be unable to determine whether the impostor's educational shortcomings " 'actually affected the adequacy of his representation.' "We would, however, surely set aside his conviction if the person who had represented him was not a real lawyer. Four compelling reasons make setting aside the conviction the proper remedy in this case.

First, it is the remedy dictated by our holdings in Holloway v. Arkansas, Cuyler v. Sullivan, and Wood v. Georgia, 450 U.S. 261 (1981). In this line of precedent, our focus was properly upon the duty of the trial court judge to inquire into a potential conflict. This duty was triggered either via defense counsel's objection, as was the case in *Holloway*, or some other "special circumstances" whereby the serious potential for conflict was brought to the attention of the trial court judge.As we unambiguously stated in *Wood*, "*Sullivan* mandates a reversal when the trial court has failed to make an inquiry even though it 'knows or reasonably should know that a particular conflict exists.' " * * *

Second, it is the only remedy that responds to the real possibility that Mickens would not have received the death penalty if he had been represented by conflict-free counsel during the critical stage of the proceeding in which he first met with his lawyer. We should presume that the lawyer for the victim of a brutal homicide is incapable of establishing the kind of relationship with the defendant that is essential to effective representation.

Third, it is the only remedy that is consistent with the legal profession's historic and universal condemnation of the representation of conflicting interests without the full disclosure and consent of all interested parties. The Court's novel and naïve assumption that a lawyer's divided loyalties are acceptable unless it can be proved that they actually affected counsel's performance is demeaning to the profession.

Finally, "justice must satisfy the appearance of justice." Setting aside Mickens' conviction is the only remedy that can maintain public confidence in the fairness of the procedures employed in capital cases. Death is a different kind of punishment from any other that may be imposed in this country. "From the point of view of the defendant, it is different in both its severity and its finality. From the point of view of society, the action of the sovereign in taking the life of one of its citizens also differs dramatically from any other legitimate state action. It is of vital importance to the defendant and to the community that any decision to impose the death sentence be, and appear to be, based on reason rather than caprice or emotion." Gardner v. Florida, 430 U.S. 349, 357–358 (1977). A rule that allows the State to foist a murder victim's lawyer onto his accused is not only capricious; it poisons the integrity of our adversary system of justice.

I respectfully dissent.

JUSTICE SOUTER, dissenting

A judge who knows or should know that counsel for a criminal defendant facing, or engaged in, trial has a potential conflict of interests is obliged to enquire into the potential conflict and assess its threat to the fairness of the proceeding. Unless the judge finds that the risk of inadequate representation is too remote for further concern, or finds that the defendant has intelligently assumed the risk and waived any potential Sixth or Fourteenth Amendment claim of inadequate counsel, the court must see that the lawyer is replaced.

The District Judge reviewing the federal habeas petition in this case found that the state judge who appointed Bryan Saunders to represent petitioner Mickens on a capital murder charge knew or should have known that obligations stemming from Saunders's prior representation of the victim, Timothy Hall, potentially conflicted with duties entailed by defending Mickens. The state judge was therefore obliged to look further into the extent of the risk and, if necessary, either secure Mickens's knowing and intelligent assumption of the risk or appoint a different lawyer. The state judge, however, did nothing to discharge her constitutional duty of care. In the one case in which we have devised a remedy for such judicial dereliction, we held that the ensuing judgment of conviction must be reversed and the defendant afforded a new trial. *Holloway*. That should be the result here.

I

The Court today holds, instead, that Mickens should be denied this remedy because Saunders failed to employ a formal objection as a means of bringing home to the appointing judge the risk of conflict.

Without an objection, the majority holds, Mickens should get no relief absent a showing that the risk turned into an actual conflict with adverse effect on the representation provided to Mickens at trial. But why should an objection matter when even without an objection the state judge knew or should have known of the risk and was therefore obliged to enquire further? What would an objection have added to the obligation the state judge failed to honor? * * *

The different burdens on the *Holloway* and *Cuyler* defendants are consistent features of a coherent scheme for dealing with the problem of conflicted defense counsel; a prospective risk of conflict subject to judicial notice is treated differently from a retrospective claim that a completed proceeding was tainted by conflict, although the trial judge had not been derelict in any duty to guard against it. When the problem comes to the trial court's attention before any potential conflict has become actual, the court has a duty to act prospectively to assess the risk and, if the risk is not too remote, to eliminate it or to render it acceptable through a defendant's knowing and intelligent waiver. This duty is something more than the general responsibility to rule without committing legal error; it is an affirmative obligation to investigate a disclosed possibility that defense counsel will be unable to act with uncompromised loyalty to his client. It was the judge's failure to fulfill that duty of care to enquire further and do what might be necessary that the *Holloway* Court remedied by vacating the defendant's subsequent conviction. The

error occurred when the judge failed to act, and the remedy restored the defendant to the position he would have occupied if the judge had taken reasonable steps to fulfill his obligation. But when the problem of conflict comes to judicial attention not prospectively, but only after the fact, the defendant must show an actual conflict with adverse consequence to him in order to get relief. Fairness requires nothing more, for no judge was at fault in allowing a trial to proceed even though fraught with hidden risk.

In light of what the majority holds today, it bears repeating that, in this coherent scheme established by *Holloway* and *Cuyler*, there is nothing legally crucial about an objection by defense counsel to tell a trial judge that conflicting interests may impair the adequacy of counsel's representation. Counsel's objection in *Holloway* was important as a fact sufficient to put the judge on notice that he should enquire. In most multiple-representation cases, it will take just such an objection to alert a trial judge to prospective conflict, and the *Cuyler* Court reaffirmed that the judge is obliged to take reasonable prospective action whenever a timely objection is made. But the Court also indicated that an objection is not required as a matter of law: "Unless the trial court knows or reasonably should know that a particular conflict exists, the court need not initiate an enquiry."

Since the District Court in this case found that the state judge was on notice of a prospective potential conflict, this case calls for nothing more than the application of the prospective notice rule announced and exemplified by *Holloway* * * * . The remedy for the judge's dereliction of duty should be an order vacating the conviction and affording a new trial.

* * *

II

Since the majority will not leave the law as it is, however, the question is whether there is any merit in the rule it now adopts, of treating breaches of a judge's duty to enquire into prospective conflicts differently depending on whether defense counsel explicitly objected. There is not. The distinction is irrational on its face, it creates a scheme of incentives to judicial vigilance that is weakest in those cases presenting the greatest risk of conflict and unfair trial, and it reduces the so-called judicial duty to enquire into so many empty words.

The most obvious reason to reject the majority's rule starts with the accepted view that a trial judge placed on notice of a risk of prospective conflict has an obligation then and there to do something about it. The majority does not expressly repudiate that duty, which is too clear for cavil. It should go without saying that the best time to deal with a known threat to the basic guarantee of fair trial is before the trial has proceeded to become unfair. It would be absurd, after all, to suggest that a judge should sit quiescent in the face of an apparent risk that a lawyer's conflict will render representation illusory and the formal trial a waste of time, emotion, and a good deal of public money. And as if that were not bad enough, a failure to act early raises the specter * * * that failures on the part of conflicted counsel will elude demonstration after the fact, simply because they so often consist of what did not happen. While a defendant can fairly be saddled with the characteristically difficult burden of proving adverse effects of conflicted decisions after the fact when the judicial system was not to blame in tolerating the risk of conflict, the burden is indefensible when a judge was on notice of the risk but did nothing.

With so much at stake, why should it matter how a judge learns whatever it is that would point out the risk to anyone paying attention? Of course an objection from a conscientious lawyer suffices to put a court on notice, as it did in *Holloway*, and probably in the run of multiple-representation cases nothing short of objection will raise the specter of trouble. But sometimes a wide-awake judge will not need any formal objection to see a risk of conflict, as the federal habeas court's finding in this very case shows. Why, then, pretend contrary to fact that a judge can never perceive a risk unless a lawyer points it out? Why excuse a judge's breach of judicial duty just because a lawyer has fallen down in his own ethics or is short on competence? Transforming the factually sufficient trigger of a formal objection into a legal necessity for responding to any breach of judicial duty is irrational.

* * *

The irrationality of taxing defendants with a heavier burden for silent lawyers naturally produces an equally irrational scheme of incentives operating on the judges. The judge's duty independent of objection * * * is made concrete by reversal for failure to honor it. The plain fact is that the specter of reversal for failure to enquire into risk is an incentive to trial judges to keep their eyes peeled for lawyers who wittingly or otherwise play loose with loyalty to their clients and the fundamental guarantee of a fair That incentive is needed least when defense counsel points out the risk with a formal objection, and needed most with the lawyer who keeps risk to himself, quite possibly out of self-interest. Under the majority's rule, however, it is precisely in the latter situation that the judge's incentive to take care is at its ebb. With no objection on record, a convicted defendant can get no relief without showing adverse effect, minimizing the possibility of a later reversal and the consequent inducement to judicial care. This makes no sense.

* * *

The Court's rule makes no sense unless, that is, the real point of this case is to eliminate the judge's constitutional duty entirely in no-objection cases, for that is certainly the practical consequence of today's holding. The defendant has the same burden to prove adverse effect (and the prospect of reversal is the same) whether the judge has no reason to know of any risk or every reason to know about it short of explicit objection. In that latter case, the duty explicitly described in *Cuyler* * * * becomes just a matter of words, devoid of sanction; it ceases to be any duty at all.

As that duty vanishes, so does the sensible regime under which a defendant's burden on conflict claims took account of the opportunities to ensure against conflicted counsel in the first place. Convicted defendants had two alternative avenues to show entitlement to relief. A defendant might, first, point to facts indicating that a judge knew or should have known of a "particular conflict," before that risk had a chance to play itself out with an adverse result. If he could not carry the burden to show that the trial judge had fallen down in the duty to guard against conflicts prospectively, the defendant was required to show, from the perspective of an observer looking back after the allegedly conflicted representation, that there was an actual conflict of interests with an adverse effect. The first route was preventive, meant to avoid the waste of costly after-the-fact litigation where the risk was clear and easily avoidable by a reasonably vigilant trial judge; the second was retrospective, with a markedly heavier burden justified when the judiciary was not at fault, but at least alleviated by dispensing with any need to show prejudice. Today, the former system has been skewed against recognizing judicial responsibility. The judge's duty applies only when a *Holloway* objection fails to induce a resolutely obdurate judge to take action upon the explicit complaint of a lawyer facing impossible demands. In place of the forsaken judicial obligation, we can expect more time-consuming post-trial litigation like this, and if this case is any guide, the added time and expense are unlikely to purchase much confidence in the judicial system.

I respectfully dissent.

JUSTICE BREYER, with WHOM JUSTICE GINSBURG joins, dissenting.

The Commonwealth of Virginia seeks to put the petitioner, Walter Mickens, Jr., to death after having appointed to represent him as his counsel a lawyer who, at the time of the murder, was representing the very person Mickens was accused of killing. I believe that, in a case such as this one, a categorical approach is warranted and automatic reversal is required. To put the matter in language this Court has previously used: By appointing this lawyer to represent Mickens, the Commonwealth created a "structural defect affecting the framework within which the trial [and sentencing] proceeds, rather than simply an error in the trial process itself." Arizona v. Fulminante, 499 U.S. 279, 310 (1991).

The parties spend a great deal of time disputing how this Court's precedents of Holloway v. Arkansas, Cuyler v. Sullivan, and Wood v. Georgia resolve the case. Those precedents involve the significance of a trial judge's "failure to inquire" if that judge "knew or should have known" of a "potential" conflict. The majority and dissenting opinions dispute the meaning of these cases as well. Although I express no view at this time about how our precedents should treat most ineffective-assistance-of-counsel claims involving an alleged conflict of interest (or, for that matter, whether *Holloway, Sullivan* and *Wood* provide a sensible or coherent framework for dealing with those cases at all), I am convinced that this case is not governed by those precedents, for the following reasons.

First, this is the kind of representational incompatibility that is egregious on its face. Mickens was represented by the murder victim's lawyer; that lawyer had represented the victim on a criminal matter; and that lawyer's representation of the victim had continued until one business day before the lawyer was appointed to represent the defendant.

Second, the conflict is exacerbated by the fact that it occurred in a capital murder case. In a capital case, the evidence submitted by both sides regarding the victim's character may easily tip the scale of the jury's choice between life or death. Yet even with extensive investigation in post-trial proceedings, it will often prove difficult, if not impossible, to determine whether the prior representation affected defense counsel's decisions regarding, for example: which avenues to take when investigating the victim's background; which witnesses to call; what type of impeachment to undertake; which arguments to make to the jury; what language to use to characterize the victim; and, as a general matter, what basic strategy to adopt at the sentencing stage. Given the subtle forms that prejudice might take, the consequent difficulty of proving actual prejudice, and the significant likelihood that it will nonetheless occur when the same lawyer represents both accused killer and victim, the cost of litigating the existence of actual prejudice in a particular case cannot be easily justified.

Third, the Commonwealth itself created the conflict in the first place. Indeed, it was the same judge who dismissed the case against the victim who then appointed the victim's lawyer to represent Mickens one business day later. In light of the judge's active role in bringing about the incompatible representation, I am not sure why the concept of a judge's "duty to inquire" is thought to be central to this case. No "inquiry" by the trial judge could have shed more light on the conflict than was obvious on the face of the matter, namely, that the lawyer who would represent Mickens today is the same lawyer who yesterday represented Mickens' alleged victim in a criminal case.

This kind of breakdown in the criminal justice system creates, at a minimum, the appearance that the proceeding will not " 'reliably serve its function as a vehicle for determination of guilt or innocence,' " and the resulting " 'criminal punishment' "will not " 'be regarded as fundamentally fair.' " This appearance, together with the likelihood of prejudice in the typical case, are serious enough to warrant a categorical rule—a rule that does not require proof of prejudice in the individual case.

The Commonwealth complains that this argument "relies heavily on the immediate visceral impact of learning that a lawyer previously represented the victim of his current client."And that is so. The "visceral impact," however, arises out of the obvious, unusual nature of the conflict. It arises from the fact that the Commonwealth seeks to execute a defendant, having provided that defendant with a lawyer who, only yesterday, represented the victim. In my view, to carry out a death sentence so obtained would invariably "diminis[h] faith" in the fairness and integrity of our criminal justice system. That is to say, it would diminish that public confidence in the criminal justice system upon which the successful functioning of that system continues to depend.

I therefore dissent.

Chapter Eleven

SENTENCING

I. INTRODUCTION

D. CONSTITUTIONAL LIMITATIONS ON PUNISHMENT

1. *Cruel and Unusual Punishment*

Page 1319. At the bottom of the page, add the following section:

Three Strikes Legislation: Ewing v. California

In the following case, the Court applies its *Rummel–Harmelin* line of Eighth Amendment jurisprudence to the California "Three Strikes" law.

EWING v. CALIFORNIA

Supreme Court of the United States, 2003.
123 S.Ct. 1179.

JUSTICE O'CONNOR **announced the judgment of the Court and delivered an opinion in which** THE CHIEF JUSTICE **and** JUSTICE KENNEDY **join.**

In this case, we decide whether the Eighth Amendment prohibits the State of California from sentencing a repeat felon to a prison term of 25 years to life under the State's "Three Strikes and You're Out" law.

I

A

California's three strikes law reflects a shift in the State's sentencing policies toward incapacitating and deterring repeat offenders who threaten the public safety. The law was designed "to ensure longer prison sentences and greater punishment for those who commit a felony and have been previously convicted of serious and/or violent felony offenses." Cal. Penal Code Ann. § 667(b) (West 1999). * * * Between 1993 and 1995, 24 States and the Federal Government enacted three strikes laws. *Ibid.* Though the three strikes laws vary from State to State, they share a common goal of protecting the public safety by providing lengthy prison terms for habitual felons.

B

* * * When a defendant [in California] is convicted of a felony, and he has previously been convicted of one or more prior felonies defined as "serious" or "violent" in Cal. Penal Code Ann. § § 667.5 and 1192.7 (West Supp. 2002), sentencing is conducted pursuant to the three strikes law. Prior convictions must be alleged in the charging document, and the defendant has a right to a jury determination that the prosecution has proved the prior convictions beyond a reasonable doubt. If the defendant has one prior "serious" or "violent" felony conviction, he must be sentenced to "twice the term otherwise provided as punishment for the current felony conviction." If the defendant has two or more prior "serious" or "violent" felony convictions, he must receive "an indeterminate term of life imprisonment." Defendants sentenced to life under the three strikes law become eligible for parole on a date calculated by reference to a "minimum term," which is the greater of (a) three times the term otherwise provided for the current conviction, (b) 25 years, or (c) the term determined by the court pursuant to § 1170 for the underlying conviction, including any enhancements.

Under California law, certain offenses may be classified as either felonies or misdemeanors. These crimes are known as "wobblers." Some crimes that would otherwise be misdemeanors become "wobblers" because of the defendant's prior record. For example, petty theft, a misdemeanor, becomes a "wobbler" when the defendant has previously served a prison term for committing specified theft-related crimes. Other crimes, such as grand theft, are "wobblers" regardless of the defendant's prior record. Both types of "wobblers" are triggering offenses under the three strikes law only when they are treated as felonies. Under California law, a "wobbler" is presumptively a felony and remains a felony except when the discretion is actually exercised to make the crime a misdemeanor.

In California, prosecutors may exercise their discretion to charge a "wobbler" as either a felony or a misdemeanor. Likewise, California trial courts have discretion to reduce a "wobbler" charged as a felony to a misdemeanor either before preliminary examination or at sentencing to avoid imposing a three strikes sentence. In exercising this discretion, the court may consider "those factors that direct similar sentencing decisions," such as "the nature and circumstances of the offense, the defendant's appreciation of and attitude toward the offense, ... [and] the general objectives of sentencing." California trial courts can also vacate allegations of prior "serious" or "violent" felony convictions, either on motion by the prosecution or *sua sponte*. In ruling whether to vacate allegations of prior felony convictions, courts consider whether, "in light of the nature and circumstances of [the defendant's] present felonies and prior serious and/or violent felony convictions, and the particulars of his background, character, and prospects, the defendant may be deemed outside the [three strikes'] scheme's spirit, in whole or in part." Thus, trial courts may avoid imposing a three strikes sentence in two ways: first, by reducing "wobblers" to misdemeanors (which do not qualify as triggering offenses), and second, by vacating allegations of prior "serious" or "violent" felony convictions.

C

On parole from a 9–year prison term, petitioner Gary Ewing walked into the pro shop of the El Segundo Golf Course in Los Angeles County on March 12, 2000. He walked out with three golf clubs, priced at $399 apiece, concealed in his pants leg. A shop employee, whose suspicions were aroused when he observed Ewing limp out of the pro shop, telephoned the police. The police apprehended Ewing in the parking lot.

Ewing is no stranger to the criminal justice system. In 1984, at the age of 22, he pleaded guilty to theft. The court sentenced him to six months in jail (suspended), three years' probation, and a $300 fine. In 1988, he was convicted of felony grand theft auto and sentenced to one year in jail and three years' probation. After Ewing completed probation, however, the sentencing court reduced the crime to a misdemeanor, permitted Ewing to withdraw his guilty plea, and dismissed the case. In 1990, he was convicted of petty theft with a prior and sentenced to 60 days in the county jail and three years' probation. In 1992, Ewing was convicted of battery and sentenced to 30 days in the county jail and two years' summary probation. One month later, he was convicted of theft and sentenced to 10 days in the county jail and 12 months' probation. In January 1993, Ewing was convicted of burglary and sentenced to 60 days in the county jail and one year's summary probation. In February 1993,

he was convicted of possessing drug paraphernalia and sentenced to six months in the county jail and three years' probation. In July 1993, he was convicted of appropriating lost property and sentenced to 10 days in the county jail and two years' summary probation. In September 1993, he was convicted of unlawfully possessing a firearm and trespassing and sentenced to 30 days in the county jail and one year's probation.

In October and November 1993, Ewing committed three burglaries and one robbery at a Long Beach, California, apartment complex over a 5–week period. He awakened one of his victims, asleep on her living room sofa, as he tried to disconnect her video cassette recorder from the television in that room. When she screamed, Ewing ran out the front door. On another occasion, Ewing accosted a victim in the mailroom of the apartment complex. Ewing claimed to have a gun and ordered the victim to hand over his wallet. When the victim resisted, Ewing produced a knife and forced the victim back to the apartment itself. While Ewing rifled through the bedroom, the victim fled the apartment screaming for help. Ewing absconded with the victim's money and credit cards.

On December 9, 1993, Ewing was arrested on the premises of the apartment complex for trespassing and lying to a police officer. The knife used in the robbery and a glass cocaine pipe were later found in the back seat of the patrol car used to transport Ewing to the police station. A jury convicted Ewing of first-degree robbery and three counts of residential burglary. Sentenced to nine years and eight months in prison, Ewing was paroled in 1999.

Only 10 months later, Ewing stole the golf clubs at issue in this case. He was charged with, and ultimately convicted of, one count of felony grand theft of personal property in excess of $400. As required by the three strikes law, the prosecutor formally alleged, and the trial court later found, that Ewing had been convicted previously of four serious or violent felonies for the three burglaries and the robbery in the Long Beach apartment complex. At the sentencing hearing, Ewing asked the court to reduce the conviction for grand theft, a "wobbler" under California law, to a misdemeanor so as to avoid a three strikes sentence. Ewing also asked the trial court to exercise its discretion to dismiss the allegations of some or all of his prior serious or violent felony convictions, again for purposes of avoiding a three strikes sentence. Before sentencing Ewing, the trial court took note of his entire criminal history, including the fact that he was on parole when he committed his latest offense. The court also heard arguments from defense counsel and a plea from Ewing himself. In the end, the trial judge determined that the grand theft should remain a felony. The court also ruled that the four prior strikes for the three burglaries and the robbery in Long Beach should stand. As a newly convicted felon with two or more "serious" or "violent" felony convictions in his past, Ewing was sentenced under the three strikes law to 25 years to life.

The California Court of Appeal affirmed in an unpublished opinion. Relying on our decision in *Rummel v. Estelle,* 445 U.S. 263

(1980), the court rejected Ewing's claim that his sentence was grossly disproportionate under the Eighth Amendment. Enhanced sentences under recidivist statutes like the three strikes law, the court reasoned, serve the "legitimate goal" of deterring and incapacitating repeat offenders. The Supreme Court of California denied Ewing's petition for review, and we granted certiorari. We now affirm.

II

A

The Eighth Amendment, which forbids cruel and unusual punishments, contains a "narrow proportionality principle" that "applies to noncapital sentences." Harmelin v. Michigan, 501 U.S. 957, 996–997 (1991) (KENNEDY, J., concurring in part and concurring in judgment). We have most recently addressed the proportionality principle as applied to terms of years in a series of cases beginning with Rummel v. Estelle, *supra.*

In *Rummel*, we held that it did not violate the Eighth Amendment for a State to sentence a three-time offender to life in prison with the possibility of parole. Like Ewing, Rummel was sentenced to a lengthy prison term under a recidivism statute. Rummel's two prior offenses were a 1964 felony for "fraudulent use of a credit card to obtain $80 worth of goods or services," and a 1969 felony conviction for "passing a forged check in the amount of $28.36.". His triggering offense was a conviction for felony theft—"obtaining $120.75 by false pretenses." This Court ruled that "having twice imprisoned him for felonies, Texas was entitled to place upon Rummel the onus of one who is simply unable to bring his conduct within the social norms prescribed by the criminal law of the State." The recidivism statute "is nothing more than a societal decision that when such a person commits yet another felony, he should be subjected to the admittedly serious penalty of incarceration for life, subject only to the State's judgment as to whether to grant him parole." We noted that this Court "has on occasion stated that the Eighth Amendment prohibits imposition of a sentence that is grossly disproportionate to the severity of the crime." . But "outside the context of capital punishment, successful challenges to the proportionality of particular sentences have been exceedingly rare." Although we stated that the proportionality principle "would . . . come into play in the extreme example . . . if a legislature made overtime parking a felony punishable by life imprisonment," we held that "the mandatory life sentence imposed upon this petitioner does not constitute cruel and unusual punishment under the Eighth and Fourteenth Amendments." * * *

Three years after *Rummel*, in Solem v. Helm, 463 U.S. 277, 279 (1983), we held that the Eighth Amendment prohibited "a life sentence without possibility of parole for a seventh nonviolent felony." The triggering offense in *Solem* was "uttering a 'no account' check for $100." We specifically stated that the Eighth Amendment's ban on cruel and unusual punishments "prohibits . . . sentences that are disproportionate to the crime committed," and that the "constitutional principle of proportionality has been recognized explicitly in this

Court for almost a century." The *Solem* Court then explained that three factors may be relevant to a determination of whether a sentence is so disproportionate that it violates the Eighth Amendment: "(i) the gravity of the offense and the harshness of the penalty; (ii) the sentences imposed on other criminals in the same jurisdiction; and (iii) the sentences imposed for commission of the same crime in other jurisdictions." Applying these factors in *Solem*, we struck down the defendant's sentence of life without parole. We specifically noted the contrast between that sentence and the sentence in *Rummel*, pursuant to which the defendant was eligible for parole. Indeed, we explicitly declined to overrule *Rummel* * * *.

Eight years after *Solem*, we grappled with the proportionality issue again in *Harmelin*, *supra*. *Harmelin* was not a recidivism case, but rather involved a first-time offender convicted of possessing 672 grams of cocaine. He was sentenced to life in prison without possibility of parole. A majority of the Court rejected Harmelin's claim that his sentence was so grossly disproportionate that it violated the Eighth Amendment. The Court, however, could not agree on why his proportionality argument failed. JUSTICE SCALIA, joined by THE CHIEF JUSTICE, wrote that the proportionality principle was "an aspect of our death penalty jurisprudence, rather than a generalizable aspect of Eighth Amendment law." He would thus have declined to apply gross disproportionality principles except in reviewing capital sentences.

JUSTICE KENNEDY, joined by two other Members of the Court, concurred in part and concurred in the judgment. JUSTICE KENNEDY specifically recognized that "the Eighth Amendment proportionality principle also applies to noncapital sentences." He then identified four principles of proportionality review—"the primacy of the legislature, the variety of legitimate penological schemes, the nature of our federal system, and the requirement that proportionality review be guided by objective factors"—that "inform the final one: The Eighth Amendment does not require strict proportionality between crime and sentence. Rather, it forbids only extreme sentences that are 'grossly disproportionate' to the crime." JUSTICE KENNEDY's concurrence also stated that *Solem* "did not mandate" comparative analysis "within and between jurisdictions."

The proportionality principles in our cases distilled in JUSTICE KENNEDY's concurrence guide our application of the Eighth Amendment in the new context that we are called upon to consider.

B

For many years, most States have had laws providing for enhanced sentencing of repeat offenders. Yet between 1993 and 1995, three strikes laws effected a sea change in criminal sentencing throughout the Nation. These laws responded to widespread public concerns about crime by targeting the class of offenders who pose the greatest threat to public safety: career criminals. * * *

Throughout the States, legislatures enacting three strikes laws made a deliberate policy choice that individuals who have repeatedly engaged in serious or violent criminal behavior, and whose conduct has not been deterred by more conventional approaches to punishment, must be isolated from society in order to protect the public safety. Though three strikes laws may be relatively new, our tradition of deferring to state legislatures in making and implementing such important policy decisions is longstanding.

Our traditional deference to legislative policy choices finds a corollary in the principle that the Constitution "does not mandate adoption of any one penological theory.". A sentence can have a variety of justifications, such as incapacitation, deterrence, retribution, or rehabilitation. Some or all of these justifications may play a role in a State's sentencing scheme. Selecting the sentencing rationales is generally a policy choice to be made by state legislatures, not federal courts.

When the California Legislature enacted the three strikes law, it made a judgment that protecting the public safety requires incapacitating criminals who have already been convicted of at least one serious or violent crime. Nothing in the Eighth Amendment prohibits California from making that choice. To the contrary, our cases establish that "States have a valid interest in deterring and segregating habitual criminals." Parke v. Raley, 506 U.S. 20, 27 (1992); Oyler v. Boles, 368 U.S. 448, 451 (1962) ("The constitutionality of the practice of inflicting severer criminal penalties upon habitual offenders is no longer open to serious challenge"). Recidivism has long been recognized as a legitimate basis for increased punishment. See Almendarez–Torres v.

United States, 523 U.S. 224, 230 (1998) (recidivism "is as typical a sentencing factor as one might imagine").

California's justification is no pretext. Recidivism is a serious public safety concern in California and throughout the Nation. According to a recent report, approximately 67 percent of former inmates released from state prisons were charged with at least one "serious" new crime within three years of their release. See U.S. Dept. of Justice, Bureau of Justice Statistics, P. Langan & D. Levin, Special Report: Recidivism of Prisoners Released in 1994, p. 1 (June 2002). In particular, released property offenders like Ewing had higher recidivism rates than those released after committing violent, drug, or public-order offenses. *Id.*, at 8. Approximately 73 percent of the property offenders released in 1994 were arrested again within three years, compared to approximately 61 percent of the violent offenders, 62 percent of the public-order offenders, and 66 percent of the drug offenders. Ibid.

* * *

The State's interest in deterring crime also lends some support to the three strikes law. We have long viewed both incapacitation and deterrence as rationales for recidivism statutes. Four years after the passage of California's three strikes law, the recidivism rate of parolees returned to prison for the commission of a new crime dropped by nearly 25 percent. California Dept. of Justice, Office of the Attorney General, "Three Strikes and You're Out"—Its Impact on the California Criminal Justice System After Four Years 10 (1998). Even more dramatically:

"an unintended but positive consequence of 'Three Strikes' has been the impact on parolees leaving the state. More California parolees are now leaving the state than parolees from other jurisdictions entering California. This striking turnaround started in 1994. It was the first time more parolees left the state than entered since 1976. This trend has continued and in 1997 more than 1,000 net parolees left California." *Ibid.*

See also Janiskee & Erler, Crime, Punishment, and Romero: An Analysis of the Case Against California's Three Strikes Law, 39 Duquesne L. Rev. 43, 45–46 ("Prosecutors in Los Angeles routinely report that 'felons tell them they are moving out of the state because they fear getting a second or third strike for a nonviolent offense.' ") (quoting Sanchez, A Movement Builds Against "Three Strikes" Law, Washington Post, Feb. 18, 2000, p. A3)).

To be sure, California's three strikes law has sparked controversy. Critics have doubted the law's wisdom, cost-efficiency, and effectiveness in reaching its goals. This criticism is appropriately directed at the legislature, which has primary responsibility for making the difficult policy choices that underlie any criminal sentencing scheme. We do not sit as a "superlegislature" to second-guess these policy choices. It is enough that the State of California has a reasonable basis for believing that dramatically enhanced sentences for habitual felons "advances the goals of [its] criminal justice system in any substantial way." See *Solem*, 463 U.S., at 297, n. 22.

III

Against this backdrop, we consider Ewing's claim that his three strikes sentence of 25 years to life is unconstitutionally disproportionate to his offense of "shoplifting three golf clubs." Brief for Petitioner 6. We first address the gravity of the offense compared to the harshness of the penalty. At the threshold, we note that Ewing incorrectly frames the issue. The gravity of his offense was not merely "shoplifting three golf clubs." Rather, Ewing was convicted of felony grand theft for stealing nearly $1,200 worth of merchandise after previously having been convicted of at least two "violent" or "serious" felonies. Even standing alone, Ewing's theft should not be taken lightly. His crime was certainly not "one of the most passive felonies a person could commit." *Solem, supra,* at 296. To the contrary, the Supreme Court of California has noted the "seriousness" of grand theft in the context of proportionality review. Theft of $1,200 in property is a felony under federal law, 18 U.S.C. § 641, and in the vast majority of States. * * *

In weighing the gravity of Ewing's offense, we must place on the scales not only his current felony, but also his long history of felony recidivism. Any other approach would fail to accord proper deference to the policy judgments that find expression in the legislature's choice of sanctions. In imposing a three strikes sentence, the State's interest is not merely punishing the offense of conviction, or the "triggering" offense: "It is in addition the interest ... in dealing in a harsher manner with those who by repeated criminal acts have shown that they are simply incapable of conforming to the norms of society as established by its criminal law." See *Rummel,* 445 U.S., at 276. To give full effect to the State's choice of this legitimate penological goal, our proportionality review of Ewing's sentence must take that goal into account.

Ewing's sentence is justified by the State's public-safety interest in incapacitating and deterring recidivist felons, and amply supported by his own long, serious criminal record. Ewing has been convicted of numerous misdemeanor and felony offenses, served nine separate terms of incarceration, and committed most of his crimes while on probation or parole. His prior "strikes" were serious felonies including robbery and three residential burglaries. To be sure, Ewing's sentence is a long one. But it reflects a rational legislative judgment, entitled to deference, that offenders who have committed serious or violent felonies and who continue to commit felonies must be incapacitated. The State of California "was entitled to place upon [Ewing] the onus of one who is simply unable to bring his conduct within the social norms prescribed by the criminal law of the State." *Rummel, supra,* at 284. Ewing's is not "the rare case in which a threshold comparison of the crime committed and the sentence imposed leads to an inference of gross disproportionality." *Harmelin,* 501 U.S., at 1005 (KENNEDY, J., concurring in part and concurring in judgment).

We hold that Ewing's sentence of 25 years to life in prison, imposed for the offense of felony grand theft under the three strikes law, is not grossly disproportionate and therefore does not violate the Eighth

Amendment's prohibition on cruel and unusual punishments. The judgment of the California Court of Appeal is affirmed.

It is so ordered.

JUSTICE SCALIA, concurring in the judgment.

In my concurring opinion in Harmelin v. Michigan, 501 U.S. 957, 985 (1991), I concluded that the Eighth Amendment's prohibition of "cruel and unusual punishments" was aimed at excluding only certain *modes* of punishment, and was not a "guarantee against disproportionate sentences." Out of respect for the principle of *stare decisis*, I might nonetheless accept the contrary holding of Solem v. Helm, 463 U.S. 277 (1983)—that the Eighth Amendment contains a narrow proportionality principle—if I felt I could intelligently apply it. This case demonstrates why I cannot.

Proportionality—the notion that the punishment should fit the crime—is inherently a concept tied to the penological goal of retribution. "It becomes difficult even to speak intelligently of 'proportionality,' once deterrence and rehabilitation are given significant weight," *Harmelin, supra,* at 989—not to mention giving weight to the purpose of California's three strikes law: incapacitation. In the present case, the game is up once the plurality has acknowledged that "the Constitution does not mandate adoption of any one penological theory," and that a "sentence can have a variety of justifications, such as incapacitation, deterrence, retribution, or rehabilitation." That acknowledgment having been made, it no longer suffices merely to assess "the gravity of the offense com-

pared to the harshness of the penalty"; that classic description of the proportionality principle (alone and in itself quite resistant to policy-free, legal analysis) now becomes merely the "first" step of the inquiry. Having completed that step (by a discussion which, in all fairness, does not convincingly establish that 25–years-to-life is a "proportionate" punishment for stealing three golf clubs), the plurality must then *add* an analysis to show that "Ewing's sentence is justified by the State's public-safety interest in incapacitating and deterring recidivist felons."

Which indeed it is—though why that has anything to do with the principle of proportionality is a mystery. Perhaps the plurality should revise its terminology, so that what it reads into the Eighth Amendment is not the unstated proposition that all punishment should be reasonably proportionate to the gravity of the offense, but rather the unstated proposition that all punishment should reasonably pursue the multiple purposes of the criminal law. That formulation would make it clearer than ever, of course, that the plurality is not applying law but evaluating policy.

Because I agree that petitioner's sentence does not violate the Eighth Amendment's prohibition against cruel and unusual punishments, I concur in the judgment.

JUSTICE THOMAS, concurring in the judgment.

I agree with JUSTICE SCALIA's view that the proportionality test announced in Solem v. Helm, 463 U.S. 277 (1983), is incapable of judicial application. Even were *Solem*'s test perfectly clear, however, I would not feel compelled by *stare decisis* to apply it. In my view, the Cruel and Unusual Punishments Clause of the Eighth Amendment contains no proportionality principle. See Harmelin v. Michigan, 501 U.S. 957, 967–985 (1991) (opinion of SCALIA, J.).

Because the plurality concludes that petitioner's sentence does not violate the Eighth Amendment's prohibition on cruel and unusual punishments, I concur in the judgment.

JUSTICE STEVENS, with whom JUSTICE SOUTER, JUSTICE GINSBURG and JUSTICE BREYER join, dissenting.

JUSTICE BREYER has cogently explained [see Justice Breyer's dissent, infra] why the sentence imposed in this case is both cruel and unusual.[1] The concurrences prompt this separate writing to emphasize that proportionality review is not only capable of judicial application but also required by the Eighth Amendment.

* * * Faithful to the Amendment's text, this Court has held that the Constitution directs judges to apply their best judgment in determining the proportionality of fines, see, *e.g.*, United States v. Bajakajian, 524 U.S. 321, 334–336 (1998), bail, see, *e.g.*, Stack v. Boyle, 342 U.S. 1, 5 (1951), and other forms of punishment, including the imposition of a death sentence, see, *e.g.*, Coker v. Georgia, 433 U.S. 584, 592 (1977). It "would be anomalous indeed" to suggest that the Eighth Amendment makes proportionality

review applicable in the context of bail and fines but not in the context of other forms of punishment, such as imprisonment. Solem v. Helm, 463 U.S. 277, 289 (1983). Rather, by broadly prohibiting excessive sanctions, the Eighth Amendment directs judges to exercise their wise judgment in assessing the proportionality of all forms of punishment.

The absence of a black-letter rule does not disable judges from exercising their discretion in construing the outer limits on sentencing authority that the Eighth Amendment imposes. After all, judges are "constantly called upon to draw ... lines in a variety of contexts," *id.*, at 294, and to exercise their judgment to give meaning to the Constitution's broadly phrased protections. For example, the Due Process Clause directs judges to employ proportionality review in assessing the constitutionality of punitive damages awards on a case-by-case basis. See, e.g., BMW of North America, Inc. v. Gore, 517 U.S. 559, 562 (1996). Also, although the Sixth Amendment guarantees criminal defendants the right to a speedy trial, the courts often are asked to determine on a case-by-case basis whether a particular delay is constitutionally permissible or not. See, e.g., Doggett v. United States, 505 U.S. 647 (1992).

Throughout most of the Nation's history—before guideline sentencing became so prevalent—federal and state trial judges imposed spe-

---

1. * * * I agree with JUSTICE BREYER that Ewing's sentence is grossly disproportionate even under *Harmelin*'s narrow proportionality framework. However, it is not clear that this case is controlled by *Harmelin*, which considered the proportionality of a life sentence imposed on a drug

offender who had *no* prior felony convictions. Rather, the three-factor analysis established in Solem v. Helm, 463 U.S. 277, 290–291 (1983), which specifically addressed recidivist sentencing, seems more directly on point.

cific sentences pursuant to grants of authority that gave them uncabined discretion within broad ranges. It was not unheard of for a statute to authorize a sentence ranging from one year to life, for example. In exercising their discretion, sentencing judges wisely employed a proportionality principle that took into account all of the justifications for punishment—namely, deterrence, incapacitation, retribution and rehabilitation. Likewise, I think it clear that the Eighth Amendment's prohibition of "cruel and unusual punishments" expresses a broad and basic proportionality principle that takes into account all of the justifications for penal sanctions. It is this broad proportionality principle that would preclude reliance on any of the justifications for punishment to support, for example, a life sentence for overtime parking.

Accordingly, I respectfully dissent.

JUSTICE BREYER, **with whom** JUSTICE STEVENS, JUSTICE SOUTER, **and** JUSTICE GINSBURG **join, dissenting.**

The constitutional question is whether the "three strikes" sentence imposed by California upon repeat-offender Gary Ewing is "grossly disproportionate" to his crime. *Ante,* at 1, 18 (plurality opinion). The sentence amounts to a real prison term of at least 25 years. The sentence-triggering criminal conduct consists of the theft of three golf clubs priced at a total of $1,197. The offender has a criminal history that includes four felony convictions arising out of three separate burglaries (one armed). In *Solem v. Helm,* 463 U.S. 277 (1983), the Court found grossly disproportionate a somewhat longer sentence imposed on a recidivist offender for triggering criminal conduct that was somewhat less severe. In my view, the differences are not determinative, and the Court should reach the same ultimate conclusion here.

I

* * *

The plurality applies JUSTICE KENNEDY's analytical framework in *Harmelin.* And, for present purposes, I will consider Ewing's Eighth Amendment claim on those terms. But see *ante,* at 1, n. 1 (STEVENS, J., dissenting). To implement this approach, courts faced with a "gross disproportionality" claim must first make "a threshold comparison of the crime committed and the sentence imposed." *Harmelin, supra,* at 1005 (KENNEDY, J., concurring in part and concurring in judgment). If a claim crosses that threshold—itself a *rare* occurrence—then the court should compare the sentence at issue to other sentences "imposed on other criminals" in the same, or in other, jurisdictions. *Solem, supra,* at 290–291; *Harmelin, supra,* at 1005 (KENNEDY, J., concurring in part and concurring in judgment). The comparative analysis will "validate" or invalidate "an initial judgment that a sentence is grossly disproportionate to a crime." Ibid.

I recognize the warnings implicit in the Court's frequent repetition of words such as "rare." Nonetheless I believe that the case before us is a "rare" case—one in which a court can say with reasonable confidence that the punishment is "grossly disproportionate" to the crime.

II

Ewing's claim crosses the gross disproportionality "threshold."

First, precedent makes clear that Ewing's sentence raises a serious disproportionality question. Ewing is [**47] a recidivist. Hence the two cases most directly in point are those in which the Court considered the constitutionality of recidivist sentencing: *Rummel* and *Solem*. Ewing's claim falls between these two cases. It is stronger than the claim presented in *Rummel*, where the Court upheld a recidivist's sentence as constitutional. It is weaker than the claim presented in *Solem*, where the Court struck down a recidivist sentence as unconstitutional.

* * * In *Rummel*, the Court held constitutional (a) a sentence of life imprisonment *with parole available within 10 to 12 years*, (b) for the offense of obtaining $120 by false pretenses, (c) committed by an offender with two prior felony convictions (involving small amounts of money). In *Solem*, the Court held unconstitutional (a) a sentence of life imprisonment *without parole*, (b) for the crime of writing a $100 check on a nonexistent bank account, (c) committed by an offender with six prior felony convictions (including three for burglary). Which of the three pertinent comparative factors made the constitutional difference?

The third factor, prior record, cannot explain the difference. The offender's prior record was *worse* in *Solem*, where the Court found the sentence too long, than in *Rummel*, where the Court upheld the sentence. The second factor, offense conduct, cannot explain the difference. The nature of the triggering offense—viewed in terms of the actual monetary loss—in the two cases was about the same. The one critical factor that explains the difference in the outcome is the length of the likely prison term measured in real time. In *Rummel*, where the Court upheld the sentence, the state sentencing statute authorized parole for the offender, Rummel, after 10 or 12 years. In *Solem*, where the Court struck down the sentence, the sentence required the offender, Helm, to spend the rest of his life in prison.

Now consider the present case. The third factor, *offender characteristics—i.e.*, prior record—does not differ significantly here from that in *Solem*. Ewing's prior record consists of four prior felony convictions (involving three burglaries, one with a knife) contrasted with Helm's six prior felony convictions (including three burglaries, though none with weapons). The second factor, *offense behavior*, is worse than that in *Solem*, but only to a degree. It would be difficult to say that the actual behavior itself here (shoplifting) differs significantly from that at issue in *Solem* (passing a bad check) or in *Rummel* (obtaining money through false pretenses). Rather the difference lies in the *value* of the goods obtained. That difference, measured in terms of the most relevant feature (loss to the victim, *i.e.*, wholesale value) and adjusted for the irrelevant feature of inflation, comes down (in 1979 values) to about $379 here compared with $100 in *Solem*, or (in 1973 values) to $232 here compared with $120.75 in *Rummel*. Alternatively, if one measures the inflation-adjusted value difference in terms of the golf clubs' sticker price, it comes down to $505 here compared to $100 in *Solem*, or $309 here compared to $120.75 in *Rummel*.

The difference in *length* of the real prison term—the first, and critical, factor in *Solem* and *Rummel*—is considerably more important. Ewing's sentence here amounts, in real terms, to at least 25 years without parole or good-time credits. That sentence is considerably shorter than Helm's sentence in *Solem*, which amounted, in real terms, to life in prison. Nonetheless Ewing's real prison term is more than twice as long as the term at issue in *Rummel*, which amounted, in real terms, to at least 10 or 12 years. And, Ewing's sentence, unlike Rummel's (but like Helm's sentence in *Solem*), is long enough to consume the productive remainder of almost any offender's life. (It means that Ewing himself, seriously ill when sentenced at age 38, will likely die in prison.).

The upshot is that the length of the real prison term—the factor that explains the *Solem/Rummel* difference in outcome—places Ewing closer to *Solem* than to *Rummel*, though the greater value of the golf clubs that Ewing stole moves Ewing's case back slightly in *Rummel*'s direction. Overall, the comparison places Ewing's sentence well within the twilight zone between *Solem* and *Rummel*—a zone where the argument for unconstitutionality is substantial, where the cases themselves cannot determine the constitutional outcome.

Ewing's sentence on its face imposes one of the most severe punishments available upon a recidivist who subsequently engaged in one of the less serious forms of criminal conduct. I do not deny the seriousness of shoplifting, which an *amicus curiae* tells us costs retailers in the range of $30 billion annually. But consider that conduct in terms of the factors that this Court mentioned in *Solem*—the "harm caused or threatened to the victim or society," the "absolute magnitude of the crime," and the offender's "culpability." In respect to all three criteria, the sentence-triggering behavior here ranks well toward the bottom of the criminal conduct scale. * * *

[Justice Breyer notes that shoplifting is not considered a serious factor for recidivist sentencing under the Federal Sentencing Guidelines].

Taken together, these * * * circumstances make clear that Ewing's "gross disproportionality" argument is a strong one. That being so, his claim *must* pass the "threshold" test. If it did not, what would be the function of the test? A threshold test must permit *arguably* unconstitutional sentences, not only *actually* unconstitutional sentences, to pass the threshold—at least where the arguments for unconstitutionality are unusually strong ones. A threshold test that blocked every ultimately invalid constitutional claim—even strong ones—would not be a *threshold* test but a *determinative* test. And, it would be a *determinative* test that failed to take account of highly pertinent sentencing information, namely, comparison with other sentences Sentencing comparisons are particularly important because they provide proportionality review with *objective* content. By way of contrast, a threshold test makes the assessment of constitutionality highly subjective. And, of course, so to transform that *threshold* test would violate this Court's earlier precedent. See 463 U.S., at 290, 291–292; *Harmelin, supra*, at

1000, 1005 (KENNEDY, J., concurring in part and concurring in judgment).

III

Believing Ewing's argument a strong one, sufficient to pass the threshold, I turn to the comparative analysis. A comparison of Ewing's sentence with other sentences requires answers to two questions. First, how would other jurisdictions (or California at other times, *i.e.*, without the three strikes penalty) punish the *same offense conduct?* Second, upon what other conduct would other jurisdictions (or California) impose the *same prison term?* Moreover, since hypothetical punishment is beside the point, the relevant prison time, for comparative purposes, is *real* prison time, *i.e.*, the time that an offender must *actually serve.* [Justice Breyer concludes that before the three strikes law, "Ewing-type prison time" for a recidivist was reserved for those convicted of serious crimes of violence. He also concluded that under the Federal Sentencing Guidelines and under the laws of most states, Ewing probably would have served substantially less time than under the California three strikes law.]

The upshot is that comparison of other sentencing practices, both in other jurisdictions and in California at other times (or in respect to other crimes), validates what an initial threshold examination suggested. Given the information available, given the state and federal parties' ability to provide additional contrary data, and given their failure to do so, we can assume for constitutional purposes that the following statement is true: Outside the California three strikes context, Ewing's recidivist sentence is virtually unique in its harshness for his offense of conviction, and by a considerable degree.

IV

This is not the end of the matter. California sentenced Ewing pursuant to its "three strikes" law. That law represents a deliberate effort to provide stricter punishments for recidivists. And, it is important to consider whether special criminal justice concerns related to California's three strikes policy might justify including Ewing's theft within the class of triggering criminal conduct (thereby imposing a severe punishment), even if Ewing's sentence would otherwise seem disproportionately harsh.

I can find no such special criminal justice concerns that might justify this sentence. The most obvious potential justification for bringing Ewing's theft within the ambit of the statute is administrative. California must draw some kind of workable line between conduct that will trigger, and conduct that will not trigger, a "three strikes" sentence. "But the fact that a line has to be drawn somewhere does not justify its being drawn anywhere." Pearce v. Commissioner, 315 U.S. 543, 558, 86 L. Ed. 1016, 62 S. Ct. 754 (1942) (Frankfurter, J., dissenting). The statute's administrative objective would seem to be one of separating more serious, from less serious, triggering criminal conduct. Yet the statute does not do that job particularly well.

The administrative line that the statute draws separates "felonies" from "misdemeanors." Those words suggest a graduated difference in degree. But an examination of how California applies these labels in practice to criminal conduct suggests that the offenses do not necessarily reflect those differences. Indeed, California uses those words in a way unrelated to the seriousness of offense conduct in a set of criminal statutes called "wobblers," one of which is at issue in this case.

Most "wobbler" statutes classify the same criminal conduct either as a felony or as a misdemeanor, depending upon the actual punishment imposed, which in turn depends primarily upon whether "the rehabilitation of the convicted defendant" either does or does not "require" (or would or would not "be adversely affected by") "incarceration in a state prison as a felon." In such cases, the felony/misdemeanor classification turns primarily upon the nature of the offender, not the comparative seriousness of the offender's conduct. * * * The result of importing this kind of distinction into California's three strikes statute is a series of anomalies. One anomaly concerns the seriousness of the triggering behavior. "Wobbler" statutes cover a wide variety of criminal behavior, ranging from assault with a deadly weapon, vehicular manslaughter, and money laundering, to the defacement of property with graffiti, or stealing more than $100 worth of chickens, nuts, or avocados. Some of this behavior is obviously less serious, even if engaged in twice, than other criminal conduct that California statutes classify as pure misdemeanors, such as reckless driving, the use of force or threat of force to interfere with another's civil rights, selling poisoned alcohol, child neglect, and manu-

facturing or selling false government documents with the intent to conceal true citizenship.

Another anomaly concerns temporal order. An offender whose triggering crime is his third crime likely will *not* fall within the ambit of the three strikes statute provided that (a) his *first* crime was chicken theft worth more than $100, and (b) he subsequently graduated to more serious crimes, say crimes of violence. That is because such chicken theft, when a first offense, will likely be considered a misdemeanor. A similar offender likely *will* fall within the scope of the three strikes statute, however, if such chicken theft was his *third* crime. That is because such chicken theft, as a third offense, will likely be treated as a felony.

A further anomaly concerns the offender's criminal record. California's "wobbler" "petty theft with a prior" statute * * * classifies a petty theft as a "felony" if, but only if, the offender has a prior record that includes at least one conviction for certain theft-related offenses. Thus a violent criminal who has committed two violent offenses and then steals $200 will *not* fall within the ambit of the three strikes statute, for his prior record reveals no similar *property* crimes. A similar offender *will* fall within the scope of the three strikes statute, however, if that offender, instead of having committed two previous violent crimes, has committed one previous violent crime and one previous petty theft. (Ewing's conduct would have brought him within the realm of the petty theft statute prior to 1976 but for inflation.)

At the same time, it is difficult to find any strong need to define the lower boundary as the State has done. The three strikes statute itself, when defining prior "strikes," simply lists the kinds of serious criminal conduct that falls within the definition of a "strike." There is no obvious reason why the statute could not enumerate, consistent with its purposes, the relevant triggering crimes. Given that possibility and given the anomalies that result from California's chosen approach, I do not see how California can justify on *administrative* grounds a sentence as seriously disproportionate as Ewing's.

* * *

Nor do the remaining criminal law objectives seem relevant. No one argues for Ewing's inclusion within the ambit of the three strikes statute on grounds of "retribution." Cf. Vitiello, Three Strikes: Can We Return to Rationality?, 87 J. Crim. L. & Criminology 395, 427 (1997) (California's three strikes law, like other "habitual offender statutes[, is] not retributive" because the term of imprisonment is "imposed without regard to the culpability of the offender or [the] degree of social harm caused by the offender's behavior," and "has little to do with the gravity of the offense"). For reasons previously discussed, in terms of "deterrence," Ewing's 25–year term amounts to overkill. And "rehabilitation" is obviously beside the point. The upshot is that, in my view, the State cannot find in its three strikes law a special criminal justice need sufficient to rescue a sentence that other relevant considerations indicate is unconstitutional.

V

JUSTICE SCALIA and JUSTICE THOMAS argue that we should not review for gross disproportionality a sentence to a term of years. Otherwise, we make it too difficult for legislators and sentencing judges to determine just when their sentencing laws and practices pass constitutional muster. I concede that a bright-line rule would give legislators and sentencing judges more guidance. But application of the Eighth Amendment to a sentence of a term of years requires a case-by-case approach. And, in my view, like that of the plurality, meaningful enforcement of the Eighth Amendment demands that application—even if only at sentencing's outer bounds.

A case-by-case approach can nonetheless offer guidance through example. Ewing's sentence is, at a minimum, 2 to 3 times the length of sentences that other jurisdictions would impose in similar circumstances. That sentence itself is sufficiently long to require a typical offender to spend virtually all the remainder of his active life in prison. These and the other factors that I have discussed, along with the questions that I have asked along the way, should help to identify "gross disproportionality" in a fairly objective way—at the outer bounds of sentencing.

In sum, even if I accept for present purposes the plurality's analytical framework, Ewing's sentence (life imprisonment with a minimum term of 25 years) is grossly disproportionate to the triggering offense conduct—stealing three golf clubs—Ewing's recidivism notwithstanding.

For these reasons, I dissent.

The Three Strikes Law on Habeas Corpus
Review: Lockyer v. Andrade

Lockyer v. Andrade, 123 S.Ct. 1166 (2003), was a companion case to *Ewing*, in which the Court considered a habeas corpus challenge to the constitutionality of the California three strikes law. Under the AEDPA (see Text, Chapter 13), a constitutional challenge on habeas corpus will be successful only if the state court's ruling was "contrary to" or "an unreasonable application of clearly established federal law" as determined by the Supreme Court. The California courts found that it did not violate the Eighth Amendment to sentence Andrade to two consecutive terms of 25 years to life for stealing videotapes worth about $150 from two stores. Andrade had previously been convicted of three counts of residential burglary. The Supreme Court, in an opinion by Justice O'Connor for five members of the Court, held that the state court's interpretation of the Eighth amendment was neither "contrary to" nor "an unreasonable application of clearly established federal law."

Justice O'Connor first analyzed the question of what had been "clearly established" in the *Rummell-Harmelin* line of cases:

* * * "[C]learly established Federal law" under § 2254(d)(1) [the habeas corpus statute, as amended by AEDPA] is the governing legal principle or principles set forth by the Supreme Court at the time the state court renders its decision. In most situations, the task of determining what we have clearly established will be straightforward. The difficulty with Andrade's position, however, is that our precedents in this area have not been a model of clarity. * * * Through this thicket of Eighth Amendment jurisprudence, one governing legal principle emerges as "clearly established" under § 2254(d)(1): A gross disproportionality principle is applicable to sentences for terms of years.

Our cases exhibit a lack of clarity regarding what factors may indicate gross disproportionality. In *Solem* (the case upon which Andrade relies most heavily), we stated: "It is clear that a 25-year sentence generally is more severe than a 15-year sentence, but in most cases it would be difficult to decide that the former violates the Eighth Amendment while the latter does not." And in *Harmelin*, both JUSTICE KENNEDY and JUSTICE SCALIA repeatedly emphasized this lack of clarity: that "*Solem* was scarcely the expression of clear ... constitutional law," 501 U.S., at 965 (opinion of SCALIA, J.), that in "adhering to the narrow proportionality principle ... our proportionality decisions have not been clear or consistent in all respects," *id.*, at 996 (KENNEDY, J., concurring in part and concurring in judgment), that "we lack clear objective standards to distinguish between sentences for different terms of years," *id.*, at 1001 (KENNEDY, J., concurring in part and concurring in judgment), and that the "precise contours" of the proportionality principle "are unclear," *id.,* at 998 (KENNEDY, J., concurring in part and concurring in judgment).

Thus, in this case, the only relevant clearly established law amenable to the "contrary to" or "unreasonable application of "framework is the gross disproportionality principle, the precise contours of which are unclear, applicable only in the "exceedingly rare" and "extreme" case.

Justice O'Connor then analyzed whether the state court's ruling was "contrary to" or an "unreasonable application of" the gross disproportionality principle that had been "clearly established" by the Supreme Court.

First, a state court decision is "contrary to our clearly established precedent if the state court applies a rule that contradicts the governing law set forth in our cases" or "if the state court confronts a set of facts that are materially indistinguishable from a decision of this Court and nevertheless arrives at a result different from our precedent." Williams v. Taylor, *supra,* at 405–406; see also Bell v. Cone, *supra,* at 694. In terms of length of sentence and availability of parole, severity of the underlying offense, and the impact of recidivism, Andrade's sentence implicates factors relevant in both *Rummel* and *Solem*. Because *Harmelin* and *Solem* specifically stated that they did not overrule *Rummel*, it was not contrary to our clearly established law for the California Court of Appeal to turn to *Rummel* in deciding whether a sentence is grossly disproportionate. Indeed, *Harmelin* allows a state court to reasonably rely on *Rummel* in determining whether a sentence is grossly disproportionate. The California Court of Appeal's decision was therefore not "contrary to" the governing legal principles set forth in our cases.

Andrade's sentence also was not materially indistinguishable from the facts in *Solem*. The facts here fall in between the facts in *Rummel* and the facts in *Solem*. *Solem* involved a sentence of life in prison without the possibility of parole. The defendant in *Rummel* was sentenced to life in prison with the possibility of parole. Here, Andrade retains the possibility of parole. *Solem* acknowledged that *Rummel* would apply in a "similar factual situation." And while this case resembles to some degree both *Rummel* and *Solem*, it is not materially indistinguishable from either. Consequently, the state court did not "confront a set of facts that are materially indistinguishable from a decision of this Court and nevertheless arrive at a result different from our precedent." Williams v. Taylor, 529 U.S., at 406. n1 * * *

Second, "under the 'unreasonable application' clause, a federal habeas court may grant the writ if the state court identifies the correct governing legal principle from this Court's decisions but unreasonably applies that principle to the facts of the prisoner's case." The "unreasonable application" clause requires the state court decision to be more than incorrect or erroneous. The state court's application of clearly established law must be objectively unreasonable. * * *

Section 2254(d)(1) permits a federal court to grant habeas relief based on the application of a governing legal principle to a set of facts different from those of the case in which the principle was announced. See, *e.g.,* Williams v. Taylor, *supra,* at 407 (noting that it is "an unreasonable application of this Court's precedent if the state court identifies the correct governing legal rule from this Court's cases but unreasonably applies it to the facts of the particular state prisoner's case"). Here, however, the governing legal principle gives legislatures broad discretion to fashion a sentence that fits within the scope of the proportionality principle—the "precise contours" of which "are unclear." Harmelin v. Michigan, 501 U.S., at 998 (KENNEDY, J., concurring in part and concurring in judgment). And it was not objectively unreasonable for the California Court of Appeal to conclude that these "contours" permitted an affirmance of Andrade's sentence.

* * *

The gross disproportionality principle reserves a constitutional violation for only the extraordinary case. In applying this principle for § 2254(d)(1) purposes, it was not an unreasonable application of our clearly established law for the California Court of Appeal to affirm Andrade's sentence of two consecutive terms of 25 years to life in prison.

Justice Souter, joined by Justices Stevens, Ginsburg and Breyer, dissented in *Lockyer.* Justice Souter compared Andrade's 50 years to life sentence to that in the companion case of *Ewing,* noting that Andrade's criminal history was less grave than Ewing's, and yet Andrade received a prison term twice as long for a less serious triggering offense. Justice Souter also argued that the state court's sentence was an "unreasonable application" of the law that he contended to be "clearly established" in Solem v. Helm.

Although *Solem* is important for its instructions about applying objective proportionality analysis the case is controlling here because it established a benchmark in applying the general principle. We specifically held that a sentence of life imprisonment without parole for uttering a $100 "no account" check was disproportionate to the crime, even though the defendant had committed six prior nonviolent felonies. In explaining our proportionality review, we contrasted the result with *Rummel*'s on the ground that the life sentence there had included parole eligibility after 12 years.

The facts here are on all fours with those of *Solem* and point to the same result. Andrade, like the defendant in *Solem,* was a repeat offender who committed theft of fairly trifling value, some $150, and their criminal records are comparable, including burglary (though Andrade's were residential), with no violent crimes or crimes against the person. The respective sentences, too, are strikingly alike. Although Andrade's petty thefts occurred on two separate occasions, his sentence can only be understood as punishment for the total amount he stole. The two thefts were separated by only two weeks; they involved the same victim; they apparently constituted parts of a single, continuing effort to finance drug sales; their seriousness is measured by the dollar value of the things taken; and the government charged both thefts in a single indictment. The state court accordingly spoke of his punishment collectively as well, carrying a 50–year minimum before parole eligibility, and because Andrade was 37 years old when sentenced, the substantial 50–year period amounts to life without parole. The results under the Eighth Amendment should therefore be the same in each case. The only ways to reach a different conclusion are to reject the practical equivalence of a life sentence without parole and one with parole eligibility at 87, or to discount the continuing authority of *Solem*'s example, as the California court did, see App. to Pet. for Cert. 76 ("The current validity of the Solem proportionality analysis is questionable.") The former is unrealistic; an 87–year-old man released after 50 years behind bars will have no real life left, if he survives to be released at all. And the latter, disparaging *Solem* as a point of reference on Eighth Amendment analysis, is wrong as a matter of law.

Page 1322. At the end of the section entitled "Note on the Death Penalty" add the following:

For recent developments in death penalty jurisprudence, *see, e.g.,* Atkins v. Virginia, 536 U.S. 304 (2002) (execution of a mentally retarded defendants is a cruel and unusual punishment prohibited by the Eighth Amendment); Ring v. Arizona, 536 U.S. 584 (2002) (Sixth Amendment right to jury trial requires that statutory aggravating factors must be determined by the jury, not the judge).

II.   GUIDELINES SENTENCING

B.   HOW THE FEDERAL GUIDELINES WORK

Page 1342. At the end of the headnote on "Acceptance of Responsibility" add

The Sentencing Commission recently eliminated from Guideline § 3E1.1 a provision under which a defendant could get an extra one-level decrease by timely providing the government with complete information about the offense.

D. SUPREME COURT CONSTRUCTION OF THE FEDERAL SENTENCING GUIDELINES

5. *Departures*

Page 1356. Add the following

In 2003, Congress passed legislation that imposes substantial changes on departures in Guidelines sentencing. The legislation, known as the Feeney amendment, and the political machinations behind that amendment, are described by Professor Frank Bowman, published in the Legal Times on April 21, 2003:

> Within the last few weeks, the Department of Justice has come very close to taking complete control of the federal criminal sentencing process, effectively eliminating the U.S. Sentencing Commission, the judiciary, and the bar from meaningful participation in making and applying sentencing rules. It may yet succeed. If it is to be stopped, the legal public must recognize what the department is doing.

> The Justice Department has three apparent objectives: (1) to eliminate or drastically reduce judicial sentencing discretion, (2) to maximize prosecutorial sentencing discretion, and (3) to marginalize the Sentencing Commission. All three objectives have been on display in the congressional debate over the Feeney Amendment.

> On April 10, Congress passed the Amber Alert Bill, which creates a national notification system for child abductions. Included in the bill was the unrelated Justice Department-sponsored add-on called the Feeney Amendment—for Rep. Tom Feeney of Florida, the Republican freshman who introduced it. The amendment has been described as a "disaster" for federal criminal sentencing; according to an April 14 New York Times editorial, it "will prevent federal judges from using their discretion to give shorter prison terms than prescribed by federal sentencing guidelines." Neither description is accurate ... yet. But disaster and the evisceration of a principal component of judicial sentencing discretion were averted, for now, only by furious opposition from the federal judiciary, the Sentencing Commission, the American Bar Association, civil rights groups, defense attorney organizations, and academics.

> In its original form, the Feeney Amendment would indeed have virtually eliminated the judicial power to depart downward from guideline sentences. The last-minute storm of opposition secured ameliorating changes in the House–Senate conference committee.

> But the Feeney Amendment still directs the Sentencing Commission to pass, within 180 days, rule changes that will "ensure that the incidence of downward departures are [sic] substantially reduced." The bill imposes a de novo standard of appellate review for departures, overturning the Supreme Court's decision in Koon v. United States (1996), and prohibits downward departures on remand on any ground not raised in the initial sentencing hearing.

The bill requires downward departures to be reported to Congress—clearly to induce judicial caution. And, in a final slap at the judiciary, the bill amends the law creating the Sentencing Commission, which had formerly required at least three of the seven commissioners to be federal judges, to state that henceforth "no more than three" commissioners may be judges.

To appreciate the significance of the battle over the Feeney Amendment, one must understand the roles of judges, prosecutors, defense attorneys, the Sentencing Commission, and Congress in making and administering federal sentencing law. In 1984, Congress created the Sentencing Commission. Lawmakers were reacting, in large part, to the perception that the previous system gave too much play to the personal idiosyncrasies of judges and produced unjustifiable disparities between the sentences of similar offenders. Therefore, the first Sentencing Commission produced a system in which each offender's sentence is determined primarily by his placement on a grid measuring the seriousness of the offense and the offender's criminal history. Judges determine offense seriousness by making findings of fact regarding offense characteristics specified in the guidelines, such as the amount of money stolen, the quantity of drugs possessed, and so forth.

On the other hand, the reformers recognized that no rigid set of national rules could prescribe the "correct" sentence for every person. While the guidelines restrict judicial discretion, they also depend on the wisdom and good sense of judges to ensure that general rules are applied sensibly in particular cases. Therefore, each position on the grid is a sentence range stated in months. The trial judge may sentence the defendant anywhere within the range.

In addition, since the inception of the guidelines the judge has had the power to "depart"—to sentence a defendant above or below the guideline range if the judge finds aggravating or mitigating factors of a kind or degree not considered by the commission. The guidelines also provide for "substantial assistance" departures, in which the government seeks a reduced sentence for a defendant who has cooperated against others. In theory, both judge-initiated downward departures and prosecution-requested substantial assistance departures should be relatively rare.

Thus, the guidelines system envisions different roles for different actors. The Sentencing Commission is to be a politically neutral body of expert rule-makers accountable to Congress. Prosecutors are to bring charges, establish guilt, and prove facts relevant to sentencing. They may request downward departures to encourage cooperation or achieve a just sentence. Judges have the dual role of finding the facts necessary to apply the guidelines and exercising their discretion to choose sentences within the guidelines range or to depart appropriately. Prosecutors, judges, and the defense bar are all to be consulted by the Sentencing Commission, but no group is to dictate the rules.

The Feeney Amendment stems from Justice Department complaints that in recent years judges have exercised their downward departure power too promiscuously. Sentencing statistics make this complaint superficially plausible. The percentage of defendants receiving downward departures for reasons other than "substantial assistance" to the government rose from less than 6 percent of federal cases in 1991 to 18.8 percent in 2001.

However, the bulk of this increase stemmed not from liberal judges run amok but from government plea-bargaining. Beginning around 1995, U.S. attorneys in the five Mexican-border districts, faced with rising caseloads, began recommending downward departures to induce fast pleas. By 2001, 59 percent of all non-substantial-assistance departures occurred in the Mexican-border districts. Substantial assistance departures requested by the government have also risen, from roughly 12 percent of federal cases in 1991 to 17 percent in 2001. By 2001, roughly 79 percent of all downward departures were requested by the Justice Department, either for substantial assistance or as part of a fast-track plea bargain.

Through the original Feeney Amendment, the Justice Department sought to eliminate the fewer than 20 percent of downward departures initiated by judges, while retaining the more than 80 percent requested by the Justice Department. Indeed, the final Feeney Amendment commands the Sentencing Commission to authorize fast-track departures, which, though increasingly common, are not now sanctioned by the guidelines and are inconsistent with their structure.

Even more troubling than the department's objectives were its methods. First, the Feeney Amendment was a deliberate end run around the Sentencing Commission. The department made no effort to work through the commission to address judicial departures. Second, the department showed utter disregard for the federal judiciary. It made no effort to consult directly with the judges. And by end-running the commission and introducing the Feeney Amendment as a floor amendment to another bill, it ensured that the judges would have no forum in which to respond to the allegations about excessive departures.

Finally, the Justice Department manipulated Congress itself, using slanted statistics, alarmist rhetoric, and the procedural dodge of a floor amendment to avoid the scrutiny of legislative hearings and debate.

In its final form, the Feeney Amendment does not directly eliminate judicial discretion. But it does direct the Sentencing Commission to study departures and to pass guideline amendments ensuring that downward departures will be "substantially reduced."

The Justice Department's next moves are predictable. First, the department will argue that the commission is now required to do through the guidelines very much what the original Feeney Amendment would have done through legislation—largely eliminate judicially initiated downward departures. Second, unless the commission complies, the department will threaten to go back to Congress for more-stringent legislation. Two weeks ago, the department used this same tactic to pressure the commission to raise economic crime sentences for the third time in 18 months in response to the Sarbanes–Oxley legislation.

In truth, the Justice Department's concerns about judicial departures are not entirely unfounded. Judicial departures have increased, and some judges seem to delight in proclaiming their disdain for the guidelines. Nonetheless, the overall rise in departure rates has been driven primarily by prosecutorial choices. The one desirable feature of the Feeney Amendment in its final form was highlighted by Sen. Edward Kennedy (D–Mass.), who observed that it calls for "a thorough and impartial review of all downward departures. . . . Only a review embracing all downward departures will provide the Commission the information necessary to fulfill the mandate of this legislation."

If the Sentencing Commission is to survive as an independent policy-making body, it must take that directive seriously. It must perform an impartial study of all types of downward departures, consulting with judges, probation officers, defense attorneys, prosecutors, and members of Congress. And its recommendations must not yield to any one view, but must instead maintain the balance of sentencing discretion between judges and prosecutors on which the guidelines are based.

For the moment at least, the Justice Department appears to have lost sight of the fact that it is only one among a group of institutions whose views must be respected in the making of sentencing policy. The other institutions, notably the judiciary and Congress, must provide a counterweight until the Justice Department rediscovers a sense of restraint.

III. SENTENCING PROCEDURES

B. PROCEDURES FOR DETERMINATE SENTENCING SYSTEMS

Page 1381. After the section on McMillan v. Pennsylvania, add the following:

Limitation on Sentencing Enhancements:
Apprendi v. New Jersey

McMillan upheld a statute that allowed the judge to impose a mandatory minimum sentence, on a showing of a particular fact by a preponderance of the evidence. The question of visible possession of a firearm was a sentencing factor rather than an element of the crime that had to be submitted to a jury. However, the defendant in *McMillan* did not receive a sentence that was higher than the prescribed range of penalties for the crime of which he was convicted—the sentencing enhancement factor established a higher "floor" for the sentence, but it did not create a higher "ceiling". In Apprendi v. New Jersey, 530 U.S. 466 (2000), a state statute permitted the judge to enhance a sentence for a weapons offense upon a finding (by a preponderance of the evidence) that the crime was committed with a racial bias. The difference from *McMillan* was that the sentence authorized, and imposed by the judge, was beyond the statutory maximum otherwise authorized for the weapons offense. The Supreme Court, in a 5–4 opinion written by Justice Stevens, struck down the statute as a violation of the defendant's constitutional right to a jury trial, as well as his constitutional right to proof beyond a reasonable doubt of every element of the crime.

Justice Stevens concluded that "it is unconstitutional for a legislature to remove from the jury the assessment of facts that increase the prescribed range of penalties to which a criminal defendant is exposed. It is equally clear that such facts must be established by proof beyond a reasonable doubt." Justice Stevens had this to say about *McMillan:*

> We do not overrule *McMillan*. We limit its holding to cases that do not involve the imposition of a sentence more severe than the statutory maximum for the offense established by the jury's verdict—a limitation identified in the *McMillan* opinion itself. Conscious of the likelihood that legislative decisions may have been made in reliance on *McMillan*, we reserve for another day the question whether *stare decisis* considerations preclude reconsideration of its narrower holding.

The majority found it unnecessary to determine whether its ruling (preventing a sentencing judge from finding facts that would increase a sentence beyond a prescribed maximum, even though the sentencing enhancement is authorized by statute), would have any effect on sentencing procedures under the Federal Sentencing Guidelines. But Justice O'Connor, for four dissenters, accused the majority of throwing all determinate sentencing systems, including the Federal Sentencing Guidelines, into disarray. The Guidelines permit enhancement, beyond the statutory maximum, for a variety of factors, including the quantity of drugs. Justice O'Connor declared as follows:

> The actual principle underlying the Court's decision may be that any fact (other than prior conviction) that has the effect, in real terms, of increasing the maximum punishment beyond an otherwise applicable range must be submitted to a jury and proved beyond a reasonable doubt. The principle thus would apply not only to schemes like New Jersey's, under which a factual determination exposes the defendant to a sentence beyond the prescribed statutory maximum, but also to all determinate-sentencing schemes in which

the length of a defendant's sentence within the statutory range turns on specific factual determinations (e.g., the federal Sentencing Guidelines). * * *

Prior to the most recent wave of sentencing reform, the Federal Government and the States employed indeterminate-sentencing schemes in which judges and executive branch officials (e.g., parole board officials) had substantial discretion to determine the actual length of a defendant's sentence. Studies of indeterminate-sentencing schemes found that similarly situated defendants often received widely disparate sentences. Although indeterminate sentencing was intended to soften the harsh and uniform sentences formerly imposed under mandatory-sentencing systems, some studies revealed that indeterminate sentencing actually had the opposite effect.

In response, Congress and the state legislatures shifted to determinate-sentencing schemes that aimed to limit judges' sentencing discretion and, thereby, afford similarly situated offenders equivalent treatment. The most well known of these reforms was the federal Sentencing Reform Act of 1984, 18 U.S.C. § 3551 et seq. In the Act, Congress created the United States Sentencing Commission, which in turn promulgated the Sentencing Guidelines that now govern sentencing by federal judges. Whether one believes the determinate-sentencing reforms have proved successful or not—and the subject is one of extensive debate among commentators—the apparent effect of the Court's opinion today is to halt the current debate on sentencing reform in its tracks and to invalidate with the stroke of a pen three decades' worth of nationwide reform, all in the name of a principle with a questionable constitutional pedigree. Indeed, it is ironic that the Court, in the name of constitutional rights meant to protect criminal defendants from the potentially arbitrary exercise of power by prosecutors and judges, appears to rest its decision on a principle that would render unconstitutional efforts by Congress and the state legislatures to place constraints on that very power in the sentencing context.

Finally, perhaps the most significant impact of the Court's decision will be a practical one—its unsettling effect on sentencing conducted under current federal and state determinate-sentencing schemes. As I have explained, the Court does not say whether these schemes are constitutional, but its reasoning strongly suggests that they are not. Thus, with respect to past sentences handed down by judges under determinate-sentencing schemes, the Court's decision threatens to unleash a flood of petitions by convicted defendants seeking to invalidate their sentences in whole or in part on the authority of the Court's decision today. Statistics compiled by the United States Sentencing Commission reveal that almost a half-million cases have been sentenced under the Sentencing Guidelines since 1989. Federal cases constitute only the tip of the iceberg. * * * Because many States, like New Jersey, have determinate-sentencing schemes, the number of individual sentences drawn into question by the Court's decision could be colossal.

The decision will likely have an even more damaging effect on sentencing conducted in the immediate future under current determinate-sentencing schemes. Because the Court fails to clarify the precise contours of the constitutional principle underlying its decision, federal and state judges are left in a state of limbo. Should they continue to assume the constitutionality of the determinate-sentencing schemes under which they have operated for so long, and proceed to sentence convicted defendants in accord with those governing statutes and guidelines? The Court provides no answer, yet its reasoning suggests that each new sentence will rest on shaky ground. The most unfortunate aspect of today's decision is that our precedents did not foreordain this disruption in the world of sentencing. Rather, our cases traditionally took a cautious approach to questions like the one presented in this case. The Court throws that caution to the wind and, in the process, threatens to cast sentencing in the United States into what will likely prove to be a lengthy period of considerable confusion.

Apprendi is set forth, in detail in this Supplement, in the section in Chapter 10 on constitutionally-based proof requirements.

Adhering to McMillan After Apprendi: Harris v. United States

In Harris v. United States, 536 U.S. 545 (2002), the Court reaffirmed *McMillan* and held that *Apprendi* does not prevent a judge from determining a fact that is the basis for a mandatory minimum sentence—so long as the sentence does not exceed the range established in the statute. *Harris* is set forth in full in this Supplement, in the section in Chapter 10 on constitutionally-based proof requirements.

C. PAROLE AND PROBATION PROCEDURES

Page 1388. At the end of the section on Black v. Romano, add the following:

3. The Relationship Between Supervised Release and Imprisonment

In Johnson v. United States, 529 U.S. 694 (2000), the defendant was convicted on a number of narcotics and firearm counts. He was sentenced to a lengthy prison term on all these sentences, as well as a mandatory 3–year term of supervised release on the narcotics offenses. But because the firearms offenses were based on an incorrect interpretation of the law, they were vacated, and the court reduced the prison sentence. By the time this happened, Johnson had already served 30 months longer than the valid sentence. He was immediately released, and filed a motion to have his term of supervised release reduced by the amount of extra prison time he had served. The district court refused to grant this motion; that court's ruling was upheld in a unanimous opinion written by Justice Kennedy. The Court held that a period of supervised release is not altered by the fact that a defendant serves excess prison time.

Justice Kennedy parsed 18 U.S.C. § 3624(e), the statutory provision governing the time at which a period of supervised release can begin. That statute provides explicitly that the term of supervised release "commences on the day the person is released from imprisonment". Justice Kennedy reasoned that "released" means what it says, and to say that Johnson "was released while still imprisoned diminishes the concept the word intends to convey."

Justice Kennedy also noted that beginning the period of supervised release upon actual release from imprisonment is consistent with Congress' purpose in establishing a system of supervised release. He explained that the "objectives of supervised release would be unfulfilled if excess prison time were to offset and reduce terms of supervised release." He noted that "Congress intended supervised release to assist individuals in their transition to community life. Supervised release fulfills rehabilitative ends, distinct from those served by incarceration." Therefore, it would be error to treat time in prison as interchangeable with a period of supervised release.

Chapter Twelve

DOUBLE JEOPARDY

II. THE EFFECT OF AN ACQUITTAL

Page 1400. Add at the end of the headnote titled "Entry of Judgment of Acquittal":

In Price v. Vincent, 123 S.Ct. 1848 (2003), the Court distinguished *Smalis* and *Martin Linen* and held that a trial judge's ruling was not sufficiently final to terminate jeopardy. The defendant was charged with murder. At the close of the government's case, defense counsel moved for a directed verdict of acquittal as to first degree murder, arguing that there was insufficient evidence of deliberation and premeditation. The trial judge stated:

> "My impression at this time is that there's not been shown premeditation or planning in the, in the alleged slaying. That what we have at the very best is Second Degree Murder.... I think that Second Degree Murder is an appropriate charge as to the defendants. Okay."

The prosecutor asked to make a brief statement regarding first-degree murder, but the defendant objected, arguing that his motion for directed verdict had been granted, and that further consideration of that charge would violate the Double Jeopardy Clause. The trial judge responded that he had "granted a motion" but had not directed a verdict. The judge noted that the jury had not been informed of his statements, and that his language indicated that he was going to reserve a ruling on the matter. Subsequently, the trial judge submitted the charge of first-degree murder to the jury and the defendant was convicted on that charge. The state courts, on review, concluded that the trial judge's comments on the directed verdict motion were not sufficiently final to constitute a judgment of acquittal terminating jeopardy.

The defendant sought habeas corpus relief, arguing that his rights under the Double Jeopardy Clause had been violated. Chief Justice Rehnquist, in an opinion for a unanimous Court, noted first that to obtain habeas relief the petitioner must show that the state court's adjudication of his claim was "contrary to, or involved an unreasonable application of, clearly established Federal law, as determined by the Supreme Court of the United States." [See the discussion of the habeas corpus statute in Chapter 13]. Thus, if reasonable minds could differ about whether the state courts were correct in finding insufficient finality to the trial court's ruling in this case, habeas relief must be denied. On the question of finality, the Court noted that in *Smalis* and *Martin Linen*, unlike in the present case, "the trial courts not only rendered statements of clarity and finality but also entered formal orders from which appeals were taken." No such order was entered in the instant case. Under these circumstances, the Michigan courts were not unreasonable in concluding that the trial judge's oral ruling was insufficiently final to terminate jeopardy.

XI. DOUBLE JEOPARDY AND REVIEW OF SENTENCING

B. REVIEW IN CAPITAL CASES

Page 1486. Add at the end of the section

Jury Deadlock on the Death Penalty and Death Penalty on a Retrial: Sattazahn v. Pennsylvania

The Court applied its *Bullington–Rumsey* line of cases in Sattazahn v. Pennsylvania, 537 U.S. 101 (2003), and found that the state could permissibly impose the death penalty on a retrial, after the defendant appealed a conviction in which life imprisonment was imposed. The jury at Sattazahn's first trial convicted him of first degree murder but then deadlocked on the death penalty. Under Pennsylvania law, if the jury deadlocks on a penalty of death, the judge must sentence the defendant to life imprisonment. Sattazahn appealed his conviction, alleging that the jury received improper instructions on certain matters. The state court agreed with Sattazahn, reversing his conviction and remanding. On retrial, the state again sought the death penalty, and this time (in part based on facts not presented previously) the jury unanimously agreed on a death sentence.

Justice Scalia, joined by the Chief Justice, Justice Thomas, and in most respects by Justice Kennedy, reasoned that Satterzahn's double jeopardy rights were not violated because he had never been "acquitted" of a death sentence. Justice Scalia first discussed the relevant case law:

> Where, as here, a defendant is convicted of murder and sentenced to life imprisonment, but appeals the conviction and succeeds in having it set aside, we have held that jeopardy has not terminated, so that the life sentence imposed in connection with the initial conviction raises no double-jeopardy bar to a death sentence on retrial. Stroud v. United States, 251 U.S. 15 (1919).

> In *Stroud*, the only offense at issue was that of murder, and the sentence was imposed by a judge who did not have to make any

further findings in order to impose the death penalty. In Bullington v. Missouri, 451 U.S. 430 (1981), however, we held that the Double Jeopardy Clause does apply to capital-sentencing proceedings where such proceedings "have the hallmarks of the trial on guilt or innocence." We identified several aspects of Missouri's sentencing proceeding that resembled a trial, including the requirement that the prosecution prove certain statutorily defined facts beyond a reasonable doubt to support a sentence of death. Such a procedure, we explained, "*explicitly requires* the jury to determine whether the prosecution has proved its case." Since, we concluded, a sentence of life imprisonment signifies that "the jury has already acquitted the defendant of whatever was necessary to impose the death sentence," the Double Jeopardy Clause bars a State from seeking the death penalty on retrial. We were, however, careful to emphasize that it is not the mere imposition of a life sentence that raises a double-jeopardy bar. We discussed *Stroud*, a case in which a defendant who had been convicted of first-degree murder and sentenced to life imprisonment obtained a reversal of his conviction and a new trial when the Solicitor General confessed error. In *Stroud*, the Court unanimously held that the Double Jeopardy Clause did not bar imposition of the death penalty at the new trial. What distinguished *Bullington* from *Stroud*, we said, was the fact that in *Stroud* "there was no separate sentencing proceeding at which the prosecution was required to prove—beyond a reasonable doubt or otherwise—additional facts in order to justify the particular sentence." We made clear that an "acquittal" at a trial-like sentencing phase, rather than the mere imposition of a life sentence, is required to give rise to double-jeopardy protections.

Later decisions refined *Bullington*'s rationale. In Arizona v. Rumsey, 467 U.S. 203 (1984), the State had argued in the sentencing phase, based on evidence presented during the guilt phase, that three statutory aggravating circumstances were present. The trial court, however, found that no statutory aggravator existed, and accordingly entered judgment in the accused's favor on the issue of death. On the State's cross-appeal, the Supreme Court of Arizona concluded that the trial court had erred in its interpretation of one of the statutory aggravating circumstances, and remanded for a new sentencing proceeding, which produced a sentence of death. In setting that sentence aside, we explained that "the double jeopardy principle relevant to [Rumsey's] case is the same as that invoked in *Bullington:* an acquittal on the merits by the sole decisionmaker in the proceeding is final and bars retrial on the same charge." * * * *Rumsey* thus reaffirmed that the relevant inquiry for double-jeopardy purposes was not whether the defendant received a life sentence the first time around, but rather whether a first life sentence was an "acquittal" based on findings sufficient to establish legal entitlement to the life sentence—*i. e.,* findings that the government failed to prove one or more aggravating circumstances beyond a reasonable doubt.

A later case in the line, Poland v. Arizona, 476 U.S. 147 (1986), involved two defendants convicted of first-degree murder and sentenced to death. On appeal the Arizona Supreme Court set aside the convictions (because of jury consideration of nonrecord evidence) and further found that there was insufficient evidence to support the one aggravating circumstance found by the trial court. It concluded, however, that there *was* sufficient evidence to support a *different* aggravating circumstance, which the trial court had thought not proved. The court remanded for retrial; the defendants were again convicted of first-degree murder, and a sentence of death was again imposed. We decided that in those circumstances, the Double Jeopardy Clause was *not* implicated. We distinguished *Bullington* and *Rumsey* on the ground that in *Poland*, unlike in those cases, neither the judge nor the jury had "acquitted" the defendant in his first capital sentencing proceeding by entering findings sufficient to establish legal entitlement to the life sentence. * * *

Justice Scalia then addressed the defendant's argument that a jury deadlock should trigger double jeopardy protection in the death penalty context:

Normally, "a retrial following a 'hung jury' does not violate the Double Jeopardy Clause." Richardson v. United States, 468 U.S. 317, 324 (1984). Petitioner contends, however, that given the unique treatment afforded capital-sentencing proceedings under *Bullington*, double-jeopardy protections were triggered when the jury deadlocked at his first sentencing proceeding and the court prescribed a sentence of life imprisonment pursuant to Pennsylvania law.

We disagree. Under the *Bullington* line of cases just discussed, the touchstone for double-jeopardy protection in capital-sentencing proceedings is whether there has been an "acquittal." Petitioner here cannot establish that the jury or the court "acquitted" him during his first capital-sentencing proceeding. As to the jury: The verdict form returned by the foreman stated that the jury deadlocked 9-to-3 on whether to impose the death penalty; it made no findings with respect to the alleged aggravating circumstance. That result—or more appropriately, that non-result—cannot fairly be called an acquittal "based on findings sufficient to establish legal entitlement to the life sentence."*Rumsey.*

The entry of a life sentence by the judge was not "acquittal," either. As the Pennsylvania Supreme Court explained:

" 'Under Pennsylvania's sentencing scheme, the judge has no discretion to fashion sentence once he finds that the jury is deadlocked. The statute directs him to enter a life sentence. The judge makes no findings and resolves no factual matter. Since judgment is not based on findings which resolve some factual matter, it is not sufficient to establish legal entitlement to a life sentence. A default judgment does not trigger a double jeopardy bar to the death penalty upon retrial.' "

It could be argued, perhaps, that the statutorily required entry of a life sentence creates an "entitlement" even without an "acquittal," because that is what the Pennsylvania Legislature intended—*i.e.*, it intended that the life sentence should survive vacation of the underlying conviction. The Pennsylvania Supreme Court, however, did not find such intent in the statute—and there was eminently good cause not to do so. A State's simple interest in closure might make it willing to accept the default penalty of life imprisonment when the conviction is affirmed and the case is, except for that issue, at an end—but unwilling to do so when the case must be retried anyway. And its interest in conservation of resources might make it willing to leave the sentencing issue unresolved (and the default life sentence in place) where the cost of resolving it is the empaneling of a new jury and, in all likelihood, a repetition of much of the guilt phase of the first trial—though it is eager to attend to that unfinished business if there is to be a new jury and a new trial anyway.

Justice Scalia, in a section of the opinion joined only by the Chief Justice and Justice Thomas, argued that the Court's jurisprudence on double jeopardy at sentencing was in need of revision in light of the Court's landmark decision in Apprendi v. New Jersey, 530 U.S. 466 (2000) [see the discussion of *Apprendi* in Chapters 10 and 11 of this Supplement]. Justice Scalia explained as follows:

When *Bullington*, *Rumsey*, and *Poland* were decided, capital-sentencing proceedings were understood to be just that: *sentencing proceedings*. Whatever "hallmarks of [a] trial" they might have borne, *Bullington*, 451 U.S., at 439, they differed from trials in a respect crucial for purposes of the Double Jeopardy Clause: They dealt only with the *sentence* to be imposed for the "offence" of capital murder. Thus, in its search for a rationale to support *Bullington* and its "progeny," the Court continually tripped over the text of the Double Jeopardy Clause.

Recent developments, however, have illuminated this part of our jurisprudence. Our decision in Apprendi v. New Jersey, 530 U.S. 466 (2000), clarified what constitutes an "element" of an offense for purposes of the Sixth Amendment's jury-trial guarantee. Put simply, if the existence of any fact (other than a prior conviction) increases the maximum punishment that may be imposed on a defendant, that fact—no matter how the State labels it—constitutes an element, and must be found by a jury beyond a reasonable doubt.

Just last Term we recognized the import of *Apprendi* in the context of capital-sentencing proceedings. In Ring v. Arizona, 536 U.S. 584 (2002), we held that aggravating circumstances that make a defendant eligible for the death penalty "operate as 'the functional equivalent of an element of a *greater offense*.' " That is to say, for purposes of the Sixth Amendment's jury-trial guarantee, the underlying offense of "murder" is a distinct, lesser included offense of "murder plus one or more aggravating circumstances": Whereas the former exposes a defendant to a maximum penalty of life imprisonment, the latter increases the maximum permissible sentence to death. Accordingly, we held that the Sixth Amendment requires that a jury, and not a judge, find the existence of any aggravating circumstances, and that they be found, not by a mere preponderance of the evidence, but beyond a reasonable doubt. We can think of no principled reason to distinguish, in this context, between what constitutes an offense for purposes of the Sixth Amendment's jury-trial guarantee and what constitutes an "offence" for purposes of the Fifth Amendment's Double Jeopardy Clause. In the post-*Ring* world, the Double Jeopardy Clause can, and must, apply to some capital-sentencing proceedings consistent with the text of the Fifth Amendment. If a jury unanimously concludes that a State has failed to meet its burden of proving the existence of one or more aggravating circumstances, double-jeopardy protections attach to that "acquittal" on the offense of "murder plus aggravating circumstance(s)." Thus, *Rumsey* was correct to focus on whether a factfinder had made findings that constituted an "acquittal" of the aggravating circumstances; but the reason that issue was central is not that a capital-sentencing proceeding is "comparable to a trial," but rather that "murder plus one or more aggravating circumstances" is a separate offense from "murder" *simpliciter*.

For purposes of the Double Jeopardy Clause, then, "first-degree murder" under Pennsylvania law—the offense of which petitioner was convicted during the guilt phase of his proceedings—is properly understood to be a lesser included offense of "first-degree murder plus aggravating circumstance(s)." Thus, if petitioner's first sentencing jury had unanimously concluded that Pennsylvania failed to prove any aggravating circumstances, that conclusion would operate as an "acquittal" of the greater offense—which would bar Pennsylvania from retrying petitioner on that greater offense (and thus, from seeking the death penalty) on retrial.

But that is not what happened. Petitioner was convicted in the guilt phase of his first trial of the lesser offense of first-degree murder. During the sentencing phase, the jury deliberated without reaching a decision on death or life, and without making any findings regarding aggravating or mitigating circumstances. After 3 1/2 hours the judge dismissed the jury as hung and entered a life sentence in accordance with Pennsylvania law. * * * [N]either judge nor jury "acquitted" petitioner of the greater offense of "first-degree murder plus aggravating circumstance(s)." Thus, when petitioner appealed and succeeded in invalidating his conviction of the lesser offense, there was no double-jeopardy bar to Pennsylvania's retrying petitioner on both the lesser and the greater offense; his "jeopardy" never terminated with respect to either.

Justice O'Connor wrote a concurring opinion. She refused to join in any opinion implying that *Apprendi* had any effect on sentencing or on double jeopardy jurisprudence, "because I continue to believe that case was wrongly decided. She did agree with Justice Scalia, however, that Satterzahn's double jeopardy rights were not violated because he had never been "acquitted" of a sentence of death. She elaborated as follows:

> Because death penalty sentencing proceedings bear the hallmarks of a trial, we held in Arizona v. Rumsey that "an acquittal on the merits by the sole decisionmaker in the proceeding is final and bars retrial on the same charge." A defendant is "acquitted" of the death penalty for purposes of double jeopardy when the sentencer "decides that the prosecution has not proved its case that the death penalty is appropriate." Poland v. Arizona, 476 U.S. 147, 155 (1986). In the absence of a death-penalty acquittal, the "clean slate" rule recognized in North Carolina v. Pearce, 395 U.S. 711, 719–721 (1969), applies and no double jeopardy bar arises.
>
> When, as in this case, the jury deadlocks in the penalty phase of a capital trial, it does not "decide" that the prosecution has failed to prove its case for the death penalty. Rather, the jury makes no decision at all. Petitioner's jury did not *"agree . . . that the prosecution had not proved its case."* *Bullington, supra,* at 443. It did not make any findings about the existence of the aggravating or mitigating circumstances. In short, the jury did not "acquit" petitioner of the death penalty under *Bullington* and *Rumsey*.

Justice Ginsburg, joined by Justices Stevens, Souter and Breyer, dissented. She argued that the policies of the Double Jeopardy Clause are at stake when the defendant is sentenced to life imprisonment rather than death and is then subject to the death penalty on retrial. She explained as follows:

> I recognize that this is a novel and close question: Sattazahn was not "acquitted" of the death penalty, but his case was fully tried and the court, on its own motion, entered a final judgment—a life sentence—terminating the trial proceedings. I would decide the double jeopardy issue in Sattazahn's favor, for the reasons herein stated, and giving weight to two ultimate considerations. First, the Court's holding confronts defendants with a perilous choice, one we have previously declined to impose in other circumstances. See Green v. United States, 355 U.S., at 193–194. Under the Court's decision, if a defendant sentenced to life after a jury deadlock chooses to appeal her underlying conviction, she faces the possibility of death if she is successful on appeal but convicted on retrial. If, on the other hand, the defendant loses her appeal, or chooses to forgo an appeal, the final judgment for life stands. In other words, a defendant in Sattazahn's position must relinquish either her right to file a potentially meritorious appeal, or her state-granted entitlement to avoid the death penalty.

We have previously declined to interpret the Double Jeopardy Clause in a manner that puts defendants in this bind. In *Green*, we rejected the argument that appealing a second-degree murder conviction prolonged jeopardy on a related first-degree murder charge. We noted that a ruling on this question in favor of the prosecutor would require defendants to "barter [their] constitutional protection against a second prosecution for an offense punishable by death as the price of a successful appeal from an erroneous conviction of another offense." "The law," we concluded, "should not ... place [defendants] in such an incredible dilemma." Although Sattazahn was required to barter a state-law entitlement to life against his right to appeal, rather than a constitutional protection, I nevertheless believe the considerations advanced in *Green* should inform our decision here.

Second, the punishment Sattazahn again faced on re-trial was death, a penalty "unique in both its severity and its finality." Monge v. California, 524 U.S. 721, 732 (1998). These qualities heighten Sattazahn's double jeopardy interest in avoiding a second prosecution. The "hazards of [a second] trial and possible conviction," *Green*, 355 U.S., at 187, the "continuing state of anxiety and insecurity" to which retrial subjects a defendant, and the "financial" as well as the "emotional burden" of a second trial, are all exacerbated when the subsequent proceeding may terminate in death. Death, moreover, makes the "dilemma" a defendant faces when she decides whether to appeal all the more "incredible." *Green*, 355 U.S., at 193.

Chapter Thirteen

POST–CONVICTION CHALLENGES

II. GROUNDS FOR DIRECT ATTACKS ON A CONVICTION

D. THE EFFECT OF ERROR ON THE VERDICT

2. *Plain Error*

Page 1509.   At the end of the section, add the following:

Plain Error Review of an Apprendi Violation: United States v. Cotton

In Apprendi v. New Jersey, 530 U.S. 466 (2000), the Court held that "[o]ther than the fact of a prior conviction, any fact that increases the penalty for a crime beyond the prescribed statutory maximum must be submitted to a jury, and proved beyond a reasonable doubt." [*Apprendi* is set forth in this Supplement, Chapter 10]. In federal prosecutions, such facts must also be charged in the indictment. In United States v. Cotton, 535 U.S. 625 (2002), the Court reviewed an *Apprendi* violation for plain error. The defendants in *Cotton* received a sentence beyond the statutory maximum, after the trial judge (rather than the jury) found that the drug offenses involved more than 50 grams of cocaine base. The indictment made no allegation as to any amount of drugs. Under *Apprendi*, the amount of drugs that triggers an enhanced sentence beyond the statutory maximum is an element of the crime that must be set forth in the indictment and proved to the jury. The government conceded that the defendants' enhanced sentence was erroneous under *Apprendi*, but pointed out that the defendants had failed to raise the *Apprendi* argument before the district court.

The Supreme Court, in an opinion by Chief Justice Rehnquist, held that the defendants were not entitled to relief because he could not meet his burden of showing plain error under the circumstances. Chief Justice Rehnquist analyzed the plain error question as follows:

[W]e proceed to apply the plain-error test of Federal Rule of Criminal Procedure 52(b) to respondents' forfeited claim. See United

States v. Olano, 507 U.S. 725, 731 (1993). "Under that test, before an appellate court can correct an error not raised at trial, there must be (1) 'error,' (2) that is 'plain,' and (3) that 'affect[s] substantial rights.'" Johnson v. United States, 520 U.S. 461, 466–467 (1997). "If all three conditions are met, an appellate court may then exercise its discretion to notice a forfeited error, but only if (4) the error seriously affect[s] the fairness, integrity, or public reputation of judicial proceedings." 520 U.S., at 467. The Government concedes that the indictment's failure to allege a fact, drug quantity, that increased the statutory maximum sentence rendered respondents' enhanced sentences erroneous under the reasoning of *Apprendi*. The Government also concedes that such error was plain. See *Johnson, supra*, at 468 ("[W]here the law at the time of trial was settled and clearly contrary to the law at the time of appeal[,] it is enough that an error be 'plain' at the time of appellate consideration").

The third inquiry is whether the plain error "affect[ed] substantial rights." This usually means that the error "must have affected the outcome of the district court proceedings." *Olano, supra*, at 734. Respondents argue that an indictment error falls within the "limited class" of "structural errors," *Johnson, supra*, at 468–469 that "can be corrected regardless of their effect on the outcome," *Olano, supra*, at 735. * * *

As in *Johnson*, we need not resolve whether respondents satisfy this element of the plain-error inquiry, because even assuming respondents' substantial rights were affected, the error did not seriously affect the fairness, integrity, or public reputation of judicial proceedings. The error in *Johnson* was the District Court's failure to submit an element of the false statement offense, materiality, to the petit jury. The evidence of materiality, however, was "overwhelming" and "essentially uncontroverted." We thus held that there was "no basis for concluding that the error 'seriously affect[ed] the fairness, integrity or public reputation of judicial proceedings.'"

The same analysis applies in this case to the omission of drug quantity from the indictment. The evidence that the conspiracy involved at least 50 grams of cocaine base was "overwhelming" and "essentially uncontroverted." Much of the evidence implicating respondents in the drug conspiracy revealed the conspiracy's involvement with far more than 50 grams of cocaine base. Baltimore police officers made numerous state arrests and seizures between February 1996 and April 1997 that resulted in the seizure of 795 ziplock bags and clear bags containing approximately 380 grams of cocaine base. A federal search of respondent Jovan Powell's residence resulted in the seizure of 51.3 grams of cocaine base. A cooperating co-conspirator testified at trial that he witnessed respondent Hall cook one-quarter of a kilogram of cocaine powder into cocaine base. Another cooperating co-conspirator testified at trial that she was present in a hotel room where the drug operation bagged one kilogram of cocaine base into ziplock bags. Surely the grand jury, having found that the conspiracy existed, would have also found that the conspiracy involved at least 50 grams of cocaine base.

Respondents emphasize that the Fifth Amendment grand jury right serves a vital function in providing for a body of citizens that acts as a check on prosecutorial power. No doubt that is true. But that is surely no less true of the Sixth Amendment right to a petit jury, which, unlike the grand jury, must find guilt beyond a reasonable doubt. The important role of the petit jury did not, however, prevent us in *Johnson* from applying the longstanding rule "that a constitutional right may be forfeited in criminal as well as civil cases by the failure to make timely assertion of the right...." In providing for graduated penalties in 21 U.S.C. § 841(b), Congress intended that defendants, like respondents, involved in large-scale drug operations receive more severe punishment than those committing drug offenses involving lesser quantities. Indeed, the fairness and integrity of the criminal justice system depends on meting out to those inflicting the greatest harm on society the most severe punishments. The real threat then to the "fairness, integrity, and public reputation of judicial proceedings" would be if respondents, despite the overwhelming and uncontroverted evidence that they were involved in a vast drug conspiracy, were to receive a sentence prescribed for those committing less substantial drug offenses because of an error that was never objected to at trial.

III. COLLATERAL ATTACK

B. THE FEDERAL HABEAS CORPUS SCHEME: THE PROCEDURAL FRAMEWORK

2. General Principles Concerning Habeas Relief After AEDPA

Page 1523. Add at the end of the section:

Certificate of Appealability

The AEDPA limits the right to appeal from a district court's denial of a state defendant's petition for a writ of habeas corpus. The Act requires that the petitioner must obtain a "certificate of appeal" from a circuit judge. In Slack v. McDaniel, 529 U.S. 473 (2000), the Court set forth the standard that circuit judges are to apply in deciding whether to issue a certificate of appealability. It declared as follows:

Where a district court has rejected the constitutional claims on the merits, the showing required to satisfy § 2253(c) is straightforward: The petitioner must demonstrate that reasonable jurists would find the district court's assessment of the constitutional claims debatable or wrong. The issue becomes somewhat more complicated where, as here, the district court dismisses the petition based on procedural grounds. We hold as follows: When the district court denies a habeas petition on procedural grounds without reaching the prisoner's underlying constitutional claim, a COA should issue when the prisoner shows, at least, that jurists of reason would find it debatable whether the petition states a valid claim of the denial of a constitutional right and that jurists of reason would find it debatable whether the district court was correct in its procedural ruling. This construction gives meaning to Congress' requirement that a prisoner demonstrate substantial underlying constitutional claims and is in conformity with the meaning of the "substantial showing" standard * * * adopted by Congress in AEDPA. Where a plain procedural bar is present and the district court is correct to invoke it to dispose of the case, a reasonable jurist could not conclude either that the district court erred in dismissing the petition or that the petitioner should be allowed to proceed further. In such a circumstance, no appeal would be warranted.

See also Miller–El v. Cockrell, 537 U.S. 322 (2003) (finding that the petitioner met the *Slack* standard by providing circumstantial evidence that the prosecutor excused jurors on racial grounds in violation of Batson v. Kentucky).

3. *Factual Findings and Mixed Questions of Law and Fact*

Page 1523. After the block quotation of section 2254(d), delete the rest of the section and add the following:

In Williams v. Taylor, 529 U.S. 362 (2000), the Court construed section 2254(d) as amended by the AEDPA, and set forth the standard for federal review of state court determinations, as mandated by that section. The case involved a claim on habeas that Williams' counsel had been ineffective at the penalty phase of his capital trial by failing to introduce evidence that Williams had been abused as a child and was borderline retarded. The State Supreme Court, applying Strickland v. Washington and subsequent Supreme Court cases, rejected Williams' ineffectiveness claim on the ground that Williams had not been prejudiced. Justice O'Connor, writing for the Court, set forth and analyzed the statutory language of the AEDPA in the following passage:

> Section 2254 now provides:
>
> > (d) An application for a writ of habeas corpus on behalf of a person in custody pursuant to the judgment of a State court shall not be granted with respect to any claim that was adjudicated on the merits in State court proceedings unless the adjudication of the claim—
> >
> > > (1) resulted in a decision that was contrary to, or involved an unreasonable application of, clearly established Federal law, as determined by the Supreme Court of the United States.

Accordingly, for Williams to obtain federal habeas relief, he must first demonstrate that his case satisfies the condition set by

§ 2254(d)(1). That provision modifies the role of federal habeas courts in reviewing petitions filed by state prisoners.

* * *

The word "contrary" is commonly understood to mean "diametrically different," "opposite in character or nature," or "mutually opposed." The text of § 2254(d)(1) therefore suggests that the state court's decision must be substantially different from the relevant precedent of this Court. * * * A state-court decision will certainly be contrary to our clearly established precedent if the state court applies a rule that contradicts the governing law set forth in our cases. Take, for example, our decision in Strickland v. Washington, 466 U.S. 668 (1984). If a state court were to reject a prisoner's claim of ineffective assistance of counsel on the grounds that the prisoner had not established by a preponderance of the evidence that the result of his criminal proceeding would have been different, that decision would be "diametrically different," "opposite in character or nature," and "mutually opposed" to our clearly established precedent because we held in *Strickland* that the prisoner need only demonstrate a "reasonable probability that ... the result of the proceeding would have been different." A state-court decision will also be contrary to this Court's clearly established precedent if the state court confronts a set of facts that are materially indistinguishable from a decision of this Court and nevertheless arrives at a result different from our precedent. Accordingly, in either of these two scenarios, a federal court will be unconstrained by § 2254(d)(1) because the state-court decision falls within that provision's "contrary to" clause.

On the other hand, a run-of-the-mill state-court decision applying the correct legal rule from our cases to the facts of a prisoner's case would not fit comfortably within § 2254(d)(1)'s "contrary to" clause. Assume, for example, that a state-court decision on a prisoner's ineffective-assistance claim correctly identifies *Strickland* as the controlling legal authority and, applying that framework, rejects the prisoner's claim. Quite clearly, the state-court decision would be in accord with our decision in *Strickland* as to the legal prerequisites for establishing an ineffective-assistance claim, even assuming the federal court considering the prisoner's habeas application might reach a different result applying the *Strickland* framework itself. It is difficult, however, to describe such a run-of-the-mill state-court decision as "diametrically different" from, "opposite in character or nature" from, or "mutually opposed" to *Strickland*, our clearly established precedent. Although the state-court decision may be contrary to the federal court's conception of how *Strickland* ought to be applied in that particular case, the decision is not "mutually opposed" to *Strickland* itself.

Thus, in Justice O'Connor's view, a state court decision cannot be overturned on habeas simply because it is incorrect—under the "contrary to" clause, the state court decision must be diametrically opposed to Supreme Court precedent in order to justify habeas relief. Justice O'Connor next took issue with the broader view of the statute posited by Justice Stevens in dissent. Justice O'Connor summarized, and criticized, Justice Stevens' view in the following passage:

> Justice Stevens would instead construe § 2254(d)(1)'s "contrary to" clause to encompass such a routine state-court decision. That construction, however, saps the "unreasonable application" clause of any meaning. If a federal habeas court can, under the "contrary to" clause, issue the writ whenever it concludes that the state court's application of clearly established federal law was incorrect, the "unreasonable application" clause becomes a nullity. We must, however, if possible, give meaning to every clause of the statute. Justice Stevens not only makes no attempt to do so, but also construes the "contrary to" clause in a manner that ensures that the "unreasonable application" clause will have no independent meaning. We reject that expansive interpretation of the statute. Reading § 2254(d)(1)'s "contrary to" clause to permit a federal court to grant relief in cases where a state court's error is limited to the manner in which it applies Supreme Court precedent is suspect given the logical and natural fit of the neighboring "unreasonable application" clause to such cases.

Justice O'Connor next construed the "unreasonable application" clause of § 2254(d)(1):

> First, a state-court decision involves an unreasonable application of this Court's precedent if the state court identifies the correct governing legal rule from this Court's cases but unreasonably applies it to the facts of the particular state prisoner's case. Second, a state-court decision also involves an unreasonable application of this Court's precedent if the state court either unreasonably extends a legal principle from our precedent to a new context where it should not apply or unreasonably refuses to extend that principle to a new context where it should apply.

> A state-court decision that correctly identifies the governing legal rule but applies it unreasonably to the facts of a particular prisoner's case certainly would qualify as a decision "involv[ing] an unreasonable application of ... clearly established Federal law."

Justice O'Connor noted that some lower courts had defined "unreasonable application of law" by determining whether any reasonable jurist would agree with the state court's determination—if so, this would preclude habeas relief. Justice O'Connor, however, rejected the "reasonable jurist" standard:

> There remains the task of defining what exactly qualifies as an "unreasonable application" of law under § 2254(d)(1). The [lower court] held * * * that a state-court decision involves an "unreasonable application of ... clearly established Federal law" only if the

state court has applied federal law "in a manner that reasonable jurists would all agree is unreasonable." * * *

Defining an "unreasonable application" by reference to a "reasonable jurist" * * * is of little assistance to the courts that must apply § 2254(d)(1) and, in fact, may be misleading. Stated simply, a federal habeas court making the "unreasonable application" inquiry should ask whether the state court's application of clearly established federal law was objectively unreasonable. The federal habeas court should not transform the inquiry into a subjective one by resting its determination instead on the simple fact that at least one of the Nation's jurists has applied the relevant federal law in the same manner the state court did in the habeas petitioner's case. The "all reasonable jurists" standard would tend to mislead federal habeas courts by focusing their attention on a subjective inquiry rather than on an objective one. For example, the Fifth Circuit appears to have applied its "reasonable jurist" standard in just such a subjective manner. See Drinkard v. Johnson, 97 F.3d 751, 769 (1996) (holding that state court's application of federal law was not unreasonable because the Fifth Circuit panel split 2–1 on the underlying mixed constitutional question). * * *

The term "unreasonable" is no doubt difficult to define. That said, it is a common term in the legal world and, accordingly, federal judges are familiar with its meaning. For purposes of today's opinion, the most important point is that an unreasonable application of federal law is different from an incorrect application of federal law. * * * In § 2254(d)(1), Congress specifically used the word "unreasonable," and not a term like "erroneous" or "incorrect." Under § 2254(d)(1)'s "unreasonable application" clause, then, a federal habeas court may not issue the writ simply because that court concludes in its independent judgment that the relevant state-court decision applied clearly established federal law erroneously or incorrectly. Rather, that application must also be unreasonable.

Justice O'Connor concluded as follows:

In sum, § 2254(d)(1) places a new constraint on the power of a federal habeas court to grant a state prisoner's application for a writ of habeas corpus with respect to claims adjudicated on the merits in state court. Under § 2254(d)(1), the writ may issue only if one of the following two conditions is satisfied—the state-court adjudication resulted in a decision that (1) "was contrary to . . . clearly established Federal law, as determined by the Supreme Court of the United States," or (2) "involved an unreasonable application of . . . clearly established Federal law, as determined by the Supreme Court of the United States." Under the "contrary to" clause, a federal habeas court may grant the writ if the state court arrives at a conclusion opposite to that reached by this Court on a question of law or if the state court decides a case differently than this Court has on a set of materially indistinguishable facts. Under the "unreasonable application" clause, a federal habeas court may grant the writ if the state court identifies the correct governing legal principle from this Court's decisions but unreasonably applies that principle to the facts of the prisoner's case.

On the merits, a majority of the Court held that the state court's decision was both "contrary to" and an "unreasonable application" of *Strickland*. The state court held that the *Strickland* prejudice prong did not focus on what the outcome might have been had defense counsel acted effectively—when in fact that is the very focus of the prejudice prong. The state court also ignored the impact that the substantial mitigating evidence might have had on the jury at the penalty phase.

In Bell v. Cone, 535 U.S. 685 (2002), the Court applied the *Williams* standard of review to reject a claim on habeas that defense counsel in a capital case acted so ineffectively as to justify a presumption of prejudice. *Cone* is set forth in Chapter 10 of this Supplement.

D. LIMITATIONS ON OBTAINING HABEAS RELIEF

3. *Procedural Default*

Page 1548. After the Section on *Frady*, add the following section:

Federal Defendant's Failure to Raise an Ineffective Assistance Claim on Direct Appeal; Is That a Procedural Default?: Massaro v. United States.

In the following case, the Court considered whether a federal defendant had procedurally defaulted an ineffective assistance of counsel claim by failing to assert it on direct review of his conviction.

MASSARO v. UNITED STATES

Supreme Court of the United States, 2003.
123 S.Ct. 1690.

JUSTICE KENNEDY delivered the opinion of the Court.

Petitioner, Joseph Massaro, was indicted on federal racketeering charges, including murder in aid of racketeering, in connection with the shooting death of Joseph Fiorito. He was tried in the United States District Court for the Southern District of New York. The day before Massaro's trial was to begin, prosecutors learned of what appeared to be a critical piece of evidence: a bullet allegedly recovered from the car in which the victim's body was found. They waited for several days, however, to inform defense counsel of this development. Not until the trial was underway and the defense had made its opening statement did they make this disclosure. After the trial court and the defense had been informed of the development but still during the course of trial, defense counsel more than once declined the trial court's offer of a continuance so the bullet could be examined. Massaro was convicted and sentenced to life imprisonment.

On direct appeal new counsel for Massaro argued the District Court had erred in admitting the bullet in evidence, but he did not raise any claim relating to ineffective assistance of trial counsel. The Court of Appeals for the Second Circuit affirmed the conviction.

Massaro later filed a motion under 28 U.S.C. § 2255, seeking to vacate his conviction. As relevant here, he claimed that his trial counsel had rendered ineffective assistance in failing to accept the trial court's offer to grant a continuance. The United States District Court for the Southern District of New York found this claim procedurally defaulted because Massaro could have raised it on direct appeal.

The Court of Appeals for the Second Circuit affirmed. The court acknowledged that ineffective-assistance claims usually should be excused from procedural default rules because an attorney who handles both trial and appeal is unlikely to raise an ineffective-assistance claim against himself. Nevertheless, it adhered to its decision in Billy–Eko v. United States, 8 F.3d 111 (1993). Under *Billy-Eko*, when the defendant is represented by new counsel on appeal and the ineffective assistance claim is based solely on the record made at trial, the claim must be raised on direct appeal; failure to do so results in procedural default unless the petitioner shows cause and prejudice. Finding that Massaro was represented by new counsel on appeal, that his trial counsel's ineffectiveness was evident from the record, and that he had failed to show cause or prejudice, the Court of Appeals held him procedurally barred from bringing the ineffec-tive-assistance claim on collateral review.

We granted certiorari. Petitioner now urges us to hold that claims of ineffective assistance of counsel need not be raised on direct appeal, whether or not there is new counsel and whether or not the basis for the claim is apparent from the trial record. The Federal Courts of Appeals are in conflict on this question, with the Seventh Circuit joining the Second Circuit, see Guinan v. United States, 6 F.3d 468 (C.A.7 1993), and 10 other Federal Courts of Appeals taking the position that there is no procedural default for failure to raise an ineffective-assistance claim on direct appeal. We agree with the majority of the Courts of Appeals, and we reverse.

The background for our discussion is the general rule that claims not raised on direct appeal may not be raised on collateral review unless the petitioner shows cause and prejudice. See United States v. Frady, 456 U.S. 152 (1982). The procedural default rule is neither a statutory nor a constitutional requirement, but it is a doctrine adhered to by the courts to conserve judicial resources and to respect the law's important interest in the finality of judgments. We conclude that requiring a criminal defendant to bring ineffective-assistance-of-counsel claims on direct appeal does not promote these objectives.

As Judge Easterbrook has noted, "rules of procedure should be designed to induce litigants to present their contentions to the right tribunal at the right time." *Guinan, supra,* at 474 (concurring opinion). Applying the usual procedural-default rule to ineffective-assistance claims would have the opposite effect, creating the risk that defendants would feel compelled to raise the issue before there has been an opportunity fully to develop the factual predicate for the claim. Furthermore, the issue would be raised for the first time in a forum not best suited to assess those facts. This is so even if the record contains some indication of deficiencies in counsel's performance. The better-reasoned approach is to permit ineffective-assistance claims to be brought in the first instance in a timely motion in the district court under § 2255. We hold that an ineffective-assistance-of-counsel claim may be brought in a collateral proceeding under § 2255, whether or not the petitioner could have raised the claim on direct appeal.

In light of the way our system has developed, in most cases a motion brought under § 2255 is preferable to direct appeal for deciding claims of ineffective-assistance. When an ineffective-assistance claim is brought on direct appeal, appellate counsel and the court must proceed on a trial record not developed precisely for the object of litigating or preserving the claim and thus often incomplete or inadequate for this purpose. Under Strickland v. Washington, 466 U.S. 668 (1984), a defendant claiming ineffective counsel must show that counsel's actions were not supported by a reasonable strategy and that the error was prejudicial. The evidence introduced at trial, however, will be devoted to issues of guilt or innocence, and the resulting record in many cases will not disclose the facts necessary to decide either prong of the *Strickland* analysis. If the alleged error is one of commission, the record may

reflect the action taken by counsel but not the reasons for it. The appellate court may have no way of knowing whether a seemingly unusual or misguided action by counsel had a sound strategic motive or was taken because the counsel's alternatives were even worse. See *Guinan, supra,* at 473 (Easterbrook, J., concurring) ("No matter how odd or deficient trial counsel's performance may seem, that lawyer may have had a reason for acting as he did.... Or it may turn out that counsel's overall performance was sufficient despite a glaring omission ..."). The trial record may contain no evidence of alleged errors of omission, much less the reasons underlying them. And evidence of alleged conflicts of interest might be found only in attorney-client correspondence or other documents that, in the typical criminal trial, are not introduced .. Without additional factual development, moreover, an appellate court may not be able to ascertain whether the alleged error was prejudicial.

Under the rule we adopt today, ineffective-assistance claims ordinarily will be litigated in the first instance in the district court, the forum best suited to developing the facts necessary to determining the adequacy of representation during an entire trial. The court may take testimony from witnesses for the defendant and the prosecution and from the counsel alleged to have rendered the deficient performance. In addition, the § 2255 motion often will be ruled upon by the same district judge who presided at trial. The judge, having observed the earlier trial, should have an advantageous perspective for determining the effectiveness of counsel's conduct and whether any deficiencies were prejudicial.

The Second Circuit's rule creates inefficiencies for courts and counsel, both on direct appeal and in the collateral proceeding. On direct appeal it puts counsel into an awkward position vis-a-vis trial counsel. Appellate counsel often need trial counsel's assistance in becoming familiar with a lengthy record on a short deadline, but trial counsel will be unwilling to help appellate counsel familiarize himself with a record for the purpose of understanding how it reflects trial counsel's own incompetence.

Subjecting ineffective-assistance claims to the usual cause-and-prejudice rule also would create perverse incentives for counsel on direct appeal. To ensure that a potential ineffective assistance claim is not waived—and to avoid incurring a claim of ineffective counsel at the appellate stage—counsel would be pressured to bring claims of ineffective trial counsel, regardless of merit.

Even meritorious claims would fail when brought on direct appeal if the trial record were inadequate to support them. Appellate courts would waste time and resources attempting to address some claims that were meritless and other claims that, though colorable, would be handled more efficiently if addressed in the first instance by the district court on collateral review. See, *e.g.,* United States v. Galloway, 56 F.3d at 1241 ("threat of ... procedural bar has doubtless resulted in many claims being asserted on direct appeal only to protect the record ... unnecessarily burdening both the parties and the court ..."). This concern is far from spec-

ulative. The Court of Appeals for the Second Circuit, in light of its rule applying procedural default to ineffective-assistance claims, has urged counsel to "err on the side of inclusion on direct appeal."

On collateral review, the Second Circuit's rule would cause additional inefficiencies. Under that rule a court on collateral review must determine whether appellate counsel is "new." Questions may arise, for example, about whether a defendant has retained new appellate counsel when different lawyers in the same law office handle trial and appeal. The habeas court also must engage in a painstaking review of the trial record solely to determine if it was sufficient to support the ineffectiveness claim and thus whether it should have been brought on direct appeal. A clear rule allowing these claims to be brought in a proceeding under § 2255, by contrast, will eliminate these requirements. Although we could "require the parties and the district judges to search for needles in haystacks—to seek out the rare claim that could have been raised on direct appeal, and deem it waived," *Guinan*, 6 F.3d at 475 (Easterbrook, J., concurring)—we do not see the wisdom in requiring a court to spend time on exercises that, in most instances, will produce no benefit. It is a better use of judicial resources to allow the district court on collateral review to turn at once to the merits.

The most to be said for the rule in the Second Circuit is that it will speed resolution of some ineffective-assistance claims. For the reasons discussed, however, we think few such claims will be capable of resolution on direct appeal and thus few will benefit from earlier resolution. And the benefits of the Second Circuit's rule in those rare instances are outweighed by the increased judicial burden the rule would impose in many other cases, where a district court on collateral review would be forced to conduct the cause-and-prejudice analysis before turning to the merits. The Second Circuit's rule, moreover, does not produce the benefits of other rules requiring claims to be raised at the earliest opportunity—such as the contemporaneous objection rule—because here, raising the claim on direct appeal does not permit the trial court to avoid the potential error in the first place.

A growing majority of state courts now follow the rule we adopt today. For example, the Supreme Court of Pennsylvania recently changed its position to hold that "a claim raising trial counsel ineffectiveness will no longer be considered waived because new counsel on direct appeal did not raise a claim related to prior counsel's ineffectiveness." Commonwealth v. Grant, 813 A.2d 726, 738 (2002); see also *id.*, at 735–738, and n. 13 (cataloging other States' case law adopting this position).

Although the Government now urges us to adopt the rule of the Court of Appeals for the Second Circuit, the Government took the opposite approach in some previous cases, arguing not only that claims of ineffective assistance of counsel could be brought in the first instance in a motion under § 2255, but that they must be brought in such a motion proceeding and not on direct appeal. See, *e.g.,* United States v. Cronic, 466 U.S. 648 (1984). We do not go this far. We do not hold that ineffective-assistance claims must be reserved for collateral review. There may be cases in which trial counsel's ineffectiveness is so apparent from the record that appellate counsel will consider it advisable to raise the issue on direct appeal. There may be instances, too, when obvious deficiencies in representation will be addressed by an appellate court *sua sponte.* In those cases, certain questions may arise in subsequent proceedings under § 2255 concerning the conclusiveness of determinations made on the ineffective-assistance claims raised on direct appeal; but these matters of implementation are not before us. We do hold that failure to raise an ineffective-assistance-of-counsel claim on direct appeal does not bar the claim from being brought in a later, appropriate proceeding under § 2255.

The judgment of the Court of Appeals is reversed, and the case is remanded for further proceedings consistent with this opinion.

It is so ordered.

c.   *The Meaning of "Cause"*

Page 1554.   After the end of the section on *Carrier*, add the following:

Suppose a state defendant fails to bring a claim on direct appeal. That claim is procedurally defaulted unless the defendant can establish "cause and prejudice". Suppose the reason for failing to bring the claim on direct appeal is that appellate counsel was constitutionally ineffective.

Under *Carrier*, this is enough to establish "cause." But suppose the state has a procedural rule that all claims of ineffective assistance must be brought within a certain time period. If the defendant fails to make that time period, then he has run into another procedural bar in his attempt to establish "cause" for his failure to comply with the first procedural bar. What happens then? Must the defendant establish "cause and prejudice" for his failure to meet the state time period? Must he prove, for instance, that his counsel was constitutionally ineffective for failing to comply with the state time period that mandates a timely complaint about an ineffective counsel?

These were the complicated questions addressed by the Court in *Edwards v. Carpenter*, 529 U.S. 446 (2000). Justice Scalia, writing for the Court, held that "an ineffective-assistance-of-counsel claim asserted as cause for the procedural default of another claim can itself be procedurally defaulted." Therefore, the petitioner was required to establish cause and prejudice for his failure to comply with the state procedural rule requiring ineffective assistance of counsel claims within a certain time period. Justice Scalia reasoned that this result is required by *Carrier's* holding that ineffective assistance of counsel claims must be exhausted at the state level before they can be heard by a federal habeas court. With the exhaustion requirement comes the need for the petitioner to comply with state procedural bars. Thus, the procedural default rule and the exhaustion requirement work together to assure respect for state interests. Justice Scalia explained the interrelationship as follows:

> The purposes of the exhaustion requirement * * * would be utterly defeated if the prisoner were able to obtain federal habeas review simply by "letting the time run" so that state remedies were no longer available. Those purposes would be no less frustrated were we to allow federal review to a prisoner who had presented his claim to the state court, but in such a manner that the state court could not, consistent with its own procedural rules, have entertained it. In such circumstances, though the prisoner would have concededly exhausted his state remedies, it could hardly be said that, as comity and federalism require, the State had been given a fair opportunity to pass upon his claims.

The Court remanded for a determination of whether counsel was ineffective for failing to file a timely claim of ineffective assistance of counsel.

Justice Breyer, joined by Justice Stevens, concurred in the judgment. He agreed that the case had to be remanded, but argued that the only determination necessary was whether the initial counsel was ineffective in failing to bring a claim on direct appeal. He argued that the majority was adding needless complexity to an already complex area of the law. He elaborated as follows:

> The added complexity resulting from the Court's opinion is obvious. Consider a prisoner who wants to assert a federal constitutional claim (call it FCC). Suppose the State asserts as a claimed

"adequate and independent state ground" the prisoner's failure to raise the matter on his first state-court appeal. Suppose further that the prisoner replies by alleging that he had "cause" for not raising the matter on appeal (call it C). After *Carrier*, if that alleged "cause" (C) consists of the claim "my attorney was constitutionally ineffective," the prisoner must have exhausted C in the state courts first. And after today, if he did not follow state rules for presenting C to the state courts, he will have lost his basic claim, FCC, forever. But, I overstate. According to the opinion of the Court, he will not necessarily have lost FCC forever if he had "cause" for not having followed those state rules (i.e., the rules for determining the existence of "cause" for not having followed the state rules governing the basic claim, FCC) (call this "cause" C*). The prisoner could therefore still obtain relief if he could demonstrate the merits of C*, C, and FCC.

I concede that this system of rules has a certain logic, indeed an attractive power for those who like difficult puzzles. But I believe it must succumb to this question: Why should a prisoner, who may well be proceeding pro se, lose his basic claim because he runs afoul of state procedural rules governing the presentation to state courts of the "cause" for his not having followed state procedural rules for the presentation of his basic federal claim? And, in particular, why should that special default rule apply when the "cause" at issue is an "ineffective-assistance-of-counsel" claim, but not when it is any of the many other "causes" or circumstances that might excuse a failure to comply with state rules? I can find no satisfactory answer to these questions.

4. *Adequate and Independent State Grounds*

Page 1567.   At the end of the section, add the following:

"Exorbitant" Application of an Adequate State Ground: Lee v. Kemna

In Lee v. Kemna, 534 U.S. 362 (2002), the Court found an exception to procedural default on an adequate state ground, for "exceptional cases in which exorbitant application of a generally sound rule renders the state ground inadequate to stop consideration of a federal question" on habeas review. Lee was being tried for murder in Missouri, and had produced alibi witnesses from California, who would have testified that Lee was with them in California on the day of the murder. When it came time to present the witnesses, however, on the third day of trial, they were not in court and Lee's counsel did not know where they were. He asked for a day's continuance so that he could locate the witnesses, and assured the court that the witnesses had not left the jurisdiction because they had business to attend to locally. The trial judge refused to continue the trial, because he wanted to be with his daughter, who was having surgery, the next day, and had other trials to attend to after that. Lee presented no witnesses and was convicted. He brought a habeas action, arguing that the refusal to grant a continuance violated his due process rights, and presented affidavits from the alibi witnesses who stated that they were not in the courtroom on the third day of trial because they had been informed by court personnel that they would not be testifying that day.

The state appellate court refused to consider the merits of Lee's due process argument, relying on a procedural bar: Missouri rules of procedure (Court Rules 24.09 and 24.10) that require a motion for continuance to be submitted in writing and set forth other requirements for a satisfactory motion for continuance. The question for the Supreme Court was whether this procedural bar prohibited a habeas action in the absence of a showing of cause and prejudice.

Justice Ginsburg, writing for six Justices, declared that this case fit into the "limited category" of exceptional cases in which a generally sound state rule of procedure must be found inadequate. She summarized as follows:

> Three considerations, in combination, lead us to conclude that this case falls within the small category of cases in which asserted state grounds are inadequate to block adjudication of a federal claim. First, when the trial judge denied Lee's motion, he stated a reason that could not have been countered by a perfect motion for continuance. The judge said he could not carry the trial over until the next day because he had to be with his daughter in the hospital; the judge further informed counsel that another scheduled trial prevented him from concluding Lee's case on the following business day. Although the judge hypothesized that the witnesses had "abandoned" Lee, he had not "a scintilla of evidence or a shred of information" on which to base this supposition.

> Second, no published Missouri decision directs flawless compliance with Rules 24.09 and 24.10 in the unique circumstances this case presents—the sudden, unanticipated, and at the time unexplained disappearance of critical, subpoenaed witnesses on what became the trial's last day. Lee's predicament, from all that appears, was one Missouri courts had not confronted before. * * *

> Third and most important, given the realities of trial, Lee substantially complied with Missouri's key Rule. As to the "written motion" requirement, Missouri's brief in this Court asserted: "Nothing would have prevented counsel from drafting a brief motion and affidavit complying with Rul[e] 24.09 in longhand while seated in the courtroom." At oral argument, however, Missouri's counsel edged away from this position. Counsel stated: "I'm not going to stand on the formality ... of a writing or even the formality of an affidavit." This concession was well advised. Missouri does not rule out oral continuance motions; they are expressly authorized, upon consent of the adverse party, by Rule 24.09. And the written transcript of the brief trial court proceedings enabled an appellate court to comprehend the situation quickly. In sum, we are

drawn to the conclusion reached by the Eighth Circuit dissenter: "[A]ny seasoned trial lawyer would agree" that insistence on a written continuance application, supported by an affidavit, "in the midst of trial upon the discovery that subpoenaed witnesses are suddenly absent, would be so bizarre as to inject an Alice-in-Wonderland quality into the proceedings."

Justice Ginsburg concluded as follows:

> We hold that the Missouri Rules, as injected into this case by the state appellate court, did not constitute a state ground adequate to bar federal habeas review. Caught in the midst of a murder trial and unalerted to any procedural defect in his presentation, defense counsel could hardly be expected to divert his attention from the proceedings rapidly unfolding in the courtroom and train, instead, on preparation of a written motion and affidavit. Furthermore, the trial court, at the time Lee moved for a continuance, had in clear view the information needed to rule intelligently on the merits of the motion. Beyond doubt, Rule 24.10 serves the State's important interest in regulating motions for a continuance—motions readily susceptible to use as a delaying tactic. But under the circumstances of this case, we hold that petitioner Lee, having substantially, if imperfectly, made the basic showings Rule 24.10 prescribes, qualifies for adjudication of his federal, due process claim. His asserted right to defend should not depend on a formal "ritual ... [that] would further no perceivable state interest." Osborne v. Ohio, 495 U.S. 103, 124 (1990) (quoting James v. Kentucky, 466 U.S. 341, 349 (1984).

Justice Kennedy, joined by Justices Scalia and Thomas, dissented. Justice Kennedy argued that a regularly followed state rule had previously been found inadequate "only when the state had no legitimate interest in the rule's enforcement." The need to provide regulations on possibly spurious motions for continuance meant that the Missouri rules were "adequate" within the meaning of Supreme Court jurisprudence. Justice Kennedy concluded that the Court's new exception "does not bode well for the adequacy doctrine or federalism."

7. *Limitations on Obtaining a Hearing*

Page 1573. At the end of the section, add the following:

Application of Evidentiary Hearing Standards Under AEDPA: Williams v. Taylor

In Williams v. Taylor, 529 U.S. 420 (2000), the Court construed and applied the limitations on evidentiary hearings established by Congress in the AEDPA. As amended by the AEDPA, 28 U.S.C. § 2254(e)(2)—the provision which controls whether petitioner may receive an evidentiary hearing in federal district court on claims that were not developed in the state court—provides as follows:

If the applicant has failed to develop the factual basis of a claim in State court proceedings, the court shall not hold an evidentiary hearing on the claim unless the applicant shows that—

(A) the claim relies on—

(i) a new rule of constitutional law, made retroactive to cases on collateral review by the Supreme Court, that was previously unavailable; or

(ii) a factual predicate that could not have been previously discovered through the exercise of due diligence; and

(B) the facts underlying the claim would be sufficient to establish by clear and convincing evidence that but for constitutional error, no reasonable factfinder would have found the applicant guilty of the underlying offense.

In his habeas petition, Williams sought an evidentiary hearing to develop three claims: 1) a claim under *Brady* that the prosecution failed to disclose a psychological report on the prosecution's star witness; 2) a claim that a juror had lied on voir dire by failing to disclose a source of bias; and 3) a related claim that the prosecutor committed misconduct because he knew that the juror was biased and failed to disclose that fact. In the Supreme Court, Williams conceded that he could not satisfy the stringent standards for relief set forth in subdivision (B) of the statute (i.e., actual innocence). Resolution of the right to an evidentiary hearing therefore depended on whether Williams had "failed to develop" the basis of the factual claim in state court. The parties agreed that the facts necessary to support Williams' habeas claims had *not* been developed in the state court. Williams argued, however, that he had not *failed* to develop the claims, because he was *unable* to pursue the claims during the state court proceeding, i.e., he was not at fault. The government argued for a no-fault interpretation of the statutory term "failed", i.e., if the claims were not developed in the state court—no matter the reason—then there is no right to an evidentiary hearing to develop the claims in the federal district court.

The Supreme Court, in a unanimous opinion by Justice Kennedy, rejected the government's no-fault construction of the AEDPA term "failed", and held that the term "failed to develop" requires some "lack of diligence" on the petitioner's part. Justice Kennedy explained this ruling in the following passage:

> Under [the government's] no-fault reading of the statute, if there is no factual development in the state court, the federal habeas court may not inquire into the reasons for the default when determining whether the opening clause of § 2254(e)(2) applies. We do not agree with the Commonwealth's interpretation of the word "failed."

> * * *

> We give the words of a statute their ordinary, contemporary, common meaning, absent an indication Congress intended them to

bear some different import. In its customary and preferred sense, "fail" connotes some omission, fault, or negligence on the part of the person who has failed to do something. To say a person has failed in a duty implies he did not take the necessary steps to fulfill it. He is, as a consequence, at fault and bears responsibility for the failure. In this sense, a person is not at fault when his diligent efforts to perform an act are thwarted, for example, by the conduct of another or by happenstance. Fault lies, in those circumstances, either with the person who interfered with the accomplishment of the act or with no one at all. We conclude Congress used the word "failed" in the sense just described. Had Congress intended a no-fault standard, it would have had no difficulty in making its intent plain. It would have had to do no more than use, in lieu of the phrase "has failed to," the phrase "did not."

Under the opening clause of § 2254(e)(2), a failure to develop the factual basis of a claim is not established unless there is lack of diligence, or some greater fault, attributable to the prisoner or the prisoner's counsel. * * *

* * *

Interpreting § 2254(e)(2) so that "failed" requires lack of diligence or some other fault avoids putting it in needless tension with § 2254(d). A prisoner who developed his claim in state court and can prove the state court's decision was "contrary to, or an unreasonable application of, clearly established federal law, as determined by the Supreme Court of the United States," is not barred from obtaining relief by § 2254(d)(1). If the opening clause of § 2254(e)(2) covers a request for an evidentiary hearing on a claim which was pursued with diligence but remained undeveloped in state court because, for instance, the prosecution concealed the facts, a prisoner lacking clear and convincing evidence of innocence could be barred from a hearing on the claim even if he could satisfy § 2254(d). See 28 U.S.C. § 2254(e)(2)(B). The "failed to develop" clause does not bear this harsh reading, which would attribute to Congress a purpose or design to bar evidentiary hearings for diligent prisoners with meritorious claims just because the prosecution's conduct went undetected in state court. We see no indication that Congress by this language intended to remove the distinction between a prisoner who is at fault and one who is not.

* * *

We are not persuaded by the Commonwealth's further argument that anything less than a no-fault understanding of the opening clause is contrary to AEDPA's purpose to further the principles of comity, finality, and federalism. There is no doubt Congress intended AEDPA to advance these doctrines. Federal habeas corpus principles must inform and shape the historic and still vital relation of mutual respect and common purpose existing between the States and the federal courts. In keeping this delicate balance we have been careful to limit the scope of federal intrusion into state criminal adjudications and to safeguard the States' interest in the integrity of their criminal and collateral proceedings.

It is consistent with these principles to give effect to Congress' intent to avoid unneeded evidentiary hearings in federal habeas corpus, while recognizing the statute does not equate prisoners who exercise diligence in pursuing their claims with those who do not. Principles of exhaustion are premised upon recognition by Congress and the Court that state judiciaries have the duty and competence to vindicate rights secured by the Constitution in state criminal proceedings. Diligence will require in the usual case that the prisoner, at a minimum, seek an evidentiary hearing in state court in the manner prescribed by state law. * * * For state courts to have their rightful opportunity to adjudicate federal rights, the prisoner must be diligent in developing the record and presenting, if possible, all claims of constitutional error. If the prisoner fails to do so, himself or herself contributing to the absence of a full and fair adjudication in state court, § 2254(e)(2) prohibits an evidentiary hearing to develop the relevant claims in federal court, unless the statute's other stringent requirements are met. Federal courts sitting in habeas are not an alternative forum for trying facts and issues which a prisoner made insufficient effort to pursue in state proceedings. Yet comity is not served by saying a prisoner "has failed to develop the factual basis of a claim" where he was unable to develop his claim in state court despite diligent effort. In that circumstance, an evidentiary hearing is not barred by § 2254(e)(2).

Justice Kennedy then applied the "diligence" test to the facts of the case. He found that Williams had not been diligent in pursuing his *Brady* claim, because the witness' psychological history had been disclosed at that witness' sentencing proceeding, well in time for Williams to use it in his state proceedings. Williams and his counsel were thus aware of the report and yet took no steps to have it produced. In contrast, Williams was not at fault for the failure to develop the claim of juror bias and the related claim of prosecutorial misconduct for failure to disclose the juror bias. The juror had misrepresented her background in answering a question on voir dire. There was no reason for Williams or his counsel to believe that the juror and the prosecutor were hiding anything. The Court noted that it would be"surprised, to say the least, if a district court familiar with the standards of trial practice were to hold that in all cases diligent counsel must check public records containing personal information pertaining to each and every juror."

Part II

EXCERPTS FROM THE CONSTITUTION OF THE UNITED STATES

Preamble

We the People of the United States, in Order to form a more perfect Union, establish Justice, insure domestic Tranquility, provide for the common defence, promote the general Welfare, and secure the Blessings of Liberty to ourselves and our Posterity, do ordain and establish this Constitution for the United States of America.

Article I

Section 1. All legislative Powers herein granted shall be vested in a Congress of the United States, which shall consist of a Senate and House of Representatives.

[6] The Senate shall have the sole Power to try all Impeachments. When sitting for that Purpose, they shall be on Oath or Affirmation. When the President of the United States is tried, the Chief Justice shall preside: And no Person shall be convicted without the Concurrence of two thirds of the Members present.

[7] Judgment in Cases of Impeachment shall not extend further than to removal from Office, and disqualification to hold and enjoy any Office of honor, Trust, or Profit under the United States: but the Party convicted shall nevertheless be liable and subject to Indictment, Trial, Judgment, and Punishment, according to Law.

Section 6. [1] The Senators and Representatives shall receive a Compensation for their Services, to be ascertained by Law, and paid out of the Treasury of the United States. They shall in all Cases, except Treason, Felony and Breach of the Peace, be privileged from Arrest during their Attendance at the Session of their respective Houses, and in going to and returning from the same; and for any Speech or Debate in either House, they shall not be questioned in any other Place.

Section 8. [1] The Congress shall have Power To lay and collect Taxes, Duties, Imposts and Excises, to pay the Debts and provide for the common Defence and general Welfare of the United States; but all

Duties, Imposts and Excises shall be uniform throughout the United States;

[6] To provide for the Punishment of counterfeiting the Securities and current Coin of the United States;

[9] To constitute Tribunals inferior to the supreme Court;

[10] To define and punish Piracies and Felonies committed on the high Seas, and Offenses against the Law of Nations;

[17] To exercise exclusive Legislation in all Cases whatsoever, over such District (not exceeding ten Miles square) as may, by Cession of particular States, and the Acceptance of Congress, become the Seat of the Government of the United States, and to exercise like Authority over all Places purchased by the Consent of the Legislature of the State in which the Same shall be, for the Erection of Forts, Magazines, Arsenals, dock-Yards, and other needful Buildings;—And

[18] To make all Laws which shall be necessary and proper for carrying into Execution the foregoing Powers, and all other Powers vested by this Constitution in the Government of the United States, or in any Department or Officer thereof.

Section 9. * * *

[2] The privilege of the Writ of Habeas Corpus shall not be suspended, unless when in Cases of Rebellion or Invasion the public Safety may require it.

[3] No Bill of Attainder or ex post facto Law shall be passed.

Section 10. [1] No State shall enter into any Treaty, Alliance, or Confederation; grant Letters of Marque and Reprisal; coin Money; emit Bills of Credit; make any Thing but gold and silver Coin a Tender in Payment of Debts; pass any Bill of Attainder, ex post facto Law, or Law impairing the Obligation of Contracts, or grant any Title of Nobility.

Article II

Section 1. [1] The executive Power shall be vested in a President of the United States of America. * * *

[8] Before he enter on the Execution of his Office, he shall take the following Oath or Affirmation: "I do solemnly swear (or affirm) that I will faithfully execute the Office of President of the United States, and will to the best of my Ability, preserve, protect and defend the Constitution of the United States."

Section 2. [1] The President shall be Commander in Chief of the Army and Navy of the United States, and of the militia of the several States, when called into the actual Service of the United States; he may require the Opinion, in writing, of the principal Officer in each of the Executive Departments, upon any Subject relating to the Duties of their respective Offices, and he shall have Power to grant Reprieves and Pardons for Offenses against the United States, except in Cases of Impeachment.

[2] He shall have Power, by and with the Advice and Consent of the Senate to make Treaties, provided two thirds of the Senators present concur; and he shall nominate, and by and with the Advice and Consent of the Senate, shall appoint Ambassadors, other public Ministers and Consuls, Judges of the supreme Court, and all other Officers of the United States, whose Appointments are not herein otherwise provided for, and which shall be established by Law; but the Congress may by Law vest the Appointment of such inferior Officers, as they think proper, in the President alone, in the Courts of Law, or in the Heads of Departments.

[3] The President shall have Power to fill up all Vacancies that may happen during the Recess of the Senate, by granting Commissions which shall expire at the End of their next Session.

Section 3. He shall from time to time give to the Congress Information of the State of the Union, and recommend to their Consideration such Measures as he shall judge necessary and expedient; he may, on extraordinary Occasions, convene both Houses, or either of them, and in Case of Disagreement between them, with Respect to the Time of Adjournment, he may adjourn them to such Time as he shall think proper; he shall receive Ambassadors and other public Ministers; he shall take Care that the Laws be faithfully executed, and shall Commission all the Officers of the United States.

Section 4. The President, Vice President and all civil Officers of the United States, shall be removed from Office on Impeachment for, and Conviction of, Treason, Bribery, or other high Crimes and Misdemeanors.

Article III

Section 1. The judicial Power of the United States, shall be vested in one supreme Court, and in such inferior Courts as the Congress may from time to time ordain and establish. The Judges, both of the supreme and inferior Courts, shall hold their Offices during good Behaviour, and shall, at stated Times, receive for their Services a Compensation, which shall not be diminished during their Continuance in Office.

Section 2. [1] The judicial Power shall extend to all Cases, in Law and Equity, arising under this Constitution, the Laws of the United States, and Treaties made, or which shall be made, under their Authority;—to all Cases affecting Ambassadors, other public Ministers and Consuls;—to all Cases of admiralty and maritime Jurisdiction;—to Controversies to which the United States shall be a Party;—to Controversies between two or more States;—between a State and Citizens of another State;—between Citizens of different States;—between Citizens of the same State claiming Lands under the Grants of different States, and between a State, or the Citizens thereof, and foreign States, Citizens or Subjects.

[2] In all Cases affecting Ambassadors, other public Ministers and Consuls, and those in which a State shall be a Party, the supreme Court

shall have original Jurisdiction. In all the other Cases before mentioned, the supreme Court shall have appellate Jurisdiction, both as to Law and Fact, with such Exceptions, and under such Regulations as the Congress shall make.

[3] The trial of all Crimes, except in Cases of Impeachment, shall be by Jury; and such Trial shall be held in the State where the said Crimes shall have been committed; but when not committed within any State, the Trial shall be at such Place or Places as the Congress may by Law have directed.

Section 3. [1] Treason against the United States, shall consist only in levying War against them, or, in adhering to their Enemies, giving them Aid and Comfort. No Person shall be convicted of Treason unless on the Testimony of two Witnesses to the same overt Act, or on Confession in open Court.

[2] The Congress shall have Power to declare the Punishment of Treason, but no Attainder of Treason shall work Corruption of Blood, or Forfeiture except during the Life of the Person attainted.

Article IV

Section 1. Full Faith and Credit shall be given in each State to the public Acts, Records, and judicial Proceedings of every other State. And the Congress may by general Laws prescribe the Manner in which such Acts, Records and Proceedings shall be proved, and the Effect thereof.

Section 2. [1] The Citizens of each State shall be entitled to all Privileges and Immunities of Citizens in the several States.

[2] A Person charged in any State with Treason, Felony, or other Crime, who shall flee from Justice, and be found in another State, shall on demand of the executive Authority of the State from which he fled, be delivered up, to be removed to the State having Jurisdiction of the Crime.

[3] No Person held to Service or Labour in one State, under the Laws thereof, escaping into another, shall, in Consequence of any Law or Regulation therein, be discharged from such Service or Labour, but shall be delivered up on Claim of the Party to whom such Service or Labour may be due.

Section 3. * * *

[2] The Congress shall have Power to dispose of and make all needful Rules and Regulations respecting the Territory or other Property belonging to the United States; and nothing in this Constitution shall be so construed as to Prejudice any Claims of the United States, or of any particular State.

Section 4. The United States shall guarantee to every State in this Union a Republican Form of Government, and shall protect each of them against Invasion; and on Application of the Legislature, or of the

Executive (when the Legislature cannot be convened) against domestic Violence.

Article V

The Congress, whenever two thirds of both Houses shall deem it necessary, shall propose Amendments to this Constitution, or, on the Application of the Legislatures of two thirds of the several States, shall call a Convention for proposing Amendments, which, in either Case, shall be valid to all Intents and Purposes, as part of this Constitution, when ratified by the Legislatures of three fourths of the several States, or by Conventions in three fourths thereof, as the one or the other Mode of Ratification may be proposed by the Congress; Provided that no Amendment which may be made prior to the Year One thousand eight hundred and eight shall in any Manner affect the first and fourth Clauses in the Ninth Section of the first Article; and that no State, without its Consent, shall be deprived of its equal Suffrage in the Senate.

Article VI

[2] This Constitution, and the Laws of the United States which shall be made in Pursuance thereof; and all Treaties made, or which shall be made, under the Authority of the United States, shall be the supreme Law of the Land; and the Judges in every State shall be bound thereby, any Thing in the Constitution or Laws of any State to the Contrary notwithstanding.

[3] The Senators and Representatives before mentioned, and the Members of the several State Legislatures, and all executive and judicial Officers, both of the United States and of the several States, shall be bound by Oath or Affirmation, to support this Constitution; but no religious Test shall ever be required as a Qualification to any Office or public Trust under the United States.

Article VII

The Ratification of the Conventions of nine States shall be sufficient for the Establishment of this Constitution between the States so ratifying the Same.

ARTICLES IN ADDITION TO, AND AMENDMENT OF, THE CONSTITUTION OF THE UNITED STATES OF AMERICA, PROPOSED BY CONGRESS, AND RATIFIED BY THE LEGISLATURES OF THE SEVERAL STATES PURSUANT TO THE FIFTH ARTICLE OF THE ORIGINAL CONSTITUTION.

Amendment I [1791]

Congress shall make no law respecting an establishment of religion, or prohibiting the free exercise thereof; or abridging the freedom of speech, or of the press; or the right of the people peaceably to assemble, and to petition the Government for a redress of grievances.

Amendment II [1791]

A well regulated Militia, being necessary to the security of a free State, the right of the people to keep and bear Arms, shall not be infringed.

Amendment III [1791]

No Soldier shall, in time of peace be quartered in any house, without the consent of the Owner, nor in time of war, but in a manner to be prescribed by law.

Amendment IV [1791]

The right of the people to be secure in their persons, houses, papers, and effects, against unreasonable searches and seizures, shall not be violated, and no Warrants shall issue, but upon probable cause, supported by Oath or affirmation, and particularly describing the place to be searched, and the persons or things to be seized.

Amendment V [1791]

No person shall be held to answer for a capital, or otherwise infamous crime, unless on a presentment or indictment of a Grand Jury, except in cases arising in the land or naval forces, or in the Militia, when in actual service in time of War or public danger; nor shall any person be subject for the same offence to be twice put in jeopardy of life or limb; nor shall be compelled in any criminal case to be a witness against himself, nor be deprived of life, liberty, or property, without due process of law; nor shall private property be taken for public use, without just compensation.

Amendment VI [1791]

In all criminal prosecutions, the accused shall enjoy the right to a speedy and public trial, by an impartial jury of the State and district wherein the crime shall have been committed, which district shall have been previously ascertained by law, and to be informed of the nature and cause of the accusation; to be confronted with the witnesses against him; to have compulsory process for obtaining witnesses in his favor, and to have the Assistance of Counsel for his defence.

Amendment VII [1791]

In Suits at common law, where the value in controversy shall exceed twenty dollars, the right of trial by jury shall be preserved, and no fact tried by jury, shall be otherwise re-examined in any Court of the United States, than according to the rules of the common law.

Amendment VIII [1791]

Excessive bail shall not be required, nor excessive fines imposed, nor cruel and unusual punishments inflicted.

Amendment IX [1791]

The enumeration in the Constitution, of certain rights, shall not be construed to deny or disparage others retained by the people.

Amendment X [1791]

The powers not delegated to the United States by the Constitution, nor prohibited by it to the States, are reserved to the States respectively, or to the people.

Amendment XIII [1865]

Section 1. Neither slavery nor involuntary servitude, except as a punishment for crime whereof the party shall have been duly convicted, shall exist within the United States, or any place subject to their jurisdiction.

Section 2. Congress shall have power to enforce this article by appropriate legislation.

Amendment XIV [1868]

Section 1. All persons born or naturalized in the United States, and subject to the jurisdiction thereof, are citizens of the United States and of the State wherein they reside. No State shall make or enforce any law which shall abridge the privileges or immunities of citizens of the United States; nor shall any State deprive any person of life, liberty, or property, without due process of law; nor deny to any person within its jurisdiction the equal protection of the laws.

Section 2. Representatives shall be apportioned among the several States according to their respective numbers, counting the whole number of persons in each State, excluding Indians not taxed. But when the right to vote at any election for the choice of electors for President and Vice President of the United States, Representatives in Congress, the Executive and Judicial officers of a State, or the members of the Legislature thereof, is denied to any of the male inhabitants of such State, being twenty-one years of age, and citizens of the United States, or in any way abridged, except for participation in rebellion, or other crime, the basis of representation therein shall be reduced in the proportion which the number of such male citizens shall bear to the whole number of male citizens twenty-one years of age in such State.

Section 3. No person shall be a Senator or Representative in Congress, or elector of President and Vice President, or hold any office, civil or military, under the United States, or under any State, who having previously taken an oath, as a member of Congress, or as an officer of the United States, or as a member of any State legislature, or as an executive or judicial officer of any State, to support the Constitution of the United States, shall have engaged in insurrection or rebellion against the same, or given aid or comfort to the enemies thereof. But Congress may by a vote of two-thirds of each House, remove such disability.

Section 4. The validity of the public debt of the United States, authorized by law, including debts incurred for payment of pensions and bounties for services in suppressing insurrection or rebellion, shall not be questioned. But neither the United States nor any State shall assume or pay any debt or obligation incurred in aid of insurrection or rebellion against the United States, or any claim for the loss or emancipation of any slave; but all such debts, obligations and claims shall be held illegal and void.

Section 5. The Congress shall have power to enforce, by appropriate legislation, the provisions of this article.

Part III

THE FEDERAL RULES OF CRIMINAL PROCEDURE

(As restylized, effective December 1, 2002)

TITLE I. APPLICABILITY

Rule 1. Scope; Definitions

(a) Scope.

(1) *In General.* These rules govern the procedure in all criminal proceedings in the United States district courts, the United States courts of appeals, and the Supreme Court of the United States.

(2) *State or Local Judicial Officer.* When a rule so states, it applies to a proceeding before a state or local judicial officer.

(3) *Territorial Courts.* These rules also govern the procedure in all criminal proceedings in the following courts:

(A) the district court of Guam;

(B) the district court for the Northern Mariana Islands, except as otherwise provided by law; and

(C) the district court of the Virgin Islands, except that the prosecution of offenses in that court must be by indictment or information as otherwise provided by law.

(4) *Removed Proceedings.* Although these rules govern all proceedings after removal from a state court, state law governs a dismissal by the prosecution.

(5) *Excluded Proceedings.* Proceedings not governed by these rules include:

(A) the extradition and rendition of a fugitive;

(B) a civil property forfeiture for violating a federal statute;

(C) the collection of a fine or penalty;

(D) a proceeding under a statute governing juvenile delinquency to the extent the procedure is inconsistent with the statute, unless Rule 20(d) provides otherwise;

(E) a dispute between seamen under 22 U.S.C. §§ 256–258; and

(F) a proceeding against a witness in a foreign country under 28 U.S.C. § 1784.

(b) Definitions. The following definitions apply to these rules:

(1) "Attorney for the government" means:

(A) the Attorney General or an authorized assistant;

(B) a United States attorney or an authorized assistant;

(C) when applicable to cases arising under Guam law, the Guam Attorney General or other person whom Guam law authorizes to act in the matter; and

(D) any other attorney authorized by law to conduct proceedings under these rules as a prosecutor.

(2) "Court" means a federal judge performing functions authorized by law.

(3) "Federal judge" means:

(A) a justice or judge of the United States as these terms are defined in 28 U.S.C. § 451;

(B) a magistrate judge; and

(C) a judge confirmed by the United States Senate and empowered by statute in any commonwealth, territory, or possession to perform a function to which a particular rule relates.

(4) "Judge" means a federal judge or a state or local judicial officer.

(5) "Magistrate judge" means a United States magistrate judge as defined in 28 U.S.C. §§ 631–639.

(6) "Oath" includes an affirmation.

(7) "Organization" is defined in 18 U.S.C. § 18.

(8) "Petty offense" is defined in 18 U.S.C. § 19.

(9) "State" includes the District of Columbia, and any commonwealth, territory, or possession of the United States.

(10) "State or local judicial officer" means:

(A) a state or local officer authorized to act under 18 U.S.C. § 3041; and

(B) a judicial officer empowered by statute in the District of Columbia or in any commonwealth, territory, or possession to perform a function to which a particular rule relates.

(c) Authority of a Justice or Judge of the United States. When these rules authorize a magistrate judge to act, any other federal judge may also act.

Rule 2.   Interpretation

These rules are to be interpreted to provide for the just determination of every criminal proceeding, to secure simplicity in procedure and fairness in administration, and to eliminate unjustifiable expense and delay.

TITLE II. PRELIMINARY PROCEEDINGS

Rule 3. The Complaint

The complaint is a written statement of the essential facts constituting the offense charged. It must be made under oath before a magistrate judge or, if none is reasonably available, before a state or local judicial officer.

Rule 4. Arrest Warrant or Summons on a Complaint

(a) Issuance. If the complaint or one or more affidavits filed with the complaint establish probable cause to believe that an offense has been committed and that the defendant committed it, the judge must issue an arrest warrant to an officer authorized to execute it. At the request of an attorney for the government, the judge must issue a summons, instead of a warrant, to a person authorized to serve it. A judge may issue more than one warrant or summons on the same complaint. If a defendant fails to appear in response to a summons, a judge may, and upon request of an attorney for the government must, issue a warrant.

(b) Form.

(1) *Warrant.* A warrant must:

(A) contain the defendant's name or, if it is unknown, a name or description by which the defendant can be identified with reasonable certainty;

(B) describe the offense charged in the complaint;

(C) command that the defendant be arrested and brought without unnecessary delay before a magistrate judge or, if none is reasonably available, before a state or local judicial officer; and

(D) be signed by a judge.

(2) *Summons.* A summons must be in the same form as a warrant except that it must require the defendant to appear before a magistrate judge at a stated time and place.

(c) Execution or Service, and Return.

(1) *By Whom.* Only a marshal or other authorized officer may execute a warrant. Any person authorized to serve a summons in a federal civil action may serve a summons.

(2) *Location.* A warrant may be executed, or a summons served, within the jurisdiction of the United States or anywhere else a federal statute authorizes an arrest.

(3) *Manner.*

(A) A warrant is executed by arresting the defendant. Upon arrest, an officer possessing the warrant must show it to the defendant. If the officer does not possess the warrant, the officer must inform the defendant of the warrant's existence and of the offense charged and, at the defendant's request, must show the warrant to the defendant as soon as possible.

(B) A summons is served on an individual defendant:

(i) by delivering a copy to the defendant personally; or

(ii) by leaving a copy at the defendant's residence or usual place of abode with a person of suitable age and discretion residing at that location and by mailing a copy to the defendant's last known address.

(C) A summons is served on an organization by delivering a copy to an officer, to a managing or general agent, or to another agent appointed or legally authorized to receive service of process. A copy must also be mailed to the organization's last known address within the district or to its principal place of business elsewhere in the United States.

(4) Return.

(A) After executing a warrant, the officer must return it to the judge before whom the defendant is brought in accordance with Rule 5. At the request of an attorney for the government, an unexecuted warrant must be brought back to and canceled by a magistrate judge or, if none is reasonably available, by a state or local judicial officer.

(B) The person to whom a summons was delivered for service must return it on or before the return day.

(C) At the request of an attorney for the government, a judge may deliver an unexecuted warrant, an unserved summons, or a copy of the warrant or summons to the marshal or other authorized person for execution or service.

Rule 5. Initial Appearance

(a) In General.

(1) Appearance Upon an Arrest.

(A) A person making an arrest within the United States must take the defendant without unnecessary delay before a magistrate judge, or before a state or local judicial officer as Rule 5(c) provides, unless a statute provides otherwise.

(B) A person making an arrest outside the United States must take the defendant without unnecessary delay before a magistrate judge, unless a statute provides otherwise.

(2) Exceptions.

(A) An officer making an arrest under a warrant issued upon a complaint charging solely a violation of 18 U.S.C. § 1073 need not comply with this rule if:

(i) the person arrested is transferred without unnecessary delay to the custody of appropriate state or local authorities in the district of arrest; and

(ii) an attorney for the government moves promptly, in the district where the warrant was issued, to dismiss the complaint.

(B) If a defendant is arrested for violating probation or supervised release, Rule 32.1 applies.

(C) If a defendant is arrested for failing to appear in another district, Rule 40 applies.

(3) *Appearance Upon a Summons.* When a defendant appears in response to a summons under Rule 4, a magistrate judge must proceed under Rule 5(d) or (e), as applicable.

(b) Arrest Without a Warrant. If a defendant is arrested without a warrant, a complaint meeting Rule 4(a)'s requirement of probable cause must be promptly filed in the district where the offense was allegedly committed.

(c) Place of Initial Appearance; Transfer to Another District.

(1) *Arrest in the District Where the Offense Was Allegedly Committed.* If the defendant is arrested in the district where the offense was allegedly committed:

(A) the initial appearance must be in that district; and

(B) if a magistrate judge is not reasonably available, the initial appearance may be before a state or local judicial officer.

(2) *Arrest in a District Other Than Where the Offense Was Allegedly Committed.* If the defendant was arrested in a district other than where the offense was allegedly committed, the initial appearance must be:

(A) in the district of arrest; or

(B) in an adjacent district if:

(i) the appearance can occur more promptly there; or

(ii) the offense was allegedly committed there and the initial appearance will occur on the day of arrest.

(3) *Procedures in a District Other Than Where the Offense Was Allegedly Committed.* If the initial appearance occurs in a district other than where the offense was allegedly committed, the following procedures apply:

1. the magistrate judge must inform the defendant about the provisions of Rule 20;

2. if the defendant was arrested without a warrant, the district court where the offense was allegedly committed must first issue a warrant before the magistrate judge transfers the defendant to that district;

3. the magistrate judge must conduct a preliminary hearing if required by Rule 5.1 or Rule 58(b)(2)(G);

4. the magistrate judge must transfer the defendant to the district where the offense was allegedly committed if:

1. the government produces the warrant, a certified copy of the warrant, a facsimile of either, or other appropriate form of either; and

2. the judge finds that the defendant is the same person named in the indictment, information, or warrant; and

5. when a defendant is transferred and discharged, the clerk must promptly transmit the papers and any bail to the clerk in the district where the offense was allegedly committed.

(d) Procedure in a Felony Case.

(1) *Advice.* If the defendant is charged with a felony, the judge must inform the defendant of the following:

(A) the complaint against the defendant, and any affidavit filed with it;

(B) the defendant's right to retain counsel or to request that counsel be appointed if the defendant cannot obtain counsel;

(C) the circumstances, if any, under which the defendant may secure pretrial release;

(D) any right to a preliminary hearing; and

(E) the defendant's right not to make a statement, and that any statement made may be used against the defendant.

(2) *Consulting with Counsel.* The judge must allow the defendant reasonable opportunity to consult with counsel.

(3) *Detention or Release.* The judge must detain or release the defendant as provided by statute or these rules.

(4) *Plea.* A defendant may be asked to plead only under Rule 10.

(e) Procedure in a Misdemeanor Case. If the defendant is charged with a misdemeanor only, the judge must inform the defendant in accordance with Rule 58(b)(2).

(f) Video Teleconferencing. Video teleconferencing may be used to conduct an appearance under this rule if the defendant consents.

Rule 5.1. Preliminary Hearing

(a) In General. If a defendant is charged with an offense other than a petty offense, a magistrate judge must conduct a preliminary hearing unless:

(1) the defendant waives the hearing;

(2) the defendant is indicted;

(3) the government files an information under Rule 7(b) charging the defendant with a felony;

(4) the government files an information charging the defendant with a misdemeanor; or

(5) the defendant is charged with a misdemeanor and consents to trial before a magistrate judge.

(b) Selecting a District. A defendant arrested in a district other than where the offense was allegedly committed may elect to have the preliminary hearing conducted in the district where the prosecution is pending.

(c) Scheduling. The magistrate judge must hold the preliminary hearing within a reasonable time, but no later than 10 days after the initial appearance if the defendant is in custody and no later than 20 days if not in custody.

(d) Extending the Time. With the defendant's consent and upon a showing of good cause—taking into account the public interest in the prompt disposition of criminal cases—a magistrate judge may extend the time limits in Rule 5.1(c) one or more times. If the defendant does not consent, the magistrate judge may extend the time limits only on a showing that extraordinary circumstances exist and justice requires the delay.

(e) Hearing and Finding. At the preliminary hearing, the defendant may cross-examine adverse witnesses and may introduce evidence but may not object to evidence on the ground that it was unlawfully acquired. If the magistrate judge finds probable cause to believe an offense has been committed and the defendant committed it, the magistrate judge must promptly require the defendant to appear for further proceedings.

(f) Discharging the Defendant. If the magistrate judge finds no probable cause to believe an offense has been committed or the defendant committed it, the magistrate judge must dismiss the complaint and discharge the defendant. A discharge does not preclude the government from later prosecuting the defendant for the same offense.

(g) Recording the Proceedings. The preliminary hearing must be recorded by a court reporter or by a suitable recording device. A recording of the proceeding may be made available to any party upon request. A copy of the recording and a transcript may be provided to any party upon request and upon any payment required by applicable Judicial Conference regulations.

(h) Producing a Statement.

(1) *In General.* Rule 26.2(a)-(d) and (f) applies at any hearing under this rule, unless the magistrate judge for good cause rules otherwise in a particular case.

(2) *Sanctions for Not Producing a Statement*. If a party disobeys a Rule 26.2 order to deliver a statement to the moving party, the magistrate judge must not consider the testimony of a witness whose statement is withheld.

TITLE III. THE GRAND JURY, THE INDICTMENT, AND THE INFORMATION

Rule 6. The Grand Jury

(a) Summoning a Grand Jury.

(1) *In General.* When the public interest so requires, the court must order that one or more grand juries be summoned. A grand jury must have 16 to 23 members, and the court must order that enough legally qualified persons be summoned to meet this requirement.

(2) *Alternate Jurors.* When a grand jury is selected, the court may also select alternate jurors. Alternate jurors must have the same qualifications and be selected in the same manner as any other juror. Alternate jurors replace jurors in the same sequence in which the alternates were selected. An alternate juror who replaces a juror is subject to the same challenges, takes the same oath, and has the same authority as the other jurors.

(b) Objection to the Grand Jury or to a Grand Juror.

(1) *Challenges.* Either the government or a defendant may challenge the grand jury on the ground that it was not lawfully drawn, summoned, or selected, and may challenge an individual juror on the ground that the juror is not legally qualified.

(2) *Motion to Dismiss an Indictment.* A party may move to dismiss the indictment based on an objection to the grand jury or on an individual juror's lack of legal qualification, unless the court has previously ruled on the same objection under Rule 6(b)(1). The motion to dismiss is governed by 28 U.S.C. § 1867(e). The court must not dismiss the indictment on the ground that a grand juror was not legally qualified if the record shows that at least 12 qualified jurors concurred in the indictment.

(c) Foreperson and Deputy Foreperson. The court will appoint one juror as the foreperson and another as the deputy foreperson. In the foreperson's absence, the deputy foreperson will act as the foreperson. The foreperson may administer oaths and affirmations and will sign all indictments. The foreperson—or another juror designated by the foreperson—will record the number of jurors concurring in every indictment and will file the record with the clerk, but the record may not be made public unless the court so orders.

(d) Who May Be Present.

(1) *While the Grand Jury Is in Session.* The following persons may be present while the grand jury is in session: attorneys for the government, the witness being questioned, interpreters when needed, and a court reporter or an operator of a recording device.

(2) *During Deliberations and Voting.* No person other than the jurors, and any interpreter needed to assist a hearing-impaired or speech-impaired juror, may be present while the grand jury is deliberating or voting.

(e) Recording and Disclosing the Proceedings.

(1) *Recording the Proceedings.* Except while the grand jury is deliberating or voting, all proceedings must be recorded by a court reporter or by a suitable recording device. But the validity of a prosecution is not affected by the unintentional failure to make a recording. Unless the court orders otherwise, an attorney for the government will retain control of the recording, the reporter's notes, and any transcript prepared from those notes.

(2) *Secrecy.*

(A) No obligation of secrecy may be imposed on any person except in accordance with Rule 6(e)(2)(B).

(B) Unless these rules provide otherwise, the following persons must not disclose a matter occurring before the grand jury:

    (i) a grand juror;

    (ii) an interpreter;

    (iii) a court reporter;

    (iv) an operator of a recording device;

    (v) a person who transcribes recorded testimony;

    (vi) an attorney for the government; or

    (vii) a person to whom disclosure is made under Rule 6(e)(3)(A)(ii) or (iii).

(3) *Exceptions.*

(A) Disclosure of a grand-jury matter—other than the grand jury's deliberations or any grand juror's vote—may be made to:

    (i) an attorney for the government for use in performing that attorney's duty;

    (ii) any government personnel—including those of a state or state subdivision or of an Indian tribe—that an attorney for the government considers necessary to assist in performing that attorney's duty to enforce federal criminal law; or

    (iii) a person authorized by 18 U.S.C. § x3322.

(B) A person to whom information is disclosed under Rule 6(e)(3)(A)(ii) may use that information only to assist an attorney for the government in performing that attorney's duty to enforce federal criminal law. An attorney for the government must promptly provide the court that impaneled the grand jury with the names of all persons to whom a disclosure has been made, and must certify that the attorney has advised those persons of their obligation of secrecy under this rule.

(C) An attorney for the government may disclose any grand-jury matter to another federal grand jury.

(D) An attorney for the government may disclose any grand-jury matter involving foreign intelligence, counterintelligence (as defined in 50 U.S.C. § a401a), or foreign intelligence information (as defined in Rule 6(e)(3)(D)(iii)) to any federal law enforcement, intelligence, protective, immigration, national defense, or national security official to assist the official receiving the information in the performance of that official's duties.

(i) Any federal official who receives information under Rule 6(e)(3)(D) may use the information only as necessary in the conduct of that person's official duties subject to any limitations on the unauthorized disclosure of such information.

(ii) Within a reasonable time after disclosure is made under Rule 6(e)(3)(D), an attorney for the government must file, under seal, a notice with the court in the district where the grand jury convened stating that such information was disclosed and the departments, agencies, or entities to which the disclosure was made.

(iii) As used in Rule 6(e)(3)(D), the term "foreign intelligence information" means:

(a) information, whether or not it concerns a United States person, that relates to the ability of the United States to protect against—actual or potential attack or other grave hostile acts of a foreign power or its agent; sabotage or international terrorism by a foreign power or its agent; or clandestine intelligence activities by an intelligence service or network of a foreign power or by its agent; or

(b) information, whether or not it concerns a United States person, with respect to a foreign power or foreign territory that relates to—the national defense or the security of the United States; or the conduct of the foreign affairs of the United States.

(E) The court may authorize disclosure—at a time, in a manner, and subject to any other conditions that it directs—of a grand-jury matter:

(i) preliminarily to or in connection with a judicial proceeding;

(ii) at the request of a defendant who shows that a ground may exist to dismiss the indictment because of a matter that occurred before the grand jury;

(iii) at the request of the government if it shows that the matter may disclose a violation of state or Indian tribal criminal law, as long as the disclosure is to an appropriate state, state-subdivision, or Indian tribal official for the purpose of enforcing that law; or

(iv) at the request of the government if it shows that the matter may disclose a violation of military criminal law under the Uniform Code of Military Justice, as long as the disclosure is to an appropriate military official for the purpose of enforcing that law.

(F) A petition to disclose a grand-jury matter under Rule 6(e)(3)(E)(i) must be filed in the district where the grand jury convened. Unless the hearing is ex parte—as it may be when the government is the petitioner—the petitioner must serve the petition on, and the court must afford a reasonable opportunity to appear and be heard to:

(i) an attorney for the government;

(ii) the parties to the judicial proceeding; and

(iii) any other person whom the court may designate.

(G) If the petition to disclose arises out of a judicial proceeding in another district, the petitioned court must transfer the petition to the other court unless the petitioned court can reasonably determine whether disclosure is proper. If the petitioned court decides to transfer, it must send to the transferee court the material sought to be disclosed, if feasible, and a written evaluation of the need for continued grand-jury secrecy. The transferee court must afford those persons identified in Rule 6(e)(3)(F) a reasonable opportunity to appear and be heard.

(4) *Sealed Indictment.* The magistrate judge to whom an indictment is returned may direct that the indictment be kept secret until the defendant is in custody or has been released pending trial. The clerk must then seal the indictment, and no person may disclose the indictment's existence except as necessary to issue or execute a warrant or summons.

(5) *Closed Hearing.* Subject to any right to an open hearing in a contempt proceeding, the court must close any hearing to the extent necessary to prevent disclosure of a matter occurring before a grand jury.

(6) *Sealed Records.* Records, orders, and subpoenas relating to grand-jury proceedings must be kept under seal to the extent and as long as necessary to prevent the unauthorized disclosure of a matter occurring before a grand jury.

(7) *Contempt.* A knowing violation of Rule 6 may be punished as a contempt of court.

(f) Indictment and Return. A grand jury may indict only if at least 12 jurors concur. The grand jury—or its foreperson or deputy foreperson—must return the indictment to a magistrate judge in open court. If a complaint or information is pending against the defendant and 12 jurors do not concur in the indictment, the foreperson must promptly and in writing report the lack of concurrence to the magistrate judge.

(g) Discharging the Grand Jury. A grand jury must serve until the court discharges it, but it may serve more than 18 months only if the court, having determined that an extension is in the public interest, extends the grand jury's service. An extension may be granted for no more than 6 months, except as otherwise provided by statute.

(h) Excusing a Juror. At any time, for good cause, the court may excuse a juror either temporarily or permanently, and if permanently, the court may impanel an alternate juror in place of the excused juror.

(i) "Indian Tribe" Defined. "Indian tribe" means an Indian tribe recognized by the Secretary of the Interior on a list published in the Federal Register under 25 U.S.C. § 479a–1.

Rule 7.   The Indictment and the Information

(a) When Used.

(1) *Felony.* An offense (other than criminal contempt) must be prosecuted by an indictment if it is punishable:

> (A) by death; or

> (B) by imprisonment for more than one year.

(2) *Misdemeanor.* An offense punishable by imprisonment for one year or less may be prosecuted in accordance with Rule 58(b)(1).

(b) Waiving Indictment. An offense punishable by imprisonment for more than one year may be prosecuted by information if the defendant—in open court and after being advised of the nature of the charge and of the defendant's rights—waives prosecution by indictment.

(c) Nature and Contents.

(1) *In General.* The indictment or information must be a plain, concise, and definite written statement of the essential facts constituting the offense charged and must be signed by an attorney for the government. It need not contain a formal introduction or conclusion. A count may incorporate by reference an allegation made in another count. A count may allege that the means by which the defendant committed the offense are unknown or that the defendant committed it by one or more specified means. For each count, the indictment or information must give the official or customary citation of the statute, rule, regulation, or other provision of law that the defendant is alleged to have violated.

(2) *Criminal Forfeiture.* No judgment of forfeiture may be entered in a criminal proceeding unless the indictment or the information provides notice that the defendant has an interest in property that is subject to forfeiture in accordance with the applicable statute.

(3) *Citation Error.* Unless the defendant was misled and thereby prejudiced, neither an error in a citation nor a citation's omission is a ground to dismiss the indictment or information or to reverse a conviction.

(d) Surplusage. Upon the defendant's motion, the court may strike surplusage from the indictment or information.

(e) Amending an Information. Unless an additional or different offense is charged or a substantial right of the defendant is prejudiced, the court may permit an information to be amended at any time before the verdict or finding.

(f) Bill of Particulars. The court may direct the government to file a bill of particulars. The defendant may move for a bill of particulars before or within 10 days after arraignment or at a later time if the court permits. The government may amend a bill of particulars subject to such conditions as justice requires.

Rule 8. Joinder of Offenses or Defendants

(a) Joinder of Offenses. The indictment or information may charge a defendant in separate counts with 2 or more offenses if the offenses charged—whether felonies or misdemeanors or both—are of the same or similar character, or are based on the same act or transaction, or are connected with or constitute parts of a common scheme or plan.

(b) Joinder of Defendants. The indictment or information may charge 2 or more defendants if they are alleged to have participated in the same act or transaction, or in the same series of acts or transactions, constituting an offense or offenses. The defendants may be charged in one or more counts together or separately. All defendants need not be charged in each count.

Rule 9. Arrest Warrant or Summons on an Indictment or Information

(a) Issuance. The court must issue a warrant—or at the government's request, a summons—for each defendant named in an indictment or named in an information if one or more affidavits accompanying the information establish probable cause to believe that an offense has been committed and that the defendant committed it. The court may issue more than one warrant or summons for the same defendant. If a defendant fails to appear in response to a summons, the court may, and upon request of an attorney for the government must, issue a warrant. The court must issue the arrest warrant to an officer authorized to execute it or the summons to a person authorized to serve it.

(b) Form.

(1) *Warrant.* The warrant must conform to Rule 4(b)(1) except that it must be signed by the clerk and must describe the offense charged in the indictment or information.

(2) *Summons.* The summons must be in the same form as a warrant except that it must require the defendant to appear before the court at a stated time and place.

(c) Execution or Service; Return; Initial Appearance.

(1) *Execution or Service.*

(A) The warrant must be executed or the summons served as provided in Rule 4(c)(1), (2), and (3).

(B) The officer executing the warrant must proceed in accordance with Rule 5(a)(1).

(2) *Return.* A warrant or summons must be returned in accordance with Rule 4(c)(4).

(3) *Initial Appearance.* When an arrested or summoned defendant first appears before the court, the judge must proceed under Rule 5.

TITLE IV.   ARRAIGNMENT AND PREPARATION FOR TRIAL

Rule 10.   Arraignment

(a) In General. An arraignment must be conducted in open court and must consist of:

(1) ensuring that the defendant has a copy of the indictment or information;

(2) reading the indictment or information to the defendant or stating to the defendant the substance of the charge; and then

(3) asking the defendant to plead to the indictment or information.

(b) Waiving Appearance. A defendant need not be present for the arraignment if:

(1) the defendant has been charged by indictment or misdemeanor information;

(2) the defendant, in a written waiver signed by both the defendant and defense counsel, has waived appearance and has affirmed that the defendant received a copy of the indictment or information and that the plea is not guilty; and

(3) the court accepts the waiver.

(c) Video Teleconferencing. Video teleconferencing may be used to arraign a defendant if the defendant consents.

Rule 11.   Pleas

(a) Entering a Plea.

(1) *In General.* A defendant may plead not guilty, guilty, or (with the court's consent) nolo contendere.

(2) *Conditional Plea.* With the consent of the court and the government, a defendant may enter a conditional plea of guilty or nolo contendere, reserving in writing the right to have an appellate court review an adverse determination of a specified pretrial motion. A defendant who prevails on appeal may then withdraw the plea.

(3) *Nolo Contendere Plea.* Before accepting a plea of nolo contendere, the court must consider the parties' views and the public interest in the effective administration of justice.

(4) *Failure to Enter a Plea.* If a defendant refuses to enter a plea or if a defendant organization fails to appear, the court must enter a plea of not guilty.

(b) Considering and Accepting a Guilty or Nolo Contendere Plea.

(1) *Advising and Questioning the Defendant.* Before the court accepts a plea of guilty or nolo contendere, the defendant may be placed under oath, and the court must address the defendant personally in open court. During this address, the court must inform the defendant of, and determine that the defendant understands, the following:

(A) the government's right, in a prosecution for perjury or false statement, to use against the defendant any statement that the defendant gives under oath;

(B) the right to plead not guilty, or having already so pleaded, to persist in that plea;

(C) the right to a jury trial;

(D) the right to be represented by counsel—and if necessary have the court appoint counsel—at trial and at every other stage of the proceeding;

(E) the right at trial to confront and cross-examine adverse witnesses, to be protected from compelled self-incrimination, to testify and present evidence, and to compel the attendance of witnesses;

(F) the defendant's waiver of these trial rights if the court accepts a plea of guilty or nolo contendere;

(G) the nature of each charge to which the defendant is pleading;

(H) any maximum possible penalty, including imprisonment, fine, and term of supervised release;

(I) any mandatory minimum penalty;

(J) any applicable forfeiture;

(K) the court's authority to order restitution;

(L) the court's obligation to impose a special assessment;

(M) the court's obligation to apply the Sentencing Guidelines, and the court's discretion to depart from those guidelines under some circumstances; and

(N) the terms of any plea-agreement provision waiving the right to appeal or to collaterally attack the sentence.

(2) *Ensuring That a Plea Is Voluntary.* Before accepting a plea of guilty or nolo contendere, the court must address the defendant personally in open court and determine that the plea is voluntary and did not result from force, threats, or promises (other than promises in a plea agreement).

(3) ***Determining the Factual Basis for a Plea.*** Before entering judgment on a guilty plea, the court must determine that there is a factual basis for the plea.

(c) Plea Agreement Procedure.

(1) ***In General.*** An attorney for the government and the defendant's attorney, or the defendant when proceeding pro se, may discuss and reach a plea agreement. The court must not participate in these discussions. If the defendant pleads guilty or nolo contendere to either a charged offense or a lesser or related offense, the plea agreement may specify that an attorney for the government will:

(A) not bring, or will move to dismiss, other charges;

(B) recommend, or agree not to oppose the defendant's request, that a particular sentence or sentencing range is appropriate or that a particular provision of the Sentencing Guidelines, or policy statement, or sentencing factor does or does not apply (such a recommendation or request does not bind the court); or

(C) agree that a specific sentence or sentencing range is the appropriate disposition of the case, or that a particular provision of the Sentencing Guidelines, or policy statement, or sentencing factor does or does not apply (such a recommendation or request binds the court once the court accepts the plea agreement).

(2) ***Disclosing a Plea Agreement.*** The parties must disclose the plea agreement in open court when the plea is offered, unless the court for good cause allows the parties to disclose the plea agreement in camera.

(3) ***Judicial Consideration of a Plea Agreement.***

(A) To the extent the plea agreement is of the type specified in Rule 11(c)(1)(A) or (C), the court may accept the agreement, reject it, or defer a decision until the court has reviewed the presentence report.

(B) To the extent the plea agreement is of the type specified in Rule 11(c)(1)(B), the court must advise the defendant that the defendant has no right to withdraw the plea if the court does not follow the recommendation or request.

(4) ***Accepting a Plea Agreement.*** If the court accepts the plea agreement, it must inform the defendant that to the extent the plea agreement is of the type specified in Rule 11(c)(1)(A) or (C), the agreed disposition will be included in the judgment.

(5) ***Rejecting a Plea Agreement.*** If the court rejects a plea agreement containing provisions of the type specified in Rule 11(c)(1)(A) or (C), the court must do the following on the record and in open court (or, for good cause, in camera):

(A) inform the parties that the court rejects the plea agreement;

(B) advise the defendant personally that the court is not required to follow the plea agreement and give the defendant an opportunity to withdraw the plea; and

(C) advise the defendant personally that if the plea is not withdrawn, the court may dispose of the case less favorably toward the defendant than the plea agreement contemplated.

(d) Withdrawing a Guilty or Nolo Contendere Plea. A defendant may withdraw a plea of guilty or nolo contendere:

(1) before the court accepts the plea, for any reason or no reason; or

(2) after the court accepts the plea, but before it imposes sentence if:

(A) the court rejects a plea agreement under Rule 11(c)(5); or

(B) the defendant can show a fair and just reason for requesting the withdrawal.

(e) Finality of a Guilty or Nolo Contendere Plea. After the court imposes sentence, the defendant may not withdraw a plea of guilty or nolo contendere, and the plea may be set aside only on direct appeal or collateral attack.

(f) Admissibility or Inadmissibility of a Plea, Plea Discussions, and Related Statements. The admissibility or inadmissibility of a plea, a plea discussion, and any related statement is governed by Federal Rule of Evidence 410.

(g) Recording the Proceedings. The proceedings during which the defendant enters a plea must be recorded by a court reporter or by a suitable recording device. If there is a guilty plea or a nolo contendere plea, the record must include the inquiries and advice to the defendant required under Rule 11(b) and (c).

(h) Harmless Error. A variance from the requirements of this rule is harmless error if it does not affect substantial rights.

Rule 12.   Pleadings and Pretrial Motions

(a) Pleadings. The pleadings in a criminal proceeding are the indictment, the information, and the pleas of not guilty, guilty, and nolo contendere.

(b) Pretrial Motions.

(1) *In General.* Rule 47 applies to a pretrial motion.

(2) *Motions That May Be Made Before Trial.* A party may raise by pretrial motion any defense, objection, or request that the court can determine without a trial of the general issue.

(3) *Motions That Must Be Made Before Trial*. The following must be raised before trial:

(A) a motion alleging a defect in instituting the prosecution;

(B) a motion alleging a defect in the indictment or information—but at any time while the case is pending, the court may hear a claim that the indictment or information fails to invoke the court's jurisdiction or to state an offense;

(C) a motion to suppress evidence;

(D) a Rule 14 motion to sever charges or defendants; and

(E) a Rule 16 motion for discovery.

(4) *Notice of the Government's Intent to Use Evidence.*

(A) *At the Government's Discretion.* At the arraignment or as soon afterward as practicable, the government may notify the defendant of its intent to use specified evidence at trial in order to afford the defendant an opportunity to object before trial under Rule 12(b)(3)(C).

(B) *At the Defendant's Request.* At the arraignment or as soon afterward as practicable, the defendant may, in order to have an opportunity to move to suppress evidence under Rule 12(b)(3)(C), request notice of the government's intent to use (in its evidence-in-chief at trial) any evidence that the defendant may be entitled to discover under Rule 16.

(c) Motion Deadline. The court may, at the arraignment or as soon afterward as practicable, set a deadline for the parties to make pretrial motions and may also schedule a motion hearing.

(d) Ruling on a Motion. The court must decide every pretrial motion before trial unless it finds good cause to defer a ruling. The court must not defer ruling on a pretrial motion if the deferral will adversely affect a party's right to appeal. When factual issues are involved in deciding a motion, the court must state its essential findings on the record.

(e) Waiver of a Defense, Objection, or Request. A party waives any Rule 12(b)(3) defense, objection, or request not raised by the deadline the court sets under Rule 12(c) or by any extension the court provides. For good cause, the court may grant relief from the waiver.

(f) Recording the Proceedings. All proceedings at a motion hearing, including any findings of fact and conclusions of law made orally by the court, must be recorded by a court reporter or a suitable recording device.

(g) Defendant's Continued Custody or Release Status. If the court grants a motion to dismiss based on a defect in instituting the prosecution, in the indictment, or in the information, it may order the defendant to be released or detained under 18 U.S.C. § 3142 for a specified time until a new indictment or information is filed. This rule does not affect any federal statutory period of limitations.

(h) Producing Statements at a Suppression Hearing. Rule 26.2 applies at a suppression hearing under Rule 12(b)(3)(C). At a suppression hearing, a law enforcement officer is considered a government witness.

Rule 12.1.   Notice of an Alibi Defense

(a) Government's Request for Notice and Defendant's Response.

(1) *Government's Request.* An attorney for the government may request in writing that the defendant notify an attorney for the government of any intended alibi defense. The request must state the time, date, and place of the alleged offense.

(2) *Defendant's Response.* Within 10 days after the request, or at some other time the court sets, the defendant must serve written notice on an attorney for the government of any intended alibi defense. The defendant's notice must state:

> (A) each specific place where the defendant claims to have been at the time of the alleged offense; and

> (B) the name, address, and telephone number of each alibi witness on whom the defendant intends to rely.

(b) Disclosing Government Witnesses.

(1) *Disclosure.* If the defendant serves a Rule 12.1(a)(2) notice, an attorney for the government must disclose in writing to the defendant or the defendant's attorney:

> (A) the name, address, and telephone number of each witness the government intends to rely on to establish the defendant's presence at the scene of the alleged offense; and

> (B) each government rebuttal witness to the defendant's alibi defense.

(2) *Time to Disclose.* Unless the court directs otherwise, an attorney for the government must give its Rule 12.1(b)(1) disclosure within 10 days after the defendant serves notice of an intended alibi defense under Rule 12.1(a)(2), but no later than 10 days before trial.

(c) Continuing Duty to Disclose. Both an attorney for the government and the defendant must promptly disclose in writing to the other party the name, address, and telephone number of each additional witness if:

(1) the disclosing party learns of the witness before or during trial; and

(2) the witness should have been disclosed under Rule 12.1(a) or (b) if the disclosing party had known of the witness earlier.

(d) Exceptions. For good cause, the court may grant an exception to any requirement of Rule 12.1(a)-(c).

(e) Failure to Comply. If a party fails to comply with this rule, the court may exclude the testimony of any undisclosed witness regarding the defendant's alibi. This rule does not limit the defendant's right to testify.

(f) Inadmissibility of Withdrawn Intention. Evidence of an intention to rely on an alibi defense, later withdrawn, or of a statement made in connection with that intention, is not, in any civil or criminal proceeding, admissible against the person who gave notice of the intention.

Rule 12.2. Notice of an Insanity Defense; Mental Examination

(a) Notice of an Insanity Defense. A defendant who intends to assert a defense of insanity at the time of the alleged offense must so notify an attorney for the government in writing within the time provided for filing a pretrial motion, or at any later time the court sets, and file a copy of the notice with the clerk. A defendant who fails to do so cannot rely on an insanity defense. The court may, for good cause, allow the defendant to file the notice late, grant additional trial-preparation time, or make other appropriate orders.

(b) Notice of Expert Evidence of a Mental Condition. If a defendant intends to introduce expert evidence relating to a mental disease or defect or any other mental condition of the defendant bearing on either (1) the issue of guilt or (2) the issue of punishment in a capital case, the defendant must—within the time provided for filing a pretrial motion or at any later time the court sets—notify an attorney for the government in writing of this intention and file a copy of the notice with the clerk. The court may, for good cause, allow the defendant to file the notice late, grant the parties additional trial-preparation time, or make other appropriate orders.

(c) Mental Examination.

(1) *Authority to Order an Examination; Procedures.*

(A) The court may order the defendant to submit to a competency examination under 18 U.S.C. § 4241.

(B) If the defendant provides notice under Rule 12.2(a), the court must, upon the government's motion, order the defendant to be examined under 18 U.S.C. § 4242. If the defendant provides notice under Rule 12.2(b) the court may, upon the government's motion, order the defendant to be examined under procedures ordered by the court.

(2) *Disclosing Results and Reports of Capital Sentencing Examination.* The results and reports of any examination conducted solely under Rule 12.2(c)(1) after notice under Rule 12.2(b)(2) must be sealed and must not be disclosed to any attorney for the government or the defendant unless the defendant is found guilty of one or more capital crimes and the defendant confirms an intent to offer during sentencing proceedings expert evidence on mental condition.

(3) *Disclosing Results and Reports of the Defendant's Expert Examination.* After disclosure under Rule 12.2(c)(2) of the results and reports of the government's examination, the defendant must disclose to the government the results and reports of any examination on mental condition conducted by the defendant's expert about which the defendant intends to introduce expert evidence.

(4) *Inadmissibility of a Defendant's Statements.* No statement made by a defendant in the course of any examination conducted under this rule (whether conducted with or without the defendant's consent), no testimony by the expert based on the statement, and no other fruits of the statement may be admitted into evidence against the defendant in any criminal proceeding except on an issue regarding mental condition on which the defendant:

(A) has introduced evidence of incompetency or evidence requiring notice under Rule 12.2(a) or (b)(1), or

(B) has introduced expert evidence in a capital sentencing proceeding requiring notice under Rule 12.2(b)(2).

(d) Failure to Comply. If the defendant fails to give notice under Rule 12.2(b) or does not submit to an examination when ordered under Rule 12.2(c), the court may exclude any expert evidence from the defendant on the issue of the defendant's mental disease, mental defect, or any other mental condition bearing on the defendant's guilt or the issue of punishment in a capital case.

(e) Inadmissibility of Withdrawn Intention. Evidence of an intention as to which notice was given under Rule 12.2(a) or (b), later withdrawn, is not, in any civil or criminal proceeding, admissible against the person who gave notice of the intention.

Rule 12.3. Notice of a Public–Authority Defense

(a) Notice of the Defense and Disclosure of Witnesses.

(1) *Notice in General.* If a defendant intends to assert a defense of actual or believed exercise of public authority on behalf of a law enforcement agency or federal intelligence agency at the time of the alleged offense, the defendant must so notify an attorney for the government in writing and must file a copy of the notice with the clerk within the time provided for filing a pretrial motion, or at any later time the court sets. The notice filed with the clerk must be under seal if the notice identifies a federal intelligence agency as the source of public authority.

(2) *Contents of Notice.* The notice must contain the following information:

(A) the law enforcement agency or federal intelligence agency involved;

(B) the agency member on whose behalf the defendant claims to have acted; and

(C) the time during which the defendant claims to have acted with public authority.

(3) *Response to the Notice.* An attorney for the government must serve a written response on the defendant or the defendant's attorney within 10 days after receiving the defendant's notice, but no later than 20 days before trial. The response must admit or deny that the defendant exercised the public authority identified in the defendant's notice.

(4) *Disclosing Witnesses.*

(A) *Government's Request.* An attorney for the government may request in writing that the defendant disclose the name, address, and telephone number of each witness the defendant intends to rely on to establish a public-authority defense. An attorney for the government may serve the request when the government serves its response to the defendant's notice under Rule 12.3(a)(3), or later, but must serve the request no later than 20 days before trial.

(B) *Defendant's Response.* Within 7 days after receiving the government's request, the defendant must serve on an attorney for the government a written statement of the name, address, and telephone number of each witness.

(C) *Government's Reply.* Within 7 days after receiving the defendant's statement, an attorney for the government must serve on the defendant or the defendant's attorney a written statement of the name, address, and telephone number of each witness the government intends to rely on to oppose the defendant's public-authority defense.

(5) *Additional Time.* The court may, for good cause, allow a party additional time to comply with this rule.

(b) Continuing Duty to Disclose. Both an attorney for the government and the defendant must promptly disclose in writing to the other party the name, address, and telephone number of any additional witness if:

(1) the disclosing party learns of the witness before or during trial; and

(2) the witness should have been disclosed under Rule 12.3(a)(4) if the disclosing party had known of the witness earlier.

(c) Failure to Comply. If a party fails to comply with this rule, the court may exclude the testimony of any undisclosed witness regarding the public-authority defense. This rule does not limit the defendant's right to testify.

(d) Protective Procedures Unaffected. This rule does not limit the court's authority to issue appropriate protective orders or to order that any filings be under seal.

(e) Inadmissibility of Withdrawn Intention. Evidence of an intention as to which notice was given under Rule 12.3(a), later withdrawn, is not, in any civil or criminal proceeding, admissible against the person who gave notice of the intention.

Rule 12.4. Disclosure Statement

(a) Who Must File.

(1) *Nongovernmental Corporate Party.* Any nongovernmental corporate party to a proceeding in a district court must file a statement that identifies any parent corporation and any publicly held corporation that owns 10% or more of its stock or states that there is no such corporation.

(2) *Organizational Victim.* If an organization is a victim of the alleged criminal activity, the government must file a statement identifying the victim. If the organizational victim is a corporation, the statement must also disclose the information required by Rule 12.4(a)(1) to the extent it can be obtained through due diligence.

(b) Time for Filing; Supplemental Filing. A party must:

(1) file the Rule 12.4(a) statement upon the defendant's initial appearance; and

(2) promptly file a supplemental statement upon any change in the information that the statement requires.

Rule 13. Joint Trial of Separate Cases

The court may order that separate cases be tried together as though brought in a single indictment or information if all offenses and all defendants could have been joined in a single indictment or information.

Rule 14. Relief from Prejudicial Joinder

(a) Relief. If the joinder of offenses or defendants in an indictment, an information, or a consolidation for trial appears to prejudice a defendant or the government, the court may order separate trials of counts, sever the defendants' trials, or provide any other relief that justice requires.

(b) Defendant's Statements. Before ruling on a defendant's motion to sever, the court may order an attorney for the government to deliver to the court for in camera inspection any defendant's statement that the government intends to use as evidence.

Rule 15. Depositions

(a) When Taken.

(1) *In General.* A party may move that a prospective witness be deposed in order to preserve testimony for trial. The court may grant the motion because of exceptional circumstances and in the interest of justice. If the court orders the deposition to be taken, it may also require the deponent to produce at the deposition any designated material that is not privileged, including any book, paper, document, record, recording, or data.

(2) *Detained Material Witness.* A witness who is detained under 18 U.S.C. § 3144 may request to be deposed by filing a written motion and giving notice to the parties. The court may then order that the deposition be taken and may discharge the witness after the witness has signed under oath the deposition transcript.

(b) Notice.

(1) *In General.* A party seeking to take a deposition must give every other party reasonable written notice of the deposition's date and location. The notice must state the name and address of each deponent. If requested by a party receiving the notice, the court may, for good cause, change the deposition's date or location.

(2) *To the Custodial Officer.* A party seeking to take the deposition must also notify the officer who has custody of the defendant of the scheduled date and location.

(c)   Defendant's Presence.

(1) *Defendant in Custody.* The officer who has custody of the defendant must produce the defendant at the deposition and keep the defendant in the witness's presence during the examination, unless the defendant:

(A) waives in writing the right to be present; or

(B) persists in disruptive conduct justifying exclusion after being warned by the court that disruptive conduct will result in the defendant's exclusion.

(2) *Defendant Not in Custody.* A defendant who is not in custody has the right upon request to be present at the deposition, subject to any conditions imposed by the court. If the government tenders the defendant's expenses as provided in Rule 15(d) but the defendant still fails to appear, the defendant—absent good cause—waives both the right to appear and any objection to the taking and use of the deposition based on that right.

(d) Expenses. If the deposition was requested by the government, the court may—or if the defendant is unable to bear the deposition expenses, the court must—order the government to pay:

(1) any reasonable travel and subsistence expenses of the defendant and the defendant's attorney to attend the deposition; and

(2) the costs of the deposition transcript.

(e) Manner of Taking. Unless these rules or a court order provides otherwise, a deposition must be taken and filed in the same manner as a deposition in a civil action, except that:

(1) A defendant may not be deposed without that defendant's consent.

(2) The scope and manner of the deposition examination and cross-examination must be the same as would be allowed during trial.

(3) The government must provide to the defendant or the defendant's attorney, for use at the deposition, any statement of the deponent in the government's possession to which the defendant would be entitled at trial.

(f) Use as Evidence. A party may use all or part of a deposition as provided by the Federal Rules of Evidence.

(g) Objections. A party objecting to deposition testimony or evidence must state the grounds for the objection during the deposition.

(h) Depositions by Agreement Permitted. The parties may by agreement take and use a deposition with the court's consent.

Rule 16.   Discovery and Inspection

(a) Government's Disclosure.

(1) *Information Subject to Disclosure.*

(A) *Defendant's Oral Statement.* Upon a defendant's request, the government must disclose to the defendant the substance of any relevant oral statement made by the defendant, before or after arrest, in response to interrogation by a person the defendant knew was a government agent if the government intends to use the statement at trial.

(B) *Defendant's Written or Recorded Statement.* Upon a defendant's request, the government must disclose to the defendant, and make available for inspection, copying, or photographing, all of the following:

(i) any relevant written or recorded statement by the defendant if: the statement is within the government's possession, custody, or control; and the attorney for the government knows—or through due diligence could know—that the statement exists;

(ii) the portion of any written record containing the substance of any relevant oral statement made before or after arrest if the defendant made the statement in response to interrogation by a person the defendant knew was a government agent; and

(iii) the defendant's recorded testimony before a grand jury relating to the charged offense.

(C) *Organizational Defendant.* Upon a defendant's request, if the defendant is an organization, the government must disclose to the defendant any statement described in Rule 16(a)(1)(A) and (B) if the government contends that the person making the statement:

(i) was legally able to bind the defendant regarding the subject of the statement because of that person's position as the defendant's director, officer, employee, or agent; or

(ii) was personally involved in the alleged conduct constituting the offense and was legally able to bind the defendant regarding that conduct because of that person's position as the defendant's director, officer, employee, or agent.

(D) *Defendant's Prior Record.* Upon a defendant's request, the government must furnish the defendant with a copy of the defendant's prior criminal record that is within the government's possession, custody, or control if the attorney for the government knows—or through due diligence could know—that the record exists.

(E) *Documents and Objects.* Upon a defendant's request, the government must permit the defendant to inspect and to copy or photograph books, papers, documents, data, photographs, tangible objects, buildings or places, or copies or portions of any of these items, if the item is within the government's possession, custody, or control and:

> (i) the item is material to preparing the defense;

> (ii) the government intends to use the item in its case-in-chief at trial; or

> (iii) the item was obtained from or belongs to the defendant.

(F) *Reports of Examinations and Tests.* Upon a defendant's request, the government must permit a defendant to inspect and to copy or photograph the results or reports of any physical or mental examination and of any scientific test or experiment if:

> (i) the item is within the government's possession, custody, or control;

> (ii) the attorney for the government knows—or through due diligence could know—that the item exists; and

> (iii) the item is material to preparing the defense or the government intends to use the item in its case-in-chief at trial.

(G) *Expert Testimony.* Upon a defendant's request, the government must give the defendant a written summary of any testimony the government intends to use in its case-in-chief at trial under Federal Rules of Evidence 702, 703, or 705. The summary must describe the witness's opinions, the bases and reasons for those opinions, and the witness's qualifications.

(2) *Information Not Subject to Disclosure.* Except as Rule 16(a)(1) provides otherwise, this rule does not authorize the discovery or inspection of reports, memoranda, or other internal government documents made by an attorney for the government or other government agent in connection with investigating or prosecuting the case. Nor does this rule authorize the discovery or inspection of statements made by prospective government witnesses except as provided in 18 U.S.C. § 3500.

(3) *Grand Jury Transcripts.* This rule does not apply to the discovery or inspection of a grand jury's recorded proceedings, except as provided in Rules 6, 12(h), 16(a)(1), and 26.2.

(b) Defendant's Disclosure.

(1) *Information Subject to Disclosure.*

(A) *Documents and Objects.* If a defendant requests disclosure under Rule 16(a)(1)(E) and the government complies, then the defendant must permit the government, upon request, to inspect and to copy or photograph books, papers, documents, data, photographs, tangible objects, buildings or places, or copies or portions of any of these items if:

    (i) the item is within the defendant's possession, custody, or control; and

    (ii) the defendant intends to use the item in the defendant's case-in-chief at trial.

(B) *Reports of Examinations and Tests.* If a defendant requests disclosure under Rule 16(a)(1)(F) and the government complies, the defendant must permit the government, upon request, to inspect and to copy or photograph the results or reports of any physical or mental examination and of any scientific test or experiment if:

    (i) the item is within the defendant's possession, custody, or control; and

    (ii) the defendant intends to use the item in the defendant's case-in-chief at trial, or intends to call the witness who prepared the report and the report relates to the witness's testimony.

(C) *Expert Witnesses.* The defendant must, at the government's request, give to the government a written summary of any testimony that the defendant intends to use under Rules 702, 703, or 705 of the Federal Rules of Evidence as evidence at trial, if—

    (i) the defendant requests disclosure under subdivision (a)(1)(G) and the government complies; or

    (ii) the defendant has given notice under Rule 12.2(b) of an intent to present expert testimony on the defendant's mental condition.

        This summary must describe the witness's opinions, the bases and reasons for those opinions, and the witness's qualifications.

(2) *Information Not Subject to Disclosure.* Except for scientific or medical reports, Rule 16(b)(1) does not authorize discovery or inspection of:

(A) reports, memoranda, or other documents made by the defendant, or the defendant's attorney or agent, during the case's investigation or defense; or

(B) a statement made to the defendant, or the defendant's attorney or agent, by:

(i) the defendant;

(ii) a government or defense witness; or

(iii) a prospective government or defense witness.

(c) Continuing Duty to Disclose. A party who discovers additional evidence or material before or during trial must promptly disclose its existence to the other party or the court if:

(1) the evidence or material is subject to discovery or inspection under this rule; and

(2) the other party previously requested, or the court ordered, its production.

(d) Regulating Discovery.

(1) *Protective and Modifying Orders.* At any time the court may, for good cause, deny, restrict, or defer discovery or inspection, or grant other appropriate relief. The court may permit a party to show good cause by a written statement that the court will inspect ex parte. If relief is granted, the court must preserve the entire text of the party's statement under seal.

(2) *Failure to Comply.* If a party fails to comply with this rule, the court may:

(A) order that party to permit the discovery or inspection; specify its time, place, and manner; and prescribe other just terms and conditions;

(B) grant a continuance;

(C) prohibit that party from introducing the undisclosed evidence; or

(D) enter any other order that is just under the circumstances.

Rule 17. Subpoena

(a) Content. A subpoena must state the court's name and the title of the proceeding, include the seal of the court, and command the witness to attend and testify at the time and place the subpoena specifies. The clerk must issue a blank subpoena—signed and sealed—to the party requesting it, and that party must fill in the blanks before the subpoena is served.

(b) Defendant Unable to Pay. Upon a defendant's ex parte application, the court must order that a subpoena be issued for a named witness if the defendant shows an inability to pay the witness's fees and the necessity of the witness's presence for an adequate defense. If the court orders a subpoena to be issued, the process costs and witness fees will be paid in the same manner as those paid for witnesses the government subpoenas.

(c) Producing Documents and Objects.

(1) *In General.* A subpoena may order the witness to produce any books, papers, documents, data, or other objects the subpoena designates. The court may direct the witness to produce the designated items in court before trial or before they are to be offered in evidence. When the items arrive, the court may permit the parties and their attorneys to inspect all or part of them.

(2) *Quashing or Modifying the Subpoena.* On motion made promptly, the court may quash or modify the subpoena if compliance would be unreasonable or oppressive.

(d) Service. A marshal, a deputy marshal, or any nonparty who is at least 18 years old may serve a subpoena. The server must deliver a copy of the subpoena to the witness and must tender to the witness one day's witness-attendance fee and the legal mileage allowance. The server need not tender the attendance fee or mileage allowance when the United States, a federal officer, or a federal agency has requested the subpoena.

(e) Place of Service.

(1) *In the United States.* A subpoena requiring a witness to attend a hearing or trial may be served at any place within the United States.

(2) *In a Foreign Country.* If the witness is in a foreign country, 28 U.S.C. § 1783 governs the subpoena's service.

(f) Issuing a Deposition Subpoena.

(1) *Issuance.* A court order to take a deposition authorizes the clerk in the district where the deposition is to be taken to issue a subpoena for any witness named or described in the order.

(2) *Place.* After considering the convenience of the witness and the parties, the court may order—and the subpoena may require—the witness to appear anywhere the court designates.

(g) Contempt. The court (other than a magistrate judge) may hold in contempt a witness who, without adequate excuse, disobeys a subpoena issued by a federal court in that district. A magistrate judge may hold in contempt a witness who, without adequate excuse, disobeys a subpoena issued by that magistrate judge as provided in 28 U.S.C. § 636(e).

(h) Information Not Subject to a Subpoena. No party may subpoena a statement of a witness or of a prospective witness under this rule. Rule 26.2 governs the production of the statement.

Rule 17.1. Pretrial Conference

On its own, or on a party's motion, the court may hold one or more pretrial conferences to promote a fair and expeditious trial. When a conference ends, the court must prepare and file a memorandum of any matters agreed to during the conference. The government may not use any statement made during the conference by the defendant or the defendant's attorney unless it is in writing and is signed by the defendant and the defendant's attorney.

TITLE V.   VENUE

Rule 18.   Place of Prosecution and Trial

Unless a statute or these rules permit otherwise, the government must prosecute an offense in a district where the offense was committed. The court must set the place of trial within the district with due regard for the convenience of the defendant and the witnesses, and the prompt administration of justice.

Rule 19.   [Reserved]

Rule 20.   Transfer for Plea and Sentence

(a) Consent to Transfer. A prosecution may be transferred from the district where the indictment or information is pending, or from which a warrant on a complaint has been issued, to the district where the defendant is arrested, held, or present if:

(1) the defendant states in writing a wish to plead guilty or nolo contendere and to waive trial in the district where the indictment, information, or complaint is pending, consents in writing to the court's disposing of the case in the transferee district, and files the statement in the transferee district; and

(2) the United States attorneys in both districts approve the transfer in writing.

(b) Clerk's Duties. After receiving the defendant's statement and the required approvals, the clerk where the indictment, information, or complaint is pending must send the file, or a certified copy, to the clerk in the transferee district.

(c) Effect of a Not Guilty Plea. If the defendant pleads not guilty after the case has been transferred under Rule 20(a), the clerk must return the papers to the court where the prosecution began, and that court must restore the proceeding to its docket. The defendant's statement that the defendant wished to plead guilty or nolo contendere is not, in any civil or criminal proceeding, admissible against the defendant.

(d) Juveniles.

(1) *Consent to Transfer.* A juvenile, as defined in 18 U.S.C. § 5031, may be proceeded against as a juvenile delinquent in the district where the juvenile is arrested, held, or present if:

(A) the alleged offense that occurred in the other district is not punishable by death or life imprisonment;

(B) an attorney has advised the juvenile;

(C) the court has informed the juvenile of the juvenile's rights—including the right to be returned to the district where the offense allegedly occurred—and the consequences of waiving those rights;

(D) the juvenile, after receiving the court's information about rights, consents in writing to be proceeded against in the transferee district, and files the consent in the transferee district;

(E) the United States attorneys for both districts approve the transfer in writing; and

(F) the transferee court approves the transfer.

(2) *Clerk's Duties.* After receiving the juvenile's written consent and the required approvals, the clerk where the indictment, information, or complaint is pending or where the alleged offense occurred must send the file, or a certified copy, to the clerk in the transferee district.

Rule 21. Transfer for Trial

(a) For Prejudice. Upon the defendant's motion, the court must transfer the proceeding against that defendant to another district if the court is satisfied that so great a prejudice against the defendant exists in the transferring district that the defendant cannot obtain a fair and impartial trial there.

(b) For Convenience. Upon the defendant's motion, the court may transfer the proceeding, or one or more counts, against that defendant to another district for the convenience of the parties and witnesses and in the interest of justice.

(c) Proceedings on Transfer. When the court orders a transfer, the clerk must send to the transferee district the file, or a certified copy, and any bail taken. The prosecution will then continue in the transferee district.

(d) Time to File a Motion to Transfer. A motion to transfer may be made at or before arraignment or at any other time the court or these rules prescribe.

Rule 22. [Transferred]

TITLE VI. TRIAL

Rule 23. Jury or Nonjury Trial

(a) Jury Trial. If the defendant is entitled to a jury trial, the trial must be by jury unless:

(1) the defendant waives a jury trial in writing;

(2) the government consents; and

(3) the court approves.

(b) Jury Size.

(1) *In General.* A jury consists of 12 persons unless this rule provides otherwise.

(2) *Stipulation for a Smaller Jury.* At any time before the verdict, the parties may, with the court's approval, stipulate in writing that:

(A) the jury may consist of fewer than 12 persons; or

(B) a jury of fewer than 12 persons may return a verdict if the court finds it necessary to excuse a juror for good cause after the trial begins.

(3) *Court Order for a Jury of 11.* After the jury has retired to deliberate, the court may permit a jury of 11 persons to return a verdict, even without a stipulation by the parties, if the court finds good cause to excuse a juror.

(c) Nonjury Trial. In a case tried without a jury, the court must find the defendant guilty or not guilty. If a party requests before the finding of guilty or not guilty, the court must state its specific findings of fact in open court or in a written decision or opinion.

Rule 24.   Trial Jurors

(a) Examination.

(1) *In General.* The court may examine prospective jurors or may permit the attorneys for the parties to do so.

(2) *Court Examination.* If the court examines the jurors, it must permit the attorneys for the parties to:

(A) ask further questions that the court considers proper; or

(B) submit further questions that the court may ask if it considers them proper.

(b) Peremptory Challenges. Each side is entitled to the number of peremptory challenges to prospective jurors specified below. The court may allow additional peremptory challenges to multiple defendants, and may allow the defendants to exercise those challenges separately or jointly.

(1) *Capital Case.* Each side has 20 peremptory challenges when the government seeks the death penalty.

(2) *Other Felony Case.* The government has 6 peremptory challenges and the defendant or defendants jointly have 10 peremptory challenges when the defendant is charged with a crime punishable by imprisonment of more than one year.

(3) *Misdemeanor Case.* Each side has 3 peremptory challenges when the defendant is charged with a crime punishable by fine, imprisonment of one year or less, or both. **(c) Alternate Jurors.**

(1) *In General.* The court may impanel up to 6 alternate jurors to replace any jurors who are unable to perform or who are disqualified from performing their duties.

(2) *Procedure.*

(A) Alternate jurors must have the same qualifications and be selected and sworn in the same manner as any other juror.

(B) Alternate jurors replace jurors in the same sequence in which the alternates were selected. An alternate juror who replaces a juror has the same authority as the other jurors.

(3) *Retaining Alternate Jurors.* The court may retain alternate jurors after the jury retires to deliberate. The court must ensure that a retained alternate does not discuss the case with anyone until that alternate replaces a juror or is discharged. If an alternate replaces a juror after deliberations have begun, the court must instruct the jury to begin its deliberations anew.

(4) *Peremptory Challenges.* Each side is entitled to the number of additional peremptory challenges to prospective alternate jurors specified below. These additional challenges may be used only to remove alternate jurors.

(A) *One or Two Alternates.* One additional peremptory challenge is permitted when one or two alternates are impaneled.

(B) *Three or Four Alternates.* Two additional peremptory challenges are permitted when three or four alternates are impaneled.

(C) *Five or Six Alternates.* Three additional peremptory challenges are permitted when five or six alternates are impaneled.

Rule 25. Judge's Disability

(a) During Trial. Any judge regularly sitting in or assigned to the court may complete a jury trial if:

(1) the judge before whom the trial began cannot proceed because of death, sickness, or other disability; and

(2) the judge completing the trial certifies familiarity with the trial record.

(b) After a Verdict or Finding of Guilty.

(1) *In General.* After a verdict or finding of guilty, any judge regularly sitting in or assigned to a court may complete the court's duties if the judge who presided at trial cannot perform those duties because of absence, death, sickness, or other disability.

(2) *Granting a New Trial.* The successor judge may grant a new trial if satisfied that:

(A) a judge other than the one who presided at the trial cannot perform the post-trial duties; or

(B) a new trial is necessary for some other reason.

Rule 26. Taking Testimony

In every trial the testimony of witnesses must be taken in open court, unless otherwise provided by a statute or by rules adopted under 28 U.S.C. §§ 2072–2077.

Rule 26.1. Foreign Law Determination

A party intending to raise an issue of foreign law must provide the court and all parties with reasonable written notice. Issues of foreign law are questions of law, but in deciding such issues a court may consider any relevant material or source—including testimony—without regard to the Federal Rules of Evidence.

Rule 26.2. Producing a Witness's Statement

(a) Motion to Produce. After a witness other than the defendant has testified on direct examination, the court, on motion of a party who did not call the witness, must order an attorney for the government or the defendant and the defendant's attorney to produce, for the examination and use of the moving party, any statement of the witness that is in their possession and that relates to the subject matter of the witness's testimony.

(b) Producing the Entire Statement. If the entire statement relates to the subject matter of the witness's testimony, the court must order that the statement be delivered to the moving party.

(c) Producing a Redacted Statement. If the party who called the witness claims that the statement contains information that is privileged or does not relate to the subject matter of the witness's testimony, the court must inspect the statement in camera. After excising any privileged or unrelated portions, the court must order delivery of the redacted statement to the moving party. If the defendant objects to an excision, the court must preserve the entire statement with the excised portion indicated, under seal, as part of the record.

(d) Recess to Examine a Statement. The court may recess the proceedings to allow time for a party to examine the statement and prepare for its use.

(e) Sanction for Failure to Produce or Deliver a Statement. If the party who called the witness disobeys an order to produce or deliver a statement, the court must strike the witness's testimony from the record. If an attorney for the government disobeys the order, the court must declare a mistrial if justice so requires.

(f) "Statement" Defined. As used in this rule, a witness's "statement" means:

(1) a written statement that the witness makes and signs, or otherwise adopts or approves;

(2) a substantially verbatim, contemporaneously recorded recital of the witness's oral statement that is contained in any recording or any transcription of a recording; or

(3) the witness's statement to a grand jury, however taken or recorded, or a transcription of such a statement.

(g) Scope. This rule applies at trial, at a suppression hearing under Rule 12, and to the extent specified in the following rules:

(1) Rule 5.1(h) (preliminary hearing);

(2) Rule 32(i)(2) (sentencing);

(3) Rule 32.1(e) (hearing to revoke or modify probation or supervised release);

(4) Rule 46(j) (detention hearing); and

(5) Rule 8 of the Rules Governing Proceedings under 28 U.S.C. § 2255.

Rule 26.3. Mistrial

Before ordering a mistrial, the court must give each defendant and the government an opportunity to comment on the propriety of the order, to state whether that party consents or objects, and to suggest alternatives.

Rule 27. Proving an Official Record

A party may prove an official record, an entry in such a record, or the lack of a record or entry in the same manner as in a civil action.

Rule 28. Interpreters

The court may select, appoint, and set the reasonable compensation for an interpreter. The compensation must be paid from funds provided by law or by the government, as the court may direct.

Rule 29. Motion for a Judgment of Acquittal

(a) Before Submission to the Jury. After the government closes its evidence or after the close of all the evidence, the court on the defendant's motion must enter a judgment of acquittal of any offense for which the evidence is insufficient to sustain a conviction. The court may on its own consider whether the evidence is insufficient to sustain a conviction. If the court denies a motion for a judgment of acquittal at the close of the government's evidence, the defendant may offer evidence without having reserved the right to do so.

(b) Reserving Decision. The court may reserve decision on the motion, proceed with the trial (where the motion is made before the close of all the evidence), submit the case to the jury, and decide the motion either before the jury returns a verdict or after it returns a verdict of guilty or is discharged without having returned a verdict. If the court reserves decision, it must decide the motion on the basis of the evidence at the time the ruling was reserved.

(c) After Jury Verdict or Discharge.

(1) *Time for a Motion.* A defendant may move for a judgment of acquittal, or renew such a motion, within 7 days after a guilty verdict or after the court discharges the jury, whichever is later, or within any other time the court sets during the 7–day period.

(2) *Ruling on the Motion.* If the jury has returned a guilty verdict, the court may set aside the verdict and enter an acquittal. If the jury has failed to return a verdict, the court may enter a judgment of acquittal.

(3) *No Prior Motion Required.* A defendant is not required to move for a judgment of acquittal before the court submits the case to the jury as a prerequisite for making such a motion after jury discharge.

(d) Conditional Ruling on a Motion for a New Trial.

(1) *Motion for a New Trial.* If the court enters a judgment of acquittal after a guilty verdict, the court must also conditionally determine whether any motion for a new trial should be granted if the judgment of acquittal is later vacated or reversed. The court must specify the reasons for that determination.

(2) *Finality.* The court's order conditionally granting a motion for a new trial does not affect the finality of the judgment of acquittal.

(3) *Appeal.*

(A) *Grant of a Motion for a New Trial.* If the court conditionally grants a motion for a new trial and an appellate court later reverses the judgment of acquittal, the trial court must proceed with the new trial unless the appellate court orders otherwise.

(B) *Denial of a Motion for a New Trial.* If the court conditionally denies a motion for a new trial, an appellee may assert that the denial was erroneous. If the appellate court later reverses the judgment of acquittal, the trial court must proceed as the appellate court directs.

Rule 29.1.   Closing Argument

Closing arguments proceed in the following order:

(a) the government argues;

(b) the defense argues; and

(c) the government rebuts.

Rule 30.   Jury Instructions

(a) In General. Any party may request in writing that the court instruct the jury on the law as specified in the request. The request must be made at the close of the evidence or at any earlier time that the court reasonably sets. When the request is made, the requesting party must furnish a copy to every other party.

(b) Ruling on a Request. The court must inform the parties before closing arguments how it intends to rule on the requested instructions.

(c) Time for Giving Instructions. The court may instruct the jury before or after the arguments are completed, or at both times.

(d) Objections to Instructions. A party who objects to any portion of the instructions or to a failure to give a requested instruction must inform the court of the specific objection and the grounds for the objection before the jury retires to deliberate. An opportunity must be given to object out of the jury's hearing and, on request, out of the jury's presence. Failure to object in accordance with this rule precludes appellate review, except as permitted under Rule 52(b).

Rule 31. Jury Verdict

(a) Return. The jury must return its verdict to a judge in open court. The verdict must be unanimous.

(b) Partial Verdicts, Mistrial, and Retrial.

(1) *Multiple Defendants.* If there are multiple defendants, the jury may return a verdict at any time during its deliberations as to any defendant about whom it has agreed.

(2) *Multiple Counts.* If the jury cannot agree on all counts as to any defendant, the jury may return a verdict on those counts on which it has agreed.

(3) *Mistrial and Retrial.* If the jury cannot agree on a verdict on one or more counts, the court may declare a mistrial on those counts. The government may retry any defendant on any count on which the jury could not agree.

(c) Lesser Offense or Attempt. A defendant may be found guilty of any of the following:

(1) an offense necessarily included in the offense charged;

(2) an attempt to commit the offense charged; or

(3) an attempt to commit an offense necessarily included in the offense charged, if the attempt is an offense in its own right.

(d) Jury Poll. After a verdict is returned but before the jury is discharged, the court must on a party's request, or may on its own, poll the jurors individually. If the poll reveals a lack of unanimity, the court may direct the jury to deliberate further or may declare a mistrial and discharge the jury.

TITLE VII. POST–CONVICTION PROCEDURES

Rule 32. Sentencing and Judgment

(a) Definitions. The following definitions apply under this rule:

(1) "Crime of violence or sexual abuse" means:

(A) a crime that involves the use, attempted use, or threatened use of physical force against another's person or property; or

(B) a crime under 18 U.S.C. §§ 2241–2248 or §§ x2251–2257.

(2) "Victim" means an individual against whom the defendant committed an offense for which the court will impose sentence.

(b) Time of Sentencing.

(1) *In General.* The court must impose sentence without unnecessary delay.

(2) *Changing Time Limits.* The court may, for good cause, change any time limits prescribed in this rule.

(c) Presentence Investigation.

(1) *Required Investigation.*

(A) *In General.* The probation officer must conduct a presentence investigation and submit a report to the court before it imposes sentence unless:

(i) 18 U.S.C. § 3593(c) or another statute requires otherwise; or

(ii) the court finds that the information in the record enables it to meaningfully exercise its sentencing authority under 18 U.S.C. § 3553, and the court explains its finding on the record.

(B) *Restitution.* If the law requires restitution, the probation officer must conduct an investigation and submit a report that contains sufficient information for the court to order restitution.

(2) *Interviewing the Defendant.* The probation officer who interviews a defendant as part of a presentence investigation must, on request, give the defendant's attorney notice and a reasonable opportunity to attend the interview.

(d) Presentence Report.

(1) *Applying the Sentencing Guidelines.* The presentence report must:

(A) identify all applicable guidelines and policy statements of the Sentencing Commission;

(B) calculate the defendant's offense level and criminal history category;

(C) state the resulting sentencing range and kinds of sentences available;

(D) identify any factor relevant to:

(i) the appropriate kind of sentence, or

(ii) the appropriate sentence within the applicable sentencing range; and

(E) identify any basis for departing from the applicable sentencing range.

(2) *Additional Information.* The presentence report must also contain the following information:

(A) the defendant's history and characteristics, including:

(i) any prior criminal record;

(ii) the defendant's financial condition; and

(iii) any circumstances affecting the defendant's behavior that may be helpful in imposing sentence or in correctional treatment;

(B) verified information, stated in a nonargumentative style, that assesses the financial, social, psychological, and medical impact on any individual against whom the offense has been committed;

(C) when appropriate, the nature and extent of nonprison programs and resources available to the defendant;

(D) when the law provides for restitution, information sufficient for a restitution order;

(E) if the court orders a study under 18 U.S.C. § x3552(b), any resulting report and recommendation; and

(F) any other information that the court requires.

(3) *Exclusions.* The presentence report must exclude the following:

(A) any diagnoses that, if disclosed, might seriously disrupt a rehabilitation program;

(B) any sources of information obtained upon a promise of confidentiality; and

(C) any other information that, if disclosed, might result in physical or other harm to the defendant or others.

(e) Disclosing the Report and Recommendation.

(1) *Time to Disclose.* Unless the defendant has consented in writing, the probation officer must not submit a presentence report to the court or disclose its contents to anyone until the defendant has pleaded guilty or nolo contendere, or has been found guilty.

(2) *Minimum Required Notice.* The probation officer must give the presentence report to the defendant, the defendant's attorney, and an attorney for the government at least 35 days before sentencing unless the defendant waives this minimum period.

(3) *Sentence Recommendation.* By local rule or by order in a case, the court may direct the probation officer not to disclose to anyone other than the court the officer's recommendation on the sentence.

(f) Objecting to the Report.

(1) *Time to Object.* Within 14 days after receiving the presentence report, the parties must state in writing any objections, including objections to material information, sentencing guideline ranges, and policy statements contained in or omitted from the report.

(2) *Serving Objections.* An objecting party must provide a copy of its objections to the opposing party and to the probation officer.

(3) *Action on Objections.* After receiving objections, the probation officer may meet with the parties to discuss the objections. The probation officer may then investigate further and revise the presentence report as appropriate.

(g) Submitting the Report. At least 7 days before sentencing, the probation officer must submit to the court and to the parties the presentence report and an addendum containing any unresolved objections, the grounds for those objections, and the probation officer's comments on them.

(h) Notice of Possible Departure from Sentencing Guidelines. Before the court may depart from the applicable sentencing range on a ground not identified for departure either in the presentence report or in a party's prehearing submission, the court must give the parties reasonable notice that it is contemplating such a departure. The notice must specify any ground on which the court is contemplating a departure.

(i) Sentencing.

(1) *In General.* At sentencing, the court:

(A) must verify that the defendant and the defendant's attorney have read and discussed the presentence report and any addendum to the report;

(B) must give to the defendant and an attorney for the government a written summary of—or summarize in camera—any information excluded from the presentence report under Rule 32(d)(3) on which the court will rely in sentencing, and give them a reasonable opportunity to comment on that information;

(C) must allow the parties' attorneys to comment on the probation officer's determinations and other matters relating to an appropriate sentence; and

(D) may, for good cause, allow a party to make a new objection at any time before sentence is imposed.

(2) *Introducing Evidence; Producing a Statement.* The court may permit the parties to introduce evidence on the objections. If a witness testifies at sentencing, Rule 26.2(a)-(d) and (f) applies. If a party fails to comply with a Rule 26.2 order to produce a witness's statement, the court must not consider that witness's testimony.

(3) *Court Determinations.* At sentencing, the court:

(A) may accept any undisputed portion of the presentence report as a finding of fact;

(B) must—for any disputed portion of the presentence report or other controverted matter—rule on the dispute or determine that a ruling is unnecessary either because the matter will not affect sentencing, or because the court will not consider the matter in sentencing; and

(C) must append a copy of the court's determinations under this rule to any copy of the presentence report made available to the Bureau of Prisons.

(4) *Opportunity to Speak.*

(A) *By a Party*. Before imposing sentence, the court must:

(i) provide the defendant's attorney an opportunity to speak on the defendant's behalf;

(ii) address the defendant personally in order to permit the defendant to speak or present any information to mitigate the sentence; and

(iii) provide an attorney for the government an opportunity to speak equivalent to that of the defendant's attorney.

(B) *By a Victim*. Before imposing sentence, the court must address any victim of a crime of violence or sexual abuse who is present at sentencing and must permit the victim to speak or submit any information about the sentence. Whether or not the victim is present, a victim's right to address the court may be exercised by the following persons if present:

a parent or legal guardian, if the victim is younger than 18 years or is incompetent; or

one or more family members or relatives the court designates, if the victim is deceased or incapacitated.

(C) *In Camera Proceedings*. Upon a party's motion and for good cause, the court may hear in camera any statement made under Rule 32(i)(4).

(j) Defendant's Right to Appeal.

(1) *Advice of a Right to Appeal.*

(A) *Appealing a Conviction*. If the defendant pleaded not guilty and was convicted, after sentencing the court must advise the defendant of the right to appeal the conviction.

(B) *Appealing a Sentence*. After sentencing—regardless of the defendant's plea—the court must advise the defendant of any right to appeal the sentence.

(C) *Appeal Costs*. The court must advise a defendant who is unable to pay appeal costs of the right to ask for permission to appeal in forma pauperis.

(2) *Clerk's Filing of Notice.* If the defendant so requests, the clerk must immediately prepare and file a notice of appeal on the defendant's behalf.

(k) Judgment.

(1) *In General*. In the judgment of conviction, the court must set forth the plea, the jury verdict or the court's findings, the adjudication, and the sentence. If the defendant is found not guilty or is otherwise entitled to be discharged, the court must so order. The judge must sign the judgment, and the clerk must enter it.

(2) Criminal Forfeiture. Forfeiture procedures are governed by Rule 32.2.

Rule 32.1. Revoking or Modifying Probation or Supervised Release

(a) Initial Appearance.

(1) Person In Custody. A person held in custody for violating probation or supervised release must be taken without unnecessary delay before a magistrate judge.

(A) If the person is held in custody in the district where an alleged violation occurred, the initial appearance must be in that district.

(B) If the person is held in custody in a district other than where an alleged violation occurred, the initial appearance must be in that district, or in an adjacent district if the appearance can occur more promptly there.

(2) Upon a Summons. When a person appears in response to a summons for violating probation or supervised release, a magistrate judge must proceed under this rule.

(3) Advice. The judge must inform the person of the following:

(A) the alleged violation of probation or supervised release;

(B) the person's right to retain counsel or to request that counsel be appointed if the person cannot obtain counsel; and

(C) the person's right, if held in custody, to a preliminary hearing under Rule 32.1(b)(1).

(4) Appearance in the District With Jurisdiction. If the person is arrested or appears in the district that has jurisdiction to conduct a revocation hearing—either originally or by transfer of jurisdiction—the court must proceed under Rule 32.1(b)–(e).

(5) Appearance in a District Lacking Jurisdiction. If the person is arrested or appears in a district that does not have jurisdiction to conduct a revocation hearing, the magistrate judge must:

(A) if the alleged violation occurred in the district of arrest, conduct a preliminary hearing under Rule 32.1(b) and either:

(i) transfer the person to the district that has jurisdiction, if the judge finds probable cause to believe that a violation occurred; or

(ii) dismiss the proceedings and so notify the court that has jurisdiction, if the judge finds no probable cause to believe that a violation occurred; or

(B) if the alleged violation did not occur in the district of arrest, transfer the person to the district that has jurisdiction if:

(i) the government produces certified copies of the judgment, warrant, and warrant application; and

(ii) the judge finds that the person is the same person named in the warrant.

(6) *Release or Detention.* The magistrate judge may release or detain the person under 18 U.S.C. § 3143(a) pending further proceedings. The burden of establishing that the person will not flee or pose a danger to any other person or to the community rests with the person.

(b) Revocation.

(1) *Preliminary Hearing.*

(A) *In General.* If a person is in custody for violating a condition of probation or supervised release, a magistrate judge must promptly conduct a hearing to determine whether there is probable cause to believe that a violation occurred. The person may waive the hearing.

(B) *Requirements.* The hearing must be recorded by a court reporter or by a suitable recording device. The judge must give the person:

(i) notice of the hearing and its purpose, the alleged violation, and the person's right to retain counsel or to request that counsel be appointed if the person cannot obtain counsel;

(ii) an opportunity to appear at the hearing and present evidence; and

(iii) upon request, an opportunity to question any adverse witness, unless the judge determines that the interest of justice does not require the witness to appear.

(C) *Referral.* If the judge finds probable cause, the judge must conduct a revocation hearing. If the judge does not find probable cause, the judge must dismiss the proceeding.

(2) *Revocation Hearing.* Unless waived by the person, the court must hold the revocation hearing within a reasonable time in the district having jurisdiction. The person is entitled to:

(A) written notice of the alleged violation;

(B) disclosure of the evidence against the person;

(C) an opportunity to appear, present evidence, and question any adverse witness unless the court determines that the interest of justice does not require the witness to appear; and

(D) notice of the person's right to retain counsel or to request that counsel be appointed if the person cannot obtain counsel.

(c) Modification.

(1) *In General.* Before modifying the conditions of probation or supervised release, the court must hold a hearing, at which the person has the right to counsel.

(2) *Exceptions.* A hearing is not required if:

(A) the person waives the hearing; or

(B) the relief sought is favorable to the person and does not extend the term of probation or of supervised release; and

(C) an attorney for the government has received notice of the relief sought, has had a reasonable opportunity to object, and has not done so.

(d) Disposition of the Case. The court's disposition of the case is governed by 18 U.S.C. § 3563 and § 3565 (probation) and § 3583 (supervised release).

(e) Producing a Statement. Rule 26.2(a)–(d) and (f) applies at a hearing under this rule. If a party fails to comply with a Rule 26.2 order to produce a witness's statement, the court must not consider that witness's testimony.

Rule 32.2. Criminal Forfeiture

(a) Notice to the Defendant. A court must not enter a judgment of forfeiture in a criminal proceeding unless the indictment or information contains notice to the defendant that the government will seek the forfeiture of property as part of any sentence in accordance with the applicable statute.

(b) Entering a Preliminary Order of Forfeiture.

(1) *In General.* As soon as practicable after a verdict or finding of guilty, or after a plea of guilty or nolo contendere is accepted, on any count in an indictment or information regarding which criminal forfeiture is sought, the court must determine what property is subject to forfeiture under the applicable statute. If the government seeks forfeiture of specific property, the court must determine whether the government has established the requisite nexus between the property and the offense. If the government seeks a personal money judgment, the court must determine the amount of money that the defendant will be ordered to pay. The court's determination may be based on evidence already in the record, including any written plea agreement or, if the forfeiture is contested, on evidence or information presented by the parties at a hearing after the verdict or finding of guilt.

(2) *Preliminary Order.* If the court finds that property is subject to forfeiture, it must promptly enter a preliminary order of forfeiture setting forth the amount of any money judgment or directing the forfeiture of specific property without regard to any third party's interest in all or part of it. Determining whether a third party has such an interest must be deferred until any third party files a claim in an ancillary proceeding under Rule 32.2(c).

(3) *Seizing Property.* The entry of a preliminary order of forfeiture authorizes the Attorney General (or a designee) to seize the specific property subject to forfeiture; to conduct any discovery the court considers proper in identifying, locating, or disposing of the property; and to commence proceedings that comply with any statutes governing third-party rights. At sentencing—or at any time before sentencing if the defendant consents—the order of forfeiture becomes final as to the defendant and must be made a part of the sentence and be included in the judgment. The court may include in the order of forfeiture conditions reasonably necessary to preserve the property's value pending any appeal.

(4) *Jury Determination.* Upon a party's request in a case in which a jury returns a verdict of guilty, the jury must determine whether the government has established the requisite nexus between the property and the offense committed by the defendant.

(c) Ancillary Proceeding; Entering a Final Order of Forfeiture.

(1) *In General.* If, as prescribed by statute, a third party files a petition asserting an interest in the property to be forfeited, the court must conduct an ancillary proceeding, but no ancillary proceeding is required to the extent that the forfeiture consists of a money judgment.

(A) In the ancillary proceeding, the court may, on motion, dismiss the petition for lack of standing, for failure to state a claim, or for any other lawful reason. For purposes of the motion, the facts set forth in the petition are assumed to be true.

(B) After disposing of any motion filed under Rule 32.2(c)(1)(A) and before conducting a hearing on the petition, the court may permit the parties to conduct discovery in accordance with the Federal Rules of Civil Procedure if the court determines that discovery is necessary or desirable to resolve factual issues. When discovery ends, a party may move for summary judgment under Federal Rule of Civil Procedure 56.

(2) *Entering a Final Order.* When the ancillary proceeding ends, the court must enter a final order of forfeiture by amending the preliminary order as necessary to account for any third-party rights. If no third party files a timely petition, the preliminary order becomes the final order of forfeiture if the court finds that the defendant (or any combination of defendants convicted in the case) had an interest in the property that is forfeitable under the applicable statute. The defendant may not object to the entry of the final order on the ground that the property belongs, in whole or in part, to a codefendant or third party; nor may a third party object to the final order on the ground that the third party had an interest in the property.

(3) *Multiple Petitions.* If multiple third-party petitions are filed in the same case, an order dismissing or granting one petition is not appealable until rulings are made on all the petitions, unless the court determines that there is no just reason for delay.

(4) *Ancillary Proceeding Not Part of Sentencing.* An ancillary proceeding is not part of sentencing.

(d) Stay Pending Appeal. If a defendant appeals from a conviction or an order of forfeiture, the court may stay the order of forfeiture on terms appropriate to ensure that the property remains available pending appellate review. A stay does not delay the ancillary proceeding or the determination of a third party's rights or interests. If the court rules in favor of any third party while an appeal is pending, the court may amend the order of forfeiture but must not transfer any property interest to a third party until the decision on appeal becomes final, unless the defendant consents in writing or on the record.

(e) Subsequently Located Property; Substitute Property.

(1) *In General.* On the government's motion, the court may at any time enter an order of forfeiture or amend an existing order of forfeiture to include property that:

(A) is subject to forfeiture under an existing order of forfeiture but was located and identified after that order was entered; or

(B) is substitute property that qualifies for forfeiture under an applicable statute.

(2) *Procedure.* If the government shows that the property is subject to forfeiture under Rule 32.2(e)(1), the court must:

(A) enter an order forfeiting that property, or amend an existing preliminary or final order to include it; and

(B) if a third party files a petition claiming an interest in the property, conduct an ancillary proceeding under Rule 32.2(c).

(3) *Jury Trial Limited.* There is no right to a jury trial under Rule 32.2(e).

Rule 33. New Trial

(a) Defendant's Motion. Upon the defendant's motion, the court may vacate any judgment and grant a new trial if the interest of justice so requires. If the case was tried without a jury, the court may take additional testimony and enter a new judgment.

(b) Time to File.

(1) *Newly Discovered Evidence.* Any motion for a new trial grounded on newly discovered evidence must be filed within 3 years after the verdict or finding of guilty. If an appeal is pending, the court may not grant a motion for a new trial until the appellate court remands the case.

(2) *Other Grounds.* Any motion for a new trial grounded on any reason other than newly discovered evidence must be filed within 7 days after the verdict or finding of guilty, or within such further time as the court sets during the 7–day period.

Rule 34. Arresting Judgment

(a) In General. Upon the defendant's motion or on its own, the court must arrest judgment if:

(1) the indictment or information does not charge an offense; or

(2) the court does not have jurisdiction of the charged offense.

(b) Time to File. The defendant must move to arrest judgment within 7 days after the court accepts a verdict or finding of guilty, or after a plea of guilty or nolo contendere, or within such further time as the court sets during the 7–day period.

Rule 35. Correcting or Reducing a Sentence

(a) Correcting Clear Error. Within 7 days after sentencing, the court may correct a sentence that resulted from arithmetical, technical, or other clear error.

(b) Reducing a Sentence for Substantial Assistance.

(1) *In General.* Upon the government's motion made within one year of sentencing, the court may reduce a sentence if:

(A) the defendant, after sentencing, provided substantial assistance in investigating or prosecuting another person; and

(B) reducing the sentence accords with the Sentencing Commission's guidelines and policy statements.

(2) *Later Motion.* Upon the government's motion made more than one year after sentencing, the court may reduce a sentence if the defendant's substantial assistance involved:

information not known to the defendant until one year or more after sentencing;

information provided by the defendant to the government within one year of sentencing, but which did not become useful to the government until more than one year after sentencing; or

information the usefulness of which could not reasonably have been anticipated by the defendant until more than one year after sentencing and which was promptly provided to the government after its usefulness was reasonably apparent to the defendant.

(3) *Evaluating Substantial Assistance.* In evaluating whether the defendant has provided substantial assistance, the court may consider the defendant's presentence assistance.

(4) *Below Statutory Minimum.* When acting under Rule 35(b), the court may reduce the sentence to a level below the minimum sentence established by statute.

Rule 36.   Clerical Error

After giving any notice it considers appropriate, the court may at any time correct a clerical error in a judgment, order, or other part of the record, or correct an error in the record arising from oversight or omission.

Rule 37.   [Reserved]

Rule 38.   Staying a Sentence or a Disability

(a) Death Sentence. The court must stay a death sentence if the defendant appeals the conviction or sentence.

(b) Imprisonment.

(1) *Stay Granted.* If the defendant is released pending appeal, the court must stay a sentence of imprisonment.

(2) *Stay Denied; Place of Confinement.* If the defendant is not released pending appeal, the court may recommend to the Attorney General that the defendant be confined near the place of the trial or appeal for a period reasonably necessary to permit the defendant to assist in preparing the appeal.

(c) Fine. If the defendant appeals, the district court, or the court of appeals under Federal Rule of Appellate Procedure 8, may stay a sentence to pay a fine or a fine and costs. The court may stay the sentence on any terms considered appropriate and may require the defendant to:

(1) deposit all or part of the fine and costs into the district court's registry pending appeal;

(2) post a bond to pay the fine and costs; or

(3) submit to an examination concerning the defendant's assets and, if appropriate, order the defendant to refrain from dissipating assets.

(d) Probation. If the defendant appeals, the court may stay a sentence of probation. The court must set the terms of any stay.

(e) Restitution and Notice to Victims.

(1) *In General.* If the defendant appeals, the district court, or the court of appeals under Federal Rule of Appellate Procedure 8, may stay—on any terms considered appropriate—any sentence providing for restitution under 18 U.S.C. § 3556 or notice under 18 U.S.C. § 3555.

(2) *Ensuring Compliance.* The court may issue any order reasonably necessary to ensure compliance with a restitution order or a notice order after disposition of an appeal, including:

(A) a restraining order;

(B) an injunction;

(C) an order requiring the defendant to deposit all or part of any monetary restitution into the district court's registry; or

(D) an order requiring the defendant to post a bond.

(f) Forfeiture. A stay of a forfeiture order is governed by Rule 32.2(d).

(g) Disability. If the defendant's conviction or sentence creates a civil or employment disability under federal law, the district court, or the court of appeals under Federal Rule of Appellate Procedure 8, may stay the disability pending appeal on any terms considered appropriate. The court may issue any order reasonably necessary to protect the interest represented by the disability pending appeal, including a restraining order or an injunction.

Rule 39.   [Reserved]

TITLE VIII.   SUPPLEMENTARY AND SPECIAL PROCEEDINGS

Rule 40.   Arrest for Failing to Appear in Another District

(a) In General. If a person is arrested under a warrant issued in another district for failing to appear—as required by the terms of that person's release under 18 U.S.C. §§ 3141–3156 or by a subpoena—the person must be taken without unnecessary delay before a magistrate judge in the district of the arrest.

(b) Proceedings. The judge must proceed under Rule 5(c)(3) as applicable.

(c) Release or Detention Order. The judge may modify any previous release or detention order issued in another district, but must state in writing the reasons for doing so.

Rule 41.   Search and Seizure

(a) Scope and Definitions.

(1) *Scope.* This rule does not modify any statute regulating search or seizure, or the issuance and execution of a search warrant in special circumstances.

(2) *Definitions.* The following definitions apply under this rule:

(A) "Property" includes documents, books, papers, any other tangible objects, and information.

(B) "Daytime" means the hours between 6:00 a.m. and 10:00 p.m. according to local time.

(C) "Federal law enforcement officer" means a government agent (other than an attorney for the government) who is engaged in enforcing the criminal laws and is within any category of officers authorized by the Attorney General to request a search warrant.

(b) Authority to Issue a Warrant. At the request of a federal law enforcement officer or an attorney for the government:

a magistrate judge with authority in the district—or if none is reasonably available, a judge of a state court of record in the district—has authority to issue a warrant to search for and seize a person or property located within the district;

a magistrate judge with authority in the district has authority to issue a warrant for a person or property outside the district if the person or property is located within the district when the warrant is issued but might move or be moved outside the district before the warrant is executed; and

a magistrate judge—in an investigation of domestic terrorism or international terrorism (as defined in 18 U.S.C. § 2331) having authority in any district in which activities related to the terrorism may have occurred, may issue a warrant for a person or property within or outside that district.

(c) Persons or Property Subject to Search or Seizure. A warrant may be issued for any of the following:

(1) evidence of a crime;

(2) contraband, fruits of crime, or other items illegally possessed;

(3) property designed for use, intended for use, or used in committing a crime; or

(4) a person to be arrested or a person who is unlawfully restrained.

(d) Obtaining a Warrant.

(1) *Probable Cause.* After receiving an affidavit or other information, a magistrate judge or a judge of a state court of record must issue the warrant if there is probable cause to search for and seize a person or property under Rule 41(c).

(2) *Requesting a Warrant in the Presence of a Judge.*

(A) *Warrant on an Affidavit.* When a federal law enforcement officer or an attorney for the government presents an affidavit in support of a warrant, the judge may require the affiant to appear personally and may examine under oath the affiant and any witness the affiant produces.

(B) *Warrant on Sworn Testimony.* The judge may wholly or partially dispense with a written affidavit and base a warrant on sworn testimony if doing so is reasonable under the circumstances.

(C) *Recording Testimony.* Testimony taken in support of a warrant must be recorded by a court reporter or by a suitable recording device, and the judge must file the transcript or recording with the clerk, along with any affidavit.

(3) *Requesting a Warrant by Telephonic or Other Means.*

(A) *In General.* A magistrate judge may issue a warrant based on information communicated by telephone or other appropriate means, including facsimile transmission.

(B) *Recording Testimony.* Upon learning that an applicant is requesting a warrant, a magistrate judge must:

    (i) place under oath the applicant and any person on whose testimony the application is based; and

    (ii) make a verbatim record of the conversation with a suitable recording device, if available, or by a court reporter, or in writing.

(C) *Certifying Testimony.* The magistrate judge must have any recording or court reporter's notes transcribed, certify the transcription's accuracy, and file a copy of the record and the transcription with the clerk. Any written verbatim record must be signed by the magistrate judge and filed with the clerk.

(D) *Suppression Limited.* Absent a finding of bad faith, evidence obtained from a warrant issued under Rule 41(d)(3)(A) is not subject to suppression on the ground that issuing the warrant in that manner was unreasonable under the circumstances.

(e) Issuing the Warrant.

(1) *In General.* The magistrate judge or a judge of a state court of record must issue the warrant to an officer authorized to execute it.

(2) *Contents of the Warrant.* The warrant must identify the person or property to be searched, identify any person or property to be seized, and designate the magistrate judge to whom it must be returned. The warrant must command the officer to:

    (A) execute the warrant within a specified time no longer than 10 days;

    (B) execute the warrant during the daytime, unless the judge for good cause expressly authorizes execution at another time; and

    (C) return the warrant to the magistrate judge designated in the warrant.

(3) *Warrant by Telephonic or Other Means*. If a magistrate judge decides to proceed under Rule 41(d)(3)(A), the following additional procedures apply:

    (A) *Preparing a Proposed Duplicate Original Warrant.* The applicant must prepare a "proposed duplicate original warrant" and must read or otherwise transmit the contents of that document verbatim to the magistrate judge.

    (B) *Preparing an Original Warrant.* The magistrate judge must enter the contents of the proposed duplicate original warrant into an original warrant.

    (C) *Modifications.* The magistrate judge may direct the applicant to modify the proposed duplicate original warrant. In that case, the judge must also modify the original warrant.

    (D) *Signing the Original Warrant and the Duplicate Original Warrant.* Upon determining to issue the warrant, the magistrate judge must immediately sign the original warrant, enter on its face the exact time it is issued, and direct the applicant to sign the judge's name on the duplicate original warrant.

(f) Executing and Returning the Warrant.

(1) *Noting the Time.* The officer executing the warrant must enter on its face the exact date and time it is executed.

(2) *Inventory.* An officer present during the execution of the warrant must prepare and verify an inventory of any property seized. The officer must do so in the presence of another officer and the person from whom, or from whose premises, the property was taken. If either one is not present, the officer must prepare and verify the inventory in the presence of at least one other credible person.

(3) *Receipt.* The officer executing the warrant must:

(A) give a copy of the warrant and a receipt for the property taken to the person from whom, or from whose premises, the property was taken; or

(B) leave a copy of the warrant and receipt at the place where the officer took the property.

(4) *Return.* The officer executing the warrant must promptly return it—together with a copy of the inventory—to the magistrate judge designated on the warrant. The judge must, on request, give a copy of the inventory to the person from whom, or from whose premises, the property was taken and to the applicant for the warrant.

(g) Motion to Return Property. A person aggrieved by an unlawful search and seizure of property or by the deprivation of property may move for the property's return. The motion must be filed in the district where the property was seized. The court must receive evidence on any factual issue necessary to decide the motion. If it grants the motion, the court must return the property to the movant, but may impose reasonable conditions to protect access to the property and its use in later proceedings.

(h) Motion to Suppress. A defendant may move to suppress evidence in the court where the trial will occur, as Rule 12 provides.

(i) Forwarding Papers to the Clerk. The magistrate judge to whom the warrant is returned must attach to the warrant a copy of the return, of the inventory, and of all other related papers and must deliver them to the clerk in the district where the property was seized.

Rule 42. Criminal Contempt

(a) Disposition After Notice. Any person who commits criminal contempt may be punished for that contempt after prosecution on notice.

(1) *Notice.* The court must give the person notice in open court, in an order to show cause, or in an arrest order. The notice must:

(A) state the time and place of the trial;

(B) allow the defendant a reasonable time to prepare a defense; and

(C) state the essential facts constituting the charged criminal contempt and describe it as such.

(2) *Appointing a Prosecutor.* The court must request that the contempt be prosecuted by an attorney for the government, unless the interest of justice requires the appointment of another attorney. If the government declines the request, the court must appoint another attorney to prosecute the contempt.

(3) *Trial and Disposition.* A person being prosecuted for criminal contempt is entitled to a jury trial in any case in which federal law so provides and must be released or detained as Rule 46 provides. If the criminal contempt involves disrespect toward or criticism of a judge, that judge is disqualified from presiding at the contempt trial or hearing unless the defendant consents. Upon a finding or verdict of guilty, the court must impose the punishment.

(b) Summary Disposition. Notwithstanding any other provision of these rules, the court (other than a magistrate judge) may summarily punish a person who commits criminal contempt in its presence if the judge saw or heard the contemptuous conduct and so certifies; a magistrate judge may summarily punish a person as provided in 28 U.S.C. § 636(e). The contempt order must recite the facts, be signed by the judge, and be filed with the clerk.

TITLE IX.   GENERAL PROVISIONS

Rule 43.   Defendant's Presence

(a) When Required. Unless this rule, Rule 5, or Rule 10 provides otherwise, the defendant must be present at:

(1) the initial appearance, the initial arraignment, and the plea;

(2) every trial stage, including jury impanelment and the return of the verdict; and

(3) sentencing.

(b) When Not Required. A defendant need not be present under any of the following circumstances:

(1) *Organizational Defendant.* The defendant is an organization represented by counsel who is present.

(2) *Misdemeanor Offense.* The offense is punishable by fine or by imprisonment for not more than one year, or both, and with the defendant's written consent, the court permits arraignment, plea, trial, and sentencing to occur in the defendant's absence.

(3) *Conference or Hearing on a Legal Question.* The proceeding involves only a conference or hearing on a question of law.

(4) *Sentence Correction.* The proceeding involves the correction or reduction of sentence under Rule 35 or 18 U.S.C. § 3582(c).

(c) Waiving Continued Presence.

(1) *In General.* A defendant who was initially present at trial, or who had pleaded guilty or nolo contendere, waives the right to be present under the following circumstances:

(A) when the defendant is voluntarily absent after the trial has begun, regardless of whether the court informed the defendant of an obligation to remain during trial;

(B) in a noncapital case, when the defendant is voluntarily absent during sentencing; or

(C) when the court warns the defendant that it will remove the defendant from the courtroom for disruptive behavior, but the defendant persists in conduct that justifies removal from the courtroom.

(2) *Waiver's Effect.* If the defendant waives the right to be present, the trial may proceed to completion, including the verdict's return and sentencing, during the defendant's absence.

Rule 44. Right to and Appointment of Counsel

(a) Right to Appointed Counsel. A defendant who is unable to obtain counsel is entitled to have counsel appointed to represent the defendant at every stage of the proceeding from initial appearance through appeal, unless the defendant waives this right.

(b) Appointment Procedure. Federal law and local court rules govern the procedure for implementing the right to counsel.

(c) Inquiry Into Joint Representation.

(1) *Joint Representation.* Joint representation occurs when:

(A) two or more defendants have been charged jointly under Rule 8(b) or have been joined for trial under Rule 13; and

(B) the defendants are represented by the same counsel, or counsel who are associated in law practice.

(2) *Court's Responsibilities in Cases of Joint Representation.* The court must promptly inquire about the propriety of joint representation and must personally advise each defendant of the right to the effective assistance of counsel, including separate representation. Unless there is good cause to believe that no conflict of interest is likely to arise, the court must take appropriate measures to protect each defendant's right to counsel.

Rule 45. Computing and Extending Time

(a) Computing Time. The following rules apply in computing any period of time specified in these rules, any local rule, or any court order:

(1) *Day of the Event Excluded.* Exclude the day of the act, event, or default that begins the period.

(2) *Exclusion from Brief Periods.* Exclude intermediate Saturdays, Sundays, and legal holidays when the period is less than 11 days.

(3) *Last Day.* Include the last day of the period unless it is a Saturday, Sunday, legal holiday, or day on which weather or other conditions make the clerk's office inaccessible. When the last day is excluded, the period runs until the end of the next day that is not a Saturday, Sunday, legal holiday, or day when the clerk's office is inaccessible.

(4) *"Legal Holiday" Defined.* As used in this rule, "legal holiday" means:

(A) the day set aside by statute for observing:

(i) New Year's Day;

(ii) Martin Luther King, Jr.'s Birthday;

(iii) Washington's Birthday;

(iv) Memorial Day;

(v) Independence Day;

(vi) Labor Day;

(vii) Columbus Day;

(viii) Veterans' Day;

(ix) Thanksgiving Day;

(x) Christmas Day; and

(B) any other day declared a holiday by the President, the Congress, or the state where the district court is held.

(b) Extending Time.

(1) *In General.* When an act must or may be done within a specified period, the court on its own may extend the time, or for good cause may do so on a party's motion made:

(A) before the originally prescribed or previously extended time expires; or

(B) after the time expires if the party failed to act because of excusable neglect.

(2) *Exceptions.* The court may not extend the time to take any action under Rules 29, 33, 34, and 35, except as stated in those rules.

(c) Additional Time After Service. When these rules permit or require a party to act within a specified period after a notice or a paper has been served on that party, 3 days are added to the period if service occurs in the manner provided under Federal Rule of Civil Procedure 5(b)(2)(B), (C), or (D).

Rule 46. Release from Custody; Supervising Detention

(a) Before Trial. The provisions of 18 U.S.C. §§ 3142 and 3144 govern pretrial release.

(b) During Trial. A person released before trial continues on release during trial under the same terms and conditions. But the court may order different terms and conditions or terminate the release if necessary to ensure that the person will be present during trial or that the person's conduct will not obstruct the orderly and expeditious progress of the trial.

(c) Pending Sentencing or Appeal. The provisions of 18 U.S.C. § 3143 govern release pending sentencing or appeal. The burden of establishing that the defendant will not flee or pose a danger to any other person or to the community rests with the defendant.

(d) Pending Hearing on a Violation of Probation or Supervised Release. Rule 32.1(a)(6) governs release pending a hearing on a violation of probation or supervised release.

(e) Surety. The court must not approve a bond unless any surety appears to be qualified. Every surety, except a legally approved corporate surety, must demonstrate by affidavit that its assets are adequate. The court may require the affidavit to describe the following:

(1) the property that the surety proposes to use as security;

(2) any encumbrance on that property;

(3) the number and amount of any other undischarged bonds and bail undertakings the surety has issued; and

(4) any other liability of the surety.

(f) Bail Forfeiture.

(1) *Declaration.* The court must declare the bail forfeited if a condition of the bond is breached.

(2) *Setting Aside.* The court may set aside in whole or in part a bail forfeiture upon any condition the court may impose if:

    (A) the surety later surrenders into custody the person released on the surety's appearance bond; or

    (B) it appears that justice does not require bail forfeiture.

(3) *Enforcement.*

    (A) *Default Judgment and Execution.* If it does not set aside a bail forfeiture, the court must, upon the government's motion, enter a default judgment.

    (B) *Jurisdiction and Service.* By entering into a bond, each surety submits to the district court's jurisdiction and irrevocably appoints the district clerk as its agent to receive service of any filings affecting its liability.

    (C) *Motion to Enforce.* The court may, upon the government's motion, enforce the surety's liability without an independent action. The government must serve any motion, and notice as the court prescribes, on the district clerk. If so served, the clerk must promptly mail a copy to the surety at its last known address.

(4) *Remission.* After entering a judgment under Rule 46(f)(3), the court may remit in whole or in part the judgment under the same conditions specified in Rule 46(f)(2).

(g) Exoneration. The court must exonerate the surety and release any bail when a bond condition has been satisfied or when the court has set aside or remitted the forfeiture. The court must exonerate a surety who deposits cash in the amount of the bond or timely surrenders the defendant into custody.

(h) Supervising Detention Pending Trial.

(1) *In General.* To eliminate unnecessary detention, the court must supervise the detention within the district of any defendants awaiting trial and of any persons held as material witnesses.

(2) *Reports.* An attorney for the government must report biweekly to the court, listing each material witness held in custody for more than 10 days pending indictment, arraignment, or trial. For each material witness listed in the report, an attorney for the government must state why the witness should not be released with or without a deposition being taken under Rule 15(a).

(i) Forfeiture of Property. The court may dispose of a charged offense by ordering the forfeiture of 18 U.S.C. § 3142(c)(1)(B)(xi) property under 18 U.S.C. § x3146(d), if a fine in the amount of the property's value would be an appropriate sentence for the charged offense.

(j) Producing a Statement.

(1) *In General.* Rule 26.2(a)-(d) and (f) applies at a detention hearing under 18 U.S.C. § 3142, unless the court for good cause rules otherwise.

(2) *Sanctions for Not Producing a Statement.* If a party disobeys a Rule 26.2 order to produce a witness's statement, the court must not consider that witness's testimony at the detention hearing.

Rule 47. Motions and Supporting Affidavits

(a) In General. A party applying to the court for an order must do so by motion.

(b) Form and Content of a Motion. A motion—except when made during a trial or hearing—must be in writing, unless the court permits the party to make the motion by other means. A motion must state the grounds on which it is based and the relief or order sought. A motion may be supported by affidavit.

(c) Timing of a Motion. A party must serve a written motion—other than one that the court may hear ex parte—and any hearing notice at least 5 days before the hearing date, unless a rule or court order sets a different period. For good cause, the court may set a different period upon ex parte application.

(d) Affidavit Supporting a Motion. The moving party must serve any supporting affidavit with the motion. A responding party must serve any opposing affidavit at least one day before the hearing, unless the court permits later service.

Rule 48. Dismissal

(a) By the Government. The government may, with leave of court, dismiss an indictment, information, or complaint. The government may not dismiss the prosecution during trial without the defendant's consent.

(b) By the Court. The court may dismiss an indictment, information, or complaint if unnecessary delay occurs in:

(1) presenting a charge to a grand jury;

(2) filing an information against a defendant; or

(3) bringing a defendant to trial.

Rule 49. Serving and Filing Papers

(a) When Required. A party must serve on every other party any written motion (other than one to be heard ex parte), written notice, designation of the record on appeal, or similar paper.

(b) How Made. Service must be made in the manner provided for a civil action. When these rules or a court order requires or permits service on a party represented by an attorney, service must be made on the attorney instead of the party, unless the court orders otherwise.

(c) Notice of a Court Order. When the court issues an order on any post-arraignment motion, the clerk must provide notice in a manner provided for in a civil action. Except as Federal Rule of Appellate Procedure 4(b) provides otherwise, the clerk's failure to give notice does not affect the time to appeal, or relieve—or authorize the court to relieve—a party's failure to appeal within the allowed time.

(d) Filing. A party must file with the court a copy of any paper the party is required to serve. A paper must be filed in a manner provided for in a civil action.

Rule 50. Prompt Disposition

Scheduling preference must be given to criminal proceedings as far as practicable.

Rule 51. Preserving Claimed Error

(a) Exceptions Unnecessary. Exceptions to rulings or orders of the court are unnecessary.

(b) Preserving a Claim of Error. A party may preserve a claim of error by informing the court—when the court ruling or order is made or sought—of the action the party wishes the court to take, or the party's objection to the court's action and the grounds for that objection. If a party does not have an opportunity to object to a ruling or order, the absence of an objection does not later prejudice that party. A ruling or order that admits or excludes evidence is governed by Federal Rule of Evidence 103.

Rule 52.   Harmless and Plain Error

(a) Harmless Error. Any error, defect, irregularity, or variance that does not affect substantial rights must be disregarded.

(b) Plain Error. A plain error that affects substantial rights may be considered even though it was not brought to the court's attention.

Rule 53.   Courtroom Photographing and Broadcasting Prohibited

Except as otherwise provided by a statute or these rules, the court must not permit the taking of photographs in the courtroom during judicial proceedings or the broadcasting of judicial proceedings from the courtroom.

Rule 54.   [Transferred]

[Editor's Note: All of Rule 54 was moved to Rule 1]

Rule 55.   Records

The clerk of the district court must keep records of criminal proceedings in the form prescribed by the Director of the Administrative Office of the United States Courts. The clerk must enter in the records every court order or judgment and the date of entry.

Rule 56.   When Court Is Open

(a) In General. A district court is considered always open for any filing, and for issuing and returning process, making a motion, or entering an order.

(b) Office Hours. The clerk's office—with the clerk or a deputy in attendance—must be open during business hours on all days except Saturdays, Sundays, and legal holidays.

(c) Special Hours. A court may provide by local rule or order that its clerk's office will be open for specified hours on Saturdays or legal holidays other than those set aside by statute for observing New Year's Day, Martin Luther King, Jr.'s Birthday, Washington's Birthday, Memorial Day, Independence Day, Labor Day, Columbus Day, Veterans' Day, Thanksgiving Day, and Christmas Day.

Rule 57.   District Court Rules

(a) In General.

(1) *Adopting Local Rules.* Each district court acting by a majority of its district judges may, after giving appropriate public notice and an opportunity to comment, make and amend rules governing its practice. A local rule must be consistent with—but not duplicative of—federal statutes and rules adopted under 28 U.S.C. § 2072 and must conform to any uniform numbering system prescribed by the Judicial Conference of the United States.

(2) *Limiting Enforcement.* A local rule imposing a requirement of form must not be enforced in a manner that causes a party to lose rights because of an unintentional failure to comply with the requirement.

(b) Procedure When There Is No Controlling Law. A judge may regulate practice in any manner consistent with federal law, these rules, and the local rules of the district. No sanction or other disadvantage may be imposed for noncompliance with any requirement not in federal law, federal rules, or the local district rules unless the alleged violator was furnished with actual notice of the requirement before the noncompliance.

(c) Effective Date and Notice. A local rule adopted under this rule takes effect on the date specified by the district court and remains in effect unless amended by the district court or abrogated by the judicial council of the circuit in which the district is located. Copies of local rules and their amendments, when promulgated, must be furnished to the judicial council and the Administrative Office of the United States Courts and must be made available to the public.

Rule 58. Petty Offenses and Other Misdemeanors

(a) Scope.

(1) *In General.* These rules apply in petty offense and other misdemeanor cases and on appeal to a district judge in a case tried by a magistrate judge, unless this rule provides otherwise.

(2) *Petty Offense Case Without Imprisonment.* In a case involving a petty offense for which no sentence of imprisonment will be imposed, the court may follow any provision of these rules that is not inconsistent with this rule and that the court considers appropriate.

(3) *Definition.* As used in this rule, the term "petty offense for which no sentence of imprisonment will be imposed" means a petty offense for which the court determines that, in the event of conviction, no sentence of imprisonment will be imposed.

(b) Pretrial Procedure.

(1) *Charging Document.* The trial of a misdemeanor may proceed on an indictment, information, or complaint. The trial of a petty offense may also proceed on a citation or violation notice.

(2) *Initial Appearance.* At the defendant's initial appearance on a petty offense or other misdemeanor charge, the magistrate judge must inform the defendant of the following:

(A) the charge, and the minimum and maximum penalties, including imprisonment, fines, any special assessment under 18 U.S.C. § 3013, and restitution under 18 U.S.C. § 3556;

(B) the right to retain counsel;

(C) the right to request the appointment of counsel if the defendant is unable to retain counsel—unless the charge is a petty offense for which the appointment of counsel is not required;

(D) the defendant's right not to make a statement, and that any statement made may be used against the defendant;

(E) the right to trial, judgment, and sentencing before a district judge—unless:

(i) the charge is a petty offense; or

(ii) the defendant consents to trial, judgment, and sentencing before a magistrate judge;

the right to a jury trial before either a magistrate judge or a district judge—unless the charge is a petty offense; and

if the defendant is held in custody and charged with a misdemeanor other than a petty offense, the right to a preliminary hearing under Rule 5.1, and the general circumstances, if any, under which the defendant may secure pretrial release.

(3) *Arraignment.*

(A) *Plea Before a Magistrate Judge.* A magistrate judge may take the defendant's plea in a petty offense case. In every other misdemeanor case, a magistrate judge may take the plea only if the defendant consents either in writing or on the record to be tried before a magistrate judge and specifically waives trial before a district judge. The defendant may plead not guilty, guilty, or (with the consent of the magistrate judge) nolo contendere.

(B) *Failure to Consent.* Except in a petty offense case, the magistrate judge must order a defendant who does not consent to trial before a magistrate judge to appear before a district judge for further proceedings.

(c) Additional Procedures in Certain Petty Offense Cases. The following procedures also apply in a case involving a petty offense for which no sentence of imprisonment will be imposed:

(1) *Guilty or Nolo Contendere Plea.* The court must not accept a guilty or nolo contendere plea unless satisfied that the defendant understands the nature of the charge and the maximum possible penalty.

(2) *Waiving Venue.*

(A) *Conditions of Waiving Venue.* If a defendant is arrested, held, or present in a district different from the one where the indictment, information, complaint, citation, or violation notice is pending, the defendant may state in writing a desire to plead guilty or nolo contendere; to waive venue and trial in the district where the proceeding is pending; and to consent to the court's disposing of the case in the district where the defendant was arrested, is held, or is present.

(B) *Effect of Waiving Venue.* Unless the defendant later pleads not guilty, the prosecution will proceed in the district where the defendant was arrested, is held, or is present. The district clerk must notify the clerk in the original district of the defendant's waiver of venue. The defendant's statement of a desire to plead guilty or nolo contendere is not admissible against the defendant.

(3) *Sentencing.* The court must give the defendant an opportunity to be heard in mitigation and then proceed immediately to sentencing. The court may, however, postpone sentencing to allow the probation service to investigate or to permit either party to submit additional information.

(4) *Notice of a Right to Appeal.* After imposing sentence in a case tried on a not-guilty plea, the court must advise the defendant of a right to appeal the conviction and of any right to appeal the sentence. If the defendant was convicted on a plea of guilty or nolo contendere, the court must advise the defendant of any right to appeal the sentence.

(d) Paying a Fixed Sum in Lieu of Appearance.

(1) *In General.* If the court has a local rule governing forfeiture of collateral, the court may accept a fixed-sum payment in lieu of the defendant's appearance and end the case, but the fixed sum may not exceed the maximum fine allowed by law.

(2) *Notice to Appear.* If the defendant fails to pay a fixed sum, request a hearing, or appear in response to a citation or violation notice, the district clerk or a magistrate judge may issue a notice for the defendant to appear before the court on a date certain. The notice may give the defendant an additional opportunity to pay a fixed sum in lieu of appearance. The district clerk must serve the notice on the defendant by mailing a copy to the defendant's last known address.

(3) *Summons or Warrant.* Upon an indictment, or upon a showing by one of the other charging documents specified in Rule 58(b)(1) of probable cause to believe that an offense has been committed and that the defendant has committed it, the court may issue an arrest warrant or, if no warrant is requested by an attorney for the government, a summons. The showing of probable cause must be made under oath or under penalty of perjury, but the affiant need not appear before the court. If the defendant fails to appear before the court in response to a summons, the court may summarily issue a warrant for the defendant's arrest.

(e) Recording the Proceedings.
The court must record any proceedings under this rule by using a court reporter or a suitable recording device.

(f) New Trial.
Rule 33 applies to a motion for a new trial.

(g) Appeal.

(1) *From a District Judge's Order or Judgment.* The Federal Rules of Appellate Procedure govern an appeal from a district judge's order or a judgment of conviction or sentence.

(2) *From a Magistrate Judge's Order or Judgment.*

(A) *Interlocutory Appeal.* Either party may appeal an order of a magistrate judge to a district judge within 10 days of its entry if a district judge's order could similarly be appealed. The party appealing must file a notice with the clerk specifying the order being appealed and must serve a copy on the adverse party.

(B) *Appeal from a Conviction or Sentence.* A defendant may appeal a magistrate judge's judgment of conviction or sentence to a district judge within 10 days of its entry. To appeal, the defendant must file a notice with the clerk specifying the judgment being appealed and must serve a copy on an attorney for the government.

(C) *Record.* The record consists of the original papers and exhibits in the case; any transcript, tape, or other recording of the proceedings; and a certified copy of the docket entries. For purposes of the appeal, a copy of the record of the proceedings must be made available to a defendant who establishes by affidavit an inability to pay or give security for the record. The Director of the Administrative Office of the United States Courts must pay for those copies.

(D) *Scope of Appeal.* The defendant is not entitled to a trial de novo by a district judge. The scope of the appeal is the same as in an appeal to the court of appeals from a judgment entered by a district judge.

(3) *Stay of Execution and Release Pending Appeal.* Rule 38 applies to a stay of a judgment of conviction or sentence. The court may release the defendant pending appeal under the law relating to release pending appeal from a district court to a court of appeals.

Rule 59. [Deleted]

Rule 60. Title

These rules may be known and cited as the Federal Rules of Criminal Procedure.

*

Part IV

PROVISIONS OF THE USA PATRIOT ACT THAT AFFECT SUBJECT MATTER DISCUSSED IN THE CASEBOOK

Editor's Note:

After the terrorist attack on September 11, 2001, Congress passed an act entitled "Uniting and Strengthening America by Providing Appropriate Tools Required to Intercept and Obstruct Terrorism." Known as the USA PATRIOT Act, the legislation contains a number of provisions that affect the subject matter addressed in the Casebook—especially the law covering warrants and grand jury secrecy. The pertinent provisions of the USA PATRIOT Act are set forth below:

PL 107–56 (HR 3162)

October 26, 2001

115 STAT. 272

An Act To deter and punish terrorist acts in the United States and around the world, to enhance law enforcement investigatory tools, and for other purposes.

Be it enacted by the Senate and House of Representatives of the United States of America in Congress assembled,

SECTION 1. SHORT TITLE AND TABLE OF CONTENTS.

(a) SHORT TITLE.—This Act may be cited as the "Uniting and Strengthening America by Providing Appropriate Tools Required to Intercept and Obstruct Terrorism (USA PATRIOT ACT) Act of 2001".

* * *

SEC. 203. AUTHORITY TO SHARE CRIMINAL INVESTIGATIVE INFORMATION.

(a) AUTHORITY TO SHARE GRAND JURY INFORMATION.—

(1) IN GENERAL.—Rule 6(e)(3)(C) of the Federal Rules of Criminal Procedure is amended to read as follows:

443

"(C)(i) Disclosure otherwise prohibited by this rule of matters occurring before the grand jury may also be made—

"(I) when so directed by a court preliminarily to or in connection with a judicial proceeding;

"(II) when permitted by a court at the request of the defendant, upon a showing that grounds may exist for a motion to dismiss the indictment because of matters occurring before the grand jury;

"(III) when the disclosure is made by an attorney for the government to another Federal grand jury;

"(IV) when permitted by a court at the request of an attorney for the government, upon a showing that such matters may disclose a violation of State criminal law, to an appropriate official of a State or subdivision of a State for the purpose of enforcing such law; or

"(V) when the matters involve foreign intelligence or counterintelligence (as defined in section 3 of the National Security Act of 1947 (50 U.S.C. 401a)), or foreign intelligence information (as defined in clause (iv) of this subparagraph), to any Federal law enforcement, intelligence, protective, immigration, national defense, or national security official in order to assist the official receiving that information in the performance of his official duties.

"(ii) If the court orders disclosure of matters occurring before the grand jury, the disclosure shall be made in such manner, at such time, and under such conditions as the court may direct.

"(iii) Any Federal official to whom information is disclosed pursuant to clause (i)(V) of this subparagraph may use that information only as necessary in the conduct of that person's official duties subject to any limitations on the unauthorized disclosure of such information. Within a reasonable time after such disclosure, an attorney for the government shall file under seal a notice with the court stating the fact that such information was disclosed and the departments, agencies, or entities to which the disclosure was made.

"(iv) In clause (i)(V) of this subparagraph, the term 'foreign intelligence information' means—

"(I) information, whether or not concerning a United States person, that relates to the ability of the United States to protect against—

"(aa) actual or potential attack or other grave hostile acts of a foreign power or an agent of a foreign power;

"(bb) sabotage or international terrorism by a foreign power or an agent of a foreign power; or

"(cc) clandestine intelligence activities by an intelligence service or network of a foreign power or by an agent of foreign power; or

"(II) information, whether or not concerning a United States person, with respect to a foreign power or foreign territory that relates to—

"(aa) the national defense or the security of the United States; or

"(bb) the conduct of the foreign affairs of the United States.".

(2) CONFORMING AMENDMENT.—Rule 6(e)(3)(D) of the Federal Rules of Criminal Procedure is amended by striking "(e)(3)(C)(i)" and inserting "(e) (3)(C)(i)(I)".

(b) AUTHORITY TO SHARE ELECTRONIC, WIRE, AND ORAL INTERCEPTION INFORMATION.—

(1) LAW ENFORCEMENT.—Section 2517 of title 18, United States Code, is amended by inserting at the end the following:

"(6) Any investigative or law enforcement officer, or attorney for the Government, who by any means authorized by this chapter, has obtained knowledge of the contents of any wire, oral, or electronic communication, or evidence derived therefrom, may disclose such contents to any other Federal law enforcement, intelligence, protective, immigration, national defense, or national security official to the extent that such contents include foreign intelligence or counterintelligence (as defined in section 3 of the National Security Act of 1947 (50 U.S.C. 401a)), or foreign intelligence information (as defined in subsection (19) of section 2510 of this title), to assist the official who is to receive that information in the performance of his official duties. Any Federal official who receives information pursuant to this provision may use that information only as necessary in the conduct of that person's official duties subject to any limitations on the unauthorized disclosure of such information.".

(2) DEFINITION.—Section 2510 of title 18, United States Code, is amended by * * * inserting at the end the following:

"(19) 'foreign intelligence information' means—

"(A) information, whether or not concerning a United States person, that relates to the ability of the United States to protect against—

"(i) actual or potential attack or other grave hostile acts of a foreign power or an agent of a foreign power;

"(ii) sabotage or international terrorism by a foreign power or an agent of a foreign power; or

"(iii) clandestine intelligence activities by an intelligence service or network of a foreign power or by an agent of a foreign power; or

"(B) information, whether or not concerning a United States person, with respect to a foreign power or foreign territory that relates to—

"(i) the national defense or the security of the United States; or

"(ii) the conduct of the foreign affairs of the United States.".

(c) PROCEDURES.—The Attorney General shall establish procedures for the disclosure of information pursuant to section 2517(6) and Rule 6(e)(3)(C)(i)(V) of the Federal Rules of Criminal Procedure that identifies a United States person, as defined in section 101 of the Foreign Intelligence Surveillance Act of 1978 (50 U.S.C. 1801)).

(d) FOREIGN INTELLIGENCE INFORMATION.—

(1) IN GENERAL.—Notwithstanding any other provision of law, it shall be lawful for foreign intelligence or counterintelligence (as defined in section 3 of the National Security Act of 1947 (50 U.S.C. 401a)) or foreign intelligence information obtained as part of a criminal investigation to be disclosed to any Federal law enforcement, intelligence, protective, immigration, national defense, or national security official in order to assist the official receiving that information in the performance of his official duties. Any Federal official who receives information pursuant to this provision may use that information only as necessary in the conduct of that person's official duties subject to any limitations on the unauthorized disclosure of such information.

(2) DEFINITION.—In this subsection, the term "foreign intelligence information" means—

(A) information, whether or not concerning a United States person, that relates to the ability of the United States to protect against—

(i) actual or potential attack or other grave hostile acts of a foreign power or an agent of a foreign power;

(ii) sabotage or international terrorism by a foreign power or an agent of a foreign power; or

(iii) clandestine intelligence activities by an intelligence service or network of a foreign power or by an agent of a foreign power; or

(B) information, whether or not concerning a United States person, with respect to a foreign power or foreign territory that relates to—

(i) the national defense or the security of the United States; or

(ii) the conduct of the foreign affairs of the United States.

[Editor's Note: The changes permitting a new exception to grand jury secrecy for terrorism cases have already been incorporated into the restylized Rule 6 of the Federal Rules of Criminal Procedure, set forth above. That Rule went into effect December 1, 2002.]

* * *

SEC. 204. CLARIFICATION OF INTELLIGENCE EXCEPTIONS FROM LIMITATIONS ON INTERCEPTION AND DISCLOSURE OF WIRE, ORAL, AND ELECTRONIC COMMUNICATIONS.

Section 2511(2)(f) of title 18, United States Code, is amended—

(1) by striking "this chapter or chapter 121" and inserting "this chapter or chapter 121 or 206 of this title"; and

(2) by striking "wire and oral" and inserting "wire, oral, and electronic".

[Editor's Note: This provision has the effect of expanding the Title III exception for foreign intelligence surveillance to permit interception of all electronic transmissions.]

* * *

SEC. 207. DURATION OF FISA SURVEILLANCE OF NON-UNITED STATES PERSONS WHO ARE AGENTS OF A FOREIGN POWER.

[This section amends the Foreign Intelligence Surveillance Act, discussed in the Casebook at page 440, n. 46, to provide for longer authorization and more liberal extension of orders permitting electronic surveillance.]

* * *

SEC. 209. SEIZURE OF VOICE–MAIL MESSAGES PURSUANT TO WARRANTS.

Title 18, United States Code, is amended—

(1) in section 2510—

(A) in paragraph (1), by striking beginning with "and such" and all that follows through "communication"; and

(B) in paragraph (14), by inserting "wire or" after "transmission of"; and

(2) in subsections (a) and (b) of section 2703—

(A) by striking "CONTENTS OF ELECTRONIC" and inserting "CONTENTS OF WIRE OR ELECTRONIC" each place it appears;

(B) by striking "contents of an electronic" and inserting "contents of a wire or electronic" each place it appears; and

(C) by striking "any electronic" and inserting "any wire or electronic" each place it appears.

[Editor's Note: These changes basically clarify that the provisions of Title III, authorizing seizure of electronic communications pursuant to a warrant, permit seizure of voicemail].

* * *

SEC. 213. AUTHORITY FOR DELAYING NOTICE OF THE EXECUTION OF A WARRANT.

Section 3103a of title 18, United States Code, is amended—

(1) by inserting "(a) IN GENERAL.—" before "In addition"; and

(2) by adding at the end the following:

"(b) DELAY.—With respect to the issuance of any warrant or court order under this section, or any other rule of law, to search for and seize any property or material that constitutes evidence of a criminal offense in violation of the laws of the United States, any notice required, or that may be required, to be given may be delayed if—

"(1) the court finds reasonable cause to believe that providing immediate notification of the execution of the warrant may have an adverse result (as defined in section 2705);

"(2) the warrant prohibits the seizure of any tangible property, any wire or electronic communication (as defined in section 2510), or, except as expressly provided in chapter 121, any stored wire or electronic information, except where the court finds reasonable necessity for the seizure; and

"(3) the warrant provides for the giving of such notice within a reasonable period of its execution, which period may thereafter be extended by the court for good cause shown.".

[Editor's Note: This provision amounts to a rule permitting the government to request, and the judge to grant, a delay in any notice to the target of a search required under Fed. R.Crim.P. 41, if the giving of that notice would lead to an adverse result. The Advisory Committee on Criminal Rules has proposed an amendment to Rule 41 that would accommodate this change.]

* * *

SEC. 216. MODIFICATION OF AUTHORITIES RELATING TO USE OF PEN REGISTERS AND TRAP AND TRACE DEVICES.

* * *

(b) ISSUANCE OF ORDERS.—

(1) IN GENERAL.—Section 3123(a) of title 18, United States Code, is amended to read as follows:

"(a) IN GENERAL.—

"(1) ATTORNEY FOR THE GOVERNMENT.—Upon an application made under section 3122(a)(1), the court shall enter an ex parte order authorizing the installation and use of a pen register or trap and trace device anywhere within the United States, if the court finds that the attorney for the Government has certified to the court that the information likely to be obtained by such installation and use is relevant to an ongoing criminal investigation. The order, upon service of that order, shall apply to any person or entity providing wire or electronic communication service in the United States whose assistance may facilitate the execution of the order. Whenever such an order is served on any person or entity not specifically named in the order, upon request of such person or entity, the attorney for the Government or law enforcement or investigative officer that is serving the order shall provide written or electronic certification that the order applies to the person or entity being served.

"(2) STATE INVESTIGATIVE OR LAW ENFORCEMENT OFFICER.—Upon an application made under section 3122(a)(2), the court shall enter an ex parte order authorizing the installation and use of a pen register or trap and trace device within the jurisdiction of the court, if the court finds that the State law enforcement or investigative officer has certified to the court that the information likely to be obtained by such installation and use is relevant to an ongoing criminal investigation.

"(3)(A) Where the law enforcement agency implementing an ex parte order under this subsection seeks to do so by installing and using its own pen register or trap and trace device on a packet-switched data network of a provider of electronic communication service to the public, the agency shall ensure that a record will be maintained which will identify—

"(i) any officer or officers who installed the device and any officer or officers who accessed the device to obtain information from the network;

"(ii) the date and time the device was installed, the date and time the device was uninstalled, and the date, time, and duration of each time the device is accessed to obtain information;

"(iii) the configuration of the device at the time of its installation and any subsequent modification thereof; and

"(iv) any information which has been collected by the device.

To the extent that the pen register or trap and trace device can be set automatically to record this information electronically, the record shall be maintained electronically throughout the installation and use of such device.

"(B) The record maintained under subparagraph (A) shall be provided ex parte and under seal to the court which entered the ex parte order authorizing the installation and use of the device within 30 days after termination of the order (including any extensions thereof).".

* * *

SEC. 219. SINGLE–JURISDICTION SEARCH WARRANTS FOR TERRORISM.

Rule 41(a) of the Federal Rules of Criminal Procedure is amended by inserting after "executed" the following: "and (3) in an investigation of domestic terrorism or international terrorism (as defined in section 2331 of title 18, United States Code), by a Federal magistrate judge in any district in which activities related to the terrorism may have occurred, for a search of property or for a person within or outside the district".

[Editor's Note: This change has already been made in the restylized Federal Rules of Criminal Procedure, which went into effect on December 1, 2002.]

†